Property and Conveyancing Library, No. 11

THE LAW OF EASEMENTS

AUSTRALIA
The Law Book Company Ltd.
Sydney : Melbourne : Brisbane

CANADA AND U.S.A.
The Carswell Company Ltd.
Agincourt, Ontario

INDIA
N. M. Tripathi Ltd.
Bombay

ISRAEL
Steimatzky's Agency Ltd.
Jerusalem : Tel Aviv : Haifa

MALAYSIA : SINGAPORE : BRUNEI
Malayan Law Journal (Pte) Ltd.
Singapore

NEW ZEALAND
Sweet & Maxwell (N.Z.) Ltd.
Wellington

PAKISTAN
Pakistan Law House
Karachi

Published in 1972 by
Sweet & Maxwell Limited of
11 New Fetter Lane, London
and printed in Great Britain by
The Eastern Press Limited of
London and Reading

PROPERTY AND CONVEYANCING LIBRARY, No. 11

GALE

on

Easements

FOURTEENTH EDITION

BY

SPENCER G. MAURICE

of Lincoln's Inn, Barrister-at-Law

ASSISTED BY

ROBERT WAKEFIELD, B.C.L. (Oxon.)

of the Middle Temple and Lincoln's Inn, Barrister-at-Law

LONDON
SWEET & MAXWELL
1972

First Edition	(1839) By Charles James Gale and Thomas Denman Whatley
Second Edition	(1849) By Charles James Gale
Third Edition	(1862) By W. H. Willes
Fourth Edition	(1868) By David Gibbons
Fifth Edition	(1876) „ „
Sixth Edition	(1888) By George Cave
Seventh Edition	(1899) „ „
Eighth Edition	(1908) By Raymond Roope Reeve
Ninth Edition	(1916) By T. H. Carson
Tenth Edition	(1925) By W. J. Byrne
Eleventh Edition	(1932) By F. Graham Glover
Twelfth Edition	(1950) By D. H. McMullen
Thirteenth Edition	(1959) By Michael Bowles
Second Impression	(1962)
Fourteenth Edition	(1972) By Spencer G. Maurice

SBN 421 15170 6

Sweet & Maxwell Limited

1972

PREFACE

IN the one hundred and thirty-three years since the publication of the first edition Mr. Gale's [1] book has been edited by many hands and its contents have undergone much revision. A new editor should approach with proper reverence the task of revising further a work of such antiquity, and eschew change for the sake of change. It so happens, however, that in the thirteen years since the thirteenth edition a good many important cases on the law of easements have been before the courts and those cases, some of which have done much to throw light on a difficult subject, have in this edition involved a sizeable amount of new matter and consequential revision. New statute law, in particular the Rights of Light Act 1959 (which reached the statute book just too late for the thirteenth edition, where the Bill alone could be considered), and the Water Resources Acts 1963 and 1968, has also required consideration at some length.

Yet the book has not been increased in size. Its restriction within its previous compass has been made possible in two ways. First, the chapter on Nuisances and their Legalisation has been omitted, as being out of place in a book on easements, except for the section on Prescriptive Right to Cause Nuisance, which now appears at the end of Chapter 4, Establishment of Easements by Prescription. Secondly, the lengthy passages from judgments, which have been a characteristic of earlier editions, have been pruned. I had originally contemplated far more drastic action, but I found that the retention of these passages had some support amongst practitioners and, in so far as their content was instructive and clear, mere paraphrase seemed to me to be a pointless exercise. Indeed, I have, in considering the recent authorities, used the method of verbatim citation whenever this seemed useful.

It is difficult in treating of the subject of easements not to stray into other cognate fields of law. For that reason *Gale* treats of various matters which are outside the strictly logical scope of a work on easements: the natural rights incidental to the ownership of land at common law, namely, the right to the support of land by other land and the right to the uninterrupted flow of water in a natural and defined channel; and the law relating to party walls (where rights are provided by statute), banks, and boundary trees and buildings. More obviously, *Gale* examines, in Chapter 2, Equitable Rights to Easements, those interests, sometimes called estoppel interests, illustrated by the recent

---

[1] As appears from the Preface to the last (thirteenth) edition, Mr. Gale had as his co-author Mr. Whatley, but little is known of him or the part which he played in authorship. Conventionally the work as a whole is ascribed to Mr. Gale.

cases of *Ward* v. *Kirkland* [2] and *E. R. Ives Investment Ltd.* v. *High.* [3]
Since the rules and principles governing the acquisition, extinguishment
and disturbance of *profits à prendre* are generally applicable to the
acquisition, extinguishment and disturbance of easements, rather more
attention is paid to profits in this edition than in the last one.

I have thought it wise to include a completely new chapter on
Easements and Registered Land (Chap. 5). Compulsory registration of
land is spreading rapidly, and the need for such a chapter was brought
to my attention by some recent cases. The convenient course seemed to
be to deal with the whole subject in a separate chapter rather than to try
to fit it in piecemeal in existing chapters.

I am conscious that radical changes in the law of easements and
generally in regard to rights appurtenant to land may not be far
distant. Indeed, at one time it appeared possible that substantial changes
might occur before this edition could be published. Recommendations
on the acquisition of easements and profits by prescription were
contained in the Fourteenth Report of the Law Reform Committee, [4]
while The Law Commission has the question of rights appurtenant to
land under active consideration and has suggested a new classification
of land obligations covering covenants both positive and restrictive as
well as easements and profits. The proposed revisions of the law have
not, however, reached such a stage as to warrant any reference to them
in the text of this edition.

In preparing this edition I have had invaluable assistance from Mr.
Robert Wakefield and I am most grateful to him for all that he has
done. He has carried out extensive research, in particular with regard
to the recent cases. The work on Chapter 5 (Easements and Registered
Land) and Chapter 16 (Remedies for Disturbance) has been mostly his.
He also prepared the section on the Rights of Light Act 1959 in
Chapter 4 and the section on the Water Resources Act 1963 in Chapter
6. Furthermore, he has compiled the index.

Lincoln's Inn,   SPENCER G. MAURICE.
January, 1972.

---

[2] [1967] Ch. 194.
[3] [1967] 2 Q.B. 379.
[4] Cmnd. 3100 (1966).

PREFACE TO THE FIRST EDITION

THE want of a treatise upon those important rights known in the Law of England by the name of "Easements" has, it is believed, been sensibly felt by the Profession.

The length of time which has elapsed without any attempt having been made to supply this want affords a sufficient reason for the appearance of the present Essay. The difficulties which arise from the abstruseness and refinements incident to the subject, have been increased by the comparatively small number of decided cases affording matter for defining and systematising this branch of the law. Upon some points, indeed, there is no authority at all in the English law; of the decisions some depend upon the circumstances of the particular case, and some are irreconcilable with each other.

Watercourses are the only class of easements with regard to which the law has been settled with any degree of precision.

A desire to remedy an admitted defect led to the passing of the Prescription Act—a statute, which has not only failed in effecting its particular object, but has introduced greater doubt and confusion than existed before its enactment. In fact, had it not been held, that the statute did not repeal the common law, many rights which have been enjoyed immemorially would have been put an end to by circumstances which never could have been intended to have that effect.

As in many other branches of the Law of England, the earlier authorities upon the law of easements appear to be based upon the civil law, modified, in some degree, probably, by a recognition of customs which existed among our Norman ancestors. The most remarkable instance of an adoption by the English law from this source is the doctrine known in the French law by the title of "Destination du père de famille."

In the majority of cases, both ancient and modern, probably from a consideration of this being the origin of the law, recourse has been had for assistance to the civil law. It has, therefore, been considered that the utility of the work would be increased by the introduction of many of the provisions of that refined and elaborate system with respect to Praedial Servitudes, and the doctrine of Prescription; as well as some of the observations of Pardessus—an eminent French writer on Servitudes.

With the same view the authority of decisions in the American courts has been called in aid upon the subject of watercourses—questions which the value of water as a moving power, and the frequent absence of ancient appropriation, have often given rise to in the United States. In those judgments the law is considered with much care and research, and the rights of the parties settled with precision. The result of the authorities is stated by Chancellor Kent, in his well-known *Commentaries*, with his usual ability.

Upon many points, particularly upon the construction of the Prescription Act, the observations contained in the following pages are, in some degree, unsupported by direct authority. It has, however, been thought better to endeavour to open the law upon the doubts which presented themselves than to pass them over in silence.

Temple,
  July, 1839

CONTENTS

Preface . . . . *page* v

Preface to the First Edition vii

Table of Cases xi

Table of Statutes xlvii

PART I

EASEMENTS GENERALLY

1. Characteristics of an Easement 3
2. Equitable Rights to Easements 61

PART II

THE ACQUISITION OF EASEMENTS

3. Creation of Easements by Known Transactions . . . 75
4. Establishment of Easements by Prescription . . . 133
5. Easements and Registered Land 193

PART III

PARTICULAR EASEMENTS AND PARTICULAR NATURAL RIGHTS OF A SIMILAR CHARACTER

6. Rights in Respect of Water 199
7. Right to Light 238
8. Air 256
9. Rights of Way 261
10. Support 287
11. Party-Walls, Banks and Boundary Trees and Buildings . 302

ix

PART IV

EXTINGUISHMENT OF EASEMENTS

12. Extinguishment of Easements by Operation of Law .   .   309
13. Extinguishment of Easements by Statute   .   .   .   314
14. Extinguishment of Easements by Release   316

PART V

DISTURBANCE OF EASEMENTS

15. What Amounts to a Disturbance   351
16. Remedies for Disturbance   356
Index   399

TABLE OF CASES

References in bold type indicate where a quotation from the case appears in the text.

PAGE

ABBOTT *v.* Holloway [1904] W.N. 124; 48 S.J. 525 .... **397**

Abingdon Corporation *v.* James [1940] Ch. 287; 109 L.J.Ch. 225; 162 L.T.
335; 56 T.L.R. 373; 104 J.P. 197; 84 S.J. 134; [1940] 1 All
E.R. 446 .... 36, 45, 46

Ackroyd *v.* Smith (1850) 10 C.B. 164; 19 L.J.C.P. 315; 15 L.T.(o.s.) 395;
14 Jur. 1047; 138 E.R. 68 .... 8, 9, 12, 13, 34, 42

Acton *v.* Blundell (1843) 12 M. & W. 324; 13 L.J.Ex. 289; 1 L.T.(o.s.)
207; 152 E.R. 1223 .... 208, **211–213**, 220

Albon *v.* Dremsall (1610) 1 Brownl. 215; *sub nom.* Alban *v.* Brounsall,
Yelv. 163 284

Aldin *v.* Latimer Clark, Muirhead & Co. [1894] 2 Ch. 437; 63 L.J.Ch.
601; 71 L.T. 119; 10 T.L.R. 452; 38 S.J. 458; 8 R. 352; 42 W.R.
553 .... 89, 92, 258, 259

Aldred's Case (1610) 9 Co.Rep. 57 (b); 77 E.R. 816 .... 26, **240**, 257, 258,
351, 352, 363

Aldridge *v.* Wright [1929] 2 K.B. 117; 98 L.J.K.B. 582; 141 L.T. 352 106,
109, **113**, 116, 118

Allan *v.* Gomme (1840) 11 Ad. & El. 759; 3 Per. & Dav. 581; 9 L.J.Q.B.
258; 113 E.R. 602 .... **274**, 275, 276, 278, 279, 347

Allen *v.* Ayres [1884] W.N. 242 391
—— *v.* Seckham (1879) 11 Ch.D. 790; 48 L.J.Ch. 611; 41 L.T. 260; 43 J.P.
685; 28 W.R. 26 66
—— *v.* Taylor (1880) 16 Ch.D. 355; 50 L.J.Ch. 178 .... 110, 111

Alston *v.* Scales (1832) 9 Bing. 3; 2 Moo. & S. 5; 1 L.J.M.C. 95; 131
E.R. 515 .... 363, 366

Ambler *v.* Gordon [1905] 1 K.B. 417; 74 L.J.K.B. 185; 92 L.T. 96; 21
T.L.R. 205 .... 179, 254, 333

Ambler (Jeremiah) & Sons Ltd. *v.* Bradford (Mayor) [1902] 2 Ch. 585;
71 L.J.Ch. 744; 87 L.T. 217; 18 T.L.R. 758; 66 J.P. 708 203

Anderson *v.* Cleland [1910] 2 Ir.R. 334 235
—— *v.* Francis [1906] W.N. 160 .... 147, 396

Andrews *v.* Paradise (1724) 8 Mod.Rep. 318; 88 E.R. 228 .... **353**
—— *v.* Waite [1907] 2 Ch. 500; 76 L.J.Ch. 676; 97 L.T. 428 .... 148, 188,
240, 329, **336**, 346, 396

Angus *v.* Dalton. *See* Dalton *v.* Angus.

Ankerson *v.* Connelly [1906] 2 Ch. 544; [1907] 1 Ch. 678; 76 L.J.Ch.
402; 96 L.T. 681; 23 T.L.R. 486 .... 57, **328, 329**, 330, 332, 336, 355

Anon. (1566) Dyer 248b, pl. 80; 73 E.R. 549 352
—— (1566) 3 Leon. 13 380
—— (1622) 2 Roll Rep. 255; 81 E.R. 783 305

Arcedeckne *v.* Kelk (1858) 2 Giff. 683; 32 L.T.(o.s.) 331; 23 J.P. 147;
5 Jur.(N.S.) 114; 66 E.R. 286; 7 W.R. 194 .... 336, 355, 380

Ardley *v.* Guardians of the Poor of St. Pancras (1870) 39 L.J.Ch. 871 ... 52, **53**

Arkwright *v.* Gell (1839) 5 M. & W. 203; 2 Horn. & H. 17; 8 L.J.Ex 201;
151 E.R. 87 .... **54**, 223, **225, 226**, 229

Armstrong *v.* Sheppard & Short Ltd. [1959] 2 Q.B. 384; [1959] 3 W.L.R.
84; 123 J.P. 401; 103 S.J. 508; [1959] 2 All E.R. 651 ...... 15, **56, 66**, 69,
316, 382

Ashby *v.* White (1704) 1 Bro.Parl.Cas. 62; *reversing* (1703) 2 Ld.Raym.
938; Holt.K.B. 524; 6 Mod.Rep. 45; 1 Salk. 19; 3 Salk. 17; 92
E.R. 126 379

Aspden *v.* Seddon, Preston *v.* Seddon (1876) 1 Ex.D. 496; *affirming*
Aspden *v.* Seddon (1875) 10 Ch.App. 394; 44 L.J.Ch. 359; 32
L.T. 415; 39 J.P. 597; 23 W.R. 580 46

Att.-Gen. *v.* Antrobus [1905] 2 Ch. 188; 74 L.J.Ch. 599; 92 L.T. 790; 21
T.L.R. 471; 69 J.P. 141; 49 S.J. 459; 3 L.G.R. 1071 .... 27, 28
—— *v.* Barnsley Corporation [1874] W.N. 37 .... 192, 231
—— *v.* Bradford Canal Proprietors (1866) L.R. 2 Eq. 71; 35 L.J.Ch. 619;
14 L.T. 248; 15 L.T. 9; 14 W.R. 579 370

PAGE

Att.-Gen. *v.* Cambridge Consumers' Gas Co. (1868) 4 Ch.App. 71; 38 L.J.Ch. 94; 19 L.T. 508; 33 J.P. 147; 17 W.R. 145 .... **381**, 382
—— *v.* Colney Hatch Lunatic Asylum (1868) 4 Ch.App. 146; 38 L.J.Ch. 265; 19 L.T. 708; 33 J.P. 196; 17 W.R. 240 397
—— *v.* Conduit Colliery Co. [1895] 1 Q.B. 301; 64 L.J.Q.B. 207; 71 L.T. 771; 11 T.L.R. 57; 59 J.P. 70; 15 R. 267; 43 W.R. 366 ...... 290, 291
—— *v.* Copeland [1902] 1 K.B. 690, C.A.; *reversing* [1901] 2 K.B. 101; 70 L.J.K.B. 512; 84 L.T. 562; 17 T.L.R. 422; 65 J.P. 581; 49 W.R. 489 .... **13**, 223
—— *v.* Dorking Guardians (1882) 20 Ch.D. 595; 51 L.J.Ch. 585; 46 L.T. 573; 30 W.R. 579 231
—— *v.* Doughty (1788) 2 Ves.Sen. 453; 28 E.R. 290 299
—— *v.* Esher Linoleum Co. Ltd. [1901] 2 Ch. 647; 70 L.J.Ch. 808; 85 L.T. 414; 66 J.P. 71; 50 W.R. 22 261
—— *v.* Gauntlett (1829) 3 Y. & J. 93 169
—— *v.* Great Central Ry. [1912] 2 Ch. 110; 81 L.J.Ch. 596; 106 L.T. 413; 28 T.L.R. 268; 76 J.P. 205; 56 S.J. 343; 10 L.G.R. 687 314
—— *v.* Great Northern Ry. [1909] 1 Ch. 775; 78 L.J.Ch. 577; 99 L.T. 69n.; 73 J.P. 41 .... 57, 168
—— *v.* Hallett (1847) 16 M. & W. 569; 16 L.J.Ex. 131; 8 L.T.(o.s.) 450; 11 J.P. 744; 153 E.R. 1316 .... 381, 387
—— *v.* Horner (1885) 11 App.Cas. 66; *affirming* (1884) 14 Q.B.D. 245; 54 L.J.Q.B. 227; 1 T.L.R. 28; 49 J.P. 326; 33 W.R. 93 143
—— *v.* —— (No. 2) [1913] 2 Ch. 140; 82 L.J.Ch. 339; 108 L.T. 609; 29 T.L.R. 451; 77 J.P. 257; 57 S.J. 498; 11 L.G.R. 784 ...... 19, 142, 143, 173, 178
—— *v.* Lonsdale (1868) L.R. 7 Eq. 377; 38 L.J.Ch. 335; 20 L.T. 64; 33 J.P. 435; 17 W.R. 219 236
—— *v.* Manchester Corporation [1893] 2 Ch. 87; 62 L.J.Ch. 459; 68 L.T. 608; 9 T.L.R. 315; 37 S.J. 325; 3 R. 427; 41 W.R. 459 384
—— *v.* Merthyr Tydfil Local Board of Health [1870] W.N. 148 397
—— *v.* Meyrick & Jones (1915) 74 J.P. 515 354
—— *v.* Queen Anne Gardens & Mansions Co. (1889) 60 L.T. 759; 5 T.L.R. 430; 37 W.R. 572 147
—— *v.* Reynolds [1911] 2 K.B. 888; 80 L.J.K.B. 1073; 104 L.T. 852 320
—— *v.* Sheffield Gas Consumers' Co. (1853) 3 De G.M. & G. 304; 22 L.J.Ch. 811; 21 L.T.(o.s.) 49; 17 Jur. 677; 43 E.R. 119; 1 W.R. 185 382
—— *v.* Simpson. *See* Simpson *v.* Att.-Gen.
—— *v.* Staffordshire County Council [1905] 1 Ch. 336; 74 L.J.Ch. 153; 92 L.T. 288; 21 T.L.R. 139; 69 J.P. 97; 53 W.R. 312; 3 L.G.R. 379 385
—— *v.* Terry (1874) 9 Ch.App. 423; 30 L.T. 215; 38 J.P. 340; 2 Asp.M.L.C. 217; 22 W.R. 395 236
—— *v.* Wright [1897] 2 Q.B. 318; 66 L.J.Q.B. 834; 77 L.T. 295; 13 T.L.R. 480; 8 Asp.M.L.C. 320; 46 W.R. 85 .... 143, 236, 237
Att.-Gen. of Southern Nigeria *v.* John Holt and Company (Liverpool) Ltd. [1915] A.C. 599; 84 L.J.P.C. 98; 112 L.T. 955 .... **31**, 35
Attwood *v.* Llay Main Collieries [1926] Ch. 444; 95 L.J.Ch. 221; 134 L.T. 268; 70 S.J. 265 .... 202, **204**, 205, **206**, 209
Austerberry *v.* Oldham Corporation (1885) 29 Ch.D. 750; 55 L.J.Ch. 633; 53 L.T. 543; 1 T.L.R. 473; 49 J.P. 532; 33 W.R. 807 ...... 38, 40, 48, 338
Austin *v.* Scottish Widows' Fund Assurance Society (1881) 8 L.R.Ir. 385 .... 273, 353
Aynsley *v.* Glover (1875) 10 Ch.App. 283; 44 L.J.Ch. 523; 32 L.T. 345; 39 J.P. 484; 23 W.R. 457; *affirming* (1874) L.R. 18 Eq. 544 ...... 134, 144, 239, 248, 346, 386, 387, 391

BACK *v.* Stacey (1826) 2 C. & P. 465 .... **241**, 245, 397
Backhouse *v.* Bonomi (1861) 9 H.L.C. 503; 34 L.J.Q.B. 181; 4 L.T. 754; 7 Jur.(N.S.) 809; 11 E.R. 825; 9 W.R. 769; *affirming sub nom.* Bonomi *v.* Backhouse (1859) E.B. & E. 646; *reversing* (1858) E.B. & E. 622 ...... 287, 290, 293, 379
Bailey *v.* Appleyard (1838) 8 Ad. & El. 161; 3 Nev. & P.K.B. 257; 7 L.J.Q.B. 145; 112 E.R. 798 .... 4, 153, 375
Bailey *v.* Icke (1891) 64 L.T. 789 102
—— *v.* Stephens (1862) 12 C.B.(N.S.) 91; 31 L.J.C.P. 226; 6 L.T. 356; 8 Jur. (N.S.) 1063; 142 E.R. 1077; 10 W.R. 868 .... 16, 59
Bailey (W. H.) & Son Ltd. *v.* Holborn & Frascati Ltd. [1914] 1 Ch. 598; 83 L.J.Ch. 515; 110 L.T. 574; 58 S.J. 321 .... 57, 328, **329**, 355

PAGE

Baily & Co. *v.* Clark, Son & Morland [1902] 1 Ch. 649; 71 L.J.Ch. 396; 86
L.T. 309; 18 T.L.R. 364; 46 S.J. 316; 50 W.R. 511 .... 204, 224, 227
Baker *v.* Turner [1950] A.C. 401; 66 T.L.R. (Pt. 1) 780; 94 S.J. 335; [1950]
1 All E.R. 834 31
Ball *v.* Derby (1874) cited in [1894] 1 Ch. at p. 281; *sub nom.* Batt *v.* Derby
cited in 63 L.T. at p. 381 391
—— *v.* Ray (1873) 8 Ch.App. 467; 28 L.T. 346; 37 J.P. 500; 21 W.R. 282   36
Ballacorkish Mining Co. *v.* Harrison (1873) L.R. 5 P.C. 49; *sub nom.*
Ballacorkish Mining Co. *v.* Dumbell, 43 L.J.P.C. 19; 29 L.T. 658;
38 J.P. 148 ...., 211, **213, 214**
Ballard *v.* Dyson (1808) 1 Taunt. 279; 127 E.R. 841 .... 262, **263, 264**
—— *v.* Tomlinson (1885) 29 Ch.D. 115; 54 L.J.Ch. 454; 52 L.T. 942; 1
T.L.R. 270; 49 J.P. 692; 33 W.R. 533 .... 211, 230
Balston *v.* Bensted (1808) 1 Camp. 463; 170 E.R. 462 220
Baltic Co. *v.* Simpson (1876) 2 Char.Pr.Cas. 119; 24 W.R. 390 397
Bankart *v.* Houghton (1860) 27 Beav. 425; 28 L.J.Ch. 473; 23 J.P. 260; 5
Jur.(N.S.) 282; 54 E.R. 167; 7 W.R. 197 66
—— *v.* Tennant (1870) L.R. 10 Eq. 141; 39 L.J.Ch. 809; 23 L.T. 137; 34
J.P. 628; 18 W.R. 639 66
Barber *v.* Whiteley (1865) 34 L.J.Q.B. 212; 29 J.P. 678; 11 Jur.(N.S.) 822;
13 W.R. 774 38
Barker *v.* Faulkner [1898] W.N. 69; 79 L.T. 24 219
—— *v.* Richardson (1821) 4 B. & Ald. 579; 106 E.R. 1048 ...... 139, **163**, 167, 294
Barkshire *v.* Grubb (1881) 18 Ch.D. 616; 50 L.J.Ch. 731; 45 L.J. 383; 29
W.R. 929 121
Barnes *v.* Allen [1927] W.N. 217; 64 L.J. 92; 164 L.T.J. 83 .... 370, 395
—— *v.* Loach (1879) 4 Q.B.D. 494; 48 L.J.Q.B. 756; 41 L.T. 278; 43 J.P.
817; 28 W.R. 32 .... 115, 127, **334**, 355
Barry *v.* Hasseldine [1952] Ch. 835; [1952] 2 T.L.R. 92; [1952] 2 All E.R.
317 .... 117, 118
Bartlett *v.* Baker (1864) 3 H. & C. 153; 34 L.J.Ex. 8; 159 E.R. 486 370
—— *v.* Downes (1825) 3 B. & C. 616; 1 C. & P. 522; 5 Dow. & Ry.K.B.
526; 3 L.J.(o.s.)K.B. 90; 107 E.R. 861 188
—— *v.* Tottenham [1932] 1 Ch. 114; 101 L.J.Ch. 160; 145 L.T. 686 ...... 54, 100,
224, 227, 229
Bass *v.* Gregory (1890) 25 Q.B.D. 481; 59 L.J.Q.B. 574; 6 T.L.R. 412; 55
J.P. 119 .... 36, 141, 142, 146, 258, 259
Bastard *v.* Smith (1837) 2 Mood. & R. 129 236
Bateman *v.* Bluck (1852) 18 Q.B. 870; 21 L.J.Q.B. 406; 17 J.P. 4; 17 Jur.
386; 118 E.R. 329 359
Baten's Case (1610) 9 Rep. 53*b*; 77 E.R. 810 .... 222, 356, 360
Batt *v.* Derby. *See* Ball *v.* Derby.
Battersea *v.* London City Sewers Commissioners [1895] 2 Ch. 708; 65 L.J..
Ch. 81; 73 L.T. 116; 59 J.P. 728; 39 S.J. 689; 13 R. 795; 44 W.R. 124   154
Battishill *v.* Reed (1856) 18 C.B. 696; 20 J.P. 775; 139 E.R. 1544; 25 L.J.
C.P. 290; 4 W.R. 603 .... 188, 369
Baxendale *v.* McMurray (1867) 2 Ch.App. 790; 31 J.P. 821; 16 W.R. 32 ... 36,
58, 231, 347
—— *v.* North Lambeth Liberal & Radical Club Ltd. [1902] 2 Ch. 427; 71
L.J.Ch. 806; 87 L.T. 161; 18 T.L.R. 700; 46 S.J. 616; 50 W.R. 650 ... **282,
283**
Baxter *v.* Bower (1875) 44 L.J.Ch. 625; 33 L.T. 41; 23 W.R. 805 .... 256, 383
—— *v.* Taylor (1832) 4 B. & Ad. 72; 1 Nev. & M.K.B. 11; 2 L.J.K.B. 65;
110 E.R. 382 .... 365, 366, **367**
Bayley *v.* Great Western Ry. (1884) 26 Ch.D. 434; 51 L.T. 337 ... 83, 94, 101, 167
Beadel *v.* Perry (1866) L.R. 3 Eq. 465; 15 L.T. 345; 15 W.R. 120 .... 252, 382
Bealey *v.* Shaw (1805) 6 East 208; 2 Smith K.B. 321; 102 E.R. 1266 ... 57, 208, 218
Beasley *v.* Clarke (1836) 2 Bing.N.C. 705; 5 Dowl. 50; 2 Hodg. 100; 3 Scott
258; 5 L.J.C.P. 281; 132 E.R. 271 .... 177, 189, 375, **376**
Beauchamp *v.* Frome R. D. C. [1938] 1 All E.R. 595; 54 T.L.R. 476; 82 S.J.
213; 36 L.G.R. 377; *reversing* [1937] 4 All E.R. 348 .... 27, 99
Beaufort (Duke) *v.* Patrick (1853) 17 Beav. 60; *affirming sub nom.* Doe *d.*
Patrick *v.* Beaufort (Duke) (1851) 6 Exch. 498; 20 L.J.Ex. 251; 155
E.R. 640 63
Beckett (Alfred F.) Ltd. *v.* Lyons [1967] Ch. 449; [1967] 2 W.L.R. 421; 110
S.J. 925; [1967] 1 All E.R. 833; 65 L.G.R. 73 .... 4, **8**, 141, 143, 173

PAGE

Beddington v. Atlee (1887) 35 Ch.D. 317; 56 L.J.Ch. 655; 56 L.T. 514; 3
  T.L.R. 363; 51 J.P. 484; 35 W.R. 799 .... 21, 77, 78, 102, **111, 112**, 115,
                                                                        124, 309
Beddow v. Beddow (1878) 9 Ch.D. 89; 47 L.J.Ch. 588; 26 W.R. 570 386
Bedford v. Dawson (1875) L.R. 20 Eq. 353; 44 L.J.Ch. 549; 33 L.T. 156;
  39 J.P. 804 315
Bedingfield v. Onslow (1685) 3 Lev. 209; 83 E.R. 654 .... 363, 365
Beeston v. Weate (1856) 5 E. & B. 986; 25 L.J.Q.B. 115; 26 L.T.(o.s.) 272;
  20 J.P. 452; 2 Jur.(N.S.) 540; 4 W.R. 325; 119 E.R. 748 ... 36, 37, 219, 222
Behrens v. Richards [1905] 2 Ch. 614; 74 L.J.Ch. 615; 93 L.T. 623; 21
  T.L.R. 705; 69 J.P. 381; 49 S.J. 685; 3 L.G.R. 1228; 54 W.R. 141 ... 382
Bell v. Midland Ry. (1861) 10 C.B.(N.S.) 287; 30 L.J.C.P. 273; 4 L.T. 293;
  7 Jur.(N.S.) 1200; 142 E.R. 462; 9 W.R. 612 .... 363, 365, 367
—— v. Twentyman (1841) 1 Q.B. 766; 1 Gal. & Dav. 223; 10 L.J.Q.B. 278;
  6 Jur. 366; 113 E.R. 1324 365
Bendall v. McWhirter [1952] 2 Q.B. 466; [1952] 1 T.L.R. 1332; 96 S.J. 344;
  [1952] 1 All E.R. 1307 56
Bendir v. Anson (1936) 80 S.J. 873; [1936] 3 All E.R. 326 363
Bennison v. Cartwright (1864) 5 B. & S. 1; 3 New Rep. 506; 33 L.J.Q.B. 137;
  10 L.T. 266; 28 J.P. 501; 10 Jur.(N.S.) 847; 122 E.R. 733; 12 W.R. 425 154
Bernard and Bernard v. Jennings and Hillaire (1968) 13 W.I.R. 501 ...... 286, 346
Betts, Frederick Ltd. v. Pickfords Ltd. [1906] 2 Ch. 87; 75 L.J.Ch. 483;
  94 L.T. 363; 22 T.L.R. 315; 54 W.R. 476 .... 90, 101, 102
Bevan v. London Portland Cement Co. (1892) 67 L.T. 615; 9 T.L.R. 12;
  3 R. 47 5
Bewley v. Atkinson (1879) 13 Ch.D. 283; 49 L.J.Ch. 153; 41 L.T. 603; 28
  W.R. 638 149
Beytagh v. Cassidy (1868) 16 W.R. 403 153
Bibby v. Carter (1859) 4 H. & N. 153; 28 L.J.Ex. 182; 32 L.T.(o.s.) 260;
  157 E.R. 795; 7 W.R. 193 .... 291, 373
Bickett v. Morris (1866) L.R. 1 Sc. & Div. 47; 14 L.T. 835; 30 J.P. 532;
  12 Jur.(N.S.) 802 .... 236, 379
Bidder v. North Staffordshire Ry. (1878) 4 Q.B.D. 412 .... 261, 273
Bidwell v. Holden (1890) 63 L.T. 104 382
Binckes v. Pash (1861) 11 C.B.(N.S.) 324; 31 L.J.C.P. 121; 6 L.T. 125; 8
  Jur.(N.S.) 360; 142 E.R. 822; 10 W.R. 424 325
Bird v. Dickinson (1701) 2 Lut. 1526 375
Birkenhead (Mayor of) v. London & North Western Ry. (1885) 15 Q.B.D.
  572; 55 L.J.Q.B. 48; 50 J.P. 84 45
Birmingham Corporation v. Allen (1877) 6 Ch.D. 284; 46 L.J.Ch. 673; 37
  L.T. 207; 42 J.P. 184; 25 W.R. 810 288
Birmingham, Dudley & District Banking Co. v. Ross (1888) 38 Ch.D. 295;
  57 L.J.Ch. 601; 59 L.T. 609; 4 T.L.R. 437; 36 W.R. 914 ...... 24, 92, 94,
                                                          101, **102–104**, 111, 124
Bishop v. Bedford Charity (1859) 1 E. & E. 697; 29 L.J.Q.B. 53; 1 L.T. 214;
  6 Jur.(N.S.) 220; 120 E.R. 1078; 8 W.R. 115 370
Black v. Ballymena Township Commissioners (1886) 17 L.R.Ir. 459 210
—— v. Scottish Temperance Assurance Co. [1908] 1 Ir.R. 541; 42 I.L.T. 194 248
Blackburne v. Somers (1879) 5 L.R.Ir. 1 224
Blair v. Deakin (1887) 57 L.T. 522; 3 T.L.R. 757; 52 J.P. 327 .... 230, 369
Blake & Lyons Ltd. v. Lewis Berger & Sons Ltd. [1951] W.N. 425; [1951] 2
  T.L.R. 605; 95 S.J. 514 149
Blakemore v. Glamorganshire Canal Navigation (1832) 1 My. & K. 154;
  2 L.J.Ch. 95; 39 E.R. 639 .... **382, 386**
Blanchard v. Bridges (1835) 4 A. & E. 176; 1 Har. & W. 630; 5 Nev. &
  M.K.B. 567; 5 L.J.K.B. 78; 111 E.R. 753 324
Bland v. Moseley (1587), cited in 9 Co.Rep. at p. 58a; 1 Bulst. at pp. 115,
  116; Hut. at p. 136; 77 E.R. 817; sub nom. Mosley v. Ball, Yelv. at
  p. 216 .... 258, 299
Bleachers' Association Ltd. v. Chapel-en-le-Frith R. D. C. [1933] Ch. 356;
  102 L.J.Ch. 17; 148 L.T. 91; 49 T.L.R. 51; 96 J.P. 515; 76 S.J. 902;
  31 L.G.R. 88 210
Bliss v. Hall (1838) 4 Bing.N.C. 183; 6 Dowl. 442; 1 Arn. 19; 5 Scott 500;
  7 L.J.C.P. 122; 2 Jur. 110; 132 E.R. 758 208
Blockley v. Slater (1693) 1 Lut., fol. 119 374
Bolton v. Bolton (1879) 11 Ch.D. 968; 48 L.J.Ch. 467; 43 J.P. 764; sub nom.
  Bolton v. London School Board, 40 L.T. 582 .... 20, 97, 98, 117, 124,
                                                                      285, 312

PAGE

Bolus v. Hinstorke. *See* Polus v. Hensock.
Bomford v. Neville [1904] 1 Ir.R. 474 143
Bond v. Nottingham Corporation [1940] Ch. 429; [1940] 2 All E.R. 12; 109
    L.J.Ch. 220; 163 L.T. 253; 56 T.L.R. 475; 104 J.P. 219; 84 S.J. 233;
    38 L.G.R. 209 .... 44, 47, 290, **301**
Bonner v. G. W. R. (1883) 24 Ch.D. 1; 48 L.T. 619; 47 J.P. 580; 32 W.R.
    190 .... 149, 238
Bonomi v. Backhouse. *See* Backhouse v. Bonomi.
Booth v. Alcock (1873) 8 Ch.App. 663; 42 L.J.Ch. 557; 29 L.T. 231; 37 J.P.
    709; 21 W.R. 743 .... 24, **78**, 83
Borman v. Griffith [1930] 1 Ch. 493; 99 L.J.Ch. 295; 142 L.T. 645 .... **95, 96**,
                                                                 97, 113, 123
Born v. Turner [1900] 2 Ch. 211; 69 L.J.Ch. 593; 83 L.T. 148; 44 S.J. 502;
    48 W.R. 697 .... 76, 101, 102, 239
Bourke v. Alexandra Hotel Co. [1877] W.N. 30; 25 W.R. 782 336
—— v. Davis (1890) 44 Ch.D. 110; 62 L.T. 34; 6 T.L.R. 87; 38 W.R. 167 ...   28
Bowen v. Anderson [1894] 1 Q.B. 164; 58 J.P. 213; 38 S.J. 131; 10 R. 47;
    42 W.R. 236 370
Bower v. Etherington (John) Ltd. (1965) 53 D.L.R. (2d) 338 .... 153, 180, 188
—— v. Hill (1835) 1 Bing.N.C. 549; 1 Hodg. 45; 1 Scott 526; 4 L.J.C.P.
    153; 131 E.R. 1229 .... 338, 343, 352, 365, 368, 379
—— v. Peate (1876) 1 Q.B.D. 321; 45 L.J.Q.B. 446; 35 L.T. 321; 40 J.P.
    789 .... 290, 293, **372**
Bowes v. Law (1870) L.R. 9 Eq. 636; 39 L.J.Ch. 483; 22 L.T. 267; 34 J.P.
    436; 18 W.R. 640 391
Bowry & Pope's Case (1588) 1 Leon. 168; 74 E.R. 155; *sub nom.* Bury v.
    Pope, Cro.Eliz. 118 .... **134**, 136
Boyce v. Paddington Borough Council [1903] 2 Ch. 556, C.A.; *reversing*
    [1903] 1 Ch. 109; 72 L.J.Ch. 28; 87 L.T. 564; 19 T.L.R. 38; 67 J.P.
    23; 47 S.J. 50; 1 L.G.R. 98; 51 W.R. 109; *sub nom.* Paddington
    Corpn. v. Att.-Gen. [1906] A.C. 1 149
Boyle v. Tamlyn (1827) 6 B. & C. 329; 9 Dow. & Ry.K.B. 430; 5 L.J.(o.s.)
    K.B. 134; 108 E.R. 473 .... 38-40, 310
Bradbee v. Christ's Hospital (1842) 4 Man. & G. 714 303
Bradburn v. Morris (1876) 3 Ch.D. 812 266
Bradbury v. Grinsell (1871) 2 Wms.Saund. 175; 85 E.R. 932 .... **163**, **164**
Bradford Corporation v. Ferrand [1902] 2 Ch. 655; 71 L.J.Ch. 859; 87 L.T.
    388; 18 T.L.R. 830; 67 J.P. 21; 51 W.R. 122 210
—— v. Pickles [1895] A.C. 587; 64 L.J.Ch. 759; 73 L.T. 353; 11 T.L.R.
    555; 60 J.P. 3; 11 R. 286; 44 W.R. 190 .... 211, 219
Brent v. Haddon (1619) Cro.Jac. 555; 79 E.R. 476 .... 357, 358, 369
Bridewell Hospital (Governors) v. Ward, Lock, Bowden & Co. (1893) 62
    L.J.Ch. 270; 68 L.T. 212; 3 R. 228 154
Bright v. Walker (1834) 1 C.M. & R. 211; 4 Tyr. 502; 3 L.J.Ex. 250; 149
    E.R. 1057 .... 144, 159, **164-166**, 170, 171, 312
Briscoe v. Drought (1860) 11 Ir.C.L.R. 250 214
British Railways Board v. Glass [1965] Ch. 538; [1964] 3 W.L.R. 913; 108
    S.J. 673; [1964] 3 All E.R. 418 .... 12, 57, 76, 262, 264, **269**, **280**
British Transport Commission v. Westmorland County Council [1958] A.C.
    126; [1957] 2 W.L.R. 1032; 121 J.P. 394; 101 S.J. 445; [1957] 2 All
    E.R. 353 76
Broadbent v. Ramsbotham (1856) 11 Exch. 602; 25 L.J.Ex. 115; 26 L.T.(o.s.)
    244; 20 J.P. 486; 156 E.R. 971; 4 W.R. 290 .... 209, 210, 220
Broder v. Saillard (1876) 2 Ch.D. 692; 45 L.J.Ch. 414; 40 J.P. 644; 24
    W.R. 1011 .... 369, 370
Brookes v. Drysdale (1877) 3 C.P.D. 52; 37 L.T. 467; 26 W.R. 331 46
Broomfield v. Williams [1897] 1 Ch. 602; 66 L.J.Ch. 305; 76 L.T. 243; 13
    T.L.R. 278; 41 S.J. 348; 45 W.R. 469 ...... 101, 102, 104, **105**, 111, 125, 131
Brotherton, *Re*, Brotherton v. Brotherton (1908) 77 L.J.Ch. 373, C.A.;
    reversing (1907) 77 L.J.Ch. 58; 97 L.T. 880; 52 S.J. 44 48
Brown v. Alabaster (1888) 37 Ch.D. 490; 57 L.J.Ch. 255; 58 L.T. 266;
    36 W.R. 155 .... 94, **96**, **97**, 117, 118
—— v. Dunstable Corporation [1899] 2 Ch. 378; 68 L.J.Ch. 498; 80 L.T.
    650; 15 T.L.R. 386; 43 S.J. 508; 63 J.P. 519; 47 W.R. 538 ... 191, 231, 378
—— v. Robins (1859) 4 H. & N. 186; 28 L.J.Ex. 250; 157 E.R. 809 291
Browne v. Flower [1911] 1 Ch. 219; 80 L.J.Ch. 181; 103 L.T. 557 ...... 26, **43**, **88**,
                                                  89, 90, 92, 94, 254, 312

PAGE

Browne's Case (1572) 3 Dyer 319b 222, 311

Brownlow v. Tomlinson (1840) 1 Man. & G. 484; 8 Dowl. 827; 1 Scott N.R. 426; 133 E.R. 423 .... 261, 339

Bryant v. Foot (1868) L.R. 3 Q.B. 497, Ex.Ch.; *affirming* (1867) L.R. 2 Q.B. 161; 7 B. & S. 725; 36 L.J.Q.B. 65; 16 L.T. 55; 31 J.P. 229; 15 W.R. 421 143

—— v. Lefever (1879) 4 C.P.D. 172; 48 L.J.Q.B. 380; 40 L.T. 579; 43 J.P. 478; 27 W.R. 612 .... 25, 186, 256, **258**

Brymbo Water Co. v. Lester's Lime Co. (1894) 8 R. 329 228

Buckby v. Coles (1814) 5 Taunt. 311; 128 E.R. 709 312

Buckingham v. Daily News Ltd. [1956] 2 Q.B. 534; [1956] 3 W.L.R. 375; 100 S.J. 528; [1956] 2 All E.R. 904 398

Buckley (R. H.) & Sons Ltd. v. Buckley (N.) & Sons [1898] 2 Q.B. 608; 67 L.J.Q.B. 953 46

Bullard v. Harrison (1815) 4 M. & S. 387; 105 E.R. 877 .... 286, 374, 378

Bullers v. Dickinson (1885) 29 Ch.D. 155; 54 L.J.Ch. 776; 52 L.T. 400; 1 T.L.R. 242; 33 W.R. 540 334

Bulstrode v. Lambert [1953] 1 W.L.R. 1064; 97 S.J. 557; [1953] 2 All E.R. 728 .... 16, 44, 80, 269, 271, **272**, 273, **274**, 345

Bunn v. Channen (1813) 5 Taunt. 244; 128 E.R. 683 60

Bunting v. Hicks (1894) 70 L.T. 455; 10 T.L.R. 360; 7 R. 293 214

Burrows v. Lang [1901] 2 Ch. 502; 70 L.J.Ch. 607; 84 L.T. 623; 17 T.L.R. 514; 45 S.J. 536; 49 W.R. 564 .... 27, 54, 100, 128, 176, 223, 225, 229

Burt v. Victoria Graving Dock Co. (1882) 47 L.T. 378 370

Bury v. Pope. *See* Bowry & Pope's Case.

Butler v. Standard Telephones & Cables Ltd. [1940] 1 K.B. 399; [1940] 1 All E.R. 121; 109 L.J.K.B. 238; 163 L.T. 145; 56 T.L.R. 273; 84 S.J. 189   306

Butt v. Imperial Gas Co. (1866) 2 Ch.App. 158; 16 L.T. 820; 31 J.P. 310; 15 W.R. 92 26

Butterknowle Colliery Co. v. Bishop Auckland Industrial Co-operative Society [1906] A.C. 305; 75 L.J.Ch. 541; 94 L.T. 795; 22 T.L.R. 516; 70 J.P. 361, H.L.; *affirming sub nom.* Bishop Auckland Industrial Co-operative v. Butterknowle Colliery Co. [1904] 2 Ch. 419 99

Butterworth v. West Riding Rivers Board [1909] A.C. 45; 78 L.J.K.B. 203; 100 L.T. 85; 25 T.L.R. 117; 73 J.P. 89; 7 L.G.R. 189 .... 191, 231

CABLE v. Bryant [1908] 1 Ch. 259; 77 L.J.Ch. 78; 98 L.T. 98 .... **90, 91,** 105, 115, 116, 256, 258–260, 398

Calcraft v. Thompson (1867) 15 W.R. 367; 31 J.P. 675 243

Caledonian Ry. v. Sprot (1856) 27 L.T.(o.s.) 264; 2 Jur.(N.S.) 623; 2 Macq. 449; 4 W.R. 659 .... 101, 287

Callard v. Beeney [1930] 1 K.B. 353; 99 L.J.K.B. 133; 142 L.T. 45 .... 9, 12, 269, 282

Campbell v. Paddington Corpn. [1911] 1 K.B. 869; 80 L.J.K.B. 739; 104 L.T. 394; 27 T.L.R. 232; 75 J.P. 277; 9 L.G.R. 387 26

—— v. Wilson (1803) 3 East 294; 102 E.R. 610 .... 137, 143, 171, 178, **190**

Canham v. Fisk (1831) 2 Cr. & J. 126; 2 Tyr. 155; 1 L.J.Ex. 61; 149 E.R. 53   312

Cannon v. Villars (1878) 8 Ch.D. 415; 47 L.J.Ch. 597; 38 L.T. 939; 42 J.P. 516; 26 W.R. 751 .... 269, **270, 271,** 272

Capel v. Buszard (1829) 6 Bing. 150; 3 Y. & J. 344; 3 Moo. & P. 480; 130 E.R. 1237; *affirming sub nom.* Buszard v. Capel (1828) 8 B. & C. 141; 6 L.J.(o.s.)K.B. 267 .... 5, 49

Cardiff Corporation v. Cardiff Waterworks Co. (1859) 4 De G. & J. 596, L.JJ. (1859); 33 L.T.(o.s.) 104; 24 J.P. 21; 5 Jur.(N.S.) 953; 7 W.R. 386 ...   380

Carlyon v. Lovering (1857) 1 H. & N. 784; 26 L.J.Ex. 251; 28 L.T.(o.s.) 356; 156 E.R. 1417; 5 W.R. 347 .... 146, 230, 236

Carr v. Foster (1842) 3 Q.B. 581; 2 Gal. & Dav. 753; 11 L.J.Q.B. 284; 6 Jur. 837; 114 E.R. 629 .... 153, 154, 155, 339, 342

Cartwright v. Last [1876] W.N. 60 .... 254, 397

Cawkwell v. Russell (1856) 26 L.J.Ex. 34 347

Central Electricity Generating Board v. Jennaway [1959] 1 W.L.R. 937; 103 S.J. 635; [1959] 3 All E.R. 409 .... 44, 76

Chadwick v. Marsden (1867) L.R. 2 Exch. 285; 36 L.J.Ex. 177; 16 L.T. 666; 31 J.P. 535; 15 W.R. 964 58

PAGE

Chadwick v. Trower (1839) 6 Bing.N.C. 1; 8 Scott 1; 8 L.J.Ex. 286; 133 E.R. 1, Ex.Ch.; *reversing on other grounds sub nom.* Trower v. Chadwick (1836) 3 Bing.N.C. 334; 2 Hodg. 267; 3 Scott 699; 6 L.J.C.P. 47; 132 E.R. 439 375

Challender v. Royle (1887) 36 Ch.D. 425; 56 L.J.Ch. 995; 57 L.T. 734; 3 T.L.R. 790; 4 R.P.C. 363; 36 W.R. 357 387

Chamber Colliery Co. v. Hopwood (1886) 32 Ch.D. 549; 55 L.J.Ch. 859; 55 L.T. 449; 2 T.L.R. 507; 51 J.P. 164 .... 54, 147, 176, 178, 222, 224

Chandler v. Thompson (1811) 3 Camp. 80 .... 26, 238, 324

Chapman, Morsons & Co. v. Auckland Union Guardians (1889) 23 Q.B.D. 294; 58 L.J.Q.B. 504; 61 L.T. 446; 53 J.P. 820 391

Chappell v. Davidson (1856) 8 De G.M. & G. 1; *varying* (1855) 2 K. & J. 123; 69 E.R. 719 387

—— v. Mason (1894) 10 T.L.R. 404 .... **120**

Charles v. Finchley Local Board (1883) 23 Ch.D. 767; 52 L.J.Ch. 554; 48 L.T. 569; 47 J.P. 791; 31 W.R. 717 347

Chasemore v. Richards (1859) 7 H.L.C. 349; 29 L.J.Ex. 81; 33 L.T.(o.s.) 350; 23 J.P. 596; 5 Jur.(N.S.) 873; 11 E.R. 140; 7 W.R. 685 .... 26, 139, 186, 199, 203, 205, 210, 219–221, 294, 299

Chastey v. Ackland [1895] 2 Ch. 389; 64 L.J.Q.B. 523; 72 L.T. 845; 11 T.L.R. 460; 39 S.J. 582; 12 R. 420; 43 W.R. 627, C.A.; *varying* [1897] A.C. 155 .... 26, 258, 259, 398

Cheater v. Cater [1918] 1 K.B. 247 .... **305**

Cheetham v. Hampson (1791) 4 T.R. 318; 100 E.R. 1041 .... 38, 370

Chelsea Waterworks Co. v. Bowley (1851) 17 Q.B. 358; 20 L.J.Q.B. 520; 17 L.T.(o.s.) 284; 15 J.P. 450; 15 Jur. 1129; 117 E.R. 1316 30

Cherrington v. Abney (1709) 2 Vern. 646; 23 E.R. 1022 324

Chesterfield (Lord) v. Harris. *See* Harris v. Chesterfield (Earl of). 59

City of London Brewery Co. v. Tennant (1873) 9 Ch.App. 212; 43 L.J.Ch. 457; 29 L.T. 755; 38 J.P. 468; 22 W.R. 172 .... 244, 245, 252, 256

City of London Commissioners v. Central London Railway. *See* Land Tax Commissioners of London (City) v. Central London Railway.

Clapman v. Edwards [1938] 2 All E.R. 507; 82 S.J. 295 .... **20**, 56

Clark v. Barnes [1929] 2 Ch. 368; 99 L.J.Ch. 20; 142 L.T. 88 .... **129, 131, 132**

—— v. Cogge (1607) Cro.Jac. 170; 79 E.R. 149 117

Clarke v. Clark (1865) 1 Ch.App. 16; 35 L.J.Ch. 151; 13 L.T. 482, 30 J.P. 20; 11 Jur.(N.S.) 914; 14 W.R. 115 .... **242**, 243–245, 252

—— v. Somersetshire Drainage Commissioners (1888) 57 L.J.M.C. 96; 59 L.T. 670; 4 T.L.R. 539; 52 J.P.Jo. 308; 36 W.R. 890 58

Clavering's Case (prior to 1800) 5 Vesp. 690; 6 Hare 304n.; L.R. 10 Eq., p. 147; 31 E.R. 807 67

Clayton v. Corby (1842) 2 Q.B. 813; 2 Gal. & Dav. 174; 11 L.J.Q.B. 239; 114 E.R. 316 .... 156, 159, 161, 376

Clifford v. Hoare (1874) L.R. 9 C.P. 362; 43 L.J.C.P. 225; 30 L.T. 465; 22 W.R. 828 .... 5, 285, 353, 379

—— v. Holt [1899] 1 Ch. 698; 68 L.J.Ch. 332; 80 L.T. 48; 15 T.L.R. 86; 63 J.P. 22; 43 S.J. 113 .... 148, 239, 383

Clippens Oil Co. v. Edinburgh District Water Trustees [1904] A.C. 64; 73 L.J.P.C. 32; 89 L.T. 589 142

Clore v. Theatrical Properties Ltd. [1936] 3 All E.R. 483 56

Clowes v. Staffordshire Potteries Waterworks Co. (1872) 8 Ch.App. 125; 42 L.J.Ch. 107; 27 L.T. 521; 36 J.P. 760; 21 W.R. 32 381

Cockburn v. Smith [1924] 2 K.B. 119; 93 L.J.K.B. 764; 131 L.T. 334; 40 T.L.R. 476; 68 S.J. 631 47

Cockrane v. Verner (1895) 29 I.L.T. 571 27

Codling v. Johnson (1829) 9 B. & C. 933; 4 Man. & Ry.K.B. 671; 8 L.J. (o.s.)K.B. 68; 109 E.R. 347 .... 137, 169

Colchester Corpn. v. Brooke (1845) 7 Q.B. 339; 15 L.J.Q.B. 59; 5 L.T.(o.s.) 192; 9 Jur. 1090; 115 E.R. 518 358

Colebeck v. Girdlers' Co. (1876) 1 Q.B.D. 234; 45 L.J.Q.B. 225; 34 L.T. 350; 40 J.P. 596; 24 W.R. 577 .... 47, 301

Collins v. Slade (1874) 23 W.R. 199 .... 261, 273

Collis v. Amphlett [1920] A.C. 271, H.L.; *reversing* [1918] 1 Ch. 232, C.A.; *reversing* 62 S.J. 37 304

—— v. Laugher [1894] 3 Ch. 659; 63 L.J.Ch. 851; 71 L.T. 226; 8 R. 760; 43 W.R. 202 .... 148, 240

PAGE

Colls v. Home & Colonial Stores [1904] A.C. 179; 73 L.J.Ch. 484; 90 L.T.
    687; 20 T.L.R. 475; 53 W.R. 30; *reversing* [1902] 1 Ch. 302 ...... 147, 148,
        152, 153, 155, 172, 177, 239, 240, 243, 245, 246,
        247–251, **252**, 253, **254**, 320, **324**, 328, 329, 331–333,
        336, 354, 375, 384, 391, 392, **393**, 394, 395, **396–398**
Colwell v. St. Pancras Borough Council [1904] 1 Ch. 707; 73 L.J.Ch. 275; 90
    L.T. 153; 20 T.L.R. 236; 68 J.P. 286; 2 L.G.R. 518; 52 W.R. 523 ...   366
Cook v. Bath Corporation (1868) L.R. 6 Eq. 177; 18 L.T. 123; 32 J.P. 741 ... 339,
        341
Cooke v. Chilcott (1876) 3 Ch.D. 694; 34 L.T. 207   38
—— v. Forbes (1867) L.R. 5 Eq. 166; 37 L.J.Ch. 178; 17 L.T. 371   382
—— v. Ingram (1893) 68 L.T. 671; 3 R. 607 ....   85, 286
Copeland v. Greenhalf [1952] Ch. 488; [1952] 1 T.L.R. 786; 96 S.J. 261;
    [1952] 1 All E.R. 809 ....   19, 31, **32, 33,** 34, 375
Cooper v. Barber (1810) 3 Taunt. 99; 128 E.R. 40   218
—— v. Crabtree (1882) 20 Ch.D. 589; 51 L.J.Ch. 544; 47 L.T. 5; 46 J.P.
    628; 30 W.R. 649, C.A.; *affirming* (1881) 19 Ch.D. 193 .... 366, 368
—— v. Hubbuck (1860) 30 Beav. 160; 31 L.J.Ch. 123; 25 J.P. 452; 7 Jur.
    (N.S.) 457; 9 W.R. 352; 54 E.R. 849 ....   325, 388
—— v. —— (1862) 12 C.B.(N.S.) 456; 31 L.J.C.P. 323; 6 L.T. 826; 9 Jur.
    (N.S.) 575; 142 E.R. 1220 ....   150, 153, 255
—— v. Straker (1888) 40 Ch.D. 21; 58 L.J.Ch. 26; 59 L.T. 849; 5 T.L.R.
    53; 37 W.R. 137 ....   148, 240
Corbett v. Hill (1870) L.R. 9 Eq. 671; 39 L.J.Ch. 547; 22 L.T. 263   306
—— v. Jonas [1892] 3 Ch. 137; 62 L.J.Ch. 43; 67 L.T. 191; 3 R. 25   92
Corby v. Hill (1858) 4 C.B.(N.S.) 556; 27 L.J.C.P. 318; 31 L.T.(O.S.) 181; 22
    J.P. 386; 4 Jur.(N.S.) 512; 6 W.R. 575; 140 E.R. 1209   369
Cordell v. Second Clanfield Properties Ltd. [1969] 1 Ch. 9; [1968] 3 W.L.R.
    864; 112 S.J. 841; [1968] 3 All E.R. 746; 19 P. & C.R. 848 ...... 16, 80, 387
Cory v. Davies [1923] 2 Ch. 95; 92 L.J.Ch. 261; 129 L.T. 208; 39 T.L.R.
    268; 67 S.J. 517 ....   21, **68, 69,** 107, 111, 163
Costagliola v. English (1969) 210 E.G. 1425   342
Cotching v. Bassett (1862) 32 Beav. 101; 32 L.J.Ch. 286; 9 Jur.(N.S.) 590; 11
    W.R. 197; 55 E.R. 40 ....   **63**
Cotterell v. Griffiths (1801) 4 Esp. 69   324
Coulson v. White (1743) 3 Atk. 21; 26 E.R. 816   382
Courtauld v. Legh (1869) L.R. 4 Exch. 126; 38 L.J.Ex. 45; 19 L.T. 737;
    17 W.R. 466 ....   148, 240
Cousens v. Rose (1871) L.R. 12 Eq. 366; 24 L.T. 820; 19 W.R. 792 ....   **271**
Coutts v. Gorham (1829) Moo. & M. 396 ....   **115**
Cowen v. Truefitt Ltd. [1899] 2 Ch. 309; 68 L.J.Ch. 563; 81 L.T. 104; 43
    S.J. 622; 47 W.R. 661, C.A.; *affirming* [1898] 2 Ch. 551   284
Cowley v. Byas (1877) 5 Ch.D. 944; 37 L.T. 238; 41 J.P. 804; 26 W.R. 1 ...   384
Cowling v. Higginson (1838) 4 M. & W. 245; 1 Horn. & H. 269; 7 L.J.Ex.
    265; 150 E.R. 1240 ....   262, **265, 266,** 268
Cowper v. Laidler [1903] 2 Ch. 337; 72 L.J.Ch. 578; 89 L.T. 469;
    sub nom. Cooper v. Laidlek, 47 S.J. 548; 51 W.R. 539 ...... 360, 381, 388,
        390, 391
Cox v. Matthews (1673) 1 Vent. 237; 3 Keb. 133; 86 E.R. 160   218
Craven v. Pridmore (1902) 18 T.L.R. 282   304
Crisp v. Martin (1876) 2 P.D. 15 ....   36, 146
Crofts v. Haldane (1867) L.R. 2 Q.B. 194; 8 B. & S. 194; 36 L.J.Q.B. 85;
    16 L.T. 116; 31 J.P. 358; 15 W.R. 444   315
Cross v. Lewis (1824) 2 B. & C. 686; 4 Dow. & Ry.K.B. 234; 2 L.J.(O.S.)
    K.B. 136; 107 E.R. 538 ....   164, **183, 184,** 185
Crossley & Sons Ltd. v. Lightowler (1867) L.R. 2 Ch.App. 478; 36
    L.J.Ch. 584; 16 L.T. 438; 15 W.R. 801; *affirming with variations*
    (1866) L.R. 3 Eq. 279 ...... 57, **106,** 109, 191, 206, 209, 229, 230, **342, 343**
Crow v. Wood [1971] 1 Q.B. 77; [1970] 3 W.L.R. 517; 114 S.J. 474;
    [1970] 3 All E.R. 425; 21 P. & C.R. 929 ....   **40–42,** 128
Crowhurst v. Amersham Burial Board (1878) 4 Ex.D. 5; 48 L.J.Q.B. 109;
    39 L.T. 355; 27 W.R. 95   305
Crumbie v. Wallsend Local Board [1891] 1 Q.B. 503; 60 L.J.Q.B. 392;
    64 L.T. 490; 7 T.L.R. 229; 55 J.P. 421 ....   290, 369
Crump v. Lambert (1867) 17 L.T. 133; *affirming* L.R. 3 Eq. 409; 15 L.T.
    600; 31 J.P. 485; 15 W.R. 417 ....   36, 191, 366

PAGE

Cubitt v. Porter (1828) 8 B. & C. 257; 2 Man. & Ry.K.B. 267; 6 L.J.(o.s.)
K.B. 306; 108 E.R. 1039 .... 302, **303**
Cummins v. Perkins [1899] 1 Ch. 16; 68 L.J.Ch. 57; 79 L.T. 456; 43 S.J.
112; 47 W.R. 214 386
Curriers' Co. v. Corbett (1865) 4 De G.J. & Sm. 764; 2 Drew. & Sm.
355; 5 New Rep. 458; 12 L.T. 169; 29 J.P. 469; 62 E.R. 656;
13 W.R. 538 .... 243, **260,** 325

DAKIN v. Cornish (1845) cited in 6 Exch. at p. 360; 155 E.R. 582 204
Dalton v. Angus (1881) 6 App.Cas. 740; 46 J.P. 132; 30 W.R. 191, H.L.;
sub nom. Public Works Commrs. v. Angus & Co., Dalton v.
Angus & Co., 50 L.J.Q.B. 639; 44 L.T. 844; affirming sub nom.
Angus v. Dalton (1878) 4 Q.B.D. 162 C.A.; reversing (1877) 3 Q.B.D.
85 .... **24,** 26, 27, 37, 101, **134,** 136, 137, **138–141,** 142–144, 146,
168, 174, 175, **179, 180,** 186, **187,** 259, 287, 290,
292–300, 324, 346, 372
Damper v. Bassett [1901] 2 Ch. 350; 70 L.J.Ch. 657; 84 L.T. 682; 17 T.L.R.
537; 45 S.J. 537; 49 W.R. 536 .... 147, 188, 367
Dances Way, West Town, Hayling Island, Re [1962] Ch. 490; [1962] 2
W.L.R. 815; sub nom. Freehold Land in Dances Way, West Town,
Hayling Island, Hants, Re [1962] 2 All E.R. 42; sub nom. Gilbert's
Application, Re, 106 S.J. 111 196
Dand v. Kingscote (1840) 6 M. & W. 174; 2 Ry. & Can.Cas. 27; 9 L.J.Ex.
279; 151 E.R. 370 .... 44, 273
Daniel v. Anderson (1861) 31 L.J.Ch. 610; 7 L.T. 183; 8 Jur.(N.S.) 328;
10 W.R. 366 77
—— v. Ferguson [1891] 2 Ch. 27; 39 W.R. 599 387
—— v. Hanslip (1672) 2 Lev. 67; sub nom. Leniel v. Harslop (1672) 3 Keb.
66; 84 E.R. 597 60
—— v. North (1809) 11 East 372; 103 E.R. 1047 ...... 161, 164, 181, **182,** 184, 368
Dare v. Heathcote (1856) 25 L.J.Ex. 245 266
Darley Main Colliery Co. v. Mitchell (1886) 11 App.Cas. 127; 55 L.J.Q.B.
529; 54 L.T. 882; 2 T.L.R. 301; 51 J.P. 148 .... 290, 369
Dartmouth v. Roberts (1812) 16 East. 334; 104 E.R. 1116 137
Davenport v. Rylands (1865) L.R. 1 Eq. 302; 35 L.J.Ch. 204; 14 L.T. 53;
12 Jur.(N.S.) 71; 14 W.R. 243 391
Davey v. Harrow Corporation [1958] 1 Q.B. 60 .... 304, 305
Davies v. Du Paver [1953] 1 Q.B. 184; [1952] 2 T.L.R. 890; 96 S.J. 849;
[1952] 2 All E.R. 991 .... 154, 158, 183, **185, 186**
—— v. Marshall (1861) 10 C.B.(N.S.) 697; 31 L.J.C.P. 61; 4 L.T. 581; 7
Jur.(N.S.) 1247; 9 W.R. 866; 142 E.R. 627 316
—— v. —— (No. 1) (1861) 1 Dr. & Sm. 557; 4 L.T. 105; 25 J.P. 548;
7 Jur.(N.S.) 720; 9 W.R. 368 .... 115, 325
—— v. Sear (1869) L.R. 7 Eq. 427; 38 L.J.Ch. 545; 20 L.T. 56; 17 W.R.
390 .... **63, 64,** 118
—— v. Stephens (1836) 7 C. & P. 570 184
—— v. Thomas [1899] W.N. 244 .... 78, 102
—— v. Williams (1851) 16 Q.B. 546; 20 L.J.Q.B. 330; 15 J.P. 550; 15 Jur.
752; 117 E.R. 988 .... 153, 356–358
Davis v. Marrable [1913] 2 Ch. 421; 82 L.J.Ch. 510; 109 L.T. 33; 29 T.L.R.
617; 57 S.J. 702 248
—— v Morgan (1825) 4 B. & C. 8; 6 Dow. & Ry.K.B. 42; 107 E.R. 962 ... 323
—— v. Treharne (1881) 6 App.Cas. 460; 50 L.J.Q.B. 665; 29 W.R. 869 287
Dawney v. Dee (1620) Cro.Jac. 605; 79 E.R. 517; sub nom. Dawtree v.
Dee, J.Brdg. 4; Palm. 46; 2 Roll.Rep. 139 380
Dawson v. M'Groggan [1903] 1 Ir.R. 92 .... 141, 178
—— v. Norfolk (1815) 1 Price 246; 145 E.R. 1391 174
Day v. Brownrigg (1878) 10 Ch.D. 294; 48 L.J.Ch. 173; 39 L.T. 553;
27 W.R. 217 386
Deacon v. South Eastern Railway (1889) 61 L.T. 377 .... 117, 285, 354
Deed (John S.) & Sons Ltd. v. British Electricity Authority (1950) 66
T.L.R. (Pt. 2) 567; 114 J.P. 533; 49 L.G.R. 107 54
De la Warr (Earl) v. Miles (1881) 17 Ch.D. 535; 50 L.J.Ch. 754; 44 L.T.
487; 29 W.R. 809 .... 139, 153, 172, 177, 178
Denaby v. Anson [1911] 1 K.B. 171; 80 L.J.K.B. 320; 103 L.T. 349; 26
T.L.R. 667; 54 S.J. 748; 11 Asp.M.L.C. 471 237

PAGE

Dent v. Auction Mart Co. (1866) L.R. 2 Eq. 238; 35 L.J.Ch. 555; 14 L.T.
  827; 30 J.P. 661; 12 Jur.(N.S.) 447; 14 W.R. 709 .... 241, 243, **248**, 256,
                                                      258, **259**, 324, 395, 398
De Romana v. Roberts [1906] P. 332 .... 14, 15
Derry v. Sanders [1919] 1 K.B. 223; 88 L.J.K.B. 410; 120 L.T. 194; 35
  T.L.R. 105; 63 S.J. 115 21
Devonshire (Duke) v. Elgin (1851) 14 Beav. 530; 20 L.J.Ch. 495; 51 E.R. 389   67
Dewell (Duell) v. Sanders (1618) Cro.Jac. 490; 2 Roll.Rep. 3; 79 E.R. 419 ... 191
Dewhirst v. Wrigley (1834) Coop.Pr.Cas. 329; 47 E.R. 529   218
Dicker v. Popham, Radford & Co. (1890) 63 L.T. 379 .... **248**, 391
Dickinson v. Grand Junction Canal Co., The (1852) 7 Exch. 282; 21 L.J.Ex.
  241; 18 L.T.(O.S.) 258; 16 Jur. 200; 155 E.R. 953 .... 210, 220
——— v. Harbottle (1873) 28 L.T. 186   253
Dimes v. Petley (1850) 15 Q.B. 276; 19 L.J.Q.B. 449; 16 L.T.(O.S.) 1; 14
  J.P. 653; 14 Jur. 1132; 117 E.R. 462 .... **358**
Dobson v. Blackmore (1847) 9 Q.B. 991; 16 L.J.Q.B. 233; 11 J.P. 601;
  11 Jur. 556; 115 E.R. 1554 365
Dodd v. Holme (1834) 1 Ad. & El. 493; 3 Nev. & M.K.B. 739; 110 E.R. 1296 175
Doe d. Putland v. Hilder (1819) 2 B. & Ald. 782; 106 E.R. 551 .... **337, 338**
——— d. Fenwick v. Reed (1821) 5 B. & Ald. 232; 106 E.R. 1177 ...... 137, 378
——— d. Egremont (Earl) v. Williams (1848) 11 Q.B. 688; 17 L.J.Q.B. 154;
  11 L.T.(O.S.) 27; 12 Jur. 455; 116 E.R. 631 235
——— d. Hanley v. Wood (1819) 2 B. & Ald. 724; 106 E.R. 529   13
Doherty v. Allman (1873) 3 A.C. 709; 39 L.T. 129; 42 J.P. 788; 26
  W.R. 513 381
——— v. Beasley (1835) 1 Jones Exch.Rep.(Ir.) 123 .... **339**
Donnelly v. Adams [1905] 1 I.R. 154 .... **98**, 284
Donoghue v. Stevenson [1932] A.C. 562; 101 L.J.P.C. 119; 147 L.T. 281;
  48 T.L.R. 494; 76 S.J. 396; 37 Com.Cas. 850 292
Dovaston v. Payne (1795) 2 H.Bl. 527; 126 E.R. 684   7
Drewell v. Towler (1832) 3 B. & Ad. 735; 1 L.J.K.B. 228; 110 E.R. 268 ...   35
Drewett v. Sheard (1836) 7 C. & P. 465 338
Dreyfus v. Peruvian Guano Co. See Peruvian Guano Co. v. Dreyfus
  Brothers & Co.
Drury v. Army & Navy Auxiliary Co-operative Society [1896] 2 Q.B.
  271; 65 L.J.M.C. 169; 74 L.T. 621; 12 T.L.R. 404; 60 J.P. 421;
  40 S.J. 545; 44 W.R. 560 302
Dudden v. Clutton Union Guardians (1857) 1 H. & N. 627; 26 L.J.Ex.
  146; 156 E.R. 1353 .... 214, 227
Dudley Corporation, Re (1881) L.R. 8 Q.B.D. 86; 51 L.J.Q.B. 121; 45
  L.T. 733; 46 J.P. 340 76
Duncan v. Louch (1845) 6 Q.B. 904; 14 L.J.Q.B. 185; 4 L.T.(O.S.) 356;
  9 Jur. 346; 115 E.R. 341 .... 28, 45, 46, 261
Dunn v. Blackdown Properties Ltd. [1961] Ch. 433; [1961] 2 W.L.R. 618;
  125 J.P. 397; 105 S.J. 257; [1961] 2 All E.R. 62 .... 16, **49–51**, 52
Dunster v. Hollis [1918] 2 K.B. 795; 88 L.J.K.B. 331; 120 L.T. 109;
  17 L.G.R. 42 47
Durell v. Pritchard (1865) 1 Ch.App. 244; 35 L.J.Ch. 223; 13 L.T. 545;
  14 W.R. 212; sub nom. Darrell v. Pritchard, 12 Jur.(N.S.) 16 ... 243, 382, 383
Durham & Sunderland Ry. v. Walker (1842) 2 Q.B. 940; 3 Ry. & Can.Cas.
  36; 2 Gal. & Dav. 326; 114 E.R. 364; sub nom. Wallis v. Harrison,
  Durham & Sunderland Ry. Co. v. Walker, 11 L.J.Ex. 440   80
Dutton v. Tayler (1700) 2 Lut. 1487; 125 E.R. 819 117
Dyce v. Lady James Hay (1852) 1 Macq. 305 .... 30, 34
Dyer v. Mousley (1962) unreported; Bar Library transcript No. 315 272
Dyer's Co. v. King (1870) L.R. 9 Eq. 438; 39 L.J.Ch. 339; 22 L.T. 120;
  34 J.P. 373; 18 W.R. 404 .... 247, 331, 336
Dysart (Earl) v. Hammerton [1916] A.C. 57; reversing [1914] 1 Ch. 822 ... 143

E. & G. C. Ltd. v. Bate (1935) 79 L.J. newspaper 203 .... 38, 48
Eaden v. Firth (1863) 1 H. & M. 573; 71 E.R. 251 380
Eagle v. Charing Cross Ry. (1867) L.R. 2 C.P. 638; 36 L.J.C.P. 297;
  16 L.T. 593; 15 W.R. 1016 315
East India Co. v. Vincent (1740) 2 Atk. 83; 26 E.R. 451 .... **67**, 324
East Stonehouse U. D. C. v. Willoughby Brothers Ltd. [1902] 2 K.B. 318;
  71 L.J.K.B. 873; 87 L.T. 366; 50 W.R. 698 .... 141, 143, **164**

PAGE

Easton v. Isted [1903] 1 Ch. 405; 72 L.J.Ch. 189; 87 L.T. 705; 47 S.J. 158; 51 W.R. 245 .... 150, 239
Eaton v. Swansea Waterworks Co. (1851) 17 Q.B. 267; 20 L.J.Q.B. 482; 17 L.T.(o.s.) 154; 15 Jur. 675; 117 E.R. 1282 .... 154, 172, 174
Ecclesiastical Commissioners for England v. Kino (1880) 14 Ch.D. 213; 49 L.J.Ch. 529; 42 L.T. 201; 28 W.R. 544 .... 22, 147, 167, 244, 252, 317, **319**, 335
Edwards (Job) v. Birmingham Navigations [1924] 1 K.B. 341; 93 L.J.K.B. 261; 130 L.T. 522; 40 T.L.R. 88; 68 S.J. 501 .... 357, 360
Egremont v. Pulman (1829) Mood & M. 404 365
Eldridge v. Knott (1774) 1 Cowp. 214; 98 E.R. 1050 137
Ellenborough Park, Re, Davies, decd., Re, Powell v. Maddison [1956] Ch. 131; [1955] 3 W.L.R. 892; 99 S.J. 870; [1955] 3 All E.R. 667 .... 6, **16–19**, 25, 27, 28, **29, 30**, 34
Elliotson v. Feetham (1835) 2 Bing.N.C. 134 .... 36, 191
Elliott v. Burn [1935] A.C. 84; 103 L.J.K.B. 578; 151 L.T. 526; 50 T.L.R. 556; 78 S.J. 550; 18 T.C. 595 37
—— v. North Eastern Ry. (1863) 10 H.L.Cas. 333; 2 New Rep. 87; 32 L.J.Ch. 402; 8 L.T. 337; 27 J.P. 564; 9 Jur.(n.s.) 555; 11 W.R. 604; 11 E.R. 1055, H.L.; verying sub nom. North Eastern Ry. v. Elliott (1860) 1 J. & H. 145; 2 De G.F. & J. 423, L.C. 227, 287, 380
Ellis v. Sheffield Co. (1853) 2 E. & B. 767; 2 C.L.R. 249; 23 L.J.Q.B. 42; 22 L.T.(o.s.) 84; 17 J.P. 823; 18 Jur. 146; 118 E.R. 955; 2 W.R. 19 371
Elmore v. Pirrie (1887) 57 L.T. 333 390
Elwood v. Bullock (1844) 6 Q.B. 383; 13 L.J.Q.B. 330; 8 J.P. 473; 8 Jur. 1044; 115 E.R. 147 339
Embrey v. Owen (1851) 6 Exch. 353; 20 L.J.Ex. 212; 17 L.T.(o.s.) 79; 15 Jur. 623; 155 E.R. 579 .... **200**, 201, 204, 205, 209, 220, 379
English v. Metropolitan Water Board [1907] 1 K.B. 588; 76 L.J.K.B. 361; 96 L.T. 573; 23 T.L.R. 313; 71 J.P. 313; 5 L.G.R. 384 ...... 211, 213
Ennor v. Barwell (1860) 2 Giff. 410; 3 L.T. 170; 25 J.P. 54; 6 Jur.(n.s.) 1233; 66 E.R. 171 214
Erskine v. Adeane (1873) 8 Ch.App. 756; 42 L.J.Ch. 835; 29 L.T. 234; 38 J.P. 20; 21 W.R. 802 305
Espley v. Wilkes (1872) L.R. 7 Exch. 298; 41 L.J.Ex. 241; 26 L.T. 918 ...... **85**
Evans' Contract, Re, Evans v. Deed [1970] 1 W.L.R. 583; 114 S.J. 189; [1970] 1 All E.R. 1236; 21 P. & C.R. 268 .... 193, 194
Ewart v. Belfast Guardians (1881) 9 L.R.Ir. 172 214
—— v. Cochrane (1861) 5 L.T. 1; 25 J.P. 612; 7 Jur.(n.s.) 925; 4 Macq. 117; 10 W.R. 3 99
—— v. Graham (1859) 7 H.L.C. 331; 29 L.J.Ex. 88; 33 L.T.(o.s.) 349; 23 J.P. 483; 5 Jur.(n.s.) 773; 11 E.R. 132; 7 W.R. 621 4
Exeter Corporation v. Devon (Earl) (1870) L.R. 10 Eq. 232; 23 L.T. 382; 34 J.P. 804; 18 W.R. 879 236

Farrell v. Coogan (1890) 12 L.R.Ir. 14 377
Fay v. Prentice (1845) 1 C.B. 828; 14 L.J.C.P. 298; 5 L.T.(o.s.) 216; 9 Jur. 876; 135 E.R. 769 .... 222, 223, 360, 363
Fear v. Morgan. See Morgan v. Fear.
Ferguson v. Wilson (1866) 2 Ch.App. 77; 15 L.T. 230; 30 J.P. 788; 12 Jur.(n.s.) 912; 15 W.R. 80 388
Finch v. Great Western Ry. (1879) 5 Ex.D. 254; 41 L.T. 731; 44 J.P. 8; 28 W.R. 229 .... 75, 262, **275, 276**, 279
Finlinson v. Porter (1875) L.R. 10 Q.B. 188; 44 L.J.Q.B. 56; 32 L.T. 391; 39 J.P. 661; 23 W.R. 315 .... 44, 235
Fishenden v. Higgs & Hill Ltd. (1935) 153 L.T. 128; 79 S.J. 434 .... 247, 252, 385, 392, **394**, 395, 397
Fisher v. Moon (1865) 11 L.T. 623 316
—— v. Winch [1939] 1 K.B. 666; 108 L.J.K.B. 473; 160 L.T. 347; 55 T.L.R. 553; 83 S.J. 192; [1939] 2 All E.R. 144 304
Fishmongers' Co. v. East India Co. (1752) 1 Dick. 163; 21 E.R. 232 ... 26, **241**
Fitzgerald v. Firbank [1897] 2 Ch. 96; 66 L.J.Ch. 529; 76 L.T. 584; 13 T.L.R. 390; 41 S.J. 490 .... 230, 374
Fitzhardinge (Lord) v. Purcell [1908] 2 Ch. 139; 77 L.J.Ch. 529; 99 L.T. 154; 24 T.L.R. 564; 72 J.P. 276 4

PAGE

Fitzwilliam's (Earl) Collieries Co. v. Phillips [1943] A.C. 570; 112 L.J.K.B. 554; 169 L.T. 242; 59 T.L.R. 389; 87 S.J. 298; 25 T.C. 430; [1943] 2 All E.R. 346 37
Flanigan & McGarvey & Thompson's Contract, Re, [1945] N.I. 32 .... **115**
Fletcher v. Bealey (1884) 28 Ch.D. 688; 54 L.J.Ch. 424; 52 L.T. 541; 1 T.L.R. 233; 33 W.R. 745 384
—— v. Rodgers (1878) 27 W.R. 97 386
Flight v. Thomas (1841) 8 Cl. & Fin. 231; affirming (1840) 11 Ad. & El. 688; 3 Per. & Dav. 442; 113 E.R. 575; affirming (1839) 10 Ad. & El. 590; 7 Dowl. 741; 2 Per. & Dav. 531; 8 L.J.Q.B. 337; 3 Jur. 822; 113 E.R. 224 .... 152, 154, 191
Flynn v. Harte [1913] 2 Ir.R. 322 .... 164, 167, 354
Foley's Charity Trustees v. Dudley [1910] 1 K.B. 317; 79 L.J.K.B. 410; 102 L.T. 1; 74 J.P. 413; 8 L.G.R. 320 143
Foster v. London, Chatham & Dover Ry. [1895] 1 Q.B. 711; 64 L.J.Q.B. 65; 71 L.T. 855; 11 T.L.R. 89; 39 S.J. 95; 14 R. 27; 43 W.R. 116 ... 149, 238
—— v. Lyons & Co. [1927] 1 Ch. 219; 96 L.J.Ch. 79; 136 L.T. 372; 70 S.J. 1182 149
—— v. Richmond (1910) 9 L.G.R. 65 35
—— v. Warblington U. D. C. [1906] 1 K.B. 648; 75 L.J.K.B. 514; 94 L.T. 876; 22 T.L.R. 421; 70 J.P. 233; 4 L.G.R. 735; 54 W.R. 575 192
Fowler v. Sanders (1618) Cro.Jac. 446; 79 E.R. 382 191
Fowlers v. Walker (1881) 51 L.J.Ch. 443 336
Fox v. Clarke (1874) L.R. 9 Q.B. 565; 43 L.J.Q.B. 178; 30 L.T. 646; 22 W.R. 774 302
Foxall v. Venables (1590) Cro.Eliz. 180; 78 E.R. 436 169
Francis v. Hayward (1882) 22 Ch.D. 177; 52 L.J.Ch. 291; 48 L.T. 297; 47 J.P. 517; 31 W.R. 488; affirming (1882) 20 Ch.D. 773 ... **34**, 35, 302, 306
Frechette v. Compagnie Manufacturière de St. Hyacinthe (1883) 9 App.Cas. 170; 53 L.J.P.C. 20; 50 L.T. 62 .... 57, **328**
Frewen v. Philipps (1861) 11 C.B.(N.S.) 449; 30 L.J.C.P. 356; 25 J.P. 676; 7 Jur(N.S.) 1246; 142 E.R. 871; 9 W.R. 786 .... 149, **183**
Fritz v. Hobson (1880) 14 Ch.D. 542; 49 L.J.Ch. 321; 42 L.T. 225; 24 S.J. 366; 28 W.R. 459 391
Frogley v. Lovelace (Earl) (1859) John. 333; 70 E.R. 450 69
Fullwood v. Fullwood (1878) 9 Ch.D. 176; 47 L.J.Ch. 459; 26 W.R. 435 ... 381

GALE v. Abbott (1862) 8 Jur.(N.S.) 987; 6 L.T. 852; 26 J.P. 563; 10 W.R. 748 .... **258**, 362
Gamble v. Birch Island Estates Ltd. (1971) 13 D.L.R. (3d) 657 .... 8, 282
Gandy v. Jubber (1864) 5 B. & S. 485; 3 New Rep. 569; 9 B. & S. 15; 33 L.J.Q.B. 151; 9 L.T. 800; 28 J.P. 517; 10 Jur.(N.S.) 652; 122 E.R. 762; 12 W.R. 526 370
Gardner v. Hodgson's Kingston Brewery Co. [1903] A.C. 229; 72 L.J.Ch. 558; 88 L.T. 698; 19 T.L.R. 458; 52 W.R. 17; affirming [1901] 2 Ch. 198; reversing [1900] 1 Ch. 592 ...... 137, 143, 144, 147, 161, 172, 177, 189, 239, 346, 375, 378
Garritt v. Sharp (1835) 3 A. & E. 325; 1 Har. & W. 220; 4 Nev. & M.K.B. 834; 111 E.R. 437 .... 239, 324, 325, 337
Gaskin v. Balls (1879) 13 Ch.D. 324; 28 W.R. 552 .... 383, 386, 388, 391
Gately v. Martin [1900] 2 Ir.R. 269 .... 175, 301
Gaved v. Martyn (1865) 19 C.B.(N.S.) 732; 34 L.J.C.P. 353; 13 L.T. 74; 11 Jur.(N.S.) 1017; 144 E.R. 974; 14 W.R. 62 .... **54**, **55**, 147, 170, 176, 177, **203**, 224, 236
Gaw v. Córas Iompair Éireann [1952] 89 I.L.T. 124; [1953] Ir.R. 232 ... 13, **48**, 49
Gayford v. Moffatt (1868) 4 Ch.App. 133; 33 J.P. 212 .... 21, **119**, 167, 170
—— v. Nicholls (1854) 9 Ex. 702; 2 C.L.R. 1066; 23 L.J.Ex. 205; 18 J.P. 441; 156 E.R. 371
General Estates Co. v. Beaver [1914] 3 K.B. 918; 84 L.J.K.B. 21; 111 L.T. 957; 30 T.L.R. 634; 79 J.P. 41; 12 L.G.R. 1146 .... 142, 143
Geoghegan v. Henry [1922] 2 Ir.R. 1 354
Gerrard v. Cooke (1806) 2 Bos. & Pul.N.R. 109; 127 E.R. 565 44
Gifford v. Dent [1926] W.N. 336; 71 S.J. 83 306
Giles v. Walker (1890) 24 Q.B.D. 656; 59 L.J.Q.B. 416; 62 L.T. 933; 54 J.P. 599; 38 W.R. 782 305

PAGE

Glover v. Coleman (1874) L.R. 10 C.P. 108; 44 L.J.C.P. 66; 31 L.T. 684;
23 W.R. 163 154
Godwin v. Schweppes Ltd. [1902] 1 Ch. 926; 71 L.J.Ch. 438; 86 L.T. 377;
50 W.R. 409 .... 4, **104,** 124
Goldberg v. Edwards [1950] Ch. 247; 94 S.J. 128 .... **96,** 124,, **127**
Goldsack v. Shore [1950] 1 K.B. 708; 66 T.L.R. (Pt. 1) 636; 94 S.J. 192;
[1950] 1 All E.R. 276 56
Goldsmid v. Great Eastern Ry. (1884) 9 App.Cas. 927; 54 L.J.Ch. 162;
52 L.T. 270; 49 J.P. 260; 33 W.R. 81; affirming (1884) 25 Ch.D. 511 189
—— v. Tunbridge Wells Improvement Commissioners (1866) L.R. 1
Ch.App. 349; 35 L.J.Ch. 382; 14 L.T. 154; 30 J.P. 419; 12 Jur.(N.S.)
308; 14 W.R. 562 .... 176, 191, 231
Gonty & Manchester, Sheffield & Lincolnshire Ry., Re [1896] 2 Q.B. 439;
65 L.J.Q.B. 625; 75 L.T. 239; 12 T.L.R. 617, 620; 40 S.J. 715;
45 W.R. 83 76
Goodhart v. Hyett (1883) 25 Ch.D. 182; 53 L.J.Ch. 219; 50 L.T. 95;
48 J.P. 293; 32 W.R. 165 .... 16, **45**
Goodman v. Saltash Corporation (1882) 7 App.Cas. 633; 52 L.J.Q.B. 193;
48 L.T. 239; 47 J.P. 276; 31 W.R. 293 .... 141, 143, 161
Goodman and Gore's Case (1653) 2 Rolle's Abr. 704; Godb. 189; 10
C.B.(N.S.) 274; 142 E.R. 457 .... **257**
Goodtitle v. Baldwin (1809) 11 East 488; 103 E.R. 1092 143
Gotobed v. Pridmore (1970) 115 S.J. 78 342
Graham v. Campbell (1878) 7 Ch.D. 490; 47 L.J.Ch. 593; 38 L.T. 195;
26 W.R. 336 387
Grand Hotel, Eastbourne Ltd. v. White (1913) 84 L.J.Ch. 938; 110 L.T. 209;
58 S.J. 117; affirming sub nom. White v. Grand Hotel, Eastbourne,
Ltd. [1913] 1 Ch. 113; affirming (1912) 106 L.T. 785 .... **68,** 274, 275,
278, 279
Grand Junction Co. v. Shugar (1871) 6 Ch.App. 483; 24 L.T. 402; 35 J.P.
660; 19 W.R. 569 213
Grant v. Edmondson [1913] 1 Ch. 1; 100 L.J.Ch. 1; 143 L.T. 749 47–49
Gray v. Bond (1821) 2 Brod. and Bing. 667; 5 Moore C.P. 527; 129 E.R.
1123 .... 35, 161, 181, 184
—— v. Pullen (1864) 5 B. & S. 970; 5 New Rep. 249; 34 L.J.Q.B. 265;
11 L.T. 569; 29 J.P. 69; 13 W.R. 257; 122 E.R. 1091 371
Great Western Ry. v. Talbot [1902] 2 Ch. 759; 71 L.J.Ch. 835; 87 L.T.
405; 18 T.L.R. 775; 51 W.R. 312 .... 76, 280
Greatrex v. Hayward (1853) 8 Exch. 291; 22 L.J.Ex. 137; 155 E.R.
1357 .... 54, 223, 227, 228
Green v. Ashco Horticulturalist Ltd. [1966] 1 W.L.R. 889; 110 S.J.
271; [1966] 2 All E.R. 232 .... 22, 128, 129, 131
—— v. Matthews & Co. (1930) 46 T.L.R. 206 .... 141, 168, 189, 190
Greenslade v. Halliday (1830) 6 Bing. 379; 4 Moo. & P. 71; 8 L.J.(O.S.)C.P.
124; 130 E.R. 1326 .... 57, 219, 357, 358
Greenwell v. Low Beechburn Coal Co. [1897] 2 Q.B. 165; 66 L.J.Q.B. 643;
76 L.T. 759; 13 T.L.R. 471 290
Greenwood v. Hornsey (1886) 33 Ch.D. 471; 55 L.J.Ch. 917; 55 L.T. 135;
35 W.R. 163 .... 319, 336, 386, 387, 391
Gregg v. Richards [1926] Ch. 521; 95 L.J.Ch. 209; 135 L.T. 75; 70 S.J. 443 **130**
Greyvenstein v. Hattingh [1911] A.C. 355; 80 L.J.P.C. 158; 104 L.T.
360; 27 T.L.R. 358 236
Griffith v. Blake (1884) 27 Ch.D. 474; 53 L.J.Ch. 965; 51 L.T. 274;
32 W.R. 833 387
—— v. Richard Clay & Sons Ltd. [1912] 2 Ch. 291; 81 L.J.Ch. 809;
106 L.T. 963 240
Grimley v. Minister of Housing and Local Government [1971] 2 Q.B. 96;
[1971] 2 W.L.R. 449; (1970) 115 S.J. 341; [1971] 2 All E.R. 431;
22 P. & C.R. 339; 69 L.G.R. 238 .... **301**
Grimstead v. Marlowe (1792) 4 Term Rep. 717; 100 E.R. 1263 .... 169, 375
Grosvenor Hotel Co. v. Hamilton [1894] 2 Q.B. 836; 63 L.J.Q.B. 661;
71 L.T. 362; 10 T.L.R. 506; 42 W.R. 626; 9 R. 819 89
Guest's Estates Ltd. v. Milner's Safes Ltd. (1911) 28 T.L.R. 59 354
Guilford (Earl) v. St. George's Golf Club Trust (1916) 85 L.J.Ch. 664;
115 L.T. 179; 32 T.L.R. 578 285
Guy v. West (1808) cited in 2 Selwyn's Nisi Prius, 13th ed., at p. 1244 304

PAGE

Gwinnell v. Eamer (1875) L.R. 10 C.P. 658; 32 L.T. 835 370
Gwynne v. Drewitt [1894] 2 Ch. 616; 63 L.J.Ch. 870; 71 L.T. 190; 60 J.P.
104; 43 W.R. 551; 8 R. 814 314

HACKETT v. Baiss (1875) L.R. 20 Eq. 494; 45 L.J.Ch. 13 252
Hale v. Oldroyd (1845) 14 M. & W. 789; 15 L.J.Ex. 4; 153 E.R. 694 ... **323,** 339, 342
Hall v. Lichfield Brewery Co. (1880) 49 L.J.Ch. 655; 43 L.T. 380; 45 J.P.
53 .... 24, **259**
—— v. Lund (1863) 1 H. & C. 676; 1 New Rep. 287; 32 L.J.Ex. 113;
7 L.T. 692; 9 Jur.(N.S.) 205; 158 E.R. 1055; 11 W.R. 271 .... **86**
—— v. Norfolk (Duke) [1900] 2 Ch. 493; 69 L.J.Ch. 571; 82 L.T. 836;
16 T.L.R. 443; 64 J.P. 710; 44 S.J. 550; 48 W.R. 565 290
—— v. Swift (1838) 4 Bing.N.C. 381; 1 Arn. 157; 6 Scott 167; 7 L.J.C.P. 209;
132 E.R. 834 .... 58, 153, 154, **322, 323, 342,** 352
Halliday v. Phillips. See Phillips v. Halliday.
Halsall v. Brizell [1957] Ch. 169; [1957] 2 W.L.R. 123; 101 S.J. 88; [1957]
1 All E.R. 371 .... 46, 65
Halsey v. Esso Petroleum Co. Ltd. [1961] 1 W.L.R. 683; [1961] 2 All
E.R. 145; 105 S.J. 209 191
Hamelin v. Bannerman [1895] A.C. 237; 64 L.J.P.C. 66; 72 L.T. 128;
60 J.P. 22; 11 R. 368; 43 W.R. 639 .... 219, 233
Hamer v. Knowles. See Stroyan v. Knowles, Hamer v. Same.
Hamilton (Duke) v. Graham (1871) L.R. 2 Sc. & Div. 166; 9 Macph.
(Ct. of Sess.) 98; 43 Sc.Jur. 491 13
Hammond v. Prentice Brothers Ltd. [1920] 1 Ch. 201; 89 L.J.Ch. 91; 122 L.T.
307; 36 T.L.R. 98; 84 J.P. 25; 64 S.J. 131; 18 L.G.R. 73 ...... **282, 283**
Hanbury v. Jenkins [1901] 2 Ch. 401; 70 L.J.Ch. 730; 17 T.L.R. 539;
65 J.P. 631; 49 W.R. 615 13
Hanmer v. Chance (1865) 4 De G.J. & Sm. 626; 6 New Rep. 4; 34 L.J.Ch.
413; 12 L.T. 163; 29 J.P. 324; 11 Jur(N.S.) 397; 46 E.R. 1061;
13 W.R. 556 .... **155**
Hanmer (Lord) v. Flight (1876) 36 L.T. 279; 24 W.R. 347 377
Hanna v. Pollock (1898) 2 Ir.R. 532; [1900] 2 Ir.R. 664 .... 165, 167, **173,**
225, 227, 368
Hansford v. Jago [1921] 1 Ch. 322; 90 L.J.Ch. 129; 125 L.T. 663; 65
S.J. 188 .... **97, 98,** 111, 118, 124, 130, 131
Hapgood v. J. H. Martin & Son Ltd. (1934) 152 L.T. 72; 51 T.L.R. 82 ... 130, 149
Harbidge v. Warwick (1849) 3 Exch. 552; 18 L.J.Ex. 245; 154 E.R.
964 .... 147, 148, 188
Hardaker v. Idle Council [1896] 1 Q.B. 335; 65 L.J.Q.B. 363; 74 L.T. 69;
12 T.L.R. 207; 60 J.P. 196; 40 S.J. 273; 44 W.R. 323 373
Harding v. Wilson (1823) 2 B. & C. 96; 3 Dow. & Ry.K.B. 287; 1 L.J.(O.S.)
K.B. 238; 107 E.R. 319 .... **84, 85,** 353
Harmer v. Jumbil (Nigeria) Tin Areas Ltd. [1921] 1 Ch. 200; 90 L.J.Ch.
140; 124 L.T. 418; 37 T.L.R. 91; 65 S.J. 93 .... **90**
Harrington (Earl) v. Derby Corporation [1905] 1 Ch. 205; 74 L.J.Ch. 219;
92 L.T. 153; 21 T.L.R. 98; 69 J.P. 62; 3 L.G.R. 321 231
Harris v. Chesterfield (Earl of) [1911] A.C. 623; affirming sub nom.
Chesterfield (Lord) v. Harris [1908] 2 Ch. 397; 77 L.J.Ch. 688;
99 L.T. 558; 24 T.L.R. 763; 52 S.J. 639 .... 59, 60
—— v. De Pinna (1886) 33 Ch.D. 238; 56 L.J.Ch. 344; 54 L.T. 770;
2 T.L.R. 529; 50 J.P. 486 .... 25, 26, 35, 146, 148, 239, 257, 259, 306
—— v. Flower & Sons (1905) 74 L.J.Ch. 127; 91 L.T. 816; 21 T.L.R.
13 .... 282, **347**
—— v. James (1876) 45 L.J.Q.B. 545; 35 L.T. 240; 40 J.P. 663 370
—— v. Jenkins (1882) 22 Ch.D. 481; 52 L.J.Ch. 437; 47 L.T. 570; 31
W.R. 137 .... 377, 378
—— v. Kinloch & Co. [1895] W.N. 60 239
Harrop v. Hirst (1868) L.R. 4 Exch. 43; 38 L.J.Ex. 1; 19 L.T. 426; 33 J.P.
103; 17 W.R. 164 .... 236, 379
Harvey v. Walters (1872) L.R. 8 C.P. 162; 42 L.J.C.P. 105; 28 L.T. 343;
37 J.P. 343 .... 36, 223, 323
Hastings (Lord) v. North Eastern Ry. Co. [1900] A.C. 260; affirming [1899]
1 Ch. 656; affirming [1898] 2 Ch. 674; 67 L.J.Ch. 590; 78 L.T. 812;
14 T.L.R. 505; 63 J.P. 36; 47 W.R. 59 .... 43, 49, 77
Hawker v. Tomalin (1969) 20 P. & C.R. 550 152

PAGE

Hawkins v. Carbines (1857) 27 L.J.Ex. 44 353
—— v. Rutter [1892] 1 Q.B. 668; 61 L.J.Q.B. 146; 36 S.J. 152; 40 W.R. 238   7
—— v. Wallis (1763) 2 Wils. 173; 95 E.R. 750 35
Haynes v. King [1893] 3 Ch. 439; 63 L.J.Ch. 21; 69 L.T. 855; 3 R. 715;
    42 W.R. 56 149
Haywood v. Brunswick Building Society (181) 8 Q.B.D. 403; 51 L.J.Q.B.
    73; 45 L.T. 699; 46 J.P. 356; 30 W.R. 299 38
Healey v. Hawkins [1968] 1 W.L.R. 1967; 112 S.J. 965; [1968] 3 All E.R.
    836; 20 P. & C.R. 69 .... 143, 149, 177
Heap v. Hartley (1882) 42 Ch.D. 461; 58 L.J.Ch. 790; 61 L.T. 538; 38 W.R.
    136; 5 T.L.R. 710; 6 R.P.C. 495 56
—— v. Ind. Coope and Allsopp Ltd. [1940] 2 K.B. 476; 109 L.J.K.B. 724;
    163 L.T. 169; 56 T.L.R. 948; 84 S.J. 536; [1940] 3 All E.R. 634 370
Heath v. Bucknall (1869) L.R. 8 Eq. 1; 38 L.J.Ch. 372; 20 L.T. 549; 33 J.P.
    532; 17 W.R. 755 336
Heather v. Pardon (1878) 37 L.T. 393 191
Heigate v. Williams (1607) Noy 119; 74 E.R. 1083 310
Hendy v. Stephenson (1808) 10 East 55; 103 E.R. 696 378
Henniker v. Howard (1904) 90 L.T. 157 304
Henning v. Burnet (1852) 8 Exch. 187; 22 L.J.Ex. 79; 155 E.R. 1313 ... 12, **275**, 347
Henry Ltd. v. M'Glade [1926] N.I. 144 19
Hervey v. Smith (1855) 1 K. & J. 389; subsequent proceedings 22 Beav.
    299; 52 E.R. 1123 .... 35, **69, 70**, 382
Herz v. The Union Bank of London (1854) 2 Giff. 686; 24 L.T.(o.s.) 137; 1
    Jur.(N.S.) 127; 3 W.R. 49; 66 E.R. 287 .... 89, 254, 380
Hetherington v. Galt (1905) 7 F. (Ct. of Sess.) 706; 42 S.L.R. 571; 13 S.L.T.
    90 305
Hewlins v. Shipman (1826) 5 B. & C. 221; 7 Dow. & Ry.K.B. 783; 4 L.J.
    (o.s.)K.B. 241; 108 E.R. 82 61
Heywood v. Mallalieu (1883) 25 Ch.D. 357; 53 L.J.Ch. 492; 49 L.T. 658;
    32 W.R. 538 .... 31, 35
Higgins v. Betts [1905] 2 Ch. 210; 74 L.J.Ch. 621; 92 L.T. 850; 21 T.L.R.
    552; 49 S.J. 535; 53 W.R. 549 .... 246, **250, 251**, 330, 396
Higham v. Rabett (1839) 5 Bing.N.C. 622 262
Hill v. Cock (1872) 26 L.T. 185; 36 J.P. 552 .... 347, 357
—— v. Prideaux (1595) Cro.Eliz. 384; 78 E.R. 630 358
—— v. Tottenham Council (1899) 79 L.T. 495; 15 T.L.R. 53 373
—— v. Tupper (1863) 2 H. & C. 121; 2 New Rep. 201; 32 L.J.Ex. 217; 8
    L.T. 792; 9 Jur.(N.S.) 725; 159 E.R. 51; 11 W.R. 784 ...... **19**, 34, 56, 233
Hilton v. Ankesson (1872) 27 L.T. 519 .... 38, 39
—— v. Granville (1841) 4 Beav. 130; Cr. & Ph. 283; 10 L.J.Ch. 398; 49
    E.R. 288 386
Hindson v. Ashby [1896] 2 Ch. 1; 65 L.J.Ch. 515; 74 L.T. 327; 12 T.L.R.
    314; 60 J.P. 484; 40 S.J. 417; 45 W.R. 252 237
Hoare v. Metropolitan Board of Works (1874) L.R. 9 Q.B. 296; 43 L.J.M.C.
    65; 29 L.T. 804; 38 J.P. 535 .... 35, 44
Hobart v. Southend-on-Sea Corpn. (1906) 22 T.L.R. 530; affirming (1906)
    75 L.J.K.B. 305; 94 L.T. 337; 22 T.L.R. 307; 70 J.P. 192; 4 L.G.R.
    757; 54 W.R 454 192
Hodgkinson v. Ennor (1863) 4 B. & S. 229; 2 New Rep. 272; 32 L.J.Q.B. 231;
    8 L.T. 451; 27 J.P. 469; 9 Jur.(N.S.) 1152; 122 E.R. 446; 11 W.R. 775   230
Hodgson v. Field (1806) 7 East 613; 3 Smith K.B. 538; 103 E.R. 238   44
Hogg v. Scott (1874) L.R. 18 Eq. 444; 43 L.J.Ch. 705; 31 L.T. 163; 22
    W.R. 640 388
Holcroft v. Heel (1799) 1 Bos. & P. 400; 126 E.R. 976 .... 135, 137
Holder v. Coates (1827) 1 Moo. & M. 112 305
Hole v. Sittingbourne & Sheerness Ry. (1861) 6 H. & N. 488; 30 L.J.Ex. 81;
    3 L.T. 750; 158 E.R. 201; 9 W.R. 274 371
Holford v. Hankinson (1844) 5 Q.B. 584; 1 Dav. & Mer. 473; 2 L.T.(o.s.)
    367; 8 Jur. 463; 114 E.R. 1370; sub nom. Halford v. Hankinson, 13
    L.J.Q.B. 115 375
Holker v. Porritt (1875) L.R. 10 Exch. 59; 44 L.J.Ex. 52; 33 L.T. 125; 39
    J.P. 196; 23 W.R. 400 .... 99, 218
Holland v. Deakin (1828) 7 L.J.(o.s.)K.B. 145 310
—— v. Worley (1884) 26 Ch.D. 578; 54 L.J.Ch. 268; 50 L.T. 526; 49 J.P.
    7; 32 W.R. 749 391

PAGE

Holliday v. National Telephone Co. [1899] 2 Q.B. 392; 68 L.J.Q.B. 1016; 81 L.T. 252; 47 W.R. 658; 15 T.L.R. 483 371

Hollins v. Verney (1884) 13 Q.B.D. 304; 53 L.J.Q.B. 430; 51 L.T. 753; 48 J.P. 58; 33 W.R. 5 .... **153, 155, 188, 189**

Holmes v. Buckley (1691) 1 Eq.Cas.Abr. 27; Prec.in Chanc. 39 .... 48, 49, **338**

—— v. Goring (1824) 2 Bing. 76; 9 Moore C.P. 166; 2 L.J.(o.s.)C.P. 134; 130 E.R. 233 .... 118, 120, 121, 309, 312

Holywell Union and Halkyn Parish v. Halkyn Drainage Co. [1895] A.C. 117; 64 L.J.M.C. 113; 71 L.T. 818; 11 T.L.R. 132; 59 J.P. 566; 11 R. 98 .... 5, 235

Hopgood v. Brown [1955] 1 W.L.R. 213; 99 S.J. 168; [1955] 1 All E.R. 550 .... 65, 69, 107

Hopwood v. Schofield (1837) 2 Mood. & R. 34 .... 363, 365

Hornby v. Silvester (1888) 20 Q.B.D. 797 314

Horton v. Tidd (1965) 196 E.G. 697 87

Hortons' Estate Ltd. v. James Beattie Ltd. [1927] 1 Ch. 75; 96 L.J.Ch. 15; 136 L.T. 218; 42 T.L.R. 701; 70 S.J. 917 247

Hoskins-Abrahall v. Paignton Urban District Council [1929] 1 Ch. 375; 98 L.J.Ch. 103; 140 L.T. 397; 45 T.L.R. 161; 93 J.P. 93; 27 L.G.R. 129 15

Hounslow London Borough Council v. Twickenham Garden Developments Ltd. [1971] Ch. 233; [1970] 3 W.L.R. 538; 114 S.J. 603; 69 L.G.R. 109; sub nom. London Borough of Hounslow v. Twickenham Garden Developments [1970] 3 All E.R. 326 387

House Property and Investment Co. v. H. P. Horse Nail Co. (1885) 29 Ch.D. 190; 54 L.J.Ch. 715; 52 L.T. 507; 33 W.R. 562 .... 362, 366

Howarth v. Armstrong (1897) 77 L.T. 62; 13 T.L.R. 529 101

Howton v. Frearson (1798) 8 Term Rep. 50; 101 E.R. 1261 117

—— v. Hawkins (1966) 110 S.J. 547; 199 E.G. 229 .... **344**

Hughes v. Percival (1883) 8 App.Cas. 443; 52 L.J.Q.B. 719; 49 L.T. 189; 47 J.P. 772; 31 W.R. 725; H.L.; affirming sub nom. Percival v. Hughes (1882) 9 Q.B.D. 441 .... 303, **372, 373**

Hughes and Ashley's Contract, Re [1900] 2 Ch. 595; 69 L.J.Ch. 741; 83 L.T. 390; 44 S.J. 624; 49 W.R. 67 97

Hulbert v. Dale [1909] 2 Ch. 570; 78 L.J.Ch. 457; 100 L.T. 777 .... 142, 143, 188, 341

Hull v. Horner (1774) Cowp. 102 .... 137, 139

Hulley v. Silversprings Bleaching & Dyeing Co. [1922] 2 Ch. 268; 91 L.J.Ch. 207; 126 L.T. 499; 86 J.P. 30; 66 S.J. 195 ...... 141, 156, 168, 188–191, 231

Humphries v. Brogden (1850) 12 Q.B. 739; 20 L.J.Q.B. 10; 16 L.T.(o.s.) 457; 116 E.R. 1048; sub nom. Humfries v. Brogden, 15 Jur. 124 ..... 287, 290

Hunt v. Peake (1860) John. 705; 29 L.J.Ch. 785; 25 J.P. 5; 6 Jur.(N.S.) 1071; 70 E.R. 603 .... 287, 290, 291, 380

Hurdman v. N. Eastern Ry. (1878) 3 C.P.D. 168; 47 L.J.Q.B. 368; 38 L.T. 339; 26 W.R. 489 26

Hurt v. Bowmer (1937) 53 T.L.R. 325; 81 S.J. 118; [1937] 1 All E.R. 797 273

Hutchinson v. Copestake (1861) 9 C.B.(N.S.) 863; 31 L.J.C.P. 19; 5 L.T. 178; 8 Jur.(N.S.) 54; 142 E.R. 340; 9 W.R. 896 .... 325, 326, 336

Hutton v. Hamboro (1860) 2 F. & F. 218 .... 285, 352

Hyman v. Van den Bergh [1908] 1 Ch. 167; 77 L.J.Ch. 154; 98 L.T. 478; 52 S.J. 114, C.A.; affirming [1907] 2 Ch. 516 .... 144, 147–149, 153, 345, 355, 377

IMPERIAL GAS LIGHT & COKE CO. v. Broadbent (1859) 7 H.L.Cas. 600; 29 L.J. Ch. 377; 34 L.T.(o.s.) 1; 23 J.P. 675; 5 Jur.(N.S.) 1319; 11 E.R. 239 ... 380, 381

Inchbald v. Robinson, Inchbald v. Barrington (1868) 4 Ch.App. 388; 20 L.T. 259; 33 J.P. 484; M.W.R. 459 362

Ingram & Morecraft (1863) 33 Beav. 49; 55 E.R. 284 .... **45, 46**

Insole v. James (1856) 1 H. & N. 243; 27 L.T.(o.s.) 223; 4 W.R. 680 207

International Tea Stores Co. v. Hobbs [1903] 2 Ch. 165; 72 L.J.Ch. 543; 88 L.T. 725; 51 W.R. 615 .... 27, 28, 126

Inwards v. Baker [1965] 2 Q.B. 29; [1965] 2 W.L.R. 212; 109 S.J. 75; [1965] 1 All E.R. 446 .... 56, 69, 362

I.R.C. v. New Sharlston Collieries Co. [1937] 1 K.B. 583; 106 L.J.K.B. 375; 156 L.T. 279; 53 T.L.R. 280; 81 S.J. 56; 21 T.C. 69; [1937] 1 All E.R. 86 37

Irving v. Turnbull [1900] 2 Q.B. 129; 69 L.J.Q.B. 593 302

PAGE

Isenberg v. East India House Estate Co. (1863) 3 De G.J. & S. 263; 3 New
   Rep. 345; 33 L.J.Ch. 392; 9 L.T. 625; 28 J.P. 228; 10 Jur.(N.S.) 221;
   46 E.R. 637; 12 W.R. 450 .... 383, 391
Ives (E. R.) Investment Ltd. v. High [1967] 2 Q.B. 379; [1967] 2 W.L.R.
   789; sub nom. Ives (E. R.) Investments Ltd. v. High, 110 S.J. 963;
   [1967] 1 All E.R. 504 .... Preface, **64**, **65**, 67, 69, **70**, **71**, 72, 374
Iveson v. Moore (1700) 1 Ld.Raym. 486; Carth. 451; Comb. 480; 1 Com.
   58; Holt K.B. 10; 1 Salk. 15; Willes 74 n.; 91 E.R. 1224; sub nom.
   Jeveson v. Moor, 12 Mod.Rep. 262 261
Ivimey v. Stocker (1866) 1 Ch.App. 396; 35 L.J.Ch. 467; 14 L.T. 427; 12
   Jur.(N.S.) 419; 14 W.R. 743 .... 170, 224, 310

JACKSON v. Newcastle (1864) 3 De G.J. & Sm. 275; 4 New Rep. 448; 33 L.J.
   Ch. 698; 10 L.T. 635, 802; 28 J.P. 516; 10 Jur.(N.S.) 810; 46 E.R.
   642; 12 W.R. 1066 .... 242, 398
—— v. Normanby Brick Co. [1899] 1 Ch. 438; 68 L.J.Ch. 407; 80 L.T. 482;
   43 S.J. 436 382
—— v. Pesked (1813) 1 M. & S. 234; 14 R.R. 417; 105 E.R. 88 ...... 363, 366, 380
—— v. Stacey (1816) Holt N.P. 455 261
Jacomb v. Knight (1863) 3 De G.J. & Sm. 533; 2 New Rep. 295; 32 L.J.Ch.
   601; 27 J.P. 547; 8 L.T. 621; 46 E.R. 743; 11 W.R. 812 .... **362**
James v. Dods (1834) 2 Cr. & M. 266; 4 Tyr. 101; 3 L.J.Ex. 47; 149 E.R. 760   261
—— v. Hayward (1630) Cro.Car. 184; W.Jo. 221; 79 E.R. 761 ...... **353, 358, 359**
—— v. Plant (1836) 4 Ad. & El. 749; 6 Nev. & M.K.B. 282; 6 L.J.Ex. 260;
   111 E.R. 967; reversing sub nom. Plant v. James (1833) 5 B. & Ad.
   791 .... 310, 353
—— v. Stevenson [1893] A.C. 162; 62 L.J.P.C. 51; 68 L.T. 539; 1 R. 324   **341**
Jarvis v. Aris (July 14, 1961), unreported 304
Jeffries v. Williams (1850) 5 Exch. 792; 20 L.J.Ex. 14; 16 L.T.(O.S.) 196;
   155 E.R. 347 .... 291, 373
Jelbert v. Davis [1968] 1 W.L.R. 589; 112 S.J. 172; [1968] 1 All E.R. 1182;
   19 P. & C.R. 383 .... **278**
Jenkins v. Harvey (1835) 1 Cr.M. & R. 877; 1 Gale 23; 5 Tyr. 326; 5 L.J.
   Ex. 17; 149 E.R. 1336 134
—— v. Jackson (1888) 40 Ch.D. 71; 58 L.J.Ch. 124; 60 L.T. 105; 4 T.L.R.
   747; 37 W.R. 253 370
Jessel v. Chaplin (1856) 27 L.T.(O.S.) 159; 2 Jur.(N.S.) 931; 4 W.R. 610 397
Jesser v. Gifford (1767) 4 Burr. 2141; 98 E.R. 116 .... 363, 365
Johnson v. Barnes (1873) L.R. 8 C.P. 527; 62 L.J.C.P. 259; 29 L.T. 65 59
—— v. Wyatt (1863) 2 De G.J. & Sm. 17; 3 New Rep. 270; 33 L.J.Ch.
   394; 9 L.T. 618; 28 J.P. 70; 9 Jur.(N.S.) 1333; 46 E.R. 281; 12 W.R.
   234 .... 258, 316, 388, 391
Johnstone v. Hall (1856) 2 K. & J. 414; 25 L.J.Ch. 462; 27 L.T.(O.S.) 230;
   20 J.P. 579; 2 Jur.(N.S.) 780; 69 E.R. 844; 4 W.R. 417 366
—— v. Holdway [1963] 1 Q.B. 601; [1963] 2 W.L.R. 147; 107 S.J. 55;
   [1963] 1 All E.R. 432 .... 8, **9**, **10**, 11, **79**, 354
Jolly v. Kine [1907] A.C. 1; 76 L.J.Ch. 1; 95 L.T. 656; 23 T.L.R. 1; 51 S.J.
   11, H.L.; affirming sub nom. Kine v. Jolly [1905] 1 Ch. 480 ...... 246, 247,
                                                                 249, 393, 394, 398
Jones v. Chappell (1875) L.R. 20 Eq. 539; 44 L.J.Ch. 658 .... **362**, 366
—— v. Jones (1862) 1 H. & C. 1; 31 L.J.Ex. 506; 8 Jur.(N.S.) 1132; 158
   E.R. 777 357
—— v. Llanrwst U.D.C. [1911] 1 Ch. 393; 80 L.J.Ch. 145; 103 L.T. 751;
   75 J.P. 68; 55 S.J. 125; 9 L.G.R. 222; sub nom. Isgoed-Jones v.
   Llanrwst U.D.C., 27 T.L.R. 133 .... 229, 230, **364**, 365, 366, 379, 381
—— v. Price (1836) 3 Bing.N.C. 52 152
—— v. —— [1965] 2 Q.B. 618; [1965] 3 W.L.R. 296; 109 S.J. 415; [1965]
   2 All E.R. 625 .... **37–40**, 41
—— v. Pritchard [1908] 1 Ch. 630; 77 L.J.Ch. 405; 98 L.T. 386; 24 T.L.R.
   309 .... 35, 44, 45, **46**, 47, **86**, 87, 88, **108**
—— v. Tapling (1862) 12 C.B.(N.S.) 826, Ex.Ch.; (1861) 11 C.B.(N.S.) 283   24
—— v. Williams (1843) 11 M. & W. 176; 12 L.J.Ex. 249; 152 E.R. 764 ... 357, 358
Jones (James) & Sons Ltd. v. Tankerville (Earl) [1909] 2 Ch. 440; 78 L.J.Ch.
   674; 101 L.T. 202; 25 T.L.R. 714 67

PAGE

Jordeson v. Sutton, Southcoates & Drypool Gas Co. [1899] 2 Ch. 217, C.A.;
   affirming [1898] 2 Ch. 614; 67 L.J.Ch. 666; 79 L.J. 478; 14 T.L.R.
   567; 63 J.P. 137; 42 S.J. 715; 47 W.R. 222 .... **149**, 168, 213, **289**, 391
Judge v. Lowe (1873) Ir.R. 7 C.L. 291 177

KAIN v. Norfolk [1949] Ch. 163; [1949] 1 All E.R. 176; sub nom. Kain v.
   Norfolk & E. Baker (Hauliers) [1949] L.J.R. 592; 93 S.J. 41 ...... **271, 272,**
   281, 282
Kay v. Oxley (1875) L.R. 10 Q.B. 360; 44 L.J.Q.B. 210; 33 L.T. 164; 40
   J.P. 277 126
Keeble v. Hickeringill (1809) 3 Salk. 9; Holt K.B. 14, 17, 19; Kelw. 273; 11
   Mod. 74, 130; 11 East 574 n.; 91 E.R. 659 363
—— v. Poole (1898) 42 S.J. 791 387
Keefe v. Amor [1965] 1 Q.B. 334; [1964] 3 W.L.R. 183; 108 S.J. 334; [1964]
   2 All E.R. 517 .... **272, 273,** 352
Keegan v. Young [1963] N.Z.L.R. 720 .... 291, 373
Keewatin Power Co. v. Lake of the Woods Milling Co. [1930] A.C. 640; 100
   L.J.P.C. 1; 143 L.T. 633 .... 37, 87, 345
Keith v. Twentieth Century Club (1904) 73 L.J.Ch. 545; 90 L.T. 775; 52
   W.R. 554; 20 T.L.R. 462; 48 S.J. 458 .... 28, **283, 284**
Kelk v. Pearson (1871) 6 Ch.App. 809; 24 L.T. 890; 36 J.P. 196; 19 W.R.
   665 .... **243,** 244, 245, 253, 383, 397
Kellett v. St. John's Burscough Bridge (1916) 32 T.L.R. 571 15
Kelly v. Battershell [1949] 2 All E.R. 830 92
—— v. Dea (1965) 100 I.L.T.R. 1 47
Kelsen v. Imperial Tobacco Co. (of Great Britain & Ireland) Ltd. [1957] 2
   Q.B. 334; [1957] 2 W.L.R. 1007; 101 S.J. 446; [1957] 2 All E.R. 343 306
Kempston v. Butler (1861) 12 Ir.C.L.R. 516; 6 Ir.Jur. 410 303
Kendrick v. Bartland (1679) 2 Mod.Rep. 253; Free.K.B. 230 360
Kennard v. Cory Bros. & Co. Ltd. [1922] 2 Ch. 1; 91 L.J.Ch. 452; 127 L.T.
   137; 38 T.L.R. 489; affirming [1922] 1 Ch. 265 .... 384, 385
Kensit v. Great Eastern Ry. (1884) 27 Ch.D. 122; 54 L.J.Ch. 19; 51 L.T.
   862; 32 W.R. 885 .... 202, 207, **234,** 379
Keppell v. Bailey (1834) 2 My. & K. 517; Coop.temp.Brough. 298; 39 E.R.
   1042 34
Key v. Neath R.D.C. (1907) 95 L.T. 771; affirming (1905) 93 L.T. 507 83
Keymer v. Summers (1769) Bull.N.P. 74 137
Kiddle v. Lovett (1885) 16 Q.B.D. 605; 34 W.R. 518 371
Kidgill v. Moor (1850) 9 C.B. 364; 1 L.M. & P. 131; 19 L.J.C.P. 177; 14
   L.T.(O.S.) 443; 14 Jur. 790; 137 E.R. 934 .... 353, 363, 365, **367, 368**
Kieffer v. Le Seminaire de Quebec [1903] A.C. 85 370
Kilgour v. Gaddes [1904] 1 K.B. 457; 73 L.J.K.B. 233; 90 L.T. 604; 20
   T.L.R. 240; 52 W.R. 438 .... 21, 162, 163, 167, 169, 172, 183, 309
Kine v. Jolly. See Jolly v. Kine.
King v. Allen (David) & Sons, Billposting Ltd. [1916] 2 A.C. 54; 85 L.J.
   P.C. 229; 114 L.T. 762 56
Kinloch v. Nevile (1840) 6 M. & W. 795; 10 L.J.Ex. 248; 151 E.R. 633 177,
   375, 376
Kirby v. Chessum (1914) 30 T.L.R. 660; 79 J.P. 81; varying on appeal (1913)
   30 T.L.R. 15 366
—— v. Harrogate School Board [1896] 1 Ch. 437; 65 L.J.Ch. 376; 74 L.T.
   6; 12 T.L.R. 175; 60 J.P. 182; 40 S.J. 239 315
Knight v. Fox (1850) 5 Ex. 721; 20 L.J.Ex. 9; 16 L.T.(O.S.) 128; 14 Jur. 963;
   14 J.P Jo. 721; 155 E.R. 316 371
Knox v. Sansom (1877) 25 W.R. 864 284
Krehl v. Burrell (1879) 11 Ch.D. 146; 40 L.T. 637; 27 W.R. 805; affirming
   (1878) 10 Ch.D. 420; (1878) 7 Ch.D. 551 .... 388, 390

LADYMAN v. Grave (1871) 6 Ch.App. 763, L.C.; reversing (1870) 24 L.T. 55;
   19 W.R. 344 .... 20, 148, 149, 312
Lagan Navigation Co. v. Lambeg Bleaching, Dyeing and Finishing Co.
   [1927] A.C. 226; 96 L.J.P.C. 25; 136 L.T. 417; 91 J.P. 46; 25
   L.G.R. 1 .... **359,** 360
Laing v. Whaley (1858) 3 H. & N. 675; 27 L.J.Ex. 422; affirming Whaley
   v. Laing (1857) 2 H. & N. 476; 26 L.J.Ex. 327; 5 W.R. 834; 157
   E.R. 196 .... **232,** 374

PAGE

Laird v. Birkenhead Ry. (1859) John. 500; 29 L.J.Ch. 218; 1 L.T. 159; 6
Jur.(N.S.) 140; 70 E.R. 519; 8 W.R. 58 67
—— v. Briggs (1881) 19 Ch.D. 22; 45 L.T. 238, C.A.; reversing (1880) 16
Ch.D. 440 159
Lambton v. Mellish [1894] 3 Ch. 163; 63 L.J.Ch. 929; 71 L.T. 385; 10 T.L.R.
600; 58 J.P. 835; 38 S.J. 647; 8 R. 807; 43 W.R. 5 369
Lancaster v. Eve (1859) 5 C.B.(N.S.) 717; 28 L.J.C.P. 235; 32 L.T.(O.S.) 278;
5 Jur.(N.S.) 683; 141 E.R. 288; 7 W.R. 260 .... 15, 35
Land Tax Commissioners of London (City) v. Central London Ry. [1913]
A.C. 364; H.L.; affirming [1911] 2 Ch. 467; reversing [1911] 1 Ch.
467; 80 L.J.Ch. 348; 104 L.T. 245; 27 T.L.R. 296; 75 J.P. 292; 9
L.G.R. 580 207
Lane v. Capsey [1891] 3 Ch. 411; 61 L.J.Ch. 55; 65 L.T. 375; 40 W.R.
87 .... 353, 356, 357, **359**, 360
—— v. Newdigate (1804) 10 Ves. 192; 32 E.R. 818 382
Lanfranchi v. Mackenzie (1867) L.R. 4 Eq. 421; 36 L.J.Ch. 518; 16 L.T. 114;
31 J.P. 627; 15 W.R. 614 253
Langbrook Properties Ltd. v. Surrey County Council [1970] 1 W.L.R. 161;
113 S.J. 983; [1969] 3 All E.R. 1424; 68 L.G.R. 268 .... **288**
Langley v. Hammond (1868) L.R. 3 Exch. 161; 37 L.J.Ex. 118; 18 L.T. 858;
16 W.R. 937 122
Large v. Pitt (1797) Peake Add.Cas. 152, N.P. 21
Lawrence v. Horton (1890) 59 L.J.Ch. 440; 62 L.T. 749; 6 T.L.R. 317; 38
W.R. 555 .... 383, 391
—— v. Jenkins (1873) L.R. 8 Q.B. 274; 42 L.J.Q.B. 147; 37 J.P. 357; 21
W.R. 577; sub nom. Laurence v. Jenkins, 28 L.T. 406 38
—— v. Obee (1814) 3 Camp. 514 318
—— v. South County Freeholds, Ltd. [1939] Ch. 656; [1939] 2 All E.R. 503;
108 L.J.Ch. 236; 161 L.T. 11; 55 T.L.R. 662; 83 S.J. 378 6
Lawson v. Langley (1836) 4 Ad. & El. 890; 6 L.J.K.B. 271; 111 E.R. 1018 ... 153,
378
Lawton v. Ward (1697) 1 Ld.Raym. 75; 91 E.R. 946; sub nom. Laughton v.
Ward, 1 Lut. 111 282
Lay v. Wyncoll (1966) 198 E.G. 887; 116 New L.J. 837 22
Layburn v. Gridley [1892] 2 Ch. 53; 61 L.J.Ch. 352; 36 S.J. 363; 40 W.R.
474 .... 302, 306
Lazarus v. Artistic Photographic Co. [1897] 2 Ch. 214; 66 L.J.Ch. 522; 76
L.T. 457; 41 S.J. 451; 45 W.R. 614 254
Leconfield v. Lonsdale (1870) L.R. 5 C.P. 657; 39 L.J.C.P. 305; 23 L.T. 155;
18 W.R. 1165 .... 191, 219
Lee v. Rural Municipality of Arthur (1964) 46 D.L.R. (2d) 448 209
—— v. Stevenson (1858) E.B. & E. 512; 27 L.J.Q.B. 263; 4 Jur.(N.S.) 950;
120 E.R. 600 .... 235, 352
Leech v. Schweder (1874) 9 Ch.App. 463; 43 L.J.Ch. 487; 30 L.T. 586; 38
J.P. 612; 22 W.R. 633; reversing on other grounds (1874) 22 W.R.
292 .... 4, 24, 26, **101**, **102**, 244, 253, 397, 398
Leeds Industrial Co-operative Society Ltd. v. Slack. See Slack v. Leeds
Industrial Co-operative Society Ltd.
Legge (George) & Son Ltd. v. Wenlock Corporation [1938] A.C. 204; 107
S.J.Ch. 72; 158 L.T. 265; 54 T.L.R. 315; 82 S.J. 133; [1938] 1 All
E.R. 37; 102 J.P. 93; 36 L.G.R. 117 231
Lemaitre v. Davis (1881) 19 Ch.D. 281; 51 L.J.Ch. 173; 46 L.T. 407; 46 J.P.
324; 30 W.R. 360 .... 37, **167**, 175, 301
Lemmon v. Webb [1895] A.C. 1, H.L.; affirming [1894] 3 Ch. 1; 63 L.J.Ch.
570; 70 L.T. 712; 58 J.P. 716; 10 T.L.R. 467, C.A. 191, 305, 306, 357,
358, 360
Le Strange v. Pettefar (1939) 161 L.T. 300 129
Levet v. Gas Light & Coke Co. [1919] 1 Ch. 24; 88 L.J.Ch. 12; 119 L.T. 761;
35 T.L.R. 47; 63 S.J. 69 239
Lewis v. Meredith [1913] 1 Ch. 571; 82 L.J.Ch. 255; 108 L.T. 549 .... 124, 224
—— v. Price (1761) 2 Wms.Saund. 504; 85 E.R. 926 137
Liddiard v. Waldron [1934] 1 K.B. 435; 103 L.J.K.B. 172; 150 L.T. 323;
50 T.L.R. 172 .... 106, **113**, **114**, **116**, 118
Liford's Case (1614) 11 Co.Rep. 46b; 77 E.R. 1206 44
Liggins v. Inge (1831) 7 Bing. 682; 5 Moo. & P. 712; 9 L.J.(O.S.)C.P. 202;
131 E.R. 263 .... 316, 319
Lineham v. Deeble (1859) 9 Ir.C.L.R. 309 368
Lister v. Rickard (1969) 113 S.J. 981 354

PAGE

Litchfield-Speer v. Queen Anne's Gate Syndicate (No. 2) [1919] 1 Ch. 407; 88
    L.J.Ch. 137; 120 L.T. 565; 35 T.L.R. 253; 63 S.J. 390 .... 384, 389
Littledale v. Lonsdale. See Lonsdale v. Littledale.
Liverpool Corporation v. Coghill & Son [1918] 1 Ch. 307; 87 L.J.Ch. 186;
    118 L.T. 336; 34 T.L.R. 159; 82 J.P. 129; 16 L.G.R. 91 ...... 161, 174, **176,**
                                                          179, 187, 191, 231
Livett v. Wilson (1825) 3 Bing. 115; 10 Moore C.P. 439; 3 L.J.(o.s.)C.P.
    186; 130 E.R. 457 .... 137, 378
Llandudno Urban Council v. Woods [1899] 2 Ch. 705; 81 L.T. 170; 63 J.P.
    775; 48 W.R. 43; 43 S.J. 689 382
Lloyds Bank, Ltd. v. Dalton [1942] Ch. 466; 112 L.J.Ch. 10; 167 L.T. 343;
    58 T.L.R. 394; 86 S.J. 282; [1942] 2 All E.R. 352 .... 175, 179, 180,
                                                                300, 301, 324
Lock v. Abercester [1939] Ch. 861; 108 L.J.Ch. 328; 161 L.T. 264; 55 T.L.R.
    948; 83 S.J. 656; [1939] 3 All E.R. 562 266
Lodie v. Arnold (1698) Salk. 458; 91 E.R. 396 .... **358,** 359
Logan v. Burton (1826) 5 B. & C. 513; 8 Dow. & Ry.K.B. 299; 4 Dow. &
    Ry.M.C. 50; 4 L.J.(o.s.)K.B. 217; 168 E.R. 191 314
London and Blackwall Ry. v. Cross (1886) 31 Ch.D. 354; 55 L.J.Ch. 313;
    54 L.T. 309; 2 T.L.R. 231; 34 W.R. 201 382
London and North Western Railway Co. v. Evans [1893] 1 Ch. 16; 62 L.J.
    Ch. 1; 67 L.T. 630; 9 T.L.R. 50; 41 W.R. 149; 2 R. 120 76
London Cemetery Co. v. Cundey [1953] 1 W.L.R. 786; 97 S.J. 421; [1953] 2
    All E.R. 257; 51 L.G.R. 493 15
London Corporation v. Pewterers' Co. (1842) 2 Mood. & R. 409 177
—— v. Riggs (1880) 13 Ch.D. 798; 49 L.J.Ch. 297; 42 L.T. 580; 44 J.P.
    345; 28 W.R. 610 .... **119, 120**
London, Tilbury & Southend Ry. and Gower's Walk Schools Trustees, Re
    (1889) 24 Q.B.D. 326; 62 L.T. 306; 38 W.R. 343; sub nom. Re
    Gower's Walk Schools Trustees v. London, Tilbury & Southend Ry.,
    59 L.J.Q.B. 162; 6 T.L.R. 120 336
Long v. Gowlett [1923] 2 Ch. 177; 92 L.J.Ch. 530; 130 L.T. 83; 22 L.G.R.
    214 .... 125, 126
Long Eaton Recreation Grounds Co. v. Midland Ry. [1902] 2 K.B. 574; 71
    L.J.K.B. 837; 86 L.T. 873; 18 T.L.R. 743; 67 J.P. 1; 50 W.R. 693 ... 315
Lonsdale (Earl) v. Littledale (1793) 5 Bro.Parl.Cas. 519; noted at [1899] 2
    Ch. 233n. 213
—— v. Nelson (1823) 2 B. & C. 302; 3 Dow. & Ry.K.B. 556; 2 L.J.(o.s.)
    K.B. 28; 107 E.R. 396 .... 357, 358
Lotus Ltd. v. British Soda Co. Ltd. [1971] 2 W.L.R. 7; (1970) 114 S.J. 885;
    [1971] 1 All E.R. 265; 22 P. & C.R. 11 .... 213, **289**
Love v. Pigott (1587) Cro.Eliz. 56 363
Lovell v. Smith (1857) 3 C.B.(N.S.) 120; 22 J.P. 787; 140 E.R. 685 ...... 316, **341**
Lowe v. Carpenter (1851) 6 Exch. 825; 20 L.J.Ex. 374; 17 L.T.(o.s.) 203;
    15 Jur. 883; 155 E.R. 779 153
Lowry v. Crothers (1872) Ir.R. 5 C.L. 98 177
Luscombe v. Steer (1867) 17 L.T. 229; 15 W.R. 1191 292
Luttrel's Case (1601) 4 Co.Rep. 86a; affirming (1601) 4 Co.Rep. 84b; 76
    E.R. 1063 .... 58, 275, 317, **320–322,** 324, 325
Lyell v. Hothfield (Lord) [1914] 3 K.B. 911; 84 L.J.K.B. 251; 30 T.L.R.
    630 .... 162, 174
Lyon v. Fishmongers' Co. (1876) 1 App.Cas. 662; 46 L.J.Ch. 68; 35 L.T. 569;
    42 J.P. 163; 25 W.R. 165 .... 207, 237
Lyons, Sons & Co. v. Gulliver [1914] 1 Ch. 631; 83 L.J.Ch. 281; 110 L.T.
    284; 30 T.L.R. 75; 78 J.P. 98; 58 S.J. 97; 12 L.G.R. 194 294
Lyttelton Times Co. Ltd. v. Warners Ltd. [1907] A.C. 476; 76 L.J.P.C. 100;
    97 L.T. 496; 23 T.L.R. 751 .... **86, 87,** 92, 108, 190

MABERLEY v. Dowson (1827) 5 L.J.(o.s.)K.B. 261 148
McBean v. Howey [1958] N.Z.L.R. 25 62
McCartney v. Londonderry & Lough Swilly Ry. [1904] A.C. 301; 73 L.J.P.C.
    73; 91 L.T. 105; 53 W.R. 385 .... 200, 201, **202,** 204, 205, 209, 224,
                                                        233, 234, 357, 379
McCombe v. Read [1955] 2 Q.B. 429; [1955] 1 W.L.R. 635; 99 S.J. 370;
    [1955] 2 All E.R. 458 306
McEvoy v. G. N. Ry. [1900] 2 Ir.R. 325 .... 224, 229
M'Glone v. Smith (1888) 22 L.R.Ir. 559 203

PAGE
McGrath v. Munster and Leinster Bank Ltd. (1959) 94 I.L.T.R. 110 .... 253, 362, 395
McIlraith v. Grady [1968] 1 Q.B. 468; [1967] 3 W.L.R. 1331; 111 S.J. 583; [1967] 3 All E.R. 625 .... **273**
McIntyre Brothers v. M'Gavin [1893] A.C. 268; 20 R. (Ct. of Sess.) 49; 30 Sc.L.R. 941; 1 S.L.T. 110 .... 57, 231
Mackey v. Scottish Widows' Fund Assurance Society (1877) Ir.R. 11 Eq. 541; reversing (1876) Ir.R. 10 Eq. 113 .... 254, 386, 387
McManus v. Cooke (1887) 35 Ch.D. 681; 56 L.J.Ch. 662; 56 L.T. 900; 3 T.L.R. 622; 51 J.P. 708; 35 W.R. 754 .... **67**
McNab v. Robertson [1897] A.C. 129; 66 L.J.P.C. 27; 75 L.T. 666; 61 J.P. 468 .... 235, 236
Macnaghten v. Baird [1903] 2 Ir.R. 731 167
Macpherson v. London Passenger Transport Board (1946) 175 L.T. 279 ... 290
Magor v. Chadwick (1840) 11 A. & E. 571; 3 Per. & Dav. 367; 9 L.J.Q.B. 159; 4 Jur. 482; 113 E.R. 532 .... 223, 229
Mallam v. Rose [1915] 2 Ch. 222; 84 L.J.Ch. 934; 113 L.T. 1106 .... 149, 177
Malone v. Laskey [1907] 2 K.B. 141; 76 L.J.K.B. 1134; 97 L.T. 324; 23 T.L.R. 399; 51 S.J. 356 362
Manchester Corpn. v. Lyons (1882) 22 Ch.D. 287; 47 L.T. 677 315
Manchester, Sheffield & Lincolnshire Ry. v. Anderson, Anderson v. Manchester, Sheffield & Lincolnshire Ry. [1898] 2 Ch. 394; 67 L.J.Ch. 568; 78 L.T. 821; 14 T.L.R. 489; 42 S.J. 609 315
Manley v. Burn [1916] 2 K.B. 121; 85 L.J.K.B. 505; 114 L.T. 127 ...... 290, 369
Manning v. Wasdale (1836) 5 A. & E. 758; 2 Har. & W. 431; 1 Nev. & P.K.B. 172; 6 L.J.K.B. 59; 111 E.R. 1353 .... 4, 36
Marshall v. Borrowdale Plumbago Mines (1892) 8 T.L.R. 275 35
—— v. Taylor [1895] 1 Ch. 641; 64 L.J.Ch. 416; 72 L.T. 670; 12 R. 310 ... 304
Martin v. Goble (1808) 1 Camp. 320 .... 248, **324**
—— v. Headon (1866) L.R. 2 Eq. 425; 35 L.J.Ch. 602; 14 L.T. 585; 30 J.P. 742; 12 Jur.(N.S.) 387; 14 W.R. 723 .... 243, 327
—— v. Price [1894] 1 Ch. 276; 63 L.J.Ch. 209; 70 L.T. 202; 10 T.L.R. 172; 38 S.J. 127; 7 R. 90; 42 W.R. 262 .... 381, 389, 391
Martyn v. Williams (1857) 1 H. & N. 817; 26 L.J.Ex. 117; 28 L.T.(O.S.) 321; 5 W.R. 351; 156 E.R. 1430 47
Martyr v. Lawrence (1864) 2 De G.J. & Sm. 261; 4 New Rep. 312; 10 L.T. 677; 28 J.P. 580; 10 Jur.(N.S.) 858; 46 E.R. 375; 12 W.R. 1043 86
Mason v. Clarke [1955] A.C. 778; [1955] 2 W.L.R. 853; 99 S.J. 274; [1955] 1 All E.R. 914; reversing [1954] 1 Q.B. 460; [1954] 2 W.L.R. 48; 98 S.J. 28; [1954] 1 All E.R. 189 .... 4, 69, 80
—— v. Hill (1833) 5 B. & Ad. 1; 2 Nev. & M.K.B. 747; 1 L.J.K.B. 118; 110 E.R. 692 .... 207, 208, 218
—— v. Shrewsbury Ry. (1871) L.R. 6 Q.B. 578; 40 L.J.Q.B. 293; 25 L.T. 239; 36 J.P. 324; 20 W.R. 14 .... 55, 178, 218, 219, 228, 229, 370
Masters v. Pollie (1620) 2 Roll.Rep. 141; 81 E.R. 712 305
Mathias v. Davies (1970) 114 S.J. 268 395
Matts v. Hawkins (1813) 5 Taunt. 20; 128 E.R. 593 302
Maxey Drainage Board v. G. N. Ry. (1912) 106 L.T. 429; 76 J.P. 236; 10 L.G.R. 248; sub nom. Massey Drainage Board v. G. N. Ry., 56 S.J. 275 236
May v. Belleville [1905] 2 Ch. 605; 74 L.J.Ch. 678; 93 L.T. 241; 54 W.R. 12; 49 S.J. 651 .... **68**, 80, 81
Mayfair Property Co. v. Johnston [1894] 1 Ch. 508; 63 L.J.Ch. 399; 70 L.T. 485; 38 S.J. 253; 8 R. 781 .... 303, 366
Medway Co. v. Romney (Earl) (1861) 9 C.B.(N.S.) 575; 30 L.J.C.P. 236; 4 L.T. 87; 25 J.P. 550; 7 Jur.(N.S.) 846; 142 E.R. 226; 9 W.R. 482 ... 200, 204
Mellor v. Walmesley [1905] 2 Ch. 164; 74 L.J.Ch. 475; 93 L.T. 574; 21 T.L.R. 591; 49 S.J. 565; 53 W.R. 581 .... 82, 85, 207
Menzies v. Breadalbane (1828) 3 Bligh (N.S.) 414; 4 E.R. 1387 236
Mercer v. Denne [1905] 2 Ch. 538, C.A.; affirming [1904] 2 Ch. 534; 74 L.J. Ch. 71; 91 L.T. 513; 20 T.L.R. 609; 68 J.P. 479; 3 L.G.R. 385; 53 W.R. 55 155
Mersey & Irwell v. Douglas (1802) 2 East 497 380
Merttens v. Hill [1901] 1 Ch. 842; 70 L.J.Ch. 489; 17 T.L.R. 289; sub nom. Marttens v. Hill, 84 L.T. 260; 65 J.P. 312; 49 W.R. 408 143
Metropolitan Association v. Petch (1858) 5 C.B.(N.S.) 504; 27 L.J.C.P. 330; 23 J.P. 119; 4 Jur.(N.S.) 1000; 141 E.R. 204 .... 363, 365, **368**

PAGE

Metropolitan Board of Works v. London & North Western Ry. (1881) 17
Ch.D. 246; 50 L.J.Ch. 409; 44 L.T. 270; 29 W.R. 693 58
Metropolitan Ry. v. Fowler [1893] A.C. 416, H.L.; *affirming* [1892] 1 Q.B.
165; 61 L.J.Q.B. 193; 65 L.T. 772; 8 T.L.R. 189; 56 J.P. 244; 36
S.J. 137; 40 W.R. 306 .... 5, 21, 30, 309
Metropolitan Water Board v. London & North-Eastern Ry. (1924) 131 L.T.
123; 40 T.L.R. 396; 88 J.P. 101; 22 L.G.R. 383 45
Mexborough (Earl) v. Bower (1843) 2 L.T.(o.s.) 205; *affirming* 7 Beav. 127;
49 E.R. 1011 382
Middleton v. Clarence (1877) Ir.R. 11 C.L. 499 35
Midland Ry. v. Gribble [1895] 2 Ch. 827; 64 L.J.Ch. 826; 73 L.T. 270;
44 W.R. 133; 12 R. 513 .... 76, 341
—— v. Miles (1886) 33 Ch.D. 632; 55 L.J.Ch. 745; 55 L.T. 428; 2 T.L.R.
775; 35 W.R. 76 118
Miles v. Tobin (1868) 17 L.T. 432; 16 W.R. 465 102
Mill v. New Forest Commissioner (1856) 18 C.B. 60; 25 L.J.C.P. 212; 20
J.P. 375; 2 Jur.(N.S.) 520; 139 E.R. 1286; 4 W.R. 508 .... **168**
Miller v. Emcer Products Ltd. [1956] Ch. 304; [1956] 2 W.L.R. 267; 100
S.J. 74; [1956] 1 All E.R. 237 .... **31**, 35
Mills v. Brooker [1919] 1 K.B. 555; 88 L.J.K.B. 950; 121 L.T. 254; 35
T.L.R. 261; 63 S.J. 431; 17 L.G.R. 238 305
—— v. Colchester Corpn. (1868) L.R. 3 C.P. 575; 37 L.J.C.P. 278; 16 W.R.
987; *affirming* (1867) L.R. 2 C.P. 476; 36 L.J.C.P. 210; 16 L.T. 626;
15 W.R. 955 172
—— v. Stokman (1967) 41 A.L.J.R. 16 69
Milner's Safe Co. Ltd. v. Great Northern & City Ry. [1907] 1 Ch. 229;
varying [1907] 1 Ch. 208; 75 L.J.Ch. 807; 95 L.T. 321; 22 T.L.R. 706;
50 S.J. 668 .... 57, 111, **281**, 286, **347**
Milnes v. Branch (1816) 5 M. & S. 411; 105 E.R. 1101 48
Miner v. Gilmour (1858) 12 Moo.P.C.C. 131; 33 L.T.(o.s.) 98; 14 E.R.
861; 7 W.R. 328 .... **200, 201,** 209
Mint v. Good [1951] 1 K.B. 517; 94 S.J. 882; [1950] 2 All E.R. 1159;
49 L.G.R. 495 370
Mitcalfe v. Westaway (1864) 17 C.B.(N.S.) 658; 34 L.J.C.P. 113; 11 L.T.
673; 10 Jur.(N.S.) 1202; 144 E.R. 264; *sub nom.* Metcalfe v. Westaway,
5 New Rep. 126; 13 W.R. 181 282
Mitchell v. Cantrill (1887) 37 Ch.D. 56; 57 L.J.Ch. 72; 58 L.T. 29; 36
W.R. 229 149
Mogul Steamship Co. v. M'Gregor (1885) 15 Q.B.D. 476; 54 L.J.Q.B. 540;
53 L.T. 268; 1 T.L.R. 664; 49 J.P. 646; 5 Asp.M.L.C. 467; 15
Cox C.C. 740 .... 381, 387
Monmouth Canal Co. v. Harford (1834) 1 Cr.M. & R. 614; 5 Tyr. 68;
4 L.J.Ex. 43; 149 E.R. 1226 .... 171, 176, 189, 375
Moody v. Steggles (1879) 12 Ch.D. 261; 48 L.J.Ch. 639; 41 L.T.
25 .... 19, 20, 35, 219
Moore v. Browne (1572) 3 Dyer 319b; 73 E.R. 723; *sub nom.* More v.
Brown, Ben. 215 352
—— v. Hall (1878) 3 Q.B.D. 178; 47 L.J.Q.B. 334; 38 L.T. 419; 42
J.P. 343; 26 W.R. 401 .... 248, 324
—— v. Rawson (1824) 3 B. & C. 332; 5 Dow. & Ry.K.B. 234;
3 L.J.(o.s.)K.B. 32; 107 E.R. 756 .... 23, 24, 238, 259, 298, **318–320,**
337, **338,** 343
Morant v. Chamberlin (1861) 6 H. & N. 541; 30 L.J.Ex. 299 339
Morgan v. Fear [1907] A.C. 425; 76 L.J.Ch. 660; 51 S.J. 702; *affirming*
[1906] 2 Ch. 406 .... 21, 149, 162, 183
—— v. Khyatt [1964] 1 W.L.R. 475; 108 S.J. 236 305
Morrice v. Baker (1616) 3 Bulst. 196; 81 E.R. 165; *sub nom.* Norris v.
Baker & Baker, J. Bridg. 47; 1 Roll Rep. 393 .... **360**
Morris v. Cartwright (1963) 107 S.J. 553; 187 E.G. 751 48
—— v. Edgington (1810) 3 Taunt. 24; 128 E.R. 10 136
—— v. Redland Bricks Ltd. *See* Redland Bricks Ltd. v. Morris.
Mosley v. Ball. *See* Bland v. Moseley.
Mostyn v. Atherton [1899] 2 Ch. 360; 68 L.J.Ch. 629; 81 L.T. 356; 48 W.R.
168 214
Mott v. Shoolbred (1875) L.R. 20 Eq. 22 .... 191, 365, 366
Mounsey v. Ismay (1865) 3 H. & C. 486; 34 L.J.Ex. 52; 12 L.T. 26;
11 Jur.(N.S.) 141; 13 W.R. 521; 159 E.R. 621 .... **29, 30**

PAGE

Mumford *v.* Oxford, Worcester & Wolverhampton Ry. (1856) 1 H. & N. 34;
25 L.J.Ex. 265; 27 L.T.(o.s.) 58; 156 E.R. 1107 .... 366, **367**

Murchie *v.* Black (1865) 19 C.B.(n.s.) 190; 34 L.J.C.P. 337; 12 L.T. 735;
11 Jur.(n.s.) 608; 144 E.R. 759; 13 W.R. 896 101

Murgatroyd *v.* Robinson (1857) 7 Ex.B. 391; 26 L.J.Q.B. 233; 29 L.J.(o.s.)
63; 3 Jur.(n.s.) 615; 5 W.R. 375; 119 E.R. 1292 .... 191, 230

Murly *v.* M'Dermott (1838) 8 A. & E. 138; 3 Nev. & P.K.B. 356; 1
Will.Woll & H. 226; 7 L.J.Q.B. 242; 112 E.R. 789; *sub nom.*
Murphy *v.* M'Dermott, 2 Jur. 806 302

Murray *v.* East India Co. (1821) 5 B. & Ald. 204; 106 E.R. 1167 136

Myers *v.* Catterson (1889) 43 Ch.D. 470; 59 L.J.Ch. 315; 62 L.T. 205;
6 T.L.R. 111; 38 W.R. 488 .... 92, **105**, 149

National Guaranteed Manure Co. *v.* Donald (1859) 4 H. & N. 8; 28
L.J.Ex. 185; 157 E.R. 737; 7 W.R. 185 .... 169, 190, 309

National Provincial Plate Glass Insurance Co. *v.* Prudential Assurance
Co. (1877) 6 Ch.D. 757; 46 L.J.Ch. 871; 37 L.T. 91; 26 W.R.
26 .... 317, **332, 333**, 391

National Trust *v.* Midlands Electricity Board [1952] Ch. 380; [1952] 1
T.L.R. 74; 116 J.P. 65; 96 S.J. 29; [1952] 1 All E.R. 298 25

Neaverson *v.* Peterborough R.D.C. [1902] 1 Ch. 557; 71 L.J.Ch. 378; 86 L.T.
738; 18 T.L.R. 360; 66 J.P. 404; 50 W.R. 549 .... 141, 168, 189, 190

Nelson *v.* Liverpool Brewery Co. (1877) 2 C.P.D. 311; 46 L.J.Q.B. 675;
25 W.R. 877 370

New River Co. *v.* Johnson (1860) 2 E. & E. 435; 29 L.J.M.C. 93; 1 L.T.
295; 24 J.P. 244; 6 Jur.(n.s.) 374; 121 E.R. 164; 8 W.R. 179 211

New Windsor Corpn. *v.* Stovell (1884) 27 Ch.D. 665; 54 L.J.Ch. 113; 51
L.T. 626; 33 W.R. 223 .... 58, 267

—— *v.* Taylor [1899] A.C. 41; 68 L.J.Q.B. 87; 15 T.L.R. 67; 63 J.P. 164;
sub nom. Windsor Corpn. *v.* Taylor, 79 L.T. 450; *affirming ibid.*, *sub*
nom. Taylor *v.* New Windsor Corpn. [1898] 1 Q.B. 186 .... **315**, 315

Newcastle-under-Lyme Corporation *v.* Wolstanton Ltd. [1947] Ch. 427;
[1947] L.J.R. 1311; 176 L.T. 242; 63 T.L.R. 162; 111 J.P. 102;
[1947] 1 All E.R. 218; *reversing in part* [1947] Ch. 92 .... 5, 16, 362

Newcomen *v.* Coulson (1877) 5 Ch.D. 133; 46 L.J.Ch. 459; 36 L.T. 385;
25 W.R. 469 .... 44, 75, 273, **276**

Newham *v.* Lawson (1971) 115 S.J. 446; 22 P. & C.R. 852 .... 52, **254**

News of the World *v.* Fairhead (Allen) & Sons [1931] 2 Ch. 402; 100 L.J.Ch.
394; 146 L.T. 11 .... 57, 328, **330–332**, 336, 355

Newson *v.* Pender (1884) 27 Ch.D. 43; 52 L.T. 9; 33 W.R. 243 ... 327, 336, 386

Nicholas *v.* Chamberlain (1606) Cro.Jac. 121; 79 E.R. 105 .... **100**, 108

Nicholls *v.* Ely Beet Sugar Factory Ltd. [1931] 2 Ch. 84, 87; 100 L.J.Ch.
259; 145 L.T. 113 230

—— *v.* —— [1936] Ch. 343; 105 L.J.Ch. 279; 154 L.T. 531; 80 S.J. 127 230

—— *v.* Nicholls (1899) 81 L.T. 811 .... 94, 96, 97, 111

Nicol *v.* Beaumont (1883) 53 L.J.Ch. 853; 50 L.T. 112 .... 285, 353

Nield *v.* London & North-Western Ry. (1874) L.R. 10 Ex. 4; 44 L.J.Ex. 15;
23 W.R. 60 236

Nisbet & Potts' Contract, *Re* [1905] 1 Ch. 391; [1906] 1 Ch. 386; 75 L.J.Ch.
238; 22 T.L.R. 233; 50 S.J. 191; *sub nom. Re* Nesbitt & Potts'
Contract, 94 L.T. 297; 54 W.R. 286 43

Nixon *v.* Tynemouth Union Rural Sanitary Authority (1888) 52 J.P. 504, D.C. 369

Norbury *v.* Meade (1821) 3 Bli. 211, 4 E.R. 582 .... 316, **344**

Norbury (Lord) *v.* Kitchin (1863) 3 F. & F. 292; 1 New Rep. 241; 7 L.T.
685; 9 Jur.(n.s.) 132 204

Norfolk (Duke) *v.* Arbuthnot (1880) 5 C.P.D. 390; 49 L.J.Q.B. 782; 43 L.T.
302; 44 J.P. 796, C.A.; *affirming* (1879) 4 C.P.D. 293 .... 134, 139, 143,
144, 147, 378

Norris *v.* Baker & Baker. *See* Morrice *v.* Baker.

North Shore Ry. *v.* Pion (1889) 14 App.Cas. 612; 59 L.J.P.C. 25; 61 L.T.
525 .... 207, 237

Northam *v.* Hurley (1853) 1 E. & B. 665; 22 L.J.Q.B. 183; 17 Jur. 672;
118 E.R. 586 .... 23, **235**, 379

North-Eastern Ry. *v.* Elliott. *See* Elliott *v.* North-Eastern Ry.

Norval *v.* Pascoe (1864) 4 New Rep. 390; 34 L.J.Ch. 82; 10 L.T. 809; 28
J.P. 548; 10 Jur.(n.s.) 792; 12 W.R. 973 47

                                                                                    PAGE
Noye v. Reed (1827) 1 Man. & Ry.K.B. 63; 6 L.J.(o.s.)K.B. 5   304
Nuneaton v. General Sewage Co. (1875) 20 Eq. 127; 44 L.J.Ch. 561   396
Nuttall v. Bracewell (1866) L.R. 2 Exch. 1; 4 H. & C. 714; 36 L.J.Ex. 1;
    15 L.T. 313; 31 J.P. 8; 12 Jur.(N.S.) 989 .... 16, 19, 34, 37

O'CEDAR LTD. v. Slough Trading Co. [1927] 2 K.B. 123; 96 L.J.K.B. 709;
    137 L.T. 208; 43 T.L.R. 382   92
O'Connor v. Walsh (1906) 42 I.L.T.R. 20   254
Olney v. Gardiner. See Onley v. Gardiner.
Onley v. Gardiner (1838) 4 M. & W. 496; 1 Horn & H. 381; 150 E.R.
    1525; sub nom. Olney v. Gardiner, 8 L.J.Ex. 102 .... 147, 156, 160,
                                                            345, 375, 376
Original Hartlepool Collieries Co. v. Gibb (1877) 5 Ch.D. 713; 46 L.J.Ch.
    311; 36 L.T. 433; 41 J.P. 660; 3 Asp.M.L.C. 411 .... 237, 353
Ormerod v. Todmorden Joint Stock Mill Co. Ltd. (1883) 11 Q.B.D. 155;
    affirming (1882) 8 Q.B.D. 664; 51 L.J.Q.B. 348; 46 L.T. 669;
    30 W.R. 805 .... 202, 203, 207, 208, 233, 379
Orr-Ewing v. Colquhoun (1877) 2 App.Cas. 839 .... 202, 203, 208, 236, 237,
Osborn v. Wise (1837) 7 Car. & P. 761   117
Ough v. King [1967] 1 W.L.R. 1547; 111 S.J. 792; [1967] 3 All E.R. 859;
    19 P. & C.R. 40 .... 246, 247, 253, 398
Outram v. Maude (1881) 17 Ch.D. 391; 50 L.J.Ch. 783; 29 W.R. 818   188
Owen v. Davies [1874] W.N. 175   204

PACKER v. Wellstead (1658) 2 Sid. 39, 111; 82 E.R. 1284   117
Paddington Corporation v. Att.-Gen. See Boyce v. Paddington Borough
    Council.
Paine & Co. v. St. Neots Gas & Coke Co. [1938] 4 All E.R. 592; [1939] 3
    All E.R. 812 .... 4, 16, 56, 77, 351, 361, 373-375
Palk v. Shinner (1852) 18 Q.B. 568; 22 L.J.Q.B. 27; 19 L.T.(o.s.) 228;
    17 Jur. 372; 118 E.R. 215 .... 157, 158, 184, 185, 366, 367
Palmer v. Fletcher (1663) 1 Lev. 122; 1 Keb. 553, 625; 1 Sid. 167; 83
    E.R. 329   101
—— v. Guadagni [1906] 2 Ch. 494; 75 L.J.Ch. 721; 95 L.T. 258   378
Parker v. First Avenue Hotel Co. (1883) 24 Ch.D. 282; 49 L.T. 318;
    32 W.R. 105   252
—— v. Mitchell (1840) 11 A. & E. 788; 3 Per. & Dav. 655; 9 L.J.Q.B. 194;
    4 Jur. 915; 113 E.R. 613   153
—— v. Smith (1832) 5 C. & P. 438 .... 241, 242, 244, 245
—— v. Stanley (W. F.) & Co. Ltd. (1902) 50 W.R. 282 .... 254, 391
Parkinson v. Reid (1966) 56 D.L.R. (2d) 315   46–48
Partridge v. Scott (1838) 3 M. & W. 229; 1 Horn & H. 31; 7 L.J.Ex. 101;
    150 E.R. 1124   174
Pattisson v. Gilford (1874) L.R. 18 Eq. 259; 43 L.J.Ch. 524; 22 W.R. 673   384
Paul v. Robson (1914) 83 L.J.P.C. 304; 111 L.T. 481; 30 T.L.R. 533 246
Payne v. Shedden (1834) 1 Mood. & R. 382 .... 153, 339
Peachey v. Lee (1964) 192 E.G. 365 ....   76, 193
Pearson v. Spencer (1861) 1 B. & S. 571; 8 L.T. 166; 122 E.R. 285; 11 W.R.
    471; sub nom. R. v. Pearson, 1 New Rep. 373 Ex.Ch. 117, 118
Pearson's Will, Re (1900) 83 L.T. 626   5
Peck & London School Board's Contract, Re [1893] 2 Ch. 315; 62 L.J.Ch.
    598; 68 L.T. 847; 41 W.R. 388; 3 R. 511; sub nom. Peck v. London
    School Board, 37 S.J. 372 .... 98, 122, 126, 129
Peech v. Best [1931] 1 K.B. 1; 99 L.J.K.B. 537; 143 L.T. 266; 46 T.L.R.
    467; 74 S.J. 520   4
Pendarves v. Monro [1892] 1 Ch. 611; 61 L.J.Ch. 494; 8 T.L.R. 388   336
Pennington v. Brinsop Hall Coal Co. (1877) 5 Ch.D. 769; 46 L.J.Ch. 773;
    37 L.T. 149; 25 W.R. 874   381
Penny v. Wimbledon Council [1899] 2 Q.B. 72; 68 L.J.Q.B. 704; 80 L.T.
    615; 47 W.R. 565, C.A.; affirming [1898] 2 Q.B. 212   373
Penruddock's Case (1598) 5 Rep. 100b; Jenk. 260; 77 E.R. 210 ...... 357, 360, 369
Penwarden v. Ching (1829) Mood. & M. 400; 173 E.R. 1203 .... 137, 238, 239
Perry v. Eames, Salaman v. Eames, Mercers' Co. v. Eames [1891]
    1 Ch. 658; 60 L.J.Ch. 345; 64 L.T. 438; 7 T.L.R. 297; 39 W.R.
    602 .... 146, 147, 190, 255

PAGE

Perry v. Fitzhowe (1846) 8 Q.B. 757; 15 L.J.Q.B. 239; 7 L.T.(o.s.) 180;
   10 J.P. 600; 10 Jur. 799; 115 E.R. 1057 .... 356, 357, 358
Peru Republic v. Dreyfus Bros. & Co. (1888) 38 Ch.D. 348; 57 L.J.Ch. 536;
   58 L.T. 433; 4 T.L.R. 333; 36 W.R. 492 387
Peruvian Guano Co. v. Dreyfus Brothers & Co. [1892] A.C. 166; 61 L.J.Ch.
   749; sub nom. Dreyfus Brothers v. Peruvian Guano Co., Peruvian
   Guano Co. v. Dreyfus Brothers, 66 L.T. 536; 8 T.L.R. 327; 7
   Asp.M.L.C. 225; varying (1889) 43 Ch.D. 316 389
Peter v. Daniel (1848) 5 C.B. 568; 17 L.J.C.P. 177; 12 Jur. 604; 136 E.R.
   1001 .... 36, 355, 365
Pettey v. Parsons [1914] 2 Ch. 653; 84 L.J.Ch. 81; 11 L.T. 1011; 30 T.L.R.
   655; 58 S.J. 721 .... **285, 286,** 352, 354
Peyton v. London Corpn. (1829) 9 B. & C. 725; 109 E.R. 269; sub nom.
   Peyton v. St. Thomas's Hospital (Governors) 7 L.J.(o.s.)K.B. 322 ... 303
Pheysey v. Vicary (1847) 16 M. & W. 484; 8 L.T.(o.s.) 451; 153 E.R.
   1280 .... 117, 310
Phillimore v. Watford R. D. C. [1913] 2 Ch. 434; 82 L.J.Ch. 514; 109 L.T.
   616; 77 J.P. 453; 57 S.J. 741; 11 L.G.R. 980 58
Phillips v. Halliday [1891] A.C. 228; 61 L.J.Q.B. 210; 64 L.T. 745;
   55 J.P. 741, H.L.; affirming sub nom. Halliday v. Phillips (1899)
   23 Q.B.D. 48 .... 36, 137, 141, **142,** 143
—— v. Low [1892] 1 Ch. 47; 61 L.J.Ch. 44; 65 L.T. 552; 8 T.L.R.
   23 .... 24, 101, 111
—— v. Thomas (1890) 62 L.T. 793; 6 T.L.R. 327 .... 370, 384
—— v. Treeby (1862) 6 L.T. 796; 8 Jur.(N.S.) 999, L.C.; affirming 3
   Giff. 632 353
Philpot v. Bath [1905] W.N. 105; 21 T.L.R. 634; 49 S.J. 618; affirming
   (1904) 20 T.L.R. 589 .... 32, 35
Phipps v. Pears [1965] 1 Q.B. 76; [1964] 2 W.L.R. 996; 108 S.J. 236;
   [1964] 2 All E.R. 35 .... 24, 26, 27, 34, 36, 128, 257, 303
Pickard v. Smith (1861) 10 C.B.(N.S.) 470; 4 L.T. 470; 142 E.R. 535 ...... **371, 372**
Pinnington v. Galland (1853) 9 Exch. 1; 1 C.L.R. 819; 22 L.J.Ex. 348;
   22 L.T.(o.s.) 41; 156 E.R. 1 .... 117, 118
Pitt v. Buxton (1969) 21 P. & C.R. 127 .... **80, 81**
Plasterers' Co. v. Parish Clerks' Co. (1851) 6 Exch. 630; 20 L.J.Ex. 362;
   17 L.T.(o.s.) 246; 15 Jur. 965; 155 E.R. 696 .... 153, 177
Pledge & Sons v. Pomfret [1905] W.N. 56; 74 L.J.Ch. 357; 92 L.T. 560 377
Polden v. Bastard (1865) L.R. 1 Q.B. 156; 7 B. & S. 130; 35 L.J.Q.B. 92;
   13 L.T. 441; 30 J.P. 73; 14 W.R. 198 .... 36, 86, 98, 222
Pollard v. Gare [1901] 1 Ch. 834; 70 L.J.Ch. 404; 84 L.T. 352; 65 J.P.
   264 .... 101, 102, 105
Polsue & Alfieri Ltd. v. Rushmer [1907] A.C. 121; 76 L.J.Ch. 365; 96 L.T.
   510; 23 T.L.R. 362; sub nom. Rushmer v. Polsue & Alfieri Ltd., 51
   S.J. 324, H.L.; affirming [1906] 1 Ch. 234 247
Polus v. Henstock (1670) 1 Vent. 97; 86 E.R. 67; sub nom. Bolus v.
   Hinstorke (1670) T.Raym. 192; 2 Keb. 686, 707 .... 40, 41
Pomfret v. Ricroft (1669) 1 Wms.Saund. 6th ed. 321; 2 Keb. 543, 569;
   1 Sid. 429; 1 Vent. 26, 44; 85 E.R. 454 .... 39, 44, 47
Ponting v. Noakes [1894] 2 Q.B. 281; 63 L.J.Q.B. 549; 70 L.T. 842; 10
   T.L.R. 444; 58 J.P. 559; 88 S.J. 438; 10 R. 265; 42 W.R. 506 305
Popplewell v. Hodkinson (1869) L.R. 4 Ex. 248; 38 L.J.Ex. 126; 20 L.T.
   578; 17 W.R. 806 .... 89, **288**
Port v. Griffith [1938] 1 All E.R. 295; 82 S.J. 154 92
Portsmouth Borough Waterworks Co. v. London, Brighton & South Soast
   Ry. (1909) 74 J.P. 61; 26 T.L.R. 173 .... **206**
Poster v. Slough Estates Ltd. [1969] 1 Ch. 495; [1968] 1 W.L.R. 1515;
   112 S.J. 705; [1968] 3 All E.R. 257; 19 P. & C.R. 841 .... 64, **71**
Potter v. North (1669) 1 Lev. 268; 2 Keb. 513, 517; 1 Saund. 346;
   1 Vent. 383; 83 E.R. 400 137
Potts v. Smith (1868) L.R. 6 Eq. 311; 38 L.J.Ch. 58; 18 L.T. 629; 33 J.P. 52;
   16 W.R. 891 .... 26, 239
Poulton v. Moore [1915] 1 K.B. 400; 84 L.J.K.B. 462; 112 L.T. 202 ... 102, 316
Powell v. Butler (1871) Ir.R. 5 C.L. 309 224
—— v. Thomas (1848) 6 Hare 300 67
Prescott v. Phillips (1798) cited 6 East at p. 213; 102 E.R. 1268 218
Presland v. Bingham (1889) 41 Ch.D. 268; 60 L.T. 433; 53 J.P. 583;
   37 W.R. 385 .... 148, 154

PAGE

Preston v. Luck (1844) 27 Ch.D. 497; 33 W.R. 317 387
—— v. Norfolk Ry. & Eastern Counties Ry. (1858) 2 H. & N. 735; 157
E.R. 303; sub nom. Preston v. Eastern Counties & Norfolk Ry. 30
L.T.(o.s.) 288 370
Pretty v. Bickmore (1873) L.R. 8 C.P. 401; 28 L.T. 704; 37 J.P. 552;
21 W.R. 733 370
Price v. Hilditch [1930] 1 Ch. 500; 99 L.J.Ch. 299; 143 L.T. 33 ...... 148, 240,
247, **248, 249**, 253, 254, 394
Prichard v. Powell (1845) 10 Q.B. 589; 116 E.R. 224; sub nom. Pritchard v.
Powell, 15 L.J.Q.B. 166; 10 Jur. 154; sub nom. Powell v. Pritchard,
5 L.T.(o.s.) 263 146
Pride of Derby & Derbyshire Angling Association v. British Celanese Ltd.
[1953] Ch. 149; [1953] 2 W.L.R. 58; 117 J.P. 52; 97 S.J. 28; [1953]
1 All E.R. 179; 51 L.G.R. 121; affirming [1952] W.N. 227; [1952] 1
T.L.R. 1013; 96 S.J. 263; [1952] 1 All E.R. 1326; 50 L.G.R. 488 ... 229, 230
Pringle v. Wernham (1836) 7 C. & P. 377 241
Prinsep v. Belgravian Estates Ltd. (1895) 39 S.J. 381; [1896] W.N. 39 69
Proctor v. Hodgson (1855) 10 Exch. 824; 3 C.L.R. 755; 24 L.J.Ex. 195;
156 E.R. 674 .... 121, 378
Proud v. Hollis (1822) 2 B. & C. 8; 107 E.R. 4; sub nom. Hollis v. Proud,
2 Dow. & Ry.K.B. 31; 1 L.J.(o.s.)K.B. 10 .... 8, 357
Prow v. Chaplin (Trading as Chaplin Bros., A Firm) (1964) 108 S.J. 463;
190 E.G. 865 395
Pugh v. Savage [1970] 2 Q.B. 373; [1970] 2 W.L.R. 634; 114 S.J. 109;
[1970] 2 All E.R. 353; 21 P. & C.R. 242 ...... 20, 164, 170, **184, 185**, 378
Pullin v. Deffel (1891) 64 L.T. 134 .... 261, 352
Pwllbach Colliery Co. Ltd. v. Woodman [1915] A.C. 634; affirming sub nom.
Woodman v. Pwllbach Colliery Co. Ltd. (1914) 111 L.T. 169 ...... **15**, 23,
44, 66, 86, **87**, 88, 108, 109, 121, 190
Pye v. Mumford (1848) 11 Q.B. 666; 5 Dow. & L. 414; 17 L.J.Q.B. 138;
11 L.T.(o.s.) 62; 116 E.R. 623 .... 35, 159, 161, 375, 376
Pyer v. Carter (1857) 1 H. & N. 916; 26 L.J.Ex. 258; 28 L.T.(o.s.) 371;
21 J.P. 247; 156 E.R. 1472; 5 W.R. 371 .... 99, **107**, 222

Quarman v. Burnett (1840) 6 M. & W. 499; 9 L.J.Ex. 308; 4 Jur. 969;
151 E.R. 509 .... 371, **372**
Quicke v. Chapman [1903] 1 Ch. 659; 72 L.J.Ch. 373; 88 L.T. 610; 51 W.R.
452; 19 T.L.R. 284 .... **78**, 104, 111, 124

R. v. Bristol Dock Co. (1810) 12 East 429 230
—— v. Chelsea Waterworks Co. (1833) 5 B. & Ad. 156; 2 Nev. & M.K.B.
767; 2 Nev. & M.M.C. 13; 2 L.J.M.C. 98; 110 E.R. 750 5
—— v. Chorley (1848) 12 Q.B. 515; 12 L.T.(o.s.) 371; 13 J.P. 136; 12 Jur.
822; 3 Cox C.C. 262; 116 E.R. 960 .... 261, **339, 340**, 343
—— v. Drucquer (Judge) ex p. Speller [1939] 2 K.B. 588; 108 L.J.K.B.
559; 160 L.T. 550; 55 T.L.R. 671; 83 S.J. 499; [1939] 2 All E.R. 473 361
—— v. Hatfield, Inhabitants of (1835) 4 A. & E. 156; 111 E.R. 746 314
—— v. Hermitage (1692) Carth. 239; 1 Show. 106; 90 E.R. 743 310
—— v. Joliffe (1823) 2 B. & C. 54; 3 Dow. & Ry.K.B. 240; 1 L.J.(o.s.)K.B.
232; 107 E.R. 303 138
—— v. Metropolitan Board of Works (1863) 3 B. & S. 710; 1 New Rep.
473; 32 L.J.Q.B. 105; 8 L.T. 238; 27 J.P. 342; 9 Jur.(N.S.) 1009;
122 E.R. 266; 11 W.R. 492 211
—— v. Pagham, Sussex, Sewers Commissioners (1828) 8 B. & C. 355 236
—— v. Pedly (1834) 1 Ad. & El. 822; 3 Nev. & M.K.B. 627; 3 L.J.M.C.
119; 110 E.R. 1422 370
—— v. Rosewell (1699) 2 Salk. 459; 91 E.R. 397 .... **356**, 357
—— v. Tindall (1837) 6 Ad. & El. 143; 1 Nev. & P.K.B. 719; Will.Woll.
& Dav. 316; 6 L.J.M.C. 97; 1 J.P. 139; 112 E.R. 55 352
—— v. Trafford (1832) 8 Bing. 204, Ex.Ch.; reversing sub nom. Trafford v.
R. (1831) 1 B. & Ad. 874; 109 E.R. 1011 236
R. C. P. Holdings Ltd. v. Rogers [1953] 1 All E.R. 1029 ...... 134, 143, 266, **268**
Race v. Ward (1857) 7 E. & B. 384; affirming (1855) 4 E. & B. 702; 3
C.L.R. 744; 24 L.J.Q.B. 153; 24 L.T.(o.s.) 270; 19 J.P. 563; 1 Jur.(N.S.)
704; 119 E.R. 259; 3 W.R. 240 .... 4, 36, 190, 222, 355

PAGE

Radstock Co-operative & Industrial Society Ltd. *v.* Norton-Radstock
U.D.C. [1968] Ch. 605; [1968] 2 W.L.R. 1214; 132 J.P. 238; 112
S.J. 135; [1968] 2 All E.R. 59; 66 L.G.R. 457 236
Raikes *v.* Townsend (1804) 2 Smith K.B. 9 .... **356**
Raine *v.* Alderson (1838) 4 Bing.N.C. 702; 1 Arn. 329; 6 Scott. 691; 7
L.J.C.P. 273; 2 Jur. 327; 132 E.R. 959 366
Rameshur *v.* Koonj (1878) 4 App.Cas. 121 .... 202, **223,** 224
Ramsden *v.* Dyson (1866) L.R. 1 H.L. 129; 12 Jur.(N.S.) 506; 14 W.R.
926, H.L.; *reversing sub nom.* Thornton *v.* Ramsden (1864) 4
Giff. 519 .... 62, 66
Ramsgate Corporation *v.* Debling (1906) 70 J.P. 132; 22 T.L.R. 369;
4 L.G.R. 495 155
Randall *v.* Hall (1851) 4 De G. & Sm. 343; 64 E.R. 861 284
Randfield *v.* Randfield (1860) 1 Drew. & Sm. 310; (1861) 3 De G.F. & J.
766, L.JJ. 357
Rangeley *v.* Midland Ry. (1868) 3 Ch.App. 306; 37 L.J.Ch. 313; 18 L.T.
69; 16 W.R. 547 .... 7, 8
Raper *v.* Fortescue [1886] W.N. 78; *affirming* [1886] W.N. 67 336
Rawstron *v.* Taylor (1855) 11 Exch. 369; 25 L.J.Ex. 33; 156 E.R. 873 ...
200, 209, 220, 235, 379
Ray *v.* Fairway Motors (Barnstaple) Ltd. (1968) 112 S.J. 925; 20 P. &
C.R. 261 .... 290, **292,** 324
—— *v.* Hazeldine [1904] 2 Ch. 17; 73 L.J.Ch. 537; 90 L.T. 703 106
Rea *v.* Sheward (1837) 2 M. & W. 424; 6 L.J.Ex. 125; 1 Jur. 433; 150 E.R.
823; *sub nom.* Ray *v.* Sheward, Murph. & H. 68 359
Read *v.* Brookman (1789) 3 T.R. 151 .... 137, 378
Redland Bricks Ltd. *v.* Morris [1970] A.C. 652; [1969] 2 W.L.R. 1437;
113 S.J. 405; [1969] 2 All E.R. 576; *reversing* [1967] 1 W.L.R.
967 .... 290, 360, 381, 383, **384,** 385
Reedie *v.* London & North-Western Ry., Hobbit *v.* Same (1849) 4 Exch. 244;
6 Ry. & Can.Cas. 184; 20 L.J.Ex. 65; 13 Jur. 659; 154 E.R. 1201 ... 371
Regis Property Co. Ltd. *v.* Redman [1956] 2 Q.B. 612; [1956] 3 W.L.R.
95; 100 S.J. 417; [1956] 2 All E.R. 335 128
Reignolds *v.* Edwards (1741) Willes 282; 125 E.R. 1173 261
Reilly *v.* Booth (1890) 44 Ch.D. 12; 62 L.T. 378; 38 W.R. 484 5
—— *v.* Orange [1955] 2 Q.B. 112; [1955] 1 W.L.R. 616; 99 S.J. 353;
[1955] 2 All E.R. 369 .... 153, 177
Remfry *v.* Natal (Surveyor-General) [1896] A.C. 558; 65 L.J.P.C. 72;
75 L.T. 58 235
Renshaw *v.* Bean (1852) 18 Q.B. 112; 21 L.J.Q.B. 219; 19 L.T.(O.S.) 22;
16 Jur. 814; 118 E.R. 42 .... 325–327, 336
Reynolds *v.* Clarke (1725) 2 Ld.Raym. 1399; 1 Stra. 634; Fortes.Rep. 212;
8 Mod.Rep. 272; 92 E.R. 410 223
Reynolds *v.* Moore [1908] 2 I.R. 641 282
Rich *v.* Basterfield (1847) 4 C.B. 783; 16 L.J.C.P. 273; 9 L.T.(O.S.) 77,
356; 11 Jur. 696; 136 E.R. 715 370
Richards *v.* Fry (1838) 7 Ad. & El. 698; 3 Nev. & P.K.B. 67; 1 Will.Woll.
& H. 116; 7 L.J.Q.B. 68; 2 Jur. 641; 112 E.R. 632 .... 152, **345,** 377
—— *v.* Jenkins (1868) 18 L.T. 437; 17 W.R. 30 .... 291, 373
—— *v.* Rose (1853) 9 Exch. 218; 2 C.L.R. 311; 23 L.J.Ex. 3; 22 L.T.(O.S.)
104; 18 J.P. 56; 17 Jur. 1036; 156 E.R. 93 .... 101, 106
Richardson *v.* Graham [1908] 1 K.B. 39; 77 L.J.K.B. 27; 98 L.T. 360 313
Rider *v.* Smith (1790) 3 Term.Rep. 766; 100 E.R. 848 .... 47, 375
Ridge *v.* Midland Ry. (1888) 53 J.P. 55 236
Rigby *v.* Bennett (1882) 21 Ch.D. 559; 48 L.T. 47; 47 J.P. 217; 31
W.R. 222 .... 101, 111
Rippon *v.* Bowles (1616) 1 Roll.Rep. 221; 81 E.R. 446; *sub nom.* Ryppon
v. Bowles, Cro.Jac. 373; 79 E.R. 318 370
Rivers (Lord) *v.* Adams (1878) 3 Ex.D. 361; 48 L.J.Q.B. 47; 39 L.T. 39;
42 J.P. 728; 27 W.R. 381 .... 143, 178
Robbins *v.* Jones (1863) 15 C.B.(N.S.) 240; 3 New Rep. 85; 33 L.J.C.P. 1;
9 L.T. 523; 10 Jur.(N.S.) 239; 143 E.R. 768; 12 W.R. 248 369
Roberts *v.* Fellowes (1906) 94 L.T. 279 .... 36, **176,** 219
—— *v.* Gwyrfai District Council [1899] 2 Ch. 608; 68 L.J.Ch. 757; 81 L.T.
465; 16 T.L.R. 2; 64 J.P. 52; 44 S.J. 10; 48 W.R. 51 ...... 202, 204, 209, 379
—— *v.* Karr (1809) 1 Taunt. 495; 127 E.R. 926; *affirming* (1807) 1 Camp.
262n. **84**

PAGE

Roberts *v*. Macord (1832) 1 Mood. & R. 230 .... **239**
—— *v*. Richards (1882) 51 L.J.Ch. 944, C.A.; *compromising on appeal*
  (1881) 50 L.J.Ch. 297; 44 L.T. 271 .... 202, 224
—— *v*. Rose (1865) L.R. 1 Exch. 82; 4 H. & C. 103; 35 L.J.Ex. 62;
  13 L.T. 471; 30 J.P. 5; 12 Jur.(N.S.) 78; 14 W.R. 225 .... 357, 358
Roberts & Lovell *v*. James (1903) 89 L.T. 282; 19 T.L.R. 573 ... 141, 163, 164, 179
Robertson *v*. Abrahams. *See* Robertson *v*. Adams.
—— *v*. Adams (1930) 69 L.J. 301; *sub nom.* Robertson *v*. Abrahams, 169
  L.T.J. 305; [1930] W.N. 79 .... 285, 353
—— *v*. Hartopp (1889) 43 Ch.D. 484; 59 L.J.Ch. 553; 62 L.T. 585;
  6 T.L.R. 126 60
Robins *v*. Evans (1863) 2 H. & C. 410; 159 E.R. 169; *sub nom.* Evans *v*.
  Robins, 33 L.J.Ex. 68; 11 L.T. 211; 10 Jur.(N.S.) 473; 12 W.R. 604 17
Robinson *v*. Bailey [1948] W.N. 402; [1948] 2 All E.R. 791 ... 271, 274, **280, 281**
—— *v*. Byron (Lord) (1785) 1 Bro.C.C. 588; 28 E.R. 1315 .... 380, 382
—— *v*. Grave (1873) 29 L.T. 7; 21 W.R. 569 102
—— *v*. Kilvert (1889) 41 Ch.D. 88; 58 L.J.Ch. 392; 61 L.T. 60; 37 W.R.
  545 .... 89, 92
Robson *v*. Edwards [1893] 2 Ch. 146; 62 L.J.Ch. 378; 68 L.T. 195; 37 S.J.
  285; 3 R. 336; 41 W.R. 569 149
—— *v*. Whittingham (1866) 1 Ch.App. 442; 35 L.J.Ch. 227; 13 L.T. 730;
  30 J.P. 179; 12 Jur.(N.S.) 40; 14 W.R. 291 243
Rochdale Canal Co. *v*. King (1851) 2 Sim.(N.S.) 78; (1853) 16 Beav. 630;
  reversing sub nom. King *v*. Rochdale Canal Co. (1851) 14 Q.B. 136;
  18 L.T.(O.S.) 5; 15 Jur. 896; 117 E.R. 55: *affirming sub nom.*
  Rochdale Canal Co. *v*. King (1849) 14 Q.B. 122 .... **62, 63,** 379
—— *v*. Radcliffe (1852) 18 Q.B. 287; 21 L.J.Q.B. 297; 19 L.T.(O.S.) 163;
  16 Jur. 1111; 118 E.R. 108 .... 168, 190
Roe *v*. Siddons (1888) 22 Q.B.D. 224; 60 L.T. 345; 53 J.P. 246; 37 W.R.
  228 .... 21, 85, 309
Rogers *v*. Hyde [1951] 2 Q.B. 923; 95 S.J. 483; [1951] 2 All E.R. 79 31
—— *v*. Taylor (1857) 1 H. & N. 706; 26 L.J.Ex. 203; 28 L.T.(O.S.) 275;
  156 E.R. 1385 35
Rolle *v*. Whyte (1868) L.R. 3 Q.B. 286; 8 B. & S. 116; 37 L.J.Q.B. 105;
  17 L.T. 560; 32 J.P. 645; 16 W.R. 593 .... 37, 154, 174, 191, 219
Rosewell *v*. Prior (1701) Holt K.B. 500; 12 Mod.Rep. 635; 90 E.R. 1175;
  sub nom. Rosewell *v*. Prior, 1 Ld.Raym. 392, 713; 6 Mod.Rep. 116;
  2 Salk. 460 .... 101, 369, 370
Roskell *v*. Whitworth (1870) 5 Ch.App. 459 (1871) 19 W.R. 804 380
Rouse *v*. Gravelworks Ltd. [1940] 1 K.B. 489; [1940] 1 All E.R. 26; 109
  L.J.K.B. 408; 162 L.T. 230; 56 T.L.R. 225; 84 S.J. 112 .... 290, 304
Rowbotham *v*. Wilson (1860) 8 H.L.Cas. 348; 30 L.J.Q.B. 49; 2 L.T. 642;
  24 J.P. 579; 6 Jur.(N.S.) 965; 11 E.R. 463; *affirming* (1857) 8
  E. & B. 123; (1856) 6 E. & B. 593 .... 23, 78, 290
Royal Mail Steam Packet Co. *v*. George & Branday [1900] A.C. 480;
  69 L.J.P.C. 107; 82 L.T. 539 191
Rudd *v*. Bowles [1912] 2 Ch. 60; 81 L.J.Ch. 277; 105 L.T. 864 ...... **85, 86**, 98
Rugby Joint Water Board *v*. Walters [1967] Ch. 397; [1966] 3 W.L.R.
  934; 131 J.P. 10; 110 S.J. 635; [1966] 3 All E.R. 497; 119 E.G.
  565 .... 201, **204,** 205, **210,** 214, 216
Runcorn *v*. (Doe d.) Cooper (1826) 5 B. & C. 696; 8 Dow. & Ry.K.B. 450;
  4 L.J.(O.S.)K.B. 281; 108 E.R. 259 163
Ruscoe *v*. Grounsell (1903) 89 L.T. 426; 20 T.L.R. 5 149
Rushmer *v*. Polsue. *See* Polsue & Alfieri Ltd. *v*. Rushmer.
Russell *v*. Harford (1866) L.R. 2 Eq. 507; 15 L.T. 171; 14 W.R. 982 81
—— *v*. Watts (1885) 10 App.Cas. 590; 55 L.J.Ch. 158; 53 L.T. 876;
  50 J.P. 68; 34 W.R. 277; *reversing* (1883) 25 Ch.D. 559 ... 23, 106, 110, **111**
Rust *v*. Victoria Graving Dock Co. & London & St. Katherine Dock Co.
  (1887) 36 Ch.D. 113; 56 L.T. 216; 35 W.R. 673 .... 364, 365
Ryder *v*. Bentham (1750) 1 Ves.Sen. 543; 27 E.R. 1194 382
Rye *v*. Rye [1962] A.C. 496; [1962] 2 W.L.R. 361; 106 S.J. 94; [1962]
  1 All E.R. 146 123
Rymer *v*. McIlroy [1897] 1 Ch. 528; 66 L.J.Ch. 336; 76 L.T. 115; 45 W.R.
  411 79
Ryppon *v*. Bowles. *See* Rippon *v*. Bowles.

PAGE

SACK v. Jones [1925] Ch. 235; 94 L.J.Ch. 229; 133 L.T. 129 290
St. John v. Moody (1675) 1 Vent. 274; 2 Lev. 148; 3 Keb. 531; 86 E.R. 184 374
Salaman v. Glover (1875) L.R. 20 Eq. 444; 44 L.J.Ch. 551; 32 L.T. 792;
    23 W.R. 722 .... 124, 316
Salmon v. Bensley (1825) Ry. & M. 189 369
Salt Union v. Brunner, Mond & Co. [1906] 2 K.B. 822; 76 L.J.K.B. 55;
    95 L.T. 647; 22 T.L.R. 835 .... 211, 213, 289
Salter's Co., London v. Jay (1842) 3 Q.B. 109 255
Salvin's Indenture, Re, Pitt v. Durham County Water Board (1938) 82 S.J.
    395; [1938] 2 All E.R. 498; 36 L.G.R. 388 .... 14, 56
Sampson v. Hoddinott 3 C.B.(N.S.) 596; Ex.Ch. affirming (1857) 1
    C.B.(N.S.) 590; 26 L.J.C.P. 148; 28 L.T.(O.S.) 304; 21 J.P. 375; 3
    Jur.(N.S.) 243; 140 E.R. 242; 5 W.R. 230 .... 200, 205, 209, 218
Sandford v. Clarke (1888) 21 Q.B.D. 398; 57 L.J.Q.B. 507; 59 L.T. 226;
    52 J.P. 773; 37 W.R. 28 370
Sands v. Trefuses (1640) Cro.Car. 575 375
Sandwich (Earl) v. Great Northern Ry. (1878) 10 Ch.D. 707; 49 L.J.Ch. 225;
    43 J.P. 429; 27 W.R. 616 .... 202, 204
Saunders v. Newman (1818) 1 B. & Ald. 258; 106 E.R. 95 .... 57, 208, 322
Sayers v. Collyer (1884) 28 Ch.D. 103; 54 L.J.Ch. 1; 51 L.T. 723; 1 T.L.R.
    45; 49 J.P. 244; 33 W.R. 91 390
Schwann v. Cotton [1916] 2 Ch. 459; 85 L.J.Ch. 689; 115 L.T. 168; 60 S.J.
    654 .... 16, 37, 54, 100, 111, 178
Scots Mines Co. v. Leadhills Mines Co. (1859) 34 L.T.(O.S.) 34 213
Scott v. Pape (1886) 31 Ch.D. 554; 55 L.J.Ch. 426; 54 L.T. 399; 2 T.L.R.
    310; 50 J.P. 645; 34 W.R. 465 .... 23, 239, 240, 244, 245, 319, 324,
                                                        327, 334, 335, 336
Scottish Vacuum Cleaner Co. Ltd. v. Provincial Cinematograph Theatres
    Ltd. (1915) 32 R.P.C. 353 56
Seaman v. Vawdry (1810) 16 Ves. 390; 33 E.R. 1032 339
Seddon v. Bank of Bolton (1882) 19 Ch.D. 462; 51 L.J.Ch. 542; 46 L.T. 225;
    30 W.R. 362 154
Sedleigh-Denfield v. O'Callaghan [1940] A.C. 880; 164 L.T. 72; 56
    T.L.R. 887; 84 S.J. 657; [1940] 3 All E.R. 349 .... 369, 371
Selby v. Crystal Palace Gas Co. (1862) 4 De G.F. & J. 246; 31 L.J.Ch.
    595; 6 L.T. 790; 26 J.P. 676; 8 Jur.(N.S.) 830; 45 E.R. 1178; 10
    W.R. 636 .... 281, 285
—— v. Nettleford (1873) 9 Ch.App. 111; 43 L.J.Ch. 359; 29 L.T. 661;
    38 J.P. 404; 22 W.R. 142 286
—— v. Whitbread & Co. [1917] 1 K.B. 736; 86 L.J.K.B. 974; 116 L.T.
    690; 33 T.L.R. 214; 81 J.P. 165; 15 L.G.R. 279 .... 301, 304
Semon (Charles) & Co. v. Bradford Corpn. [1922] 2 Ch. 737; 91 L.J.Ch.
    602; 127 L.T. 800; 66 S.J. 648 .... 240, 252
Senhouse v. Christian (1787) 1 T.R. 560; 99 E.R. 1251 .... 42, 44, 273
Senior v. Pawson (1866) L.R. 3 Eq. 330; 15 W.R. 220 391
Serff v. Acton Local Board (1886) 31 Ch.D. 679; 55 L.J.Ch. 569; 54 L.T.
    379; 2 T.L.R. 284; 34 W.R. 563 119
Serrao v. Noel (1885) 15 Q.B.D. 549; 1 T.L.R. 581 390
Shadwell v. Hutchinson (1831) 2 B. & Ad. 97; 9 L.J.(O.S.)K.B. 142; 109
    E.R. 1079; affirming (1830) 4 C. & P. 334; reversing (1829) 3 C. & P.
    615; Mood. & M. 350 .... 364, 365, 369
Shannon Ltd. v. Venner Ltd. [1965] Ch. 682; [1965] 2 W.L.R. 718;
    109 S.J. 12; [1965] 1 All E.R. 590 .... 10, 11
Sharp v. Wilson, Rotheray & Co. (1905) 93 L.T. 155; 21 T.L.R. 679 ... 204, 209
Sharpe v. Durrant [1911] W.N. 158; affirming (1911) 55 S.J. 423 .... 50, 51
Shayler v. Woolf [1946] Ch. 320; [1947] L.J.R. 71; 175 L.T. 170; 90
    S.J. 357; [1946] 2 All E.R. 54 56
Sheffield Masonic Hall Co. v. Sheffield Corporation [1932] 2 Ch. 17; 101
    L.J.Ch. 328; 147 L.T. 474; 48 T.L.R. 336 .... 250, 253
Shelfer v. City of London Electric Lighting Co., Meux's Brewery Co. v.
    City of London Electric Lighting Co. [1895] 1 Ch. 287; 64 L.J.Ch.
    216; 72 L.T. 34; 11 T.L.R. 137; 39 S.J. 132; 12 R. 112; 43 W.R.
    238 .... 360, 364, 366, 390–393, 394, 395
Shepherd Homes v. Sandham [1971] Ch. 340; [1970] 3 W.L.R. 348;
    114 S.J. 636; [1970] 3 All E.R. 402; 21 P. & C.R. 863 .... 382, 387
Sheringham U. D. C. v. Holsey (1904) 91 L.T. 225; 20 T.L.R. 402;
    68 J.P. 395; 48 S.J. 416; 2 L.G.R. 744 191

PAGE

Shiel v. Godfrey [1893] W.N. 115 383
Shiloh Spinners Ltd. v. Harding [1971] 3 W.L.R. 34; 115 S.J. 248;
   [1971] 2 All E.R. 307; 22 P. & C.R. 447 71
Shirvell v. Hackwood Estates Co. [1938] 2 K.B. 577; 107 L.J.K.B. 713;
   159 L.T. 49; 54 T.L.R. 554; 82 S.J. 271; [1938] 2 All E.R. 1 305
Shoesmith v. Byerley (1873) 28 L.T. 553; 21 W.R. 668 353
Shrewsbury's (Earl) Case (1610) 9 Co.Rep. 46b; 77 E.R. 798 361
Shubrook v. Tufnell (1882) 46 L.T. 886; sub nom. Sherbrooke v. Tufnell,
   46 J.P. 694 101
Shury v. Piggot (1626) 3 Bulst. 339; 81 E.R. 280; sub nom. Sury v. Pigott,
   Palm. 444; Poph. 166; Benl. 188; sub nom. Surrey v. Piggot,
   Lat. 153; Noy. 84; sub nom. Shewry v. Pigott, W.J. 145 ...... 222, 310, **311**
Shuttleworth v. Le Fleming (1865) 19 C.B.(N.S) 687; 34 L.J.C.P. 309;
   11 Jur.(N.S.) 841; 14 W.R. 13; 144 E.R. 956 .... 59, 155
Siddons v. Short (1877) 2 C.P.D. 572; 46 L.J.Q.B. 795; 37 L.T. 230 ... 101, 384
Simcox v. Yardley Rural District Council (1905) 69 J.P. 66; 3 L.G.R. 1350 304
Simeon, Re [1937] Ch. 525; varying [1935] 2 K.B. 183; sub nom. Simeon
   v. Minister of Health, 104 L.J.K.B. 330; 152 L.T. 372; 51 T.L.R.
   235; 99 J.P. 167; 79 S.J. 109; 33 L.G.R. 75 .... 4, 35, 219
Simmons v. Midford [1969] 2 Ch. 415; [1969] 3 W.L.R. 168; 113 S.J. 566;
   [1969] 2 All E.R. 1269; 20 P. & C.R. 758 15
Simper v. Foley (1862) 2 J. & H. 555; 5 L.T. 669; 70 E.R. 1179 .... 148, 149,
                                                            312, 362
Simpson v. Att.-Gen. [1904] A.C. 476; 74 L.J.Ch. 1; 91 L.T. 610; 20 T.L.R.
   761; 69 J.P. 85; 3 L.G.R. 190, H.L.; reversing sub nom. Att.-Gen. v.
   Simpson [1901] 2 Ch. 671; 85 L.T. 325; 16 T.L.R. 47 ... 137, 141, 143, 237
—— v. Godmanchester Corporation [1897] A.C. 696; 66 L.J.Ch. 770; 77 L.T.
   409; 13 T.L.R. 544; affirming [1896] 1 Ch. 214 ...... **16**, 19, 34, 36, 142, 146,
                                                            219, 259
—— v. Lewthwaite (1832) 3 B. & Ad. 226; 1 L.J.K.B. 126; 110 E.R. 85 378
—— v. Savage (1856) 1 C.B.(N.S.) 347; 26 L.J.C.P. 50; 28 L.T.(O.S.) 204;
   21 J.P. 279; 3 Jur.(N.S.) 161; 140 E.R. 143; 5 W.R. 147 ...... 364–366, **367**
—— v. Weber (1925) 133 L.T. 46; 41 T.L.R. 302 .... 108, 110
Sitwell v. Londesborough [1905] 1 Ch. 460; 53 W.R. 445; sub nom., Re
   Sitwell, Sitwell v. Londesborough (Earl) 74 L.J.Ch. 254 77
Sketchley v. Berger (1893) 69 L.T. 754 .... 269, 285, 286
Skull v. Glenister (1864) 16 C.B.(N.S.) 81; 3 New Rep. 389; 33 L.J.C.P.
   185; 91 L.T. 763; 143 E.R. 1055; 12 W.R. 554 .... 8, 282
Slack v. Hancock (1912) 107 L.T. 14 .... **132**
—— v. Leeds Industrial Co-operative Society Ltd. [1924] 2 Ch. 475;
   reversing sub nom. Leeds Industrial Co-operative Society Ltd. v.
   Slack [1924] A.C. 851; 93 L.J.Ch. 436; 131 L.T. 710; 40 T.L.R.
   745; 68 S.J. 715; reversing sub nom. Slack v. Leeds Industrial
   Co-operative Society Ltd. [1923] 1 Ch. 431 .... 388, **389, 390**, 393
Sloan v. Holliday (1874) 30 L.T. 757; 38 J.P. 662 268
Smeteborn v. Holt (1347) Y.B. 21 Edw. 3, fo. 2, pl. 5 79
Smith v. Baxter [1900] 2 Ch. 138; 69 L.J.Ch. 437; 82 L.T. 650; 44 S.J.
   393; 48 W.R. 458 .... 58, 148, 153, 188, 240, 319, 327, 336, 346, 377, 378
—— v. Colbourne [1914] 2 Ch. 533; 84 L.J.Ch. 112; 111 L.T. 927; 58
   S.J. 783 .... **52, 53**
—— v. Day (1882) 21 Ch.D. 421; affirming (1880) 13 Ch.D. 651; 28 W.R.
   712 .... 383, 386, 387
—— v. Evangelization Society Trust [1933] Ch. 515; 102 L.J.Ch. 275;
   149 L.T. 6; 49 T.L.R. 262 .... 57, 239, 247
—— v. Gates [1952] C.P.L. 814; 160 E.G. 512 .... 32, 35
—— v. Giddy [1904] 2 K.B. 448; 73 L.J.K.B. 894; 91 L.T. 296; 20 T.L.R.
   596; 48 S.J. 589; 53 W.R. 207 .... 305, 360
—— v. Jones [1954] 1 W.L.R. 1089; 98 S.J. 540; [1954] 2 All E.R. 823 132
—— v. Owen (1866) 35 L.J.Ch. 317; 14 W.R. 422 26
—— v. Smith (1875) L.R. 20 Eq. 500; 44 L.J.Ch. 630; 32 L.T. 787; 23
   W.R. 771 .... 382, 383, 388, 391
—— v. Thackerah (1866) L.R. 1 C.P. 564; Har. & Ruth. 615; 35 L.J.C.P.
   276; 14 L.T. 761; 12 Jur.(N.S.) 545; 14 W.R. 832 291
Smith & Co. (Orpington) v. Morris (1962) 112 L.J. 702 148
Smith (James) & Co. v. West Derby Board (1878) 3 C.P.D. 423; 47 L.J.Q.B.
   607; 38 L.T. 716; 42 J.P. 615; 27 W.R. 137 373

PAGE

Smith & Snipes Hall Farm Ltd. *v.* River Douglas Catchment Board [1949]
2 K.B. 500; *sub nom.* Smith *v.* River Douglas Catchment Board,
65 T.L.R. 628; 113 J.P. 388; 93 S.J. 525; [1949] 2 All E.R. 179;
47 L.G.R. 627 46
Smith's Case (1633) W.Jones 272 370
Snark, The [1900] P. 105; 69 L.J.P. 41; 82 L.T. 42; 16 T.L.R. 160;
44 S.J. 209; 9 Asp.M.L.C. 50; 48 W.R. 279 371
Solomon *v.* Vintners' Co. (1859) 4 H. & N. 585; 28 L.J.Ex. 370; 33
L.T.(o.s.) 224; 23 J.P. 424; 5 Jur.(n.s.) 1177; 157 E.R. 970; 7
W.R. 613 .... 29, 175, 301
Soltau *v.* De Held (1852) 2 Sim.(n.s.) 133; 21 L.J.Ch. 153; 16 Jur. 326;
61 E.R. 291 381
Somersetshire Drainage Commissioners *v.* Bridgwater Corpn. (1899) 81
L.T. 729 .... 143, 192
South Eastern Ry. *v.* Associated Portland Cement Manufacturers (1900)
Ltd. [1910] 1 Ch. 12; 79 L.J.Ch. 150; 101 L.T. 865; 26 T.L.R. 61;
74 J.P. 21; 54 S.J. 80 .... 5, **50, 51**
—— *v.* Cooper [1924] 1 Ch. 211; [1923] 93 L.J.Ch. 292; 22 L.G.R. 109;
87 J.P.Jo. 816 .... **279,** 280
South Metropolitan Cemetery Co. *v.* Eden (1855) 16 C.B. 42; 25 L.T.(o.s.)
69, 100; 139 E.R. 670 .... **275,** 286, 337
Southport Corporation *v.* Ormskirk Union Assessment Committee [1894]
1 Q.B. 196; 63 L.J.Q.B. 250; 69 L.T. 852; 10 T.L.R. 34; 58 J.P. 212;
9 R. 46; Ryde Rat.App. [1891–93] 438; 42 W.R. 153 5
Southwark & Vauxhall Water Co. *v.* Wandsworth Board of Works [1898]
2 Ch. 603; 67 L.J.Ch. 657; 79 L.T. 132; 14 T.L.R. 576; 62 J.P. 756;
47 W.R. 107 .... **301,** 303
Southwark's (Prior of) Case, 13 Hen. 7, 26 363
Spedding *v.* Fitzpatrick (1888) 38 Ch.D. 410; 58 L.J.Ch. 139; 59 L.T. 492;
4 T.L.R. 505; 37 W.R. 20 377
Spencer's Case (1583) 5 Co.Rep. 16a; 77 E.R. 72; *sub nom.* Anon., Moore,
K.B. 159 40
Sports & General Press Agency Ltd. *v.* "Our Dogs" Publishing Co Ltd.
[1917] 2 K.B. 125; 86 L.J.K.B. 702; 116 L.T. 626; 33 T.L.R. 204;
61 S.J. 299 56
Stacey *v.* Sherrin (1913) 29 T.L.R. 555 286
Stafford (Marquis) *v.* Coyney (1827) 7 B. & C. 257; 5 L.J.(o.s.)K.B. 285;
108 E.R. 719 261
Staffordshire & Worcestershire Canal Navigation *v.* Birmingham Canal Navi-
gation (1866) L.R. 1 H.L. 254; *affirming* (1865) as reported in 11 L.T.
647; 11 Jur.(n.s.) 71; 13 W.R. 358 .... 146, 168, 178, 190, 219, 228
—— *v.* Bradley [1912] 1 Ch. 91; 81 L.J.Ch. 147; 106 L.T. 215; 56 S.J. 91;
75 J.P.J. 555 60
Staight *v.* Burn (1869) 5 Ch.App. 163; 39 L.J.Ch. 289; 22 L.T. 831; 34 J.P.
212; 18 W.R. 243 .... 317, 319, 327, 336, 355
Stait *v.* Fenner [1912] 2 Ch. 504; 56 S.J. 669; *sub nom.* Stait *v.* Fenner,
Fenner *v.* McNab, 81 L.J.Ch. 710; 107 L.T. 124 131
Standard Bank of British South America (Africa) *v.* Stokes (1878) 9 Ch.D.
68; 47 L.J.Ch. 554; 38 L.T. 672; 43 J.P. 91; 26 W.R. 492 302
Stanley of Alderly (Lady) *v.* Shrewsbury (Earl) (1875) L.R. 19 Eq. 616;
44 L.J.Ch. 389; 32 L.T. 248; 23 W.R. 678 391
Star *v.* Rookesby (1710) 1 Salk 335; 91 E.R. 295 39
Stileman-Gibbard *v.* Wilkinson [1897] 1 Q.B. 749; 66 L.J.Q.B. 749; 76 L.T.
90; 61 J.P. 214; *sub nom.* Wilkinson, Jarvis & Clode *v.* Stileman-
Gibbard, *Re* an Application in, 13 T.L.R. 145 .... 36, 143
Stockport Waterworks Co. *v.* Potter (1864) 3 H. & C. 300; 4 New Rep. 441;
10 L.T. 748; 10 Jur.(n.s.) 1005; 159 E.R. 545 .... 14, 207, **232, 233**
Stokes *v.* City Offices Co. (1865) 13 L.T. 81, L.C.; *affirming* (1865) 2 Hem.
& M. 650; 12 L.T. 602; 29 J.P. 708; 11 Jur.(n.s.) 560; 71 E.R. 616;
13 W.R. 537 .... 396, 397
Stokoe *v.* Singers (1857) 8 E. & B. 31; 26 L.J.Q.B. 257; 29 L.T.(o.s.) 263;
3 Jur.(n.s.) 1256; 120 E.R. 12; 5 W.R. 756 .... 319, 320, 340
Stourcliffe Estates Co. Ltd. *v.* Bournemouth Corporation [1910] 2 Ch. 12;
79 L.J.Ch. 455; 102 L.T. 629; 26 T.L.R. 450; 74 J.P. 289; 8 L.G.R.
595 76
Stratford (J. T.) & Son Ltd. *v.* Lindley [1965] A.C. 269; [1964] 3 W.L.R.
541; 108 S.J. 636; [1964] 3 All E.R. 102; [1964] 2 Lloyd's Rep. 133 387

PAGE

Strick (F. C.) & Co. Ltd. *v.* City Offices Ltd. (1906) 22 T.L.R. 667 .... **285,** 353
Stroyan *v.* Knowles, Hamer *v.* Same (1861) 6 H. & N. 454; 30 L.J.Ex. 102;
    3 L.T. 746; 9 W.R. 615; 158 E.R. 186 291
Sturges *v.* Bridgman (1879) 11 Ch.D. 852; 48 L.J.Ch. 785; 41 L.T. 219;
    43 J.P. 716; 28 W.R. 200 .... 167, **179, 186,** 191, 208
Suffield *v.* Brown (1864) 4 De G.J. & Sm. 185; 3 New Rep. 340; 33 L.J.Ch.
    249; 9 L.T. 627; 10 Jur.(N.S.) 111; 46 E.R. 888; 12 W.R. 356 ...... 35, 93,
                                           106, 107, 109, 111
Suffolk's (Earl) Case, 13 Hen. 4, 11; 1 Rolle, Ab. 107, pl. 7 363
Sury *v.* Pigott. *See* Shury *v.* Piggot.
Sutcliffe *v.* Booth (1863) 32 L.J.Q.B. 136; 27 J.P. 613; 9 Jur.(N.S.) 1037 ... 224
—— *v.* Holmes [1947] K.B. 147; [1947] L.J.R. 415; 175 L.T. 487; 62 T.L.R.
    733; [1946] 2 All E.R. 599 38
Sutherland (Duke) *v.* Heathcote [1892] 1 Ch. 475; 61 L.J.Ch. 248; 66 L.T.
    210; 8 T.L.R. 272; 36 S.J. 231 4
Swaine *v.* Great Northern Ry. (1864) 4 De G.J. & Sm. 211; 3 New Rep.
    399; 33 L.J.Ch. 399; 9 L.T. 745; 10 Jur.(N.S.) 191; 46 E.R. 899;
    12 W.R. 391 382
Swan *v.* Sinclair [1925] A.C. 227; 94 L.J.Ch. 104; 132 L.T. 577; 41 T.L.R.
    158; 89 J.P. 38; [1924] All E.R. 277; 22 L.G.R. 705; *affirming* [1924]
    1 Ch. 254 .... 343, 344
Swansborough *v.* Coventry (1832) 9 Bing. 305; 2 Moo. & S. 362; 2 L.J.C.P.
    11; 131 E.R. 629 .... **101, 105,** 111
Sweet & Maxwell *v.* Michael-Michaels (Advertising) (December 9, 1965);
    [1965] C.L.Y. 2192 129
Swindon Waterworks Co. *v.* Wilts & Berks Canal Navigation Co. (1875)
    L.R. 7 H.L. 697; 45 L.J.Ch. 638; 33 L.T. 513; 40 J.P. 804; 24 W.R.
    284, H.L.; *varying ibid., sub nom.* Wilts & Berks Canal Navigation
    Co. *v.* Swindon Water Works Co. (1874) 9 Ch.App. 451 ... **201,** 203–205, 379
Symons *v.* Leaker (1885) 15 Q.B.D. 629; 54 L.J.Q.B. 480; 53 L.T. 227;
    1 T.L.R. 564; 49 J.P. 775; 33 W.R. 875 159

TAFF VALE RY. *v.* Cardiff Ry. [1917] 1 Ch. 299; 86 L.J.Ch. 129; 115 L.T.
    800 .... 5, 7, 31
—— *v.* Gordon Canning [1909] 2 Ch. 48; 78 L.J.Ch. 492; 100 L.T. 845 ... 76, 280
Tapling *v.* Jones (1865) 20 C.B.(N.S.) 166; 11 H.L.Cas. 290; 5 New Rep.
    493; 34 L.J.C.P. 342; 12 L.T. 555; 29 J.P. 611; 11 Jur.(N.S.) 309;
    144 E.R. 1067; 13 W.R. 617; H.L.; *affirming* (1862) 12 C.B.(N.S.)
    affirming (1861) 11 C.B.(N.S.) 283 .... 26, 66, 144, 149, 168, 238, 239,
                                325–327, 328, 331, 333, 337
Taws *v.* Knowles [1891] 2 Q.B. 564; 60 L.J.Q.B. 641; 65 L.T. 124; 56 J.P.
    68; *sub nom.* Tawes *v.* Knowles, 39 W.R. 675 106
Taylor *v.* St. Helens Corporation (1877) 6 Ch.D. 264; 46 L.J.Ch. 857;
    37 L.T. 253; 25 W.R. 885 .... 57, 58, 235, 236
—— *v.* Whitehead (1781) 2 Doug.K.B. 745; 99 E.R. 475 .... 45, 47, 286
Tebbutt *v.* Selby (1837) 6 A. & E. 786 .... 374, 380
Tehidy Minerals Ltd. *v.* Norman [1971] 2 Q.B. 528; [1971] 2 W.L.R. 711;
    (1970) 115 S.J. 59; [1971] 2 All E.R. 475; 22 P. & C.R. 371 ...... 133, 138,
                                141, **142,** 144, 317, 377
Tenant *v.* Goldwin (1704) 1 Salk. 21, 360; Holt K.B. 500; 2 Ld.Raym.
    1089; 6 Mod.Rep. 311; 91 E.R. 20, 314 .... 351, 375
Theed *v.* Debenham (1876) 2 Ch.D. 165; 24 W.R. 775 .... 252, 254
Thomas *v.* Owen (1888) 20 Q.B.D. 225; 57 L.J.Q.B. 198; 58 L.T. 162; 52
    J.P. 516; 36 W.R. 440 .... **113,** 114–116, 124
—— *v.* Sorrell (1673) Vaugh. 330; 1 Lev. 217; 1 Freem.K.B. 85, 137;
    3 Keb. 264; 124 E.R. 1098 56
—— *v.* Thomas (1835) 2 C.M. & R. 34; 1 Gale 61; 5 Tyr. 804; 4 L.J.Ex.
    179; 150 E.R. 15 .... 222, **312,** 323
Thompson *v.* Eastwood (1852) 8 Exch. 69; 19 L.T.(O.S.) 313 357
—— *v.* Gibson (1841) 7 M. & W. 456; 10 L.J.Ex. 330; 151 E.R. 845 369
Thornton *v.* Little (1907) 97 L.T. 24; 23 T.L.R. 357 .... **283**
Thorpe *v.* Brumfitt (1873) L.R. 8 Ch.App. 650; 37 J.P. 742 ...... 9, 10, 13, 352,
                                              380, 381
Thrupp *v.* Scruton [1872] W.N. 60 302
Tickle *v.* Brown (1836) 4 A. & E. 369; 1 Har. & W. 769; 6 Nev. & M.K.B.
    230; 5 L.J.K.B. 119; 111 E.R. 826 .... 171, 172, 177, 189, 367, 375

PAGE

Tilbury *v.* Silva (1890) 45 Ch.D. 98; 63 L.T. 141 .... 143, 152
Tipping *v.* Eckersley (1855) 2 K. & J. 264; 69 E.R. 779 229
Tisdall *v.* McArthur & Co. (Steel & Metal) Ltd. [1951] Ir.R. 228 .... 142, 144,
148, 149, 239
Titchmarsh *v.* Royston Water Co. (1899) 81 L.T. 673; 64 J.P. 56; 44 S.J.
101; 48 W.R. 201 .... 118, 125
Titterton *v.* Conyers (1813) 5 Taunt. 465; 1 Marsh 140; 128 E.R. 770 315
Todd *v.* Flight (1860) 9 C.B.(N.S.) 377; 30 L.J.C.P. 21; 3 L.T. 325;
7 Jur.(N.S.) 291; 142 E.R. 148; 9 W.R. 145 370
Todrick *v.* Western National Omnibus Co. [1934] Ch. 561; 103 L.J.Ch.
224; 151 L.T. 163; 78 S.J. 318; *reversing on other grounds* [1934]
Ch. 190 .... **13, 20, 271, 277, 278**
Tomlin *v.* Fuller (1681) 1 Mod.Rep. 27; 2 Keb. 575, 583; 1 Vent. 48; 86
E.R. 705 261
Tone *v.* Preston (1883) 24 Ch.D. 739; 53 L.J.Ch. 50; 49 L.T. 99; 32
W.R. 166 .... 176, 301
Trahern's Case (1613) Galb. 233; 78 E.R. 135 .... **257**
Traill *v.* McAllister (1890) 25 L.R.Ir. 524 169
Trinidad Asphalt Co. *v.* Ambard [1899] A.C. 594; 68 L.J.P.C. 114; 81
L.T. 132; 48 W.R. 116 .... **289**
Trower *v.* Chadwick. *See* Chadwick *v.* Trower.
Truckell *v.* Stock [1957] 1 W.L.R. 161; 101 S.J. 108; [1957] 1 All E.R.
74 .... 100, 306
Truscott *v.* Merchant Tailors' Co. (1856) 11 Exch. 855; 26 L.T.(O.S.) 283;
20 J.P. 132; 2 Jur.(N.S.) 356; 4 W.R. 295; 156 E.R. 1079; *sub nom.*
Merchant Taylors' Co. *v.* Truscott, 25 L.J.Ex. 173 .... 66, 150, 255
Tucker *v.* Newman (1839) 11 Ad. & El. 40; 3 Per. & Dav. 14; 9 L.J.Q.B.
1; 3 Jur. 1145; 113 E.R. 327 .... 223, 363, 367
Turner *v.* Crush (1879) 4 App.Cas. 221; 48 L.J.Q.B. 481; 40 L.T. 661; 43
J.P. 540; 27 W.R. 553; *affirming sub nom.* Crush *v.* Turner (1878)
3 Ex.D. 303 314
—— *v.* Mirfield (1865) 34 Beav. 390; 55 E.R. 685 .... 230, 388
—— *v.* Spooner (1861) 1 Dr. & Sm. 467; 30 L.J.Ch. 801; 4 L.T. 732; 25 J.P.
467; 7 Jur.(N.S.) 1068; 62 E.R. 457; 9 W.R. 684 .... 57, 325
Turner's Will Trusts, *Re*, District Bank Ltd. *v.* Turner [1937] Ch. 15; 106
L.J.Ch. 58; 155 L.T. 266; 52 T.L.R. 713; 80 S.J. 791; [1936] 2 All
E.R. 1435 156
Tyler *v.* Wilkinson, 4 Mason (U.S.) 400 211
Tyne Improvement Commissioners *v.* Imrie. Att.-Gen. *v.* Tyne Improvement
Commissioners (1899) 81 L.T. 174 141
Tyrringham's Case (1584) 4 Co.Rep. 36b; 76 E.R. 973 60

UNION LIGHTERAGE Co. *v.* London Graving Dock Co. [1902] 2 Ch. 557; 71
L.J.Ch. 791; 87 L.T. 381; 18 T.L.R. 754 .... 107, 108, 118, **175, 176,**
180, 300, 301
United Land Co. *v.* Great Eastern Ry. (1875) 10 Ch.App. 586; 44 L.J.Ch.
685; 33 L.T. 292; 40 J.P. 37; 23 W.R. 896; *affirming with variation*
(1873) L.R. 17 Eq. 158 .... **276, 277,** 279
Universal Permanent Building Society *v.* Cooke [1952] Ch. 95; [1951] 2
T.L.R. 962; [1951] 2 All E.R. 893 78
Upjohn *v.* Seymour Estates Ltd. (1938) 54 T.L.R. 465; [1938] 1 All E.R. 614 303
Urich *v.* Local Health Authorities for St. Andrew-St. David (1964) 7
W.I.R. 482 47

V.T. ENGINEERING LTD. *v.* Barland (Richard) & Co. Ltd. (1968) 19 P. &
C.R. 890; 207 E.G. 247 .... 44, 272, 285, 353
Vanderpant *v.* Mayfair Hotel Co. [1930] 1 Ch. 138; 99 L.J.Ch. 84; 142 L.T.
198; 94 J.P. 23 87
Vere *v.* Minter [1914] W.N. 89; 49 L.Jo. 129 396
Vickers' Lease, *Re*, Pocock *v.* Vickers [1947] Ch. 420; [1948] L.J.R. 69; 177
L.T. 637; 91 S.J. 294; [1947] 1 All E.R. 707 .... 56, 282
Villers *v.* Ball (1689) 1 Show. 7 375
Von Joel *v.* Hornsey [1895] 2 Ch. 774; 65 L.J.Ch. 102; *sub nom.* Van Joel
v. Hornsey, 73 L.T. 372 387
Vooght *v.* Winch (1819) 2 B. & Ald. 662; 106 E.R. 507 218
Vowles *v.* Miller (1810) 3 Taunt. 137; 128 E.R. 54 304

PAGE

WADDINGTON v. Naylor (1889) 60 L.T. 480 .... 37, 301
Wade & English Ltd. v. Dixon & Cardus Ltd. (1937) 81 S.J. 703; [1937]
    3 All E.R. 900 .... 142, 378
Wake v. Hall (1883) 8 App.Cas. 195; 52 L.J.Q.B. 494; 48 L.T. 834; 47 J.P.
    548; 31 W.R. 585 15
Wallington v. Townsend [1939] Ch. 588; 108 L.J.Ch. 305; 160 L.T. 537;
    55 T.L.R. 531; 83 S.J. 297; [1939] 2 All E.R. 225 131
Walmesley & Shaw's Contract, Re [1917] 1 Ch. 93; 86 L.J.Ch. 120; 115
    L.T. 670; 61 S.J. 86 .... 98, 129
Walsh v. Oates [1953] 1 Q.B. 578; [1953] 2 W.L.R. 835; 117 J.P. 223; 97
    S.J. 281; [1953] 1 All E.R. 963 261
Warburton v. Parke (1857) 2 H. & N. 64; 26 L.J.Ex. 298; 29 L.T.(O.S.) 127   375
Ward v. Kirkland [1967] Ch. 194; [1966] 1 W.L.R. 601; 110 S.J. 289; [1966]
    1 All E.R. 609 .... Preface, 33, 34, 36, **64**, 66, 69, 83, **91, 94,** 126,
                                                                         127, 154, 177, 374
—— v. Ward (1852) 7 Exch. 838; 21 L.J.Ex. 334; 155 E.R. 1189 .... **340,** 343
Ward (Thomas W.) Ltd. v. Bruce (Alexander) (Grays) Ltd. [1959] 2 Lloyd's
    Rep. 472 .... 32, 36, 44, 57, 178
Wardle v. Brocklehurst (1859) 1 E. & E. 1058; 29 L.J.Q.B. 145; 1 L.T. 519;
    6 Jur.(N.S.) 319; 120 E.R. 1209; 8 W.R. 241 .... **125,** 228
Waring v. Griffiths (1758) 1 Burr. 440; 2 Keny. 183; 97 E.R. 392 15
Warner v. McBryde (1877) 36 L.T. 360 115
Warren v. Brown [1902] 1 K.B. 15; 71 L.J.K.B. 12; 85 L.T. 444; 18 T.L.R.
    55; 46 S.J. 50; 50 W.R. 97; reversing [1900] 2 Q.B. 722 .... **244, 245**
Warrick v. Queen's College, Oxford (1871) 6 Ch.App. 716; 40 L.J.Ch. 780;
    25 L.T. 254; 19 W.R. 1098 .... 144, 346
Waterlow v. Bacon (1866) L.R. 2 Eq. 514; 35 L.J.Ch. 643; 14 L.T. 724; 12
    Jur.(N.S.) 614; 14 W.R. 855 316
Waterman v. Soper (1697) 1 Ld.Raym. 737; 91 E.R. 1393 305
Waterpark (Lord) v. Fennell (1859) 7 H.L.C. 650; 33 L.T.(O.S.) 374; 23 J.P.
    643; 5 Jur.(N.S.) 1135; 7 W.R. 634; 11 E.R. 259 10
Watson v. Gray (1880) 14 Ch.D. 192; 49 L.J.Ch. 243; 42 L.T. 294; 44 J.P.
    537; 28 W.R. 438 302
Watts v. Kelson (1870) 6 Ch.App. 166; 40 L.J.Ch. 126; 24 L.T. 209; 35
    J.P. 422; 19 W.R. 338 .... 57, **99,** 114, 271, **278,** 323
Weatherley v. Ross (1862) 1 Hem. & M. 349; 1 New Rep. 228; 32 L.J.Ch.
    128; 27 J.P. 388; 71 E.R. 152 325
Webb v. Bird (1861) 10 C.B.(N.S.) 268; (1862) 13 C.B.(N.S.) 841; 31 L.J.C.P.
    335; 8 Jur.(N.S.) 621; 143 E.R. 332 .... 25, 139, 146, **257, 258,** 294, 299
Webb's Lease, Re [1951] Ch. 808; 95 S.J. 367; sub nom. Re Webb, Sandom
    v. Webb [1951] 2 All E.R. 131; sub nom. Sandom v. Webb [1951] 2
    T.L.R. 530 .... 56, 106, 107, **108–110**
Webber v. Lee (1882) 9 Q.B.D. 315; 51 L.J.Q.B. 485; 47 L.T. 215; 47 J.P.
    4; 30 W.R. 866 .... 59, 60, 69
Wells v. London, Tilbury and Southend Rail Co. (1877) 5 Ch.D. 126; 37 L.T.
    302; 41 J.P. 452; 25 W.R. 325 .... 261, 315
—— v. Ody (1836) 1 M. & W. 452; 7 C. & P. 410; 5 Dowl. 95; 2 Gale 12;
    Tyr. & Ger. 715; 5 L.J.Ex. 199; 150 E.R. 512 .... 242, 315
West Leigh Colliery Co. v. Tunnicliffe & Hampson Ltd. [1908] A.C. 27; 77
    L.J.Ch. 102; 98 L.T. 4; 24 T.L.R. 146; sub nom. Tunnicliffe & Hamp-
    son Ltd. v. West Leigh Colliery Co. Ltd., 52 S.J. 93, H.L.; reversing
    sub nom. Tunnicliffe & Hampson Ltd. v. West Leigh Colliery Co.
    Ltd. [1906] 2 Ch. 22 290
Westhoughton Urban District Council v. Wigan Coal & Iron Co. [1919] 1
    Ch. 159; 88 L.J.Ch. 60; 120 L.T. 242 46
Westminster Brymbo, etc., Co. v. Clayton (1867) 36 L.J.Ch. 476 382
Weston v. Arnold (1873) 8 Ch.App. 1084; 43 L.J.Ch. 123; 22 W.R. 284 ... 302, 315
—— v. Weaver (Lawrence) Ltd. [1961] 1 Q.B. 402; [1961] 2 W.L.R. 192;
    105 S.J. 155; [1961] 1 All E.R. 478 .... 304, 353
Westwood v. Heywood [1921] 2 Ch. 130; 90 L.J.Ch. 515; 125 L.T. 761; 37
    T.L.R. 851; 65 S.J. 753 .... 100, **114,** 115
Wettor v. Dunk (1864) 4 F. & F. 298 369
Whaley v. Laing. See Laing v. Whaley.
Whalley v. Lancashire Ry. (1884) 13 Q.B.D. 131; 53 L.J.Q.B. 285; 50 L.T.
    472; 48 J.P. 500; 32 W.R. 711 .... 236, 237
—— v. Tompson (1799) 1 Bos. & P. 375; 126 E.R. 959 312

PAGE
Wheaton v. Maple & Co. [1893] 3 Ch. 48; 62 L.J.Ch. 963; 69 L.T. 208; 9
T.L.R. 559; 37 S.J. 615; 2 R. 549; 41 W.R. 677 .... 21, 134, 146, 147,
162, 163, 169
Wheeldon v. Burrows (1879) 12 Ch.D. 31; 48 L.J.Ch. 853; 41 L.T. 327;
28 W.R. 196 .... 43, 75, 82, 84, 88, **92–94,** 95, 96, 100, 106, 107, 109,
115, 116, 195
White v. Grand Hotel, Eastbourne. *See* Grand Hotel, Eastbourne v. White.
—— v. Jameson (1874) L.R. 18 Eq. 303; 38 J.P. 694; 22 W.R. 761 369
—— v. London General Omnibus Co. [1914] W.N. 78; 58 S.J. 339 ..... 364, 366
—— v. Reeves (1818) 2 Moore C.P. 23 314
—— v. Taylor (No. 2) [1969] 1 Ch. 160; [1967] 3 W.L.R. 1246; 111 S.J.
585; [1967] 3 All E.R. 349 .... 4, 21, 44, 60, 69, **88,** 111, **112,** 124, 128,
129, 142, 153, 189
—— v. Williams [1922] 1 K.B. 727; 91 L.J.K.B. 721; 127 L.T. 231; 38
T.L.R. 419; 66 S.J. 505 .... 4, 124, 127
White (John) & Sons v. White [1906] A.C. 72; 75 L.J.P.C. 14; 94 L.T. 65 ... 218
Whitehead v. Parks (1858) 2 H. & N. 870; 27 L.J.Ex. 169; 157 E.R. 358 ... 211,
214, 235
Whitmores (Edenbridge), Ltd. v. Stanford [1909] 1 Ch. 427; 78 L.J.Ch. 144;
99 L.T. 924; 25 T.L.R. 169; 53 S.J. 134 224
Whitton v. Crompton (1568) 3 Dyer 278a 136
Wickham v. Hawker (1840) 7 M. & W. 63; 10 L.J.Ex. 153; 151 E.R. 679 ... 4
Wicks v. Hunt (1859) John. 372; 70 E.R. 466 388
Wigford v. Gill (1592) Cro.Eliz. 269; 78 E.R. 524 303
Wigram v. Fryer (1887) 36 Ch.D. 87; 56 L.J.Ch. 1098; 57 L.T. 255; 3
T.L.R. 652; 36 W.R. 100 315
Wilchick v. Marks & Silverstone [1934] 2 K.B. 56; 103 L.J.K.B. 372; 151
L.T. 60; 50 T.L.R. 281; 78 S.J. 277 370
Wilde v. Minsterley (1640) 2 Rolle Abr. 564; tit. Trespass I, pl. 1; cited 12
Q.B. at p. 743 .... **291**
Wilkes v. Greenway (1890) 6 T.L.R. 449 43
Wilkins v. Leighton [1932] 2 Ch. 106; 101 L.J.Ch. 385; 147 L.T. 495; 76
S.J. 232 370
Wilkinson v. Proud (1843) 11 M. & W. 33; 12 L.J.Ex. 227; 7 Jur. 284 13
Williams v. James (1867) L.R. 2 C.P. 577; 36 L.J.C.P. 256; 16 L.T. 664;
15 W.R. 928 .... 266, **267,** 268, 269
—— v. Jersey (Earl) (1841) Cr. & Ph. 91; 10 L.J.Ch. 149; 5 Jur. 426; 41
E.R. 424 .... **63**
—— v. Morland (1824) 2 B. & C. 910; 4 Dow. & Ry.K.B. 583; 2 L.J.(O.S.)
K.B. 191; 107 E.R. 620 .... 208, 379
Willmott v. Barber (1880) 15 Ch.D. 96; 49 L.J.Ch. 792; 43 L.T. 95; 28
W.R. 911 .... 62, 66
Willoughby v. Eckstein (No. 2) [1937] Ch. 167; 106 L.J.Ch. 86; 156 L.T. 187;
53 T.L.R. 251; 81 S.J. 98; [1937] 1 All E.R. 257 149
Wills v. May [1923] 1 Ch. 317; 92 L.J.Ch. 253; 128 L.T. 826; 67 S.J. 350 ... 240
Wilson v. Newberry (1871) L.R. 7 Q.B. 31; 41 L.J.Q.B. 31; 25 L.T. 695; 36
J.P. 215; 20 W.R. 111 305
—— v. Peto (1821) 6 Moore C.P. 47 369
—— v. Townend (1860) 1 Dr. & Sm. 324; 30 L.J.Ch. 25; 3 L.T. 352; 25 J.P.
116; 6 Jur.(N.S.) 1109; 9 W.R. 30; 62 E.R. 403 ..... 325, 362, 365, 380, 387
Wilts & Berks Canal Navigation Co. v. Swindon Waterworks Co. *See*
Swindon Waterworks Co. v. Wilts & Berks Canal Navigation Co.
Wiltshire v. Sidford (1827) 8 B. & C. 259n; 1 Man. & Ry.K.B. 404; 6 L.J.
(O.S.)K.B. 151; 108 E.R. 1040 302
Wimbledon & Putney Commons Conservators v. Dixon (1875) 1 Ch.D. 362;
45 L.J.Ch. 353; 33 L.T. 679; 40 J.P. 102; 24 W.R. 466 ...... **267, 268, 284**
Winford v. Wollaston (1689) 3 Lev. 266; 83 E.R. 682 374
Winship v. Hudspeth (1854) 10 Exch. 5; 2 C.L.R. 1042; 23 L.J.Ex. 268; 23
L.T.(O.S.) 162; 156 E.R. 332; 2 W.R. 523 .... 136, 171
Winter v. Baker (1887) 3 T.L.R. 569 370
—— v. Brockwell (1807) 8 East 308; 103 E.R. 359 316
Winter Garden Theatre (London) Ltd. v. Millenium Productions Ltd. [1948]
A.C. 173; [1947] L.J.R. 1422; 177 L.T. 349; 63 T.L.R. 529; 91 S.J.
504; [1947] 2 All E.R. 331 56
Withers v. Purchase (1889) 60 L.T. 819; 5 T.L.R. 399 236
Wong v. Beaumont Property Trust Ltd. [1965] 1 Q.B. 173; [1964] 2 W.L.R.
1325; 108 S.J. 237; [1964] 2 All E.R. 119 .... 36, **121, 122,** 260, 361

PAGE

Wood v. Hewett (1846) 8 Q.B. 913; 15 L.J.Q.B. 247; 7 L.T.(o.s.) 109; 10
    Jur. 390; 115 E.R. 1118 .... 36, 219
—— v. Leadbitter (1845) 13 M. & W. 838; 14 L.J.Ex. 161; 4 L.T.(o.s.) 433;
    9 J.P. 312; 9 Jur. 187; 153 E.R. 351 69
—— v. Saunders (1875) 10 Ch.App. 582; affirming 10 Ch.App. 583n; 44 L.J.
    Ch. 514; 32 L.T. 363; 23 W.R. 514 .... **58**, 269
—— v. Stourbridge Ry. (1864) 16 C.B.(N.S.) 222; 143 E.R. 1111 284
—— v. Sutcliffe (1851) 2 Sim.(N.S.) 165; 21 L.J.Ch. 253; 18 L.T.(o.s.) 194;
    16 Jur. 75; 61 E.R. 303 382
—— v. Waud (1849) 3 Exch. 748; 18 L.J.Ex. 305; 13 L.T.(o.s.) 212; 13 Jur.
    472; 154 E.R. 1047 .... 54, **178**, 199, 205, 209, 223, **226–228**, 229, 311
Woodhouse v. Newry Navigation Co. [1898] 1 I.R. 161 385
Woodhouse & Co. Ltd. v. Kirkwood (Derby) Ltd. [1970] 1 W.L.R. 1185; 2
    All E.R. 587 .... 57, **91, 92**, 269
Woodman v. Pwllbach Colliery Co. Ltd. See Pwllbach Colliery Co. Ltd.
    v. **Woodman**.
Woollerton and Wilson Ltd. v. Costain (Richard) Ltd. [1970] 1 W.L.R. 411;
    114 S.J. 170 360
Wright v. Howard (1823) 1 Sim. & St. 190; 57 E.R. 76; sub nom. Wright v.
    Howard, Howard v. Wright, 1 L.J.(o.s.)Ch. 94 208
—— v. Macadam [1949] 2 K.B. 744; 93 S.J. 646; [1949] 2 All E.R. 565 ... 33, 35,
                                                123, **126, 127**, 229
—— v. Williams (1836) 1 M. & W. 77; 1 Gale 410; Tyr. & Gr. 375; 5 L.J.
    Ex. 107; 150 E.R. 353 .... 36, 146, 152, **158**, 166, 168, 191, 230
Wringe v. Cohen [1940] 1 K.B. 229; 109 L.J.K.B. 227; 161 L.T. 366; 56
    T.L.R. 101; 83 S.J. 923; [1939] 4 All E.R. 241 370
Wyatt v. Harrison (1832) 3 B. & Ad. 871; 1 L.J.K.B. 237; 110 E.R. 320 ... **291**,
                                                292, 374
Wynne v. Pope 1960 (3) S.A. 37 .... 117, 285
Wynstanley v. Lee (1818) 2 Swan. 333; 36 E.R. 643 .... 190, 255, 386

YARMOUTH CORPORATION v. Simmons (1878) 10 Ch.D. 518; 47 L.J.Ch. 792;
    38 L.T. 881; 26 W.R. 802 314
Yates v. Jack (1866) L.R. 1 Ch. 295; 35 L.J.Ch. 539; 14 L.T. 151; 30 J.P. 324;
    12 Jur.(N.S.) 305; 14 W.R. 618 .... **242**, 243, 245, 246, **396**
Young (John) & Co. v. Bankier Distillery Co. [1893] A.C. 698; 69 L.T.
    838; 58 J.P. 100 229
Young (Trustees of Young, Deceased) v. Star Omnibus Co. (1902) 86 L.T.
    41 .... **341**, 388, 391
Ystradyfodwg & Pontypridd Main Sewerage Board v. Bensted [1907] A.C.
    264; 76 L.J.K.B. 876; 97 L.T. 141; 23 T.L.R. 621; 71 J.P. 425; 51 S.J.
    588; 5 L.G.R. 865; 5 T.C. 230; affirming [1907] 1 K.B. 490 5

TABLE OF STATUTES

References in bold type indicate where the text of the section appears.

PAGE

1275 Limitation of Prescription
Act (3 Edw. 1, c. 39) 133,
134

1540 Limitation of Prescription
Act (32 Hen. 8, c. 2) 134–
136

1623 Limitation Act (21 Jac. 1,
c. 16) 134–137

1801 Inclosure (Consolidation)
Act (41 Geo. 3, c.
109) 75, 190
s. 8 314

1832 Prescription Act (2 & 3
Will. 4, c. 71) 30, 133,
142–145, 151, 160, 162,
164–167, 169, 170, 177,
182, 188, 218, 225, 226,
239, 240, 243, 250, 251,
253, 255, 294, 299, 300,
317, 335, 336, 345, 346,
355, 375, 377
s. 1 .... 138, **145**, 147, 152,
156, 157, 160, 168,
185, 189, 346
s. 2 ...... 21, 25, 29, 145, **146**,
147, 148, 152, 154, 156–
158, 160, 162, 167, 168,
172, 177, 219, 230, 259,
266, 296, 298, 346, 376
s. 3 ... 21, 23, 144, 146, **147**,
148–150, 152, 156, 157,
161, 168, 172, 173, 177,
239, 244, 249, 255, 260,
326, 328, 334, 346
s. 4 ...... 144, 147, **152**, 153,
173, 187, 188, 328, 346
s. 5 ...... **154, 155**, 169, 170,
172, 375–377
s. 6 .... 150, **155**
s. 7 ...... 147, 152, **155, 156**,
159–162, 168, 183,
375, 376
s. 8 ... 147, 156, **157**, 158–162,
166, 168, 183, 376

1835 Highway Act (5 & 6 Will.
4, c. 50)—
s. 67 13
s. 91 261

1845 Lands Clauses Consolidation Act (8 & 9 Vict.
c. 18) 75, 315
s. 84 7
Railway Clauses Consolid-
ation Act (8 & 9 Vict.
c. 20), s. 68 ... 75, 76, 280
Inclosure Act (8 & 9 Vict.
c. 118), ss. 62–68 314

PAGE

1847 Cemeteries Clauses Act
(10 & 11 Vict. c. 65),
s. 40 15

1852 Burial Act (15 & 16 Vict.
c. 85), s. 33 15

1853 Burial Act (16 & 17 Vict.
c. 134), s. 4 15

1855 Metropolitan Building Act
(18 & 19 Vict. c. 122) 63
ss. 83, 85 315

1858 Chancery Amendment Act
(21 & 22 Vict. c. 27) ... 359,
362, 383, 385, 390, 394
s. 2 .... **388**

1862 Metropolis Management
Amendment Act (25 &
26 Vict. c. 102), s. 85 251

1873 Judicature Act (36 & 37
Vict. c. 66) 380, 390
s. 16 388
s. 25 (8) 386

1875 Explosives Act (38 & 39
Vict. c. 17) 90

1876 Rivers Pollution Prevention Act (39 & 40
Vict. c. 75), ss. 3, 4 ... 231

1881 Conveyancing Act (44 &
45 Vict. c. 41)—
s. 6 ... 27, 95, 105, 122, 129
s. 62 (1) 80

1883 Statute Law Revision and
Civil Procedure Act
(46 & 47 Vict. c. 49),
ss. 3, 5 388

1888 County Courts Act (51 &
52 Vict. c. 43), s. 60 7

1889 Interpretation Act (52 & 53
Vict. c. 63), s. 38 (2)
(a) 314

1891 Brine Pumping (Compensation for Subsidence)
Act (54 & 55 Vict.
c. 40) 213, 289

1894 Copyhold Act (57 & 58
Vict. c. 46), s. 23 ... 21
London Building Act (57
& 58 Vict. c. ccxiii),
s. 49 251

1898 Statute Law Revision Act
(61 & 62 Vict. c. 22),
s. 1 388

1899 Commons Act (62 & 63
Vict. c. 30), s. 23,
Sched. 2 314

1918 Income Tax Act (8 & 9
Geo. 5, c. 40), Sched.
A, No. 1, r. 7 37

PAGE

1919 Ministry of Health Act (9
& 10 Geo. 5, c. 21),
s. 3 (1) (a) 213
1922 Law of Property Act (12
& 13 Geo. 5, c. 16)—
ss. 12, 31 156
Sched. 12, para. 5 21
1924 Law of Property (Amendment) Act (15 & 16
Geo. 5, c. 5), s. 9,
Sched. 9, para. 3 82
1925 Settled Land Act (15 & 16
Geo. 5, c. 18) 156
ss. 38, 39, 41, 42, 49 (1)
(a), 59 (2), 61 (2) (e) ... 77
s. 73 (1) (xii) 79
Law of Property Act (15
& 16 Geo. 5, c. 20)—
Part I, ss. 1–39 ...... 144, 156
s. 1 (2) 61
(a) 69, 70
(3) 70
(6) 156, 302
ss. 2 (3) (iii), 4 (1) 70
s. 12 .... 144, 156
s. 19 156
s. 28 77
s. 38 (1) 303
s. 39 156
s. 40 .... 67, 69
s. 51 (2) 80
s. 52 (1) 61, 69
(2) (a) (d), ... 61
s. 54 (2) 61
s. 60 80
s. 62 ... 27, 33, 40, 41, 59, 75,
83, 91, 95, 125–132,
194, 195
(1) **122**, 129, 304
(2) 100, **122**, 129
(3) **123**
(4) **123**, 130
(5)–(6) **123**
s. 65 80
s. 72 (3) 20
s. 101 76
s. 149 159
s. 162 .... 50, **52**
s. 187 (1) 4, 8
(2) 37
s. 199 70
(1) 79
s. 200 82
s. 205 (1) (ii) ... 95, 123, 124
(ix) 69, 123
(x) 69
Sched. 1, Pt. V, para. 1 303
Land Registration Act (15
& 16 Geo. 5, c. 21) ... 71, 76
ss. 3 (xxiv), 5–7, 9, 11, 12 193
s. 18 (1) 194
(d) (e) 195
(2) 194, 195
s. 19 (2) 72, 194, 196
(3) 194
s. 20 194
(1) 194, 195
(a) 72

PAGE

1925 Land Registration Act—cont.
s. 20 (1) (c) 72, 195
(d) 195
s. 21 (1) 194
s. 22 (2) 72, 194, 196
(3) 194
s. 23 194
(1) 194, 195
(a) (c) 72
ss. 49 (1) (c), 54 72
s. 59 (2) 72, 214
s. 70 (1) (a) 72, 196
(2) 196
(3) 195, 196
s. 72 .... 193, 194
s. 75 (5) 195
s. 141 (1) (xx) 194
s. 144 (1) (xx) 193
Land Charges Act (15 &
16 Geo. 5, c. 22) ... 70, 71
s. 10 (1), Class C (iv). 72, 79
Class D (iii) ... 72
s. 13 65
(2) 70, 72, 78, 79
Administration of Estates
Act (15 & 16 Geo. 5,
c. 23)—
s. 36 82
(2) 112
s. 39 77
Supreme Court of Judica-
ture (Consolidation)
Act (15 & 16 Geo. 5,
c. 49) 380
s. 18 388
s. 45 .... 361, 386
1930 London Building Act (20
& 21 Geo. 5, c. clviii),
s. 53 251
1934 County Courts Act (24 &
25 Geo. 5, c. 53)—
s. 51 (a) 361
1936 Housing Act (26 Geo. 5 &
1 Edw. 8, c. 51)—
s. 26 301
s. 46 (3) 315
1938 Coal Act (1 & 2 Geo. 6, c.
52), Sched. 2, Pt. II ... 99
1939 Limitation Act (2 & 3 Geo.
6, c. 21) 43
Compensation (Defence)
Act (2 & 3 Geo. 6,
c. 75) 6
London Building Acts
(Amendment) Act (2
& 3 Geo. 6, c. xcvii) 304
s. 54 315
1946 Ministers of the Crown
(Transfer of Functions)
Act (9 & 10 Geo. 6,
c. 31), s. 1 215
Acquisition of Land
(Authorisation Pro-
cedure) (9 & 10 Geo.
6, c. 49), s. 8 (1) 301
Sched. 1, para. 3 (1) (b) 301

PAGE

1948 Requisitioned Land and
War Works Act (11 &
12 Geo. 6, c. 17), s. 7 315
1949 Civil Aviation Act (12 &
13 Geo. 6, c. 67), s. 26 315
1951 Rivers (Prevention of Pollution) Act (14 & 15
Geo. 6, c. 64) 231
ss. 7, 12 (2), Sched. 3 ... 231
1954 Landlord and Tenant Act
(2 & 3 Eliz. 2, c. 56) 71
1956 Copyright Act (4 & 5 Eliz.
2, c. 74), s. 19 56
1957 Occupiers' Liability Act (5
& 6 Eliz. 2, c. 31) ... 47
Housing Act (5 & 6 Eliz.
2, c. 56)—
s. 44 301
s. 64 (3) 315
Pt. III 315
Coal-Mining (Subsidence)
Act (5 & 6 Eliz. 2,
c. 59) 300
1959 County Courts Act (7 & 8
Eliz. 2, c. 22), ss. 51,
361 361
s. 197 361
Highways Act (7 & 8 Eliz.
2, c. 25) 314
s. 108 261
Rights of Light Act (7 &
8 Eliz. 2, c. 56) 150
ss. 1, 2 151
s. 3 (1) (2) 151
(3)–(6) 152
s. 4 150
s. 7 151
1960 Clean Rivers (Estuaries
and Tidal Waters) Act
(8 & 9 Eliz. 2, c. 54) 231
Church Property (Mis-
cellaneous Provisions)
Measure (8 & 9 Eliz.
2, No. 1), s. 9 (1)–(3) 77
1961 Rivers (Prevention of Pollution) Act (9 & 10
Eliz. 2, c. 50), s. 1 ... 231
1963 County Courts (Jurisdiction) Act (c. 5) 361
London Government Act
(c. 33), s. 43 304
Water Resources Act (c.
38) 199, 214–218, 231
s. 2 (1) (2) (b) (3) 215

PAGE

1963 Water Resources Act—cont.
s. 3 214
s. 4 215
s. 23 (1) 215, 217
s. 24 .... 216, 217
(1) 216
(2) (3) 216–218
s. 25 216
s. 26 (1) 217
(a) 217
(b) 218
(2) 217, 218
s. 27 (2) (3) 215
s. 29 (2) 217
(3) (5)–(8) 215
s. 30 216
s. 31 (1) 216, 217
(2) (3) 216
ss. 32–35 216
s. 39 215
ss. 49, 50 (1) (3) (4) 217
ss. 55, 56 (5) 216
s. 81 (4) (5) 214
s. 117 215
s. 135 (1) 215, 216
Part IV 215
1964 Perpetuities and Accumulations Act (c. 55),
ss. 3, 15 (3) 50
Ministers of the Crown
Act (c. 98), s. 4 215
1965 New Towns Act (c. 59)—
s. 18 (3) 76
s. 19 315
Commons Registration Act
(c. 64) 59
1966 Land Registration Act
(c. 39) 76
Liverpool Corporation
(General Powers) Act
(c. xl), s. 3 (2) 301
1967 Leasehold Reform Act
(c. 58), s. 10 (2) 76
1968 Water Resources Act
(c. 35) 199, 214
s. 1 (1) 215
1970 Income and Corporation
Taxes Act (c. 10),
ss. 156, 157 37
1971 Animals Act (c. 22), s. 5 (6) 40
Town and Country Plan-
ning Act (c. 78), ss.
117–127 315

PART I

EASEMENTS GENERALLY

CHAPTER 1

CHARACTERISTICS OF AN EASEMENT

1.—INTRODUCTION

Ownership of land and easements

The ownership of land consists of a limited right to use it. Subject to general statutory restrictions, not here in point (such as those imposed by planning legislation), the owner of land in fee simple free from incumbrances has the exclusive right to do on it anything that does not so affect other land, or its occupiers, as to cause a nuisance or some other injury of which the law takes notice. This limitation on the right of a landowner to use his land as he pleases is reflected in a corresponding right in neighbouring landowners, and in the landowner himself, *vis-à-vis* other landowners, to immunity. The law recognises a situation in which some natural right incident to the ownership of a piece of land (the servient tenement) is, *quoad* other land (the dominant tenement), curtailed and, as a result, a corresponding artificial right is added to the rights naturally incident to the dominant tenement. This situation may come about in three classes of case. First, the natural right of the servient owner to exclude others from the use of his land may, in some respect, be curtailed, giving place to a corresponding right in the dominant owner to invade, or encroach on, the servient tenement. Secondly, the natural right of the servient tenement to immunity may, in some respect, be curtailed in favour of a corresponding increase in the limited rights of user naturally incident to the ownership of the dominant tenement. Thirdly, the natural limited right of the servient owner to use his land as he pleases may be curtailed, in some respect, by an increase in the ordinary rights, incident to the ownership of the dominant land, of immunity against nuisance and the like. If and so long as such a situation exists, the dominant tenement has an easement over the servient tenement. Easements in the first and second classes, that is, those conferring a right to invade or encroach on the servient tenement, and those conferring a special right in respect of the user of the dominant tenement, are affirmative or positive easements. Those in the third class, that is, those conferring some special right of immunity, are negative easements, or easements of immunity.

It is of the essence of an easement that, as between two pieces of land, there is a shift in the equilibrium of natural rights incident to their ownership, a diminution in the natural rights of one being accompanied by a corresponding artificial addition to the natural rights of the other; the result being that a conveyance of either operates automatically,[1] and can only operate, as a transfer of natural rights diminished, or of natural rights plus an additionally acquired right.

Easements and profits à prendre

An easement relates only to user of land, that is, it merely confers a right to utilise the servient tenement in a particular manner, or to prevent the commission of some act on that tenement, whereas a *profit à prendre in solo alieno* confers a right to take from the servient tenement some part of the soil of that tenement or minerals under it or some of its natural produce or the animals *ferae naturae* existing upon it.[2] For example, the right to depasture cattle,[3] or to graze sheep[4] is a profit, and so is the right to take sea-washed coal from the foreshore.[5] The subject-matter of a profit must be something which is capable of ownership.[6] Hence the right to take water (except water appropriated or confined in some receptacle) is not a profit, for water (unless so confined) is not capable of being owned,[7] but the right is or may be an easement.[8]

While the nature of a profit is thus essentially different from that of an easement, the rules and principles governing the acquisition, extinguishment and disturbance of profits are generally applicable to the acquisition, extinguishment and disturbance of easements. For this reason, although this work is not one on the law of profits,[9] reference will be made to the classification of profits[10] and the subject of profits will

1 See the Law of Property Act 1925, s. 187 (1); Co.Litt. 121b; Shep.Touchstone 189; *Leech* v. *Schweder* (1874) 9 Ch.App. 463, 474–476; *Godwin* v. *Schweppes Ltd.* [1902] 1 Ch. 926, 932. A servient owner can only convey such rights of ownership as he has, and where an easement has been created for a legal estate and the servient tenement has been shorn of one of its natural rights, a purchaser, with or without notice, must take it as it is.

2 *Alfred F. Beckett Ltd.* v. *Lyons* [1967] Ch. 449, 482, per Winn L.J., approving the statement in Halsbury's *Laws of England*, 3rd ed., Vol. 12, p. 522, para. 1129; and see *Sutherland* v. *Heathcote* [1892] 1 Ch. 475, 484.

3 *Bailey* v. *Appleyard* (1838) 8 A. & E. 161.

4 *White* v. *Taylor* (*No. 2*) [1969] 1 Ch. 160, 177.

5 *Alfred F. Beckett Ltd.* v. *Lyons* [1967] Ch. 449, 474, per Harman L.J.; 482, per Winn L.J. In the expression *profit à prendre in alieno solo* the words *in solo alieno* are not equivalent to *ex solo alieno*: per Winn L.J. 480.

6 *Ibid.* 481, 482, per Winn L.J. The nature of *profits à prendre* (including the right to kill and carry away game and fish) is discussed in *Wickham* v. *Hawker* (1840) 7 M. & W. 63; *Ewart* v. *Graham* (1859) 7 H.L.C. 344; *Fitzhardinge* v. *Purcell* [1908] 2 Ch. 163; *White* v. *Williams* [1922] 1 K.B. 727; *Peech* v. *Best* [1931] 1 K.B. 1; *Mason* v. *Clarke* [1955] A.C. 778.

7 *Alfred F. Beckett Ltd.* v. *Lyons* [1967] Ch. 449, 481, per Winn L.J.

8 *Race* v. *Ward* (1855) 4 E. & B. 702; *Manning* v. *Wasdale* (1836) 5 A. & E. 758; *Paine and Co.* v. *St. Neots Gas and Coke Co.* [1939] 3 All E.R. 812, 823; *Re Simeon* [1937] Ch. 525.

9 As will be seen (p. 59, *post*), a profit may be a " sole " or " several " profit, or a profit " in common " or right of common. For a detailed discussion of the law of profits and commons, see, *e.g.* Hall, *Law of Profits à Prendre and Rights of Common*; *Williams on Commons*; *Woolrych on Commons*; Harris and Ryan, *An Outline of the Law Relating to Common Land*; Halsbury's *Laws of England*, 3rd ed., Vol. 5, pp. 295 *et seq.*

10 See in particular section 8 of this chapter, p. 59, *post*.

be referred to whenever to do so appears to be helpful in expounding the law of easements.

A possessory right cannot be an easement

The grantee of the exclusive use of land has an estate in the land and not an easement. So Lopes L.J. in *Reilly* v. *Booth* said [11]:

" The exclusive or unrestricted use of a piece of land, I take it, beyond all question passes the property or ownership in that land, and there is no easement known to the law which gives exclusive and unrestricted use of a piece of land."

The status, for rating and similar purposes, of railway tunnels, gas mains, and the like, belonging to statutory undertakers, has been considered in a number of cases in which no question arose as to the rights of the undertakers *vis-à-vis* the owners of the surrounding soil, but the distinction between easement and ownership was referred to. Such cases appear to be *sui generis*, and it is difficult, for instance, to find a dominant tenement.[12] Usually no easement is created.[13] In *South Eastern Railway* v. *Associated Portland Cement Manufacturers (1900) Limited* [14] the reservation, in a conveyance to a railway company, of the right for the conveying party, his heirs and assigns, to make a tunnel under the land conveyed (the proposed railway) was treated by Swinfen Eady J. as a reservation of an easement, but by the Court of Appeal as an assignable personal contract. The owner of an exclusive right to use a tunnel is in fact, almost certainly, the owner of the tunnel itself.[15]

2.—ESSENTIAL CHARACTERISTICS OF AN EASEMENT

Definition of an easement

An easement was defined by Lord Esher M.R. in *Metropolitan Railway* v. *Fowler* [16] as " some right which a person has over land which is not his own," but this definition lacks precision, as not every right which one has over another's land is necessarily an easement, and perhaps no precise definition is possible. The question of easement or no easement usually arises where (1) a right has been granted and (a) the allegedly dominant tenement or the allegedly servient tenement has since changed

---

[11] (1890) 44 Ch.D. 12, 26. See also *Capel* v. *Buszard* (1829) 6 Bing. 150, 159; *Clifford* v. *Hoare* (1874) L.R. 9 C.P. 362, 371.

[12] *Metropolitan Railway* v. *Fowler* [1892] 1 Q.B. 165; [1893] A.C. 416; *Holywell Union and Halkyn Parish* v. *Halkyn Drainage Co.* [1895] A.C. 117; *R.* v. *Chelsea Waterworks Co.* (1833) 5 B. & Ad. 156; *Southport Corporation* v. *Ormskirk Union Assessment Committee* [1894] 1 Q.B. 196; *Ystradyfodwg and Pontypridd Main Sewerage Board* v. *Bensted* [1907] 1 K.B. 490, 497; *Taff Vale Railway* v. *Cardiff Railway* [1917] 1 Ch. 299, 317.

[13] *Newcastle-under-Lyme Corporation* v. *Wolstanton Ltd.* [1947] Ch. 427, 456–457. It seems clear, however, that a particular house or piece of land can have an easement to maintain and use a drain on other land : see pp. 15, 30, *post*.

[14] [1910] 1 Ch. 12.

[15] *Bevan* v. *London Portland Cement Co.* (1892) 67 L.T. 615; *Re Pearson's Will* (1900) 83 L.T. 626; and see (1916) 32 *Law Quarterly Review* 70.

[16] [1892] 1 Q.B. 165, 171.

hands or (b) the grantee of the right seeks to restrain obstruction by a
stranger to the allegedly servient tenement; or (2) a " right " long enjoyed
is alleged to have been acquired, by prescription, or lost grant, as an
easement. In such cases it is safer to try to discover the essential
characteristics of an easement, and see whether the right in question
has them, than to rely on some pretended definition which may or may
not be wholly accurate.

Essential characteristics

The essential characteristics of an easement appear from *Re Ellenborough Park.*[17]   In that case the question arose whether the owners of
certain houses in Ellenborough Park, which is an open space, comparable
with the garden of a London " square," in Weston-super-Mare, had any
right to participate in a compensation rental and dilapidations payment
received by the owners of the Park under the Compensation (Defence)
Act 1939. Such a right could only exist if the house-owners had some
interest in the Park; their only possible interest was an easement, and the
question thus became one of easement or no easement. The facts were
shortly as follows: Ellenborough Park is a rectangular piece of land [18]
surrounded by a road, on three sides of which (the fourth faces the sea)
are rows of houses. In or about 1864 the sites of the houses, and also
of other houses further away, formed part of a building estate which was
sold in plots. The conveyance of one of these plots, which was accepted
as typical, contained a grant of the plot, together with the dwelling-house
in course of erection thereon, and together with easements over the roads
and drains in the estate,

> " And also the full enjoyment . . . at all times hereafter in common
> with the other persons to whom such easements may be granted of
> the pleasure ground . . . [Ellenborough Park] . . . but subject to the
> payment of a fair and just proportion of the costs charges and
> expenses of keeping in good order and condition the said pleasure
> ground." [19]

There was a detailed covenant by the purchaser to complete the house
in accordance with specifications and plans, similar in every respect
externally and in a uniform manner with a particular house already
built, and a covenant by him against alteration of the external elevation
or structure, and against user for commercial purposes. The vendors
covenanted with the purchaser, and his successors in title and all other
persons to whom the right of enjoyment of the Park might be granted,
to keep the Park as an ornamental pleasure ground, and not at any time
to " erect or permit to be erected any dwelling-house and other building

---

[17] [1956] Ch. 131.
[18] More exactly, it is two pieces of land, intersected by a main road.
[19] It may be observed that the grant of a similar right was provided for in an agree-
    ment, made in 1843, for a lease of a house in a similar crescent in Brighton.
    Lawrence v. *South County Freeholds Ltd.* [1939] Ch. 656, 660.

(except any grotto bower summer-house . . . or other ornamental erection) within or on any part of the " Park, but that the same should at all times remain as an ornamental garden or pleasure ground. A similar right of user was granted in respect of some nine or ten other plots, not actually fronting the Park but separated from the road round it only by houses so fronting. The right to use the Park was held by the Court of Appeal,[20] affirming Danckwerts J., to be an easement, and for the purposes of the decision it was agreed between counsel, and accepted by the court, that the following four characteristics [21] are essential to an easement:

1. There must be a dominant and a servient tenement.[22]
2. An easement must accommodate the dominant tenement.[23]
3. Dominant and servient owners must be different persons.[24]
4. A right over land cannot amount to an easement, unless it is capable of forming the subject-matter of a grant.[25]

These four characteristics to some extent overlap, but it will be convenient to consider each of them separately.

1. There must be a dominant and a servient tenement

In other words, an easement requires that some diminution of the natural rights incident to the ownership of an estate in one piece of land be reflected in a corresponding artificial right superimposed on the natural rights incident to another piece of land. Lord Cairns in *Rangeley* v. *Midland Railway Company* [26] said:

" There can be no easement properly so called unless there be both a servient and a dominant tenement. . . . There can be no such thing according to our law, or according to the civil law, as what I may term an easement in gross. An easement must be connected with a dominant tenement."

Again, Lord Coleridge C.J. in *Hawkins* v. *Rutter* [27] said:

" No doubt the term ' easement ' has, somewhat loosely and inaccurately perhaps,[28] but still with sufficient accuracy for some pur-

---

[20] The judgment of the court was delivered by Sir Raymond Evershed M.R.
[21] As formulated in Cheshire's *Modern Real Property*, 10th ed., pp. 469 *et seq.*
[22] See *infra*.   [23] See pp. 16 *et seq.*, *post*.
[24] See pp. 20 *et seq.*, *post*.   [25] See pp. 22 *et seq.*, *post*.
[26] (1868) 3 Ch.App. 306, 310–311. The question here was whether a railway company could divert a public footpath without acquiring and paying for the new site, and the passage quoted was dealing with an argument that this would not be permanently used, within s. 84 of the Lands Clauses Consolidation Act 1845, and that the company would have a mere easement, the ownership of the site remaining as before.
[27] [1892] 1 Q.B. 668, 671, deciding that the right of a member of the public to ground his barge on the bed of a navigable river was not an " easement " for the purposes of the County Courts Act 1888, s. 60.
[28] For instance, in *Dovaston* v. *Payne* (1795) 2 H.Bl. 527, the soil of a highway was said to be subject to an easement for the benefit of the public, but a public right of way cannot be an easement, for there is no dominant tenement. In *Taff Vale Railway* v. *Cardiff Railway* [1917] 1 Ch. 299, 317, Scrutton L.J. pointed out that " Parliament and parliamentary draftsmen have used the term ' easement ' in relation to various rights which no lawyer would describe as ' easements.' "

poses, been said to define the case of a public right of way, in which case there exists no dominant and servient tenement; but in strictness, and according to the proper use of legal language, the term 'easement' does imply a dominant tenement in respect of which the easement is claimed, and a servient tenement upon which the right claimed is exercised."

Recently Winn L.J. in *Alfred F. Beckett Ltd.* v. *Lyons* [29] said:

" I think it is an essential element of any easement that it is annexed to land, and that no person can possess an easement otherwise than in respect of and in amplification of his enjoyment of some estate or interest in a piece of land: compare *Rangeley* v. *Midland Railway Company.*" [30]

It follows that an easement, being annexed to the dominant tenement, cannot be separated from it by being assigned to a stranger.[31] This does not mean, however, that the use of the dominant tenement is confined to the dominant owner personally. It seems clear, in the first place, that a lease or tenancy of dominant land operates as a lease or tenancy of the land plus the easement, and that anyone for the time being entitled to an interest in the land which, *vis-à-vis* the owner, gives him the right to possession is entitled, *vis-à-vis* whoever is in possession of the servient land, to use the easement.[32] Secondly, the grant of an easement normally operates as a grant of the right to such user as the enjoyment of the dominant land reasonably requires, and this includes user by strangers.[33] In *Proud* v. *Hollis* [34] it was said that the landlord of land to which a right of way is annexed may use the way to view waste, or to demand rent, or to remove an obstruction. Perhaps the true view is that user by a landlord for any purpose connected with the dominant tenement could be justified as had under the licence, express or implied, of the tenant.

Dominant tenement

A dominant tenement can usually be identified without much difficulty. Although it is obviously good conveyancing practice in a deed granting an easement to specify the dominant tenement clearly, failure so to do is not necessarily fatal to the grant, for extrinsic evidence, including evidence of the manner in which a purchaser intends to use land in the future, is admissible to identify the dominant tenement when its identity does not appear clearly from the deed. This rule is illustrated by two recent cases.[34a]

[29] [1967] Ch. 449, 483.
[30] (1868) 3 Ch.App. 306.
[31] *Cf. Ackroyd* v. *Smith* (1850) 10 C.B. 164, 188.
[32] *Skull* v. *Glenister* (1864) 16 C.B.(N.S.) 81 (parol letting from year to year). *Cf.* Law of Property Act 1925, s. 187 (1). On the other hand it seems that, in the absence of clear words enabling him to do so, the owner of a dominant tenement could not authorise the public to use a right of way annexed thereto: see *Johnstone* v. *Holdway* [1963] 1 Q.B. 601, 613.
[33] See *post*, p. 282.   [34] (1822) 2 B. & C. 8.
[34a] See also *Gamble* v. *Birch Island Estates Ltd.* (1971) 13 D.L.R. (3d) 657.

In *Johnstone* v. *Holdway*[35] a vendor held certain land, including a quarry, in trust for a company. The vendor as trustee and the company as beneficial owner conveyed part of that land to a purchaser, who was the defendant's predecessor in title. The quarry was not included in the land conveyed, but was adjacent to it on its north-western boundary. There was a public highway on the south-eastern boundary of the land conveyed, and the conveyance contained a reservation and exception in favour of the company and its successors in title of a right of way for use " at all times and for all purposes (including quarrying) " over the land conveyed from a point on its north-western boundary to a point on its south-eastern boundary. The reservation did not specify the dominant tenement for the benefit of which the right of way was given, but it was intended to be the quarry. The plaintiffs became the owners of the quarry as the company's successors in title, and they claimed a declaration that they had a right of way over the defendant's land from the highway to the quarry. For the defendant it was submitted that it was not permissible to identify the dominant tenement by inferences from facts and circumstances which must have been known to the parties at the time of the conveyance. Delivering the judgment of the Court of Appeal, Upjohn L.J. referred to *Thorpe* v. *Brumfitt*.[36] In that case, in the course of a rearrangement of boundaries a triangular piece of land, containing five and a half square yards and intended to be thrown into the yard of an inn to which a right of way had previously been enjoyed, was conveyed with a right of way at all times and for all purposes over a passage described as being " between " the highway and the north side of the piece of land conveyed. In an action for obstruction, it appears to have been argued, in reliance on *Ackroyd* v. *Smith*,[37] that the right was in gross. Rejecting this, Mellish L.J. said that the words " between," etc., might fairly be construed as making the right appurtenant to the five and a half square yards. James L.J. went further, and said that the right to and from the five and a half square yards must be construed reasonably, in the circumstances, as meaning a right of way between the highway and the yard, of which the five and a half square yards were to form part, and that the right would therefore pass as appurtenant to the inn.

Upjohn L.J. said[38] that it was quite plain that James L.J. took the view that you must look at the whole of the relevant facts which must have been known to the grantor and the grantee at the time of the grant and take into consideration the whole object of the transaction. Upjohn L.J. referred[39] to *Callard* v. *Beeney*[40] in which a vendor conveyed a farm to a purchaser together with a right of way over a field No. 171

35 [1963] 1 Q.B. 601.
36 (1873) 8 Ch.App. 650.
37 (1850) 10 C.B. 164; see p. 12, *post*.
38 [1963] 1 Q.B. 611.
39 *Ibid*.
40 [1930] 1 K.B. 353.

belonging to the vendor " for the purpose of access to and from the point marked ' X ' on the said plan to the field numbered 169," and the Divisional Court held as a matter of construction that the dominant tenement was the whole of the seventy acres or so of land conveyed by the deed and that the right of way was appurtenant to those lands and not limited to use for purposes connected with field 169 only. Upjohn L.J. pointed out that Wright J. in his judgment [41] dealt with the matter purely as a matter of construction and cited the observations of Lord Wensleydale in *Lord Waterpark* v. *Fennell* [42] that:

> " The construction of a deed is always for the court but in order to apply its provisions evidence is in every case admissible of all material facts existing at the time of the execution of the deed so as to place the court in the situation of the grantor."

In the light of those authorities Upjohn L.J. said [43]:

> " In our judgment, it is a question of the construction of the deed creating a right of way as to what is the dominant tenement for the benefit of which the right of way is granted and to which the right of way is appurtenant. In constructing the deed the court is entitled to have evidence of all material facts at the time of the execution of the deed, so as to place the court in the situation of the parties."

It seemed to the Court of Appeal perfectly plain that in the case before it the dominant tenement was the land and quarry.

The Shannon Limited v. *Venner Limited*,[44] in which the Court of Appeal applied *Thorpe* v. *Brumfitt* [45] and *Johnstone* v. *Holdway*,[46] not only is authority on the admissibility of extrinsic evidence but also shows that the easement granted may, when the dominant tenement is not specified in the deed of grant, be appurtenant to other land besides that conveyed by the deed. In 1927 the plaintiff company bought certain land in Surrey on which they built a factory so constructed that it could be extended. In 1930 adjoining land, described as land " to the north of land recently sold by the vendor to the company," was conveyed to it by the same vendor " together with a right of way for all purposes for the company and their successors in title their tenants and servants and all persons authorised by the company in common with the vendor and all others authorised by him over and along the private estate drive of the vendor as " identified on a plan. There was no physical division between the land conveyed and the land acquired by the company in 1927. The company claimed a declaration that the right of way was appurtenant to the adjacent land which it had previously acquired. Pennycuick J. admitted evidence that at the time of its purchase the company intended

41 [1930] 1 K.B. 360.
42 (1859) 7 H.L.C. 650, 684.
43 [1963] 1 Q.B. 612.
44 [1965] Ch. 682.
45 (1873) 8 Ch.App. 650.
46 [1963] 1 Q.B. 601.

to use the further land in connection with its factory, and that that intention was communicated to the vendor before the execution of the conveyance, but, founding his conclusion on the reference to the company and its successors in title and the inclusion of the grant of the right of way between the parcels and the *habendum,* held that the words of the conveyance were clear and that the right of way was not appurtenant to the land previously acquired by the company. The Court of Appeal allowed an appeal from Pennycuick J.'s decision, holding that proper conveyancing practice required not merely a reference to " successors in title " but an identification of the owner or occupier of identified dominant land for the benefit of which an easement was created; that the identification of the dominant tenement was not clear or sufficient in the conveyance, which did not in terms identify the dominant tenement at all; and that extrinsic evidence was therefore admissible concerning the circumstances in which the conveyance was executed.

Danckwerts L.J., delivering the judgment of the Court of Appeal, said [47]:

" It is one thing to allow a party to say: ' By the words in the deed, I meant this meaning ' (which is not admissible), and quite another thing to advance evidence that, in acquiring a particular piece of land, the purchaser had certain plans for the use of that land which may explain the form which the document took. The evidence was rightly admitted as throwing light upon the circumstances in which the document came to be executed.

" It is sufficient to refer to the words of Upjohn L.J., giving the judgment of the court, in *Johnstone* v. *Holdway*." [48]

Having cited the words from the judgment in *Johnstone* v. *Holdway* [48] quoted above, Danckwerts L.J. continued [49]:

" That is the situation in the present case, and we are entitled to have the benefit of the evidence of the surrounding circumstances. A document intended to have legal effect is not executed in a vacuum. It is drafted and executed to deal with the situation in which the parties find themselves. Of course, if the words used in the deed are perfectly clear, they must be given their meaning, and extrinsic evidence is not admissible, because that would be contradicting the terms of the deed.

" . . . Of course the deed must be looked at, and then, if the meaning is not plain, the court is entitled to consider the surrounding circumstances so as to see whether light as to the construction is to be gained from these."

It had been submitted for the defendant company that, in the absence of a statement identifying the dominant tenement, there must be a pre-

[47] [1965] Ch. 691.
[48] [1963] 1 Q.B. 601, 612; see p. 10, *ante.*
[49] [1965] Ch. 691, 692.

sumption, and possibly an inference, that the land actually conveyed by the deed must be the dominant tenement, and reliance was placed upon *Callard* v. *Beeney*,[50] as support for the proposition to that effect on page 8 of the thirteenth edition of this work. The Court of Appeal thought [1] that that might be so in the absence of evidence causing an inference that some other land was the dominant tenement for the benefit of which the easement was created, but held that it could not be an irrebuttable presumption. *Callard* v. *Beeney*[50] was a case where the contest was between the whole of the land conveyed and a single field forming part of it. It did not seem to be the same point as that which the court had to consider in the case then before it.

The description of a right of way may limit the dominant tenement to some part only of the land conveyed. In *Henning* v. *Burnet*[2] a conveyance of a house and a field beyond it contained a grant of a right of way over a road which was described as " leading " to the house; in fact it passed alongside it and then turned in so as to divide the house from the field. It was held that the way was to the house only, and was not annexed to the field also. In *British Railways Board* v. *Glass*,[3] on the other hand, a conveyance of land acquired for the construction of a railway line contained an exception in favour of the grantor and his heirs and assigns of " a right of crossing the said railway to the extent of twelve feet in width on the level thereof with all manner of cattle to and from one part of the said close of land hereinbefore described and called Cowshed or Cowleaze . . . to the other part of the said close severed by the said . . . railway " and it was held that the reference to the field called Cowshed as containing the two ends of the crossing place was merely used so as to identify the position of the crossing; that is to say, the description of a part of the dominant land was not restrictive of the dominant tenement but merely intended to show where the right of way would be exercised.

In *Ackroyd* v. *Smith*,[4] where a close and other lands were conveyed, together with the right for the grantee, his heirs and assigns, owners and occupiers for the time being of the said close and other lands, of passing and repassing, with or without horses, cattle, carts, and carriages, *for all purposes*, in, over, along and through a certain road described as running between a certain turnpike road and a certain lane called Legram's Lane, or through some other road in the same direction to be formed by the grantee, the court expressed the opinion that the grant, on its true construction, was not only for the purposes of the land conveyed but also for purposes unconnected with it, and was therefore a grant of a right in gross, not appurtenant to the land conveyed and not capable of passing

50 [1930] 1 K.B. 353.
1 [1965] Ch. 692, 693.
2 (1852) 8 Exch. 187.
3 [1965] Ch. 538.
4 (1850) 10 C.B. 164.

by a subsequent conveyance of it with its appurtenances. It seems reasonable to suppose, however, that a right granted in the same quite common form would now be treated as annexed to the land conveyed. In *Todrick* v. *Western National Omnibus Co.*[5] Romer L.J. said: " I doubt however whether at the present day any judge would hold that the right granted in that case was as a matter of construction a grant of a right of way for all purposes whether connected or unconnected with the land in question." The topography of *Ackroyd* v. *Smith* is obscure, but it seems [6] that the land to which it was sought to make the way appurtenant was not at the end of the road. So far as can be gathered,[7] this road either led into or passed the end of an accommodation road, part of the " lands " granted and leading to other of these lands.

The dominant tenement usually consists of corporeal property. It was, however, held by Buckley J. in *Hanbury* v. *Jenkins*[8] that a right of way can be appurtenant to a right of fishing. He adopted note 7 to Hargrave and Butler's edition of Co.Litt. 121b, that the true test of appurtenancy was the propriety of relation between the principal and the adjunct, which might be found out by considering whether they so agreed in nature and quality as to be capable of union without incongruity.

In *Att.-Gen.* v. *Copeland*,[9] a highway authority claimed an easement of discharging water on the defendant's land by means of a pipe running from a highway. The action was dismissed by Lord Alverstone C.J. on the ground that the public right of passage over the road was not such a right as was capable of having the easement claimed attached to it, and that therefore the claim to the easement failed for want of a dominant tenement. This decision was reversed by the Court of Appeal, on the ground that the pipe in question was a " drain " within the meaning of section 67 [10] of the Highway Act 1835; Collins M.R. adding " that a legal origin was possible, and ought to be presumed," for the right claimed, and the Lords Justices apparently concurring.

Applying the above-mentioned test, it is submitted that if the owner of a right to take certain minerals [11] under close A obtained from the owner of an adjacent close, B, a grant of a way over the close B, or a right to discharge water over it, for him, his heirs and assigns, as appurtenant to the right of mining, an easement would undoubtedly be created

---

5 [1934] Ch. 561, 583; and *cf. Thorpe* v. *Brumfitt* (1873) 8 Ch.App. 650, 658; *Gaw* v. *Córas Iompair Éireann* [1953] I.R. 232.

6 See *Thorpe* v. *Brumfitt* (1873) 8 Ch.App. 650, 657; *Todrick* v. *Western National Omnibus Co.* [1934] Ch. 561, 590–591.

7 See 10 C.B. 176.

8 [1901] 2 Ch. 422.

9 [1901] 2 K.B. 101. On appeal [1902] 1 K.B. 690.

10 Now repealed.

11 The right to take minerals out of the soil of another is an incorporeal right; the right to a stratum of minerals is a corporeal right: *Doe* d. *Hanley* v. *Wood* (1819) 2 B. & Ald. 724; *Wilkinson* v. *Proud* (1843) 11 M. & W. 33; *Hamilton* v. *Graham* (1871) L.R. 2 Sc. & Div. 166.

and would be appurtenant to the incorporeal right already vested in the grantee. It is clear that, if the grantee, in the case above supposed, was already the owner, not merely of the incorporeal hereditament, but of the substratum itself containing the minerals, and obtained such a grant from the owner of B, he would thus become entitled to an easement appurtenant to his soil; and what reason is there for holding that such would not also be the result in the case first put? If the question were raised in the form above suggested, the difficulty could not be evaded by holding that the first incorporeal right is enlarged by the grant of the second, and that both together form one entire right, as they would do if they had originally been conferred by the same grantor in one grant.[12]

Re Salvin's Indenture[13] indicates that a dominant tenement may consist of both corporeal and incorporeal hereditaments. The defendants were the water authority for an important area in the county of Durham. The plaintiff's predecessors in title had some years before purported to grant to the defendants' predecessors in title (who were at that time the water authority for the area in question) " the free and uninterrupted right easement liberty leave and authority " in consideration of a small yearly rentcharge " to make and from time to time lay . . . enlarge alter . . . cleanse drain and repair all or any mains and pipes necessary for the conveyance or transit of water for the purposes of " the water authority. The plaintiff took out an originating summons for the construction of this grant, and on his behalf it was contended unsuccessfully that it had not operated as the grant of an easement, but only as the grant of a licence, on the ground that the defendants' system of pipes was not a dominant tenement to which the right of conveying water could have been annexed. Dealing with this argument, Farwell J. said[14]:

> " In my judgment that is not sound. The undertaking in this case, which is now vested in the defendants, consists of corporeal hereditaments, and incorporeal hereditaments, the corporeal hereditaments being the lands which the company acquired for the purpose of its object—that is to say, lands for the erection of reservoirs and other similar purposes—and the incorporeal hereditaments being the rights which it acquired in land of others to lay pipes and for other purposes. The undertaking, in my judgment, being composed of corporeal and incorporeal hereditaments, is capable of being the dominant tenement in respect of such a grant as this." [15]

The exclusive right of burial may be granted in perpetuity, under a faculty if the vault is in a church or churchyard[16]; otherwise under the

---

12 The instance given above, with substantially the conclusions stated, was originally from the hand of Mr. W. H. Willes, the editor of the 3rd edition (1862).
13 [1938] 2 All E.R. 498. Farwell J.'s decision is criticised in an article, " The Dominant Estate," by Mr. Peter Brett in 14 *Conveyancer* (N.S.) 264, 267 *et seq.*
14 [1938] 2 All E.R. 506.
15 But see *Stockport Waterworks Co.* v. *Potter* (1864) 3 H. & C. 300, 327.
16 *De Romana* v. *Roberts* [1906] P. 332.

Burial Act 1852, s. 33, or the Cemetery Clauses Act 1847, s. 40,[17] or under some private Act. The validity of a non-statutory perpetual grant of this kind appears to be undoubted,[18] but the nature of the right created is questionable, and it is submitted that no easement is created,[19] for there is no dominant tenement. A true easement, of burying in the chancel of a church any person dying in a certain house, was recognised in *Waring* v. *Griffiths*.[20]

Servient tenement

If no servient tenement is ascertainable there is, of course, no easement. In *Woodman* v. *Pwllbach Colliery Co. Ltd.*,[21] where a lessee claimed, unsuccessfully, that his lease contained an implied grant of the right to cause a nuisance by allowing coal dust to dissipate itself over adjoining land of the lessor (to which no reference was made in the lease), the Court of Appeal,[22] who refused to infer any such grant, intimated that the right, if granted, could not be an easement, for no servient tenement was ascertainable. Cozens Hardy M.R. said[23]:

> " If it is an easement it is elementary to say that you must have a dominant and a servient tenement. You cannot have a dominant tenement without some definition of what is the tenement that goes by the name of the servient tenement. There is no reference whatever to be found in this deed which enables one to answer that question. . . . It may have been [the lessor's] whole property for all I know. . . . You cannot have a servient tenement without an area. You must have lines defining some area."

Swinfen Eady L.J. said[24]: " It is necessary for an easement that there should be a servient tenement that can be defined and pointed out."

Difficulty in identifying the servient tenement, though not any doubt as to its existence, may arise where, for instance, a house is granted with the right to receive water, or discharge drainage, through a pipe in adjoining property retained by the grantor. In such a case the servient tenement may be thought to consist of the adjoining property or some part of it, or of the pipe itself, if this is not part and parcel of the dominant land,[25] or of the adjoining property and the pipe.[26] For most

---

17 See *Hoskins-Abrahall* v. *Paignton U.D.C.* [1929] 1 Ch. 375.
18 See *e.g. De Romana* v. *Roberts, supra*; *Kellett* v. *St. John's, Burscough* (1916) 32 T.L.R. 571, and *cf.* the Burial Act 1853, s. 4.
19 This was conceded in *London Cemetery Co.* v. *Cundey* [1953] 1 W.L.R. 786, but on the ground that there was no servient tenement. See *Kellett* v. *St. John's, Burscough, supra*, 572.
20 (1758) 1 Burr. 440.   21 (1914) 111 L.T. 169; *affd.* [1915] A.C. 634.
22 And see *per* Lord Sumner [1915] A.C. 634, 648–649.
23 111 L.T. 172.   24 111 L.T. 174.
25 If a pipe is laid in the land of another, then, in the absence of express agreement, the application of the maxim *quicquid plantatur solo solo cedit* depends upon the circumstances and the language of the grant: *Simmons* v. *Midford* [1969] 2 Ch. 415, where *Lancaster* v. *Eve* (1859) 5 C.B.(N.S.) 717; *Wake* v. *Hall* (1883) 8 App.Cas. 195 and *Armstrong* v. *Sheppard & Short Ltd.* [1959] 2 Q.B. 384, 401, *per* Lord Evershed

---

26 For footnote, see p. 16.

practical purposes the question is of little importance, for it is clear that such a right is an easement,[27] and that, whatever the servient tenement may be, the pipe is entitled to protection from interference,[28] including, presumably, interference by withdrawal of support.[29] Furthermore, in cases of doubt the deed will be construed against the grantor.[30] In other similar cases the identity of the servient tenement may bear on the question whether the so-called easement is not repugnant to the proprietary rights of the servient owner.[31]

2. An easement must accommodate the dominant tenement

This and the first condition mean, in effect, that no right over land can be an easement unless it in fact [32] accommodates other land (the dominant tenement). It is no objection that other land, or other people, could equally be accommodated by the same right,[33] or that the grant of the right has the effect of conferring some benefit on other land also.[34]

As Lord Evershed M.R. said delivering the judgment of the Court of Appeal in *Re Ellenborough Park* [35] what is required is that the right " accommodates and serves the dominant tenement, and is reasonably necessary for the better enjoyment of that tenement, for if it has no necessary connection therewith, although it confers an advantage upon the owner and renders his ownership of the land more valuable, it is not an easement at all, but a mere contractual right personal to and only enforceable between the two contracting parties." In applying this to the grant of " the full enjoyment " of Ellenborough Park, the Court of

M.R. are considered; see also *Goodhart* v. *Hyett* (1883) 25 Ch.D. 182, 186; *Newcastle-under-Lyme Corporation* v. *Wolstanton Ltd.* [1947] Ch. 427, 439.

[26] *Paine & Co.* v. *St. Neots Gas & Coke Co.* [1939] 3 All E.R. 812, 823.

[27] " The right to the free passage of water through my neighbour's land, and for that purpose to maintain a pipe or other channel therein, is one of the commonest forms of easement " (Warrington L.J., *Schwann* v. *Cotton* [1916] 2 Ch. 459, 474); and see *Nuttall* v. *Bracewell* (1866) L.R. 2 Exch. 1, 10.

[28] *Schwann* v. *Cotton, supra.*

[29] The pipe has, however, no right to participate in any right of support which the soil enclosing it may itself have; *Newcastle-under-Lyme Corporation* v. *Wolstanton, Ltd.* [1947] Ch. 427.

[30] *Dunn* v. *Blackdown Properties Ltd.* [1961] Ch. 433; *Cordell* v. *Second Clanfield Properties Ltd.* [1969] 1 Ch. 9; but *cf. Bulstrode* v. *Lambert* [1953] 1 W.L.R. 1064, 1068; see *post*, p. 80.

[31] See *post*, p. 30.

[32] " An incident of this nature cannot, even by express words in a deed, be connected with the estate by the mere acts of the parties "; *per* Byles J. in *Bailey* v. *Stephens* (1862) 12 C.B.(N.S.) 91, 115, pointing out that a grant to the owner of land in Kent of a right of way over land in Northumberland would not create an easement.

[33] *Re Ellenborough Park* [1956] Ch. 131, 172, explaining a dictum of Willes J. in *Bailey* v. *Stephens, supra.*

[34] *Simpson* v. *Godmanchester Corporation* [1897] A.C. 696, 702, 703. " It is, no doubt, one of the essential characteristics of an easement that its exercise shall be for the use and benefit of the dominant estate. But there is no law to the effect that an easement, which is serviceable and beneficial to that estate, shall cease to exist whenever, from the very nature of the right, its exercise by the dominant estate confers. or tends to confer, some benefit upon other lands or tenements " (Lord Watson at p. 703).

[35] [1956] Ch. 131, 170; quoting and adopting Cheshire's *Modern Real Property*, 7th ed., p. 457. See p. 6, *ante.*

Appeal decided that the right did " accommodate and serve " each of the houses with which it was granted, in that the use of the park was an extension of the normal use of the house. The court recognised that mere increase in value is not decisive, and that some rights, granted with a house, may fail to qualify as easements because they are not connected, or are too remotely connected, with the normal enjoyment of the house; on the other hand they intimated that a grant to each owner or lessee of a separate part of a house (as where a house is converted into flats) of the right to use the garden in common with the others does create an easement.[36] The material part of the judgment is as follows [37]:

> " It is clear that the right did, in some degree, enhance the value of the property, and this consideration cannot be dismissed as wholly irrelevant. It is, of course, a point to be noted; but we agree with Mr. Cross's submission that it is in no way decisive of the problem; it is not sufficient to show that the right increased the value of the property conveyed, unless it is also shown that it was connected with the normal enjoyment of that property. It appears to us that the question whether or not this connection exists is primarily one of fact, and depends largely on the nature of the alleged dominant tenement and the nature of the right granted. As to the former, it was in the contemplation of the parties to the conveyance of 1864 that the property conveyed should be used for residential and not commercial purposes. That appears from the conveyance itself, and the covenant by the purchaser already quoted, that the dwelling-house, etc., which he bound himself to build should not ' be occupied or used as an open or exposed shop for any purpose of trade or commerce other than a lodging-house or private school or seminary ' without the vendor's written consent. Since it . . . has been conceded that all the conveyances of plots for building purposes fronting or near Ellenborough Park were as regards (*inter alia*) user substantially the same as the conveyance of 1864, the inevitable inference is that the houses, which were to be built upon the plots were to constitute a residential estate. As appears from the map, the houses, which were built upon the plots around and near to Ellenborough Park varied in size, some being large detached houses and others smaller and either semi-detached or in a row. We have already stated that the purchasers of all the plots, which actually abutted on the park were granted the right to enjoy the use of it, as were also the purchasers of some of the plots which, although not fronting upon the park, were only a short distance away from it. As to the nature of the right granted, the conveyance of 1864 shows that the park was to be kept and maintained as a pleasure ground or ornamental garden, and that it was contem-

---

[36] *Cf. Robins* v. *Evans* (1863) 2 H. & C. 410.
[37] [1956] Ch. 173.

plated that it should at all times be kept in good order and condition and well stocked with plants and shrubs; and the vendors covenanted that they would not at any time thereafter erect or permit to be erected any dwelling-house or other building (except a grotto, bower, summer-house, flower-stand, fountain, music-stand or other ornamental erection) within or on any part of the pleasure ground. On these facts Mr. Cross submitted that the requisite connection between the right to use the park and the normal enjoyment of the houses which were built around it or near it had not been established. He likened the position to a right granted to the purchaser of a house to use the Zoological Gardens free of charge or to attend Lord's Cricket Ground without payment. Such a right would undoubtedly, he said, increase the value of the property conveyed but could not run with it at law as an easement, because there was not sufficient nexus between the enjoyment of the right and the use of the house. It is probably true, we think, that in neither of Mr. Cross's illustrations would the supposed right constitute an easement, for it would be wholly extraneous to, and independent of, the use of the house as a house, namely, as a place in which the householder and his family live and make their home; and it is for this reason that the analogy which Mr. Cross sought to establish between his illustrations and the present case cannot, in our opinion, be supported. A much closer analogy, as it seems to us, is the case of a man selling the freehold of part of his house and granting to the purchaser, his heirs and assigns, the right, appurtenant to such part, to use the garden in common with the vendor and his assigns. In such a case, the test of connection, or accommodation, would be amply satisfied; for just as the use of a garden undoubtedly enhances, and is connected with, the normal enjoyment of the house to which it belongs, so also would the right granted, in the case supposed, be closely connected with the use and enjoyment of the part of the premises sold. Such, we think, is in substance the position in the present case. The park became a communal garden for the benefit and enjoyment of those whose houses adjoined it or were in its close proximity. Its flower beds, lawns and walks were calculated to afford all the amenities which it is the purpose of the garden of a house to provide; and, apart from the fact that these amenities extended to a number of householders instead of being confined to one (which on this aspect of the case is immaterial), we can see no difference in principle between Ellenborough Park and a garden in the ordinary signification of that word. It is the collective garden of the neighbouring houses, to whose use it was dedicated by the owners of the estate, and as such amply satisfied, in our judgment, the requirement of connection with the dominant tenements to which it is appurtenant. The result is not affected by the circumstance that the right to the park is in this case enjoyed by some few houses which are not immediately fronting on the park. The test for present purposes, no doubt, is that the park should constitute in a real and intelligible sense the garden (albeit the communal garden) of the houses to which its enjoyment is annexed. But we think that the test is satisfied as regards these few neighbouring, though not adjacent, houses. We think that the extension of the right of enjoyment to these few houses does not negative the presence of the necessary 'nexus' between the subject-matter enjoyed and the premises to which the enjoyment is expressed to belong."

In *Hill* v. *Tupper* [38] the plaintiff, to whom a canal company had granted a lease of land adjoining the canal, together with " the sole and exclusive right or liberty to put or use boats on the said canal, and let the same for the purposes of pleasure only," sued the defendant, who also had premises on the canal, for damages for letting out pleasure boats and so infringing the plaintiff's alleged right. The action failed, on the ground that the " exclusive right " granted had no connection with the use and enjoyment of the plaintiff's land, and was unknown to the law.[39] The grant operated as a licence or covenant on the part of the company, and was binding as between the company and the plaintiff, but gave him no right of action in his own name for any infringement of the supposed exclusive right. Of this case it was said in *Re Ellenborough Park* [40] that

" what the plaintiff was trying to do was to set up, under the guise of an easement, a monopoly which had no normal connection with the ordinary use of his land, but was merely an independent business enterprise. So far from the right claimed sub-serving or accommodating the land, the land was but a convenient incident to the exercise of the right." [41]

The mere fact that an easement is acquired for the purposes of a business carried on on the dominant tenement does not disqualify it under this head.[42]

In *Simpson* v. *Godmanchester Corporation* [43] the corporation established, by prescription, alternatively under a lost grant, an easement to open lock gates in times of flood. It was admitted that there was some municipal land which was thereby protected from floodwater.

---

[38] (1863) 2 H. & C. 121.
[39] *Cf. Att.-Gen.* v. *Horner* [1913] 2 Ch. 140, 180, 196–197.
[40] [1956] Ch. 131, 175.
[41] Interference with the right to put boats on the canal would, however, have been actionable; see *per* Bramwell B. in *Nuttall* v. *Bracewell* (1866) L.R. 2 Exch. 1, 11, 12.
[42] *Moody* v. *Steggles* (1879) 12 Ch.D. 261 (right to fix a signboard on adjoining property); *Henry Ltd.* v. *M'Glade* [1926] N.I. 144 (stationary sandwich-man); *Copeland* v. *Greenhalf* [1952] Ch. 488 (claim to keep things for business purposes on neighbouring land).
[43] [1897] A.C. 696.

In *Clapman* v. *Edwards* [44] a ninety-nine-year lease of a petrol station to the defendant included " the right to use the flank walls of [certain adjoining premises of the lessor] for advertising purposes." The defendant granted to a bill-posting company the right, for a year, to post bills, etc., on these premises, whereupon the plaintiff, who derived title to both properties under the lessor, sought to restrain the defendant from permitting any other person to use the flank walls for advertising, his contention being that the right granted was an easement appurtenant to the petrol station and therefore could not be assigned separately from the station; alternatively, that any advertisements must be confined to advertisements relating to the business of the station. Bennett J. held that there was nothing in the words quoted to confine the permitted advertisements to advertisements connected with the petrol station, and that the right of advertising, not being connected with the station or any other land, was not an easement but a licence.

If land to which a right purports to be annexed is in fact accommodated by the use of the right, the right qualifies as an easement whether the dominant and servient tenements are contiguous or not.[45] A right of way, not ending anywhere on the land to which it is annexed, will be a valid easement if the owner of the land owns, or otherwise has the right to pass over, the intervening land.[46]

3. Dominant and servient owners must be different persons

The meaning is, that the owner and occupier of land cannot subject it to an easement in favour of other land also owned and occupied by himself.[47] It is obvious that if A owns and occupies a piece of land (or several pieces of land) any use made by him of part in connection with another part is referable to his rights of ownership,[48] and does not involve any diminution of, or accretion to, natural rights. " In order to obtain an easement over land you must not be the possessor of it, for you cannot have the land itself and also an easement over it." [49] " You

---

44 [1938] 2 All E.R. 507.
45 *Todrick* v. *Western National Omnibus Co.* [1934] Ch. 561; *cf. Moody* v. *Steggles* (1879) 12 Ch.D. 261, 267.
46 *Todrick* v. *Western National Omnibus Co., supra*; *Pugh* v. *Savage* [1970] 2 Q.B. 373, where there was a right of way to and from field C over field A, passing over an intervening field B with the consent of the tenant of field B: the right subsisted after the owner of field C became the owner of field B.
47 This proposition is thought not to be affected by s. 72 (3) of the Law of Property Act 1925, which provides that a person may convey land (which is defined to include, unless the context otherwise requires, an easement) to himself. The question might conceivably arise if the owner-occupier of land purported to grant to himself an easement over part of it, and then disposed of that part. In such a case, however, an easement might well be held to have been granted *de novo*, by implication, under the disposition.
48 It is pointed out in *Bolton* v. *Bolton* (1879) 11 Ch.D. 971, that user of part in connection with another part is referable to the ownership of the part used, and not necessarily to the ownership of the other part, and therefore that the right could not pass, under a conveyance of the other part, as " appurtenant " to it.
49 *Ladyman* v. *Grave* (1871) 6 Ch.App. 763, 767, *per* Lord Hatherley L.C.

cannot have an easement over your own land." [50] " Of course, strictly speaking, the owner of two tenements can have no easement over one of them in respect of the other. When the owner of Whiteacre and Black-acre passes over the former to Blackacre, he is not exercising a right of way in respect of Blackacre; he is merely making use of his own land to get from one part of it to another." [1]

Accommodations enjoyed by an owner or occupier of land over part of it are usually described as " quasi-easements," and may become actual easements if the part accommodated is disposed of separately.[2]

An owner of two pieces of land can, of course, grant, expressly or impliedly, an easement over one to a tenant of the other. Such grants constantly arise by implication.[3] A tenant cannot, however, obtain an easement over other land of his landlord, either under section 2 of the Prescription Act 1832[4] or by prescription at common law,[5] or (apparently) under the doctrine of lost modern grant.[6] This is because a tenant can only prescribe in right of his landlord,[7] and because an easement cannot be obtained by prescription for a limited time only.[8] A tenant can, however, under section 3 of the Prescription Act, prescribe against his landlord for an easement of light.[9]

It appears from *Derry* v. *Sanders*,[10] that, by the custom of the manor, a copyhold tenant could prescribe for an easement against another copy-hold tenant, or against the lord. Such a right would [11] survive enfranchisement under the Copyhold Act 1894 (see s. 23), and if so, would, it seems, survive enfranchisement under the Law of Property Act 1922 (see Sched. 12, para. (5))[12]; but it would not, unless expressly reserved, survive a common law enfranchisement of the servient tenement. In *White* v. *Taylor* (*No. 2*)[13] (where the right claimed was a *profit à*

---

[50] *Metropolitan Ry. Co.* v. *Fowler* [1892] 1 Q.B. 165, 171, *per* Lord Esher M.R.
[1] *Roe* v. *Siddons* (1888) 22 Q.B.D. 224, 236, *per* Fry L.J.
[2] See *post,* p. 92.
[3] See *e.g. Beddington* v. *Atlee* (1887) 35 Ch.D. 317, 322. An easement granted expressly or impliedly to a tenant determines with the expiration or determination by any means of the tenancy (*ibid.*).
[4] *Kilgour* v. *Gaddes* [1904] 1 K.B. 457; *Gayford* v. *Moffatt* (1868) 4 Ch.App. 133, 135.
[5] *Large* v. *Pitt* (1797) Peake Add.Cas. 152.
[6] *Wheaton* v. *Maple & Co.* [1893] 3 Ch. 48, 63, where Lindley L.J. said " The whole theory of prescription at common law is against presuming any grant or covenant not to interrupt, by or with anyone except an owner in fee. A right claimed by prescription must be claimed as appendant or appurtenant to land, and not as annexed to it for a term of years. Although, therefore, a grant . . . might be inferred as a fact, if there was evidence to justify the inference, there is no legal presumption, as distinguished from an inference in fact, in favour of such a grant." See also *Cory* v. *Davies* [1923] 2 Ch. 95, 107, 108.
[7] *Gayford* v. *Moffatt, supra.*
[8] *Wheaton* v. *Maple & Co.* [1893] 3 Ch. 48, 63; *Kilgour* v. *Gaddes* [1904] 1 K.B. 457, 460, 466, 467.
[9] *Morgan* v. *Fear* [1907] A.C. 425; see p. 149, *post.*
[10] [1919] 1 K.B. 223.
[11] *Ibid.* 239, 243, *per* Scrutton L.J.
[12] *Quaere,* however, whether the " other easements " referred to in para. (5) are not confined to mining easements.
[13] [1969] 1 Ch. 160, 185.

prendre) Buckley J. held that enjoyment of grazing facilities by tenants of the lord of the manor holding under leases or tenancy agreements, could not establish a reputation of rights appurtenant to the lands comprised in their holdings.

The question whether land owned by a person as trustee can have or be subject to an easement over or in favour of other land owned by the same person beneficially was touched on in *Ecclesiastical Commissioners for England* v. *Kino*,[14] but does not appear to have arisen for decision. In that case, where the owners of a church, until recently owned by the rector, sought an interim injunction to restrain a threatened obstruction of light to the church by the then owners of adjoining land, until recently part of the glebe and also owned by the rector, it was objected that the unity of possession prevented the acquisition of a right to light. The Court of Appeal doubted this; at least they thought the point not so clearly sound as to justify the refusal of an interim injunction, and Brett L.J. said that his present inclination of opinion was that the rector, as beneficial owner of the glebe, might make it a servient tenement to the church of which he was only trustee.

4. A right over land cannot amount to an easement unless it is capable of forming the subject-matter of a grant

Positive rights

It is thought that the right to do any definite positive thing can be the subject-matter of a grant, and that such a right, if the other three conditions mentioned above are satisfied, will rank as an easement; but that the negative rights, or rights of immunity, capable of being the subject-matter of a grant (as distinct from a restrictive covenant) are strictly limited. On the other hand, a right which depends upon the exigencies of the other owner's use of his land at any time, and therefore his consent, cannot be the subject of a legal grant.[15]

It is difficult to imagine any right to do some positive act on servient land that could not, by the use of intelligible words, be the subject of a grant. If a right of way over A's land can be granted, why should the right to do any other positive act on A's land not be capable of being granted? Although the right to do, on dominant land, a positive act infringing the natural rights of the servient land (for instance to create a nuisance) is seldom, if ever, granted expressly, but is more usually acquired (if at all) by prescription, which presumes a grant, or under the doctrine against derogation from grant, there is no reason to suppose that any particular right to do a positive act on dominant land is incap-

---

14 (1880) 14 Ch.D. 213.
15 *Green* v. *Ashco Horticulturalist Ltd.* [1966] 1 W.L.R. 889; *Lay* v. *Wyncoll* (1966) 198 E.G. 887.

able of being granted.[16] "No particular words are necessary to a grant," [17] and words of covenant or agreement may operate as a grant. Thus an agreement between A, owner of land, and B, owner of mines beneath it, that the owners of the mines should not be liable for (in effect) damage to the surface, was construed as a grant of the right to let down the surface,[18] and an agreement between A and B that A and his successors in title should have the control of a stream on B's land, and that such stream should be allowed to flow in a free and uninterrupted course into A's land, was held to be an easement of the watercourse.[19] In *Russell* v. *Watts*,[20] Lord Blackburn said that a covenant may, if it is necessary to carry out the intention, operate as a grant.

Negative rights

Negative rights, or rights of immunity, stand on a different footing. Such rights are naturally acquired by means of covenants; and a *grant* to the owners of Whiteacre that it shall not be lawful for the owners of Blackacre to do on Blackacre some particular thing that might otherwise be lawfully done is a doubtful conception. Even in regard to the right to light, which undoubtedly is an easement, and, like all other easements, must originate (at common law [21]) in a grant, express, implied or pre-sumed, it has been repeatedly said that this cannot be the subject of a grant; and indeed the judicial utterances to that effect are almost as num-erous as those which support the contrary view. Thus, in *Moore* v. *Rawson*,[22] Littledale J. said:

"Although a right of way, being a privilege of something positive to be done or used in the soil of another man's land, may be the sub-ject of legal grant, yet light and air, not being to be used in the soil of the land of another, are not the subject of actual grant, but the right to insist upon the non-obstruction and non-interruption of them more properly arises by a covenant which the law would imply, not to interrupt the free use of the light and air."

In *Rowbotham* v. *Wilson*,[23] Cresswell J. said that "rights, such as the right to light and air, are not the subject-matter of a grant." In *Scott* v. *Pape*,[24] Bowen L.J. said that before the Prescription Act the right to light depended "on the implication, derived from user, of some sup-posed covenant by the owner of the servient tenement." In *Birmingham*,

---

16 In *Pwllbach Colliery Co. Ltd.* v. *Woodman* [1915] A.C. 634, 649, Lord Sumner said that a right for A to spread coal dust, emanating from his land, anywhere on adjoin-ing land can be the subject of a grant, but he also expressed the opinion that it is too indeterminate to be an easement proper.
17 *Rowbotham* v. *Wilson* (1860) 8 H.L.C. 348, 362, *per* Lord Wensleydale.
18 *Rowbotham* v. *Wilson* (1860) 8 H.L.C. 348.
19 *Northam* v. *Hurley* (1853) 1 E. & B. 665.
20 (1885) 10 App.Cas. 590, 611.
21 No presumption of grant is required for the purposes of s. 3 of the Prescription Act 1832; see *post*, p. 149.
22 (1824) 3 B. & C. 332, 340.
23 (1857) 8 E. & B. 123, 143.
24 (1886) 31 Ch.D. 554, 571.

Dudley and District Banking Co. v. *Ross*,[25] Lindley L.J. said that " the grant of an easement of this kind [light] is, properly speaking, an implied covenant by the grantor not to use his own land so as to injure the rights of [the dominant owners] "; and in *Hall* v. *Lichfield Brewery Co.*,[26] Fry J., in awarding damages for obstruction of the access, long enjoyed, of air through windows of a slaughterhouse, expressed the opinion that the right so recognised could not be claimed by grant, and therefore (prescription being the implication of a grant) could not be the subject of prescription, but must rest on implied covenant.

On the other hand, in *Dalton* v. *Angus*,[27] Lord Selborne, after stating his opinion that a right of support can be gained by prescription, proceeded :

> " Some of the learned judges " (*i.e.* those who were summoned to give their opinion) " appear to think otherwise, and to doubt whether it could be the subject of grant. For that doubt I am unable to perceive any sufficient foundation. Littledale J. in *Moore* v. *Rawson*,[28] spoke of the right to *light* as being properly the subject, not of grant, but of covenant. If he had said (which he did not), that a right to light could not be granted, in the sense of the word ' grant ' necessary for prescription, I should have doubted the correctness of the opinion, notwithstanding the great learning of that eminent judge. . . . The light which enters a building by particular apertures does and must pass over the adjoining land in a course which, though not visibly defined, is really certain, and, in that sense, definite. Why should it be impossible for the owner of the adjoining land to grant a right of unobstructed passage over it for that light in that course? "

There are many other judicial references to a " grant " of light,[29] and it is thought that, provided that the channel is sufficiently defined, the right to an uninterrupted flow or passage of light, water, or anything else can be granted as a negative easement. Even so, no right, except the right of support,[30] of immunity against the doing on servient land of some otherwise lawful act (not involving interference with the flow of something), appears to have been accepted as an easement, and it is thought that the class of negative easements is now closed. In *Phipps* v. *Pears*,[31] in which the Court of Appeal held that there was no such

---

25 (1888) 38 Ch.D. 295, 312. See also *per* Bowen L.J. at p. 313.
26 (1880) 49 L.J.Ch. 655. See also the opinion of the same judge in *Dalton* v. *Angus* (1881) 6 App.Cas. 740, 771, 773, 776.
27 (1881) 6 App.Cas. 740, 794; see also 823, *per* Lord Blackburn.
28 (1824) 3 B. & C. 332, 340.
29 See *e.g. Jones* v. *Tapling* (1862) 12 C.B.(N.S.) 826, 864; *Booth* v. *Alcock* (1873) 8 Ch.App. 663, 665, 666; *Leech* v. *Schweder* (1874) 9 Ch.App. 463, 474; *Phillips* v. *Low* [1892] 1 Ch. 47, 50.
30 It is a question whether the right of support is purely negative. Regarded as the right to exert thrust on the supporting land or buildings, it is positive: *Dalton* v. *Angus* (1881) 6 App.Cas. 740, 793.
31 [1965] 1 Q.B. 76.

easement known to the law as an easement to be protected from the weather, Lord Denning M.R. said [32] that a negative easement must be looked at with caution, because the law has been very chary of creating any new negative easements. The question is important, for although, by taking a restrictive covenant, a man can acquire for his land immunity from almost anything,[33] a restrictive covenant is not enforceable against a purchaser for value without notice, whereas an easement is valid against all comers.[34]

Significance of the fourth characteristic

In *Re Ellenborough Park*,[35] the court, after remarking [36] that the exact significance of this fourth and last characteristic [37] is, at first, perhaps, not entirely clear, said that, for the purposes of that case, the cognate questions involved under it were (a) whether the rights purported to be given were expressed in terms of too wide and vague a character (or [38] whether the right conferred was too wide and vague); (b) whether, if and so far as effective, such rights would amount to rights of joint occupation or would substantially deprive the park owners of proprietorship or legal possession; (c) whether, if and so far as effective, such rights constituted mere rights of recreation, possessing no quality of utility or benefit, and on such grounds could not qualify as easements. It is convenient to consider (a) and (c) together and then (b).

Easements which are not recognised

As to (a) and (c) there appears to be no reported case in which an express grant of a supposed easement has been held to create no easement because the wording of the grant is too vague, but to this head may be referred the cases in which a prescriptive right to the unobstructed general flow of air from an allegedly servient tenement over an allegedly dominant tenement has been rejected. In *Webb* v. *Bird*,[39] it was decided that the owner of a windmill could not become entitled, either under section 2 of the Prescription Act, or by presumed grant, to the general flow of air from adjoining land; the reason being that the right claimed was, in the nature of things, incapable of being interrupted. This was followed in *Bryant* v. *Lefever*,[40] and *Harris* v. *De Pinna*,[41] where a build-

---

[32] [1965] 1 Q.B. 82, 83.

[33] In *National Trust* v. *Midlands Electricity Board* [1952] Ch. 380, a covenant, intended to preserve the view from certain land of the Trust, that " no act or thing shall be done or placed or permitted to remain upon [certain land of the covenantors] which shall injure prejudice affect or destroy the natural aspect and condition of the land " was held void for uncertainty.

[34] A right in the nature of an easement and enforceable against successors in title without notice may arise, under the doctrine forbidding derogation from grant, from an express grant for a particular purpose. *Post*, p. 89.

[35] [1956] Ch. 131; see p. 6, *ante*.

[36] [1956] Ch. 164.

[37] See pp. 7, 22, *ante*.

[38] [1956] Ch. 175.

[39] (1861) 10 C.B.(N.S.) 268; (1862) 3 C.B.(N.S.) 841.

[40] (1879) 4 C.P.D. 172.

[41] (1886) 33 Ch.D. 238.

ing erected on adjoining land affected the draught of the plaintiff's chimneys, and in *Chastey* v. *Ackland* [42] where the erection of a building on adjoining land prevented the dissipation of foul air coming from the plaintiff's premises. It appears to be undoubted that an express grant of a *general* right to receive air from adjoining premises would not create an easement.[43] It has been repeatedly said that a grant will not be presumed when the grantor could not have reasonably prevented the enjoyment of the subject of the grant,[44] and it may be true to say that a grant of the right to receive what the grantee must inevitably receive in any case is a grant of nothing; but the general passage of air can be at least partially obstructed, as appears from the cases just cited, and probably the true reason for refusing to recognise an easement of the general flow of air is that the subject-matter is too vague, and that it would be inconvenient to do so.[45]

For the same or similar reasons the law does not recognise an easement of prospect,[46] or privacy.[47] That there is no natural right to either is clear,[48] and it is thought that the cases in the footnotes,[46,47] sufficiently establish that no such right can be acquired as an easement. It seems also that, except by agreement, there can be no separate right to have maintained unobstructed the view of premises by (*e.g.*) prospective customers.[49]

In *Phipps* v. *Pears* [50] the Court of Appeal held that there was no right to be protected from the weather and Lord Denning M.R. (with whom Pearson and Salmon L.JJ. agreed), having referred to cases dealing with prospect and air coming through an undefined channel, said [1]:

> "The reason underlying these instances is that if such an easement were to be permitted, it would unduly restrict your neighbour in his enjoyment of his own land. It would hamper legitimate

---

[42] [1895] 2 Ch. 389; compromised on appeal [1897] A.C. 155.

[43] " The principle . . . I conceive to be that, until defined and confined, there is in those cases [water], as in light and air in its natural state, no subject-matter capable of being the subject of a lawful grant." *Dalton* v. *Angus* (1881) 6 App.Cas. 740, 759, *per* Field J.

[44] See *e.g. per* Wightman J., *Chasemore* v. *Richards* (1859) 7 H.L.C. 349, 370; Fry J., *Dalton* v. *Angus* (1881) 6 App.Cas. 740, 776; Lopes L.J., *Chastey* v. *Ackland* [1895] 2 Ch. 389, 397.

[45] See *per* Lindley L.J., *Harris* v. *De Pinna* (1886) 33 Ch.D. 238, 262; but *cf.* the view of Lord Denning M.R. in *Phipps* v. *Pears* [1965] 1 Q.B. 76, 83.

[46] *Aldred's Case* (1610) 9 Co.Rep. 57 (b), 58 (b); *Harris* v. *De Pinna* (1886) 33 Ch.D. 238, 262; *Dalton* v. *Angus* (1881) 6 App.Cas. 740, 824; *Browne* v. *Flower* [1911] 1 Ch. 219, 225; *Campbell* v. *Paddington Corporation* [1911] 1 K.B. 869, 875–876; *Leech* v. *Schweder* (1874) 9 Ch.App. 463, 475, where " attach . . . to the land " clearly means " attach as an easement."

[47] *Chandler* v. *Thompson* (1811) 3 Camp. 80; *Dalton* v. *Angus* (1881) 6 App.Cas. 740, 764; *Browne* v. *Flower* [1911] 1 Ch. 219, 225.

[48] *Tapling* v. *Jones* (1865) 11 H.L.C. 290, 305; *Fishmongers' Co.* v. *East India Co.* (1752) 1 Dick. 163; *Potts* v. *Smith* (1868) L.R. 6 Eq. 311, 318; *Campbell* v. *Paddington Corporation* [1911] 1 K.B. 869, 878–879; *Hurdman* v. *North Eastern Railway Co.* (1878) 3 C.P.D. 168, 174.

[49] *Smith* v. *Owen* (1866) 35 L.J.Ch. 317; *Butt* v. *Imperial Gas Co.* (1866) 2 Ch.App. 158.

[50] [1965] 1 Q.B. 76. This decision is criticised in (1964) 80 *Law Quarterly Review* 318.

[1] [1965] 1 Q.B. 83

development: see *Dalton* v. *Angus*, *per* Lord Blackburn.[2] Likewise here, if we were to stop a man pulling down his house, we would put a brake on desirable improvement. Every man is entitled to pull down his house if he likes.[3] If it exposes your house to the weather, that is your misfortune. It is no wrong on his part. Likewise every man is entitled to cut down his trees if he likes,[3] even if it leaves you without shelter from the wind or shade from the sun; see the decision of the Master of the Rolls in Ireland in *Cockrane* v. *Verner*.[4] There is no such easement known to the law as an easement to be protected from the weather."

It has been held that, if A sends water, for his own purposes, from one part of his land to another, a right in an adjoining owner to take from the latter part such water as happens to be there from time to time (the amount, if any, depending on the will of A) cannot arise by implication.[5]

Jus spatiandi

In *Re Ellenborough Park*,[6] it was further argued that the grant of a right to full enjoyment of the park was too wide and vague, was a right of mere recreation and amusement and not of utility and benefit, and was a *jus spatiandi*, and, on each of those grounds, failed to rank as an easement. The court decided that the right, on its proper interpretation, was a right well defined and commonly understood; and that, assuming that a mere right of recreation and amusement is capable of ranking as an easement,[7] this was not such a right, but was a beneficial attribute of the houses in respect of which it was granted. In regard to *jus spatiandi*, the argument was based on certain dicta of Farwell J. in *International Tea Stores Co.* v. *Hobbs*[8] and *Att.-Gen.* v. *Antrobus*.[9] In the first case the learned judge expressed the opinion that if a house or lodge at the vendor's park gates were conveyed with the rights conferred by section 6 of the Conveyancing Act 1881,[10] the purchaser would not acquire a right to use the garden and park, because such a right " being a mere *jus spatiandi*, is unknown to the law." [11] This was *obiter dictum*. In the second case, the learned judge declined to presume a lost grant or lost statute creating a public right to visit Stonehenge, because the public as such cannot prescribe, " nor is *jus spatiandi* known to our law as a pos-

2 (1881) 6 App.Cas. 740, 824.
3 This is not, of course, entirely accurate because he may be prevented from doing so by statute.
4 (1895) 29 I.L.T. 571.
5 *Burrows* v. *Lang* [1901] 2 Ch. 502. The case is otherwise if the right to the water is expressly granted; *Beauchamp* v. *Frome R. D. C.* [1937] 4 All E.R. 348, 357; [1938] 1 All E.R. 595, 599.
6 [1956] Ch. 131.
7 See *post*, p. 29.
8 [1903] 2 Ch. 165.
9 [1905] 2 Ch. 188.
10 See now the Law of Property Act 1925, s. 62.
11 [1903] 2 Ch. 172.

sible subject-matter of grant or prescription." [12]   The court in *Re Ellen-borough Park* doubted whether the right which it was there considering could be said to constitute a mere *jus spatiandi*, for the essence and main purpose of *jus spatiandi* is wandering at large, whereas a private garden is an ordinary attribute of the residence to which it is attached, and the right of wandering in it is only one method of enjoying it.   On the assumption, however, that the right there in question did constitute a *jus spatiandi*, or that it was analogous thereto, the court put to itself the question " Whether the right which is in question in these proceedings is, for that reason, incapable of ranking in law as an easement."   After considering the judgments of Farwell J., and pointing out that he cited no authority for his proposition that *jus spatiandi* is unknown to the law and incapable of being granted, and after considering *Duncan* v. *Louch*,[13] the court concluded that (a) while the decision in *Att.-Gen.* v. *Antrobus* was unquestionably right, for no public right of wandering at will over an undefined open space can be granted or prescribed for, the dictum in *International Tea Stores Co.* v. *Hobbs* could not be accepted as an exhaustive statement of the law, and, in reference at least to such a case as was being considered in *Re Ellenborough Park*, could not be regarded as authoritative; (b) the reasoning of the decision in *Duncan* v. *Louch*, and the circumstances of the case, no less than the language used, involved " acceptance as an easement of a right such as that with which, according to our interpretation of the effect of the relevant deeds, we are here concerned."   It was also pointed out that *Keith* v. *Twentieth Century Club* [14] had, in the peculiar circumstances of that case which need not here be stated, no authoritative force.   The court was careful to confine its decision to the case before it, and it did not, at any rate in terms, address itself to the abstract question whether a *jus spatiandi* is capable of ranking as an easement; but the decision at least establishes that there is no authority against this view, and it seems safe to assume that, while in some cases a *jus spatiandi* might possibly fail as an ease-ment because it does not accommodate the supposedly dominant tene-ment, such a right will not fail merely on the ground of vagueness.   It is possible, however, that a *jus spatiandi* alleged to have been acquired by mere user might be more difficult to establish than a right acquired by express grant capable of being read and construed.   Mere user, more-over, might well be assumed to have been had by permission, and not as of right.[15]

In *Duncan* v. *Louch*,[16] the plaintiff declared for a right of passing and repassing into a certain close called Terrace Walk, and of walking

---

12 [1905] 2 Ch. 198.

13 (1845) 6 Q.B. 904; see *infra*.

14 (1904) 73 L.J.Ch. 545.

15 *Cf. Bourke* v. *Davis* (1890) 44 Ch.D. 110, 121.   The *jus spatiandi* is considered in an article, " What is an Easement? " by Michael A. Peel in 28 *Conveyancer* (N.S.) 450, 460 *et seq*.

16 (1845) 6 Q.B. 904.

there, and of passing and repassing into and upon a certain erection at
the other end called the Water Gate. He proved a grant to a predecessor
of " the free liberty, use, benefit and privilege of the Terrace Walk." An
objection that a right so granted was not a right of way, but a right to
use the walk for pleasure only, and was therefore improperly stated in the
declaration, was overruled, on the ground that the right claimed, namely,
a right of way from one end of the walk to the other, was less than, but
included in, the right proved, namely, a right of passage backwards and
forwards over every part of the walk. Such a right was evidently
regarded as a valid easement.

Recreation and amusement

The proposition [17] that a right of mere recreation and amusement cannot rank as an easement was founded, in argument in Re Ellenborough
Park [18] on a passage in Theobald's The Law of Land, 2nd ed., p. 263,
where two cases are referred to. One, Solomon v. Vintners' Co.,[19] which
relates to support, contains, on this point, nothing more than two interlocutory and inconclusive observations [20] which seem, if anything, to
negative the proposition, and in Re Ellenborough Park were regarded
as unimportant. In the other, Mounsey v. Ismay,[21] it was decided that
a customary public right to hold horse races was not an " easement "
within section 2 of the Prescription Act. Martin B., delivering the judgment of the court, considered, without deciding, whether an easement in
gross was within the statute,[22] and proceeded,[23]

> " But however this may be, we are of opinion that to bring the
> right within the term ' easement ' in the second section it must be
> one analogous to that of a right of way which precedes it and a
> right of watercourse which follows it, and must be a right of utility
> and benefit, and not one of mere recreation and amusement."

Of this, the Court of Appeal in Re Ellenborough Park said [24]:

> " The words which we have quoted were used in reference to a
> claim for a right to conduct horse races and, in our judgment, the
> formula adopted by Theobald should be used in the light of that
> circumstance. In any case, if the proposition be well-founded, we
> do not think that the right to use a garden of the character with
> which we are concerned in this case can be called one of mere
> recreation and amusement, as those words were used by Martin

17 Ante, p. 27.
18 [1956] Ch. 131.
19 (1859) 5 H. & N. 585.
20 " Pollock C.B.—If I build a wall at the extremity of my land, and my neighbour
plays racquets against it for twenty years, is it contended that he would acquire a
right to have it kept up? Bramwell B.—Probably a right not to have it pulled down,
if he had used it for that purpose as of right " (p. 593).
21 (1865) 3 H. & C. 486.
22 It is now clear that there cannot be an easement in gross. Ante, p. 7.
23 (1865) 3 H. & C. 498.
24 [1956] Ch. 179.

B. . . . We think that the statement of Baron Martin must at least be confined to exclusion of rights to indulge in such recreations as were in question in the case before him, horse racing or perhaps playing games, and has no application to the facts of the present case."

The decision in *Mounsey* v. *Ismay* was that the Prescription Act does not apply to customary rights acquired by the inhabitants of a district. The last sentence of the judgment [24a]: " What we think [the Prescription Act] contemplated were incorporeal rights, incident to and annexed to property for its more beneficial and profitable enjoyment, and not customs for mere pleasure," might be taken to indicate that a right of mere pleasure cannot accommodate land, but the case is some way from being an authority on this point, or for the general proposition asserted by Theobald. In practice, rights of playing games on another's land are usually enjoyed by permission; express grants of such rights, or circumstances in which the user " as of right " required by the Prescription Act could be alleged with any prospect of success, must be rare.

Rights amounting to joint occupation, etc.

As to (b).[25] An easement, as already mentioned, involves a diminution of natural rights of ownership, and a grant under which the proprietary rights of the so-called servient owner are either shared or usurped cannot create an easement. For instance, " no man can be considered to have a right of property, worth holding, in a soil over which *the whole world* has the privilege to walk and disport itself at pleasure." [26] The line is difficult to draw, and each new case would probably be decided on its own facts in the light of common sense. It is obvious that the identity of the servient tenement is, at least in theory, a relevant consideration. If Blackacre has a right to receive water through a pipe laid under A's field, the right is clearly not repugnant to A's proprietary rights in the field, and if the servient tenement is considered to be the field, there is no difficulty on principle in establishing an easement. A, however, could sell the greater part of the field entirely free from the easement; the servient tenement must, it is thought, consist at most of the space occupied by the pipe and so much of the soil on each or one side as is necessary for access for repair. Of the servient tenement so constituted A is very nearly (and certainly of the space occupied by the pipe) deprived of possession; yet the validity of an easement of this kind is undoubted.[27] On the other hand, a right to make and use on another's land an embankment for the purpose of a railway or tramway cannot,

---

[24a] (1865) 3 H. & C. 486, 499.

[25] *Ante*, p. 25.

[26] Lord St. Leonards, *Dyce* v. *Lady James Hay* (1852) 1 Macq. 305, 309, negativing an alleged public *jus spatiandi* over private property; and see *Metropolitan Ry.* v. *Fowler* [1893] A.C. 416, 426, *per* Lord Watson.

[27] *Ante*, p. 16, note 27; and see *Chelsea Waterworks Co.* v. *Bowley* (1851) 17 Q.B. 358.

it seems, be an easement, for the proprietary rights of the landowner in the embankment and its site are entirely excluded.[28]

If the possession of the supposedly servient tenement is truly shared, there can be no easement, but " sharing " in the popular sense is not necessarily on equal terms; there can be a " sharer " and a " sharee." If A grants or lets to B part of a house together with the right to use, in common with A or others, a particular room of which A retains control, then, while in a sense B " shares " with A, A does not share with B,[29] and in such a case there is no difficulty in establishing an easement. In *Heywood* v. *Mallalieu* [30] an alleged right to use the kitchen of a house for washing and drying clothes was assumed, in proceedings for specific performance of an agreement for sale of the house, to be an easement. In *Miller* v. *Emcer Products, Ltd.*[31] a grant to the lessee of an office of the right to use a lavatory in common with the landlords and others was held to create an easement. Romer L.J. said [32]:

> " In my judgment the right had all the requisite characteristics of an easement. There is no doubt as to what were intended to be the dominant and servient tenements respectively, and the right was appurtenant to the former and calculated to enhance its bene-ficial use and enjoyment. It is true that during the times when the dominant owner exercised the right the owner of the servient tene-ment would be excluded, but this in greater or less degree is a common feature of many easements (for example, rights of way) and does not amount to such an ouster of the servient owner's rights as was held by Upjohn J. to be incompatible with a legal easement in *Copeland* v. *Greenhalf.*" [33]

In *Att.-Gen. of Southern Nigeria* v. *John Holt and Company (Liver-pool) Ltd.*[34] the Judicial Committee expressed the opinion that a right to store goods on the land of another could be created as an easement. " There is nothing in the purposes for which the easement is claimed inconsistent in principle with a right of easement as such." [35]

---

[28] *Taff Vale Railway* v. *Cardiff Railway* [1917] 1 Ch. 299, 316, 317.
[29] *Rogers* v. *Hyde* [1951] 2 Q.B. 923, 931, 932; *Baker* v. *Turner* [1950] A.C. 401, 415–416, 422, 432–433, 437–438 (both cases on the Rent Acts).
[30] (1883) 25 Ch.D. 357.
[31] [1956] Ch. 304.
[32] [1956] Ch. 316.
[33] [1952] Ch. 488; see page 32, *post.*
[34] [1915] A.C. 599.
[35] [1915] A.C. 617. In this case the land over which the easement was claimed (by prescription) was held to belong to the Crown, subject to a perpetual right in the company, under an implied licence, to use it for their business purposes. There could be no easement properly so called, because during the period of user the company had thought itself to be, as in effect it was, the owner of the land. A claim to an easement by prescription which fails because the right claimed is too wide may succeed as a claim to title by adverse possession, and a claim to title which fails may succeed as a claim to an easement: see an article, " Adverse Possession or Prescription? Problems of Conflict," by Michael J. Goodman in 32 *Conveyancer* (N.S.) 270.

In *Smith* v. *Gates*[36] a prescriptive right to keep chicken coops on a common was established. In *Philpot* v. *Bath*[37] the grant of an easement was inferred from an act which might, if an intention to dispossess had been established, have operated to dispossess the servient owner and give the dominant owner a statutory title to the servient tenement. The defendant, who had recently erected certain works on the foreshore on which his premises abutted, and was defending an action for an order on him to remove the works, sought to establish a statutory title on the ground that his predecessors had dispossessed the owner of the foreshore by bringing onto it a number of large boulders. It was held that these boulders had been installed for the purpose, not of dispossessing the owner but of protecting the defendant's premises from the sea, and that the defendant had not acquired a statutory title, but had acquired an easement. An order made against him to remove the works was expressed to be without prejudice to his right to an easement over the foreshore for the purpose of protecting his premises from encroachment by the sea by means of rocks, stones or piles placed on the foreshore. In *Thomas W. Ward Ltd.* v. *Alexander Bruce (Grays) Ltd.*[38] on the other hand, the Court of Appeal held that, even though there may be a prescriptive right to break up vessels in a dock, that does not include the right to maintain the silt over the area in question. Such a right cannot be the subject-matter of a legal easement, because it involves the almost complete exclusion of the alleged servient owner.

In *Copeland* v. *Greenhalf*[39] the defendant claimed a prescriptive right to deposit and repair vehicles on a strip of land varying in width from fifteen to thirty-five feet, and leading from a village street to an orchard. Upjohn J. found[40] that

> " the practice established [by the evidence] is this, that for fifty years past the defendant and his predecessor, his father, have been in the habit of storing on the south-east side of the strip vehicles awaiting repair to their woodwork, and that they have been stored on any part of the south-east side of the strip provided that an adequate means of access to Barebones orchard is left, such adequate means being a width of something like ten feet. Subject to that, the defendant and his predecessors have for the last fifty years used the south-east side of the strip for depositing vehicles awaiting repair, for putting vehicles there which have been repaired and were awaiting collection, and for repairing them there themselves. The nature of the vehicles placed on the strip has, of course, changed with changing conditions of life. Lorries and other vehicles of that sort are now placed there and repaired, or while awaiting

36 [1952] C.P.L. 814.
37 [1905] W.N. 105.
38 [1959] 2 Lloyd's Rep. 472.
39 [1952] Ch. 488.
40 *Ibid.* 491.

repair. I am fully satisfied that that is what the defendant and his father have done for fifty years."

On these facts the learned judge decided that no easement had been acquired. He said [41]

" I think that the right claimed goes wholly outside any normal idea of an easement, that is, the right of the owner or the occupier of a dominant tenement over a servient tenement. This claim (to which no closely related authority has been referred to me) really amounts to a claim to a joint user of the land by the defendant. Practically, the defendant is claiming the whole beneficial user of the strip of land on the south-east side of the track there; he can leave as many or as few lorries there as he likes for as long as he likes; he may enter on it by himself, his servants and agents to do repair work thereon. In my judgment, that is not a claim that can be established as an easement. It is virtually a claim to possession of the servient tenement, if necessary to the exclusion of the owner; or, at any rate, to a joint user, and no authority has been cited to me which would justify the conclusion that a right of this wide and undefined nature can be the proper subject-matter of an easement. It seems to me that to succeed, this claim must amount to a successful claim of possession by reason of long adverse possession. I say nothing, of course, as to the creation of such rights by deed or covenant; I am dealing solely with a right acquired by prescription."

Such questions must be questions of degree. A prescriptive claim based on user, where a grant has to be invented or imagined by the court, may well have more difficulty in qualifying as an easement than a right actually granted and capable of being scrutinised; and it is not inconceivable that the right asserted by the defendant in *Copeland's* case might be acquired, as a valid easement, under a judiciously worded express grant. Moreover, in *Wright* v. *Macadam* [42] (which was not cited in *Copeland* v. *Greenhalf* [43]), the plaintiff established a right, under section 62 of the Law of Property Act 1925, to use a coal-shed on the defendant's land, although the practical effect was to exclude the defendant from the coal-shed.

Copeland v. *Greenhalf* [43] was distinguished by Ungoed-Thomas J. in *Ward* v. *Kirkland*.[44] The plaintiff in that case owned a cottage the northern wall of which was built on his boundary and abutted onto the defendant's farmyard. The plaintiff claimed a right to go onto the defendant's land to do maintenance work on the side of his cottage. It appeared that there had been no case in which such a right had been accepted as an easement, and it was objected that such a right constituting an easement would amount to an exclusion of the servient owner

[41] *Ibid.* 498.
[42] [1949] 2 K.B. 744; see p. 126, *post.*
[43] [1952] Ch. 488. [44] [1967] Ch. 194, 222–223.

from possession of his land. Ungoed-Thomas J. pointed out that the facts of the case were very different from those of *Copeland* v. *Greenhalf*.[43] Dealing with the argument that such a right as that claimed would in effect exclude the defendant from the use of part of the farmyard next to the cottage or interfere substantially with such use, his Lordship pointed out that similar considerations arose even in cases of rights of way, because the owner of the servient tenement cannot exercise his property rights in such a manner as to defeat the easement which exists over the way, and had no difficulty in coming to the conclusion that such a right as the plaintiff claimed was not a right which would be defeated upon the ground that it would amount to the possession or joint possession of part of the defendant's property, that is to say, that part over which the plaintiff would be exercising his right to maintain his wall.

It may happen that what appears to be the subject of an easement is in fact part and parcel of the dominant tenement. Thus in *Francis* v. *Hayward* [45] a fascia on one (A) of two houses, A and B, in common ownership, had at all material times been used to advertise the business of the tenant for the time being of B. B was let in 1855 for twenty-one years, and in 1874 A was let to the defendant. At the expiration of the lease of B, and during the lease of A, B was let to the plaintiff, who claimed a right to use the fascia. It was argued that the defendant's lease was granted subject, at most, to a reservation of an easement for the term of the then existing, and since expired, lease of B, and that no grant could be implied in the plaintiff's existing lease, in derogation of the pre-existing lease to the defendant, which contained no express reservation. The court was inclined to think that A was let subject to, and B was let with, a right to use the fascia, but the decision was that the fascia was part of B and included in the demise to the plaintiff.

Class of possible easements not closed

Such, then, are the essential characteristics of an easement. Notwithstanding certain nineteenth-century dicta to the effect that rights of a novel kind cannot be annexed to land,[46] it is clear that any right having these characteristics will rank as an easement, and that, while the category of negative easements is, in the nature of things, limited, so that a negative easement must be looked at with caution,[47] and it is unlikely that any new negative easements will be recognised, the class of possible easements is not closed.[48]

---

[45] (1882) 20 Ch.D. 773; (1882) 22 Ch.D. 177; and see *post*, p. 306.
[46] *Keppell* v. *Bailey* (1834) 2 My. & K. 517, 535; *Ackroyd* v. *Smith* (1850) 10 C.B. 164, 188; *Hill* v. *Tupper* (1863) 2 H. & C. 121, 127; *Nuttall* v. *Bracewell* (1866) L.R. 2 Exch. 1, 10.
[47] *Phipps* v. *Pears* [1965] 1 Q.B. 76, 82–83, *per* Lord Denning M.R.
[48] *Ward* v. *Kirkland* [1967] Ch. 194, 222; and see *Re Ellenborough Park* [1956] Ch. 131; *Simpson* v. *Godmanchester Corporation* [1896] 1 Ch. 214, 219; *Dyce* v. *Lady James Hay* (1852) 1 Macq. 305, 309.

3.—EXAMPLES OF EASEMENTS

The following among other rights have been recognised by the courts, in many cases inferentially or by tacit assumption, as easements:

Positive Easements

Rights of way.

Right to place over neighbouring land clothes on lines.[49]

Right to move a timber traveller through and over neighbouring land [50]; or to cause bowsprits of vessels in dock to project over adjoining land.[1]

Right in working mines,[2] or quarries,[3] to make spoil banks on surface.

Right to mix muck on a neighbour's land.[4]

Right to deposit on a neighbour's land house refuse, or trade goods.[5]

Right to place a signpost,[6] or chicken-coops,[7] on a common.

Right to nail fruit trees on a neighbour's wall.[8]

Right to use a fascia on a neighbour's house.[9]

Right to fix a signboard on a neighbour's house.[10]

Right to use the chimney of a neighbour's house for the passage of smoke.[11]

Right to use the kitchen of a neighbour's house for washing.[12]

Right to use a lavatory.[13]

Right to use a coal-shed.[14]

Right of landing nets on another's land.[15]

All necessary rights to enable the grantee to obtain water from the land of the grantor.[16]

Right to place a pile in the bed of a river.[17]

Right to place stones on the foreshore for protection of adjoining land.[18]

---

[49] *Drewell* v. *Towler* (1832) 3 B. & Ad. 735.

[50] *Harris* v. *De Pinna* (1886) 33 Ch.D. 251.

[1] *Suffield* v. *Brown* (1864) 4 De G. J. & Sm. 185.

[2] *Rogers* v. *Taylor* (1857) 1 H. & N. 706; see *Marshall* v. *Borrowdale Plumbago Mines* (1892) 8 T.L.R. 275.

[3] *Middleton* v. *Clarence* (1877) Ir.R. 11 C.L. 499.

[4] *Pye* v. *Mumford* (1848) 11 Q.B. 666.

[5] *Foster* v. *Richmond* (1910) 9 L.G.R. 65; *Att.-Gen. for S. Nigeria* v. *Holt* [1915] A.C. 617.

[6] *Hoare* v. *Metropolitan Board of Works* (1874) L.R. 9 Q.B. 296.

[7] *Smith* v. *Gates* [1952] C.P.L. 814.

[8] *Hawkins* v. *Wallis* (1763) 2 Wils. 173.

[9] *Francis* v. *Hayward* (1882) 22 Ch.D. 177, 182, *per* Bowen L.J.

[10] *Moody* v. *Steggles* (1879) 12 Ch.D. 261.

[11] *Hervey* v. *Smith* (1855) 1 K. & J. 389; 22 Beav. 299; see *Jones* v. *Pritchard* [1908] 1 Ch. 630.

[12] *Heywood* v. *Mallalieu* (1883) 25 Ch.D. 357.

[13] *Miller* v. *Emcer Products Ltd.* [1956] Ch. 304.

[14] *Wright* v. *Macadam* [1949] 2 K.B. 744.

[15] *Gray* v. *Bond* (1821) 2 Brod. & Bing. 667.

[16] *Re Simeon* [1937] Ch. 525, 537.

[17] *Lancaster* v. *Eve* (1859) 5 C.B.(N.S.) 717.

[18] *Philpott* v. *Bath* [1905] W.N. 114.

Right to go on the land of another to clear a mill-stream and repair its banks [19]; or to open locks in time of flood.[20]

Right for the occupier of a messuage to water cattle at a pond and take water for domestic purposes.[21]

Right to go on a neighbour's land and draw water from a spring there,[22] or from a pump.[23]

Right to discharge rainwater by a spout or projecting eaves.[24]

Right to discharge polluted water into another's watercourse.[25]

Right to send water across a neighbour's land by an artificial watercourse.[26]

Right to use or affect the water of a natural stream in manner not justified by a natural right, e.g. by damming it.[27]

Right to place a fender in mill-stream to prevent waste of water.[28]

Right to commit a private nuisance by creating noise [29]; or by polluting water [30]; or by polluting air by smoke or smell.[31]

Right to a pew in a church.[32]

Right to construct and maintain a ventilation duct.[33]

Right to enter on adjoining land to repair an outside wall.[34]

Right to use the area alongside a wharf for the loading and unloading of vessels, and possibly for breaking up vessels.[35]

Negative easements

Right to receive light for a building.

Right to receive air by a defined channel.[36]

---

[19] *Beeston* v. *Weate* (1856) 5 E. & B. 986; *Peter* v. *Daniel* (1848) 5 C.B. 568; *Roberts* v. *Fellowes* (1906) 94 L.T. 279.

[20] *Simpson* v. *Godmanchester Corpn.* [1897] A.C. 696.

[21] *Manning* v. *Wasdale* (1836) 5 A. & E. 758.

[22] *Race* v. *Ward* (1855) 4 E. & B. 702.

[23] *Polden* v. *Bastard* (1865) L.R. 1 Q.B. 156 (but in that case the right was not proved).

[24] *Harvey* v. *Walters* (1872) L.R. 8 C.P. 162.

[25] *Wright* v. *Williams* (1836) 1 M. & W. 77.

[26] *Beeston* v. *Weate* (1856) 5 E. & B. 986; *Abingdon Corpn.* v. *James* [1940] Ch. 287.

[27] *Beeston* v. *Weate* (1856) 5 E. & B. 986.

[28] *Wood* v. *Hewett* (1846) 8 Q.B. 913.

[29] *Elliotson* v. *Feetham* (1835) 2 Bing.N.C. 134; *Ball* v. *Ray* (1873) 8 Ch.App. 467, 471.

[30] *Baxendale* v. *McMurray* (1867) 2 Ch.App. 790.

[31] *Crump* v. *Lambert* (1867) L.R. 3 Eq. 409, 413.

[32] " There may be annexed to a house, as appurtenant to it, by means of a faculty, the exclusive right to use a pew ": *Phillips* v. *Halliday* [1891] A.C. 228, 233. A lost faculty will be presumed in appropriate circumstances, but for this purpose evidence is required of acts of user, e.g. repair, which are more consistent with a right under a faculty than with occupation by permission of or arrangement with the church authorities: *Halliday* v. *Phillips* (1889) 23 Q.B.D. 48; *Stileman-Gibbard* v. *Wilkinson* [1897] 1 Q.B. 749; *Crisp* v. *Martin* (1876) 2 P.D. 15.

[33] *Wong* v. *Beaumont Property Trust Ltd.* [1965] 1 Q.B. 173.

[34] *Ward* v. *Kirkland* [1967] Ch. 194; but there is no right to have a structure protected from the weather (which would be a negative easement): *Phipps* v. *Pears* [1965] 1 Q.B. 76.

[35] *Thomas W. Ward Ltd.* v. *Alexander Bruce (Grays) Ltd.* [1959] 2 Lloyd's Rep. 472, C.A.; but there is no right to maintain silt; see p. 44, *post.*

[36] *Bass* v. *Gregory* (1890) 25 Q.B.D. 481.

Right of support of buildings from land [37]; or from buildings.[38]
Right to receive a flow of water in an artificial stream.[39]

In *Elliott* v. *Burn* [40] where surface owners had granted to mineral owners the right to let down the surface on terms of paying a tonnage rent and compensation for any damage, it was held by the House of Lords, negativing a claim for income tax on the tonnage rents as profits arising from an easement ("hereditament") under the Income Tax Act 1918, Sched. A, No. I, r. 7,[41] that what was granted was not an easement at all, but (it seems) [42] merely a release from the liability of being sued on letting down the surface, for damages for a nuisance, or for an injunction.

Qualified easements

A qualified easement may exist; as, for instance, the right of a land-owner to dam up a stream running through the servient land, and divert it into an artificial cut through the servient land to the dominant land, subject to the right of the servient owner to use the water in the cut for irrigation, when required,[43] or a right to enclose part of a river into a fishing-weir, subject to the right of a mill-owner on the opposite side to open the weir when water is scarce.[44]

Easements in common

Section 187 (2) of the Law of Property Act 1925 provides that nothing in the Act affects the right of a person to hold or exercise an easement, right or privilege over or in relation to land for a legal estate in common with any other person, or the power of creating or conveying such an easement, right or privilege. The meaning appears to be that several pieces of land in different ownership can have an easement, *e.g.* a right of way, over the same site.

4.—RIGHTS ANALOGOUS TO EASEMENTS

Fencing easements

The following statement of the law, taken from the 13th edition of this work, was quoted with approval by Willmer L.J. in the Court of Appeal in *Jones* v. *Price* [45]:

> "A true easement, as has been seen, is either a right to do something or a right to prevent something. A right to have something done is not an easement, nor is it an incident of an easement;

---

[37] *Dalton* v. *Angus* (1881) 6 App.Cas. 740.
[38] *Lemaitre* v. *Davis* (1881) 19 Ch.D. 281; *Waddington* v. *Naylor* (1889) 60 L.T. 480.
[39] *Keewatin Power Co.* v. *Lake of the Woods Milling Co.* [1930] A.C. 640; *Schwann* v. *Cotton* [1916] 2 Ch. 459; *Nuttall* v. *Bracewell* (1866) L.R. 2 Exch. 1, 10.
[40] [1935] A.C. 84.
[41] See now the Income and Corporation Taxes Act 1970, ss. 156 and 157; *Earl Fitz-william's Collieries Co.* v. *Phillips* [1943] A.C. 570.
[42] See *I. R. C.* v. *New Sharlston Collieries Co.* [1937] 1 K.B. 583, 605.
[43] *Beeston* v. *Weate* (1856) 5 E. & B. 986.
[44] *Rolle* v. *Whyte* (1868) L.R. 3 Q.B. 286.   [45] [1965] 2 Q.B. 618.

for instance, the owner of the site of a right of way is not bound to keep the way in repair.[46] An obligation to do something on one's own land can only arise, speaking generally, by statute or contract,[47] and the burden of a contractual obligation of that kind does not run with the land.[48] Anomalously, however, the courts have recognised what has been called a prescriptive obligation on the owners and occupiers of a piece of land to maintain a fence thereon for the benefit of the owners and occupiers of adjoining land.[49] The obligation has been established by proof of long usage under which the quasi-servient owner or occupier has consistently repaired the fence when told to do so by the quasi-dominant owner or occupier,[50] and therefore inferentially in performance of a binding obligation. The legal justification for subjecting private land to a positive burden does not appear to have been questioned or explained; the right so recognised is not an easement, but if it may be assumed to be enforceable against a purchaser without notice its existence produces the same situation as if an easement had been created. Probably it rests on the presumption of a contract,[1] which is considered or assumed, contrary to modern principle, to be binding on successors in title.[2]

" When land has been enclosed from a common and the person taking it has maintained a fence against the rest of the common, an obligation to do so for the benefit of the commoners and their successors has been inferred." [3]

In *Jones* v. *Price* [4] the plaintiff claimed damages for cattle trespass and the defendant by way of defence alleged an obligation on the part of the plaintiff to maintain part of a hedge which the judge of the Llanidloes County Court found was on the defendant's land but which the Court of Appeal found was a boundary fence. The Court of Appeal found that there was no evidence to establish against the plaintiff a prescriptive right to keep the hedge in repair, either by immemorial user or

---

46 *Post*, p. 47.
47 *Cf. Hilton* v. *Ankesson* (1872) 27 L.T. 519.
48 *Austerberry* v. *Oldham Corporation* (1885) 29 Ch.D. 750; *E. & G. C. Ltd.* v. *Bate* (1935) 79 L.Journal 203.
49 *Lawrence* v. *Jenkins* (1873) L.R. 8 Q.B. 274, where earlier cases are referred to. The obligation is on the occupier, not on the owner if not in occupation: *Cheetham* v. *Hampson* (1791) 4 Term Rep. 318.
50 *Hilton* v. *Ankesson, supra; Boyle* v. *Tamlyn* (1827) 6 B. & C. 329.
1 *Boyle* v. *Tamlyn, supra.*
2 As late as 1876 it was considered that a covenant to pump water from a well on land of the covenantor to houses on the land of the covenantee bound successors in title of the covenantor (*Cooke* v. *Chilcott* (1876) 3 Ch.D. 694). See now *Haywood* v. *Brunswick Building Society* (1881) 8 Q.B.D. 403; *Austerberry* v. *Oldham Corporation* (1885) 29 Ch.D. 750.
3 *Barber* v. *Whiteley* (1865) 34 L.J.Q.B. 212; *cf. Sutcliffe* v. *Holmes* [1947] K.B. 147. Such cases are in a special category: *Jones* v. *Price* [1965] 2 Q.B. 618, 647, *per* Winn L.J.
4 [1965] 2 Q.B. 618.

by the doctrine of a lost grant. Their Lordships uttered valuable dicta on the nature of the obligation to fence.

Willmer L.J. said [5]:

"It is clear that the right to require the owner of adjoining land to keep the boundary fence in repair is a right which the law will recognise as a quasi-easement. . . .

"That such a right can arise by prescription is well recognised in a number of cases to which we were referred. In the report of *Pomfret* v. *Ricroft* [6] there is a useful note setting out the ancient practice for the enforcement of such a right as follows: 'The ancient remedy was by the writ *de curia claudenda*, which lay for the tenant of the freehold against another tenant of land adjoining to compel him to make a fence or wall, which he ought, by prescription, to make between his land and the plaintiff's.'

"Such a prescriptive right was commonly established by proof of immemorial usage. This is shown by *Star* v. *Rookesby*,[7] a case of error brought before the Court of Exchequer Chamber on a judgment by default. The plaintiff declared that the tenants and occupiers of the defendant's close had, time out of mind, made and repaired the fence between the plaintiff's and the defendant's close, and that, for want of repair, the defendant's cattle came into the plaintiff's close. It was held: 'The plaintiff has made himself a sufficient title in this declaration, by showing the defendant bound to this charge by prescription; which prescription is sufficiently alleged.'

"*Boyle* v. *Tamlyn*,[8] as I understand the report, was a case which proceeded on similar lines."

Having considered *Hilton* v. *Ankesson*,[9] Willmer L.J. said [10] that he was reluctant to accept a contention that a prescriptive right to have a boundary fence maintained could be proved only by showing that repairs had consistently been carried out at request, adding that he would hesitate to hold that a plaintiff was necessarily limited to only one method of proof. His Lordship said that he did, however, accept that it was necessary to prove in one way or another that the repairs had been consistently carried out by the alleged quasi-servient owner as a matter of obligation.

Diplock L.J. expressed the view [11] that the right of the occupier of the dominant tenement to have work done upon his tenement by the occupier of the servient tenement was not an obligation capable of running with the land in law or in equity. He continued:

[5] [1965] 2 Q.B. 633, 634.
[6] (1669) 1 Saund. 321, 322a.
[7] (1710) 1 Salk. 335.
[8] (1827) 6 B. & C. 329.
[9] (1872) 27 L.T. 519.
[10] [1965] 2 Q.B. 636.
[11] [1965] 2 Q.B. 639, 640.

"On the other hand, an obligation to maintain a cattle-proof boundary fence upon one's own land to keep out the cattle of one's neighbour is capable of running with the land as servient tenement in favour of the neighbouring land as dominant tenement. . . .

"Such an obligation . . . is anomalous. It is of very ancient origin, and was originally enforceable by the writ *de curia claudenda*. It is by no means clear whether such an obligation can today be newly created so as to run with the land, except by Act of Parliament. It can undoubtedly exist by immemorial usage. It is tempting to think that its real origin lies in local custom, but this explanation was rejected in 1670 in *Polus* v. *Henstock*.[12] The rationalisation which has been current since then is that it can arise by prescription at common law, from which it must follow that, in theory, it is capable of being created by covenant or grant. In 1827, the Court of King's Bench was prepared to assume that it could be created by covenant (see *Boyle* v. *Tamlyn*[13]), but, since it is a positive obligation, this assumption cannot survive the decision of the Court of Appeal in *Austerberry* v. *Oldham Corporation*.[14] It was not, in any event, easy to reconcile with *Spencer's Case*.[15] In theory, therefore, it can lie only in grant. There is no precedent in the books for such a grant. I find it difficult to envisage its form. It would be interesting to consider whether the doctrine of lost modern grant is applicable to such an obligation, as well as common law prescription. Most enclosures and their boundary hedges can be proved to have been created after 1183,[16] so that, if the obligation exists at all, it must be by virtue of a lost modern grant. Much as I have enjoyed the erudite argument of counsel, however, I see no need to decide this question on the present appeal. There was, in my view, no evidence before the county court judge from which either a prescriptive obligation or a lost modern grant could be inferred."

Winn L.J. said [17] that the supposed lost grant would in the circumstances of the case before the court have had a substance of an agreement: only a duty independent of any contract or covenant and existing immemorially could prevail.

In *Crow* v. *Wood* [18] the Court of Appeal held that a right to have one's neighbour keep up fences was a right which lay in grant and was of such a nature that it could pass under section 62 of the Law of Property Act 1925. A large sheep moor with several adjoining farms remained for many years in common occupation. The farms were

---

12 (1670) 1 Vent. 97; reported as *Bolus* v. *Hinstorke* (1670) 2 Keb. 686.
13 (1827) 6 B. & C. 329.
14 (1885) 29 Ch.D. 750.   15 (1583) 5 Co.Rep. 16a.
16 It is thought that his Lordship meant 1189.   17 [1965] 2 Q.B. 647.
18 [1971] 1 Q.B. 77. By s. 5 (6) of the Animals Act 1971, the existence of a duty on the part of a landowner to fence provides a defence to an action by such a person for trespass by livestock.

let to individual farmers who had the right to stray a certain number of sheep on the moor and who agreed to keep their fences and walls in good repair. In 1951 one of the farms was sold together with the right to stray forty sheep on the moor. That right was let in 1962 to the defendant, who put forty sheep on the moor. In 1956 and 1966 respectively two other adjacent farms were sold to the plaintiff together with rights of stray which she did not exercise. From 1966 the plaintiff ceased to keep up the walls and fences on her farm against sheep from the moor and in consequence sheep, and in particular the defendant's sheep, often got into her farm. In an action by the plaintiff against the defendant for damages for cattle trespass and an injunction, the defendant claimed that the plaintiff was under a duty by implied grant at common law and/or by section 62 of the Law of Property Act 1925 to keep up her fences and walls for the benefit of holders of grazing rights on the moor; and that his sheep had only entered her land because of her failure to do so. The judge of the Malton County Court awarded the plaintiff damages and an injunction but the Court of Appeal allowed the defendant's appeal.

The defendant's plea that a duty to fence arose at common law failed because, as Lord Denning M.R. pointed out,[19] prescription at common law is of avail only as between adjoining owners, not where, as in the present case, the lands had been in common ownership until recent years. The county court judge had, however, held that there was a custom of the moor by which each of the farmers adjoining the moor was bound to keep up the fences and walls of his own farm. Lord Denning pointed out that this was not by itself sufficient to put an obligation on the plaintiff to fence, and he referred to *Polus* v. *Henstock*.[20] On the other hand the custom was of importance because of section 62. Having referred to the judgments of Willmer L.J. and Diplock L.J. in *Jones* v. *Price*,[21] Lord Denning said [22]:

" It seems to me that it is now sufficiently established—or at any rate, if not established hitherto, we should now declare—that the right to have your neighbour keep up the fences is a right in the nature of an easement which is capable of being granted by law so as to run with the land and to be binding on successors. It is a right which lies in grant and is of such a nature that it can pass under section 62 of the Law of Property Act 1925."

Lord Denning also said,[23] *obiter*, that there was in every conveyance to a farmer who bought his farm from a common owner, and who had a right to put sheep on the moor and to have his neighbour repair fences, implied an obligation, ancillary to that right, to keep up his own fences.

19 [1971] 1 Q.B. 77, 83–84.
20 (1670) 1 Vent. 97; reported as *Bolus* v. *Hinstorke* (1670) 2 Keb. 686.
21 [1965] 2 Q.B. 618; see pp. 39, 40, *ante*.
22 [1971] 1 Q.B. 77, 84–85.
23 [1971] 1 Q.B. 77, 85.

Edmund Davies L.J. said [24] that it seemed clear that a duty to fence against trespassers could be created by express or implied grant, but he declined to give a final decision as to the exact legal nature of the duty. Whatever might be the legal basis of a duty to fence, the balance of authorities for centuries favoured the view that the obligation, when it existed, arose from proof that the land was *accustomed* to be fenced and that it was immaterial that a party had voluntarily fenced his premises simply for, it might be, his own protection.

Ways in gross

There is no doubt that in former times a grant of a perpetual right of way in gross was considered to be valid, in the sense that it created a heritable and presumably assignable right which the owners for the time being of the quasi-servient tenement were bound to recognise. For instance, in *Senhouse* v. *Christian*,[25] which was an action of trespass, the defendant pleaded that in 1722 H. Senhouse (the plaintiff's father) granted by deed to John Christian (the defendant's grandfather), his heirs and assigns, a way over a certain slip of land; that John Christian by virtue of this deed became seised of the said way *in gross*; that the same on his death descended to Evan Christian, as his son and heir, and on the death of Evan, to one John Christian, as the brother and heir of Evan; and from the last-mentioned John Christian, upon his death, to the present defendant Christian, as his son and heir, who justified, under that deed, the acts complained of. The question argued and decided was whether the defendant's acts were within the terms of the grant; no suggestion was made that he had no right, and it was evidently assumed without question that he and the plaintiff had the same rights and obligations as the original grantor and grantee; in other words, that the right granted had descended to the defendant and bound the plaintiff. A right of this kind is clearly not an easement, for there is no dominant tenement; but why, if at all, it should not be possible now, as it was before, to grant, for an interest equivalent to an estate in fee simple, an assignable and transmissible right binding the land over which it is exercised, and comparable with a *profit à prendre* in gross, it would be difficult to explain. As was pointed out in early editions of this work,[26] *Ackroyd* v. *Smith* [27] is no authority against this possibility. All that was decided there is that a right of way for purposes not connected with the land to which it was supposed to be appurtenant did not pass to successive owners of the land. As late as 1911 the late Mr. Charles Sweet wrote [28] " It is possible to create a perpetual way in gross by grant, if the

24 [1971] 1 Q.B. 77, 86–87.
25 (1787) 1 T.R. 560.
26 See *e.g.* the 3rd ed., by Mr. W. H. Willes, p. 13.
27 (1850) 10 C.B. 164.
28 Challis' *Real Property*, 3rd ed., p. 55; and see his article in (1908) 24 *Law Quarterly Review* 259.

deed is clearly expressed and proper words of limitation are used." If that statement was true then, it is true now.[29] The question need not be merely academic; the court may yet be confronted with a grant by A to B in fee simple of the right to land helicopters on A's land.

Special immunities under the doctrine of non-derogation from grant

The same situation as if an easement had been created, although none has been, can arise from the doctrine that no one can derogate from, that is to say, impede the purpose of, his grant. The principle was stated by Parker J. in *Browne* v. *Flower*[30] as follows:

" If a grant or demise be made for a particular purpose, the grantor or lessor comes under an obligation not to use the land retained by him in such a way as to render the land granted or demised unfit or materially less fit for the particular purpose for which the grant or demise was made."

The immunity obtained may be of a special kind not recognised as an easement. On the other hand, it may have all the qualities of a recognised easement. Furthermore, the rule in *Wheeldon* v. *Burrows*,[31] under which a positive right may be acquired, is a branch of the general rule against derogation from grant. Accordingly, the acquisition of rights by reference to the doctrine will be considered[32] on the basis that those rights are easements, although strictly they are not.

5.—INCIDENTS OF EASEMENTS

Easements and the Limitation Act

A person who acquires a statutory title to land does not thereby acquire a way of necessity to it over adjoining land of the dispossessed person.[33] The reason is that while the title of the former owner is extinguished, the Limitation Act does not operate as a statutory conveyance; and hence it must follow that no new easement of any kind can arise in such a case, for there is no disposition by the common owner[34] under which an easement can arise by implication.

The question whether a person who acquires a statutory title to land becomes entitled to an easement[35] which is already annexed to it does not appear to have arisen for decision.

Such a person is bound by an easement[35] already affecting the land which he acquires.[36]

29 See also *Lord Hastings* v. *North Eastern Railway Co.* [1898] 2 Ch. 674; and *cf. ante*, p. 14, as to rights of burial.
30 [1911] 1 Ch. 219, 226.
31 (1879) 12 Ch.D. 31, 49, *per* Thesiger L.J.
32 See pp. 88 *et seq., post.*
33 *Wilkes* v. *Greenway* (1890) 6 T.L.R. 449.
34 See *post*, p. 83.
35 Or restrictive covenant.
36 *Re Nisbet and Potts' Contract* [1905] 1 Ch. 391, 400; [1906] 1 Ch. 386, 401.

Ancillary easements

The grant of an easement is also the grant of such ancillary rights as are reasonably necessary to its exercise or enjoyment.[37] Where the use of a thing is granted, everything is granted by which the grantee may have and enjoy such use.[38] The ancillary right arises because it is necessary for the enjoyment of the right expressly granted.[39]

In *Central Electricity Generating Board* v. *Jennaway*,[40] in which the plaintiff had under statutory powers a wayleave to place electric lines above the ground over the defendant's land, Lloyd-Jacob J. held that the wayleave carried with it the right to place in the defendant's land towers to support the lines. In *White* v. *Taylor* (*No.* 2)[41] Buckley J. held that the plaintiffs, who had a profit of grazing sheep on the defendant's down, were entitled, as an ancillary right under an implied grant, to water their sheep on the down by means of suitably located troughs supplied by carted water.

The question of ancillary easements commonly arises in connection with repairs. Thus the grantee of an easement for a watercourse through his neighbour's land may, when reasonably necessary, enter his neighbour's land for the purpose of repairing, and may repair, such watercourse.[37] If a man gives me a licence to lay pipes on his land to convey water to my cistern, I may afterwards enter and dig the land to mend the pipes, though the soil belongs to another and not to me.[38] The owner of a building entitled to support from an adjoining building is entitled to enter and take the necessary steps to ensure that the support continues by effecting repairs, and so forth, to the part of the building which gives the support.[42]

Repair for this purpose includes making and improving the subject of the easement[43]; alteration to meet altered conditions[44]; also replacement.[45]

---

[37] Parker J., *Jones* v. *Pritchard* [1908] 1 Ch. 630, 638; and see *Bulstrode* v. *Lambert* [1953] 1 W.L.R. 1064. *Cf. Thomas W. Ward Ltd.* v. *Alexander Bruce* (*Grays*) *Ltd.* [1959] 2 Lloyd's Rep. 472, C.A.: a prescriptive right to break up vessels and scuttle them on a bed of silt does not carry a right to maintain the silt so as to prevent the servient owner from dredging. See also *V. T. Engineering Ltd.* v. *Richard Barland & Co. Ltd.* (1968) 19 P. & C.R. 890: a grant of a right of way over a road for all purposes includes a right to halt vehicles on the way while being loaded or unloaded, but does not entitle the grantee to station loading equipment on the way.

[38] *Pomfret* v. *Ricroft* (1669) 1 Wms.Saund. 6th ed., 321, 323. And see *Liford's Case* (1614) 11 Co.Rep. 46b, 52a; *Gerrard* v. *Cooke* (1806) 2 Bos. & Pul.N.R. 109; *Senhouse* v. *Christian* (1787) 1 Term Rep. 560; *Dand* v. *Kingscote* (1840) 6 M. & W. 174; Shep.Touch. 100.

[39] Lord Parker, *Pwllbach Colliery Co. Ltd.* v. *Woodman* [1915] A.C. 634, 646, and see p. 643. The principle is expressed in the maxim " *Lex est cuicunque aliquis quid concedit concedere videtur et id sine quo res esse non potuit.*"

[40] [1959] 1 W.L.R. 937.

[41] [1969] 1 Ch. 160.

[42] *Bond* v. *Nottingham Corporation* [1940] Ch. 429, 439.

[43] *Newcomen* v. *Coulson* (1877) 5 Ch.D. 133, 144 (way); *cf. Hodgson* v. *Field* (1806) 7 East 613.

[44] *Finlinson* v. *Porter* (1875) L.R. 10 Q.B. 188.

[45] *Hoare* v. *Metropolitan Board of Works* (1874) L.R. 9 Q.B. 296.

The dominant owner, having a right to enter and repair, is entitled to prevent anything being done which substantially interferes with the exercise of that right. Thus in *Goodhart* v. *Hyett* [46] the owner of a pipe easement in another's land, and in *Abingdon Corporation* v. *James* [47] a local authority with a statutory duty to maintain a pipe, laid and owned by it, obtained in the one case an injunction restraining the erection of a proposed building, and in the other a mandatory order for the removal of an existing building, over the line of the pipe. The limit up to which interference remains not actionable, *i.e.* whether the exercise of the right must be made practically impossible,[48] or merely substantially more difficult, has not been precisely determined.[49] In *Goodhart* v. *Hyett* [50] North J. said: " The question is not whether [repair] can be done as a matter of engineering skill, but whether practically the plaintiff will have the same opportunity of enjoying the right as before," but the proposed building in that case would clearly have made access for repair underneath it practically impossible.

Obligation to repair—dominant owner

Generally speaking, a dominant owner is not bound to keep the subject of his easement in repair. In *Taylor* v. *Whitehead* [1] where the owner of a right of way unsuccessfully asserted a right to deviate on the way becoming flooded, Lord Mansfield said,[2] that by common law he who has the use of a thing ought to repair it; but this means that the servient owner is not bound to repair,[3] and if the dominant owner wants the way repaired he must repair it himself.[4]

Nevertheless a dominant owner, though not compellable to repair, may be practically obliged to do so in order to avoid committing a trespass or nuisance. In *Ingram* v. *Morecraft* [5] Sir John Romilly M.R. said *obiter*: " If I grant a man a right to lay pipes over my land, it

46 (1883) 25 Ch.D. 182.
47 [1940] Ch. 287.
48 Cf. *Mayor of Birkenhead* v. *London and North Western Railway Co.* (1885) 15 Q.B.D. 572, 580.
49 *Abingdon Corporation* v. *James* [1940] Ch. 287.
50 (1883) 25 Ch.D. 187. And see *Metropolitan Water Board* v. *L.N.E. Ry.* (1924) 131 L.T. 123.
1 (1781) 2 Doug.K.B. 745.
2 *Ibid.*, 749.
3 *Jones* v. *Pritchard* [1908] 1 Ch. 630, 638, *per* Parker J.
4 *Duncan* v. *Louch* (1845) 6 Q.B. 904, 909–910, *per* Coleridge J.
5 (1863) 33 Beav. 49, 51, 52. This was directed to the point that it is for the grantee of a right of way, and not the grantor, to do what is necessary to make the right available. The defendant had granted to the plaintiff the right to use a way, not yet made up and crossed at one point by a fence. The plaintiff having knocked down the fence in order to pass, and the defendant having put it up again, an injunction restraining this alleged obstruction was refused. The Master of the Rolls was not satisfied that the defendant was not entitled to have the fence, provided it did not prevent the use of the way. The real question, he said, was, who was to make a gate in the fence, and his impression was that it was for the plaintiff to do this, but the question who was to be at the expense of £1 for a gate was not, he thought, a fit subject for a Chancery suit.

follows that he must keep them watertight, for otherwise the escape of water is a trespass." This situation [6] was explained by Parker J.[6a] as follows:

> " There is undoubtedly a class of cases in which the nature of the easement is such that the owner of the dominant tenement not only has the right to repair the subject of the easement, but may be liable to the owner of the servient tenement for damages due to any want of repair. Thus, if the easement be to take water in pipes across another man's land and pipes are laid by the owner of the dominant tenement and fall into disrepair, so that water escapes on to the servient tenement, the owner of the dominant tenement will be liable for damage done by such water. Strictly speaking, I do not think that even in this case the dominant owner can be said to be under any duty to repair. I think the true position is that he cannot, under the circumstances mentioned, plead the easement as justifying what would otherwise be a trespass, because the easement is not, in fact, being fairly or properly exercised."

The fact that the pipe also serves the servient tenement, and that the servient owner has thus a right of repair, does not, it seems, make any difference.[7]

It is a common practice to grant a right of way to a purchaser " the purchaser and his successors in title contributing " some proportion of the cost of keeping the way in repair. There is a curious dearth of authority as to the effect of such a provision. It seems reasonable to suppose that the dominant owner for the time being could be restrained from using the way while the stipulated obligation remained unperformed; but whether the right determines on default once occurring, or is merely suspended until the default is made good, is not known.[8] It is thought also that the stipulation would be regarded as a covenant,[9] and that, as such, it could be enforced against the original grantee of the easement by the servient owner for the time being,[10] but not (if the easement were perpetual) against a successor of the original grantee. A successor in title of the original grantee could, however, it seems, be held liable to make the prescribed contribution under the principle *qui sentit commodum sentire debet et onus*.[11]

---

[6] See also *Abingdon Corporation* v. *James* [1940] Ch. 287, 295.

[6a] *Jones* v. *Pritchard* [1908] 1 Ch. 638.

[7] *Buckley (R. H.) & Sons Ltd.* v. *Buckley (N.) & Sons* [1898] 2 Q.B. 608.

[8] See *Duncan* v. *Louch* (1845) 6 Q.B. 904, *per curiam*.

[9] *Cf. Brookes* v. *Drysdale* (1877) 3 C.P.D. 52.

[10] *Cf. Smith and Snipes Hall Farm, Ltd.* v. *River Douglas Catchment Board* [1949] 2 K.B. 500.

[11] *Cf. Aspden* v. *Seddon* (1876) 1 Ex.D. 496; *Westhoughton U.D.C.* v. *Wigan Coal & Iron Co.* [1919] 1 Ch. 159, 171, establishing that any person having a right to let down the surface subject to making compensation for damage must, if he exercises the right, pay the compensation; *Halsall* v. *Brizell* [1957] Ch. 169; *Parkinson* v. *Reid* (1966) 56 D.L.R. (2d) 315, 319–320.

If such a provision were contained in a grant of an easement for a term of years, its benefit and burden would run, no doubt, in accordance with the rules applicable to covenants in leases. In such cases the grantor is considered to have the reversion to the easement which he created *de novo* himself.[12]

Obligation to repair—servient owner

Apart from any special local custom or express contract, the owner of a servient tenement is not bound to execute any repairs necessary to ensure the enjoyment of the easement by the owner of the dominant tenement. The grantor of a way over a bridge is not by common law liable, nor does he impliedly contract, to keep the bridge in repair for the convenience of the grantee.[13]

It was said by Mr. Serjeant Williams in the note to *Pomfret* v. *Ricroft*,[14] that " the grantor of a right of way may be bound either by express stipulation or prescription to repair it," and he cites *Rider* v. *Smith* [15] in which, on demurrer in an action against the owner of a close for not keeping in repair a footway running across it, the court held that a declaration alleging that by reason of his possession the defendant ought to repair was good, and that the special matter of the objection might be given in evidence, thus recognising, at all events, the possibility of such an obligation being established. But the only surviving trace of a prescriptive obligation to keep anything in repair for the benefit of a private individual is the fencing obligation mentioned above.[16]

A lessor who lets part of a building with a right to use a staircase, or other common part, retained by himself is under an obligation to the tenant to take reasonable care to keep the staircase in a reasonably safe condition.[17] Whether this obligation rests on implied contract or arises at common law is not entirely clear,[18] but it is thought that the duty, however arising, is owed to the tenant as tenant of the demised premises rather than as a dominant owner.[19]

---

[12] *Martyn* v. *Williams* (1857) 1 H. & N. 817, where, a right (*profit à prendre*) to get china clay in certain land having been granted to the defendant for a term of years, a successor in title to the land successfully enforced a covenant by the defendant to deliver up works in repair. And see *Grant* v. *Edmondson* [1931] 1 Ch. 1, 33. A converse case (assignee of the right held liable) is *Norval* v. *Pascoe* (1864) 34 L.J.Ch. 82.

[13] Parker J., *Jones* v. *Pritchard* [1908] 1 Ch. 630, 637; and see *Pomfret* v. *Ricroft* (1669) 1 Wms.Saunders, 6th ed., 321, 322a; *Taylor* v. *Whitehead* (1781) 2 Doug. K.B. 745, 749; *Colebeck* v. *Girdlers' Company* (1876) 1 Q.B.D. 234, 243; *Bond* v. *Nottingham Corporation* [1940] Ch. 429, 438; *Urich* v. *Local Health Authorities for St. Andrew-St. David* (1964) 7 W.I.R. 482; *Kelly* v. *Dea* (1965) 100 I.L.T.R. 1; *Parkinson* v. *Reid* (1966) 56 D.L.R. (2d) 315, 319.

[14] (1669) 1 Wms.Saunders, 6th ed., 322a.

[15] (1790) 3 Term Rep. 766.

[16] See p. 37.

[17] *Dunster* v. *Hollis* [1918] 2 K.B. 795.

[18] *Cockburn* v. *Smith* [1924] 2 K.B. 119.

[19] As to the statutory liability to visitors, which has, of course, nothing to do with the law of easements, see the Occupiers' Liability Act 1957.

It seems clear on principle [20] that if a servient owner covenants to keep in repair the subject of a perpetual easement, the covenant, being a positive covenant, cannot be enforced against a successor in title. The devolution of the benefit of such a covenant was considered in *Gaw* v. *Córas Iompair Eireann*.[21] There a railway company, in making, more than a hundred years ago, the Dublin-Wicklow line along the seashore, had acquired a strip of land from A, who owned a house on the top of a cliff and land, including the strip, extending down the cliff to the sea, and had granted to A a right of way over this strip, which it covenanted to keep in repair. The plaintiff, on whom the house, land and right of way had devolved without any express assignment of the benefit of the covenant, successfully enforced this against the defendant, who had succeeded by statute to the obligations of the original railway company, and was thus practically in the position of an original covenantor. Dixon J. decided two things: first that the covenant did not touch and concern the house and land so as to run with them, but ran, if at all, with the easement; and, secondly, that there is no clear authority that the benefit of a covenant cannot run with an incorporeal hereditament in the same manner as a corporeal one; furthermore, that the old case of *Holmes* v. *Buckley*,[22] properly understood, is some authority that it can; and that the covenant touched and concerned, and therefore its benefit ran with, the right of way. The learned judge made a careful and informative review of the authorities, and concluded that *Milnes* v. *Branch* [23] did not decide that the benefit of a covenant to pay a rentcharge does not run with the rentcharge, and did not prevent him from deciding that the benefit of a covenant to repair the subject of an easement can run with the easement. Unfortunately the case of *Grant* v. *Edmondson*,[24] in which the English Court of Appeal followed *Milnes* v. *Branch*, and decided the very point that Dixon J. thought was not decided there, was not cited, and this omission deprives the conclusion of Dixon J. of most of its authority. There has been much learned discussion [25] as to whether an easement, incapable as it is, or was, of descending independently of the land to which it is appurtenant, can properly be described, as a rentcharge can, as an incorporeal hereditament; and even if it can, a decision on a covenant to pay a rent-

---

[20] *Austerberry* v. *Oldham Corpn.* (1885) 29 Ch.D. 750; *E. & G. C. Ltd.* v. *Bate* (1935) 79 L.Journal 203; and see *Morris* v. *Cartwright* (1963) 107 S.J. 553; *Parkinson* v. *Reid* (1966) 56 D.L.R. (2d) 315.

[21] [1953] I.R. 232.

[22] (1691) Prec. in Chanc. 39; doubted in *Austerberry* v. *Oldham Corpn.* (1885) 29 Ch.D. 750. In this case a covenant, by a grantor of a watercourse, to clean it was enforced by an assignee of the watercourse against an assignee of the land through which it ran. The explanation, so far as the benefit of the covenant is concerned, may be that the watercourse served adjoining land of the covenantee, and the benefit of the covenant ran with that land (*per* Cotton L.J., 777), but " the case is too loosely reported to be a guide on the point " (*per* Lindley L.J., 782).

[23] (1816) 5 M. & S. 411.   [24] [1931] 1 Ch. 1.

[25] See *e.g.* Challis's *Real Property*, 3rd ed., p. 55; *Re Brotherton's Estate* (1907) 77 L.J.Ch. 58.

charge, or to build for the better security of a rentcharge, does not necessarily apply to a covenant to repair the subject of an easement[26]; but
however that may be, the decision in *Gaw's* case, *supra*, cannot be
regarded as authoritative, and *Holmes* v. *Buckley*,[22] which appears to
be the only other reported case on the same point, is of doubtful
authority also.

The burden and benefit of a covenant entered into by the grantor of
an easement for a term of years devolves, no doubt, in accordance with
the rules applicable as between landlord and tenant.[27]

" Rent " for easements

Rent, properly so called, cannot be reserved on the grant of an
easement.[28] A covenant by a dominant owner to make some payment
for the use of the easement must depend on the same considerations
as a covenant by him to repair.[29] In *Lord Hastings* v. *North Eastern
Railway*[30] the owner of land demised to a railway company a wayleave or right to make and use a railway over the land, reserving to himself, his heirs and assigns, a periodical payment calculated on the tonnage
of coal, etc., carried to a certain port over any part of the railways comprised in the company's special Act. The right to recover the payments
was held to have devolved on a successor in title to the land, as the
owner of the reversion to the right, but this right cannot have been an
easement, for there was no dominant tenement.

Easements and the rule against perpetuities

The rule against perpetuities in relation to the creation of easements
was examined by Cross J. in *Dunn* v. *Blackdown Properties Ltd.*[31] In
that case two plots of land were, by two conveyances dated respectively
December 17, 1926, and January 11, 1938, conveyed to the plaintiff's
predecessors in title, together with the right for the grantees, their heirs
and assigns to use the sewers and drains " now passing or hereafter to
pass " under a private road on which the plots abutted and belonging to
the defendant's predecessors in title. At some date after January 11,

---

26 As pointed out by Romer L.J. in *Grant* v. *Edmondson* [1931] 1 Ch. 1, 28–29, it is
impossible to reason on these questions by analogy. " Apart from decisive authority
one way or another, it seems to me that it is impossible to answer the question
whether a covenant to pay runs with a rentcharge one way or the other. The question
' Why should it? ' cannot be answered by reference to principles with any greater
conviction than can the question ' Why should it not? ' "

27 See *ante*, p. 47.

28 Co.Litt. 47a; *Capel* v. *Buszard* (1829) 6 Bing. 150 (affirming (1828) 8 B. & C. 141),
where a distress on barges lying on land between high- and low-water mark in the
Thames, of which land the plaintiffs were found by special verdict to have " the
exclusive use " (which was treated for the present purpose as an easement and not
as a demise of the land itself) was held bad.

29 *Ante*, p. 46.

30 [1898] 2 Ch. 674; affd. [1899] 1 Ch. 656; [1900] A.C. 260.

31 [1961] Ch. 433. This decision is discussed in an article, " Easements and the Rule
against Perpetuities," by G. Battersby in 25 *Conveyancer* (N.S.) 415.

1938, the defendant's predecessors in title constructed a surface water sewer along the road and a soil sewer which passed from their land lying north of the road, ran under the road for some distance, and turned onto other land of theirs. The two plots together with the foregoing right were conveyed to the plaintiff on September 20, 1945. The plaintiff claimed a declaration that she was entitled to the right to use the sewers and drains then passing or thereafter to pass under the road in connection with the two plots, and Cross J. held that since no sewers or drains were in existence at the date of the conveyance to the plaintiff's predecessors in title the grant of the right to use the sewers and drains " hereafter to pass " was a grant of an easement to arise at an uncertain date in the future not limited to take effect within the perpetuity period and was therefore, void.

Cross J. said [32] that, subject to the operation of section 162 of the Law of Property Act 1925 (which contains restrictions on the rule), there was no doubt that the rule applied to grants of easements. It followed that, where the grant was not immediate but was of an easement to arise in the future, it would be void unless it were limited to take effect only within the perpetuity period. It seems clear, however, that the " wait and see " rule introduced by section 3 of the Perpetuities and Accumulations Act 1964 might save a grant made on or after the date of commencement of that Act (June 16, 1964: see section 15 (3)) and not expressly confined within the perpetuity period.

Cross J. continued by saying that it was not always easy to decide whether the grant in question was of an immediate right or of a right to arise in the future. He illustrated the difficulty by comparing *South Eastern Railway Co.* v. *Associated Portland Cement Manufacturers (1900) Ltd.*[33] with *Sharpe* v. *Durrant.*[34]

In *S.E. Railway Co.* v. *Associated Portland Cement Manufacturers (1900) Ltd.*[35] an agreement under hand between the plaintiff's agent and A, a landowner, and made in contemplation of the acquisition by the plaintiff of a strip of the land for a railway, provided that A, his heirs and assigns, should have the right to make a tunnel under the proposed railway, and this was followed by a grant of the strip which reserved a like right. An action by the plaintiff to restrain the assignees of the lessees of the devisee of the grantor from doing so was dismissed by Swinfen Eady J., who, treating the right reserved as an easement, held that this was an immediate right, and that there was no question as to the validity of a grant *in futuro*. An appeal was dismissed on the ground that the agreement was a personal contract which the defendant company, which held under a lease containing an assignment of the benefit of the agreement, was entitled to enforce. The Court of Appeal did not

[32] [1961] Ch. 438.
[33] [1910] 1 Ch. 12.
[34] (1911) 55 S.J. 423; [1911] W.N. 158, C.A.
[35] [1910] 1 Ch. 12.

express any view on the question whether the reservation was of an immediate or a future easement.

In *Sharpe* v. *Durrant* [36] a conveyance of a strip of land for a tramway contained a reservation to the vendors of the right of passing over the tramway by crossings to be made by the purchaser, who covenanted to make crossings as, and at any two places that, the vendors should require. One crossing-place was selected, but it was held by Warrington J. that the reservation was void for remoteness, for until the selection was made there was no easement. His Lordship also held that the personal covenant to make crossings, involving as it did an obligation not to interfere with the passage across, was, although " a personal agreement not creating any interest in land," a negative covenant which the defendants could enforce against the plaintiff who had acquired the tramway, with notice, after the selection of the crossing-place; consequently there was a declaration that the defendants were entitled to a right of way over the crossings. An appeal was dismissed, but the appeal is not reported, and it is of course possible that the Court of Appeal differed from the opinion of Warrington J. as to the validity of the reservation.

Cross J. in *Dunn* v. *Blackdown Properties Ltd.* said [37] :

"I do not find the views expressed by Swinfen Eady J. and Warrington J. as to the effect from the point of view of perpetuity of a right given to the grantee to select the site of an easement at all easy to reconcile. I do not think, however, that I am compelled to choose between them in this case. If there had been a sewer under [the defendant's road] at the dates of the grants to her predecessors in title the plaintiff could have claimed, on authority of the *Associated Portland Cement* case,[38] that the owners of [her land] had from the first a right exercisable at any time to make connections with and use that sewer or any sewer substituted for it, but, as there was no sewer under the road, the plaintiff must rely on the words ' or hereafter to pass.' It is not for the owners of the [plaintiff's land] to decide whether or not a sewer will or will not pass under the road in future. That is for the owner of the road to decide, and I do not see how this part of the right granted can be treated as anything but the grant of an easement to arise at an uncertain date in the future.

"Counsel for the plaintiff submitted that in the *Associated Portland Cement* case [38] the right to construct the tunnel only arose if the railway company decided to build the railway and that Swinfen Eady J. must have thought that this fact did not make the reservation bad for perpetuity. I do not so read the facts or the judgment. It is to my mind reasonably clear that the reservation in question

---

[36] (1911) 55 S.J. 423; [1911] W.N. 158, C.A.
[37] [1961] Ch. 440.
[38] [1910] 1 Ch. 12.

was of an immediate right to build a tunnel exercisable as from the date of the conveyance to the railway company, whether or not a railway was built."

It was also argued for the plaintiff in *Dunn* v. *Blackdown Properties Ltd.*,[39] that, assuming that the grants would have been void at common law, they were saved by section 162 of the Law of Property Act 1925. That section provides:

(1) For removing doubts, it is hereby declared that the rule of law relating to perpetuities does not apply and shall be deemed never to have applied—

(*d*) to any grant, exception or reservation of any right of entry on, or user of, the surface of land or of any easements, rights, or privileges over or under land for the purpose of—

(i) winning, working, inspecting, measuring, converting, manufacturing, carrying away, and disposing of mines and minerals;

(ii) inspecting, grubbing up, felling and carrying away timber and other trees, and the tops and lops thereof;

(iii) executing repairs, alterations, or additions to any adjoining land, or the buildings and erections thereon;

(iv) constructing, laying down, altering, repairing, renewing, cleansing and maintaining sewers, watercourses, cesspools, gutters, drains, water-pipes, gas-pipes, electric wires or cables or other like works.

(2) This section applies to instruments coming into operation before or after the commencement of this Act.

This argument also failed because Cross J. held[40] that on its true construction section 162 (1) (*d*) (iv) was only intended to make it clear that if a basic right of sewage was not itself void for perpetuity an ancillary right to construct works to make the basic right effective was not to be treated as void for perpetuity because it might be exercised outside the perpetuity period.

Two further cases which illustrate the operation of the rule in regard to easements are *Smith* v. *Colbourne*[41] and *Ardley* v. *Guardians of the Poor of St. Pancras.*[42]

In *Smith* v. *Colbourne*,[41] where a purchaser objected to title on the ground that a former owner, A, had agreed with a neighbour, B, that the light to a certain window in the property was enjoyed by the revocable licence of B and his successors, and that, if the licence were revoked, A or his successors would block up the window, and, if they did not, B or his successors might do so, the Court of Appeal intimated that if the conditional right last mentioned was an easement, which they thought it

---

[39] [1961] Ch. 433.
[40] [1961] Ch. 441, 442.
[41] [1914] 2 Ch. 533; and see *Newham* v. *Lawson* (1971) 22 P. & C.R. 852.
[42] (1870) 39 L.J.Ch. 871.

was not, it was void for remoteness, the reason being, no doubt, that it would not arise until A or his successors had failed to block up after revocation of the licence, neither of which events would necessarily occur in due time, or at all.

In *Ardley* v. *Guardians of the Poor of St. Pancras* [42] an underlease of land reserved to the underlessor and his heirs a right of way over the east side of the land to the other land comprised in the lease, during such time as they should hold such other land, and, if they disposed of it, then there was reserved to the underlessor, his heirs and assigns, a right of ingress and egress over the same east part for the purpose of building or repairing on a different piece of land belonging to the underlessor in fee. The defendants, who were assignees of that other land, claimed to be entitled to the right first reserved, and contended that a right of way granted or reserved until alienation of the dominant tenement is absolute, the attempted limitation being void as a restraint on alienation. Lord Romilly M.R., after rejecting this contention and holding that the first right had ceased, added that the second right (not belonging to the defendants) still continued; *i.e. semble*, had begun on the cesser of the first. His Lordship said [43]:

> " I do not think there is anything illegal in a man reserving to himself and his heirs a right of way for a limited purpose, and when that purpose is accomplished to say that the right of way shall cease, reserving to himself after that a different and distinct right of way for another and separate purpose.
>
> " I am of opinion, therefore, that when the houses [on the other land] were built, the right of way into [that land] ceased. The right of ingress and egress still continues for the purpose of repairing and rebuilding any of the houses [on the underlessor's own land]. That, however, is not what the defendants claim, and I am of opinion they have no right of way over the eastern portion of the [land underleased]."

The validity of the reservation of the second right was not questioned in argument, nor was it material. This case may perhaps support the view that the grant of a right for a certain purpose until a certain event, and then for a different purpose, is valid if the dominant tenement is the same throughout, for such a grant might well be regarded as an immediate grant of a single but variable right.

No easement on easement

A servient owner as such has no right to have an easement continued. This is particularly illustrated by drainage easements. If A, in order to drain his land or mines, sends water through the land of B, B can either prevent this, or, if the water is useful to him, accept the water. If A, by grant or prescription, acquires a right to send the water, B has no

[43] (1870) 39 L.J.Ch. 874.

rights at all; he must accept the water but he cannot demand it; and a right to demand it, or to prevent A from turning it off, cannot be acquired by prescription.

So Lord Abinger C.B. in *Arkwright* v. *Gell* said [44]:

" Several instances were put in the course of the argument of cases analogous to the present in which it could not be contended for a moment that any right was acquired. A steam-engine is used by the owner of a mine to drain it, and the water pumped up flows in a channel to the estate of the adjoining landowner, and there is used for agricultural purposes for twenty years. Is it possible, from the fact of such a user to presume the grant by the owner of a steam-engine of the right to the water in perpetuity, so as to burden himself and the assigns of his mine with the obligation to keep a steam-engine for ever, for the benefit of the landowner? Or, if the water from the spout of the eaves of a row of houses were to flow into an adjoining yard, and be there used by its occupiers for twenty years for domestic purposes, could it be successfully contended that the owners of the houses had contracted an obligation not to alter their construction so as to impair the flow of water? Clearly not. In all the nature of the case distinctly shows that no right is acquired as against the owner of the property from which the course of water takes its origin; though, as between the first and any subsequent appropriator of the water course itself, such a right may be acquired."

So also Erle C.J. in *Gaved* v. *Martyn* said [45]:

" If there is uninterrupted user of the land of the neighbour for receiving the flow as a right for twenty years, such user is evidence that the land from which the water is sent into the neighbour's land has become the dominant tenement, having a right to the easement of so sending the water, and that the neighbour's land has become subject to the easement of receiving that water. But such user of the easement of sending on the water of an artificial stream is of itself alone no evidence that the land from which the water is sent has become subject to the servitude of being bound to send on the water to the land of the neighbour below. The enjoyment of the easement is of itself no evidence that the party enjoying it has become subject to the servitude of being bound to exercise the easement for the benefit of the neighbour. A right of way is no evidence

---

[44] (1839) 5 M. & W. 203, 232. The effect of the final sentence (" though . . .") is not entirely clear. It was adopted by Lord Cozens-Hardy M.R., in *Schwann* v. *Cotton* [1916] 2 Ch. 459 (see p. 100, *post*), and applied to a case where water flowed through a pipe not for the purpose of draining the property in which it arose, but for supplying other property: see also *per* Warrington L.J. 475. See also *Chamber Colliery Co.* v. *Hopwood* (1886) 32 Ch.D. 549, 558; *Wood* v. *Waud* (1849) 3 Exch. 748, 777; *Greatrex* v. *Hayward* (1853) 8 Exch. 291; *Burrows* v. *Lang* [1901] 2 Ch. 502, 509; *Bartlett* v. *Tottenham* [1932] 1 Ch. 114, 129; *Deed (John S.) & Sons Ltd.* v. *British Electricity Authority* (1950) 66 T.L.R. (Pt. 2) 567.

[45] (1865) 19 C.B.(N.S.) 732, 758.

that the party entitled thereto is under a duty to walk; nor a right of eaves-dropping on the neighbour's land that the party is bound to send on his rainwater to that land. In like manner, we consider that a party by the mere exercise of a right to make an artificial drain into his neighbour's land either from mine or surface does not raise any presumption that he is subject to any duty to continue his artificial drain, by twenty years' user, although there might be additional circumstances by which that presumption would be raised or the right proved."

The proposition is, however, subject to the qualification that " if it be proved that the stream was originally intended to have a permanent flow, or if the party by whom or on whose behalf the artificial stream was caused to flow is shown to have abandoned permanently without intention to resume the works by which the flow was caused, and given up all right to and control over the stream, such stream may become subject to the laws relating to natural streams." [46]

In *Mason v. Shrewsbury and Hereford Railway Co.*[47] a canal company, acting under statutory powers, had diverted to its canal, over a period of about sixty years, most of the water in a natural stream, from a point above the land of the plaintiff, who was a riparian owner. The defendant company, having acquired power to buy the canal and discontinue it, restored the water to its natural course, which by then had become silted up and incapable of holding the water, which thus flooded the plaintiff's land. The plaintiff unsuccessfully claimed damages for causing the flood, and for disturbance of an alleged easement to have the water diverted. Cockburn C.J. said [48]:

" I am far from saying that the grant of an easement might not be accompanied by stipulations on the part of the grantor, as, for instance, that the easement should not be discontinued without his consent, or that on its discontinuance certain things should be done. I am far from saying that such a stipulation would not give a right of action. My observations are intended to apply to a case in which nothing appears beyond the existence of an easement. In such a case, it appears to be beyond doubt that the servient owner acquires no right to the continuance of the easement and the incidental advantages arising to him from it, if the dominant owner thinks proper to abandon it."

6.—LICENCES

A right of user not annexed to land and not incident to a tenancy is (subject to what is said above, p. 42, as to ways in gross) a personal licence. A mere permission, given voluntarily and not coupled with a

[46] *Gaved* v. *Martyn* (1865) 19 C.B.(N.S.) 759, *per* Erle C.J.
[47] (1871) L.R. 6 Q.B. 578.
[48] *Ibid*. 588.

grant, that is, not being a licence to enter and take away (which will usually be a *profit à prendre*) is revocable by the licensor [49] and is not assignable by the licensee [50] who, indeed, like a tenant at will, would have nothing substantial to assign. A licence granted on terms of payment is treated as part of the contract under which it is given, and it is (prima facie) revocable on such notice as the nature of the case requires.[1]

In *Armstrong* v. *Sheppard & Short Ltd.*,[2] the Court of Appeal held that if A gives authority to B for the doing of an act on his land, and the act is done and completed, then whatever be the description of the authority, it is generally too late for A to complain and, accordingly, the plaintiff could not complain of a sewer which the defendant had constructed on the plaintiff's land after the plaintiff had informed the defendant orally that he did not object to the construction of it. On the other hand the Court of Appeal held that an oral licence to discharge water through another's land, to be irrevocable during the licensor's tenure of the land, must have the necessary qualities of a contract binding on the parties, and be supported by consideration, and that, there being no consideration for the licence granted by the plaintiff to the defendant, the plaintiff was entitled to revoke the licence and had, on the facts, done so.

It is submitted that a licence, unless clearly personal to the licensee, is assignable.[3] The traditional view was that, being only a contractual and not a proprietary right, it was not binding on a successor in title of the licensor,[4] and that accordingly the licensee could not sue a stranger for disturbance.[5] In *Inwards* v. *Baker*,[6] however, where a father had encouraged his son to build a bungalow on the father's land, the Court of

---

[49] *Thomas* v. *Sorrell* (1673) Vaugh. 330; *Goldsack* v *Shore* [1950] 1 K.B. 708, 713, 714.
[50] Shep.Touch. 238. " If licence be granted to me to walk in another man's garden, or to go through another man's ground, I may not give or grant this to another."
[1] *Winter Garden Theatre (London) Ltd.* v. *Millennium Productions Ltd.* [1948] A.C. 173.
[2] [1959] 2 Q.B. 384. This decision is discussed in an article, " The Executed Licence," by Maurice C. Cullity in 29 *Conveyancer*(N.S.) 19.
[3] See *Clapman* v. *Edwards* [1938] 2 All E.R. 507; and *cf. Shayler* v. *Woolf* [1946] Ch. 320; *Re Vickers' Lease* [1947] Ch. 420.
[4] *King* v. *David Allen & Sons, Billposting Ltd.* [1916] 2 A.C. 54; *Clore* v. *Theatrical Properties Ltd.* [1936] 3 All E.R. 483; *Re Salvin's Indenture* [1938] 2 All E.R. 498, 506. See, however, *Re Webb's Lease* [1951] Ch. 808, 821, 830, 831, where it was evidently thought that the plaintiff (lessee of the defendant) was bound by an advertising licence granted by the defendant before the lease; and *Bendall* v. *McWhirter* [1952] 2 Q.B. 466, 482. See also an article by Dr. Cheshire in 16 M.L.R. 1, and articles in 64 L.Q.R. 67, 68 L.Q.R. 337, and 16 *Conveyancer*(N.S.) 323. In *Clapman* v. *Edwards* [1938] 2 All E.R. 507, where a lease contained a licence to use adjoining property of the lessor for advertising, it was not disputed that the assignee of the reversion to the demised premises and of the adjoining land was bound by the licence.
[5] *Heap* v. *Hartley* (1882) 42 Ch.D. 461, 468; *Paine & Co.* v. *St. Neots Gas & Coke Co.* [1939] 3 All E.R. 812, 823; *cf. Sports and General Press Agency, Ltd.* v. " *Our Dogs* " *Publishing Co. Ltd.* [1917] 2 K.B. 125; *Hill* v. *Tupper* (1863) 2 H. & C. 121. The rights in this respect of exclusive licensees of patents and copyrights depend on different considerations; *Scottish Vacuum Cleaner Co. Ltd.* v. *Provincial Cinematograph Theatres Ltd.* (1915) 32 R.P.C. 353; *Heap* v. *Hartley, supra*; Copyright Act 1956, s. 19.
[6] [1965] 2 Q.B. 29.

Appeal found that there was an equitable estoppel in favour of the son to protect his occupation of the land, and that the equity bound the successors in title of the father and would bind anyone taking the land with notice of the son's interest.

7.—EXTENT AND MODE OF ENJOYMENT

As every easement is a restriction upon the rights of property of the owner of the servient tenement, no alteration can be made in the mode of enjoyment by the owner of the dominant tenement, the effect of which will be to increase such restriction beyond its legitimate limit.[7] In the case of an express grant of the easement the limit depends on the words used.[8] Supposing no express grant to exist, the right must be limited and defined by the user proved.[9]

In the case of the easement of light, the dominant owner may obtain increase of light by altering his mode of framing and glazing.[10] On the other hand, a dominant tenement, having ancient windows overlooking the servient tenement, may not be so altered as to make the unobstructed access of light to the ancient windows more necessary to the enjoyment of the dominant tenement than they were before the alteration, so as to render actionable an obstruction which would not, before the alteration, have been an illegal interference with the light.[11]

In the case of water rights, a mill-owner who has the right of diverting water cannot alter his sluice so as to divert more water.[12] Nor can a riparian owner who has acquired a prescriptive right to pollute water increase the pollution to the prejudice of others.[13] Nor can a riparian owner increase the burden of the lower riparian owner by making structures which increase the flow of water.[14] But where the burden is not increased, trifling variations can be made in the user of the easement. Thus, where a right existed to supply cattle-sheds by a watercourse, the dominant owner could erect cottages in the place of the cattle-sheds.[15]

---

[7] e.g. as to light: *Ankerson* v. *Connelly* [1906] 2 Ch. 544; [1907] 1 Ch. 678; *News of the World* v. *Allen Fairhead & Sons* [1931] 2 Ch. 402.

[8] See, for instance, in the case of an express grant of a watercourse, the judgment of Jessel M.R. in *Taylor* v. *St. Helens Corpn.* (1877) 6 Ch.D. 271; and in the case of grants of rights of way, Chap. 9, *post*.

[9] *Milner's Safe Co.* v. *G.N. & City Railway* [1907] 1 Ch. 229; *Att.-Gen.* v. *G.N. Ry.* [1909] 1 Ch. 775; *British Railways Board* v. *Glass* [1965] Ch. 538; *Thomas W. Ward Ltd.* v. *Alexander Bruce (Grays) Ltd.* [1959] 2 Lloyd's Rep. 472; *Woodhouse & Co. Ltd.* v. *Kirkwood (Derby) Ltd.* [1970] 1 W.L.R. 1185; see further p. 281, *post*.

[10] *Turner* v. *Spooner* (1861) 1 Dr. & Sm. 467.

[11] *Ankerson* v. *Connelly, supra*; *News of the World* v. *Allen Fairhead & Sons* [1931] 2 Ch. 402; *Smith* v. *Evangelization Society Trust* [1933] Ch. 515. See *Bailey (W. H.) & Sons Ltd.* v. *Holborn and Frascati Ltd.* [1914] 1 Ch. 598.

[12] *Bealey* v. *Shaw* (1805) 6 East 208.

[13] *Crossley & Sons Ltd.* v. *Lightowler* (1867) 2 Ch.App. 478; *McIntyre Bros.* v. *M'Gavin* [1893] A.C. 268.

[14] *Frechette* v. *Compagnie Manufacturière de St. Hyacinthe* (1883) 9 App.Cas. 170.

[15] *Watts* v. *Kelson* (1870) 6 Ch.App. 166. See also *Saunders* v. *Newman* (1818) 1 B. & Ald. 258; *Greenslade* v. *Halliday* (1830) 6 Bing. 379.

On the construction of grants, it has been held that a grantee of a watercourse could not enlarge the channel.[16] A grant of the running of water, etc., from land did not authorise the discharge of a sewage effluent,[17] or of the refuse of tan pits.[18]

In *Wood* v. *Saunders* [19] the plaintiff, being entitled by express grant to a mansion with the free passage of water and soil to a cesspool on the defendant's land, enlarged the mansion so as to increase the amount of soil. The defendant having stopped the drains leading to the cesspool, the case came before Hall V.-C., who restrained the defendant from preventing the free use and passage of water and soil in and to the cesspool, but added that his order was only to protect the plaintiff in the reasonable use of such cesspool to the extent to which the same was used prior to the date of the grant. On appeal the decree was varied, the plaintiff submitting to be restrained from allowing the drainage from the additional buildings erected by him to go into the cesspool, and the defendant being restrained from preventing the free passage of water and soil into the cesspool. The court apparently treated the drainage from the additional buildings as severable from the drainage from the original building; and thus the case became a question of " excess " rather than of construction.

The pulling down of a house for the purpose of repair does not, by the law of England, even when construed most strictly, cause the loss of any easement attached to it, if it be accompanied by an intention, acted upon within a reasonable time, of rebuilding it.[20] This intention will be presumed.[21] The reason is that it is incidental to all houses to be repaired and at some time to be rebuilt, and the right when acquired is acquired for the tenement with such incidents. If this were not so, no prescriptive right could be acquired in respect of a messuage or any other artificial structure.[22]

A mere alteration in the mode of enjoyment, as the change of a mill from a fulling to a grist mill, or the like,[23] whereby no injury is caused to the servient tenement, or a trifling alteration in the course of a watercourse,[24] does not destroy the right. On the other hand in *Clarke* v. *Somersetshire Drainage Commissioners* [25] it was held that an easement to pollute a stream with the refuse of a fellmongery and with the waste dyes used in making coloured rags had been lost by the place in which those businesses had been carried on being utilised as a leather-board

---

16 *Taylor* v. *St. Helens Corpn.* (1877) 6 Ch.D. 264.
17 *Phillimore* v. *Watford R. D. C.* [1913] 2 Ch. 434.
18 *Chadwick* v. *Marsden* (1867) L.R. 2 Exch. 285.
19 (1875) 10 Ch.App. 582. See *New Windsor (Mayor)* v. *Stovell* (1884) 27 Ch.D. 665; *Metropolitan Board of Works* v. *L. & N.W. Ry.* (1881) 17 Ch.D. 246.
20 *Luttrel's Case* (1602) 4 Rep. 86.
21 *Smith* v. *Baxter* [1900] 2 Ch. 138.
22 See further p. 318, *post.*
23 *Luttrel's Case* (1602) 4 Rep. 86; *Baxendale* v. *McMurray* (1867) 2 Ch.App. 790.
24 *Hall* v. *Swift* (1838) 4 Bing.N.C. 381.
25 (1888) 57 L.J.M.C. 96.

factory, because the resulting pollution was of a different kind, although less objectionable.

8.—CLASSIFICATION OF PROFITS

Profits and rights of common

The nature of a *profit à prendre* and the essential differences between an easement and a profit have already been noticed.[26] The classification of profits will now be briefly considered.

A *profit à prendre* may be enjoyed to the exclusion of all other persons, in which case it is termed a " sole " or " several " profit. On the other hand, a profit may be enjoyed in common with one or more persons, including the owner of the servient land, when it is called a profit " in common " or right of common.[27] Every right of common is, therefore, a *profit à prendre*, but not every *profit à prendre* is a right of common.

Historically, rights of common came first, being based upon the former system of landholding which gave rise to the communal enjoyment of certain types of *profits à prendre*, e.g. rights of pasture. The enjoyment of profits in severalty was a later development and indeed most modern instances of profits are also of rights of common.[28]

Appurtenant or in gross

As with an easement, a *profit à prendre* may be appurtenant to a dominant tenement. Unlike an easement, however, a profit may also exist in gross, that is, it may be unconnected with the ownership of any dominant tenement.[29] If a profit is appurtenant to land it will run with the dominant tenement into the hands of successive owners thereof.[30] A profit which is appurtenant cannot be unlimited in its extent; it must have either a definite limit (or " stint ") or be limited by reference to the needs of the dominant tenement.[31] Thus, the common of pasture appurtenant must be limited to a definite number of cattle or to cattle *levant* and *couchant*, that is, the number that the dominant tenement is capable of supporting in winter.[32] Generally, a profit appurtenant cannot

---

[26] See p. 4, *ante*.

[27] For the distinction between a profit in common and a profit sole or several profit, see Harris and Ryan, *An Outline of the Law relating to Common Land*, pp. 34, 35. The general principles referred to in the present work relate to all profits, whether in common or in severalty.

[28] All rights of common should now be registered: Commons Registration Act 1965. For the effects of the Act, see Harris and Ryan, *An Outline of the Law relating to Common Land*.

[29] *Lord Chesterfield* v. *Harris* [1908] 2 Ch. 397, 421, *per* Buckley L.J. And see *Shuttleworth* v. *Le Fleming* (1865) 19 C.B.(N.S.) 687; *Johnson* v. *Barnes* (1873) L.R. 8 C.P. 527; *Webber* v. *Lee* (1882) 9 Q.B.D. 315, C.A.

[30] The general words of the Law of Property Act 1925, s. 62, will apply to profits upon a conveyance of the dominant land.

[31] *Bailey* v. *Stephens* (1862) 12 C.B.(N.S.) 91; *Lord Chesterfield* v. *Harris* [1908] 2 Ch. 397, C.A. (affirmed *sub nom. Harris* v. *Earl of Chesterfield* [1911] A.C. 623).

[32] *Lord Chesterfield* v. *Harris* [1908] 2 Ch. 397, C.A., 421, *per* Buckley L.J.

be severed or enjoyed apart from its dominant tenement, although where the right has a definite limit, not by reference to the needs of the dominant tenement, it may be severed, at least in the case of the common of pasture.[33]

A profit in gross, however, is not limited by the needs of any dominant tenement and can exist without a definite limit. There may be a right in gross to take the proceeds of another man's land without stint.[34] A profit in gross is an interest in land and can be dealt with and will devolve in the same way as other interests in land.[35]

There may also exist a profit appendant, that is, annexed to land by operation of law. This type of right arose when the lord of the manor subinfeudated arable land. The feoffee would take a right to pasture on the manorial waste animals necessary to plough and manure the land granted to him. The Statute of *Quia Emptores* 1289–90,[36] ended subinfeudation, so that a profit appendant must have come into existence before the Statute. The right was limited to animals *levant* and *couchant*.[37]

A profit may also exist in the form of a common *pur cause de vicinage*, which is restricted to rights of pasture. The right arises where there is inter-commoning between two contiguous pieces of common land.[38]

[33] *Bunn* v. *Channen* (1813) 5 Taunt. 244; *Daniel* v. *Hanslip* (1672) 2 Lev. 67; and see discussion on this point in *White* v. *Taylor* (*No.* 2) [1969] 1 Ch. 160, 189–190, *per* Buckley J. and authorities therein cited. This probably applies to all profits where the limit is fixed, *e.g.* rights to take a fixed amount of turves, wood or fish.
[34] *Lord Chesterfield* v. *Harris* [1908] 2 Ch. 397, C.A., 421, *per* Buckley L.J.; *Staffordshire and Worcestershire Canal Navigation* v. *Bradley* [1912] 1 Ch. 91.
[35] *Staffordshire and Worcestershire Canal Navigation* v. *Bradley* [1912] 1 Ch. 91, where the right to take fish could have been the subject of a lease; and see *Webber* v. *Lee* (1882) 9 Q.B.D. 315.
[36] 18 Edw. 1, c. 1.
[37] *Robertson* v. *Hartopp* (1889) 43 Ch.D. 484, 516–517.
[38] *Tyrringham's Case* (1584) 4 Co.Rep. 37.

CHAPTER 2

EQUITABLE RIGHTS TO EASEMENTS

A LEGAL easement is one which is created for an interest equivalent to a fee simple absolute in possession or a term of years absolute,[1] and is either so created by statute, or is the subject of an assent, which need not be under seal, made to give effect to a devise, or is created *inter vivos* by a deed.[2]

Inasmuch as an easement attaches to the dominant tenement in respect of which it is granted, it is obvious that an easement already in existence as a legal easement cannot be disposed of separately, and that there can be no question of creating an interest in an existing easement apart from the land to which it belongs. If an easement over Whiteacre is granted by deed to A, owner of Blackacre, in fee simple, and C afterwards becomes entitled in equity to Blackacre (as for instance by paying his purchase-money under an agreement for sale, but not taking a conveyance), then C, it is thought, could exercise the easement to which Whiteacre has already been subjected, although his interest in Blackacre and the easement is only equitable. But it would be impossible for A to create an equitable interest in the easement as a separate thing; no one could claim a right to the easement otherwise than by virtue of an interest in Blackacre. Questions seldom arise as to the rights of a person entitled to an equitable interest in an existing legal easement. There are, however, many cases, difficult to classify, in which a right to an easement has been established by one to whom no easement has been actually granted by deed or acquired by him by prescription. Most of these depend on some form of equitable estoppel. Some recent decisions provide guidance in establishing the principles involved, but the subject of equitable rights to easements remains a difficult one.

Agreement presumed from acquiescence

There are a number of cases in which natural rights of immunity against nuisance or the like, or against trespass, have been abrogated by an agreement inferred from acquiescence. The principle appears to be that A cannot restrain B from doing something that invades a natural

---

[1] Law of Property Act 1925, s. 1 (2).
[2] *Ibid*. s. 52 (1) (2) (*a*); *Hewlins* v. *Shippam* (1826) 5 B. & C. 221. Possibly a parol lease of land plus an easement, taking effect in possession for a term not exceeding three years, and at the best rent reasonably obtainable, would create a legal easement (L.P. Act 1925, ss. 52 (2) (*d*), 54 (2)).

right incident to A's land if what is done is, or is the reasonable consequence of, something that has been encouraged or countenanced by A,
but mere abstinence by A from legal proceedings does not amount to
acquiescence.   There is no element of mistake in these cases, which
should be distinguished from those [3] in which it has been said that a man
is not entitled to take the benefit of improvements made on his own land
by someone who, to his knowledge, believes himself to be the owner of
it.   B knows, or may be assumed to know, of A's rights, but is led to
believe that they will not be asserted, and thus he acquires, by imputed
agreement, something in the nature of an equitable easement.

In *Rochdale Canal Co.* v. *King*,[4,5] the company, which had obtained
a decision at law that the defendant, the owner of a mill adjoining the
company's canal, was not entitled to use the water for generating steam,
applied first for an interim injunction,[4] and then for a perpetual injunction,[5] restraining the defendant from doing so.   Both were refused.   Lord
Cranworth said [6]:

> "The defendants by their answer swear that, to their belief,
> when the mill was originally built by James King [their father] in
> 1830, express notice was given by him to the canal company of his
> intention to make a communication with the canal in order to draw
> from it water, not only for the purpose of condensing steam [which
> was allowed], but also for the purpose of raising it, and for other
> purposes; that the servants and agents of the company superintended
> the laying down of the pipes, and were aware of the uses to which
> they were to be applied, and made no objection, although they were
> cognisant of the great expense incurred.   Now, unquestionably, if
> this be true, the plaintiffs can have no relief in this court. . . .   I
> entirely assent to the argument . . . that mere acquiescence (if by
> acquiescence is to be understood only the abstaining from legal
> proceedings) is unimportant.   Where one party invades the rights of
> another, that other does not, in general, deprive himself of the right
> of seeking redress merely because he remains passive . . .   But the
> evidence of long-continued use of the water for all purposes, by the
> adjacent mill-owners, may be very important, as tending to satisfy
> this court that when the mill of the defendants was erected the
> plaintiffs must have known that King, who was building it, was lay-
> ing out his money in the expectation that he would have the same
> privilege of using the water as was enjoyed by all his neighbours."

On the later motion Sir John Romilly M.R. said [7]:

> "I am of opinion that, so far as concerns this mill, which was

---

[3] See *e.g. Ramsden* v. *Dyson* (1866) L.R. 1 H.L. 129, 140; *Willmott* v. *Barber* (1880)
15 Ch.D. 96; and see *McBean* v. *Howey* [1958] N.Z.L.R. 25.
[4] (1851) 2 Sim.(N.S.) 78.
[5] (1853) 16 Beav. 630.
[6] (1851) 2 Sim.(N.S.) 88.
[7] (1853) 16 Beav. 641.

constructed in 1829, I must on this evidence come to the conclusion that the company have encouraged James King in so constructing his mill as to derive, from the canal, water for the purposes of steam, and that they cannot now, after the lapse of eighteen years, dispute his right to do so . . .[8]: I think that the plaintiffs had then distinct notice that James King intended to employ the water of the canal for the purpose of steam, in addition to the condensation thereof, and having sent their engineer to inspect the laying down of the pipes for this purpose from the canal, I am of opinion that they must be held to have assented to the use of the water for such purposes relating to the generation or employment of steam, as the construction of his mill would manifestly and plainly have disclosed to anyone conversant in such matters."

In a judgment delivered two days later in another case,[9] Sir John Romilly referred to " the principle . . . that he who stands by and encourages an act, cannot afterwards complain of it."

In *Cotching* v. *Bassett* [10] the plaintiffs had pulled down a building, which had windows with an easement of light over the defendants' adjoining property, and built another, which, by arrangement made between them and the defendants for the benefit of the defendants, was no higher than a line of light drawn from the top of a wall at the back to the top of a party-wall, belonging to the plaintiffs and the defendants, in front. The defendants, having given notice under the Metropolitan Building Act 1855 [11] of intention to raise the party-wall, and so to deprive the new building of light, were restrained from doing so.

In *Williams* v. *Earl of Jersey* [12] the plaintiffs sought to restrain the defendant from proceeding with an action at law for alleged nuisance caused by copper works on the plaintiffs' land. The bill alleged that the defendant was well aware of the works being erected and the purpose for which they were intended, and of the deleterious effect on vegetation produced by the manufacture of copper, but nevertheless he acquiesced in and encouraged their erection and the expenditure of money thereon. A demurrer was overruled.

The defendant in *Davies* v. *Sear* [13] took from A an assignment of a lease, granted to A, of a house under which was an arch, marked " gateway " on the plan, and leading to a mews. At this time the mews was not fully enclosed, but A was under contract to build round it so as to leave no other means of access than under the arch, and this the plaintiff, A's successor in title to the mews and surrounding land, did. The defendant, after the mews had been completely enclosed, was restrained from

---

[8] The defendants were his successors in title.
[9] *Duke of Beaufort* v. *Patrick* (1853) 17 Beav. 60, 74. Not a case of easement.
[10] (1862) 32 Beav. 101.
[11] Now repealed.
[12] (1841) Cr. & Ph. 91.
[13] (1869) L.R. 7 Eq. 427.

depriving it of all means of access by blocking up the arch, on the ground [14] that the physical appearance of the arch put him on inquiry as to how the land surrounding the mews was intended to be developed.

In *Ward* v. *Kirkland* [15] the plaintiff's predecessor in title had in 1928 purchased a cottage which was part of the glebe. The cottage was built on the northern boundary of the land conveyed and abutted onto a yard of a farm which was also part of the glebe. In 1942 the defendant's husband became tenant of the farm. In 1954 the cottage was conveyed to the plaintiff. In 1955 the plaintiff wished to instal a bathroom and water closets in the cottage and he asked for, and was given, permission by the defendant to lay drains. He then advised the rector of his plans and asked permission from him to lay drains through the farmyard and to connect them to the septic tank on his own premises. The rector gave permission for the bath water to be so drained without imposing any limit on the time during which the drains might remain. Nothing was said about effluent from the water closets. The plaintiff did the work, laying drains for the effluent and bath water and constructing his septic tank so as to take both and also surface water, which since before 1928 had come through the defendant's land onto his. In 1958 the defendant purchased the freehold of the farm. The defendant alleged that the drains laid under the farmyard constituted a trespass and she purported to terminate any licence which might have been given to the plaintiff and demanded that they should be removed.

Ungoed-Thomas J. found that the drains in the farmyard had been laid at the plaintiff's expense in reliance on the permission given by the fee simple owner without any stipulation as to period, and, in those circumstances, the plaintiff had an equitable right to keep the drains in position permanently for the purpose of draining off the bath water, and he was accordingly entitled to an injunction restraining the defendant from interfering with that right. Furthermore, Ungoed-Thomas J. held that although the plaintiff's equity related only to the drainage of bath water, the defendant's claim for an injunction to restrain the drainage of effluent failed, because she had herself given consent to the installation of the drains and had stood by while they were put in, not objecting until much later; and that, although the plaintiff had trespassed in using the drains in excess of the permission granted, that was an insubstantial and trivial trespass entitling the defendant to nominal damages only.

Ward v. *Kirkland* [16] was applied in *E. R. Ives Investment Limited* v. *High*.[17] The defendant, who was a builder, bought in 1949 the site of a

---

[14] It was also held that a way of necessity arose. See *post*, p. 118.
[15] [1967] Ch. 194. This case and also the other recent case on equitable easements *E.R. Ives Investment Ltd.* v. *High* [1967] 2 Q.B. 379 (see *infra*) together with *Poster* v. *Slough Estates Ltd.* [1969] 1 Ch. 495 have been discussed in the *Conveyancer*; see " Estoppel Interests in Land " by Mr. F. R. Crane, 31 *Conveyancer* 332; " Equities in the Making " by Mr. R. E. Poole, 32 *Conveyancer* 90; and " Equitable Easements " by Mr. Paul Jackson, 33 *Conveyancer* 135.
[16] [1967] Ch. 194.
[17] [1967] 2 Q.B. 379.

bombed house and started to build a house on it. At about the same time one Westgate bought an adjoining double site and started to build on it a block of flats. Westgate encroached on the defendant's site, putting the foundations of the flats about a foot over the boundary into the defendant's land some feet below ground level. The defendant objected to this trespass but at a meeting between the parties it was orally agreed between them that Westgate was to be allowed to keep the foundations of the flats on the defendant's land and that the defendant was to have a right of way from the back of his house across the yard of Westgate's flats so as to get access to a side road. There were letters evidencing the agreement, which was acted upon by both sides. In 1950 Westgate sold his site to a Flight Lieutenant and Mrs. Wright, who knew of the agreement. Soon afterwards both the defendant's house and the block of flats were finished. The defendant used the way across the yard and, in 1959, relying on the right of way, he built a garage which was so constructed that it could only be used by means of the yard. The Wrights raised no objection to the building of the garage or to the defendant's use of the yard for access to it. Moreover, in 1960, the Wrights got the defendant to re-surface the yard and he paid one-fifth of the cost of so doing. In 1962 the Wrights put up the flats for sale by auction, the particulars of sale referring to the defendant's right of way over the yard. The plaintiff company bought this property at the auction and the conveyance to the company from the Wrights stated that the property was conveyed subject to the right of way. The right of way was never registered as a land charge and the plaintiff claimed that it was void against it under section 13 of the Land Charges Act 1925. The plaintiff brought an action for damages and trespass and an injunction restraining the defendant from trespassing on the yard. The judge of the Norwich County Court dismissed the claim and an appeal by the plaintiff to the Court of Appeal failed. Lord Denning M.R. and Danckwerts L.J.[18] held that the defendant had in equity a good right of way across the yard arising in two ways, first by reason of the mutual benefit and burden under the agreement made between Westgate and the defendant in 1949, and secondly, by reason of the acquiescence of the plaintiff's predecessors in the rights thereby acquired. Winn L.J.[19] put the defendant's rights slightly differently, saying that a very clear equity and also an estoppel arose against the plaintiff preventing it from denying the defendant's use of the right of way.

It is not, however, possible to acquire on the basis of acquiescence a

---

[18] Danckwerts L.J. referred (at p. 399) with approval to Snell's *Equity* (26th ed., 1966), pp. 629–633, where the equitable ground in question is discussed under the name of " proprietory estoppel " and the comment is made (at p. 633) that " the doctrine thus displays equity at its most flexible." Both Lord Denning M.R. and Danckwerts L.J. applied *Hopgood* v. *Brown* [1955] 1 W.L.R. 213 and *Halsall* v. *Brizell* [1957] Ch. 169.

[19] Winn L.J. referred (at p. 405) to *Halsall* v. *Brizell* [1957] Ch. 169, 182, *per* Upjohn J.

right to do something, or to produce a result, not reasonably capable of being supposed to have been contemplated by the acquiescing party.

In *Bankart* v. *Houghton* [20] Sir John Romilly M.R. thought it "impossible to be reasonably contended that, because a man has acquiesced in the erection of certain works which have produced little or no injury, he is not afterwards to have any remedy if, by the increase of the works at a subsequent period, he sustains a serious injury." In *Bankart* v. *Tennant*,[21] where a tenant under an agreement for a lease had started a copper factory and for a time, without objection by the lessor, had used surplus water from the lessor's canal, no agreement for the use of this was imputed to the lessor, for the canal water was not essential to the factory.[22]

In *Armstrong* v. *Sheppard & Short Limited* [23] the plaintiff owned a small strip of land at the rear of his premises on which the defendant company had entered and constructed a sewer for the discharge of sewage and effluent. The plaintiff claimed damages for trespass and an injunction to restrain the discharge of effluent through the sewer. The judge of the Willesden County Court found as a fact that the plaintiff had orally informed the defendant that he did not object to the construction of the sewer; but he also found that the plaintiff, when he so informed the defendant, was not aware that he was the owner of the strip of land or that he had a right to object to the construction of the sewer. In those circumstances the Court of Appeal held that the plaintiff was not debarred from asserting his legal right against one who was shown to have infringed it on the ground of acquiescence, unless it was clear that at the time when he acquiesced he was aware of his proprietory right and, accordingly, that there was no equity which barred the plaintiff from asserting his legal title, though in the circumstances he should not be granted an injunction.

There is no reported case in which a man, merely because he has encouraged the erection of a building by his neighbour, has had imputed to him an agreement that the light to the windows of the building shall not be obstructed. As a general rule it is clear that the right to build on land is one of the natural rights of ownership, and that one who builds on the edge of his land takes his chance of his neighbour doing the same, to his prejudice.[24]

There are cases in which a man has executed works, etc., on the understanding that he is to have an easement on terms, but no terms have

[20] (1860) 27 Beav. 425.
[21] (1870) L.R. 10 Eq. 141.
[22] *Cf. Pwllbach Colliery Co.* v. *Woodman* [1915] A.C. 634.
[23] [1959] 2 Q.B. 384. The Court of Appeal applied *Ramsden* v. *Dyson* (1865) L.R. 1 H.L. 129 and *Willmott* v. *Barber* (1880) 15 Ch.D. 96; see also *Ward* v. *Kirkland* [1967] Ch. 194, 235–241.
[24] *Tapling* v. *Jones* (1865) 11 H.L.C. 290, 305; *Allen* v. *Seckham* (1879) 11 Ch.D. 790, 792, 797; *Truscott* v. *Merchant Tailors' Co.* (1856) 11 Exch. 855, 864–865.

been agreed. In such cases interference with the intended right has been restrained, the terms being settled by the court.[25]

Actual agreement

It appears that an agreement made for valuable consideration for the grant of an easement, or to the effect that some easement shall be exercisable, creates in equity a valid easement which can be exercised against the servient party and his successors in title, not being a purchaser for value without notice[26]; and that the same result follows[27] from an agreement not made for valuable consideration but involving expenditure or work actually incurred or done by the dominant party, as, for instance, an agreement, oral or under hand only, made between A and B and acted on by B, that B shall have the right to lay and maintain a pipe in A's land for the use of B's land.[28] In *McManus* v. *Cooke*,[29] the plaintiff and defendant, being owners of adjoining houses, had entered into an oral agreement, under which a party-wall was to be pulled down and rebuilt at their joint expense, and each party was to be at liberty to make a lean-to skylight resting on the new party-wall and running up to the sill of the first-floor window of his own building. The defendant having shaped his skylight so as to show above the wall and obstruct some of the light coming to the plaintiff's skylight, Kay J. granted an injunction, holding that the agreement was for an easement of light, and that if the Statute of Frauds[30] applied, as in his opinion it did, the plaintiff, having provided the defendant with the benefit intended for him, was entitled to the benefit intended for himself. The order, after reciting that the alleged agreement as to pulling down and rebuilding the party-wall, and the position of the skylights on each side of it, had been proved, restrained the defendant from permitting his skylight to remain, and from placing any other skylight which would obstruct the light to the plaintiff's skylight more than the skylight which the defendant agreed to erect would have done, the plaintiff giving a corresponding undertaking as to his skylight; and it directed, if necessary, the execution of a proper deed to secure these easements to both parties.

---

25 *Laird* v. *Birkenhead Ry. Co.* (1859) John. 500; *Powell* v. *Thomas* (1848) 6 Hare 300; *Duke of Devonshire* v. *Eglin* (1851) 14 Beav. 530; *cf. Clavering's Case*, referred to by Lord Loughborough, 5 Ves. 690; 6 Hare 304n.; L.R. 10 Eq. 147. In *East India Co.* v. *Vincent* (1740) 2 Atk. 83, where the defendant agreed, in return for a promise by the company to employ him, that certain proposed new windows in the company's building should have a right of light (both agreements being oral), and on the faith of this the windows were put in but the company did not employ as agreed, whereupon the defendant built a wall obstructing the light, Lord Hardwicke ordered the defendant to pull down the wall, and the company to perform its agreement.
26 See *post*, p. 69.
27 *Cf.* the cases referred to *ante*, pp. 62 *et seq.*; *Jones (James) & Sons Ltd.* v. *Tankerville (Earl)* [1909] 2 Ch. 440, 443.
28 In *E.R. Ives Investment* v. *High* [1967] 2 Q.B. 379, see p. 64, *ante*, the Court of Appeal found that there was a concluded agreement which the parties contemplated would be put into force, but this was not the *ratio decidendi* in that case.
29 (1887) 35 Ch.D. 681.
30 Now s. 40 of the L.P. Act 1925.

In *May* v. *Belleville* [31] a right of way reserved to the plaintiff, pursuant to a sale agreement, in a conveyance by him not executed by the purchaser and so not operating as a legal grant of the way,[32] was enforced against a successor in title of the purchaser taking with notice of the agreement.

In *White* v. *Grand Hotel, Eastbourne*,[33] where it was proved that P and F, predecessors in title of the parties, had made and acted on a verbal arrangement under which F was to set back into his land a boundary wall between his land and a passage belonging to P, so widening the passage, and in return was to be allowed to open a gateway in the new wall and have a right of way over the passage, the rights of the parties in regard to the passage were determined exactly as they would have been if the right had been actually granted.

In *Cory* v. *Davies* [34] three adjoining pieces of land, west, middle and east, fronting on a road, had been demised in 1857 separately to three related persons called Cory, each of whom covenanted with the lessor to develop in accordance with plans and specifications said in the lease to have been agreed. A terrace of seven houses, standing back from the road, was built, two (W 1 and 2) on the west plot, three on the middle plot, and two (E 1 and 2) on the east plot. A wall was built along the side of the road, with a gate at each end, opposite W 1 and E 2. Inside was a roadway, suitable for vehicles but without turning space, the result being that a vehicle going to any of the houses had to use both gates and the whole of the roadway. The defendant, who had taken an assignment of E 2, the piece of roadway in front of it and the east gateway, refused to allow vehicles to pass his house, and unsuccessfully defended an action by the assignees of the leasehold interest in the other six houses. Judgment was given on alternative grounds, one of which was that the circumstances justified the inference that the three original lessees, before building the houses and making the roadway and gates, had mutually agreed that each should grant the others the easements required for vehicular access, that the Statute of Frauds was no defence, for each intended grantee had performed his part by making, or contributing to the expense of his portion of, the terrace, roadway and gates, and that each of the three plots thus acquired in equity the requisite easement over the others. The defendant took (as it was held) with notice of the easement acquired by the other two plots, and was thus bound by them. An argument that the assignee of E 1, which had been leased together with E 2, had no rights against E 2, because the assignment of E 2 contained no express reservation in favour of E 1, was rejected on the ground that, as the assignment of E 2 carried inferentially a right over the portion

31 [1905] 2 Ch. 605.
32 See *post*, p. 80.
33 (1912) 106 L.T. 785; [1913] 1 Ch. 113; 82 L.J.Ch. 57 (C.A.); 110 L.T. 209 (H.L.).
34 [1923] 2 Ch. 95.

of roadway belonging to E 1, it could be considered to reserve by implication a similar right over the roadway belonging to E 2; alternatively an actual verbal agreement to that effect could be assumed to have been made. The same conclusion was reached on the alternative ground that, in the circumstances, there ought to be implied in each of the three leases a grant of the right to use the roadway and gates not included in the demise, and a reservation to the lessor and his lessees, owners and occupiers of the other plots, of the right to use the roadway and gates, so far as constructed on the demised plot.

The same principle is applied in the case of a *profit à prendre* which, to exist as a legal interest, must be granted by deed.[35] An enforceable contract will give the grantee an equitable right to a profit.[36] If not supported by part performance, there must be a sufficient memorandum in writing to satisfy section 40 of the Law of Property Act 1925.[37] If there is evidence in writing, or if the grant is supported by acts of part performance, the grantee may sue for interference with the right.[38]

Devolution of easements to which the right is equitable only

An easement to which an equitable right has arisen in any of the ways mentioned in this section enures, it is thought, like a legal easement, for the benefit of the dominant tenement,[39] but it does not bind a purchaser of the servient tenement for value without notice. Thus, in *Prinsep* v. *Belgravian Estate Ltd.*,[40] a house built under a building agreement eventually followed by a lease was held not to have an easement of light against adjoining property which had been sold by the lessor, after the agreement but before the lease, to a purchaser without notice of the agreement.

In *Hervey* v. *Smith*,[41] where the outside wall of a new house contained two flues reserved for the use of an adjoining house which was afterwards built and connected with them, the adjoining owner making a payment under the London Building Act and so becoming entitled in equity to an easement, a subsequent purchaser for value of the first house, who blocked up the flues and claimed to have taken without notice, was held to be put on inquiry by the mere existence of the flues.

---

35 Law of Property Act 1925, s. 52 (1); see *Mason* v. *Clarke* [1955] A.C. 778, 798, *per* Lord Morton of Henryton. This was also the case at common law: *Wood* v. *Leadbitter* (1845) 13 M. & W. 838, 842–843. Moreover, to create a legal interest, the grant must be for an interest equivalent to an estate in fee simple absolute in possession on a term of years absolute. Law of Property Act 1925, ss. 1 (2) (*a*), 205 (1) (ix), (x).
36 *White* v. *Taylor* (*No.* 2) [1969] 1 Ch. 160, 181; see also *Mills* v. *Stokman* (1967) 41 A.L.J.R. 16 (contract to sell slate).
37 *Webber* v. *Lee* (1882) 9 Q.B.D. 315.
38 *Frogley* v. *Earl of Lovelace* (1859) John. 333; *Mason* v. *Clarke* [1955] A.C. 778.
39 *E. R. Ives Investment* v. *High* [1967] 2 Q.B. 379; and see *Inwards* v. *Baker* [1965] 2 Q.B. 29, 37, *per* Lord Denning M.R.; also *Hopgood* v. *Brown* [1955] 1 W.L.R. 213; *Armstrong* v. *Sheppard & Short Ltd.* [1959] 2 Q.B. 384; *Ward* v. *Kirkland* [1967] Ch. 194.
40 [1896] W.N. 39.
41 (1855) 1 K. & J. 389; subsequent proceedings, 22 Beav. 299.

Page Wood V.-C. said [42] that the question of notice concerning the right
to an easement of this kind is like those cases in which notice of
possession by a tenant is notice of the terms of his holding.

In *E. R. Ives Investment Ltd.* v. *High* [43] it was part of the plaintiff's
case that as a right of way was never registered as a land charge under
Class C (iv) as an estate contract or under Class D (iii) as an equitable
easement, it was void against the plaintiff under section 13 (2) of the
Land Charges Act 1925. It was said that the right was an " equitable
easement " within Class D (iii). This class is defined as " Any easement right or privilege over or affecting land created or arising after
the commencement of this Act, and being merely an equitable interest."
Lord Denning M.R. pointed out [44] that those words were almost
identical with those used in subsection (3) (iii) of section 2 of the Law
of Property Act 1925, which is concerned with equitable interests which
cannot be overreached. He said that the words should be given the
same meaning and must be read in conjunction with sections 1 (2) (*a*),
(3) and 4 (1) of the Law of Property Act. It then appeared that an
" equitable easement " was a proprietory interest in land such as would
before 1926 have been recognised as capable of being conveyed or
created at law, but which since 1926 only took effect as an equitable
interest. An instance of such a proprietory interest was a *profit à
prendre* for life. It did not include a right, liberty or privilege arising
in equity by reason of " mutual benefit and burden," or arising out of
" acquiescence," or by reason of a contractual licence, because before
1926 these were not proprietory interests such as were capable of
being conveyed or created at law; they only subsisted in equity.
Accordingly they did not need to be registered as land charges, so as
to bind successors, but took effect in equity without registration. [45]
Danckwerts L.J. also held [46] that the charge in question was not a
registrable charge; accordingly section 199 of the Law of Property Act
1925, which provides that a purchaser shall not be prejudicially affected
by notice of any instrument or matter capable of registration under
the provisions of the Land Charges Act 1925 which is void or not
enforceable against him under that Act, had no application. Winn L.J.
said [47] that such equities as arose from merely standing by whilst
expenditure was incurred under a mistake of fact or law, or from
attempts both to approbate and reprobate a deed, always supposing
them to be capable of registration (which was, he thought, on the whole
an open question), might not survive the lethal effect of the Land
Charges Act unless they had been registered. On the other hand he

---

42 (1855) 1 K. & J. 394.
43 [1967] 2 Q.B. 379.
44 *Ibid.* 395.
45 In so holding, Lord Denning M.R. adopted the views expressed by Mr. C. V. Davidge
   in an article, " Equitable Easements " in 59 *Law Quarterly Review* 259 and of
   Professor H. W. R. Wade in [1956] *Cambridge Law Journal* 225, 226.
46 [1967] 2 Q.B. 400.   47 *Ibid.* 405.

could not see that the statute had any impact upon an estoppel, nor did he think that an estoppel could be registrable under its provisions.

In *Poster* v. *Slough Estates Ltd.*[48] (which was concerned with the question of a right to remove tenant's fixtures) Cross J. referred to the views expressed by Lord Denning M.R. in *E. R. Ives Investment Ltd.* v. *High*[49] and pointed out that there was nothing in the judgments of Danckwerts L.J. and Winn L.J. to suggest that they agreed with the view that equitable easements comprised only those equitable interests which before 1926 could have subsisted as legal estates in easements or profits. Cross J. said, however, that, even if Lord Denning's view was not strictly binding on him, he would, naturally, follow it unless he was clearly of opinion that it was wrong, and he said that in this field he was not clear about anything. He would, had the plaintiffs not been precluded by the effects of the Landlord and Tenant Act 1954 from exercising their right to remove the fixtures, have held that they could enforce the right against the second defendant (a tenant by virtue of that Act), although it was not registered under the Land Charges Act. Cross J. went on, however, to refer to some consequences which might flow from the acceptance of the view that "equitable easements" for the purposes of the Land Charges Act comprised only those equitable interests which could before 1926 have subsisted as legal estates in easements or profits. He said[50]:

"So long as one is dealing with unregistered land, all is plain sailing, for the judge can apply the doctrine of notice to the unregistrable equities in question. This may enable him to arrive at a fairer result in the particular case than he could have reached had the equity been registrable but unregistered. But if he is dealing with registered land the position may be different. The general principle of the Land Registration Act is that a purchaser of registered land takes free from any unregistered rights which are not 'overriding interests.' The sort of right with which we are concerned in this case is not an overriding interest, and the result of holding that it is not registrable as an equitable easement may, in the case of registered land, be that there is no way of making it bind a purchaser. This would be unfortunate. On the whole, the modern law of real property works well, but 'equitable easements' seem to be a weak spot in it which might with advantage receive the attention of the Law Commission."

The position of a person who claims in respect of registered land such an equitable right as Lord Denning took to be outside Class D (iii), is,

48 [1969] 1 Ch. 495.
49 [1967] 2 Q.B. 379. Both *E. R. Ives Investments Ltd.* v. *High* and *Poster* v. *Slough Estates Ltd.* were referred to in *Shiloh Spinners Ltd.* v. *Harding* [1971] 3 W.L.R. 34, 41–42, 54. In the latter case the Court of Appeal held (Sachs L.J. dissenting) that the right of the assignor of a lease to re-enter the premises under a clause in the assignment was registrable as a Class D (iii) land charge, but (Russell L.J. dissenting) was not registrable as a Class D (iv) land charge.   50 [1969] 1 Ch. 495, 507.

as Cross J. indicated, in a position of difficulty. As *E. R. Ives Investment Ltd.* v. *High*[1] and *Poster* v. *Slough Estates Ltd.*[2] appear to leave the legal position in some doubt, perhaps the best course for such a person to adopt would be to apply for the right to be protected by notice, as a land charge, or by a caution. If the application were refused, the matter might be brought before the court for its decision.

Where there is a specifically enforceable contract to grant a legal easement over unregistered land the purchaser has an equitable right to a legal grant. This right would seem to fall outside the Land Charges Act 1925, s. 10 (1), Class D (iii); it is not an " equitable easement " because there is no easement presently exercisable. In any event, the remarks in *E. R. Ives Investments Ltd.* v. *High*[3] would preclude its registration under Class D (iii) because it is an interest which even before 1926 would not have taken effect at law. It is, however, probably registrable as an estate contract under Class C (iv), and if not so registered would not bind a purchaser for money or money's worth of the servient land.[4] If the contract were to grant an easement over registered land, it would presumably not be an overriding interest within the class of rights included in the Land Registration Act 1925, s. 70 (1) (*a*), not being an existing easement but merely a right to a grant of such. If it is to bind a purchaser of the servient tenement it should therefore be protected by notice,[5] as a land charge, or by a caution.[6]

Where registered land is subject to equitable easements, which are equitable by reason only of their being for less than a fee simple absolute in possession or a term of years absolute, there is some doubt as to whether they are overriding interests or whether they should be protected by notice on the register. Overriding interests include equitable easements not " required to be protected by notice on the register." [7] As there is no provision in the Land Registration Act 1925 requiring equitable easements to be protected by notice on the register, it is arguable that all equitable easements must be overriding interests and therefore will bind subsequent proprietors of the servient land whether protected by notice or not. The requirement of entering a notice seems, however, to be envisaged by the Act; if so, equitable easements would not bind subsequent proprietors if entry were not made on the register.[8]

---

[1] [1967] 2 Q.B. 379.   [2] [1968] 1 W.L.R. 1515.
[3] [1967] 2 Q.B. 379, *ante*, p. 70.   [4] Land Charges Act 1925, s. 13 (2).
[5] Land Registration Act 1925, ss. 49 (1) (*c*), 59 (2). Even if a contract to grant an easement does give rise to an " equitable easement " it may nevertheless be prudent to protect it by notice or caution; see *infra*.
[6] Land Registration Act 1925, s. 54.   [7] *Ibid.* s. 70 (1) (*a*).
[8] *Ibid.* ss. 20 (1) (*a*), 23 (1) (*a*). Equitable *profits à prendre* would appear to be overriding interests, there being no limitation to legal *profits à prendre* in the Land Registration Act 1925, s. 70 (1) (*a*). An easement granted by a registered proprietor which is to be appurtenant to registered land must be registered before it becomes a legal easement: *ibid.* ss. 19 (2), 22 (2); until registration it will take effect in equity only and the same doubt exists as to whether it is an overriding interest or required to be protected by notice.

PART II

THE ACQUISITION OF EASEMENTS

CHAPTER 3

CREATION OF EASEMENTS BY KNOWN TRANSACTIONS

AN easement may be created by a particular statute, or *inter partes* by a private grant or a testamentary disposition. It may be granted expressly by the terms of the conveyance and it may be expressly reserved over land granted. It may be created by the general words contained in the conveyance or imported into it by section 62 of the Law of Property Act 1925. It may arise by implication, founded on presumed intention, under a grant or an agreement for a grant of land, as where land is disposed of for a particular purpose, or the ownership of land becomes divided and continuous and apparent easements pass in accordance with the rule in *Wheeldon* v. *Burrows*.[1] Only exceptionally can an easement be reserved by implication. The express grant or reservation of an easement is a conveyancing matter which, given a competent grantor and a competent grantee, should present no difficulty. The creation of easements by implication and by general words is considered below.[2] An easement may also be established under the doctrine of prescription or lost modern grant, as to which see the next chapter.[3]

1.—CREATION BY STATUTE

There are, or have been, very many public and private Acts, under which, or by the exercise or performance of powers or obligations contained in them, easements or rights analogous thereto, can arise.[4] Private inclosure Acts, and awards made under the Inclosure Acts 1801 and 1845, whereby land subject to rights of common was parcelled out in severalty, nearly always created rights of way and other easements.[5] The owner of land severed by a railway acquires the right to pass over level crossings and other accommodation works made under section 68

---

1 (1879) 12 Ch.D. 31, 49.
2 See pp. 82 *et seq.*, 122 *et seq.*, *post.*
3 *Cf.* those cases where special immunities arise under the doctrine of non-derogation from grant, pp. 88 *et seq.*, *post*, and those cases where rights to easements arise in equity, pp. 61 *et seq.*, *ante.*
4 For a discussion of this subject, see an article, " Statutory Easements " by J. F. Garner, in 20 *Conveyancer* (N.S.) 208.
5 See *e.g. Newcomen* v. *Coulson* (1877) 5 Ch.D. 133; *Finch* v. *G.W. Railway* (1880) 5 Ex.D. 254.

of the Railway Clauses Consolidation Act 1845.[6] Government depart-
ments and public boards also have various powers to acquire and
grant easements. Thus, section 18 (3) of the New Towns Act 1965
empowers a development corporation to create easements over land
which it acquires. The empowering statute may grant the right by
implication to the public body. Thus, the simultaneous provision of a
power to construct works and of a right to compensation in respect of
consequent damage raises the implication that the empowering statute
gives a right of support to the works after construction.[7] A statutory
power to acquire an easement may impliedly include necessary ancillary
rights.[8] Land, the title to which has been registered under the Land
Registration Acts 1925 and 1966, may have an easement by reason
of the registration.[9] By virtue of section 10 (2) of the Leasehold
Reform Act 1967, easements may arise under a conveyance executed
to give effect to an obligation to enfranchise under that Act. *Profits à
prendre* may also be created by statute. When land was allotted to
commoners under the Inclosure Acts, shooting rights were frequently
reserved to the lord of the manor.

2.—CREATION INTER PARTES

Competent grantors

An individual owner of land can subject it to an easement for any
estate or interest for which he could alienate it; and a corporation
whose power to alienate its land is restricted can grant an easement
which is not inconsistent with the purposes for which it holds the land.[10]

The statutory power of sale of a mortgagee includes power, if the
mortgage was executed after 1911,[11] and does not provide to the
contrary, to sell part of the mortgaged property with a grant or reservation of a right of way or other easement over either the part retained
or the part sold.[12]

---

[6] See *e.g. G.W. Railway* v. *Talbot* [1902] 2 Ch. 759; *Taff Vale Railway* v. *Gordon
Canning* [1909] 2 Ch. 48; *Midland Railway* v. *Gribble* [1895] 2 Ch. 827. In *British
Railways Board* v. *Glass* [1965] Ch. 538 a conveyance to a railway company
operated as a grant of a right of way for all purposes to the owner of the fields
severed by the railway line and not merely as a grant of an accommodation way
under s. 68 of the Railway Clauses Consolidation Act 1845.

[7] *Re Corporation of Dudley* (1881) L.R. 8 Q.B.D. 86, 93, *per* Brett L.J.; *London and
North Western Railway Co.* v. *Evans* [1893] 1 Ch. 16, 31, *per* A. L. Smith L.J.

[8] *Central Electricity Generating Board* v. *Jennaway* [1959] 1 W.L.R. 937; see p. 44,
ante.

[9] *Peachey* v. *Lee* (1964) 192 E.G. 365 (rights of way).

[10] *Re Gonty and Manchester, Sheffield and Lincolnshire Railway Co.* [1896] 2 Q.B.
439; *cf. Stourcliffe Estates Co. Ltd.* v. *Bournemouth Corporation* [1910] 2 Ch. 12;
and see *British Transport Commission* v. *Westmorland County Council* [1958] A.C.
126.

[11] In *Born* v. *Turner* [1900] 2 Ch. 211, where the mortgage was executed before 1912,
and the mortgagee sold part of the mortgaged property, a right of light over the
retained part was held to pass by implication. Whether the mortgagee could have
expressly granted a right which would not arise by implication was not decided.

[12] Law of Property Act 1925, s. 101.

Similarly, on any sale or other disposition or dealing under the powers conferred by the Settled Land Act 1925 (which are exercisable by trustees for sale and personal representatives [13]), an easement, right or privilege of any kind may be reserved or granted over or in relation to the settled land or any part thereof or other land, including the part disposed of, and, in the case of an exchange, the land taken in exchange.[14]   A person exercising Settled Land Act powers can also (apparently) sell [15] or lease [16] an easement over his land as an independent transaction, *i.e.* to a person already the owner of the dominant tenement. In the case of a lease in such circumstances, the " best rent " required by section 42 (1) (ii) is presumably recoverable by the estate owner for the time being.[17]   The requirement of a proviso for re-entry (s. 42 (1) (iii)), does not apply.[18]   Such a person may also subject his land to an easement in exchange for the grant of an easement over other land,[19] or, with or without consideration, including the release of an easement over his land,[20] release other land from an easement accommodating his land.[21]   The incumbent of a benefice, or during a vacancy the bishop of the diocese in which the benefice is situated, has power to take an easement for the benefit of any land which forms part of the property of the benefice and to grant an easement over such land, but the exercise of such powers requires the consent of the Church Commissioners, the patron, the diocesan dilapidations board and, where the power is exercised by the incumbent, the bishop.[22]   The grant or taking of an easement in such a case may be made or done either without monetary consideration or in consideration of the payment of a capital sum, any capital sum payable in respect of the grant of an easement being payable to the Commissioners to be applied for the purposes for which the proceeds of sale of the land over which the easement is granted would be applicable.[23]

Persons entitled to rights of common have no power, prima facie, to grant an easement over the common.[24]

Clearly a person entitled to land cannot subject it to an easement more extensive than his own interest.[25]   If, however, a person expressly

[13] *Ibid.* s. 28; Administration of Estates Act 1925, s. 39.
[14] Settled Land Act 1925, s. 49 (1) (*a*).
[15] *Ibid.* ss. 38, 39.
[16] *Ibid.* ss. 41, 42.
[17] *Lord Hastings* v. *North Eastern Railway* [1898] 2 Ch. 674; *ante,* p. 49.
[18] *Sitwell* v. *Londesborough (Earl)* [1905] 1 Ch. 460, 465.
[19] S.L. Act 1925, s. 38 (1) (iii).
[20] *Ibid.* s. 61 (2) (*e*).
[21] s. 59 (2).
[22] Church Property (Miscellaneous Provisions) Measure 1960, s. 9 (1).
[23] *Ibid.* s. 9 (2) (3).
[24] *Paine & Co.* v. *St. Neots Gas & Coke Co.* [1938] 4 All E.R. 592; [1939] 3 All E.R. 812.
[25] *Beddington* v. *Atlee* (1887) 35 Ch.D. 317, 327; and *cf. Daniel* v. *Anderson* (1861) 31 L.J.Ch. 610.

grants an easement over land to which he has no title, and then acquires the fee, the land will be bound by estoppel.[26]   On the other hand, no grant will be implied, or arise from general words, in excess of the interest of the grantor at the time of the grant.   In *Booth* v. *Alcock*[27] where the defendant, being lessee of land and owner of a house adjoining it, granted to the plaintiff a lease of the house with its appurtenances, including " lights," and then acquired the reversion in fee of the land, it was held that the plaintiff acquired a right to light for the residue of the term of the lease of the land, and that the defendant's acquisition of the reversion made no difference.   " General words in a grant must be restricted to that which the grantor had then power to grant, and will not extend to anything which he might subsequently acquire."[28]   In *Quicke* v. *Chapman*,[29] where the defendant, having entered into a building agreement under which he was to build houses on a number of plots, and was to have a lease of each house on completion and in the meantime a licence to enter only, took and assigned to the plaintiff a lease of a completed house before completing and acquiring a lease of the adjoining house, the plaintiff was held not entitled to restrain interference with the light of his house by the adjoining house when completed.   The implication of a grant of right to light was negatived by the consideration that the defendant, when he assigned the lease to the plaintiff, had no interest in the adjoining land which would have enabled him to grant the right expressly.

Similarly, no easement will arise by implication, or under general words in a conveyance, if the vendor, before agreeing to sell the supposedly dominant tenement (A), has agreed to sell the supposedly servient tenement (B), without reserving the alleged easement.   The reason is that the vendor, on agreeing to sell B, becomes a trustee of B for his purchaser, and a subsequent contract by him to sell A cannot be assumed to include a contract to create an incumbrance on B.[30] Hence it appears to follow that if the owner of two properties, A and B, agrees to sell B, and then agrees to sell A, with an express grant of an easement over B, the grant of the easement will be ineffectual unless the grantee is a purchaser for money or money's worth without notice of the contract to sell B.   As the purchaser of A is presumably a purchaser of " an interest in " B, within section 13 (2) of the Land

---

26 *Rowbotham* v. *Wilson* (1857) 8 El. & Bl. 123, 145; (1860) 8 H.L.C. 348, 364. *Quaere* as to the position if the grantor, having some interest in the land, expressly grants an easement in excess of the interest, and afterwards acquires the excess interest.   See *Booth* v. *Alcock* (1873) 8 Ch.App. 663; *Universal Permanent Building Society* v. *Cooke* [1952] Ch. 95, 102; Co.Litt. 47b; 2 Wms.Saund. (1871) 829, 830.
27 (1873) 8 Ch.App. 663.
28 *Per* Mellish L.J. (1873) 8 Ch.App. 667.
29 [1903] 1 Ch. 659.
30 *Beddington* v. *Atlee* (1887) 35 Ch.D. 317; and see *Davies* v. *Thomas* [1899] W.N 244, where the purchaser of property having an apparent pipe easement over adjoining property, belonging to the vendor but then mortgaged, failed to establish the easement against a subsequent purchaser from the mortgagee.

Charges Act 1925, it seems to follow that if the contract to sell B has not been registered as a land charge (Class C (iv)) under section 10 (1) of that Act, the contract will be void under section 13 (2) against the purchaser of A, and by virtue of section 199 (1) of the Law of Property Act 1925 he will not be prejudicially affected by notice of it.

Competent grantees

It seems that no easement can be effectually granted in excess of the interest, if any, of the grantee in the dominant tenement.[31] However, if, on the grant of a perpetual easement to one who is only tenant for years of the dominant tenement, it appears to have been contemplated that the grantee will acquire the fee, and he does so, the grant may take effect according to its tenor.[32]

A grant to an equitable owner may be construed as a grant of a legal easement. In *Johnstone* v. *Holdway*[33] a vendor held land, including a quarry, in trust for a company and on a sale of part of the land, not including the quarry, the conveyance contained an exception and reservation in favour of the company and its successors in title of a right of way for the benefit of the quarry over the land sold. The exception and reservation operated by way of regrant by the purchaser to the vendor and the question arose whether, as a matter of construction, the purchaser granted to the company a legal easement or an equitable easement. The Court of Appeal held that it would be unreasonable to suppose that the parties intended that the purchaser should grant an equitable easement to the company, retaining a bare legal right in himself to be held upon trust for the company. The company was the beneficial owner of the quarry and the party interested to preserve its right to go to the quarry; the vendor was not interested. The court accordingly held that the exception and reservation operated as a grant at law and not only in equity.

An authorised mode of application of capital money is the purchase in fee simple, or for a term of sixty years or more, of any easement convenient to be held with the settled land for mining or other purposes.[34]

Grant inter vivos

As already mentioned,[35] a legal easement cannot be created *inter vivos* otherwise than by deed. An easement so otherwise granted or agreed to be granted takes effect, if at all, in equity, and does not bind a purchaser for value of the servient tenement without notice.[36]

31 *Smeteborn* v. *Holt* (1347) Y.B. 21 Edw. 3, fo. 2, pl. 5.
32 *Rymer* v. *McIlroy* [1897] 1 Ch. 528, where the grant also operated as a covenant; the circumstances were unusual.
33 [1963] 1 Q.B. 601, 612–613; see also p. 9, *ante*.
34 S.L. Act 1925, s. 73 (1) (xii).
35 *Ante*, p. 61.
36 *Ante*, pp. 69 *et seq.*

It is not necessary to use the word "grant"[37] or, since 1925 at any rate, to use words of limitation.[38]

Before 1926 an easement purporting to be reserved by the grantor was in truth granted by the grantee,[39] and for this reason an easement reserved to the vendor in a conveyance not executed by the purchaser took effect in equity only.[40] Section 65 of the Law of Property Act 1925 provides,[41] however, that after 1925, (1) a reservation of a legal estate operates at law without any execution of the conveyance by the grantee of the legal estate out of which the reservation is made, or any regrant by him, and operates to create the legal estate reserved, and to vest the same in possession in the person (whether being the grantor or not) for whose benefit the reservation is made, and (2) a conveyance of a legal estate expressed to be made subject to another legal estate not in existence immediately before the date of the conveyance is to operate as a reservation, unless a contrary intention appears. In *Cordell* v. *Second Clanfield Properties Ltd.*[42] Megarry J. held that as the reservation of an easement no longer required a regrant, the rule that an exception out of a grant is to be construed against the grantor should be applied to the reservation, so that it, too, should be construed against the vendor or grantor and in favour of the purchaser or grantee.

If a vendor wishes to reserve an easement over the land conveyed in favour of the land which he retains he should do so in specific terms. It may, however, be possible to construe a reservation from general words which refer to current user of the land conveyed for the benefit of the land retained.[43] In *Pitt* v. *Buxton*[44] this question was considered by the Court of Appeal. In 1946 one of the plaintiff's predecessors in title purchased certain fields, adjoining a public road, through which passed a roadway. There was no mention of the roadway in the conveyance which was expressed to be "subject to all rights of way . . . (including all quasi-easements and methods of user hitherto used or enjoyed by the vendor in connection with his adjoining or

---

37 Law of Property Act 1925, s. 51 (2).
38 *Ibid.* s. 60. The necessity for the use of words of limitation before 1926 was considered in three articles in (1908) 24 L.Q.R. 199, 259, 264.
39 "It is neither parcel of the thing granted, nor is it issuing out of the thing granted, the former being essential to an exception, and the latter to a reservation": Tyndal C.J., *Durham and Sunderland Railway* v. *Walker* (1842) 2 Q.B. 940, 967. In the years 1882–1925 a conveyance to the use that the vendor or some other person might have, for an estate not exceeding in duration the estate conveyed in the land, an easement over the land conveyed operated to vest the easement in that person for that estate: Conveyancing Act 1881, s. 62 (1).
40 *May* v. *Belleville* [1905] 2 Ch. 605.
41 See also *Mason* v. *Clarke* [1954] 1 Q.B. 460, 466, *per* Denning L.J.; [1955] A.C. 778, 786, *per* Viscount Simonds (a case of a *profit à prendre*).
42 [1969] 1 Ch. 9; not following dicta of Upjohn J. in *Bulstrode* v. *Lambert* [1953] 1 W.L.R. 1064, 1068 and Denning L.J. in *Mason* v. *Clarke* [1954] 1 Q.B. 460, 467.
43 This should not be confused with implied reservation, as to which see p. 106, *post.* Here the surrounding circumstances are giving meaning to expressions in the conveyance.
44 (1970) 21 P. & C.R. 127.

neighbouring property) if any . . . existing over or affecting [the property conveyed] . . . and to all occupation and other roads." The property conveyed adjoined a small enclosure which itself adjoined a lake, both the properties of the vendor. In 1953 another of the plaintiff's predecessors in title purchased the small enclosure from the owner of the lake, the conveyance again being made subject to " quasi-easements," " methods of user " and " occupation ways " affecting the property conveyed. The defendant, who was the present owner of the lake, claimed a right of way on foot or by vehicle, for himself, his tenants and licensees for the purpose of passing from the public road to the lake to fish. The question on appeal was whether the general words in the 1946 and 1953 conveyances operated as grants of rights of way over the roadway and the enclosure for access to the lake for fishing. Russell L.J. said [45] :

> " I do not see, in principle, that it is not possible to constitute an express regrant by the use of general words referring to current *de facto* accommodation of the latter by the former. Whether there is a grant must be a question of the intention of the parties to be gathered from the language of the instrument in the circumstances in which that language was used. If land is conveyed subject to ' rights ' of way hitherto enjoyed, it may well be that mere accommodations or quasi-easements are not by such language elevated to the status of an easement: see, for example, *Russell* v. *Harford*,[46] but see also *May* v. *Belleville*.[47] If, however, express reference is made to all quasi-easements and methods of user hitherto enjoyed, it seems to me that the proper conclusion is that a grant by the purchaser is intended, the nature and extent of the easement being determined (if at all) by the facts of user which obtained, though it must be for the vendor (or his successors) to establish with some precision what were the facts and, consequently, what was the right said to be created."

There was some evidence that at the time of the two conveyances persons were permitted to use the roadway and the small enclosure, on foot and with vehicles, to reach the lake from the public road for the purpose of fishing. The evidence, however, was exiguous and it could not be said that there was such a regular and established method of user of or quasi-easement over the roadway in favour of the lake for fishing purposes as would support the view that an easement was created by the language of the 1946 conveyance. There was even less evidence in support of the necessary extent of user at the time of the 1953 conveyance.

[45] *Ibid.* 133. Sachs L.J. assumed, without deciding, that general words may give rise to a reservation: *ibid.* 135–136. Phillimore L.J. did not add to the judgments.
[46] (1866) L.R. 2 Eq. 507.
[47] [1905] 2 Ch. 605.

Grant by will

Easements may be created in a will where the testator owns and makes separate dispositions of the dominant and servient tenements. Until the personal representative gives a written assent,[48] the easement takes effect in equity only.[49] There is apparently nothing to prevent a testator from subjecting, by his will, land owned by him to a new easement in favour of land not owned by him.

Indorsement of memorandum

Section 200 of the Law of Property Act 1925 provides that (1) where land (other than registered land) having a common title with other land is disposed of to a purchaser (other than a lessee or mortgagee) who does not hold or obtain possession of the documents forming the common title, such purchaser, notwithstanding any provision to the contrary, may require that a memorandum giving notice of any provision contained in the disposition to him restrictive of the user of, or giving rights over, any other land comprised in the common title, shall, where practicable, be written or indorsed on, or, where impracticable, be permanently annexed to some one document selected by the purchaser but retained in the possession or power of the person who makes the disposition, and being or forming part of the common title; but (2) the title of a person who omits to do so is not to be prejudiced.

3.—CREATION BY IMPLICATION

An easement may arise by implication under a grant, including a lease and a testamentary gift,[50] of land if an intention to grant it can properly be inferred. This intention may be inferred:

    1. Where the grant contains particular words of description. Alternatively, in such a case, the easement may be created by estoppel.[1]

    2. Where the circumstances indicate that it was contemplated that the land granted would be used in some particular manner. The easement may be implied by the necessity of the case.

    3. Under the doctrine of non-derogation from grant, by virtue of which, as already noticed,[2] there may be acquired not only easements but also immunities of a special kind not recognised as easements.

    4. Under the rule in *Wheeldon* v. *Burrows*,[3] which is a branch

---

48 Administration of Estates Act 1925, s. 36. Where the easement arises by implication, it should be expressly included in the assent relating to the dominant tenement, and the assent relating to the servient tenement should be expressed to be subject to it.

49 Law of Property (Amendment) Act 1924, s. 9, Sched. 9, para. 3.

50 Where an easement created by will arises by implication, it should be expressly included in the assent relating to the dominant tenement, and the assent relating to the servient tenement should be expressed to be subject to it.

1 See *Mellor* v. *Walmesley* [1905] 2 Ch. 164, 175–176.

2 See p. 43, *ante.*

3 (1879) 12 Ch.D. 31.

of the general rule against derogation from grant, but which is commonly considered under a separate head.[4]

The occasion on which an easement most commonly arises without being granted or reserved in express terms is when the owner, or lessee,[5] of land sells or lets [6] part of it and retains the rest; or disposes of both parts to different persons at the same time. An easement impliedly agreed to be granted or reserved in such a case takes effect as an equitable easement pending the execution of the conveyance or lease, and thereafter, whether expressly granted or not, takes effect as a legal easement.[7]

At this point it should be observed that an easement arising or acquired by implication may at the same time arise under general words, either set out in the conveyance or, as is more probable today, imported into it by section 62 of the Law of Property Act 1925.[8] The two classes of obligations, the one implied from the surrounding circumstances and the fact of the grant, and the other found as a matter of construction from the words of the grant, are quite distinct from one another, as appears from the judgment of Bowen L.J. in the Court of Appeal in *Bayley* v. *Great Western Railway Company*.[9]

In many cases in which the question arises it is sufficient, for practical purposes, to see whether the right in question is included in the general words, for if it is, it will have arisen and can be enforced. Nevertheless, it is thought that the first question in such cases is whether the right would have arisen apart from the general words, for if it would, it will have passed under the conveyance or other disposition whether it is included in the general words or not, unless the disposition shows a contrary intention; and if it would not, then, although it may be included in the general words, these may be liable to rectification on the ground of mutual mistake. Moreover, the question may arise between contract and conveyance, as when it is sought to modify the general words in a proposed conveyance so as to exclude the grant of

---

4 See, for example, *Ward* v. *Kirkland* [1967] Ch. 194. This case is considered further at p. 94, *post.*

5 For the present purpose it makes no difference whether the disposing party is owner in fee, or lessee or tenant (see *Key* v. *Neath R.D.C.* (1905) 93 L.T. 507, affd. (1907) 95 L.T. 771); but an easement created or a disposition by a lessee will not, of course, bind the reversion, nor will it do so if the reversion is afterwards acquired by the lessee, see *Booth* v. *Alcock* (1873) 8 Ch.App. 663, *ante*, p. 78.

6 The case of a voluntary conveyance of part does not seem to have come before the courts.

7 Inasmuch as the rights of the purchaser or lessee arise from the contract, he is, it is thought, clearly entitled to have an express grant, in his conveyance or lease, of the easement which would otherwise be implied. See *Williams on Vendor and Purchaser*, 4th ed., pp. 659–660.

8 In *Ward* v. *Kirkland* [1967] Ch. 194 the plaintiff claimed an easement by implication of law, by the application of the doctrine of derogation from grant, by general words under s. 62 of the Law of Property Act 1925 and by prescription. General words are considered at pp. 122 *et seq., post.*

9 (1883) 26 Ch.D. 434, 452. See " Non-Derogation from Grant " by Mr. D. W. Elliott (1964) 80 *Law Quarterly Review* 224 *et seq.* for an interesting discussion of the distinction.

an easement which the contract does not import; or to include in the conveyance an express grant of an easement which the contract does import. Furthermore, where the owner of the land disposed of and the land retained is also the occupier of both, no right can arise under general words which is not imported by the contract.

An easement may also arise if an intention to reserve it can properly be inferred, but the general rule is that a grantor who intends to reserve a right over the tenement granted must do so expressly, so that it is only in exceptional cases that an easement can be reserved by implication.[10]

1. From description in parcels

In *Roberts* v. *Karr*,[11] Pratt had released to Compigné land of unequal width, described as abutting east on a new road on Pratt's own land. It abutted in the widest part on the road; but in the narrower part a strip of the grantor's land (which he alleged that he had intended to reserve) intervened between the road and the premises granted. It was held that, even admitting that Pratt had intended to reserve the land, yet he and those claiming under him were precluded by the description in Compigné's release from preventing Compigné or his assigns from coming out into the road over the strip of land. "Is it not," asked Lord Mansfield C.J.,[12] "a sufficient answer to say, you have told me in your lease, 'this land abuts on the road': you cannot now be allowed to say that the land on which it abuts is not the road."

In *Harding* v. *Wilson*[13] a lease of premises to one Bolton described them as abutting on "an *intended* way of thirty feet wide," the soil on that side of the premises demised being the property of one Sloane, the lessor. The defendant, as tenant of the adjoining land under a subsequent demise from Sloane, afterwards built to within twenty-seven feet of the land demised to Bolton. The plaintiff, an underlessee from Bolton, having brought his action claiming a right of way over the whole thirty feet, it was admitted that he was entitled (independently, as it seems, of the description) to a convenient way, his premises not being otherwise accessible from the high road; but it was held that he was not entitled to more. "Adverting," said Abbott C.J.,[14] "to the lease from Sloane to Bolton, the former does not grant a way thirty feet wide, but only described the land demised as bounded by an intended way of that width. There is merely an expression and declaration of intention." The argument was somewhat complicated by the fact that the plaintiff's underlease did not specify any particular width;

---

10 *Wheeldon* v. *Burrows* (1879) 12 Ch.D. 31, 49, *per* Thesiger L.J.; see pp. 106 *et seq.*, *post*.
11 (1809) 1 Taunt. 495.
12 *Ibid.* 503.
13 (1823) 2 B. & C. 96.
14 *Ibid.* 98.

but this was held to be immaterial. This case does not seem to have received very much consideration.

In *Espley* v. *Wilkes*[15] the defendant's lease described the premises demised as " bounded on the east and north by newly-made streets," and the new streets were shown on the plan indorsed. The lessee covenanted to kerb the causeways adjoining the land demised. The way to the east was never made or marked out, and the site was subsequently leased by the same landlord to the plaintiff. It was held that the effect of the defendant's lease was to give him a private right of way over both streets; for the lessor was by his own description estopped from denying that there were streets which were in fact ways. Kelly C.B. relied on *Harding* v. *Wilson*[16] as an authority for the defendant, apparently treating that decision, so far as it affirmed the plaintiff's right to a convenient way, as proceeding on estoppel. But it is difficult to understand why, if the lessor in that case was estopped from denying that the plaintiff was entitled to some way, he was not equally estopped from denying that the way should be thirty feet wide. It is conceived that the " convenient way " in *Harding* v. *Wilson* was a way of necessity.[17]

In *Mellor* v. *Walmesley*,[18] where land conveyed was described with full dimensions and reference to a plan and also, inconsistently with these, as " bounded on the west by the ' seashore ' " (which was construed as " foreshore," *i.e.* the land between ordinary high- and low-water marks), it was held by Vaughan Williams and Stirling L.JJ. that if, as they thought, the western boundary was in fact, on the proper construction of the conveyance, east of the foreshore, the defendants as successors in title of the grantor were estopped as against the plaintiffs, as successors in title of the grantees, from denying that the intervening land west of this boundary was part of the " seashore "; and that the plaintiffs were entitled to unrestricted access over the intervening land to the sea.

In *Rudd* v. *Bowles*[19] leases of four new houses with back gardens, bounded at the rear by land of the lessor, were granted by reference to a plan, on which a strip, part of the lessor's land at the back and running along the boundaries of the gardens, but not mentioned in the body of the lease, was shown coloured. Except through the houses themselves there was no other means of access to the gardens, and each garden had a gate opening into the strip. In the circumstances it was held that each lease contained an implied grant of a right of way

15 (1872) L.R. 7 Exch. 298.
16 (1823) 2 B. & C. 96.
17 *Harding* v. *Wilson* and *Espley* v. *Wilkes* were referred to by Cave and A. L. Smith JJ. in *Roe* v. *Siddons* (1888) 22 Q.B.D. 224, but the decision ultimately turned on another point. See also *Cooke* v. *Ingram* (1893) 68 L.T. 671.
18 [1905] 2 Ch. 164.
19 [1912] 2 Ch. 60.

over the strip, the grounds being that, reading the leases in the light of the surrounding circumstances, an intention to grant such a right must necessarily be inferred, and that the colouring on the plan was intended to denote a way or passage, either made or intended to be made, along the backs of the gardens.

It is sometimes a question whether, in parcels, such words as " as the same was late in the occupation of X " are merely additional words of identification, or import that the property is to be held with or subject to the rights that affected it when occupied by X. It seems that such words will generally be regarded as words of identification.[20]

2. From special circumstances

In *Hall* v. *Lund* [21] the owner of two mills had leased one to the defendant. In the lease he was described as a bleacher, and the premises leased as lately occupied by Pullan. Pullan had formerly carried on the business of a bleacher in this mill, and had drained his refuse into a watercourse which supplied the other mill. The lessor having afterwards sold the mills to the plaintiff, it was held that there had been an implied grant to the defendant of the right to use the watercourse as Pullan had used it,[22] for the purposes of the bleaching business, notwithstanding that such user caused a nuisance.

Parker J. said in *Jones* v. *Pritchard* [23]:

" If a man grant a divided moiety of an outside wall of his own house, with the intention of making such a wall a party-wall between such house and an adjoining house to be built by the grantee, the law will, I think, imply the grant and reservation in favour of the grantor and grantee respectively of such easements as may be necessary to carry out what was the common intention of the parties with regard to the user of the wall; the nature of those easements varying with the particular circumstances of the case."

On the other hand, in *Lyttelton Times Co. Ltd.* v. *Warners Ltd.*,[24] which was an action by a lessee of part of a building to restrain the commission by the lessor of a nuisance by noise on the rest, it appeared that, when the lease was negotiated, both parties had agreed to a

---

20 *Martyr* v. *Lawrence* (1864) 2 De G.J. & S. 261 (not in fact a case of easement); *Polden* v. *Bastard* (1865) L.R. 1 Q.B. 156.

21 (1863) 1 H. & C. 676.

22 The grant would not, *semble*, have extended to a nuisance caused by some different method of working afterward adopted; see *Pwllbach Colliery Co.* v. *Woodman* [1915] A.C. 634, 648.

23 [1908] 1 Ch. 630, 635. Subject, however, to such easements, the owner of each moiety may deal with it as he pleases, and if he does with it only what it was at the time of the grant in the contemplation of the parties that he should do, and is guilty of no negligence or want of reasonable care or precaution, he cannot be liable for nuisance entailed on the grantee (*ibid.* p. 636). In this case there was an implied reservation as well as an implied grant; see p. 108, *post.*

24 [1907] A.C. 476.

rebuilding of the premises on the terms that the lessee company was to rent from the lessor the upper floors as additional bedrooms for its adjoining hotel, and the lessor was to use the ground floor as a printing works, both parties believing, wrongly as it turned out, that this would not cause any nuisance. There was no evidence that the printing works were carried on improperly, and the action failed because the lessor company was doing nothing more than what had been contemplated, and so must be taken to have impliedly reserved the right to do what it was doing. "If it be true that neither has done or asks to do anything which was not contemplated by both, neither can have any right against the other." [25] This case is authority for the proposition that a nuisance may be legalised by grant.

In *Pwllbach Colliery Co.* v. *Woodman* [26] Lord Parker said: "The law will readily imply the grant or reservation of such easements as may be necessary to give effect to the common intention of the parties to a grant of real property, with reference to the manner or purposes in and for which the land granted or some land retained by the grantor is to be used." [27] Lord Parker referred to *Jones* v. *Pritchard* [28] and *Lyttelton Times Co. Ltd.* v. *Warners Ltd.* [24] He added:

> "It is essential for this purpose that the parties should intend that the subject of the grant or the land retained by the grantor should be used in some definite and particular manner. It is not enough that the subject of the grant or the land retained should be intended to be used in a manner which may or may not involve this definite and particular use."

In that case it was held that a lease which recognised that the lessee would, or might, carry on mining operations did not grant by implication the right to create a nuisance by dissipating coal dust over the lessor's land by the use of screening plant installed for the purposes of mining operations begun after the date of the lease. There was no evidence that the trade could not be carried on otherwise.

In *Keewatin Power Co.* v. *Lake of the Woods Milling Co.* [29] a grant by the Crown of land which included a mill and artificial channels from a lake was held to include, by implication from the circumstances, the

---

25 [1907] A.C. 481, *per* Lord Loreburn.
26 [1915] A.C. 634, 646.
27 In *Vanderpant* v. *Mayfair Hotel Co.* [1930] 1 Ch. 138, which was an action for nuisance by noise from, *inter alia*, the kitchen of a large hotel, the defendant attempted, unsuccessfully on the facts, to apply this principle to a case where, before the hotel was built, the plaintiff had secured, by agreement, immunity from the obstruction of light to his house by any future building other than the hotel, and certain other rights, all of which it was alleged were granted on the understanding that the part of the hotel opposite should be used as a kitchen. See also *Horton* v. *Tidd* (1965) 196 E.G. 697; the grant of a lease to a cricket club did not carry an implied right to hit cricket balls into adjoining premises.
28 [1908] 1 Ch. 630.
29 [1930] A.C. 640.

right to use, for the purposes of the mill, all the water that the channels, at the time of the grant, could bring.

In *White* v. *Taylor* (*No.* 2)[1] in which the plaintiffs claimed a *profit à prendre* of grazing sheep, Buckley J. also referred to Lord Parker's dictum in *Pwllbach Colliery Co.* v. *Woodman*[2] and said that the court should be no less ready to give effect to the common intention of the parties in resolving a latent ambiguity in the language than in perfecting the transaction by implying what they had omitted to say. Buckley J. held, applying Lord Parker's dictum and also *Jones* v. *Pritchard*,[3] that the plaintiffs, who had established their right to depasture sheep, were entitled, as an ancillary right under an implied grant, to water the sheep so depastured by means of troughs supplied by carted water and to do anything else necessary for the proper care and maintenance of the sheep.

3. Special immunities under the doctrine of non-derogation from grant

Reference has already been made, in considering in Chapter 1 the characteristics of an easement, to the doctrine of non-derogation from grant from which can arise the same situation as if an easement had been granted, although none has been.[4] The doctrine is most conveniently considered by reference to the judgment of Parker J. in *Browne* v. *Flower*.[5] His Lordship said[6]:

" The plaintiffs next relied on the maxim that no one can be allowed to derogate from his own grant. This maxim is generally quoted as explaining certain implications which may arise from the fact that, or the circumstances under which, an owner of land grants or demises part of it, retaining the remainder in his own hands. The real difficulty is in each case to ascertain how far such implications extend. It is well settled that such a grant or demise will (unless there be something in the terms of the grant or demise or in the circumstances of the particular case rebutting the implication) impliedly confer on the grantee or lessee, as appurtenant to the land granted or demised to him, easements over the land retained corresponding to the continuous or apparent quasi-easements enjoyed at the time of the grant or demise by the property granted or demised over the property retained."

Parker J. was here referring to the rule in *Wheeldon* v. *Burrows*[7] and he proceeded to give examples of the manner in which the easements might arise by reference to the rule and to point out that the terms of

1 [1969] 1 Ch. 160, 183, 184.
2 [1915] A.C. 634, 646.
3 [1908] 1 Ch. 630.
4 *Ante*, p. 43.
5 [1911] 1 Ch. 219.
6 [1911] 1 Ch. 224, 225.
7 (1879) 12 Ch.D. 31. See *post*, pp. 92–94.

the grant or demise or the special circumstances of the case might, on the other hand, rebut the implication. His Lordship then continued [8]:

" But the implications usually explained by the maxim that no one can derogate from his own grant do not stop short with easements. Under certain circumstances there will be implied on the part of the grantor or lessor obligations which restrict the user of the land retained by him further than can be explained by the implication of any easement known to the law. Thus, if the grant or demise be made for a particular purpose, the grantor or lessor comes under an obligation not to use the land retained by him in such a way as to render the land granted or demised unfit or materially less fit for the particular purpose for which the grant or demise was made."

His Lordship went on to refer to examples as follows [9]:

" In *Aldin* v. *Latimer Clark, Muirhead & Co.*,[10] land having been demised for the purpose of carrying on the business of a timber merchant, the lessor came under an obligation not to build on land retained by him so as to interrupt the access of air to sheds on the demised property used for drying timber, although the law does not recognise any easement of air unless it comes through or to some defined passage or aperture. Similarly in the case of *Grosvenor Hotel Co.* v. *Hamilton* [11] the lessee was held entitled to prevent the lessor from using property retained by him in such a way as to cause on the demised property vibrations which did not amount to a legal nuisance, though there is no such easement known to the law as an easement of freedom from vibration any more than there is an easement of freedom from noise. Once again, though possibly there may not be known to the law any easement of light for special purposes, still the lease of a building to be used for a special purpose requiring an extraordinary amount of light might well be held to preclude the grantor from diminishing the light passing to the grantee's windows, even in cases where the diminution would not be such as to create a nuisance within the meaning of the recent decisions: see *Herz* v. *Union Bank of London*.[12] In none of these cases would any easement be created, but the obligation implied on the part of the lessor or grantor would be analogous to that which arises from a restrictive covenant. It is to be observed that in the several cases to which I have referred the lessor had done or proposed to do something which rendered or would render the demised

---

[8] [1911] 1 Ch. 225, 226. See also *Popplewell* v. *Hodkinson* (1869) L.R. 4 Ex. 248, *post*, p. 288; *Robinson* v. *Kilvert* (1889) 41 Ch.D. 88.
[9] [1911] 1 Ch. 226.
[10] [1894] 2 Ch. 437.
[11] [1894] 2 Q.B. 836.
[12] (1854) 2 Giff. 686.

premises unfit or materially less fit to be used for the particular purpose for which the demise was made." [13]

In *Harmer* v. *Jumbil (Nigeria) Tin Areas Ltd.*[14] it was established that the application of the rule against derogation from grant is not confined to physical interference with the land granted. Land was leased with the express purpose that it should be used for the purposes of an explosives magazine, and further land was held under a tenancy agreement which permitted the erection thereon of a shed for packing explosives. Subsequently adjoining land was leased to the defendant company by a lessor who was the successor in title of both the grantor of the lease of the site of the explosives magazine and the grantor of the tenancy of the land on which the shed was sited. The defendant proposed to erect buildings which would have occasioned the withdrawal of the plaintiff's licence for the magazine and packing shed under the Explosives Act 1875. The Court of Appeal held that in the circumstances in which the lease was granted there must be implied on the part of the lessor an obligation not to do anything which would violate the conditions under which the licence was held, so as to cause a forfeiture of it; that the acts of the defendant would, if done by the lessor, have been in derogation of his grant; and that inasmuch as the defendant was for this purpose in the same position as the lessor, the acts of the defendant must be regarded as being done by him. This case is not only authority for the proposition that a successor in title of the grantor may be restrained from acting in derogation of the grant; it is also apparently the only case in which a right of immunity acquired under the doctrine of non-derogation has been successfully asserted by a successor in title of the grantee. It is thought, however, that, at least so long as the original purpose of the grant is adhered to,[15] the right, even if it is of a kind not recognised as an easement, attaches to the premises granted in the same way as an easement.

The statement by Parker J. in *Browne* v. *Flower*[16] that the obligation implied on the part of the lessor or grantor would be analogous to that which arises from a restrictive covenant requires qualification, for unlike the obligation which arises under a restrictive covenant, the obligation implied on the part of the lessor or grantor binds successors without notice. This appears from *Cable* v. *Bryant*.[17] A stable and an adjoining yard were in common ownership, the yard being subject to a lease. The freeholder let the stable, in which were two windows or ventilators, to the plaintiff. A few months later the freeholder conveyed the yard to the defendant, the lessee joining to surrender the lease. The

13 See also *Frederick Betts Ltd.* v. *Pickfords Ltd.* [1906] 2 Ch. 87.
14 [1921] 1 Ch. 200.
15 If the premises were used for some different purpose, the right might well be considered to have been abandoned.
16 [1911] 1 Ch. 219, 226.
17 [1908] 1 Ch. 259.

defendant then erected a hoarding in the yard close to the stable, so blocking the windows or the ventilators; and the plaintiff obtained an injunction. The immunity, so recognised, of interference with air and light appears to have had the characteristics of an easement, but it was argued that as the yard was let when the plaintiff took his lease, no implication of the grant of an easement could arise, because the easement could not have taken effect in possession. Neville J. expressed no opinion as to this, and decided the case on the principle of non-derogation from grant; that is, on the ground that the lessor, having let the stable, was under an obligation not to interfere with its reasonable use for the purposes of a stable for which it was granted. He held that the rule against derogation from grant did not depend on implied covenant but was a rule of law and that the obligation to which it gave rise affected a successor in title, with or without notice.

In *Ward* v. *Kirkland*,[18] in which the plaintiff claimed a right to go onto the defendant's property for the purpose of doing certain works to the advantage of the plaintiff's property, Ungoed-Thomas J. said [19] that the question of derogation from grant generally arose in cases where the grantor did something on his own property which defeated the enjoyment of the property granted as it existed and was contemplated at the time of the grant. His Lordship said that clearly there was a distinction between the two categories of case, but it seemed to him that the underlying principle of the doctrine applied to both categories. It was (he said) with hesitation and with an appreciation of the difficulties that he came to that conclusion, and he preferred, in upholding the plaintiff's claim, to rely upon the operation of the general words under section 62 of the Law of Property Act 1925; so that his views on the operation of the doctrine were *obiter dictum*.

In *Woodhouse & Co. Ltd.* v. *Kirkland (Derby) Ltd.*,[20] however, Plowman J. held, distinguishing *Cable* v. *Bryant*,[21] that, although a purely negative right over the servient or quasi-servient tenement might be acquired under the doctrine forbidding derogation from grant in a manner which was indistinguishable from an implied grant, this was not true of a positive right, such as a right of way. The plaintiff company's premises enjoyed a right of way over a passageway belonging to the defendant company which gave access from the plaintiff's yard to the public highway. In 1965 the plaintiff acquired from the defendant company a small strip of land near the entrance to the passageway from the yard in order to improve the access from the yard. The plaintiff, having acquired the strip of land, increased the width of the gateway leading into its yard. The plaintiff alleged that the defendant was aware

18 [1967] Ch. 194.
19 [1967] Ch. 227.
20 [1970] 1 W.L.R. 1185. Rather surprisingly, *Ward* v. *Kirkland* [1967] Ch. 194 was not cited in argument.
21 [1908] 1 Ch. 259.

of the plaintiff's intention to increase the width of the gateway and must be taken to have increased the width of the right of way by opening it out at the end where the plaintiff's gates were situated. The defendant erected posts so as to bar entry to the yard except over the original width of the passageway. Plowman J. held that the 1965 conveyance did not operate as an implied grant of an extended right of way, though he did find that the erection of the posts amounted to a derogation from grant in that they rendered the land conveyed in 1965 materially less fit for the purpose for which the grant was made, namely, to improve the access to the yard.

The immunities acquired by virtue of the doctrine depend upon the common intention, to be gathered either from the express words of the grant or the circumstances in which the grant was made.[22] Prima facie the obligation involved in the grant for use for a particular business is confined to the ordinary purposes of that business, and does not extend to special branches of it which require extraordinary protection.[23] Furthermore, no act can be complained of, under the doctrine, which does not make the land granted unfit for the particular purpose for which it was granted. In *Browne* v. *Flower*,[24] for example, where the plaintiff was tenant of a residential flat, and the landlords and those representing them had erected a staircase leading from the outside to the flat above, so affecting the plaintiff's privacy, the plaintiff's action failed because, although there had been interference with her amenities, the land was still no less capable of being used as a flat than it had been before.

4. The rule in Wheeldon v. Burrows

The rule in *Wheeldon* v. *Burrows*[25] is limited to continuous and apparent easements impliedly granted when the owner of a piece of land grants away part of it. As appears from the judgment of Thesiger L.J. in that case, this common law rule for determining what easements are implied in favour of the grantee against the grantor is really a branch of the general rule against derogation from grant. The facts of the case are less important than the rule but may be shortly stated. A workshop and an adjacent piece of land belonging to the same owner were put up for sale by auction. The workshop was not then sold, but the piece of

---

[22] *Birmingham, Dudley and District Banking Co.* v. *Ross* (1888) 38 Ch.D. 295; *Myers* v. *Catterson* (1889) 43 Ch.D. 470; *Corbett* v. *Jonas* [1892] 3 Ch. 137; *Lyttelton Times Co.* v. *Warners Ltd.* [1907] A.C. 476, 481.

[23] *Aldin* v. *Latimer Clark, Muirhead & Co.* [1894] 2 Ch. 437, 444; *Robinson* v. *Kilvert* (1889) 41 Ch.D. 88.

[24] [1911] 1 Ch. 219; see *ante*, p. 43. See also *O'Cedar Ltd.* v. *Slough Trading Co.* [1927] 2 K.B. 123 (use of adjoining land in a manner calculated to raise the fire insurance premium for the demised building held not to be a derogation); *Port* v. *Griffith* [1938] 1 All E.R. 295 (similar decision as to a lease of adjoining premises for a business which the plaintiff was bound to carry on under her lease); *Kelly* v. *Battershell* [1949] 2 All E.R. 830 (similar decision as to the incorporation of the rest of a house, in which the plaintiff had a flat, into a hotel on adjoining premises).

[25] (1879) 12 Ch.D. 31.

land was, and it was soon afterwards conveyed to the purchaser. A month after this the vendor agreed to sell the workshop to another person, and in due course conveyed it to him. The workshop had windows overlooking and receiving their light from the piece of land first sold, and Bacon V.-C. and the Court of Appeal held that, as the vendor had not when he conveyed the piece of land reserved the right of access of light to the windows, no such right passed to the purchaser of the workshop, and that the purchaser of the piece of land could build so as to obstruct the windows of the workshop. The case was thus itself concerned with an alleged implied reservation, but Thesiger L.J.'s judgment (which was the judgment of the court) stated the rules governing implied grant as well as implied reservation. His Lordship said [26]:

> " We have had a considerable number of cases cited to us, and out of them I think that two propositions may be stated as what I may call the general rules governing cases of this kind. The first of these rules is, that on the grant by the owner of a tenement of part of that tenement as it is then used and enjoyed, there will pass to the grantee all those continuous and apparent easements (by which, of course, I mean quasi-easements), or, in other words, all those easements which are necessary to the reasonable enjoyment of the property granted, and which have been and are at the time of the grant used by the owners of the entirety for the benefit of the part granted. The second proposition is that, if the grantor intends to reserve any right over the tenement granted, it is his duty to reserve it expressly in the grant. Those are the general rules governing cases of this kind, but the second of those rules is subject to certain exceptions. One of those exceptions is the well-known exception which attaches to cases of what are called ways of necessity; and I do not dispute for a moment that there may be, and probably are, certain other exceptions, to which I shall refer before I close my observations upon this case.
>
> " Both of the general rules which I have mentioned are founded upon a maxim which is as well established by authority as it is consonant to reason and common sense, *viz.* that a grantor shall not derogate from his grant."

Thesiger L.J. proceeded to review the leading cases on the subject,[27] including those dealing with ways of necessity, and then continued [28]:

> " These cases . . . support the propositions that in the case of a grant you may imply a grant of such continuous and apparent ease-

---

[26] (1879) 12 Ch.D. 49.

[27] See in particular *Suffield* v. *Brown* (1864) 4 De G.J. & S. 185 and the speech of Lord Westbury at p. 194, from which Thesiger L.J. in the passage cited above freely quoted.

[28] (1879) 12 Ch.D. 58, 59.

ments or such easements as are necessary to the reasonable enjoyment of the property conveyed, and have in fact been enjoyed
during the unity of ownership, but that, with the exception which I
have referred to of easements of necessity, you cannot imply a
similar reservation in favour of the grantor of land." [29]

In *Ward* v. *Kirkland* [30] in which the plaintiff, as stated above,[31]
claimed the right to go onto the defendant's property for the purpose of
doing certain works for the advantage of the plaintiff's cottage, Ungoed-
Thomas J. referred to the passage in *Wheeldon* v. *Burrows* [32] last quoted
and said that, reading that passage on its own, on first impression, it
would appear that the " easements which are necessary to the reasonable enjoyment of the property conveyed " might be a separate class
from " continuous and apparent easements." His Lordship said that it
had been recognised that there was some difficulty in those descriptions,
and that it had been suggested that perhaps the " easements necessary to
the reasonable enjoyment of the property conveyed " might refer to negative easements, whereas the case with which his Lordship was dealing
was concerned with positive easements. However that might be, there is
no reported case in which positive easements not " continuous and
apparent " has been held to come within the doctrine of *Wheeldon* v.
Burrows.[33] Ungoed-Thomas J. took the words " continuous and apparent " to be directed to there being on the servient tenement a feature
which would be seen on inspection and which was neither transitory nor
intermittent; for example, drains and paths, as contrasted with the bowsprits of ships overhanging a piece of land. On the facts of the case
before him, his Lordship held that there was no continuous and
apparent easement within the requirements of *Wheeldon* v. *Burrows*,[33]
and so the easement claimed was not created by implication of law.

It is suggested that a negative easement acquired on the disposition
of part of a tenement is more correctly attributed to the operation of the
rule that no one can be allowed to derogate from his grant than to an
implied grant.[34] In other words, while the owner of a house served by
a drive and overlooking a field can fairly be said, on selling the house
without the drive, to have intended to grant with the house a right of
way over the drive, it seems more natural, if he sells the house and retains
the field, to ascribe to him the intention, not actually to grant with the

---

[29] See also *Bayley* v. *Great Western Railway* (1884) 26 Ch.D. 434, 452, *per* Bowen L.J.;
Brown v. *Alabaster* (1888) 37 Ch.D. 490; *Birmingham, Dudley and District Banking
Co.* v. *Ross* (1888) 38 Ch.D. 295, 308, *per* Cotton L.J.; *Nicholls* v. *Nicholls* (1899)
81 L.T. 811; *Browne* v. *Flower* [1911] 1 Ch. 219, 225, when Parker J. tacitly converted " continuous and apparent " into " continuous or apparent."

[30] [1967] Ch. 194, 224–226.

[31] See *ante*, p. 91.

[32] (1879) 12 Ch.D. 31, 58–59.

[33] (1879) 12 Ch.D. 31.

[34] See *ante*, p. 88. Although the principle of derogation from grant applies to both
positive and negative easements, generally it is applied to negative easements: *Ward*
v. *Kirkland* [1967] Ch. 194, 226–227, *per* Ungoed-Thomas J.

house a right to light, but to charge the field with the uninterrupted passage of light to the house. The result, however, appears to be the same on either view. The manner in which different types of positive and negative easements are acquired on a disposition of part will now be considered.

Positive easements

(a) *Rights of way.* *Borman* v. *Griffith* [35] provides a clear formulation of the principles under consideration and shows that the rule in *Wheeldon* v. *Burrows* [36] remains of importance in spite of the statutory importation of general words by section 6 of the Conveyancing Act 1881, and its successor, section 62 of the Law of Property Act 1925, if only because the general words will not always be imported. In *Borman* v. *Griffiths* [35] A had been the owner of a private park, in which a drive ran from the main road past the front door of a house (formerly a gardener's lodge) called The Gardens, and on to another house called The Hall. In 1923 A agreed under hand to demise to the plaintiff for seven years The Gardens with the adjoining paddock, orchard and gardens, but not the drive. At this time the plaintiff was making, and he afterwards completed, an unmetalled way leading from the main road to the paddock at the rear; but there was no road across the paddock, and the plaintiff used the drive, which was the natural way of approaching The Gardens, until it was obstructed by the defendant, who had taken a lease of The Hall and the rest of the park, including the drive, in 1926. Maugham J., giving judgment for the plaintiff, decided, first, that no general words were to be imported into the agreement, for an agreement for a lease exceeding a term of three years is not, for the purposes of section 62 of the Law of Property Act 1925, a " conveyance " as defined in section 205 (1) (ii) [37]; and he proceeded [58]:

> " In my opinion, however, the position of the court in granting specific performance of a contract such as this is the same in effect, so far as regards rights of way, as if there had been, before the coming into force of the Conveyancing Act 1881,[39] a conveyance of this property with no mention of rights of way: in other words, the doctrine that a grantor may not derogate from his own grant would apply in the circumstances of this case. The plaintiff being entitled to specific performance, the court would decide that he must be given all such rights of way as, according to the doctrine of the court in regard to implied grants, would pass upon a conveyance or demise. In my view, the principles laid down in such

[35] [1930] 1 Ch. 493.
[36] (1879) 12 Ch.D. 31.
[37] See *post*, pp. 122 *et seq.*
[38] [1930] 1 Ch. 493, 498. The italics are the editor's.
[39] *i.e.* s. 6, repealed and reproduced, as to conveyances made after 1881, by s. 62 of the L.P. Act 1925.

cases as *Wheeldon* v. *Burrows*,[40] *Brown* v. *Alabaster*,[41] and *Nicholls* v. *Nicholls*,[42] are applicable. Without going through all the cases in detail, I may state the principle as follows—namely, that *where, as in the present case, two properties belonging to a single owner and about to be granted are separated by a common road, or where a plainly visible road exists over the one for the apparent use of the other, and that road is necessary for the reasonable enjoyment of the property, a right to use the road will pass with the quasi-dominant tenement, unless by the terms of the contract that right is excluded*: and in my opinion, if the present position were that the plaintiff were claiming against the lessor specific performance of the agreement of October 10, 1923, he would be entitled to be given a right of way for all reasonable purposes along the drive, including the part that passes the farm on the way to the orchard.

" It is true that the easement, or, rather, quasi-easement, is not continuous. But the authorities are sufficient to show that a grantor of property in circumstances where an obvious, *i.e.*, visible and made road is necessary for the reasonable enjoyment of the property by the grantee, must be taken prima facie to have intended to grant a right to use it."

In *Goldberg* v. *Edwards*[43] the formula italicised above was accepted by the Court of Appeal, subject to the possible addition[44] of the words " and convenient " after " reasonable." In that case, where an annexe to a house was let separately from the house and access to the annexe was either through the house or (much less conveniently) along a passage outside, it was held on the facts that access through the house was not necessary for the reasonable or convenient enjoyment of the annexe. Evershed M.R. said[45]:

" In my judgment it does not follow that a way through the front door of another's premises and through the ground floor and passages is even prima facie necessary for the reasonable or convient enjoyment of the premises behind. It would take strong evidence to show that it was so, for the right to pass through another's premises, particularly when they are business premises, is, I think, a considerable burden upon the servient tenement in any case."

In *Brown* v. *Alabaster*[46] the lessee of two plots of land, A and B, had built on B two houses, *Westbourne* and *Cottisbrook,* each with a

40 (1879) 12 Ch.D. 31.
41 (1888) 37 Ch.D. 490.
42 (1899) 81 L.T. 811.
43 [1950] Ch. 247.
44 Taken from a passage in previous editions of this book.
45 [1950] Ch. 247, 254.
46 (1888) 37 Ch.D. 490.

garden to which the only means of access, except through the houses themselves or a narrow passage with two steps down into the garden, was through a gate at the back and thence along an enclosed way, part of A, to a street. It was held that an assignment of the lease of the two houses included a right of way over the way on A. Kay J. said [47]:

"It seems to me that the law is this—that a particular formed way to an entrance to premises like these ' Westbourne ' and ' Cottis-brook ' which leads to gates in a wall, part of these demised premises, and without which those gates would be perfectly useless, may pass . . . by implied grant without any large general words, or indeed without any general words at all . . . That it was intended, looking at all the facts that the persons to whom ' Westbourne ' and ' Cottisbrook ' were conveyed should have the use of those two gates and of this back-way, is, to my mind, beyond all doubt. Then although I agree that it is not for all purposes a way of necessity, do I want an express grant? It seems to me to be clear on the authorities that an express grant is not wanted in such a case as this."

In Nicholls v. Nicholls [48] an agreement for the partition of two houses behind which was a formed road was held to include an agreement to grant to each house a right of way over the road. Stirling J. said that although in general a way not being a way of necessity does not pass by implication, still it was established by many cases that a formed road over one tenement to and for the apparent use of the other does.

If the land disposed of can be reached by two formed ways over the land retained, and has no other means of access, the purchaser is entitled to a way of necessity over one of them, to be selected by the grantor.[49]

Maugham J., in Borman v. Griffith,[50] referred to a " road," but the implication can equally apply to a passage or path if the use of this appears to be necessary for the reasonable or convenient enjoyment of the property. In Hansford v. Jago,[1] where a right of way was held to have passed, by implication, over an enclosed strip of land, not made up but constituting, as in Brown v. Alabaster,[2] practically the only means of access to the backyards of the cottages in respect of which the right was claimed, Russell J. said [3]:

"What is required in the case of a quasi-easement is the quality of being apparent. That quality may be arrived at in different ways, and, no doubt, the easiest case is that of a made-up road; it is most

[47] (1888) 37 Ch.D. 507.
[48] (1899) 81 L.T. 811.
[49] Bolton v. Bolton (1879) 11 Ch.D. 968; and see Re Hughes and Ashley's Contract [1900] 2 Ch. 595.
[50] [1930] 1 Ch. 493; see p. 95, ante.
[1] [1921] 1 Ch. 322.
[2] (1888) 37 Ch.D. 490; see p. 96, ante.
[3] [1921] 1 Ch. 342.

important, if not essential, that the road should be made up when it is sought to establish the apparency of a quasi-easement of way over an unenclosed piece of land. But when every other possible indication is present as here, and they all point to a defined and enclosed strip having been set aside to provide an access to the rear of certain houses, I certainly decline to hold, unless compelled to do so by authority, that the absence of a made-up road prevented the establishment of an implied grant. . . . It is often very important that there should be a made-up road, especially where the right is claimed over unenclosed land, but, where there are other indicia to show that a strip of land was intended to be used as a way, it is not necessary that there should be a made-up road to establish the right." [4]

It appears moreover from *Donnelly* v. *Adams* [5] that if the termini of the alleged way raise the obvious inference that a way between them was intended to be included, the way itself need not be marked out at all. In that case, where a lease had been granted of a house with a back garden and a garden wall, in which was a door opening on a piece of waste ground which was retained by the lessor and had on its further side a wall in which were two gates opening on public passages, the Irish Court of Appeal inferred, from the circumstances and evidence, an intention to grant a right of way for the purpose of carrying coal across the waste land between the garden door to one of the passages, by such route and through such of the two gates as the lessor should from time to time appoint.[6]

In *Re Walmsley and Shaw's Contract* [7] where a plot of land was sold under a contract not referring, either expressly or generally, to rights of way, Eve J. held that the vendor was entitled to exclude from the conveyance the statutory general words and to substitute " together with all . . . easements rights and appurtenances . . . appertaining or appurtenant thereto "; so (presumably), in effect, excluding all rights not already appurtenant, including a right of way, which the purchaser claimed, over a farm cart-track, not made up and not in any sense constructed as a means of access to the property sold. This case, *Bolton* v. *Bolton* [8] and *Re Peck and London School Board*,[9] which the learned judge followed, may appear to be authorities for the proposition that a contract to sell a piece of land " with its appurtenances " is a contract to

---

[4] See also *Rudd* v. *Bowles* [1912] 2 Ch. 60, referred to *ante*, p. 85, where the further side of the strip was not fenced off from the remaining land of the lessor.

[5] [1905] 1 I.R. 154.

[6] Whether *Polden* v. *Bastard* (1865) L.R. 1 Q.B. 156, where it was decided that a devise of a house did not include the right to go from it (whether by a formed or visible path does not appear) across the garden of an adjoining house of the testatrix to fetch water from a pump there, would be decided in the same way now, *quaere*.

[7] [1917] 1 Ch. 93.

[8] (1879) 11 Ch.D. 968.

[9] [1893] 2 Ch. 315.

sell the land with such easements, if any, as are already appurtenant to it (these would pass automatically) and nothing else, but it is thought that they are not. Eve J. said that he thought that the contract was, as in the other cases just referred to, a contract for the sale of the premises with such rights of way only as were legally appendant or appurtenant to them; and this part of the judgment, taken by itself, appears to suggest that a contract for sale, at any rate a contract to sell " with appurtenances," negatives any implication of intention to grant *de novo* a right not already appurtenant; but, if that is what is meant, the learned judge would not have gone on to point out, as he did, that when a property with a particular mode of access apparently and actually constructed as a means of access to it is contracted to be sold, there is a strong presumption that the means of access is included in the sale, but that the farm track there in question was not so constructed.

(b) *Drainage.* Where the property disposed of is drained through a pipe or the like in the property retained, the right to continue to drain will pass by implication.[10] The same, no doubt, applies to eavesdrop.[11]

(c) *Right to withdraw support.* The grant of minerals separately from the surface does not, under the general law, include by implication the right to withdraw support from the surface.[12]

Negative easements

(a) *Water supply.* It appears to be undoubted that where water is conveyed to the property granted through a pipe or the like in the land retained, the right to the continued flow of water through the pipe will pass by implication. In *Watts* v. *Kelson*[13] the owner of two pieces of land having made on one a tank, fed by a natural stream, from which two pipes carried water to cattle sheds on the other, sold first the land with the cattle sheds to the plaintiff, and then the land with the tank to a predecessor in title of the defendant. The plaintiff was held entitled to the same flow of water through the pipes as was enjoyed at the time of the sale to him, and this notwithstanding that at the time of the action the sheds had been replaced by a house and the water was used for domestic purposes. In this case the land first sold appears to have had the exclusive right to the water in the tank, and in such a case the use to which the water is put from time to time is plainly immaterial.[14]

---

[10] *Pyer* v. *Carter* (1857) 1 H. & N. 916; *Ewart* v. *Cochrane* (1861) 4 Macq. 117; 10 W.R. 3.

[11] See *Pyer* v. *Carter, supra.*

[12] *Butterknowle Colliery Co.* v. *Bishop Auckland Industrial Co-operative Society* [1906] A.C. 305. The rights in this respect of the National Coal Board are set out in Part II of Sched. 2 to the Coal Act 1938.

[13] (1870) 6 Ch.App. 166.

[14] *Cf. Holker* v. *Porritt* (1875) L.R. 10 Exch. 59, 62. As to the effect of a grant of the right " as now enjoyed in common with others having the same right " to receive spring water through a pipe, see *Beauchamp* v. *Frome R.D.C.* [1938] 1 All E.R. 595.

In *Schwann* v. *Cotton* [15] at the death of a testator there were three adjoining properties, Nugent's, Malta and Braxton. An underground pipe conveyed water from a well in Nugent's, through Braxton, which belonged to the testator, to Malta, which also belonged to him. The testator having left a will giving Malta and Braxton respectively to the predecessors in title of the plaintiff and the defendant, it was held that Malta had acquired, by implication, against Braxton the right to the uninterrupted flow of such water as came through the pipe. The possibility that the owner of Nugent's, who was not a party, might have the right to stop the water at the well made no difference.

In *Nicholas* v. *Chamberlain* [16] " It was held by all the Court upon demurrer, that if one erect a house and build a conduit thereto in another part of his land, and convey water by pipes to the house, and afterwards sell the house with the appurtenances, excepting the land, or sell the land to another, reserving to himself the house, [17] the conduit and pipes pass with the house; because it is necessary, *et quasi* appendant thereto; and he shall have liberty by law to dig in the land for amending the pipes, or making them new, as the case may require." In *Wheeldon* v. *Burrows* [18] James L.J. suggested that what was thought by the court to pass was not merely the right to the passage of water, but the conduit itself as a corporeal part of the house [19]; and thus it may be that on a conveyance of a house, cisterns, sewers, gutters, drains, etc., serving the property conveyed exclusively may pass as part and parcel of that property under the general words imported by section 62 (2) of the Law of Property Act 1925. In *Schwann* v. *Cotton* [20] it was thought unnecessary to consider whether the property in the pipe itself, so far as it passed through Malta, vested in the devisee of Braxton.

No right will be implied, however, where the water is sent on the land granted for the purpose of draining the land retained, and not for the purpose of supplying the land granted [21]; and where the owner of land made a conduit conducting the water to a mill-pond on his land, and sold land abutting on the pond, no right passed by implication, or under the statutory general words, to have the flow to the pond continued, or to take water from the pond for the purpose of watering cattle if there should be any water to take. [22]

(b) *Support.* Where one of two buildings in common ownership and supporting each other is disposed of and the other retained, or both are disposed of at the same time, each acquires, by implied grant or reser-

15 [1916] 2 Ch. 459. See also *Westwood* v. *Heywood* [1921] 2 Ch. 130.
16 (1606) Cro.Jac. 121, 122 (Court of King's Bench).
17 See *post*, p. 108.
18 (1879) 12 Ch.D. 31.
19 *Cf. Truckell* v. *Stock* [1957] 1 W.L.R. 161, where the footings and eaves of a house, extending beyond the boundary shown on the plan, were held to have been included in the conveyance of the house. And see p. 15, *ante.*
20 [1916] 2 Ch. 459, see p. 16, *ante.*
21 *Bartlett* v. *Tottenham* [1932] 1 Ch. 114.
22 *Burrows* v. *Lang* [1901] 2 Ch. 502.

vation, a right of continued support against the other.[23] It seems that a right of support arises also where a building is disposed of separately from vacant land adjoining.[24] Furthermore, where the owner of land sells or leases part of it to someone who is known to be acquiring it for building purposes, the building when erected acquires, prima facie, by implication a right of support against the adjoining land, or the sub-jacent minerals if these are owned and reserved by the grantor.[25] This implication may, however, as always, be negatived by the circumstances. It seems that if, at the time of a contract for the grant of land, it is known to the purchaser that the grantor, or a purchaser from him, intends to build in a certain way on adjoining land of the grantor, the grantor or his purchaser is entitled to build as intended, and in so doing to let down the surface of the land granted, whether built on or not [26]; and that if the grantee has notice of a general intention to build on the retained land, the land granted is liable to such deprivation of support as reasonable building on the land retained entails.[27]

(c) *Light.* It is settled that, on a disposition of a building deriving light from adjoining land [28] of the disposing party, the building acquires prima facie, by implication, a right to light over the adjoining land. Thus in *Swansborough* v. *Coventry* [29] Tindall C.J. said:

" It is well established by the decided cases, that where the same person possesses a house, having the actual use and enjoyment of certain lights, and also possesses the adjoining land, and sells the house to another person, although the lights be new, he cannot, nor can anyone who claims under him, build upon the adjoining land so as to obstruct or interrupt the enjoyment of those lights."

So again, in *Leech* v. *Schweder* [30] Mellish L.J. said:

" It is perfectly established that if a man owns a house, and owns property of any other kind adjoining that house, and then

---

[23] *Richards* v. *Rose* (1853) 9 Exch. 218; *Dalton* v. *Angus* (1881) 6 App.Cas. 740, 792–793. No implication was made from a reversionary lease taking effect in possession 24 years after its date; *Howarth* v. *Armstrong* (1897) 77 L.T. 62.
[24] See *Shubrook* v. *Tufnell* (1882) 46 L.T. 886, and the cases in the next note.
[25] *Caledonian Ry.* v. *Sprot* (1856) 2 Macq. 449; *Rigby* v. *Bennett* (1882) 21 Ch.D. 559; *Siddons* v. *Short* (1877) 2 C.P.D. 572.
[26] *Murchie* v. *Black* (1865) 19 C.B.(N.S.) 190.
[27] *Rigby* v. *Bennett* (1882) 21 Ch.D. 559, *per* Cotton L.J. In this case the plaintiff agreed to take, and afterwards took, a lease requiring him to build to the satisfaction of the lessor. After the agreement by the plaintiff, the defendant entered into a similar agreement relating to adjoining land. The defendant then started to excavate for his building, and in so doing let down the house built by the plaintiff. The plaintiff had notice that some building was to be erected on the defendant's land, but there was no evidence that it was not possible to build on it without affecting the plaintiff's house. The defendant was held liable.
[28] The land need not be immediately adjoining; *Birmingham, Dudley and District Banking Co.* v. *Ross* (1888) 38 Ch.D. 295, 300, 312, 314.
[29] (1832) 9 Bing. 305, 309.
[30] (1874) 9 Ch.App. 463, 472. See also *Palmer* v. *Fletcher* (1663) 1 Lev. 122; *Rosewell* v. *Prior* (1701) 6 Mod.Rep. 116; *Bayley* v. *Great Western Ry.* (1884) 26 Ch.D. 434; *Myers* v. *Catterson* (1890) 43 Ch.D. 470; *Phillips* v. *Low* [1892] 1 Ch. 47; *Broom-field* v. *Williams* [1897] 1 Ch. 602; *Born* v. *Turner* [1900] 2 Ch. 211; *Pollard* v. *Gare* [1901] 1 Ch. 834; *Frederick Betts Ltd.* v. *Pickfords Ltd.* [1906] 2 Ch. 87.

either conveys the house in fee simple or demises it for a term of years to another person, a right to light unobstructed by anything to be erected on any land which at the time belonged to the grantor passes to the grantee."

This principle applies where at the time of the disposition, or, if this is preceded by an agreement, the agreement for it, the grantor knows that the land is being acquired for building purposes. In such a case the right attaches to the buildings when built.[31]

Where the building and the land are included in a mortgage, the implication arises on a mortgagee's authorised disposition of the building [32]; and also, it is submitted, on a similar disposition by the mortgagor, *e.g.* a lease granted under statutory powers, or otherwise binding on the mortgagee. It seems that a disposition, not binding on a mortgagee of a quasi-servient building, would carry a right to light against the mortgagor and his successors,[33] but not against the mortgagee and his successors.[34]

The implication, however, based as it is on intention, may be negatived or modified by the circumstances. It will not be made so as to deprive the grantor of the right to do anything which at the date of the grant (or, it is submitted,[35] at the date of the contract for it if there was one, and if on the facts the choice of date is material) it was in the contemplation of both parties that he should do. A leading case on this topic is *Birmingham, Dudley and District Banking Co.* v. *Ross.*[36] There the plaintiffs were assignees of a lease granted by the Birmingham Corporation to one, Daniell, and the defendant was a lessee from the corporation of neighbouring land. Both properties were included in an area which was subject to an improvement scheme made some years previously by the corporation under statutory powers, and this scheme included a new main street called Corporation Street. In 1880 the corporation agreed to grant to Daniell, on the completion of certain buildings which he thereby agreed to build, a lease of a piece of land fronting on the proposed site of Corporation Street on the west, and on another proposed new street or passage, to be called Warwick Passage, on the south. The corporation undertook to make these new streets. In 1883, Daniell's buildings being completed, he was granted a lease. In 1886 the corporation agreed to grant to the defendant a lease, for building purposes, of a piece of land bounded on the north by Warwick Passage and also fronting on Corporation Street. At this time

---

31 *Miles* v. *Tobin* (1868) 17 L.T. 432; *Robinson* v. *Grave* (1873) 21 W.R. 569; *Bailey* v. *Icke* (1891) 64 L.T. 789; *Pollard* v. *Gare* [1901] 1 Ch. 834; *Frederick Betts Ltd.* v. *Pickfords Ltd.* [1906] 2 Ch. 87.

32 *Born* v. *Turner* [1900] 2 Ch. 211.

33 *Beddington* v. *Atlee* (1887) 35 Ch.D. 317, 322; see *post*, pp. 111–112, and *cf. Poulton* v. *Moore* [1915] 1 K.B. 400 (release by mortgagor).

34 *Davies* v. *Thomas* [1899] W.N. 244.

35 See *Broomfield* v. *Williams* [1897] 1 Ch. 602, 616; and *post*, p. 111.

36 (1888) 38 Ch.D. 295.

there was a low building on the defendant's land, and this he proceeded (evidently in pursuance of his agreement) to demolish and replace by a larger one which materially affected the light coming to the plaintiffs' building. It appeared from the evidence that it was well known to Daniell, when his lease was granted, that the land afterwards agreed to be leased to the defendant belonged to the corporation, was included in the improvement scheme, was a valuable site, and would sooner or later be built on. It also appeared that the plaintiffs' buildings were lower than the average of those fronting Corporation Street, while the height of the defendant's building, having regard to the importance of Corporation Street, was not unreasonable. In these circumstances the Court of Appeal, affirming Kekewich J., decided that no right to light had passed by implication [37] to Daniell. Cotton L.J. said [38]:

> "When the question is as to an implied obligation we must have regard to all the circumstances which existed at the time when the conveyance was executed which brought the parties into that relation from which the implied obligation results; I quite agree that we ought not to have regard to any agreement during the negotiations entered into between the plaintiffs and the corporation; except in this way; if we find that any particular space in fact was left open at the time when the lease was granted, and that that open space was contracted to be left open during the negotiation which took place, and is not referred to in the lease, we must have regard to the fact of that open space being left, and we must have regard to the fact that by agreement between the parties the lessor had bound himself not to build upon that space; and also we must, in my opinion, in determining what obligation results from the position in which the parties have put themselves, have regard to all the other facts which existed at the time when the conveyance was made, or when the lease was granted, and which were known to both parties."

Lindley L.J. said [39] that the only implied grant that he could infer from the terms of the deed and the surrounding circumstances was of a right to such an amount of light as would come over the corporation land to Daniell's house after the corporation had built what they liked on the other side of the twenty-foot street, Warwick Passage; and Bowen L.J. said [40]:

> "Coming to the amount of enjoyment of light that is supposed by the law to accompany in an ordinary case the lease or the grant of a house which is erected with window-lights, where the grantor of the house is also the owner of premises either adjoining or

[37] Or under the statutory general words: see *post*, p. 122.
[38] (1888) 38 Ch.D. 308, 309.
[39] (1888) 38 Ch.D. 311, 312.
[40] (1888) 38 Ch.D. 313, 315.

neighbouring, then this presumption arises, that the grantor intends the grantee to enjoy so much light unobstructed as must under the circumstances have been assumed by both parties to be reasonably necessary for the fair and comfortable use of the premises which are the subject of the grant. That seems to me to be the real definition and measure of the ordinary implication that arises. . . . [The obligation] must be measured by all the surrounding circumstances. The presumption that arises in favour of the ordinary measure can be rebutted by showing that the circumstances are not ordinary circumstances, or, to speak more accurately, it is not a case of rebutting a presumption, it is a question of the proper inference to be drawn from a consideration of all the facts. I do not think any hard and fast line can be laid down beyond which you are not to admit evidence to rebut the presumption, or rather—as I should prefer to say—to measure the implication itself. Here we have some salient facts which seem to me to prove to demonstration that the plaintiffs are not entitled to the right which they claim. . . . All the parties here knew and intended that there should be buildings on the opposite side of Warwick Passage; and that the parties, when they negotiated for this grant, left the height of these buildings undefined. If Daniell had desired to protect himself further than by the width of the passage, in my opinion, he ought to have done so expressly. . . . I will not say what would be the case if the light had been absolutely destroyed."

The same principle was applied by Joyce J. in *Godwin* v. *Schweppes Ltd.*[41] In that case, at the time of the conveyance by A to B of the building, now owned by the plaintiffs, in respect of which the implied right was claimed, the adjoining land over which the right was claimed was the subject of an agreement for the grant by A to B of a building lease, in pursuance of which B had made plans for the erection, and had laid the foundations, of a building which would leave a well or area, shown on the plan to the conveyance, between it and the plaintiffs' building. These plans were afterwards abandoned, and the defendants, successors in title to A of the adjoining land, built on it a building which obstructed the plaintiffs' lights to a lesser extent than the building originally intended would have done, and did not impinge on the site of the proposed area. It was held that, in the circumstances, B did not acquire against A any right to have his lights unobstructed by any future building on the adjoining ground, not being a building within the contemplated area.

The onus of negativing the implication that prima facie arises is on the grantor.[42] It will not necessarily be negatived or limited by the fact that the grantee knows of a general intention on the part of the grantor

41 [1902] 1 Ch. 926. A somewhat similar case is *Quicke* v. *Chapman* [1903] 1 Ch. 659; see p. 78, *ante*.
42 *Broomfield* v. *Williams* [1897] 1 Ch. 602, 610, 613.

to build somewhere on the land retained. In *Broomfield* v. *Williams*,[42] where in the conveyance to the plaintiff the adjoining land was described as " building land," it was held that the implication was not negatived, but having regard to the circumstances it was conceded by the plaintiff, and would probably have been held, that he would not be entitled to complain of obstruction by a building erected (as the building in fact erected was not) more than four feet nine inches away from his boundary. Lindley and Rigby L.JJ. decided the case on the ground that a right to light passed under the general words imported by section 6 of the Conveyancing Act 1881 and that the reference to " building land " did not show an intention to exclude them. In *Pollard* v. *Gare* [43] knowledge on the part of the purchaser that the adjoining land was part of a building estate marked out on a plan in lots, with a building line, did not affect the implication. The vendor remained entitled to build, but there was no inference that he was to be entitled to build so as to obstruct the plaintiff's light. But in *Swansborough* v. *Coventry* [44] where a house conveyed " with all lights and easements to the same belonging " was described as bounded by " a piece of freehold building ground " and on this ground had stood a low building, recently demolished, the vendor and his successors were held entitled to build to the extent of the former building, but no further.

In *Myers* v. *Catterson*,[45] where the plaintiff had acquired his land from a railway company with knowledge that the adjoining land would be required for the purposes of the railway, it was held that the company entered into an implied obligation not to interfere with the plaintiff's lights by anything not necessarily required for those purposes. The plaintiff's house enjoyed light through arches in the railway viaduct, and accordingly the defendant, who had taken a lease of the arches from the company, was restrained from blocking them up.

(d) *Other negative rights.* It has already been pointed out that, where land is granted for a special purpose, the operation of the rule against derogation from grant prevents the grantor, or his successors, with or without notice, from anything that interferes with that purpose.[46] Where a building is granted without any intention, known to the grantor, to use it for any special purpose, the parties will be supposed to have intended that it shall remain capable of use and enjoyment for ordinary purposes, and on this ground the grantor and his successors will be restrained from interfering with the access of air through existing apertures in the building.[47] Whether in such a case the grantee could acquire immunity, not being one of those already considered, against interference, not actionable as between strangers,

43 [1901] 1 Ch. 834.
44 (1832) 9 Bing. 305.
45 (1890) 43 Ch.D. 470.
46 *Ante*, p. 88.
47 *Cable* v. *Bryant* [1908] 1 Ch. 259; *ante*, p. 90.

of any kind not noticed in this section seems doubtful, for the reason that it is difficult to envisage any other immunity that could be required, and it is thought that the class of negative easements is confined to those here mentioned.[48]

Implied reservation on disposition of part

After some fluctuation in the earlier authorities, it is now settled [49] that prima facie, on a disposition of part of the land of the disposing party, no reservation of any easement in favour of the part retained will be implied. In *Suffield* v. *Brown* [50] Lord Westbury said:

> "When the owner of two tenements sells and conveys one for an absolute interest therein,[1] he puts an end, by contract, to the relation which he had himself created between the tenement sold and the adjoining tenement; and discharges the tenement so sold from any burden imposed on it during his joint occupation; and the condition of such tenement is thenceforth determined by the contract of alienation and not by the previous user of the vendor during such joint ownership."

In *Crossley & Sons Ltd.* v. *Lightowler* [2] Lord Chelmsford said:

> "It appears to me to be an immaterial circumstance that the easement should be apparent and continuous, for *non constat* that the grantor does not intend to relinquish it unless he shows the contrary by expressly reserving it."

If the grantor intends to reserve any right over the tenement granted, it is his duty to reserve it expressly in the grant.[3]

Accordingly, rights of light [4] and rights of way [5] enjoyed or used by the common owner and not reserved on the severance will be lost.

The exceptions to the prima facie rule have never been exhaustively stated. One is where the property retained is landlocked, and a case for a way of necessity arises.[6] Again if one of two houses supporting each other is granted, and thus obtains by implication a right of continued support against the house retained,[7] the one retained acquires by implied reservation a similar right against the house granted.[8] " Rights will

---

48 See p. 34, *ante*.
49 *Wheeldon* v. *Burrows* (1879) 12 Ch.D. 31; *Re Webb's Lease* [1951] Ch. 808.
50 (1864) 4 De G.J. & S. 185, 195. Thesiger L.J. in *Wheeldon* v. *Burrows* (1879) 12 Ch.D. 31 freely quoted from Lord Westbury's speech.
1 The same principle applies when a term of years is granted (*Re Webb's Lease, supra*), or assigned (*Aldridge* v. *Wright* [1929] 2 K.B. 117), and on a mortgage of the property at least if the mortgagee takes possession (*Taws* v. *Knowles* [1891] 2 Q.B. 564).
2 (1867) 2 Ch.App. 478, 486.
3 Thesiger L.J., *Wheeldon* v. *Burrows* (1879) 12 Ch.D. 31, 49.
4 *Wheeldon* v. *Burrows, supra*; *Ray* v. *Hazeldine* [1904] 2 Ch. 17.
5 *Liddiard* v. *Waldron* [1934] 1 K.B. 435; *Aldridge* v. *Wright* [1929] 2 K.B. 117; *Taws* v. *Knowles* [1891] 2 Q.B. 564.
6 *Post*, p. 117.
7 See *ante*, p. 100.
8 *Richards* v. *Rose* (1853) 9 Exch. 218; *Wheeldon* v. *Burrows* (1879) 12 Ch.D. 31, 59; *Russell* v. *Watts* (1884) 25 Ch.D. 559, 573; *Aldridge* v. *Wright* [1929] 2 K.B. 129, 134.

be impliedly reserved which are in their nature reciprocal to rights which
the grant must be taken to have conferred on the grantee." [9] In *Pyer*
v. *Carter*,[10] at the time of the sale of one (A) of two adjoining houses
(A and B), water from the eaves of A fell on B, and then flowed down
a spout into a drain which ran under B, and thence under A, to the
common sewer. B was drained through this drain. A and B having
been successively sold, the owner of B obtained a verdict in an action
against the owner of A for stopping the drain where it entered A. The
Court of Exchequer, making no distinction between implied grant and
implied reservation, decided that the owner of B was, by implied grant,[11]
entitled to have the use of the drain for the purpose of conveying the
water from his house, as it was used at the time of the defendant's
purchase. It seemed in accordance with reason that, on a sale of one
of two or more adjoining houses, that house should be entitled to the
benefit of all the drains from it, and be subject to all the drains then
necessarily used for the enjoyment of the adjoining house, and that
without express reservation or grant. This decision, so far as it implies
that there is no difference between implied reservation and implied grant,
was dissented from by Lord Westbury in *Suffield* v. *Brown* [12] and is
contrary to modern principle; but it can perhaps be supported on the
ground that the drain in respect of which the right was sought was used
by both properties in common. In *Wheeldon* v. *Burrows* [13] Thesiger
L.J. said that he could see nothing unreasonable in supposing that in
such a case as *Pyer* v. *Carter*,[14] where the defendant under his grant
was to take the easement, which had been enjoyed during the unity of
ownership, of pouring his water on the grantor's land, he should also
be held to take it subject to the mutual and reciprocal easement by which
that very same water was carried into the drain on that land and then
back through the land of the person from whose land the water came.
It is curious that the Lord Justice made no reference to the water
coming from the plaintiff's land, but that no doubt is implicit.

In *Wheeldon* v. *Burrows* [15] Thesiger L.J. mentioned that easements
of necessity are excepted from the general rule; but it is questionable
whether any easement, other than access and support, can be " of
necessity." In *Union Lighterage Co.* v. *London Graving Dock Co.*[16]
Stirling L.J. expressed the opinion that an easement of necessity, in this
context, is one without which the property retained cannot be used at all,
and not one merely necessary to the reasonable enjoyment of the pro-

---

[9] Evershed M.R., *Re Webb's Lease* [1951] Ch. 808, 814. *Cf. Hopgood* v. *Brown*
[1955] 1 W.L.R. 213; *Cory* v. *Davies* [1923] 2 Ch. 95.
[10] (1857) 1 H. & N. 916.
[11] *i.e.* implied reservation.
[12] (1864) 4 De G.J. & S. 185.
[13] (1879) 12 Ch.D. 31, 59.
[14] (1857) 1 H. & N. 916.
[15] (1879) 12 Ch.D. 31, 50, 59.
[16] [1902] 2 Ch. 557.

perty. The status of *Nicholas* v. *Chamberlain* [17] so far as it decided that the reservation of the right to use a conduit supplying water to a house will be implied on a sale of the land in which the conduit is, without the house, and of *Simpson* v. *Weber*,[18] where it was held that, on the sale of one of two houses, a right was impliedly reserved to maintain on the wall of the house sold a creeper growing on the property retained and extending up that wall, and also certain plugs in the same wall which supported a gate-post belonging to the property retained, is doubtful. It does not appear that a right to light has ever been regarded as an easement of necessity.

In *Jones* v. *Pritchard*,[19] where a house had been built with fire-places and flues in the outside wall, some connected with and used by the house, and others useless for it but capable of being used by an adjoining house if built, and the plaintiff, owner of the house, granted to the adjoining owner, who intended to build and afterwards built a house connecting with the fireplaces and flues designed for it, the outside moiety of the wall, including a moiety of the flues, it was held by Parker J. that there must be implied a reservation to the grantor and a grant to the grantee of such easements as would be necessary to enable each to use the flues connected with the fireplaces on his side of the wall.[20] The case must be rare in which a grantee can be shown positively, or, for instance, by necessary inference from the effect on the property granted or some physical characteristic of the property retained, to have recognised and acquiesced in an intention on the part of the grantor to use his retained property, or part of it, in some definite manner detracting from the natural rights incident to the ownership of the property granted. Clearly it is not enough that the grantee knows that the grantor retains adjoining land and would probably wish to use it in the same way as before.

The subject was considered in *Re Webb's Lease*.[21] There the plaintiff, owner of a building, painted on one of its outside walls an advertisement of a business carried on by him on the ground floor, and granted to a company a licence, which was exercised, to use another outside wall as an advertising site. He then, first in 1939 and afterwards in 1949, let the first and second floors to the defendant, and,

[17] (1606) Cro.Jac. 121; *ante*, p. 100; and see comments of Vaughan Williams L.J. in *Union Lighterage Co.* v. *London Graving Dock Co.* [1902] 2 Ch. 565–566.
[18] (1925) 133 L.T. 46.
[19] [1908] 1 Ch. 630. See also *Lyttelton Times Co. Ltd.* v. *Warners Ltd.* [1907] A.C. 476. Both these cases were referred to by Lord Parker when, in *Pwllbach Colliery Co.* v. *Woodman* [1915] A.C. 634, 646, he said that the law will readily imply the grant or reservation of such easements as may be necessary to give effect to the common intention of the parties; see p. 87, *ante*.
[20] The point in the case was that, as a result of a defect in the plaintiff's half of one of the flues used by the adjoining house, smoke from that house found its way into the plaintiff's house and damaged his decorations and furniture. It was held that the adjoining owner, not having been guilty of negligence or want of reasonable care and precaution, was not liable. The subject of reservations in leases is considered in " Reservations and Exceptions of Easements and Similar Rights by Landlords " by Alec Samuels in 27 *Conveyancer* (N.S.) 187.   [21] [1951] Ch. 808.

disputes having arisen after a long period of acquiescence by the defendant, he issued an originating summons asking whether, in the circumstances, he was entitled, without the defendant's consent, to continue to use the two outside walls, comprised in the lease, for advertising. The Court of Appeal answered this question in the negative, on the ground that the circumstances did not justify a departure from the general rule. The burden which faces a grantor who seeks to show an implied reservation is readily apparent from the judgment of Jenkins L.J. who said [22]:

"That question must be approached with the following principles in mind: (i) If the landlord intended to reserve any such rights over the demised premises it was his duty to reserve them expressly in the lease of August 11, 1949 (*Wheeldon* v. *Burrows* [23]); (ii) The landlord having failed in this duty, the onus was upon him to establish the facts to prove, and prove clearly, that his case was an exception to the rule (*Aldridge* v. *Wright* [24]); (iii) The mere fact that the tenant knew at the date of the lease of August 11, 1949, that the landlord was using the outer walls of the demised premises for the display of the advertisements in question did not suffice to absolve the landlord from his duty of expressly reserving any rights in respect of them he intended to claim, or to take the case out of the general rule; see *Suffield* v. *Brown* [25]; *Crossley & Sons Ltd.* v. *Lightowler.* [26]

"Applying these principles to the present case, I ask myself whether the landlord has on the meagre facts proved discharged the onus which lies on him of proving it an exception to the general rule. He can, so far as I can see, derive no assistance from the passage quoted above from Lord Parker's speech in the *Pwllbach Colliery* case. [27] It might, I suppose, be said to have been in the contemplation of the parties that the landlord would continue to use the ground floor of the premises for the purposes of his business as a butcher and provision merchant, but it cannot in my view be contended that the maintenance during the term of the lease of his advertisement over the door was a necessary incident of the user so contemplated. This applies *a fortiori* to the ' Brymay ' advertisement, the display of which on the outer wall of the demised premises by the . . . licensees of the landlord was, so far as I can see, not related in any way to the use or occupation of the ground floor for the existing or any other purpose. . . .

"The mere fact that the tenant knew of the presence of the

22 *Ibid.* 828–830.
23 (1879) 12 Ch.D. 31.
24 [1929] 2 K.B. 117; see p. 113, *post.*
25 (1864) 4 De G.J. & S. 185.
26 (1867) 2 Ch.App. 478.
27 [1915] A.C. 634, 646; *i.e.* the passage quoted *ante*, p. 87.

advertisements at the date when the lease of August 11, 1949, was granted being, as stated above, beside the point, nothing is left beyond the bare circumstance that the advertisements were not only present at the date of the grant but had been continuously present without objection by the tenant since the commencement of the original tenancy in 1939. Does this circumstance suffice to raise a necessary inference of an intention common to both parties at the date of the lease that the landlord should have reserved to him the right to maintain these advertisements throughout the twenty-one years' term thereby granted? I cannot see that it does. The most that can be said is that the facts are consistent with such a common intention. But that will not do. The landlord must surely show at least that the facts are not reasonably consistent with any other explanation. Here he manifestly fails. . . .

" In short, I can hold nothing more established by the facts proved than permissive user of the outer walls by the landlord for the display of the advertisements during the original tenancy and thereafter from the granting of the lease until the tenant's objection in January, 1950; with nothing approaching grounds for inferring, as a matter of necessary inference, an intention common to both parties that such permissive user should be converted by the lease into a reservation to the landlord of equivalent rights throughout the twenty-one years' term thereby granted."

In regard to *Simpson* v. *Weber* [28] Evershed M.R. said [29] that he would not criticise the decision in it, and Jenkins L.J.[30] expressed the opinion that the physical circumstances might perhaps have sufficed to support an implication of an intention common to the parties that the easements in question should be reserved; but both expressed disapproval of the grounds on which the decision was apparently arrived at, namely, that in a case where an easement might reasonably have been reserved if the parties had thought of it, it will be taken to have been impliedly reserved unless there is evidence of an intention not to do so.

Easements acquired on simultaneous dispositions

Where separate parts of land held by the same person are disposed of at the same time, each part acquires by implication the same easements over any other part as it would if that other part had been retained, and the other part becomes subject to the easement so acquired. In *Russell* v. *Watts* Fry L.J. said [31]:

[28] (1925) 133 L.T. 46; see p. 108, *ante.*
[29] [1951] Ch. 808, 820.
[30] *Ibid.* 827.
[31] (1884) 25 Ch.D. 559, 584. The majority decision in this case was reversed ((1885) 10 App.Cas. 590) on consideration of the very special documents and circumstances. In the passage quoted it is assumed (and see *Allen* v. *Taylor* (1880) 16 Ch.D. 355, 358) that each purchaser or grantee knows that the other land is being disposed of. If either does not, then it would seem that, as between the purchasers, the rule applies; and each acquires by implication the appropriate easements over the part taken by the

" As the same vendor is selling to two persons at the same time, each purchaser is entitled, in favour of the house he buys, to the benefit of the maxim that no man shall derogate from his own grant but, at the same time, he has the burden of the same maxim in favour of his neighbour's house; and the result is, that all the quasi-easements which existed between the two lots in the hands of the one owner, the vendor, are perpetuated by way of implied grant, in the hands of the respective purchasers."

This rule applies not only where the dispositions are for value,[32] but also where they are testamentary,[33] or voluntary conveyances *inter vivos*.[34] Where the dispositions are testamentary, it makes no difference that one is specific and the other residuary, or that one disposition is expressed to be free from incumbrances.[35]

Where dispositions are preceded by contracts, the rights of the parties depend on the circumstances in which, including the dates on which, the contracts were made, and not on the dates of the conveyances. Any doubt which was previously thought to exist as to the accuracy of this proposition appears to have been removed by the judgment of Buckley J. in *White* v. *Taylor* (*No. 2*)[36] (a case concerned with *profits à prendre*) where his Lordship followed *Beddington* v. *Atlee*,[37] in which an unsuccessful claim to light was made in the following circumstances. In 1881, A, the owner of the equity of redemption in a house and adjoining land, leased the house for twenty-one years, thereby, as it was held, conferring on the lessee by implication (although A had not the legal estate), a right to light for the term of the lease. Afterwards, on January 19, 1882, he agreed to sell the house, subject to the lease, to a nominee of the plaintiff, and this contract was completed in February, 1882, by a conveyance of the house by A and his mortgagees to the plaintiff, subject to the lease. In May, 1882, A conveyed the adjoining land on sale to the defendant. In September the plaintiff determined the

---

other; but *quaere* whether, as between the ignorant purchaser and the owner, a reservation of the right acquired by the other purchaser can be implied, and whether the owner could not be made liable on covenants for title. The case does not seem to have arisen.

32 As in *Swansborough* v. *Coventry* (1832) 9 Bing. 305, *ante*, p. 105 (light), and *Nicholls* v. *Nicholls* (1899) 81 L.T. 811; *Hansford* v. *Jago* [1921] 1 Ch. 322; *Cory* v. *Davies* [1923] 2 Ch. 95 (rights of way).

33 *Allen* v. *Taylor* (1880) 16 Ch.D. 355; and *Phillips* v. *Low* [1892] 1 Ch. 47 (light); *Milner's Safe Co. Ltd.* v. *Great Northern and City Railway* [1907] 1 Ch. 208 (right of way); *Schwann* v. *Cotton* [1916] 2 Ch. 459 (water supply).

34 *Phillips* v. *Low* [1892] 1 Ch. 47, 51. The case of a common owner making a voluntary conveyance of part only, retaining the rest, does not appear to have come before the court.

35 *Phillips* v. *Low*, *supra*.

36 [1969] 1 Ch. 160.

37 (1887) 35 Ch.D. 317. See also *Birmingham, Dudley and District Banking Co.* v. *Ross* (1888) 38 Ch.D. 295; *Quicke* v. *Chapman* [1903] 1 Ch. 659; *Broomfield* v. *Williams* [1897] 1 Ch. 602, *per* Rigby L.J. at p. 616 (the dates of the contracts do not appear); the reference to " the contract " in *Rigby* v. *Bennett* (1882) 21 Ch.D. 559, 567 *ad fin.*; and *per* Lord Westbury in *Suffield* v. *Brown* (1864) 4 De G.J. & S. 185, 195, p. 106, *ante*.

lease under a proviso for re-entry, and in 1885 he commenced these proceedings to restrain the defendant from obstructing the light to the house by building on the adjoining land. If these had been the only material facts, A would have been considered to have granted to the plaintiff, with the house, a right to light against the adjoining land retained by A, and the defendant, who took his conveyance after the plaintiff took his, would have taken subject to the plaintiff's right. In fact, however, the conveyance to the defendant was made in pursuance of a contract made on January 4, 1882, before the contract with the plaintiff; and it was held that inasmuch as A was not in a position to grant an easement over the adjoining land which he had agreed to sell, the plaintiff was not entitled, either by implied grant or under the statutory general words, to the right which he claimed. As the plaintiff's contract and conveyance were both later in date than the contract with the defendant, the date of the plaintiff's conveyance might, equally with the date of his contract, have been regarded as the date when the plaintiff's rights crystallised; but it is implicit in the judgment that the question depended on the relative dates of the contracts, and that, if the plaintiff's contract had preceded the defendant's, and the course of events had been—contract with plaintiff, contract with defendant, conveyance to defendant, conveyance to plaintiff, the result would have been different. It was further held that the right to light impliedly granted by the lease of the house, which was for twenty-one years from August 1881, did not survive the actual determination of the lease.

In *White* v. *Taylor* (*No.* 2) [38] lots carrying grants of sheep rights were sold at auction. All the contracts were entered into on the same day and the purchasers thereupon became entitled in equity to the rights as appurtenances to the land which they bought. Buckley J. held that each purchaser must be taken to have known that the vendor was at the same time selling the other lots to the other purchasers upon the terms of the conditions of sale. As in *Beddington* v. *Atlee*,[39] the state of affairs upon which the language employed in the conveyances operated was governed by the contracts for sale.

In regard to assents by personal representatives, no question can arise, for an assent relates back to the death, unless a contrary intention appears.[40] It is suggested that, where different parts of an estate devolve separately, the easements with and subject to which each part is to be held ought to be specified in the assents.

Easements acquired on grant of lease

Questions of difficulty often arise where properties, originally in common ownership, are let, or one of them is. If an owner (or lessee) of land grants a lease of part of it, his lessee will acquire by implica-

---

[38] [1969] 1 Ch. 160, 181–183.
[39] (1887) 35 Ch.D. 317.
[40] Administration of Estates Act 1925, s. 36 (2).

tion, for the term of the lease, any easement over the part retained that would be acquired by a grantee in fee simple.[41] During the term of the lease, any later lease or grant of the part retained must take effect subject to the right so acquired; and in that sense the right, if not expressly reserved in the later lease or grant, will be impliedly reserved. In *Aldridge* v. *Wright*[42] Greer L.J. stated (referring to *Thomas* v. *Owen*[43]) that

"If the owner of two adjoining properties, A and B, grants to the tenant of A a tenancy from year to year with a right of way during his tenancy over B, and subsequently leases B, the lease of B is subject to a reservation of the right of way which has *ex hypothesi* been granted to the tenant of A if it is shown that the lessee of B was aware of a long continued exercise of the right by the tenant of A ";

but it is submitted that the reference to notice on the part of the subsequent lessee does not imply that an easement granted by implication is only binding on a successor in title of the grantor with notice. If the previous disposition was only equitable, if, for instance, it was an agreement for a lease, then notice is no doubt material, but if it created a legal estate or interest, and the easement is thus a legal easement, the easement must, so it is submitted, bind all persons interested in the servient tenement, with or without notice. The reference to notice on the part of the subsequent lessee perhaps imports that, admitting that this lessee takes subject to the right already acquired by the other, a reservation will be implied, if the subsequent lessee has notice, as between him and the landlord, so as to absolve the landlord from liability on covenants for title.

In *Thomas* v. *Owen*[43] the plaintiff, lessee of a farm, established against the defendant, lessee under the same landlord of an adjoining farm, a right of way over a lane through the defendant's land. This lane was in a cutting, with steep banks on each side; it had no communication with the defendant's land, and its only visible purpose was to give access from and to the high road to and from the plaintiff's farm. In 1873, when each party was a yearly tenant of his farm, the landlord granted a lease of the defendant's farm, including the site of the lane, to the defendant; and in 1878 he granted a lease of the plaintiff's farm to the plaintiff. The grounds of the decision of the Court of Appeal in favour of the plaintiff have never been considered clear; but the decision was summarised by Lawrence L.J. in *Liddiard* v. *Waldron*[44] as follows:

"The Court of Appeal came to the conclusion, paying special regard to the fact that the lane was of no use to the defendant

41 *Borman* v. *Griffith* [1930] 1 Ch. 493; *ante*, p. 95; in fact an equitable easement arising under an agreement for a lease.
42 [1929] 2 K.B. 117, 130, 131; see also *Liddiard* v. *Waldron* [1934] 1 K.B. 435, 447, *per* Greer L.J.; and see p. 116, *post*.
43 (1888) 20 Q.B.D. 225.   44 [1934] 1 K.B. 435, 444.

as a road and that it had been used and repaired exclusively by the plaintiff for many years, that a grant of a right of way over the lane was included in his yearly tenancy and that a reservation of that right ought to be implied in the 1873 lease because at the date of [that] lease . . . it had already been granted to the plaintiff, the tenant of the quasi-dominant tenement."

If the court in *Thomas* v. *Owen* had merely implied a reservation from the defendant's lease of the right then incident to the plaintiff's yearly tenancy, that reservation, it might be supposed, would have been co-terminous with the tenancy; but the court went further, and held that the lease granted in 1878 to the plaintiff included the right of way; and thus they must have regarded the reservation from the defendant's lease as a reservation for the whole of its term. *Thomas* v. *Owen* was followed in *Westwood* v. *Heywood* [45] where the plaintiff established, as incident to the land (D) conveyed to him, a right to the flow of water through a pipe from a source on adjoining land (S) belonging at the time of the conveyance to his vendor, and at the time of the action to a successor in title of the vendor. If S had been unlet at the time of the plaintiff's purchase, the right would clearly have passed by implication [46]; but S had been let, to the defendant, without reservation. If that had been all, the conveyance of D could not have conferred any right against the tenant of S; but D was also let, and this letting was earlier than the letting of S and was still on foot at the time of the conveyance. Astbury J. held that the letting of D carried the water right, that the letting of S was subject to an implied reservation of the right so granted to the tenant of D, and that at the date of the plaintiff's conveyance there was nothing to prevent the vendor from granting the water right in fee simple. It was in fact unnecessary to decide this question, because after the date of the plaintiff's conveyance, and before the action, the defendant acquired the fee simple of S, and in these circumstances it was held that, even if the defendant, as tenant of S, was not bound by the right, the conveyance of it to the plaintiff, made while the defendant was tenant, carried the right against the reversion of S subsequently acquired by the defendant.

It may, perhaps, be suggested that *Thomas* v. *Owen* should be regarded as an isolated case so far as it decides, if it does, that an owner who grants first a lease of dominant land of his, and then a longer lease, without any express reservation, of the servient land, is able to make another disposition of the dominant land which will bind the servient land during the subsistence of the servient lease and after the determination of the dominant lease; and that it is more in accordance with principle to suppose that if a lease of the dominant land is followed by a

---

[45] [1921] 2 Ch. 130.
[46] *Watts* v. *Kelson* (1870) 6 Ch.App. 166, see *ante*, p. 99.

lease or conveyance of the servient land not containing any reservation, the servient land will not be bound after the determination of the dominant lease. That was decided in *Warner* v. *McBryde*.[47]

In *Re Flanigan and McGarvey and Thompson's Contract*[48] the owner of land who, having let the dominant part on a quarterly tenancy protected by the Rent Acts, agreed to sell the servient part, was held entitled to have the conveyance so worded as to convey the property subject, during the existing tenancy of the dominant part and any tenancy that might supersede it, to such right of way as was incident to the tenancy; and not to reserve in perpetuity in the conveyance the right of way enjoyed by the tenant. Black J. expressed the opinion that that result would have followed if the conveyance had been executed without any express reservation.

In *Coutts* v. *Gorham*,[49] where the owner of two houses, D and S, leased S, and then leased D, which had windows overlooking S, to the plaintiff, and then granted a new lease of S to the defendant, it was held that the lease of D to the plaintiff carried the right to light against S, except during the original lease of S, and that, the lease of S to the defendant having been granted out of a reversion which was subject to the right already granted by the lease of D, the defendant was not entitled to obstruct D's light.

If the owner of two properties, D and S, grants a lease of D with a right to light over S, and then conveys D subject to the lease, S being all the time in hand, the conveyance of the D reversion will carry the right to light on ordinary principles, the result being, it seems, that the right is annexed to the estate or interest of both the lessee and the reversioner.[50]

If S is leased without any reservation of an easement in favour of D, and D is then granted, the grantee of D cannot, of course, have any easement over S during the lease of S. Any *negative* right over S which would pass by implication on the grant of D if S were on hand will, it seems, be acquired by D on the expiration of the lease of S, under the doctrine forbidding derogation from grant[1]; but it is questionable

---

47 (1887) 36 L.T. 360. See also *Beddington* v. *Atlee* (1887) 35 Ch.D. 317, p. 111, *ante*.
48 [1945] N.I. 32. Black J. said (43): " I have read and re-read *Thomas* v. *Owen,* and I think all the subsequent reported cases in which *Thomas* v. *Owen* has been referred to, in an earnest endeavour to see if I could formulate the precise principle in a logical framework of exceptions to the principle of *Wheeldon* v. *Burrows.* I cannot profess to have succeeded."
49 (1829) Moo. & M. 396. A similar case is *Davies* v. *Marshall (No.* 1) (1861) 1 Dr. & Sm. 557; see also *Westwood* v. *Heywood* [1921] 2 Ch. 130, p. 114, *ante,* and *Cable* v. *Bryant* [1908] 1 Ch. 259, p. 90, *ante,* where an owner having (i) leased the servient part of his land, (ii) conveyed the dominant part to the plaintiff and then (iii) conveyed the servient part to the defendant, the lessee joining to surrender the term, the plaintiff was held to have acquired a right to air against the defendant.
50 *Barnes* v. *Loach* (1879) 4 Q.B.D. 494.
1 *Cable* v. *Bryant* [1908] 1 Ch. 259.

whether a positive right, such as a right of way, will be so acquired; at any rate, there seems to be no decision that it will.[2]

Where two lessees or tenants of property, formerly owned by the same person but since conveyed separately, are in dispute as to an alleged easement of one of them, and it is not shown that the easement has been granted by one tenant to another, the proper approach would seem to be to investigate the history of the tenancies, and see whether they or either of them were granted by the common owner, and if so, which was granted first; and, if neither was granted by the common owner, to see whether the claiming lessee's landlord became entitled, under his conveyance from the common owner, to the easement claimed.

In *Aldridge* v. *Wright*,[3] which was an action to restrain trespass, the defendant, who was lessee of a house, No. 28, sought to establish against the plaintiff, who was lessee of the house next door, No. 30, a right of way over that house's garden. The two houses had been the subject of separate contemporaneous leases granted to the same person, whose successor to both houses had first assigned the lease of No. 30 to A, without reserving any rights, and afterwards assigned the lease of No. 28 to B. The plaintiff and defendant became tenants of A and B respectively, and afterwards acquired the leasehold reversions. It was held that, as the lease of the allegedly servient tenement, No. 30, had been assigned first, no right was impliedly reserved to the assignor, and that the defendant, deriving title under him, had no easement.

A similar case is *Liddiard* v. *Waldron*[4] where the plaintiff, owner of a house, No. 22, claimed against the defendant, owner of the next house, No. 21, a right of way over a path behind and belonging to No. 21. No. 21 had been conveyed by the common owner first, without reservation, and it was held that no easement passed on the later conveyance of No. 22. It appeared that, at the time of the conveyance of No. 21, the right claimed was being used by the weekly tenant of No. 22; and hence it was argued, in reliance on *Thomas* v. *Owen*[5] (and this argument succeeded in the Divisional Court[6]), that the common owner, having granted a right to the tenant of No. 22, must be taken to have reserved that right in perpetuity in the subsequent conveyance of No. 21. The Court of Appeal reversed the Divisional Court on the ground that there was no evidence that the user by the weekly tenant of No. 22 was of right, and that the case depended on *Wheeldon* v. *Burrows*.[7] The tenancy of No. 22 appears to have determined before the conveyance

---

[2] *Cf.* the argument, as to which the court expressed no opinion, in *Cable* v. *Bryant*, *supra*.
[3] [1929] 2 K.B. 117.
[4] [1934] 1 K.B. 435.
[5] (1888) 20 Q.B.D. 225; *ante*, p. 113.
[6] [1933] 2 K.B. 319.
[7] (1879) 12 Ch.D. 31.

of No. 22, and it is submitted that, even if the right had been annexed to that tenancy, the result would have been the same.

Easements of necessity

A way of necessity arises where, on a disposition by a common owner [8] of part of his land, either the part disposed of or the part retained is left without any legally enforceable means of access. In such a case the part so left inaccessible is entitled, as of necessity, to a way over the other part. The principle no doubt applies where both parts are disposed of simultaneously, either by grant *inter vivos*,[9] or by will.[10]

> " If I have a field enclosed by my land on all sides, and I alien this close to another, he shall have a way to this close over my land, as incident to the grant; for otherwise he cannot have any benefit from the grant. And the grantor shall assign the way where he can best spare it." [11]

> "Where a man having a close surrounded with his own land, grants the close to another in fee, for life or for years, the grantee shall have a way to the close over the grantor's land, as incident to the grant, for without it he cannot derive any benefit from the grant. So it is where he grants the land, and reserves the close to himself." [12]

The principle appears to be based on the idea that the neglect of agricultural land is contrary to public policy.[13] The law on the subject is antiquated and, in some respects, not fully developed.

Where a way of necessity arises, whether in favour of the grantee of the enclosed land,[14] or of the grantor retaining the enclosed land,[15] its line is to be chosen by the grantor [16]; but it is for the person entitled to it to make it up.[17] It has been said that the line, once established, cannot be altered by the servient owner.[18]

---

[8] Including a trustee; *Howton* v. *Frearson* (1798) 8 Term Rep. 50.

[9] See *ante*, p. 111.

[10] See *ante*, p. 111; *Pearson* v. *Spencer* (1861) 1 B. & S. 571; *Pheysey* v. *Vicary* (1847) 16 M. & W. 484.

[11] Rolle's Abridgment, tit. Graunt, pl. 17.

[12] 1 Wms.Saund. (1871 ed.) 570; adopted in *Pinnington* v. *Galland* (1853) 9 Exch. 1, 12.

[13] *Packer* v. *Wellstead* (1658) 2 Sid. 39, 111; *Dutton* v. *Tayler* (1701) 2 Lut. 1487.

[14] *Clark* v. *Cogge* (1607) Cro.Jac. 170; *Brown* v. *Alabaster* (1888) 37 Ch.D. 490, 500; *Barry* v. *Hasseldine* [1952] Ch. 835, 838.

[15] *Packer* v. *Wellstead*, supra.

[16] *Bolton* v. *Bolton* (1879) 11 Ch.D. 968. Only one way is allowed, and it must be a convenient way; *ibid.*, and see *Pinnington* v. *Galland* (1853) 9 Exch. 1, 12.

[17] *Osborn* v. *Wise* (1837) 7 Car. & P. 761, 764; *cf. ante*, p. 44.

[18] *Pearson* v. *Spencer* (1861) 1 B. & S. 571, 584, *per* Blackburn J.; affd. 3 B. & S. 761. In this case a right over an existing defined way appears to have passed by implication under the will. *Cf. Deacon* v. *S.E. Ry.* (1889) 61 L.T. 377. In *Wynne* v. *Pope* (1960) 3 S.A. 37, however, it was held by the Supreme Court of South Africa that an easement of necessity can be altered by the owner of the servient tenement if he can afford to the owner of the dominant tenement another route as convenient as the original route. See also " Ways of Necessity," by Mr. J. R. Garner in 24 *Conveyancer* (N.S.) 205.

It has been seen [19] that if a house or land with a drive or other obvious means of approach is granted without the drive or any right over it, a right over the drive will arise by implication. No case of necessity arises, because a right over a defined way is impliedly granted, and in this sense it is true to say [20] that a way of necessity is not a defined way. Whether, if the drive is granted and the (otherwise inaccessible) house retained, the grantor obtains a right over the drive, by implication, because it is a necessary means of access to the house,[21] or a right over *some* way, to be chosen by him, as of necessity, does not seem clear [22]; but the question can seldom be a live one, for if in such a case a true way of necessity arises, the grantor will presumably choose the existing way.

Clearly no way of necessity arises if, at the time of the grant, the claiming party owned other land which gave access,[23] but merely permissive user of other land as a means of access is disregarded [24]; and where a building, under which was an archway leading to a mews retained by the lessor, was demised to a lessee who had notice that the lessor intended to develop his retained land in such a way as to leave it inaccessible except through the archway, the lessee was restrained from blocking this up, on the ground, among others, that a way through the archway was reserved as a way of necessity.[25]

It is not essential that the inaccessibility of the land granted (or retained) be due to the fact that it is surrounded by land of the grantor (or grantee) and no other person [26]; but speaking generally it does appear to be essential that the land is absolutely inaccessible or useless.[27] If, however, a particular part of the property cannot, without the right claimed, be used for its designed purpose, then it is probably true to say that a right of access for that purpose will arise as of necessity. For instance, in *Hansford* v. *Jago*,[28] where earth closets belonging to the cottages sold could not be emptied without either infringing a local by-law or passing over the strip of land over which the right of way was claimed, Russell J. would probably have decided, if it had been necessary, that a way of necessity for this purpose had been made out. On the other hand the use of an adjoining passage for carrying coals or other things which can, though not conveniently, be carried through a house is not necessary in this sense.[29] Moreover in *Titchmarsh* v.

---

19 *Ante*, p. 95.
20 See *Brown* v. *Alabaster* (1888) 37 Ch.D. 490; p. 96, *ante*.
21 See *Pinnington* v. *Galland* (1853) 9 Exch. 1, 12.
22 See *Pearson* v. *Spencer* (1861) 1 B. & S. 571, 584, 585; *Holmes* v. *Goring* (1824) 2 Bing. 76, 84.
23 See *e.g. Midland Ry.* v. *Miles* (1886) 33 Ch.D. 632, 644.
24 *Barry* v. *Hasseldine* [1952] Ch. 835.
25 *Davies* v. *Sear* (1869) L.R. 7 Eq. 427; *ante*, p. 63.
26 *Barry* v. *Hasseldine* [1952] Ch. 835.
27 *Union Lighterage Co.* v. *London Graving Dock Co.* [1902] 2 Ch. 557, 573.
28 [1921] 1 Ch. 322; *ante*, p. 97; *post*, p. 124.
29 *Aldridge* v. *Wright* [1929] 2 K.B. 117; *cf. Liddiard* v. *Waldron* [1934] 1 K.B. 435.

Royston Water Co.[30] where land, otherwise inaccessible, adjoined a highway lying in a cutting twenty feet below, it was held that no way of necessity arose over other adjoining land.

It seems that a way acquired as of necessity, whether by the grantee or the grantor, is such a way as is necessary for the use of the servient land as it is at the time of the grant, or for such use as is then contemplated by both parties. In *Gayford* v. *Moffatt*[31] where a lease had been granted of a counting-house and vaults, to which the only means of access was over a courtyard held by the lessor, and the lessor afterwards began to build on part of the courtyard, it was held that the lessee became entitled to a way of necessity over the courtyard,

> " and that way must be a way suitable to the business to be carried on on the premises demised, namely, the business of a wine and spirit merchant. That is the position in which the tenant stood after the lease was granted, and is the position in which he now stands. The question is therefore reduced to this, whether there remained, after the building was erected, such a way as the plaintiff would have been entitled to the day after the lease was granted." [32]

It was decided that enough room was left for the plaintiff to bring pipes of wine in wagons to the vault entrance in the courtyard, and the bill was dismissed. In *Serff* v. *Acton Local Board*[33] where land acquired by the defendant Board under compulsory powers for the purpose of sewage works was conveyed to it by the plaintiff, who held that and adjoining land under a building agreement, by a conveyance containing full recitals of the proposed works, the Board was held entitled, as of necessity, to the use of a way over the plaintiff's retained land for all purposes for which it could be required for sewage works.

In *Corporation of London* v. *Riggs*[34] the defendant had conveyed to the corporation the outer part of a piece of agricultural land in Epping Forest, retaining a part which was entirely surrounded by the land conveyed. There was no defined means of access to the part retained, which was used solely for agricultural purposes. The defendant having started to build a public tea-room on the part retained, the corporation brought this action, alleging that he had unlawfully drawn timber and other building materials across the land conveyed, and that he threatened to continue to do so and to attract and cause the public to cross the land conveyed, both in carriages and on foot; and it claimed a declaration that the defendant was entitled to no more than a way of necessity over the land conveyed, sufficient for its use for agricultural purposes only; that, if necessary, the position and other particulars of that way might be set out and defined; and an injunction in accordance with the declaration.

30 (1899) 81 L.T. 673.
31 (1868) 4 Ch.App. 133.
32 (1868) 4 Ch.App. 136, *per* Lord Cairns.
33 (1886) 31 Ch.D. 679.
34 (1880) 13 Ch.D. 798.

The defendant demurred to the statement of claim, except so far as it claimed to have the way set out, and he alleged that, except as aforesaid, the claim was bad in law on the ground that he was entitled to a way for all purposes, and not for agricultural purposes only. Jessel M.R., after observing that the point did not appear to be covered by authority, overruled the demurrer, on the ground that a way of necessity must be limited by the necessity at the time of the grant. He said [35] :

> " The object of implying the re-grant, as stated by the older judges, was that if you did not give the owner of the reserved close some right of way or other, he could neither use nor occupy the reserved close, nor derive any benefit from it. But what is the extent of the benefit he is to have? Is he entitled to say, I have reserved to myself more than that which enables me to enjoy it as it is at the time of the grant? And if that is the true rule, that he is not to have more than necessity requires, as distinguished from what convenience may require, it appears to me that the right of way must be limited to that which is necessary at the time of the grant; that is, he is supposed to take a re-grant to himself of such a right of way as will enable him to enjoy the reserved thing as it is. . . . If you imply more, you reserve to him not only that which enables him to enjoy the thing he has reserved as it is, but that which enables him to enjoy it in the same way and to the same extent as if he reserved a general right of way for all purposes: that is—as in the case I have before me—a man who reserves two acres of arable land in the middle of a large piece of land is to be entitled to cover the reserved land with houses, and call on his grantee to allow him to make a wide metalled road up to it. I do not think that is a fair meaning of a way of necessity : I think it must be limited by the necessity at the time of the grant."

The Master of the Rolls added that, where the grant is of the enclosed piece, it might be that the grantee obtains a larger way of necessity than the grantor does under the implied regrant; but he did not think so.

In *Chappell* v. *Mason* [36] the lessee of a house, A, took a lease from a different landlord of the top part of the adjoining house, B, not including the stairs from the street. By permission of the landlords the party wall was opened, on the top floor, so as to give communication between the two premises, and the lessee afterwards took a lease of the top part of B for a further term. While B was so leased the landlord of A took possession (the lease of A having evidently come to an end by effluxion of time or otherwise), and blocked up the opening, so leaving the demised part of B inaccessible except by the stairs. It was held nevertheless that the lessee had no right to use the stairs.

In *Holmes* v. *Goring* [37] the Court of Common Pleas considered that

[35] (1880) 13 Ch.D. 798, 806–807.
[36] (1894) 10 T.L.R. 404.
[37] (1824) 2 Bing. 76.

a way of necessity does not survive the necessity under which it arose, and that, if the person entitled to it acquires adjoining land which gives access to the dominant tenement, the right will cease. The case is not clear, however, and it may be that, at the time of the grant of the allegedly servient tenement, the necessity for a way over it had already ceased.[38]

Easements of necessity most often arise in connection with access. In *Wong* v. *Beaumont Property Trust Limited*,[39] however, the plaintiff successfully claimed a right to construct a ventilation duct on the defendant's land. The tenant under a lease covenanted to keep the demised premises open as a popular restaurant, to control and eliminate all smells and odours caused by such use of the premises and to comply with the health regulations so that they should not become or cause an annoyance or nuisance to the landlord or to the tenants and occupiers of adjacent buildings belonging to the landlord. At the time of the execution of the lease the covenants as to ventilation could not be complied with unless a ventilation system were installed with a duct fixed to the outside back wall of the landlord's building. That fact was not then appreciated by the parties to the lease, so that this case is also authority for the proposition that an easement of necessity may impliedly be granted even though the parties do not realise that necessity at the time of the grant. The judge of the Exeter County Court granted the plaintiff, who had bought the remainder of the lease, a declaration that he was entitled to enter the landlord's premises for the purpose of constructing, maintaining and repairing a ventilation system for use in connection with the restaurant. The Court of Appeal, dismissing the landlord's appeal and applying the dictum of Lord Parker in *Pwllbach Colliery Company* v. *Woodman*,[40] held that since at the time of the grant of the lease and thereafter a ventilation system with an air duct on the wall of the landlord's premises was necessary in order that the business of a popular restaurant could legally be carried on in the demised premises in accordance with the terms of the lease, the plaintiff had established an easement of necessity and was entitled to the declaration. Lord Denning M.R. said[41]:

> "There is one point in which this case goes further than the earlier cases which have been cited. It is this. It was not realised by the parties, at the time of the lease, that this duct would be necessary. But it was in fact necessary from the very beginning. That seems to me sufficient to bring the principle into play. In

---

[38] See *per* Fry J., *Barkshire* v. *Grubb* (1881) 18 Ch.D. 616, 620. The facts in *Holmes* v. *Goring* were unusual and complicated, and the leading judgment is difficult to analyse. The decision was doubted by Parke B. and Alderson B. in *Proctor* v. *Hodgson* (1855) 10 Exch. 824, 828.

[39] [1965] 1 Q.B. 173.

[40] [1915] A.C. 634, 646.

[41] [1965] 1 Q.B. 181.

order to use this place as a restaurant, there must be implied an easement, by the necessity of the case, to carry a duct up this wall."

Pearson L.J. said [42] that the choice was either to say that the provisions of the lease could not be carried out and must remain inoperative, or to imply an easement of necessity into the lease. The court should read the lease in such a way that *res magis valeat quam pereat*, and therefore the right course was to imply an easement of necessity. Salmon L.J. said [43] that it seemed to be plain on the authorities that if a lease were granted which imposed a particular use on the tenant and it was impossible for the tenant so to use the premises legally unless an easement were granted, the law did imply such an easement as of necessity.

4.—CREATION BY GENERAL WORDS

Law of Property Act 1925, s. 62

Prior to the coming into force, on January 1, 1882, of section 6 of the Conveyancing Act 1881, it was common to set out in a conveyance "general words," operating as a species of express grant, by virtue of which easements could be claimed as being established for the benefit of the land granted. The court was not, however, inclined to establish the easement claimed unless it had previously existed and afterwards became extinguished through unity of ownership, and then only if the subsequent conveyance by the common owner contained some such general words as "together with all ways (etc.) used or enjoyed therewith." [44]

Statute has, as a matter of conveyancing, eliminated the necessity of setting out the general words by deeming them to be set out. [45] By section 62 of the Law of Property Act 1925 (which re-enacts section 6 of the Conveyancing Act 1881) it is provided that:

" (1) A conveyance of land shall be deemed to include and shall by virtue of this Act operate to convey, with the land, all buildings, erections, fixtures, commons, hedges, ditches, fences, ways, waters, watercourses, liberties, privileges, easements, rights, and advantages whatsoever, appertaining or reputed to appertain to the land, or any part thereof, or, at the time of conveyance, demised, occupied, or enjoyed with, or reputed or known as part or parcel of or appurtenant to the land or any part thereof.

" (2) A conveyance of land, having houses or other buildings thereon, shall be deemed to include and shall by virtue of this Act operate to convey, with the land, houses, or other buildings, all outhouses, erections, fixtures, cellars, areas, courts, courtyards, cisterns, sewers, gutters, drains, ways, passages, lights, watercourses,

---

[42] [1965] 1 Q.B. 183.
[43] [1965] 1 Q.B. 189.
[44] See *e.g. Langley* v. *Hammond* (1868) L.R. 3 Exch. 161, 168.
[45] *Re A Contract between Peck and the School Board for London* [1893] 2 Ch. 315, 318.

liberties, privileges, easements, rights and advantages whatsoever, appertaining or reputed to appertain to the land, houses, or other buildings conveyed, or any of them, or any part thereof, or, at the time of conveyance, demised, occupied, or enjoyed with, or reputed or known as part or parcel of or appurtenant to, the land, houses, or other buildings conveyed, or any of them, or any part thereof.

" (3) A conveyance of a manor shall be deemed to include and shall by virtue of this Act operate to convey, with the manor, all pastures, feedings, wastes, warrens, commons, mines, minerals, quarries, furzes, trees, woods, underwoods, coppices, and the ground and soil thereof, fishings, fisheries, fowlings, courts leet, courts baron, and other courts, view of frankpledge and all that to view of frankpledge doth belong, mills, mulctures, customs, tolls, duties, reliefs, heriots, fines, sums of money, amerciaments, waifs, estrays, chief-rents, quit-rents, rentscharge, rents seck, rents of assize, fee farm rents, services, royalties, jurisdictions, franchises, liberties, privileges, easements, profits, advantages, rights, emoluments, and hereditaments whatsoever, to the manor appertaining or reputed to appertain, or, at the time of conveyance, demised, occupied, or enjoyed with the same, or reputed or known as part, parcel, or member thereof. . . .

" (4) This section applies only if and as far as a contrary intention is not expressed in the conveyance, and has effect subject to the terms of the conveyance and to the provisions therein contained.

" (5) This section shall not be construed as giving to any person a better title to any property, right, or thing in this section mentioned than the title which the conveyance gives to him to the land or manor expressed to be conveyed, or as conveying to him any property, right, or thing in this section mentioned, further or otherwise than as the same could have been conveyed to him by the conveying parties.

" (6) This section applies to conveyances made after the 31st day of December, 1881."

" Conveyance " includes (s. 205 (1) (ii)) a mortgage, charge, lease, assent, vesting declaration, vesting instrument, disclaimer, release, and every other assurance of property or an interest therein by any instrument, except a will. It includes a tenancy agreement for a term not exceeding three years,[46] but not an agreement for a lease exceeding three years,[47] nor a mere oral tenancy.[48]

" Land " includes (s. 205 (1) (ix)) land of any tenure, and mines and minerals, whether or not held apart from the surface, and buildings or parts of buildings (whether the division is horizontal, vertical or made in any other way), and other corporeal hereditaments.

[46] *Wright* v. *Macadam* [1949] 2 K.B. 744.
[47] *Borman* v. *Griffith* [1930] 1 Ch. 493; see *ante*, p. 95.
[48] *Rye* v. *Rye* [1962] A.C. 496.

The words " appertaining . . . to " refer, in their strict meaning,[49] to easements already existing and annexed to the estate granted. In that sense they are superfluous,[50] and it does not seem that an easement could ever arise under the statutory words " appertaining . . . to." On the other hand " appurtenances " easily admits a secondary meaning, such as " usually occupied," [1] and in a conveyance will carry a right of way used by a tenant over adjoining land of the vendor.[2] Such a right would also pass as a right " enjoyed with " the property. In *White* v. *Taylor* (*No.* 2) [3] the tenants of the vendor, the common owner of a number of properties which were offered for sale by auction, had sheep grazing rights over one of the properties. These rights could not be appurtenant to the other properties and the purchasers had notice of this fact. Buckley J. accordingly held that the rights were not " reputed or known as part or parcel of or appurtenant to the land or any part thereof," and in so holding distinguished *White* v. *Williams*,[4] where a reference to particulars of sale operated to grant a sheepwalk by reason of admissions in the particulars.

The modern tendency, as has been seen,[5] is to rest the right to an easement on the supposed intention of the parties to the contract, or, if there was no contract, on the intention of the testator or grantor, irrespectively of the presence or absence of general words in the conveyance. Often an easement which arises by implication is created also by the operation of the statutory general words. It is uncommon, on the other hand, for an easement to arise solely under the general words and not also by implication. It is thought that the only rights, not being rights arising by implication, which pass under the statutory words in a conveyance (as defined by section 205 (1) (ii)) are rights, advantages, etc., enjoyed at the time of the conveyance [6] by an occupier of the land conveyed [7] over other land of the grantor, and rights " reputed to appertain " to such other land.[8]

---

[49] *Bolton* v. *Bolton* (1879) 11 Ch.D. 968, 970; *Thomas* v. *Owen* (1888) 20 Q.B.D. 225, 231.

[50] *Beddington* v. *Atlee* (1887) 35 Ch.D. 317, 326.

[1] *Thomas* v. *Owen* (1888) 20 Q.B.D. 225, 231–232.

[2] *Hansford* v. *Jago* [1921] 1 Ch. 322, 329–331, following on this point *Thomas* v. *Owen, supra*. No question was raised as to the power of the vendor to grant the right as against the adjoining property. Both were sold at one auction, and at that time were occupied by tenants who (apparently) became the purchasers.

[3] [1969] 1 Ch. 160, 186–189.   [4] [1922] 1 K.B. 727.

[5] *Ante*, pp. 82 *et seq.*

[6] Where a common owner sells his land in lots at one sale, the conveyances are for this purpose regarded, irrespective of their actual dates, as contemporaneous; see *Lewis* v. *Meredith* [1913] 1 Ch. 571.

[7] Including a purchaser who takes possession between contract and conveyance: *Goldberg* v. *Edwards* [1950] Ch. 247.

[8] In *Beddington* v. *Atlee* (1887) 35 Ch.D. 317 (see *ante*, p. 111); *Birmingham, Dudley and District Banking Co.* v. *Ross* (1888) 38 Ch.D. 295 (see *ante*, p. 102); *Godwin* v. *Schweppes Ltd.* [1902] 1 Ch. 926 (see *ante*, p. 104) and *Quicke* v. *Chapman* [1903] 1 Ch. 659 (see *ante*, pp. 78, 104), which have all been considered above in connection with claims to light by implication, and in all of which the claim by implication failed, a claim under the statutory general words also failed. See also *Salaman* v. *Glover* (1875) L.R. 20 Eq. 444.

What categories of easements are capable of passing under the general words imported by section 62, and whether the section is capable of operating where there is no diversity of occupation of the allegedly dominant and servient tenements before the conveyance (or lease), are questions of considerable difficulty to which the reported cases do not present a certain answer.[9] In *Titchmarsh* v. *Royston Water Company Limited*[10] and *Long* v. *Gowlett*[11] there are suggestions that the operation of section 62 is limited, where there is unity of occupation, to continuous and apparent quasi-easements. While it is clear that where there is such unity the right claimed cannot be "appurtenant" to the grantee's land, it is a question of fact whether it is "enjoyed with" it. If it is so enjoyed (and in the two cases last referred to it was found that the right claimed was not enjoyed with the land conveyed), there seems to be no reason why the right should not pass, although it is not a continuous and apparent easement.[12] So in *Wardle* v. *Brocklehurst*[13] Williams J. in the Court of Exchequer Chamber said:

". . . Inasmuch as the unity of ownership extinguishes the easement, the right of way cannot pass as simply appurtenant to the land to which it was formerly attached, though it continues to exist in point of user. But, though it does not exist as a right, it will pass by a conveyance of the land, if proper words be used to pass it, as, if all ways 'used and enjoyed' with the land are conveyed."

Moreover, *Broomfield* v. *Williams*,[14] a decision of the Court of Appeal, contradicts the contention that, where there is unity of occupation, section 62 is limited to continuous and apparent quasi-easements. Sargant J. in *Long* v. *Gowlett*[15] sought to explain *Broomfield* v. *Williams*[14] as involving a right to light which he said[16] was "extremely similar to a continuous and apparent easement," but there is nothing in the judgments in *Broomfield* v. *Williams*[14] to suggest that the statutory words should be confined in the way suggested by Sargant J.

There is a difference between the case where, for example, the common owner of Blackacre and Whiteacre exercises acts of ownership over Blackacre which are not attributable to his ownership of Whiteacre,

---

[9] In the 13th edition of this work the view was expressed that if a landowner has been in the habit of using some part of the land for the benefit or purposes of another part the right to continue such user will not pass under the general words. A more cautious view is now expressed in view of the doubt cast upon this proposition in "Easements and General Words," an article by Mr. Paul Jackson in (1966) 30 *Conveyancer* 340 *et seq.*

[10] (1899) 81 L.T. 673.

[11] [1923] 2 Ch. 177, 202–204.

[12] This accords with the views expressed by the learned editors of Megarry and Wade's *Law of Real Property* (3rd ed.), p. 832, and Foa's *Law of Landlord and Tenant* (8th ed.), pp. 75, 76.

[13] (1860) 1 E. & E. 1058, 1065–1066.

[14] [1897] 1 Ch. 602; see *ante*, p. 105.

[15] [1923] 2 Ch. 177.

[16] [1923] 2 Ch. 202.

as in *Long* v. *Gowlett*,[17] and the case where, for example, such a common owner walks regularly across Blackacre to reach Whiteacre so that the way across Blackacre is enjoyed with Whiteacre.[18] In *Ward* v. *Kirkland*[19] Ungoed-Thomas J. considered *Long* v. *Gowlett*[20] and explained it as turning on the "distinction . . . between enjoyment exclusively for the purposes of the alleged dominant tenement or enjoyment of an advantage which might be attributable to the possession and ownership of the alleged servient tenement." Ungoed-Thomas J. rejected the view that a right to pass under section 62 must be continuous and apparent, but he did not accept that every *de facto* advantage would pass. He accepted as correct the objection of Sargant J. in *Long* v. *Gowlett*[20] to the creation under section 62 of rights involving user which was both intermittent and non-apparent. In *Ward* v. *Kirkland*[21] the right claimed was to enter the farmyard included in the alleged servient tenement to carry out repairs to the cottage on the alleged dominant tenement. The right claimed was apparent, because it was obvious that the only possible and practicable way of maintaining the wall was by using the farmyard to obtain access to it.

It is settled that general words in a conveyance to a sitting tenant will operate to grant to him, as an easement, any right or advantage which is exercised by him, as tenant, over other land of the grantor, and is capable of being granted as an easement, including "rights" exercised by permission and not of right. In such cases the general words appear to operate automatically and independently of intention. The conversion, under general words, of permissive user into a legal right was first illustrated in *International Tea Stores Co.* v. *Hobbs*,[22] where Farwell J. held that the statutory general words in a conveyance to a tenant operated to grant, as an easement, a right of access to and from adjoining land retained by the vendor, which the tenant at the time of the conveyance was exercising by permission of the vendor. The access was in fact "enjoyed with" the property conveyed, and the statutory general words therefore operated. Again, in *Wright* v. *Macadam*,[23] where, at the time of the grant by the defendant to the plaintiffs of a tenancy for one year of a flat in the defendant's house, one of the plaintiffs was statutory tenant of the flat and used a shed in the garden, by permission of the defendant, for the purpose of storing coal, it was held by the Court of Appeal that, the tenancy agreement being a "conveyance" as defined for the purposes of section 62,[24] and the right to use the shed for storing coal for the purposes of

[17] [1923] 2 Ch. 177. See Jackson, *op. cit.*, 344, 345.
[18] See *Kay* v. *Oxley* (1875) L.R. 10 Q.B. 360; *Re A Contract between Peck and the School Board for London* [1893] 2 Ch. 315.
[19] [1967] Ch. 194, 228.
[20] [1923] 2 Ch. 177.
[21] [1967] Ch. 194.
[22] [1903] 2 Ch. 165.
[23] [1949] 2 K.B. 744.
[24] See *ante*, p. 123.

the flat being a right or easement recognised by the law and capable of being granted expressly, and being a right *de facto* exercised at the time of the tenancy agreement, and the case not being one in which it could be said to have been in the contemplation of the parties that the enjoyment of the right (*i.e., semble*, the existence of the shed) should be purely temporary, the general words imported into the tenancy agreement operated to grant, as part of the tenancy, the right to use the shed for the purpose of storing coal, together with the necessary means of access to it. In *Ward* v. *Kirkland* [25] Ungoed-Thomas J. said that the plaintiff's claim to a right to enter the defendant's farmyard to maintain the wall of the plaintiff's cottage would not be defeated by reason of permission to do so being given on each occasion of user while the farmyard and the cottage were in common ownership; hence the right was by the operation of section 62 transformed into an easement on the cottage being conveyed to the plaintiff.

The principle applies equally where the right is exercised by a tenant or some other person who is not the grantee under the conveyance.[26] In such a case, if the right is incident to the tenancy, the general words in the conveyance would appear to annex the right to the estate or interest granted as well.[27]

It seems that general words will carry a privilege or advantage not amounting to an easement. In *Goldberg* v. *Edwards* [28] the first defendant, in pursuance of an oral agreement made in January, granted to the plaintiffs, in July 1947, a lease of the annexe to a house for two years from January 1947. The plaintiffs had taken possession in January, and at the date of the lease they were using the house, by permission of the defendant landlord, as a means of access to the annexe, but this permission was personal to them, in the sense that it did not extend to servants and the like, or (apparently) assignees. The Court of Appeal, following *Wright* v. *Macadam*,[29] held that the rights so enjoyed at the date of the lease passed under the statutory general words, and, further, that the relevant date for this purpose, *i.e.* " the time of the conveyance," was the date (July) when the lease was granted, and not the date (in January) from which the term granted was calculated. Evershed M.R. said that he guarded himself from saying that rights which were purely personal, in the strict sense of that word, would necessarily in every case be covered by section 62, and he based himself on the view that the right there given, though limited to the lessees, was given to them *qua* lessees, and as such it was covered by the principle of *Wright* v. *Macadam*,[29] and by section

---

[25] [1967] Ch. 194, 230; see p. 64, *ante*. In fact Ungoed-Thomas J. held that the user had been enjoyed by the separate occupier of the cottage without his having obtained his neighbour's permission.

[26] *White* v. *Williams* [1922] 1 K.B. 727.

[27] *Cf. Barnes* v. *Loach* (1879) 4 Q.B.D. 494.

[28] [1950] Ch. 247; p. 96, *ante*.

[29] [1949] 2 K.B. 744.

62. If it is right to suppose that the privilege was not to be exercisable by assignees, it is difficult to see how it could have been annexed to the tenancy as an easement, and questionable whether it would bind an assign of the reversion. Nevertheless the right, whatever it was, was held to pass under the general words.

In *Crow* v. *Wood* [30] the Court of Appeal held that a right to have one's neighbour keep up fences, though not an easement strictly so called, because it involved the servient owner in the expenditure of money, was a right which was capable of being granted by law, because it was in the nature of an easement. Accordingly, it was of such a nature that it could pass under section 62 when, as in that case, it was " enjoyed with " the dominant tenement.

In *Regis Property Co. Ltd.* v. *Redman*,[31] on the other hand, the Court of Appeal held that an obligation to supply constant hot water or central heating, which involved the performance of services and was essentially a matter of personal contract, was not a right, easement or privilege capable of being granted by lease or conveyance so as to pass under section 62. In *Green* v. *Ashco Horticulturist Ltd.*[32] permission was given to the plaintiff to use a way intermittently, subject to the exigencies of the owner's business and the requirements of the owner's tenants, and Cross J. held that the right over the way which the plaintiff claimed could not have been the subject of a legal grant; accordingly, section 62 could not operate. In *White* v. *Taylor* (*No.* 2) [33] Buckley J. said that to prove that grazing rights for sheep were at the time of the conveyance " enjoyed with " the land sold, it had to be shown that a particular number of sheep was being depastured on the land retained.

In *Burrows* v. *Lang* [34] Farwell J. held that a right to take from a mill pond such water as its owner, being competent to cut off the supply, might allow to be there was a right unknown to the law, incapable of passing under general words. So, too, in *Phipps* v. *Pears* [35] the Court of Appeal held that there was no such easement known to the law as an easement to be protected from the weather.

A facility of parking cars on waste land, enjoyed by the public at large, including a neighbouring tenant of the owner of the land, without protest by the owner, was held not to pass under the statutory general words in a conveyance to the tenant of the reversion to his property. The user, being open to anyone, in the sense that the owner had never stopped anyone from trespassing by parking his car, was considered not to be enjoyed with the tenant's particular property. The same result

[30] [1971] 1 Q.B. 77; see p. 40, *ante.*
[31] [1956] 2 Q.B. 612.
[32] [1966] 1 W.L.R. 889; see p. 22, *ante.*
[33] [1969] 1 Ch. 160, 185, 186; see p. 88, *ante.*
[34] [1901] 2 Ch. 502.
[35] [1965] 1 Q.B. 76; see p. 24, *ante.*

was reached on the alternative ground that, before the conveyance, the owner had told the tenant that such user would no longer be allowed.[36]

Reputed rights

Rights which are reputed to appertain to property conveyed will pass under the statutory general words.[37] The necessary degree of "reputation," and the persons among whom it must be had, do not seem to have been defined. In *Clark* v. *Barnes*[38] a right of way over a barely visible track, which right had been annexed to plot A, but became extinguished in 1925 (subject to the rights of a tenant of plot A) on the plaintiff, owner of the site, acquiring also plot A, and at the time of the conveyance to the defendant was still used by the tenant, was held, on the evidence, to pass[39] as a right "reputed to be enjoyed with" plot A under a conveyance of that plot to the defendant in 1926; but the words quoted do not appear in section 62,[40] and it seems more probable[41] that the right was considered to be "[occupied or] enjoyed with" the plot. Similarly in *Re A Contract between Peck and the School Board for London*[42] a way over waste land, which "had been," and perhaps was being, used for convenience by tenants of property agreed to be sold would have passed, under the conveyance, if the statutory general words had been left to operate, as a right either "reputed to appertain to" or "enjoyed with" the property. It may be that the farm track in *Re Walmsley and Shaw's Contract*,[43] which had formerly been used permissively by occupiers of the property agreed to be sold, would have passed under the conveyance as a reputed right, had the wording of the conveyance not excluded it. In *White* v. *Taylor (No. 2)*[44] Buckley J. held that the enjoyment of grazing facilities by former copyholders could not establish a reputation of rights appurtenant to their lands, and thus the grazing facilities could not be said to be "appertaining or reputed to appertain to the land or any part thereof" within section 6 of the Act of 1881. In *Green* v. *Ashco Horticulturist Ltd.*,[45] Cross J. said that, in considering whether the user was such that section 62 would operate, one ought to look at a reasonable period of time before the grant in question in order to see whether there was anything over that period which could be called a pattern of regular user in any particular way or ways.

---

[36] *Le Strange* v. *Pettefar* (1939) 161 L.T. 300; *cf. Sweet & Maxwell* v. *Michael-Michaels (Advertising)* [1965] C.L.Y. 2192. Before the grant of a lease, the lessee was permitted to park a vehicle in the lessor's car park. Judge Block in the Mayor's and City of London Court held that, although the licence was revocable at will, the right passed under s. 62, and thus ceased to be revocable.

[37] See subss. (1) and (2) of s. 62, *ante*, p. 122.   [38] [1929] 2 Ch. 368.

[39] According to the report in [1929] 2 Ch. 380.   [40] See *ante*, p. 122.

[41] See the argument [1929] 2 Ch. 378.

[42] [1893] 2 Ch. 315.

[43] [1917] 1 Ch. 93; see *ante*, p. 98.

[44] [1969] 1 Ch. 160, 185, see p. 88, *ante*.

[45] [1966] 1 W.L.R. 889, 898, see p. 22, *ante*.

Contrary intention

Section 62 applies only if and as far as a contrary intention is not expressed in the conveyance, and it has effect subject to the terms of the conveyance and to the provisions therein contained.[46] The few cases on the subject show that, in order to negative the creation, under the statutory general words, of an easement which, apart from the section, would arise by implication, clear words are required. In *Gregg* v. *Richards* Sargant L.J. said:

> " It is to be noticed that it is by way of express grant that [the section] operates and not by way of implied grant, and that it is for the grantor who seeks to show that that express grant is limited to prove affirmatively that there is some limitation of that express grant." [47]

The use of the words " with the appurtenances " is not in itself an indication of a contrary intention.[48]

In *Gregg* v. *Richards* [49] the plaintiff had purchased a house and land. The conveyance contained an express grant to the plaintiff of the right to use a way described as coloured green on the plan indorsed on the deed. The part coloured green was a foot-way four feet wide, part of a wider way running along the farther side and back of the adjoining premises to the back premises of the plaintiff's house. At the time of the conveyance a right of access for vehicles to the plaintiff's back premises over the whole way was enjoyed with her house. The *habendum* in the conveyance was " to hold the same with the benefit of all such easements and privileges in the nature of easements as are now subsisting in respect of the property hereby conveyed." The plaintiff claimed that the right to use the whole width of the way for the purpose of access of vehicles to her back premises passed to her under the statutory general words. It was held by the Court of Appeal, reversing the decision of Russell J., that the maxim *expressio unius exclusio alterius* did not apply, and that no contrary intention, within subsection (4) of section 62, had been expressed. Warrington L.J. attached importance to the wording of the *habendum*, but Pollock M.R. and Sargant L.J. did not base their judgments on this narrow ground, and Sargant L.J. expressed the opinion [50] that even if there had been a more limited grant of way and nothing else, that would not of itself have been sufficient to exclude the larger right of way which was given by the Act.[1]

It has been seen [2] that easements may arise by implication, apart from the general words imported by the section. If the section is in

---

46 Subs. (4), *ante*, p. 123.
47 [1926] Ch. 521, 535.
48 *Hansford* v. *Jago* [1921] 1 Ch. 322.
49 [1926] Ch. 521.
50 [1926] Ch. 535.
1 And see *Hapgood* v. *J. H. Martin & Son Ltd.* (1934) 152 L.T. 72, where Horridge J. treated *Gregg* v. *Richards* as having been decided on the broader ground.
2 *Ante*, pp. 82 *et seq.*

some respect negatived by words in the conveyance, the question whether the words prevent the easement so negatived from arising by implication must, it is thought, depend on the circumstances. Words in a conveyance to the effect that the section is not to apply, or that a particular easement is not included, or reserving to the grantor the right to build on adjoining land as he pleases [3] would, no doubt, prevent any easement, or the easement excluded, from arising at all; but that result does not necessarily follow. In *Broomfield* v. *Williams* [4] Lindley L.J., after deciding that the description in a conveyance of adjoining land as " building land " did not show an intention to exclude the section so far as it related to light, added that, even if it did, he would still hold that the grantee had a prima facie unrestricted right to light. In *Hansford* v. *Jago* [5] Russell J., after deciding that section 62 was not excluded by the use of the word " appurtenances " in the conveyance, proceeded to hold that, if he were wrong in that, a right of way still passed, on the sale, by implication. In *Green* v. *Ashco Horti-culturist Ltd.*,[6] Cross J. held that a clause in a lease which reserved to the lessor unlimited power to deal with the land and premises adjoining that demised, including power to build without regard to the diminution of light or air enjoyed by the lessee which might result, was not applicable to rights of way.

Rectification

In many cases the creation of an easement by the statutory general words is contrary to the intention of the grantor. If such creation is the result of a mistake common to both parties, the conveyance can be rectified on ordinary principles; but it is a question what amounts, for this purpose, to a mutual mistake. Clearly, if the court is satisfied that both parties positively did not intend the conveyance to include the easement, and that the omission to modify or exclude the statutory general words was, in this sense, due to their mutual mistake, a case for rectification arises. The purchaser in such a case may, however, have had no definite ideas about the included easement, or he may not have been aware of its potential existence, and it is not entirely clear whether proof of mere lack of intention to include, as distinct from a positive intention not to include, is sufficient.[7] Again, the contract on its proper construction may not have included the right in fact created by the general words. In such a case it would seem reasonable to suppose that the contract ought to be rectified as a matter of course, but the rectification would be based, not on actual intention, but on imputed intention. In *Clark* v. *Barnes* [8] where the conveyance to the defendant was rectified, Luxmoore J. said:

---

[3] See *e.g.* Key and Elphinstone's *Conveyancing Precedents*, 15th ed., Vol. I, p. 1033.
[4] [1897] 1 Ch. 606, 610. *Ante*, p. 105.   [5] [1921] 1 Ch. 322; *ante*, pp. 97, 124.
[6] [1966] 1 W.L.R. 889, see p. 22, *ante*.
[7] The language of Morton J. in *Wallington* v. *Townsend* [1939] 2 All E.R. 225, 237, may be thought to imply that it is. In that case a strip of land was in dispute.
[8] [1929] 2 Ch. 368, 380–381. *Cf. Stait* v. *Fenner* [1912] 2 Ch. 504.

" The contract itself does not include any provision which will entitle the defendant to claim to have such a right of way as he claims, granted to him.   The question then is, is the plaintiff entitled to have words inserted in the deed of conveyance, to limit the operation of the Law of Property Act 1925, s. 62; and to prevent the grant of such a right of way by implication?   It is plain that if this point had been raised before the conveyance had been executed and the court had been asked to determine what the form of the conveyance would be, such a limitation would undoubtedly have been inserted, and on this ground the plaintiff is entitled to have the conveyance rectified ";

but the learned judge went on to find as a fact that the right of way to which the action related had been the subject of a conversation between the parties, and that it was understood and agreed between them that there should be no such right.   In *Slack* v. *Hancock* [9] where the plaintiff, owner of land over which the occupier of adjoining land of his exercised certain rights, agreed to sell the first land to the defendant, who did not know of these rights, subject to all rights exercised over it by occupiers of the adjoining land, but omitted to reserve any rights in the conveyance, a claim to have the conveyance rectified on the ground of mutual mistake was not established.

The equity of a party to a grant to have this rectified is not enforceable against a purchaser for value from the other party without notice.[10]

[9] (1912) 107 L.T. 14.   [10] *Smith* v. *Jones* [1954] 1 W.L.R. 1089.

CHAPTER 4

ESTABLISHMENT OF EASEMENTS BY PRESCRIPTION

Definition of prescription

Prescription may be defined to be: A title acquired by use or enjoyment had during the time and in the manner fixed by law. "Prescriptio est titulus ex usu et tempore substantiam capiens ab authoritate legis."[1]

Modes of acquiring title

The mode of acquiring title to an easement by prescription may be considered with respect—

First.—To the length of time during which the enjoyment must continue, whether for the purpose of prescription at common law or under the doctrine of lost grant, or by reference to the Prescription Act 1832.[2]

Second.—To the persons against and by whom the enjoyment must be had.

Third.—To the qualities of that enjoyment.

1.—THE LENGTH OF TIME DURING WHICH THE ENJOYMENT MUST BE HAD

(1) Prescription at Common Law

Time of legal memory

By the common law an enjoyment to confer a title to an easement must have continued during a period co-extensive with the memory of man; or, in a legal phrase, "during the time whereof the memory of man runneth not to the contrary."[3] To this expression a definite meaning is attached, as comprising the period elapsed since the year 1189, that year, the first of the reign of Richard I, having been fixed by the Statute of Westminster 1275, 3 Edw. 1, c. 39, and never since altered.[4]

Presumption from long enjoyment

The extreme difficulty of giving proof of enjoyment for so long a period was lessened by its being held that evidence of enjoyment for so long as anyone could remember raised a presumption that such

---

[1] Co.Litt. 133b.
[2] In *Tehidy Minerals Ltd.* v. *Norman* [1971] 2 Q.B. 528, 543, the Court of Appeal expressed the view that the co-existence of three separate methods of prescribing is anomalous and undesirable, for it results in much unnecessary complication and confusion.
[3] Co.Litt. 114b.
[4] Blackstone's *Commentaries*, Vol. II. The date was also fixed by the statute as the date for alleging seisin in a real action.

133

enjoyment had existed for the period of legal memory.[5] In *Angus* v. *Dalton*[6] Lush J. said: "Theoretically an ancient house at this period was a house which had existed from the time of Richard I. Practically, it was a house which had been erected before the time of living memory, and the origin of which could not be proved." The evidence in such a case need not cover any particular continuous period.[7]

Where, on the other hand, the actual origin of the enjoyment was shown to have been of more recent date than the time of legal memory, the right was held to be defeated. Thus, in *Bury* v. *Pope*,[8]

> "It was agreed by all the justices, that if two men be owners of two parcels of land adjoining, and one of them doth build a house upon his land, and makes windows and lights looking into the other's lands, and this house and the lights have continued by the space of thirty or forty years, yet the other may upon his own land and soil lawfully erect a house or other thing against the said lights and windows, and the other can have no action; for it was his folly to build his house so near to the other's land: and it was adjudged accordingly."

Effect of statutes of limitation

This doctrine appears to have been held down to the passing of the Statute of Limitations, 21 Jac. 1, c. 16, and is still held.[9]

> "When, by the Statute of Limitations, 3 Edw. 1, c. 39, the seisin in a writ of right was limited to the time of Richard I, so that none could count of an older seisin, this writ being the highest writ; it was taken to be also within the equity of the statute, that though a man might prove the contrary of a thing of which prescription was made, still this should not destroy the prescription, if the proof were of a thing beyond the time of limitation. For it was reasonable that the inquiry in a prescription should be limited as well as in a writ of right, being lower than that, for it was very hard to put juries to inquire of things so old." [10]

When [wrote Mr. Gale], the shorter time of sixty years was fixed for a writ of right, and fifty years for a possessory action by 32 Hen. 8,

---

[5] *Jenkins* v. *Harvey* (1835) 1 Cr.M. & R. 877, 894.
[6] (1877) 3 Q.B.D. 85, 89.
[7] *R. C. P. Holdings Ltd.* v. *Rogers* [1953] 1 All E.R. 1029, 1031, 1032.
[8] (1586) Cro.Eliz. 118. And see *Norfolk (Duke)* v. *Arbuthnot* (1880) 5 C.P.D. 390, 392, 393; *Wheaton* v. *Maple & Co.* [1893] 3 Ch. 48, 62, 67, 69.
[9] See *Aynsley* v. *Glover* (1875) 10 Ch.App. 283, where the court presumed a pre-1189 grant of light to cottages (date of building not proved) on evidence of enjoyment for so long as living memory went; and *R. C. P. Holdings Ltd.* v. *Rogers, supra* (right of way). A claim under the Prescription Act would have failed, in the former case, because of unity of possession during the statutory period; and in the latter case, because no user could have been proved in the years immediately before the commencement of the action. "When the existence of a way is spoken to over a period extending as far back as living memory goes, and there is nothing to show that there must have been a time when it did not exist, a case of prescription at common law is made out" (*per* Harman J. [1953] 1 All E.R. 1031).
[10] 2 Roll.Abr., tit. Prescription, 269, pl. 14.

it has been said that a similar extension of the statute was not made by the courts of law, and that the time of prescription for incorporeal rights remained as before.[11] It is difficult to see upon what ground this distinction could have been made, as the enacting words of the two statutes are almost identical in expression, and the latter has been considered only as an addition to the former, restricting the period of prescription to sixty years before the action brought, and making no other alteration. Accordingly, following out this doctrine, the courts, upon the fixing of a shorter period of limitation in possessory actions, ought to have diminished the length of enjoyment, from which a prescriptive right might be inferred, in all like actions to the period of twenty years, fixed by statute 21 Jac. 1.

The opinion of Serjeant Williams, supported by high authority, seems [12] to have been that:

"An action on the case, being a possessory action, was, it is presumed, considered by the court to be in the nature of an ejectment; and as no one can recover in an ejectment unless he, or those under whom he claims have been in possession within twenty years; or rather as an adverse uninterrupted possession by another for twenty years is a bar to an ejectment, so an uninterrupted possession of an easement for the same time is considered as a bar to *an action on the case,* which has for its object, in common with an ejectment, the object of the possession, or at least the dispossessing the defendant of it. . . . From . . . *Holcroft* v. *Heel,*[13] it seems necessarily to follow, that where a person has used and enjoyed an easement for twenty years and upwards, though it was a wrongful user at first, he thereby gains such a right, that if he be disturbed in the enjoyment of it, he may maintain an action on the case for the disturbance and it is no answer to show that the plaintiff originally obtained the use and possession of it by usurpation and wrong." [14]

There appears, therefore, some reason to doubt the correctness of the generally received opinion, that the equitable analogy above mentioned was not extended to the more recent statutes, 32 Hen. 8 and 21 Jac. 1, as well as to the earlier statute of Edward I. The only direct authority against this extension appears to be the opinion of Sir R. Brooke, as given in his reading on the statute of 32 Hen. 8 which is not stated to be founded on any decided case, while it is expressly laid down in Brooke's *Abridgment* that 32 Hen. 8 " entirely repealed the ancient

---

[11] See also First Report of Real Property Commissioners, p. 51.
[12] In eds. before the 13th ed. Serjeant Williams was misrepresented. In the passage cited the decision of the court in *Holcroft* v. *Heel* is being considered and a number of cases are then referred to in which the new periods of limitation were not applied to prescriptive claims. Previous editions cited this passage as a general statement of the law. This was pointed out in the 13th ed. of this work p. 118, note 7.
[13] (1799) 1 Bos. & P. 400.
[14] 2 Wms.Saund. (1845 ed.) 175; (1871 ed.) 503.

Statute of Limitations, and that it extended equally with the former statutes to copyholds as well as to freeholds; for the new statute is, that a man shall not make prescription, title, or claim, etc.; and those who claim by copy make prescription, title, and claim, etc.; also the plaints are in nature and form of a writ of our lord the king at common law, etc.; and those writs which have been brought at common law are ruled by the new limitation, and therefore the plaints of copyhold shall be of the same nature and form." [15]

In *Bury* v. *Pope*,[16] which was decided during the period which intervened between the passing of the two statutes of 32 Hen. 8 and 21 Jac. 1, sufficient time had not elapsed to confer a title by the former statute, even supposing the equitable analogy to have existed. *Whitton* v. *Crompton*,[17] which appears to be the only case decided expressly upon the statute of 32 Hen. 8, and which is at the most but a doubtful authority, turned upon the point that a formedon, having been given since the passing of the Statute of Westminster, was not within the 32 Hen. 8 which was but a mere continuation of it; and ultimately the case appears to have been compromised.

The opinion of Serjeant Williams [18] is in accordance with the expression of Lord Mansfield [19] that "an incorporeal right, which, if existing, must be in constant use, ought to be decided by analogy to the Statute of Limitations." "The several Statutes of Limitations," said Abbott C.J., "being all *in pari materia* ought to receive a uniform construction, notwithstanding any slight variation of phrase, the object and intention being the same." [20] The view of Serjeant Williams, above cited, is, however, at variance with the generally received opinions upon this subject.[21]

Effect of unity of possession

In a claim to prescription at common law, unity of possession without unity of ownership may not prevent its establishment. "If a man have common by prescription, unity of possession *of as high and perdurable estate* is an interruption of the right." [22] It is in the last-mentioned sense that "unity of possession" is used by Lord Mansfield in *Morris* v. *Edgington*,[23] where he speaks of a right of way or common extinguished by "unity of possession," that is, unity of ownership. The dictum of Martin B. in *Winship* v. *Hudspeth*,[24] that a claim by

15 Tit. Limitations, pl. 2.
16 (1586) Cro.Eliz. 118; see p. 134, *supra.*
17 (1568) 3 Dyer 278a.
18 But see note 12, *ante,* p. 135.
19 In an anonymous case cited in 2 Evans' Pothier, 136.
20 *Murray* v. *East India Co.* (1821) 5 B. & Ald. 204, 215.
21 See *e.g. Angus* v. *Dalton* (1878) 4 Q.B.D. 170, 199, *per* Thesiger and Brett L.JJ., and (1881) 6 App.Cas. 778, *per* Fry J.: and the First Report of the Real Property Commissioners, p. 51.
22 Co.Litt. 114b.
23 (1810) 3 Taunt. 24, 30.
24 (1854) 10 Exch. 8.

immemorial prescription at the common law would be defeated by proof of unity of possession at any time, must not be taken as applying to mere unity of possession without unity of ownership, which did not exist in that case.

(2) *Lost Grant*

Presumption of modern lost grant

Although the courts refused in form to shorten the time of legal memory by analogy to the later Statutes of Limitation, they obviated the inconvenience which must have arisen from allowing long enjoyment to be defeated by showing that it had not had a uniform existence during the whole period required, by introducing a new kind of title by presumption of a grant made and lost in modern times.[25]   On this ground, although it appeared that a right of way which existed formerly had been extinguished by unity of possession,[26] or even by an Act of Parliament,[27] it was held that a new title might be obtained by an enjoyment for twenty years.   In a later case, where windows were shown to have existed twenty years, proof that they did not exist twenty-two years before the obstruction was insufficient to defeat an action.[28]

This was in reality prescription shortened in analogy to the limitation of the 21 Jac. 1, and introduced into the law under a new name; for " the law allows prescription only in supply of the loss of a grant, and therefore every prescription presupposes a grant to have existed." [29] The expedient "is ancillary to the doctrine of prescription at common law, and applicable in cases where something prevents the operation of the common law prescription from time immemorial, and is therefore only applicable when the right claimed is such as, if immemorial, might have been the subject of prescription." [30]

The gist of the principle upon which a modern lost grant is presumed is that the state of affairs is otherwise unexplained.   " When the court finds an open and uninterrupted enjoyment of property for a long period unexplained, *omnia praesumuntur rite esse acta*, and the court will, if reasonably possible, find a lawful origin for the right in question." [31]

---

[25] The earliest reported decision to this effect is that of *Lewis* v. *Price* in 1761 (2 Wms. Saund. (1871 ed.) p. 504) *per* Lord Blackburn in *Dalton* v. *Angus* (1881) 6 App.Cas. 812.

[26] *Keymer* v. *Summers*, cited in *Read* v. *Brookman* (1789) 3 T.R. 151, 157.

[27] *Campbell* v. *Wilson* (1803) 3 East 294; see also *Hull* v. *Horner* (1774) 1 Cowp. 102; *Eldridge* v. *Knott* (1774) *ibid.* 214; *Holcroft* v. *Heel* (1799) 1 Bos. & P. 400; *Dartmouth* v. *Roberts* (1812) 16 East 334; *Livett* v. *Wilson* (1825) 3 Bing. 115; *Doe* d. *Fenwick* v. *Reed* (1821) 5 B. & Ald. 232; *Codling* v. *Johnson* (1829) 9 B. & C. 933.   As to the rule that a man cannot prescribe against a public Act of Parliament, see p. 189, *post*.

[28] *Penwarden* v. *Ching* (1829) Moo. & Mal. 400.   In *Phillips* v. *Halliday* [1891] A.C. 228, a faculty for a pew was presumed after long possession.

[29] 2 Bl.Com. 265, citing *Potter* v. *North* (1669) 1 Vent. 387; see *Gardner* v. *Hodgson's Kingston Brewery Co.* [1903] A.C. 229.

[30] *Dalton* v. *Angus* (1881) 6 App.Cas. 740, 816, *per* Lord Blackburn.

[31] *Att.-Gen.* v. *Simpson* [1901] 2 Ch. 671, 698, *per* Farwell J.

In *Tehidy Minerals Ltd.* v. *Norman* [32] the Court of Appeal, observing that " in the case of an easement it has long been recognised as the law that twenty years' enjoyment is or may be sufficient to give rise to a presumption of a lost grant," proceeded on that basis in considering a claim on the part of the defendants that they had acquired rights of common of grazing. The defendants could not show that they had enjoyed the rights claimed for more than thirty years before action brought, and so could not make out a case under section 1 of the Prescription Act 1832,[33] but some were on the facts able to show prescription at common law and under the doctrine of lost grant.

Objections to doctrine of lost grant

The introduction of this doctrine was attended with considerable opposition, and it was contended [34] that to sustain a claim founded upon such a lost grant the jury must actually believe in its existence, or, at all events, they must find it as a fact, though they did not believe it. Doubts and difficulties arose from the vague and uncertain language frequently made use of by judges in leaving questions to the jury— enjoyment being sometimes treated as affording a conclusive presumption, whilst at others such user was only considered to be " cogent evidence " of prescription,[35] the presumption of which judges were in the habit of recommending juries to adopt.

Dalton v. *Angus: In the Queen's Bench Division*

In *Dalton* v. *Angus,*[36] where the subject was fully considered, all the judges appear to have been of opinion that the presumption was capable of being rebutted by some means or other [37]; but they differed upon the question, what evidence or admission was sufficient for the purpose.

The plaintiffs had proved enjoyment of the support claimed for their factory since its erection twenty-seven years before the accident which gave rise to the action, and claimed the right under the doctrine of lost grant; but it was either proved or admitted at the trial that no grant had ever in fact been made. Notwithstanding this admission, Lush J. at the

---

32 [1971] 2 Q.B. 528, 546.

33 See p. 145, *post.*

34 By Sir W. D. Evans, 2 Evans' Pothier 136.

35 *R.* v. *Joliffe* (1823) 2 B. & C. 54. See *Best on Presumptions* (1844), p. 103; and *per* Bowen J. in *Dalton* v. *Angus* (1881) 6 App.Cas. 781: " The twenty years' rule . . . in truth . . . was nothing but a canon of evidence."

36 (1877) 3 Q.B.D. 85; (1878) 4 Q.B.D. 162; (1881) 6 App.Cas. 740. This case is now a leading authority upon several branches of the law of easements, and notably upon the following points, each of which is considered in its place: (1) the presumption of lost grant and the evidence admissible to rebut it; (2) the acquisition of negative easements under Lord Tenterden's Act; (3) secrecy of enjoyment; (4) the effect of an enjoyment which it is impossible or difficult to interrupt; (5) the characteristics of the easement of support generally; and (6) the liability of an employer for the acts of his contractor.

37 See especially the cases collected by Cockburn C.J. (1877) 3 Q.B.D. 106; and the observations of Brett L.J. (1878) 4 Q.B.D. 200.

trial directed a verdict for the plaintiffs; and, on the motion for judgment, he adhered to his opinion " that the mere absence of assent, or
even the express dissent of the adjoining owner, would not prevent the
right to light and support from being acquired by uninterrupted enjoyment, and that nothing short of an agreement, either express or to be
implied from payment or other acknowledgement, that the adjoining
owner shall not be prejudiced by abstaining from the exercise of his
right, would suffice to rebut the presumption.   In other words, that it
would be presumed, after the lapse of twenty years, that the easement had
been enjoyed by virtue of some grant or agreement, unless it were proved
that it had been enjoyed by sufferance." [38]   Cockburn C.J., on the contrary, held that when it was proved or admitted that the assent of the
defendant's predecessor was not asked for or obtained, by grant or in
any other way, to any support being derived from the soil, the presumption was at an end.[39]   He was also of opinion that, the enjoyment of
the support claimed not being capable of being interrupted, no grant
could be implied from the failure to interrupt it.   Mellor J. agreed
on both points with Cockburn C.J., and judgment was given for the
defendants.

Dalton v. Angus: In the Court of Appeal

The Court of Appeal was also divided upon the question now under
consideration.   Brett L.J. considered that the question of grant or no
grant was a pure question of fact to be found by the jury, and that to
exclude evidence tending to show that there never was a grant would
be to usurp the functions of the legislature [40]; quoting the observation
of Lord Mansfield in Hull v. Horner [41] that " length of time, used merely
by way of evidence, may be left to the consideration of the jury to be
credited or not, and to draw their inference one way or the other according to circumstances."   Thesiger L.J., while holding that the presumption
of lost grant might be negatived by showing " a legal incompetence as
regards the owner of the servient tenement to grant an easement,[42] or a
physical incapacity of being obstructed as regards the easement itself,[43]
or an uncertainty and secrecy of enjoyment putting it out of the category
of all known easements," [44] was of opinion that the presumption could
not be rebutted by mere proof that no grant had in fact been made.
" The presumption of acquiescence," he said, " and the fiction of an
agreement or grant deduced therefrom, in a case where enjoyment of an
easement had been for a sufficient period uninterrupted, is in the nature

[38] (1877) 3 Q.B.D. 93.
[39] (1877) 3 Q.B.D. 117, 120.
[40] (1878) 4 Q.B.D. 201.   Compare the observations of the same judge in Norfolk
    (Duke) v. Arbuthnot (1880) 5 C.P.D. 393; and in De la Warr (Earl) v. Miles (1881)
    17 Ch.D. 590.
[41] (1774) Cowp. 102.
[42] See Barker v. Richardson (1821) 4 B. & Ald. 579; post, p. 163.
[43] See Webb v. Bird (1863) 13 C.B.(N.S.) 841.
[44] See Chasemore v. Richards (1859) 7 H.L.C. 349.

of an estoppel by conduct which, while it is not conclusive so far as to prevent denial or explanation of the conduct, presents a bar to any simple denial of the fact, which is merely the legal inference drawn from the conduct." [45]   Cotton L.J. agreed with Thesiger L.J.[46]   In the result, the court directed that the defendants should elect within fourteen days whether they would take a new trial, which the court thought them entitled to upon the point of notice, and that, if they did not so elect, judgment should be entered for the plaintiff.

Dalton v. Angus: In the House of Lords

The defendants did not elect to take a new trial, but appealed to the House of Lords,[47] where the case was twice argued, and the questions were put to seven judges of the High Court. Of the judges, three [48] based their opinions upon grounds which rendered it unnecessary for them to consider in what manner the presumption of lost grant might be rebutted; three [49] in effect agreed with Thesiger and Cotton L.JJ. that the presumption could not be rebutted merely by showing that no grant had in fact been made; while the seventh [50] was of opinion that proof by the defendants that the right claimed had not been granted either by deed or by equitable agreement was sufficient to rebut the presumption.

The opposite points of view of the last four-named judges on this question are fully expressed in the opinions of Lindley and Bowen JJ., respectively. "The theory of implied grant," said Lindley J., "was invented as a means to an end. It afforded a technical common law reason for not disturbing a long-continued open enjoyment. But it appears to me contrary to the reason for the theory itself to allow such an enjoyment to be disturbed simply because it can be proved that no grant was ever in fact made. If any lawful origin for such an enjoyment can be suggested, the presumption in favour of its legality ought to be made." [1]   Bowen J., on the other hand, treated the rule as to presuming a grant or agreement from twenty years' enjoyment as nothing more than a canon of evidence, similar to the presumption of death arising from seven years' absence without news received, or to the presumption of the satisfaction of a bond after twenty years, and similarly liable to be displaced by counter-evidence. "It seems a contradiction in terms to maintain that the rebuttable presumption of the existence of a grant would not at any time have been necessarily counteracted by actual proof that no such grant had ever been made. . . . But . . . it would not now be sufficient to disprove a legal origin, unless

45 (1878) 4 Q.B.D. 173.
46 (1878) 4 Q.B.D. 186.
47 (1881) 6 App.Cas. 740.
48 Pollock B., and Field and Manisty JJ.
49 Lindley, Lopes and Fry JJ., the last-named bowing to authority, but questioning the principle of the decided cases.
50 Bowen J.
1 (1881) 6 App.Cas. 765.

the possibility of an equitable origin were negatived as well." [2]   Lindley and Lopes JJ. agreed with Bowen J. that the question of notice should have been submitted to the jury; but, the defendants having rejected a new trial, this was now immaterial to the particular case.

The House,[3] after hearing the judges, unanimously affirmed the decision of the Court of Appeal, Lord Penzance alone questioning the principle, but following the previous decisions.   Lord Blackburn appears to have proceeded on the grounds which influenced Pollock B. and Field and Manisty JJ., looking upon the right claimed as springing directly from the long enjoyment, without the interposition of a grant inferred or imputed; and he did not therefore consider the question here discussed.   Lord Selborne, while expressing an opinion that the right claimed was conferred by the Prescription Act,[4] thought that the same result could be reached by the doctrine of presumed grant, and expressed his concurrence with the majority of the Court of Appeal.[5]   Lord Watson in effect agreed with Lord Selborne, and Lord Coleridge concurred generally.

Effect of Dalton v. Angus

Although the Lords do not expressly discuss the general question as to what evidence is admissible to rebut the presumption of lost grant, the effect of their judgment is to affirm the opinion of Thesiger and Cotton L.JJ.   It follows that the presumption cannot be displaced by merely showing that no grant was in fact made; the long enjoyment either estops the servient owner from relying on such evidence or over-rides it when given,[6] and the court will make any possible presumption necessary to give that long enjoyment a legal origin.[7]   It appears, however, to be still the law that an incapacity to grant the easement will rebut the presumption in question and negative the claim so far as it rests on the fiction of a lost grant.[8]   It would not be reasonable to presume a grant when the evidence of user does not support in extent the right claimed.[9]   It is clear that the claim may be resisted on any ground which would prevent the right from being acquired by prescription from time immemorial.[10]

In *Tehidy Minerals Ltd.* v. *Norman* [11] Buckley L.J., delivering the

---

[2] (1881) 6 App.Cas. 779 to 783.

[3] Lord Selborne L.C. and Lords Penzance, Blackburn, Watson and Coleridge.

[4] See *post*, p. 146; *ante*, p. 24, n. 30.

[5] (1881) 6 App.Cas. 800.

[6] *Cf. Goodman* v. *Saltash Corporation* (1882) 7 App.Cas. 633; *Bass* v. *Gregory* (1890) 25 Q.B.D. 481; *Phillips* v. *Halliday* [1891] A.C. 228.

[7] *Att.-Gen.* v. *Simpson* [1901] 2 Ch. 671, 698; *East Stonehouse U.D.C.* v. *Willoughby Brothers Ltd.* [1902] 2 K.B. 318, 332; *Dawson* v. *M'Groggan* [1903] 1 I.R. 92, 98.

[8] See the opinion of Thesiger L.J. in *Angus* v. *Dalton* (1878) 4 Q.B.D. 173–175 and the cases there quoted: *Tyne Improvement Commissioners* v. *Imrie* (1899) 81 L.T. 174; *Neaverson* v. *Peterborough R.D.C.* [1902] 1 Ch. 557; *Hulley* v. *Silversprings Bleaching and Dyeing Co.* [1922] 2 Ch. 268; *Green* v. *Matthews* (1930) 46 T.L.R. 206.

[9] *Alfred F. Beckett* v. *Lyons* [1967] Ch. 449.

[10] See *e.g. Roberts & Lovell* v. *James* (1903) 89 L.T. 282.

[11] [1971] 2 Q.B. 528; see p. 138, *ante*.

judgment of the Court of Appeal, stated the effect of *Angus* v. *Dalton* [12] as follows [13]:

> " In our judgment *Angus* v. *Dalton* [12] decides that, where there has been upwards of twenty years' uninterrupted enjoyment of an easement, such enjoyment having the necessary qualities to fulfil the requirements of prescription, then unless, for some reason such as incapacity on the part of the person or persons who might at some time before the commencement of the twenty-year period have made a grant, the existence of such a grant is impossible, the law will adopt a legal fiction that such a grant was made, in spite of any direct evidence that no such grant was in fact made.
>
> " If this legal fiction is not to be displaced by direct evidence that no grant was made, it would be strange if it could be displaced by circumstantial evidence leading to the same conclusion, and in our judgment it must follow that circumstantial evidence tending to negative the existence of a grant (other than evidence establishing impossibility) should not be permitted to displace the fiction. Precisely the same reasoning must, we think, apply to a presumed lost grant of a *profit à prendre* as to an easement."

Application of doctrine of lost grant

It should be noted here that in modern times the courts have had frequent recourse to this doctrine and have repeated and applied in various ways the words of Lord Herschell in *Phillips* v. *Halliday* [14]:

> " Where there has been long-continued possession in assertion of a right, it is a well-settled principle of English law that the right should be presumed to have had a legal origin if such a legal origin was possible, and the courts will presume that those acts were done and those circumstances existed which were necessary to the creation of a valid title."

The doctrine of modern lost grant has been resorted to as an alternative not only to prescription at common law but also to prescription under the Prescription Act 1832. [15] The courts have presumed a lost grant of a right to ventilate a cellar through adjoining property [16]; a

---

[12] (1877) 3 Q.B.D. 85; (1878) 4 Q.B.D. 162; (1881) 6 App.Cas. 740.

[13] [1971] 2 Q.B. 552. Buckley L.J. went on to say that in *White* v. *Taylor* (*No.* 2) [1969] 1 Ch. 160 (in which *Angus* v. *Dalton* (1877) 3 Q.B.D. 85; (1878) 4 Q.B.D. 162; (1881) 6 App.Cas. 740 was not cited to him) he was wrong when he refused to presume a grant: see [1969] 1 Ch. 195.

[14] [1891] A.C. 228, 231. Those words were repeated, by Lord Halsbury in *Clippens Oil Co.* v. *Edinburgh District Water Trustees* [1904] A.C. 69; by Joyce J. in *Hulbert* v. *Dale* [1909] 2 Ch. 578; by Buckley L.J. in *Att.-Gen.* v. *Horner* [1913] 2 Ch. 177; and by Lord Reading in *General Estates Co.* v. *Beaver* [1914] 3 K.B. 926. The court will not order particulars of a lost grant: *Gabriel Wade & English Ltd.* v. *Dixon & Cardus Ltd.* [1937] 3 All E.R. 900.

[15] *Simpson* v. *Godmanchester Corporation* [1897] A.C. 696. In *Tisdall* v. *McArthur & Co.* (*Steel and Metal*) *Ltd.* [1951] I.R. 228, it was contended that a prescriptive right to light cannot arise under a presumption of modern lost grant, but this was not accepted.

[16] *Bass* v. *Gregory* (1890) 25 Q.B.D. 481.

grant in the nature of an agreement substituting one way for another[17]; and as to paying a quit rent.[18] The court will presume not only a grant from an individual but an award[19] or a faculty from the ordinary[20]; or a regulation of a port authority.[21] As regards the Crown, the courts have presumed a grant of a lost charter.[22] They have presumed a grant from the Crown to a corporation of the right to discharge sewage into a tidal river.[23] They have also presumed the grant of a manor,[24] or of a several fishery in tidal waters.[25] Lost grants by the Crown have also been presumed of a franchise ferry, whether from point to point[26] or from vill to vill.[27]

At the time of the passing of the Prescription Act 1832, a "twenty years' rule" had become established, whereby a presumption of lost grant was raised by user as of right for twenty years.[28] Since the Act this rule has become blurred. The doctrine must not be applied blindly or unrealistically.[29] The presumption of a legal grant should be applied only when no other explanation is forthcoming; when another explanation is equally possible, the court should not presume a legal origin.[30] In *Healey* v. *Hawkins*[31] Goff J., on the basis that enjoyment for twenty years might not have continued right down to the time of action brought (so that the Prescription Act was not available), presumed on the facts before him a lost modern grant. If evidence is given of user as of right during living memory and there is nothing to rebut the consequent[32] presumption of a pre-1189 grant, no presumption of a modern grant is required.[33]

17 *Hulbert* v. *Dale* [1909] 2 Ch. 570.
18 *Bomford* v. *Neville* [1904] 1 I.R. 474; *Foley's Charity Trustees* v. *Dudley* [1910] 1 K.B. 317.
19 *East Stonehouse U.D.C.* v. *Willoughby Brothers Ltd.* [1902] 2 K.B. 332.
20 *Phillips* v. *Halliday* [1891] A.C. 228; *Stileman-Gibbard* v. *Wilkinson* [1897] 1 Q.B. 749.
21 *Att.-Gen.* v. *Wright* [1897] 2 Q.B. 318.
22 *Goodtitle* v. *Baldwin* (1809) 11 East 490; *Lord Rivers* v. *Adams* (1878) 3 Ex.D. 365. As to a lost grant by the Crown of a market, see *Att.-Gen.* v. *Horner* (1885) 11 App.Cas. 66; [1913] 2 Ch. 140.
23 *Somersetshire Drainage Commissioners* v. *Bridgwater Corporation* (1904) 81 L.T. 729.
24 *Merttens* v. *Hill* [1901] 1 Ch. 851.
25 *Goodman* v. *Saltash Corporation* (1882) 7 App.Cas. 633.
26 *Dysart* v. *Hammerton* [1914] 1 Ch. 822. See also the same case in the House of Lords [1916] A.C. 57, 80.
27 *General Estates Co.* v. *Beaver* [1914] 3 K.B. 918.
28 See *e.g. Dalton* v. *Angus* (1881) 6 App.Cas. 740, 780–812; *Bryant* v. *Foot* (1867) L.R. 2 Q.B. 161, 181; *Campbell* v. *Wilson* (1803) 3 East 294.
29 *Norfolk (Duke)* v. *Arbuthnot* (1880) 5 C.P.D. 390, 394; *Tilbury* v. *Silva* (1890) 45 Ch.D. 98; *Att.-Gen.* v. *Simpson* [1901] 2 Ch. 673, 698; *Gardner* v. *Hodgson's Kingston Brewery Co.* [1903] A.C. 229, 235.
30 *Alfred F. Beckett Ltd.* v. *Lyons* [1967] Ch. 449, 473–476, C.A.
31 [1968] 1 W.L.R. 1967, 1976. Goff J. did not, however, accept as a principle of general application the suggestion in the 13th ed. of this work, at p. 126, that it would seem right to expect the doctrine to be applied where enjoyment for a period of twenty years has not continued right down to the time of action brought.
32 See *ante*, p. 133.
33 *R. C. P. Holdings Ltd.* v. *Rogers* [1953] 1 All E.R. 1029, 1031.

(3) *The Prescription Act 1832*

Purpose and effect

The real intention behind the Prescription Act 1832 [34] is a matter of speculation. The preamble suggests an intention to prevent claims " at common law," *i.e.* based on immemorial user, from being defeated by evidence of commencement of user after 1189; but this object had been achieved by the doctrine of modern lost grant, above referred to; and it seems that the chief purpose was to found on a statutory presumption the grant which, under that doctrine, unbelieving juries were required to find, as a fact, to be the basis of long user. [35] The Act, however, contains enactments much more extensive than would be necessary for the attainment of this object merely. [36]

The Act has not superseded either of the pre-existing methods of claiming by prescription. An easement is still capable of being established by prescription at common law, or under the doctrine of modern lost grant, [37] and it is not unusual to plead all three methods alternatively. [38] The Act merely provides a statutory method of establishing an easement in some cases. It is not affected by anything in Part I of the Law of Property Act 1925. [39]

It should be noticed that in *Hyman* v. *Van den Bergh* [40] Farwell L.J., basing himself on *Tapling* v. *Jones*, [41] expressed (*obiter*) his personal opinion that (a) the doctrine of modern lost grant is no longer applicable to claims to *light*, and that (b) in regard to *light*, a defence based on agreement in writing (s. 3 of the Act), or interruption (s. 4) cannot be evaded by setting up a claim otherwise than under the Act. The first proposition was considered and not accepted by Kingsmill Moore J. in *Tisdall* v. *McArthur & Co.* (*Steel and Metal*) *Ltd.* [42] The second seems inconsistent with *Norfolk* (*Duke*) v. *Arbuthnot*, [43] where the Court of Appeal, after negativing, on the ground of interruption, a claim to light under the Act, proceeded to negative, on the facts, an alternative claim

---

[34] 2 & 3 Will. 4, c. 71, formerly known as Lord Tenterden's Act.
[35] The Act, said Parke B. (referring to the relief of the consciences of jurymen), " was intended to accomplish this object by shortening in effect the period of prescription, and making that possession a bar or title of itself which was so before only by the intervention of the jury " (*Bright* v. *Walker* (1834) 1 C.M. & R. 211, 218); and *per* Cockburn C.J., in *Angus* v. *Dalton* (1877) 3 Q.B.D. 85, 105–106; and Lord Macnaghten, in *Gardner* v. *Hodgson's Kingston Brewery Co.* [1903] A.C. 229, 236.
[36] Mr. Gale added " and it certainly is to be lamented that its provisions were not more carefully framed."
[37] " The statute only applies where you want to stand upon thirty years' user; but here, where the title is one of 200 or 300 years, that statute is not needed, and the title can be rested on the original right before the passing of the statute " (*per* Lord Hatherley L.C. in *Warrick* v. *Queen's College, Oxford* (1871) 6 Ch.App. 716, 728); see also *Aynsley* v. *Glover* (1875) 10 Ch.App. 283; *Gardner* v. *Hodgson's Kingston Brewery Co.* [1903] A.C. 229, 238.
[38] See *Tehidy Minerals Ltd.* v. *Norman* [1971] 2 Q.B. 528 and *post*, p. 377.
[39] Law of Property Act 1925, s. 12.
[40] [1908] 1 Ch. 167, 176–178.
[41] (1865) 11 H.L.C. 290.
[42] [1951] I.R. 228. The Court of Appeal in Ireland expressed no opinion on the point.
[43] (1880) 5 C.P.D. 390.

under the doctrine of modern lost grant, from which it may be inferred that the claim might, on other facts, have been established.

Long title and preamble

The long title to the Prescription Act 1832 is " An Act for shortening the Time of Prescription in certain cases." The preamble is as follows:

> " Whereas the expression ' time immemorial, or time whereof the memory of man runneth not to the contrary,' is now by the law of England in many cases considered to include and denote the whole period of time from the reign of King Richard the First, whereby the title to matters that have been long enjoyed is sometimes defeated by showing the commencement of such enjoyment, which is in many cases productive of inconvenience and injustice; for remedy thereof be it enacted. . . ."

Claims to profits à prendre

Section 1 of the Prescription Act 1832 is as follows:

> " 1. No claim which may be lawfully made at the common law, by custom, prescription, or grant, to any right of common or other profit or benefit to be taken and enjoyed from or upon any land of our sovereign lord the King, his heirs or successors, or any land being parcel of the Duchy of Lancaster, or the Duchy of Cornwall, or of any ecclesiastical or lay person, or body corporate (except such matters and things as are herein specially provided for, and except tithes, rent, and services), shall, where such right, profit, or benefit shall have been actually taken and enjoyed by any person claiming right thereto without interruption for the full period of thirty years, be defeated or destroyed by showing only that such right, profit or benefit, was first taken or enjoyed at any time prior to such period of thirty years, but nevertheless such claim may be defeated in any other way by which the same is now liable to be defeated; and when such right, profit or benefit, shall have been so taken and enjoyed as aforesaid for the full period of sixty years, the right thereto shall be deemed absolute and indefeasible, unless it shall appear that the same was taken and enjoyed by some consent or agreement expressly made or given for that purpose by deed or writing."

This section concerns rights of the nature of *profits à prendre*, not easements, but its terms are similar to those of section 2 below which does concern easements. Its interpretation and effect on the acquisition of *profits à prendre* are therefore of relevance also to the law of easements.[44]

---

[44] Profits annexed to a dominant tenement and also profits in gross may be claimed by prescription at common law and under the doctrine of modern lost grant in the same manner as easements. On the other hand, s. 1 of the Prescription Act 1832 almost certainly does not apply to profits in gross, which appear to be

Rights of way, etc.

Section 2 of the Prescription Act 1832 is as follows:

> " 2. No claim which may be lawfully made at the common law, by custom, prescription or grant, to any way or other easement, or to any watercourse or the use of any water to be enjoyed or derived upon, over, or from any land or water of our said lord the King, his heirs or successors, or being parcel of the Duchy of Lancaster or of the Duchy of Cornwall, or being the property of any ecclesiastical or lay person, or body corporate, when such way or other matter as herein last before mentioned shall have been actually enjoyed by any person claiming right thereto without interruption for the full period of twenty years, shall be defeated or destroyed by showing only that such way or other matter was first enjoyed at any time prior to such period of twenty years, but nevertheless such claim may be defeated in any other way by which the same is now liable to be defeated; and where such way or other matter, as herein last before mentioned, shall have been so enjoyed as aforesaid for the full period of forty years, the right thereto shall be deemed absolute and indefeasible, unless it shall appear that the same was enjoyed by some consent or agreement expressly given or made for that purpose by deed or writing."

This section applies to all positive easements [45] and is not, as suggested in *Webb* v. *Bird*,[46] confined to rights of way and water.[45] A right to adulterate the water of a natural stream has been held to be a watercourse [47] but not a claim to water occasionally escaping from a lock.[48] The section does not apply to easements of light,[49] which is separately dealt with by section 3, nor was it apparently regarded in *Dalton* v. *Angus* [50] as applying to other purely negative easements. It was, however, evidently assumed in *Harris* v. *De Pinna* [1] that the section would apply to a negative easement in the form of a right to the passage of air through a defined channel.

Apart from the temporal limits expressed, the section does not appear to alter the common law. User for either of the two periods of

---

excluded from its operation by s. 5. In other respects, and apart from the different periods of enjoyment which are requisite, the Act applies the same rules to easements and to profits. It applies to profits *pur cause de vicinage*: see *Prichard* v. *Powell* (1845) 10 Q.B. 589.

45 *Dalton* v. *Angus* (1881) 6 App.Cas. 740, 798; *Bass* v. *Gregory* (1890) 25 Q.B.D. 481; *Simpson* v. *Godmanchester Corporation* [1897] A.C. 696, 709. It was suggested *obiter* in *Crisp* v. *Martin* (1876) 2 P.D. 15, 28, that the Act did not apply to the right to use a pew in the parish church.

46 (1861) 10 C.B.(N.S.) 268, 283.

47 *Wright* v. *Williams* (1836) 1 M. & W. 77; *Carlyon* v. *Lovering* (1857) 1 H. & N. 784, 797–798.

48 *Staffordshire & Worcestershire Canal Co.* v. *Birmingham Canal Co.* (1866) L.R. 1 H.L. 254.

49 *Perry* v. *Eames* [1891] 1 Ch. 658; *Wheaton* v. *Maple & Co.* [1893] 3 Ch. 48. See s. 3 below.

50 (1881) 6 App.Cas. 740, 798 *et seq.* As to the distinction between positive and negative easements, see p. 3, *ante.*   1 (1886) 33 Ch.D. 250.

twenty and forty years must be " as of right," that is, *nec vi, nec clam, nec precario*,[2] and the right enjoyed must have been enjoyed as an easement.[3] A claim based on user during either period (extended or not extended by s. 7 or s. 8 [4]) can be defeated by proof of unity of possession of both tenements at any time during the period, for during such unity the user cannot be " as of right " in the sense intended, *i.e.* as an easement.[5] A claim based on enjoyment for the shorter period can be defeated in any way (except proof of commencement of enjoyment within the time of legal memory) in which a claim could be defeated before the Act. A claim based on user for the longer period is prima facie capable of being defeated only by proof of consent in writing, but it is open to question [6] whether the positive enactment that the right is to be deemed absolute makes it unnecessary to presume a grant, and so enables a right to be established, by forty years' user of the kind required by the Act, against a servient owner who was incapable of granting it.

Right of light

Section 3 of the Prescription Act 1832, is as follows:

" 3. When the access and use of light to and for any dwelling-house, workshop, or other building shall have been actually enjoyed therewith for the full period of twenty [7] years without interruption, the right thereto shall be deemed absolute and indefeasible, any local usage or custom to the contrary notwithstanding, unless it shall appear that the same was enjoyed by some consent or agreement [7] expressly made or given for that purpose by deed or writing."

This section is concerned exclusively with easements of light.[8] Unlike sections 1 and 2, it does not name or bind the Crown.[9] It must be read with section 4, so that no right can become absolute and indefeasible until called in question in some action or suit.[10] The words " other building " do not necessarily include any structure.[11] They have been held to include a church,[12] an unconsecrated chapel,[13]

---

[2] *Harbidge* v. *Warwick* (1849) 3 Exch. 552; *Gaved* v. *Martyn* (1865) 19 C.B.(N.S.) 732; *Chamber Colliery Co.* v. *Hopwood* (1886) 32 Ch.D. 549; *Gardner* v. *Hodgson's Kingston Brewery Co.* [1903] A.C. 229. As to enjoyment as of right and generally as to the qualities and character of the necessary enjoyment, see pp. 170 *et seq., post.*
[3] *Onley* v. *Gardiner* (1838) 4 M. & W. 496. [4] See pp. 155–157, *post.*
[5] *Damper* v. *Bassett* [1901] 2 Ch. 350; *Onley* v. *Gardiner, supra.*
[6] See pp. 168–169, *post.* [7] See *post*, p. 150.
[8] The special characteristics of easements of light are considered in Chap. 7, *post.*
[9] *Perry* v. *Eames* [1891] 1 Ch. 658; *Wheaton* v. *Maple & Co.* [1893] 3 Ch. 48.
[10] *Colls* v. *Home and Colonial Stores* [1904] A.C. 179, 189; *Hyman* v. *Van den Bergh* [1908] 1 Ch. 167, 172. [11] See *post*, p. 239.
[12] *Ecclesiastical Commissioners* v. *Kino* (1880) 14 Ch.D. 213; *Anderson* v. *Francis* [1906] W.N. 160. A contrary view is suggested in *Norfolk (Duke)* v. *Arbuthnot* (1880) 5 C.P.D. 392, but that decision seems to turn rather on the unusual nature of the aperture, evidence of interruption, and the known history of the buildings concerned.
[13] *Att.-Gen.* v. *Queen Anne Gardens and Mansions Co.* (1889) 60 L.T. 759.

a picture gallery,[13] a greenhouse,[14] and an open-sided garage,[15] but not a structure for storing timber,[16] nor does it seem that they would apply to a trade fixture removable by a tenant at the end of his tenancy.[17] The quantum of light that can be claimed is not diminished by the user of a room for purposes requiring less than a normal amount of light, e.g. as a scullery [18]; nor is the claim affected by the fact that the light is transmitted through the glass roof of an adjacent yard,[19] or that the light, if apparently capable of being admitted, has not been admitted continuously,[20] or that the dominant house has been unoccupied.[21]

It is not necessary that the claim to light should be exercised " as of right " [22] for, unlike section 2, section 3 does not contain the words " claiming right thereto." There must, however, be evidence on which " actual enjoyment " can be found as a fact [23] and the access of light must be enjoyed in the character of an easement, and therefore enjoyment while the dominant and servient tenements are in the same occupation is not sufficient.[24]

No alteration of a building, which would not involve the loss of a right to light when indefeasibly acquired, will, if made during the currency of the statutory period, prevent the acquisition of the light.[25]

The interruption of light is subject to the same general considerations as the interruption of other easements.[26] In particular it has been held that a fluctuating or temporary obstruction caused, for instance, by the stacking of empty packing cases which are removed from time to time is not of itself an interruption within the section [27] nor is the installation of a glass roof.[28] The conventional method of interrupting the access of light, in order to prevent the acquisition of an easement,

---

[14] Clifford v. Holt [1899] 1 Ch. 698.
[15] Smith & Co. (Orpington) v. Morris (1962) 112 L.J. 702, County Court.
[16] Harris v. De Pinna (1886) 33 Ch.D. 238.
[17] Maberley v. Dowson (1827) 5 L.J.(o.s.)K.B. 261.
[18] Price v. Hilditch [1930] 1 Ch. 500.
[19] Tisdall v. McArthur & Co. (Steel and Metal) Ltd. [1951] I.R. 228.
[20] Cooper v. Straker (1888) 40 Ch.D. 21; Collis v. Laugher [1894] 3 Ch. 659; Smith v. Baxter [1900] 2 Ch. 138.
[21] Courtauld v. Legh (1869) L.R. 4 Exch. 126.
[22] Colls v. Home and Colonial Stores [1904] A.C. 179, 205.
[23] Smith v. Baxter [1900] 2 Ch. 138.
[24] Harbidge v. Warwick (1849) 3 Exch. 552, where unity of possession existed throughout the whole period relied on. The decision of Lord Hatherley (Page Wood V.-C.) in Simper v. Foley (1862) 2 J. & H. 555, that s. 3 is satisfied by enjoyment for twenty years, followed by a period of unity of possession, and his dictum in Ladyman v. Grave (1871) 6 Ch.App. 763, 768, that a right can be established under s. 3 by enjoyment for two periods, together making twenty years but separated by a period of unity of possession, would not, it is thought, now be followed; see Hyman v. Van den Bergh [1907] 2 Ch. 525–528; [1908] 1 Ch. 176.
[25] Andrews v. Waite [1907] 2 Ch. 500.
[26] Smith v. Baxter [1900] 2 Ch. 138. See post, pp. 152–154.
[27] Presland v. Bingham (1889) 41 Ch.D. 268. The temporary nature of such an obstruction shifts the onus on to the defendant. (Per Lindley L.J., ibid. 276.)
[28] Tisdall v. McArthur & Co. (Steel and Metal) Ltd. [1951] I.R. 228.

is by the erection of a screen or hoarding near the boundary of the prospectively servient property.[29]

It is settled that enjoyment as against an owner of the servient tenement who cannot dispose of the fee may be sufficient, for it is not necessary to presume an absolute grant. This result follows from the words of section 3, as to which Lord Westbury laid down in the House of Lords that the right to light now depends on positive enactment. " It is a matter *juris positivi*, and does not require, and therefore ought not to be rested on, any presumption of grant." [30]

Where the servient tenement is in the occupation of a lessee for years, the right is under section 3 of the Act acquired as against all persons interested in the servient tenement, including owners in fee,[31] even if the owner of the servient tenement be also the owner of the dominant tenement.[32]

A claim will be defeated by written consent or agreement affecting the enjoyment during any part of the period of twenty years preceding action brought.[33] An agreement not in writing is ineffective to prevent the acquisition of the right,[34] but the signature of the servient owner is unnecessary, and an agreement signed by the dominant owner [35] or his tenant [36] or any person in actual occupation,[37] is sufficient, provided it clearly refers to light.[38] If a lease or conveyance excepts the right to light in such a way as merely to negative the implication of a grant, the exception does not constitute an agreement within the section [39] but the case is otherwise, and an " agreement " is constituted, if the instrument contains words which positively authorise the grantor to build as he pleases.[40]

---

[29] Corporations holding their land for special purposes have usually the same rights in this respect as individuals; see *Bonner* v. *G.W.R.* (1883) 24 Ch.D. 1; *Myers* v. *Catterson* (1889) 43 Ch.D. 470; *Foster* v. *London, Chatham & Dover Ry.* [1895] 1 Q.B. 711; *Paddington Corporation* v. *Att.-Gen.* [1906] A.C. 1.

[30] *Tapling* v. *Jones* (1865) 11 H.L.C. 290, 304. See *Jordeson* v. *Sutton Co.* [1898] 2 Ch. 614, 618, 626, where the servient tenement belonged to a gas company, as to whom it was objected that they were under a statutory incapacity to grant a right of light, and North J. overruled the objection, holding that no presumption of grant was necessary. The fact that a presumption of grant is not required for the purposes of the Act does not import that a grant cannot be presumed independently of it: *Tisdall* v. *McArthur & Co.* (*Steel and Metal*) *Ltd.* [1951] I.R. 228, where *Tapling* v. *Jones* is explained. See also *Healey* v. *Hawkins* [1968] 1 W.L.R. 1967.

[31] *Simper* v. *Foley* (1862) 2 J. & H. 555, 564; *Ladyman* v. *Grave* (1871) 6 Ch.App. 763, 769.

[32] *Morgan* v. *Fear* [1907] A.C. 429, affg. C.A. [1906] 2 Ch. 406. This decision seems to have been arrived at in deference to the following earlier authorities, *viz.*: *Frewen* v. *Philipps* (1861) 11 C.B.(N.S.) 449; *Mitchell* v. *Cantrill* (1887) 37 Ch.D. 56; *Robson* v. *Edwards* [1893] 2 Ch. 146.

[33] *Hyman* v. *Van den Bergh* [1908] 1 Ch. 167.

[34] *Mallam* v. *Rose* [1915] 2 Ch. 222.

[35] *Bewley* v. *Atkinson* (1879) 13 Ch.D. 283.

[36] *Hyman* v. *Van den Bergh* [1908] 1 Ch. 167.   [37] *Ibid.* 179.

[38] Thus a stone placed to perpetuate the right to build has been held not to refer unequivocally to light (*Ruscoe* v. *Grounsell* (1903) 89 L.T. 426).

[39] *Mitchell* v. *Cantrill* (1887) 37 Ch.D. 56; *Hapgood* v. *Martin* (1934) 51 T.L.R. 82.

[40] *Haynes* v. *King* [1893] 3 Ch. 439; *Foster* v. *Lyons & Co.* [1927] 1 Ch. 219; *Willoughby* v. *Eckstein* [1937] Ch. 167; *Blake and Lyons Ltd.* v. *Lewis Berger & Sons Ltd.* [1951] 2 T.L.R. 605.

The application of a written agreement to given circumstances will ordinarily be a question of construction; thus a reference to a " window " has been held to include a skylight.[41]

The section effectively destroys local customs by which the right to light might be defeated.[42]

The Rights of Light Act

In March 1957, a Committee, presided over by Mr. Justice Harman, was appointed to consider whether legislation was desirable (*inter alia*) to amend the law relating to rights of light in relation to war-damaged sites or sites whose development was prevented or impeded by reason of restrictions or controls imposed during or after the 1939–1945 war.

In their Report [43] the Committee, by way of preface to their recommendations, said (1) that it would be a mistake to suppose that planning legislation has deprived the right of light of its former practical importance, in the sense that permission is unlikely now to be given for any building which would obstruct light to the point of nuisance; (2) that between 1938 and 1954 the development of all vacant sites was more or less hampered by matters outside the control of their owners, and that particularly hard hit in this respect are the owners of bombed buildings who have been unable to prevent the enjoyment by neighbouring buildings of light over the space left vacant by the bombing; (3) that the conventional erection of a screen to interrupt the flow of light was prevented by war-time restrictions, and is sometimes refused planning permission even now; and (4) that there is thus a real practical problem calling for a remedy in favour of prospectively servient property, whether damaged in the war or not. Nothing, however (the Committee thought), was required, or could usefully be done, to preserve the rights of destroyed or damaged dominant or prospectively dominant buildings.

The recommendations of the Committee have been embodied in the Rights of Light Act 1959, which provides for the notional interruption of light as an alternative to actual interruption; and for the temporary extension of the statutory twenty-year period. The Act applies to Crown land while preserving the general immunity of Crown land from section 3 of the Prescription Act 1832.[44]

The period of twenty years referred to in sections 3 and 6 of the Act of 1832 is extended to twenty-seven years for the purposes of the following proceedings: (i) proceedings in any action begun after July 16, 1959, and before January 1, 1963, except an action which has been finally disposed of before July 14, 1958, and (ii) proceedings in any action begun on or after January 1, 1963, in so far as it falls to be deter-

---

41 *Easton* v. *Isted* [1903] 1 Ch. 405.
42 *Cooper* v. *Hubbuck* (1862) 12 C.B.(N.S.) 456; *Truscott* v. *Merchant Tailors' Co.* (1856) 11 Exch. 855.
43 The Report of the Committee on the Law Relating to Rights of Light (Cmnd. 473), published on May 12, 1958.
44 Rights of Light Act 1959, s. 4.

mined in those proceedings whether (a) a person is entitled to an absolute and indefeasible right to light to a building, and (b) anything done on or before January 1, 1963 (whether by a notional obstruction or otherwise) constitutes, or if continued or completed would constitute, an infringement of that right.[45] Thus, until the end of 1962, a servient owner might obstruct the light being received by a building on adjoining land which had not enjoyed the access of light for more than twenty-six years. These temporary provisions have, however, no longer any practical importance.

The Act [46] enables the owner [47] of land over which light passes to a dwelling-house, workshop or other building to apply to the local authority for the registration of a notice in the register of local land charges.[48] The application must identify the servient land and the dominant building and specify the position and dimensions of an opaque structure to which the notice is intended to be equivalent. The Lands Tribunal, before the application is made, must have certified [49] either that adequate notice has been given to all persons who appear to the Lands Tribunal to be likely to be affected by the registration of such a notice or that the case is one of exceptional urgency. (In this latter case the certificate must specify the length of time for the notice to be on the register.) When an application has been properly made a notice should then be registered by the local authority.

A notice has effect until the expiry of one year beginning with the date of registration or, where the certificate of the Lands Tribunal certifies the case to be one of exceptional urgency, at the end of the period specified in the certificate, whichever event occurs first. In either case the notice may cease to have effect on an earlier date if the registration is cancelled.[50]

Where a notice is registered then, for the purposes of determining whether any person is entitled (by virtue of the Prescription Act 1832 or otherwise) to a right to the access of light to the dominant building across the servient land, the access of light to that building shall be treated as obstructed to the same extent as if an opaque structure of the specified dimensions had on the date of registration of the notice been erected by the applicant in the specified position, and had remained in that position only during the period for which the notice has effect.[1]

Any person who would have had a right of action in respect of the erection of such a structure as is specified in the application, as infringing a right to the access of light to the dominant building, has the like

---

[45] *Ibid*. s. 1.   [46] *Ibid*. s. 2.
[47] " Owner " includes a lessee where the lease has not less than seven years unexpired and a mortgagee in possession: s. 7.
[48] The Local Land Charges Rules 1966 (S.I. No. 579), regulate the registration of light obstruction notices in Part XI of the register of local land charges under s. 2 of the Act of 1959: see rule 16.
[49] The Lands Tribunal Rules 1963 (S.I. No. 483), Part VI, regulate applications to the Lands Tribunal for a certificate under s. 2 of the Act of 1959.
[50] s. 3 (2).   [1] s. 3 (1).

right of action in respect of the registration of the notice.[2] He may be granted such declaration as the court considers appropriate, and an order cancelling or varying the registration.[3] In order to avoid the problem of an interruption during the final year of the prescriptive period under section 3 of the Prescription Act 1832, it is provided in the Act of 1959 that the dominant owner may treat his enjoyment as having begun one year earlier than it did.[4]

For the purposes of section 4 of the Prescription Act 1832 (under which a period of enjoyment is not to be treated as interrupted except by a matter submitted to or acquiesced in for one year after notice thereof) persons interested in the dominant building are deemed to have notice of the registration and of the applicant, and until an action is brought in respect of the registration all such persons are deemed to acquiesce in the notional obstruction. If the action fails the court may direct that such persons shall continue to be deemed to acquiesce in the notional obstruction as if the action had not been brought.[5]

Periods of enjoyment: Interruption

Section 4 of the Prescription Act 1832 is as follows:

> " 4. Each of the respective periods of years hereinbefore mentioned shall be deemed and taken to be the period next before some suit or action wherein the claim or matter to which such period may relate shall have been or shall be brought into question, and that no act or other matter shall be deemed to be an interruption within the meaning of this statute, unless the same shall have been or shall be submitted to or acquiesced in for one year after the party interrupted shall have had or shall have notice thereof, and of the person making or authorising the same to be made."

This section is qualified by the provisions as to disability in section 7.[6] The enjoyment which gives an easement under the Act is enjoyment (" as of right " under sections 1 and 2 but not necessarily so under section 3)[7] during a period, of the prescribed length, running back from the commencement of an action; and not during any period of the specified length, whenever occurring.[8] Consequently, unless or until the claim or matter is brought into question in some action, the right under the Act

---

2 s. 3 (3).
3 s. 3 (5). See *Hawker* v. *Tomalin* (1969) 20 P. & C.R. 550, as to the desirable form of declaration and as to the exercise of the court's discretion under s. 3 (5).
4 s. 3 (4).
5 s. 3 (6).
6 See p. 155, *post*.
7 See p. 148, *ante*.
8 *Colls* v. *Home and Colonial Stores* [1904] A.C. 179, 189; *Wright* v. *Williams* (1836) 1 M. & W. 77; *Richards* v. *Fry* (1838) 7 A. & E. 698; *Flight* v. *Thomas* (1841) 8 Cl. & Fin. 231; *Tilbury* v. *Silva* (1890) 45 Ch.D. 98; *Jones* v. *Price* (1836) 3 Bing.N.C. 52.

remains inchoate[9]; but the commencement of such an action fixes the period and enables the right to be established.[10]

The actual user is only sufficient to satisfy the statute if during the whole of the statutory period (whether acts of user be proved in each year or not) the user is enough at any rate to carry to the mind of a reasonable person who is in possession of the servient tenement the fact that a continuous right to enjoyment is being asserted and ought to be resisted if such right is not recognised and if resistance to it is intended.[11] Whether the actual user is thus sufficient is a question of fact.[12]   Suggestions that actual user in the first and last years of the period relied on [13] or in every year of such a period [14] must necessarily be proved have not been adopted or followed by the Court of Appeal.[15]   In *Hollins* v. *Verney* [16] Lindley L.J. said that

"a cessation of user which excludes an inference of actual enjoyment as of right for the full statutory period will be fatal at whatsoever portion of the period the cessation occurs; and, on the other hand, a cessation of user which does not exclude such inference is not fatal, even although it occurs at the beginning, or the end of, the period."

An "interruption" within the section may arise from any actual discontinuance of enjoyment by reason of an obstruction acquiesced in for one year. It may result from adverse [17] obstruction by the servient owner [18] or by a stranger [19]; but the commencement of proceedings by the servient owner is not an "interruption." [20]

Since an interruption is required by section 4 to be acquiesced in for one year, it follows that an enjoyment for a period exceeding nineteen years which is then obstructed can be protected if proceedings are brought after twenty years have run and before the obstruction

9 *Colls* v. *Home and Colonial Stores* [1904] A.C. 179, 189; *Hyman* v. *Van den Bergh* [1907] 2 Ch. 516, 524–525; [1908] Ch. 167, 171, 175.
10 *Cooper* v. *Hubbuck* (1862) 12 C.B.(N.S.) 456; *Beytagh* v. *Cassidy* (1868) 16 W.R. 403.
11 *Hollins* v. *Verney* (1884) 13 Q.B.D. 304, 315; see also *Bower* v. *John Etherington Ltd.* (1965) 53 D.L.R. (2d) 338, Nova Scotia Supreme Court.
12 *Smith* v. *Baxter* [1900] 2 Ch. 138. In *White* v. *Taylor* (*No. 2*) [1969] 1 Ch. 160 non-user for two periods, each of five or six years, defeated a claim under the Act; see [1969] 1 Ch. 194.
13 See *Carr* v. *Foster* (1842) 3 Q.B. 581; *Bailey* v. *Appleyard* (1838) 8 A. & E. 161; *Parker* v. *Mitchell* (1840) 11 A. & E. 788.
14 Per Parke B. in *Lowe* v. *Carpenter* (1851) 6 Exch. 825.
15 *Hollins* v. *Verney* (1884) 13 Q.B.D. 304, 313, 314 (approving *Hall* v. *Swift*, 4 Bing.N.C. 381; *Lawson* v. *Langley*, 4 A. & E. 890); *De la Warr* (*Earl*) v. *Miles* (1881) 17 Ch. 535, 600.
16 13 Q.B.D. 314. The dictum of Patteson J. in *Payne* v. *Shedden* (1834) 1 M. & Rob. 383, that the use of a way for ten years, and an agreement for the next ten to discontinue the user, retaining the right, would be sufficient under the Act appears to be inconsistent with the cases cited above.
17 The party's own obstruction of his light does not defeat him (*Smith* v. *Baxter* [1900] 2 Ch. 138, 143).
18 *Plasterers' Co.* v. *Parish Clerks' Co.* (1851) 6 Exch. 630.
19 *Davies* v. *Williams* (1851) 16 Q.B.D. 558.
20 *Reilly* v. *Orange* [1955] 2 Q.B. 112.

has lasted one year.[21] If, however, the proceedings are brought before the twenty years have run, the plaintiff's right is still inchoate and he has no protection by injunction or otherwise.[22]

An interruption from natural causes of the flow of a stream will not prevent prescription,[23] nor will a fluctuating interruption.[24] Repeated interruptions, each for less than a year, may be evidence of contentious user so as to show that the enjoyment is not " as of right " under section 2 [25] or they may result in the acquisition of a qualified easement only.[26]

A person asserting an interruption must prove that some notice other than the mere existence of a physical obstruction was given to the person interrupted.[27] Acquiescence is then a question of fact.[28] It may be negatived by evidence of protests made in anticipation of the interruption even if not subsequently renewed during the year following its completion.[29] In order to negative submission or acquiescence, it is not essential to bring an action or to remove the obstruction.[30] There is no acquiescence in an interruption when the owner of the dominant tenement refuses to exercise his right under a permission given by the owner of the servient tenement.[31]

What the claimant may allege

Section 5 of the Prescription Act 1832 is as follows:

> " 5. In all actions upon the case and other pleadings, wherein the party claiming may now by law allege his right generally, without averring the existence of such right from time immemorial, such general allegation shall still be deemed sufficient, and if the same shall be denied, all and every the matters in this Act mentioned and provided which shall be applicable to the case, shall be admissible in evidence to sustain or rebut such allegation; and in all pleadings to actions of trespass, and in all other pleadings wherein, before the passing of this Act, it would have been necessary to allege the right to have existed from time immemorial, it shall be sufficient to allege the enjoyment thereof as of right by the occupiers of the tenement in respect whereof the same is claimed for and during such of the periods mentioned in this Act as may be

---

21 *Flight* v. *Thomas* (1841) 1 A. & E. 688; 8 Cl. & Fin. 231; see this case explained by Lord Campbell in *Eaton* v. *Swansea Waterworks Co.* (1851) 17 Q.B. 267, 272. Enjoyment continues, though interrupted, unless the interruption be acquiesced in for a year.
22 *Bridewell Hospital (Governors)* v. *Ward, Lock, Bowden & Co.* (1893) 62 L.J.Ch. 270; *Battersea* v. *London City Sewers Commissioners* [1895] 2 Ch. 708.
23 *Hall* v. *Swift* (1838) 4 Bing.N.C. 381; see *Carr* v. *Foster* (1842) 3 Q.B. 581.
24 *Presland* v. *Bingham* (1889) 41 Ch.D. 268.
25 *Eaton* v. *Swansea Waterworks Co.* (1851) 17 Q.B. 267.
26 *Rolle* v. *Whyte* (1868) L.R. 3 Q.B. 286.
27 *Seddon* v. *Bank of Bolton* (1882) 19 Ch.D. 462; *Glover* v. *Coleman* (1874) L.R. 10 C.P. 108.
28 *Bennison* v. *Cartwright* (1864) 5 B. & S. 1.
29 *Davies* v. *Du Paver* [1953] 1 Q.B. 184.
30 *Glover* v. *Coleman* (1874) L.R. 10 C.P. 108.
31 *Ward* v. *Kirkland* [1967] Ch. 194, 231–232.

applicable to the case, and without claiming in the name or right of the owner of the fee, as is now usually done; and if the other party shall intend to rely on any proviso, exception, incapacity, disability, contract, agreement, or other matter hereinbefore mentioned, or on any cause or matter of fact or of law not inconsistent with the simple fact of enjoyment, the same shall be specially alleged and set forth in answer to the allegation of the party claiming, and shall not be received in evidence on any general traverse or denial of such allegation."

This section relates to pleading, as to which see the observations *post*, pp. 375 *et seq.* The requirement that enjoyment must be alleged to have been " as of right " does not apply where an easement of light is being claimed.[32] The reference to " the tenement in respect whereof the same is claimed " shows that the Act does not apply to *profits à prendre* in gross.[33]

No presumptions to be allowed

Section 6 of the Prescription Act 1832 is as follows:

" 6. In the several cases mentioned in and provided for by this Act, no presumption shall be allowed or made in favour or support of any claim, upon proof of the exercise or enjoyment of the right or matter claimed for any less period of time or number of years than for such period or number mentioned in this Act as may be applicable to the case and to the nature of the claim."

In *Hanmer* v. *Chance* [34] Lord Westbury said:

" The meaning appears to be, that no presumption or inference in support of the claim shall be derived from the bare fact of user or enjoyment for less than the prescribed number of years; but where there are other circumstances in addition, the statute does not take away from the fact of enjoyment for a shorter period its natural weight as evidence, so as to preclude a jury from taking it, along with other circumstances, into consideration as evidence of a grant."

Proviso for disabilities

Section 7 of the Prescription Act 1832 is as follows:

" 7. Provided also that the time during which any person, other-wise capable of resisting any claim to any of the matters before mentioned, shall have been or shall be an infant, idiot, non compos mentis, feme covert, or tenant for life, or during which any

---

32 *Colls* v. *Home and Colonial Stores* [1904] A.C. 179, 205. See p. 148, *ante*.
33 *Shuttleworth* v. *Le Fleming* (1865) 19 C.B.(N.S.) 687; *Mercer* v. *Denne* [1904] 2 Ch. 534 (affd. [1905] 2 Ch. 538, 586); *Ramsgate Corporation* v. *Debling* (1906) 22 T.L.R. 369.
34 (1865) 4 De G.J. & S. 631; and see *Hollins* v. *Verney* (1884) 13 Q.B.D. 304; *Carr* v. *Foster* (1842) 3 Q.B. 581.

action or suit shall have been pending, and which shall have been diligently prosecuted until abated by the death of any party or parties thereto, shall be excluded in the computation of the periods hereinbefore mentioned, except only in cases where the right or claim is hereby declared to be absolute and indefeasible."

Where the person, against whom a period of enjoyment is running, is under one of the disabilities here mentioned, the period of such disability is to be excluded in computing the shorter periods specified in sections 1 and 2; but not in computing any period after which a right is declared to be absolute and indefeasible.[35] A woman married since 1882 is not a " feme covert " within the section, for she is not in the class of persons whose rights it was intended to preserve, that is, " persons incapable of making the grant on the presumption of which the whole structure of statutory prescription is founded, or of suing to prevent an invasion of their rights and property." [36] Inasmuch as land belonging to an infant must now be vested in trustees for him,[37] and a tenant for life under a settlement holds the legal estate in fee simple on the trusts of the settlement, it would seem reasonable to suppose that, by analogy, the protection given by the section no longer extends to infants and tenants for life; but their rights are probably preserved by s. 12 of the Law of Property Act 1925, which enacts that " nothing in Part I [38] of this Act affects the operation of any statute, or the general law . . . with reference to the acquisition of easements or rights over or in respect of land."

No provision is made for absence beyond the seas, but in such a case, although the time of such absence could not be excluded under this section, it might be used to show ignorance on the part of the servient owner of the enjoyment, so as to bring the case within the rule as to knowledge stated *post*, p. 179.

The effect of the section is to prolong the specified period, down to the time of action brought, of continuous enjoyment as of right and as an easement, by so long a time as the disability has lasted; in other words, enjoyment of the necessary character must be shown for a period of twenty (or, in the case of a profit, thirty) years, either wholly before the disability, if it is still subsisting, or partly before and partly after, if it has ended [39]; and also during the period of disability.[40]

---

[35] These are: sixty years under section 1; forty years under section 2; and twenty years under section 3.   As to the effect of ignorance or notice of dissent on the part of the reversioner, see pp. 180 *et seq., post.*

[36] *Hulley* v. *Silversprings Bleaching and Dyeing Co.* [1922] 2 Ch. 268, 281, *per* Eve J.

[37] Law of Property Act 1925, ss. 1 (6), 19.

[38] Part I consists of ss. 1–39.   The position of a tenant for life is created directly by the Settled Land Act 1925, but it could perhaps be considered to originate in s. 1 (6) (*cf.* also s. 39) of the Law of Property Act 1925.   *Cf.* ss. 12 and 31 of the Law of Property Act 1922, and *Re Turner's Will Trusts* [1937] Ch. 15.

[39] *Clayton* v. *Corby* (1842) 2 Q.B. 813.

[40] *Clayton* v. *Corby, supra; Onley* v. *Gardiner* (1838) 4 M. & W. 496.   The same considerations apply where the period of a lease is excluded under s. 8.

Extension of the period of forty years

Section 8 of the Prescription Act 1832 is as follows:

" 8. Provided always, that when any land or water upon, over, or from which any such way or other convenient watercourse or use of water shall have been or shall be enjoyed or derived, hath been or shall be held under or by virtue of any term of life, or any term of years exceeding three years from the granting thereof, the time of the enjoyment of any such way or other matter as herein last before mentioned, during the continuance of such term, shall be excluded in the computation of the said period of forty years in case the claim shall within three years next after the end or sooner determination of such term be resisted by any person entitled to any reversion expectant on the determination thereof."

The full meaning and effect of this section have never been authoritatively decided. It is intended to protect the reversioner on a tenancy for life, or for more than three years, by conditionally excluding the period of the tenancy.

The section is expressly confined to " the said period of forty years," which is the longer period mentioned in section 2.[41] It clearly cannot therefore apply to profits, etc., under section 1, or to easements of light under section 3. Its application to the twenty-year period under section 2 was considered in *Palk* v. *Shinner* [42] where the Court of Queen's Bench held that the eighth section applies only to the period of forty years, and therefore that the time during which the premises are under lease for a term exceeding three years is not to be excluded in the computation of the period of twenty years' enjoyment of a right of way. But the question whether the tenancy for years, though *not to be absolutely excluded* under section 8, might not be made use of in another way to defeat the user, is a different matter.

In *Palk* v. *Shinner* a way had been used for twenty years, during the first fifteen of which the servient tenement had been under lease; it did not appear whether the reversioner knew of the user during the lease, but at all events no resistance was made either during the fifteen years or the remaining years for which the land was in possession of the reversioner. Erle J. told the jury that the fact of the land having been in lease for the fifteen years would not defeat the user; and, upon a rule nisi for a new trial for misdirection, the question principally argued was whether section 8 of the statute applied to a twenty years' user, so that the tenancy should be *excluded*, and the court expressed a clear opinion that it did not; but Erle J. said [42a] that if this case had arisen before the statute, " there would have been good evidence to go to the jury of a user as of right for twenty years, notwithstanding the existence of the tenancy."

[41] See p. 146, *ante.*
[42] (1852) 18 Q.B. 568.   [42a] *Ibid.* 575.

It would seem that any objection in respect of the land having been in lease which might have been taken at the common law may still be taken to a user for twenty years under section 2 of the statute, although the statutory process of excluding the time of the lease is not open except in the case of forty years' user.

On the other hand, in the case of forty years' user, unless the reversioner should resist the claim within three years from the termination of the tenancy, he could not set up the existence of the lease in any way. He could not set it up by way of exclusion from the computation by reason of the express condition, imposed by section 8, of resisting within the three years above mentioned. Nor could he set it up as at the common law by reason of the provisions of section 2, which, though they allow a twenty years' user to be defeated "*in any other way*" in which the same at the common law might be defeated, do not allow the forty years' user to be so defeated, but only by showing that the enjoyment was had under a written agreement. So that but for section 8 the reversioner could make no use of the fact of the tenancy at all.

In short, there are two distinct ways in which the existence of a term of years may be taken advantage of:

1. As showing, in connection with the other circumstances of the case, that there has not been enjoyment binding against the reversioner, *e.g.* as in the case of an enjoyment for twenty years, commencing during the tenancy and continuing through it, and unknown to him and his agents.

2. As entitling the reversioner to have the period of enjoyment during the term *excluded* from the period of computation, so as virtually to extend the period of enjoyment required to be proved.

The first way was open at the common law, and is left untouched by the statute in so far as the period of twenty years' user under section 2 is concerned, but is not left in the case of the forty years' user. The second way is the creature of the statute, and, according to the case of *Palk* v. *Shinner* is only applicable to a case of forty years' user. But if the person resisting the claim does not, by resisting it within three years from the end of the term, comply with the condition upon which alone he can under section 8 take advantage of the period of enjoyment, he is debarred from setting up the fact of the existence of the tenancy for years at all, except [43] in so far as it may assist him in showing his ignorance of the claimant's enjoyment or some defect in the character of that enjoyment.

Two questions arise from the wording of the section. In the first place, the section applies only to "a way or other convenient watercourse or use of water."

"No doubt," said Parke B., in *Wright* v. *Williams*,[44] "there is a

---

[43] See *Davies* v. *Du Paver* [1953] 1 Q.B. 184 and pp. 180 *et seq., post.*
[44] (1836) 1 M. & W. 77. The suggestion does not appear by the report to have been made by the judge in this case; but it is found in counsel's argument, as reported in 1 Tyr. & G. 375 at p. 390.

mistake in the eighth section, probably a miscopying in the insertion of the word ' convenient ' instead of ' easement.' " In *Laird* v. *Briggs* [45] Fry J. adopted this construction *sub silentio*, but the Court of Appeal in the same case [46] expressly left the point open.

In the second place, the section refers to resistance by " any person entitled to any reversion expectant on the determination " of the term of life or term of years previously mentioned. This has been held not to apply to a person entitled on remainder expectant on a life estate.[47] It seems, however, questionable whether the section could now apply to any period of life tenancy, even if no other interest were created and a reversion remained in the settlor; for freehold life interests now take effect as equitable interests, and it is difficult to see how land could be said to be " held " under an equitable interest. Moreover it may be suggested that the expression " term of life " was intended to connote, as in *Bright* v. *Walker*,[48] a lease for life or lives, now capable of taking effect only as a lease for ninety years determinable.[49]

After an enjoyment of forty years, the extent of the exemption contained in the eighth section appears to amount to this:

The period during which the owner of the servient inheritance has not been *valens agere*, in consequence of the existence of a lease for life or for more than three years, is altogether excluded in the computation of the forty years, provided such owner contests the claim within three years after the lease expires. If the first twenty of the forty years' enjoyment occurred at a time when the servient tenement was not held under lease, it seems that the owner of the servient inheritance (even though he brought his action within three years from the expiration of the lease) would be prevented by a twenty years' valid enjoyment from successfully challenging the claim to an easement. Again, if the servient tenement had been held without lease during the first eighteen and the last two of the forty years, it would seem that the owner of the servient inheritance would be equally prevented by a twenty years' valid enjoyment from successfully challenging the claim. The time of enjoyment during the leases is simply to be excluded, and there appears to be nothing to prevent the tacking together of the two periods of eighteen and two years during which there has been a valid enjoyment. The case appears by the express enactment of the statute—that the time during which the property was so held on lease shall be excluded from the computation of the period of forty years—to be exempted from the rule requiring twenty years' enjoyment next before action brought.[50]

---

45 (1880) 16 Ch.D. 440.
46 (1881) 19 Ch.D. 22.
47 *Symons* v. *Leaker* (1885) 15 Q.B.D. 629.
48 (1834) 1 Cr.M. & R. 211.
49 Law of Property Act 1925, s. 149.
50 The views of Mr. Gale are confirmed by *Clayton* v. *Corby* (1842) 2 Q.B. 813, and *Pye* v. *Mumford* (1848) 11 Q.B. 675 (upon the effect of excluding the periods of disability under s. 7). See also the text to notes 39 and 40, *ante*.

Effect of Prescription Act 1832

The general effect of the Act is to confront the claimant with two difficulties which do not exist at common law. First, the user must be proved for the period computed next before the commencement of the action in which the claim is contested. Secondly, there must be nothing in the facts inconsistent with the continuous enjoyment of the easement as such during the whole period. Thus, unity of possession at any time during the period is fatal under the Act,[1] however small the claimant's interest may be. This is not so at common law, though a claim resting on a presumed pre-1189 grant can be defeated by proof of such unity of possession *and ownership* as would extinguish the right so presumed to have been granted.[2] On the other hand, the Act does not, except as to light, assist mere enjoyment *per se*. A claim based on enjoyment for one of the shorter periods specified in section 1 or 2 is liable to be defeated on any ground which would defeat it at common law; and while a claim based on enjoyment for one of the longer periods is declared to be absolute unless it was had by written consent or agreement, the enjoyment must still have been " as of right."

Difficulties have arisen as to the relationship between sections 7 and 8. If a servient tenement has been subject to a lease during which, under section 8, the forty-year period does not run, the question arises whether user for twenty years when there was no such lease can be defeated as in ordinary cases; for instance, by showing that the owner of the inheritance was during the whole or part of that time under disability. By the seventh section, the provision in favour of disabilities does not apply to the cases " where the right or claim is declared to be absolute and indefeasible "; and it may be urged that the policy of the law is, after so long an enjoyment, to clothe such user with the legal right without allowing the general object to be defeated by too minute provisions. To this, however, it may be replied that if the period of the subsistence of the lease is to be excluded, the reversioner does not obtain complete protection unless he stands in the same position to all intents and purposes as he would do in the ordinary case of a user of twenty years, when the servient tenement was not under lease; and that the words of the seventh section of the statute may be satisfied by supposing it to mean only that, in the computation of the period of forty years, for the purpose of throwing upon the owner of the inheritance the onus of showing that he was under the particular disability of a reversioner, no time of general disability is to be deducted; but that the fact of his being a reversioner being once established, and the question, therefore, then being whether there has been a valid user of twenty years, that must be decided as if it stood completely

---

[1] See *Onley* v. *Gardiner* (1838) 4 M. & W. 496, and pp. 147, 148, *ante*.
[2] See p. 137, *ante*.

abstracted from the time during which the servient tenement was in lease; or that, in other words, in computing the period of forty years, disability under section 7 shall never be deducted—in computing that of twenty years, always, if properly set up in the pleading.[3]

In considering the general effect of the Act it should be noted that the claim to light under section 3 differs from claims to other easements in that the claim need not be as of right, cannot be defeated by pleas of disability or a lease under sections 7 and 8 respectively, and cannot be claimed as against the Crown.

2.—THE PERSONS AGAINST WHOM AND BY WHOM THE ENJOYMENT MUST BE HAD TO GIVE RISE TO A PRESCRIPTIVE TITLE

(1) Against whom the Enjoyment must be had

Presumed grant by owner of servient tenement

As it is essential, wrote Mr. Gale, to the existence of an easement, that one tenement should be made subject to the convenience of another, and as the right to the easement can exist only in respect of such tenement, the continued user by which the easement is to be acquired must be by a person in possession of the dominant tenement. And as such user is only evidence of a previous grant—and as the right claimed is in its nature not one of a temporary kind, but one which permanently affects the rights of property in the servient tenement—it follows that by the common law such grant can only have been legally made by a party capable of imposing such a permanent burden upon the property—that is, the owner of an estate of inheritance.[4] Further, in order that such user may confer an easement, the owner of the servient inheritance must have known that the easement was enjoyed, and also have been in a situation to interfere with and obstruct its exercise, had he been so disposed. His abstaining from interference will then be construed as an acquiescence.[5] *Contra non valentem agere non currit praescriptio.*

In the above paragraph Mr. Gale referred to two distinct points, *viz.*: (1) the servient owner's interest in the servient tenement; and (2) such owner's knowledge of the user of the easement. In the present section it is proposed to consider the first of these points; the second will be considered in section 3.

According to the common law, all prescription presupposes a grant,[6] and (apart from the special case of light claimed under section 3 of the Act, and apart also from the doubtful question whether

---

[3] The judgments in *Clayton* v. *Corby* (1842) 2 Q.B. 813 and *Pye* v. *Mumford* (1848) 11 Q.B. 675 (see note 50, *supra*) establish these propositions.

[4] *Daniel* v. *North* (1809) 11 East 372.

[5] *Gray* v. *Bond* (1821) 2 Brod. & Bing. 667; *Liverpool Corporation* v. *Coghill* [1918] 1 Ch. 307.

[6] *Gardner* v. *Hodgson's Kingston Brewery Co.* [1903] A.C. 229, 239; *Goodman* v. *Saltash Corporation* (1882) 7 App.Cas. 654, 655.

a grant must be presumed in the case where an easement is claimed under section 2 of the Act on the ground of an enjoyment for the forty years mentioned in that section) the general rule is that, to establish a prescriptive title to an easement, the court must presume a grant of the easement by the absolute owner of the servient tenement to the absolute owner of the dominant tenement.[7] Furthermore for the purpose of such grant it must be shown that there was a capable grantor and a capable grantee. An enjoyment of the easement as against an owner of the servient tenement who could not dispose of the fee will not be sufficient.

In connection with this question the provisions in sections 7 and 8 of the Prescription Act 1832, in relation to tenants for life and for years and to persons under disability must, where the claim is made under the Act, be carefully borne in mind. For instance, disability on the part of the servient owner might prevent the presumption of a grant. But the general doctrine requires to be considered in more detail.

We have seen that the Prescription Act 1832 has not taken away any of the methods of claiming easements which previously existed.[8] In considering the present question it is important to distinguish the method in which the particular easement is claimed, and as to this it is to be remembered that there are three legal methods by which prescriptive rights can be claimed, *viz.* (1) prescription at common law; (2) claims based on lost grant; and (3) prescription under the Act.

1. Claims based on prescription at common law

In the case of an easement claimed by prescription at common law there must have been enjoyment as against an absolute owner of the servient tenement. It was laid down by Lindley L.J. in *Wheaton* v. *Maple & Co.*[9] (a case where the easement of light was in question) that a right claimed by prescription must be claimed as appendant or appurtenant to land and not as annexed to it for a term of years; also that an easement for a limited time only cannot be gained by prescription at common law. Vaughan Williams J. in *Fear* v. *Morgan*[10] seems to have been of opinion that by prescription at common law a right to light can only be acquired between absolute owners. Again, it was said by Mathew L.J. in *Kilgour* v. *Gaddes*[11] (referring to a right of way) that such an easement can only be acquired by prescription at common law where the dominant and servient tenements respectively belong to different owners in fee. It results from the words of Mathew L.J. last quoted, that where the fee simple in both dominant and servient

[7] *Wheaton* v. *Maple & Co.* [1893] 3 Ch. 63; *Kilgour* v. *Gaddes* [1904] 1 K.B. 466.
[8] *Ante*, p. 144.
[9] [1893] 3 Ch. 63, 65.
[10] [1906] 2 Ch. 415, 416.
[11] [1904] 1 K.B. 467.

tenements belongs to the same owner no easement can be acquired by prescription at common law.[12]

2. Claims based on lost grant

Where the claim to an easement is based on the doctrine of lost grant, it would seem to follow from the language used by Lindley L.J. in *Wheaton* v. *Maple & Co.*[13] that the same rule should apply, and that an enjoyment as against an owner of the servient tenement who cannot dispose of the fee is not sufficient. In *Barker* v. *Richardson*,[14] where the light of a presumably modern house had been enjoyed for more than twenty years over land which during part of that period had been glebe land, no easement was acquired; the ground of the decision being thus stated by Abbott C.J.[15]:

> "Admitting that twenty years' uninterrupted possession of an easement is generally sufficient to raise a presumption of a grant, in this case, the grant, if presumed, must have been made by a tenant for life, who had no power to bind his successor; the grant, therefore, would be invalid. . . ."

Again, in *Bradbury* v. *Grinsell*,[16] Serjeant Williams says:

> "Though an uninterrupted possession for twenty years or upwards should be sufficient evidence to be left to a jury to presume a grant; yet the rule must ever be taken with this qualification, that the possession was with the acquiescence of him who was seised of an estate of *inheritance*: for a tenant for life or years has no power to grant such right for a longer period than during the continuance of his particular estate. If such a tenant permits another to enjoy an easement on his estate for twenty years or upwards, without interruption, and then the particular estate determines, such user will not affect him who has the inheritance in reversion or remainder; but when it vests in possession the reversioner may dispute the right to the easement, and the length of possession will be no answer to his claim. Thus, where A, being a tenant for life, with a power to make a jointure, which he afterwards executed, gave licence to B, in 1747, to

---

12 " It is well settled that a lessee cannot acquire a right of way over the land of another lessee under the same lessor either by prescription at common law, or under the doctrine of a lost grant, or by prescription under the Prescription Act 1832 ": *per* P. O. Lawrence J. in *Cory* v. *Davies* [1923] 2 Ch. 95, 107, citing *Wheaton* v. *Maple & Co.* (*supra*) and *Kilgour* v. *Gaddes* (*supra*).

13 [1893] 3 Ch. 69; see p. 162, *ante.*

14 (1821) 4 B. & Ald. 579. Compare *Runcorn* v. *Doe* d. *Cooper* (1826) 5 B. & C. 696 (a case of adverse possession under the old Statutes of Limitation). It should be noted that in *Barker* v. *Richardson* the incapacity of the owner of the servient tenement to make an absolute grant covered only part of the period of enjoyment. So, again, in *Roberts & Lovell* v. *James* (1903) 89 L.T. 287, an absolute grant could at one time during the enjoyment have been made by the owners of the servient tenement. In both cases, however, the court refused to presume a grant.

15 (1821) 4 B. & Ald. 579, 582.

16 2 Wms.Saund. (1871 ed.) 175.

erect a wear on the river T. in A's soil, for the purpose of watering B's meadows, and then A died, and the jointress entered and
continued seised down to the year 1799, when the tenant of A's
farm diverted the water of the river from the wear; upon which
the tenant of B's farm brought an action on the case for diverting
the water; it was held by the Court of King's Bench that the
uninterrupted possession of the wear for so many years with
acquiescence of the particular tenants for life did not affect him
who had the inheritance in reversion."

The ruling in *Bradbury* v. *Grinsell* [17] was applied by the Court of
Appeal in the modern case of *Roberts* v. *James*,[18] where it was laid
down by Romer L.J. as clear law that, where a tenant for life is in
possession of the servient tenement, a lost grant of a right of way
cannot be implied as against the reversioner merely from the user
of the way during the life tenancy. The same doctrine was applied
where the easement of light was claimed over a servient tenement in
the possession of a tenant for years.[19]

On the other hand, in *Bright* v. *Walker*,[20] where a lessee holding
the dominant tenement claimed a right of way on the ground of user
over a servient tenement also held by a lessee, Parke B., referring to
the old doctrine of lost grant, stated that user for twenty years would
before the Prescription Act have been evidence to support a claim by
a non-existing grant from the termor in the *locus in quo* to the termor
under whom the plaintiff claimed, although such a claim was by no
means a matter of ordinary occurrence, and in practice the usual
course was to state a grant by an owner in fee to an owner in fee.
Again, in referring to the doctrine of lost grant, it was said by Channell
J. in *East Stonehouse U.D.C.* v. *Willoughby Brothers Ltd.*,[21] that in
recent times the doctrine had been applied more widely than formerly.

"In particular it can be applied between termors when there
is a difficulty in applying the statute owing to the freeholder not
being bound."

Very recently, in *Pugh* v. *Savage*,[22] the Court of Appeal held that
the fact that a tenancy of the servient tenement came into existence
during the course of the period of user was not, in the absence of
evidence that the servient owner had no knowledge of the user while
the tenant was in possession, fatal to the presumption of a lost grant,

---

17 2 Wms.Saund. (1871 ed.) 175.
18 (1903) 89 L.T. 287.
19 *Daniel* v. *North* (1809) 11 East 372. Compare *Cross* v. *Lewis* (1824) 2 B. & C. 686.
20 (1834) 1 Cr.M. & R. 211, 221.
21 [1902] 2 K.B. 318, 332. In Ireland it has been held in a series of cases that there
   may be a presumption of a lost grant which is binding on termors, and on termors
   only. See *Flynn* v. *Harte* [1913] 2 Ir.R. 326, where the decisions are reviewed by
   Dodd J.
22 [1970] 2 Q.B. 373, considered further, p. 184, *post*, in connection with claims
   under the Prescription Act 1832.

although it was a matter to be considered. On the other hand, a distinction could properly be drawn between cases where the tenancy was in existence at the beginning of the period of user and cases where the tenancy came into existence in the course of the period of user; and in the former type of case it might well be unreasonable to imply a lost grant by the owner at the beginning of the user. He might not have been able to stop the user, even if he knew about it.

The case where the fee simple in both dominant and servient tenements belongs to the same owner is a special one. The question of presuming a lost grant in such a case is in England governed by the rules that a lessee for years must prescribe in right of his lessor and not in right of himself; and that the lessor cannot have an easement over his own land.[23] The rule in Ireland is discussed in *Hanna* v. *Pollock*.[24]

3. Claims under the Prescription Act

Here it is necessary to make a further distinction between the cases where a claim is made to an easement other than light and the case where a claim is made to light. Claims to light have already been considered.[25]

(a) *On the ground of twenty years' enjoyment*

A claim under the Act to an easement other than light may be based on twenty years' enjoyment; and upon such a claim the leading authority is the above-mentioned case of *Bright* v. *Walker*,[26] where for more than twenty years the plaintiff, holding Blackacre under a lease for lives from a bishop, enjoyed without interruption a way over Whiteacre held by the defendant under a lease for lives from the same bishop. An action was subsequently brought in which the plaintiff claimed the right of way under the Prescription Act, but the claim failed. Parke B. delivered the judgment of the Court of Exchequer, in which he said [27]:

> "The important question is, whether this enjoyment, as it cannot give a title against all persons having estates in the *locus in quo*, gives a title as against the lessee and the defendants claiming under him, or not at all? We have had considerable difficulty in coming to a conclusion on this point; but, upon the fullest consideration, we think that no title at all is gained by an user which does not give a valid title against all, and permanently affect the See. Before the statute, this possession would indeed have been evidence to support a plea or claim by a non-existing grant from the termor, in the *locus in quo*, to the termor under

23 See *ante*, p. 21.
24 [1900] 2 Ir.R. 664.
25 See p. 149, *ante*.
26 (1834) 1 Cr.M. & R. 211; see *ante*, p. 164.
27 1 Cr.M. & R. 220–221.

whom the plaintiff claims, though such a claim was by no means a matter of ordinary occurrence; and in practice the usual course was to state a grant by an owner in fee to an owner in fee. But, since the statute, such a qualified right, we think, is not given by an enjoyment for twenty years. For, in the first place, the statute is 'for shortening the time of prescription'; and if the periods mentioned in it are to be deemed new times of prescription, it must have been intended that the enjoyment for those periods should give a good title against all, for titles by immemorial prescription are absolute and valid against all. They are such as absolutely bind the fee in the land. And, in the next place, the statute nowhere contains any intimation that there may be different classes of rights, qualified and absolute—valid as to some persons, and invalid as to others. From hence we are led to conclude, that an enjoyment of twenty years, if it give not a good title against all, gives no good title at all; and as it is clear that this enjoyment, whilst the land was held by a tenant for life, cannot affect the reversion in the bishop now, and is therefore not good as against every one, it is not good as against any one, and, therefore, not against the defendant."

It is, of course, to be observed that in this case the fee simple in both the dominant and the servient tenement belonged to the same owner (the bishop). It was this fact, not the existence of a tenancy of the servient tenement, which was fatal to the existence of an easement.

(b) *On the ground of forty years' enjoyment*

In *Bright* v. *Walker*,[26] the enjoyment had continued during twenty years only. The claim, however, may be based on a forty years' enjoyment. And as to this Mr. Gale expressed the opinion, that such an enjoyment would confer a right to the easement subject to the condition only that the reversioner interfered within three years after the determination of the particular estate; as in the cases of conditional estates, a valid right is given as against all the world, until by the happening of the conditions the estate is defeated.

In *Wright* v. *Williams* [28] (a case relating to water rights which was argued on demurrer) Parke B. during the course of the argument said that it was the intention of the Prescription Act that an enjoyment of twenty years should be of no avail against an idiot or other person labouring under incapacity, but that one of forty years should confer an absolute title even as against parties under disabilities. He said also, that a user for forty years confers a prima facie title which is good, unless the reversioner pursues his remedy within the three years mentioned in section 8. And, in delivering the judgment of the Court of Exchequer, Lord Abinger held that, even where a

[28] (1836) Tyr. & G. 376 (see in particular pp. 392, 393, 400).

tenancy for life existed, the enjoyment of an easement for forty years gave an indefeasible title. It seems to follow that, in the opinion of the then judges of the Court of Exchequer, it was not necessary to presume an absolute grant where a claim under the Act to an easement other than light was based on a forty years' enjoyment. This question is further discussed later on (pp. 168–169).

Where the fee simple in both the dominant and servient tenements belongs to the same owner, it is clear that (except in the case of light) the tenant of one close cannot as such acquire under the Act a prescriptive easement over another close belonging to the same landlord either by twenty years' user,[29] or by forty years' user.[30]

Incompetent grantors

It will have been seen above (pp. 161 *et seq.*) that as a general rule the enjoyment of an easement as against an owner of the servient tenement who is unable to dispose of the fee is not sufficient to give rise to a prescriptive title. The ordinary cause of such an inability arises from a deficiency of estate, as where a servient owner is tenant for life or tenant for years. The inability, however, to dispose of the fee may arise from other causes, *e.g.* where the owner of the servient tenement is restrained from alienation. In *Lemaitre* v. *Davis*[31] a right of support was claimed under section 2 of the Prescription Act. The fee simple in the servient tenement belonged to the rector and churchwardens of a parish—an ecclesiastical corporation—who were restrained from alienation. Hall V.-C. held that the fact that the servient tenement was held by such a corporation did not prevent a title to the easement being acquired under the Act. If the claim there was based upon an enjoyment for the shorter period of twenty years mentioned in section 2, the soundness of the decision seems doubtful. If, on the other hand, the claim was based upon an enjoyment for the longer period of forty years mentioned in the same section, and if the true view of the Act be that in such a case it is unnecessary to presume an absolute grant,[32] the decision was right.[33]

Again, the inability of the servient owner to dispose of the fee simple of the servient tenement may arise from the doctrine of *ultra vires.* Thus, where the owner of the servient tenement is a company whose powers of disposition are limited, and a grant of the easement by such

---

29 *Gayford* v. *Moffatt* (1868) 4 Ch.App. 133; *Bayley* v. *G.W. Ry.* (1884) 26 Ch.D. 434, 441; *Sturges* v. *Bridgman* (1879) 11 Ch.D. 852, 855.
30 *Kilgour* v. *Gaddes* [1904] 1 K.B. 457. The rule stated above is the result of the decisions of the courts in England. The rule in Ireland may be different: see *Hanna* v. *Pollock* [1900] 2 Ir.R. 664; *Macnaghten* v. *Baird* [1903] 2 Ir.R. 731; *Flynn* v. *Harte* [1913] 2 Ir.R. 326.
31 (1881) 19 Ch.D. 281, 291.
32 As to this, see pp. 168–169, *post.*
33 As to acquiring by prescription an easement over ecclesiastical property, see *Barker* v. *Richardson* (1821) 4 B. & Ald. 579; *Ecclesiastical Commissioners* v. *Kino* (1880) 14 Ch.D. 213.

company would be *ultra vires*, it seems that no prescriptive title will arise either where an easement of any kind is claimed by prescription at common law or under the doctrine of lost grant, or where an easement other than light is claimed on the ground of a twenty years' enjoyment under section 2 of the Prescription Act. The prescriptive title will not arise, because the necessary grant cannot be presumed.[34]

If, however, a claim were made to the easement of light over land owned by a disabled company on the ground of twenty years' enjoyment under section 3 of the Prescription Act, it is clear that it would not be necessary to presume a grant, and a right to the easement might be established.[35]

Lastly, if an easement other than light were claimed under section 2 of the Prescription Act on the ground of a forty years' enjoyment over land owned by a disabled company, the question whether a prescriptive title would arise is not free from doubt. Would it, or would it not, be necessary in this case to presume an absolute grant? The words which in section 2 are applied to a forty years' enjoyment of an easement other than light are identical with the words which in section 3 are applied to a twenty years' enjoyment of light. And it would seem that the same result which in the latter case was held to follow as regards light should also in the former case follow as regards easements other than light— *viz.* that it is not necessary to presume an absolute grant.[36]

Again, the words of sections 7 and 8 of the Prescription Act 1832 appear to have a material bearing on the question. If where an easement is claimed under section 2 of the Act on the ground of a forty years' enjoyment it is necessary to presume an absolute grant, this alone would, where the servient tenement is owned by a tenant for life or for years, prevent a prescriptive title from arising, and the special provisions as to exclusion which in fact are contained in sections 7 and 8 would seem inappropriate. In *Wright* v. *Williams*,[37] which was decided under section 8, a question arose as to the effect of a forty years' enjoyment of an easement other than light, the servient tenement being held by a tenant for life. The language used by the judges in that case seems to show that in their opinion it was not necessary in such a case to presume an absolute grant.

On the other hand, in *Staffordshire and Worcestershire Canal Navigation (Proprietors)* v. *Birmingham Canal Navigation (Proprietors)*,[38]

---

34 *Rochdale Co.* v. *Radcliffe* (1852) 18 Q.B. 287, 315; *Att.-Gen.* v. *G.N. Ry.* [1909] 1 Ch. 775, 778. Compare *Neaverson* v. *Peterborough R.D.C.* [1902] 1 Ch. 557; *Hulley* v. *Silversprings Bleaching and Dyeing Co.* [1922] 2 Ch. 268; *Green* v. *Matthews*, 46 T.L.R. 206; and *Mill* v. *New Forest Commissioner* (1856) 18 C.B. 60, in which last case a *profit à prendre* was enjoyed as against the Crown for thirty years, and a claim made under s. 1 of the Prescription Act was defeated on the ground that the Crown was by statute incapacitated from making a grant.
35 *Tapling* v. *Jones* (1865) 11 H.L.C. 304; *Jordeson* v. *Sutton, Southcoates and Drypool Gas Co.* [1898] 2 Ch. 614, 618, 626.
36 See the words of Lord Selborne in *Dalton* v. *Angus* (1881) 6 App.Cas. 800.
37 (1836) Tyr. & G. 375.
38 (1866) L.R. 1 H.L. 254 (see pp. 260, 262, 268 and 278).

where an easement was claimed on the ground of a forty years' enjoyment, and it was objected that the servient tenement was owned by a company which had no power to make a grant, it was said in the House of Lords that, if the Prescription Act 1832 applied to the case, it would be necessary to show that the right claimed could have been granted, and it was said, further, that under the circumstances a grant would have been *ultra vires* and void.

(2) *By whom the Enjoyment must be had*

Capable grantee

Upon the question by whom the enjoyment must be had Mr. Gale wrote as follows :

> " Although the user by which it is sought to acquire an easement must be that of the party in possession of the dominant tenement, yet any user under a claim of right in respect of such tenement will be in contemplation of law user by such possessor. Hence it appears that there is no disability of any kind to destroy the effect of such user."

These words of Mr. Gale must now, however, be read subject to the following remarks.

According to the general rule requiring the presumption of an absolute grant which is applicable in the establishment of a prescriptive title to an easement,[39] it is not only necessary to show that there was a capable grantor as regards the servient tenement, but it is also necessary to show that there was a capable grantee as regards the dominant tenement. Thus it seems that a statutory company cannot by prescription acquire rights more extensive than are conferred upon it by the legislature; and accordingly a company which has been reconstituted as a railway company could not by prescription acquire water rights.[40] So, again, the " inhabitants " of a village cannot *eo nomine* acquire by prescription a right of way, " inhabitants " not being capable grantees.[41]

While a prescriptive easement must be claimed as appurtenant to the fee simple of the dominant tenement,[42] it is sufficient in pleading to claim it on the ground of an enjoyment as of right by the occupiers of such tenement.[43]   Accordingly, the enjoyment of an easement by a tenant for life in possession of the dominant tenement will enure for the benefit of the fee simple and be a sufficient foundation for presuming an absolute grant.[44]

---

[39] *Ante,* pp. 161 *et seq.*
[40] *National Guaranteed Manure Co.* v. *Donald* (1859) 4 H. & N. 8. See *Traill* v. *McAllister* (1890) 25 L.R.Ir. 524, where it was held that a prescriptive title to an easement cannot result from acts of the dominant owner which are prohibited by statute.
[41] *Foxall* v. *Venables* (1590) Cro.Eliz. 180.
[42] *Wheaton* v. *Maple & Co.* [1893] 3 Ch. 63; *Kilgour* v. *Gaddes* [1904] 1 K.B. 466.
[43] Prescription Act 1832, s. 5.
[44] As to the rules laid down before the Prescription Act, see *Grimstead* v. *Marlowe*

As regards the enjoyment of an easement by a tenant for years, the possession of the tenant is the possession of his landlord.[45] Thus where Blackacre, the dominant tenement, is demised by A to B, and B enjoys an easement over the adjoining Whiteacre, B's enjoyment enures for the benefit of A's fee. But where Whiteacre also belongs to A in fee, no easement is acquired by B's enjoyment.[46]

Where a permanent artificial stream in Cornwall had been used from time immemorial by tin-bounders (who merely were entitled by custom to work tin on the dominant tenement), such user was sufficient to give water rights by immemorial prescription to the owner in fee of the dominant tenement; the presumption being that the privilege was originally acquired by arrangement with such owner as well as with the tin-bounders.[47]

3.—QUALITIES AND CHARACTER OF THE NECESSARY ENJOYMENT

(1) *In General*

Enjoyment as of right

In order that the enjoyment, which is the quasi-possession of an easement, may confer a right to it by length of time, it must have had certain qualities and been of a certain character. This character will be discussed in the present section.

In delivering the judgment of the Court of Exchequer in *Bright* v. *Walker*,[48] in which a right of way was claimed under the Prescription Act 1832, and the qualities of an enjoyment necessary to clothe it with right by lapse of time were considered, Parke B. made the following general remarks[49]:

> "In order to establish a right of way, and to bring the case within this section (2nd), it must be proved that the claimant has enjoyed it for the full period of twenty years, and that he has done so 'as of right,' for that is the form in which by section 5 such a claim must be pleaded; and the like evidence would have been required before the statute to prove a claim by prescription or non-existing grant. Therefore, if the way shall appear to have been enjoyed by the claimant, not openly and in the manner that a person rightfully entitled would have used it, but by stealth, as a trespasser would have done—if he shall have occasionally asked the permission of the occupier of the land—no title would be acquired, because

(1792) 4 T.R. 717; *Att.-Gen.* v. *Gauntlett* (1829) 3 Y. & J. 93; *Codling* v. *Johnson* (1829) 9 B. & C. 933.
[45] *Gayford* v. *Moffatt* (1868) 4 Ch.App. 133, 135; *Pugh* v. *Savage* [1970] 2 Q.B. 373, 383, *per* Cross L.J.
[46] *Ante*, p. 167.
[47] *Ivimey* v. *Stocker* (1866) 1 Ch.App. 396. Compare *Gaved* v. *Martyn* (1865) 19 C.B. (N.S.) 732.
[48] 1 Cr.M. & R. 211.
[49] 1 Cr.M. & R. 219.

it was not enjoyed, ' as of right.' For the same reason it would not, if there had been unity of possession during all or part of the time: for then the claimant would not have enjoyed ' as of right ' the easement, but the soil itself. So it must have been enjoyed without interruption. Again, such claim may be defeated in any other way by which the same is now liable to be defeated; that is, by the same means by which a similar claim, arising by custom, prescription or grant, would now be defeasible; and, therefore, it may be answered by proof of a grant, or of a licence, written or parol, for a limited period, comprising the whole or part of the twenty years, or of the absence or ignorance of the parties interested in opposing the claim, and their agents, during the whole time that it was exercised."

The authority of this case, and the doctrines laid down by the court in it, were fully recognised in *Monmouthshire Canal Co.* v. *Harford* [50] and *Tickle* v. *Brown.*[1]

Knowledge of user

The effect of the enjoyment, wrote Mr. Gale, being to raise the presumption of a consent on the part of the owner of the servient tenement, it is obvious that no such inference of consent can be drawn, unless it be shown that he was aware of the user, and, being so, made no attempt to interfere with its exercise.[2]   Still less can such consent be implied, but rather the contrary, where he has contested the right to the user, or where, in consequence of such opposition, an interruption in the user has actually taken place. Even supposing those defects of the user not to exist, still the effect of the user would be destroyed if it were shown that it took place by the express permission of the owner of the servient tenement, for in such a case the user would not have been had with the intention of acquiring or exercising a right. The presumption, however, is that a party enjoying an easement acted under a claim of right until the contrary is shown.[3]

User nec vi, nec clam, nec precario

The civil law expressed the essential qualities of the user, by the clear and concise rule that it should be " nec vi, nec clam, nec precario." [4] The law of England, as cited by Coke, from Bracton, exactly agrees with the civil law.

" Both to customs and prescriptions these two things are incidents inseparable, *viz.* possession, or usage, and time. Possession must have three qualities. It must be long, continual and peaceable—

---

50 (1834) 1 Cr.M. & R. 614.
1 (1836) 4 A. & E. 369; and see *Winship* v. *Hudspeth* (1854) 10 Ex. 5.
2 See pp. 179 *et seq., post.*
3 *Campbell* v. *Wilson* (1803) 3 East 294.
4 Cod. 3, 34, 1, *de serv.*; Dig. 8, 5, 10, *si serv. vind.*

'longa, continua et pacifica.' For it is said: Transferuntur dominia sine titulo et traditione per usucaptionem, scilicet per longam, continuam et pacificam possessionem. Longa, *i.e.*, per spatium temporis per legem definitum. Continuam dico, ita quod non sit legitime interrupta. Pacificam dico, quia si contentiosa fuerit, idem erit quod prius, si contentio fuerit justa. Ut si verus dominus, statim cum intrusor vel disseissor ingressus fuerit seisinam, nitatur tales viribus repellere et expellere, licet id quod inceperit perducere non possit ad effectum, dum tamen cum defecerit, diligens sit ad impetrandum et prosequendum. Longus usus nec per vim, nec clam, nec precario, etc." [5]

The words of Coke have been repeated by modern judges in stating the present rule. Thus it was said by Willes J.:

"In the case of prescription, long enjoyment in order to establish a right must have been as of right, and therefore, neither by violence, nor by stealth nor by leave asked from time to time." [6]

"An enjoyment as of right," said Lord Davey, "must be ' nec vi, nec clam, nec precario.' " [7]

Lord Davey's concise explanation will suffice for our present purpose; but reference may be made to the longer explanations given by Lord Denman in *Tickle* v. *Brown*,[8] by Brett L.J. in *De la Warr* (*Earl*) v. *Miles*,[9] and by Cozens-Hardy J. in *Gardner* v. *Hodgson's Kingston Brewery Co.*[10]

Proof of enjoyment as of right

The words " as of right " occur in section 5 of the Prescription Act; and the modern rules as to the necessity of proving an enjoyment of this character appear to be as follows: Where light is claimed under section 3 of the Act, it is not necessary that the enjoyment should have been as of right,[11] but where an easement other than light is claimed under section 2 of the Act, it is settled that the enjoyment on which the claim is based (whether for the period of twenty years or for that of forty years) must be shown to have been " as of right." [12]   In the case of claims by prescription at common law or under the doctrine of lost grant, whether to light or to any other kind of easement, it is also necessary to show an enjoyment as of right.[13]   Thus, in referring to the doctrine of lost grant, it was said by Fitzgibbon L.J.:

5 Co.Litt. 113b; Bracton, lib. 2, f. 51b, 52a, 222b.
6 *Mills* v. *Colchester Corporation* (1867) L.R. 2 C.P. 476, 486.
7 *Gardner* v. *Hodgson's Kingston Brewery Co.* [1903] A.C. 229, 238.   Lord Davey was repeating the words used by Erle J. in *Eaton* v. *Swansea Waterworks Co.* (1851) 17 Q.B. 275.
8 (1836) 4 A. & E. 369
9 (1881) 17 Ch.D. 591.
10 [1900] 1 Ch. 592, 597.
11 *Colls* v. *Home and Colonial Stores* [1904] A.C. 179, 205.
12 *Kilgour* v. *Gaddes* [1904] 1 K.B. 462.
13 See the above words of Willes J. in *Mills* v. *Colchester Corporation, supra.*

" The whole doctrine of presumed grant rests upon the desire of the law to create a legal foundation for the long-continued enjoyment, as of right, of advantages which are prima facie inexplicable in the absence of legal title. In cases such as this, where the grant is admittedly a fiction, it is all the more incumbent on the judge to see, before the question is left to the jury, that the circumstances and character of the user import that it has been ' as of right.' It appears to me, in the present case, that the evidence is inconsistent with right, and that the user is consistent only with permission to enjoy what the supposed grantor did not want, if and so long as that user might be consistent with the rights of third parties, and also with the grantor's right to use his own property from time to time in a reasonable manner. Such a user never could have been ' as of right' in its inception; it could never acquire during its continuance any higher than a permissive character, and it therefore never could be, or become, a foundation for the presumption of a grant." [14]

In *Alfred F. Beckett Ltd.* v. *Lyons*,[15] in which local inhabitants had collected and carried away sea-washed coal from the foreshore without believing that what they did was done as of right, the practice was not sufficient to support a claim as of right such as to require the court to find a legal origin for it in the fiction of a lost grant.

(2) *Rules for Acquisition of Easements by Prescription*

The following rules may be laid down as applying to the acquisition by prescription of easements generally; though not (except where otherwise stated) to the acquisition of the right to light under section 3 of the Prescription Act.

1. Nec vi
The enjoyment must not be by violence.

At common law any acts of interruption or opposition from which a jury might infer that the enjoyment was not rightful were sufficient to defeat the effect of the enjoyment, the question being whether, under all the facts of the case, such enjoyment had been under a concession of right. By the fourth section of the Prescription Act, it is enacted that nothing shall be deemed to be an interruption, unless it shall be submitted to or acquiesced in for the space of a year after the party interrupted shall have had notice thereof, and of the person making or authorising the same. It is certainly by no means clear what the precise intention of the legislature was; but it appears hardly possible that it

---

[14] *Hanna* v. *Pollock* [1900] 2 I.R. 671; see *per* Buckley L.J. in *Att.-Gen.* v. *Horner* [1913] 2 Ch. 140, 178.
[15] [1967] Ch. 449.

should have been intended to confer a right by user during the prescribed period, however " contentious " or " litigious " such user may have been.

In *Eaton* v. *Swansea Waterworks Co.*[16] the question was raised as to what would be the effect in law of a state of " perpetual warfare " between the dominant and servient owners?   And it was held by the Court of Queen's Bench that interruptions acquiesced in for less than a year might show that the enjoyment never was of right.   The inference drawn from this decision by Bowen J.[17] was that the user ought to be neither violent nor contentious.   The neighbour, without actual interruption of the user, ought perhaps, on principle, to be enabled by continuous and unmistakable protests to destroy its peaceful character, and so to annul one of the conditions upon which the presumption of right is raised.

An act of partial interruption, instead of destroying the easement claimed, may qualify it, and be evidence of another easement.   Thus, where a weir across a river was claimed by prescription, and a miller, whose mill was on its banks, had caused a fender to be shut down, the court held this not fatal to the claimant's right, thinking that there was nothing to prevent a second easement being acquired, as subordinate to that already existing, if the subject-matter admitted of it.[18]

2. Nec clam

The enjoyment must not be secret.

The user of an easement may be secret, either by reason of the mode in which a party enjoys it, or by reason of the nature of the easement itself.

Instances of the former kind are where the right is exercised by stealth, or in the night.[19]   Instances of the latter kind occur where a man who secretly excavates his own land on which a house is standing subsequently and in consequence of the excavation claims an extraordinary degree of support for the house from the neighbouring soil,[20] or where extraordinary support is claimed in consequence of a peculiarity in the internal structure of the house,[21] not visible to the neighbour.

A consideration of this rule would, it appears, afford an answer in

16 (1851) 17 Q.B. 267.
17 *Dalton* v. *Angus* (1881) 6 App.Cas. 786.   See *Lyell* v. *Hothfield* [1914] 3 K.B. 916.
18 *Rolle* v. *Whyte* (1868) L.R. 3 Q.B. 302.
19 Talis usus non valebit, cum sit clandestinus, et idem erit si nocturnus.—Bracton, Lib. 2, f. 52b.   Aut in absentia domini.—*Ibid.*, Lib. 4, f. 221a.   See *Dawson* v. *Norfolk* (1815) 1 Price 246; *Liverpool Corporation* v. *Coghill* [1918] 1 Ch. 307.
20 *Partridge* v. *Scott* (1838) 3 M. & W. 229.
21 *Angus* v. *Dalton* (1878) 4 Q.B.D. 162; see *per* Thesiger L.J. at pp. 181–183 and *per* Cotton L.J. at p. 187.   The defendants elected not to take a new trial, so that the decision on this point of the Court of Appeal was not, strictly speaking, open to review by the House of Lords; but the point was referred to on the appeal; see the same case in 6 App.Cas. 751 (Pollock B.), 757 and 760 (Field J.), 766 and 767 (Lindley L.J.), 777 and 779 (Fry J.), 787 and 789 (Bowen J.), 801 (Lord Selborne), 807 (Lord Penzance), 827 and 828 (Lord Blackburn).

the affirmative to the question incidentally raised in *Dodd* v. *Holme* [22]—whether, in order to acquire a right to support for a house by antiquity of possession, it must originally have been built with that degree of strength and coherence which may reasonably be expected to be found in a well-built house. For as there might be nothing in the external appearance of the house to give notice to the owner of the adjoining land that the weakness with which it was built caused it to require a greater degree of support from his soil than a well-built house would have required, and as *quoad* such additional support the enjoyment would have been secret, no presumption of a grant of it on his part could be implied. The same reasoning would also apply to the case of an ancient house, originally well built, becoming weaker from the want of proper repair. A man believing there were no minerals on his own land might be willing to subject it to the easement of support to a well-built house, which would diminish the value of his property only in the event of his wishing to mine in it, although he would refuse to restrict himself from digging a foundation for any building he might require; which would possibly be the case were he bound to afford the support necessary to sustain a rickety and ill-built edifice. There is also the case of a house originally requiring no more than an ordinary degree of support, but subsequently altered so as to require an unusual amount of lateral pressure to support it. But here, it seems that, if the alteration be openly and honestly made, the servient owner is fixed with notice that an additional burden of some kind is being imposed upon his tenement, and, if he makes no inquiry, will in time become subject to the obligation of increased support.[23] This reasoning also applies to the claim of an extraordinary degree of support from adjoining houses.[24]

Secrecy of enjoyment was one of the difficulties in establishing the easement of support considered in the leading case of *Dalton* v. *Angus.*[25] It was established by that decision that there must be some knowledge or means of knowledge on the part of the servient owner against whom the right is claimed.[26] In the simple case where a prescriptive easement of support is claimed by the owner of one of two adjoining houses against the owner of the other, it must be shown that the owner of the servient tenement knew or had the means of knowing that his house was affording support to the other.[27] Again, in *Union Lighterage Co.* v. *London Graving Dock Co.*[28] where the sides of a wooden dock had

---

[22] (1834) 1 A. & E. 493.
[23] *Dalton* v. *Angus* (1881) 6 App.Cas. 740; *per* Lord Selborne at p. 801.
[24] See *per* Bramwell B. in *Solomon* v. *Vintners' Co.* (1859) 4 H. & N. 601. In *Angus* v. *Dalton*, Cockburn C.J. appears to have considered that the very possibility of acquiring any prescriptive right to support was excluded by the secrecy of the enjoyment (3 Q.B.D. 117), but this opinion was negatived by the Court of Appeal and the House of Lords. See *Lloyds Bank* v. *Dalton* [1942] Ch. 466.
[25] (1881) 6 App.Cas. 740.
[26] *Union Lighterage Co.* v. *London Graving Dock Co.* [1902] 2 Ch. 557.
[27] *Gately* v. *Martin* [1900] 2 Ir.R. 269. See *Lemaitre* v. *Davis* (1881) 19 Ch.D. 291.
[28] [1902] 2 Ch. 557.

for more than twenty years been supported by underground rods which were not themselves visible, but certain nuts which fastened them were visible, claim to support for the dock from the rods was defeated on the ground that the enjoyment had been *clam*. It was held by Romer and Stirling L.JJ. that, on the facts, knowledge of the rods ought not to be attributed to the servient owner; Vaughan Williams L.J. holding, on the other hand, that there was sufficient means of knowledge.

In *Liverpool Corporation* v. *Coghill* [29] it was held that the claimants' intermittent discharge, at night, of borax solution into the plaintiffs' sewers without their knowledge was a secret enjoyment which did not entitle them to an easement although practised for more than twenty years before proceedings were brought in May 1917. Moreover, time would not have commenced to run against the plaintiffs until there had been an invasion of a legal right [30] and, as the effluent was innocuous prior to the year 1908, the requisite period had not elapsed. In any case it was doubtful if the plaintiffs in view of their statutory duties, could have made such a grant as the prescriptive right contended for implied.

In connection with the rule that enjoyment as of right must not be *clam*, reference should be made to the cases quoted later (pp. 179 *et seq.*) laying down that the user on which a claim to a prescriptive easement is based must be a user of which the servient owner has knowledge either actual or constructive.

3. Nec precario

The enjoyment must not be permissive. It must not be *precario*.

What is precarious? "That which depends not on right, but on the will of another person." [31] " Si autem," says Bracton, " (seisina) precaria fuerit et de gratia, quae tempestive revocari possit et intempestive, ex longo tempora non acquiritur jus." [32]

Enjoyment had under a licence or permission from the owner of the servient tenement confers no right to the easement. Each renewal of the licence rebuts the presumption which would otherwise arise, that such enjoyment was had under a claim of right to the easement.[33] Permission granted by a tenant who is in occupation of the servient

---

[29] [1918] 1 Ch. 307.
[30] See *Goldsmid* v. *Tunbridge Wells Improvement Commissioners* (1866) 1 Ch.App. 349.
[31] *Per* Farwell J., *Burrows* v. *Lang* [1901] 2 Ch. 502, 510.
[32] Lib. 4, f. 221a.
[33] *Monmouthshire Canal Co.* v. *Harford* (1834) 1 C.M. & R. 614; *Tone* v. *Preston* (1883) 24 Ch.D. 739; *Chamber Colliery Co.* v. *Hopwood* (1886) 32 Ch.D. 549.
    If the enjoyment commenced by permission, it is a question for the jury whether it did not continue by permission: *Gaved* v. *Martyn* (1865) 19 C.B.(N.S.) 732. The fact that a gate, through which a right of way was claimed, had always been kept locked, the key having been kept by the proprietor of the servient tenement, but always having been asked for by the proprietor of the dominant tenement as a matter of right, when it was required, and never having been refused, did not prevent the acquisition, by prescription, of the easement: *Roberts* v. *Fellowes* (1906) 94 L.T. 279.

tenement is sufficient to defeat a claim under the doctrine of lost grant or on the basis of section 2 of the Prescription Act.[34]

Before the Prescription Act, any admission, whether verbal or otherwise, that the enjoyment had been had by permission of the owner of the servient tenement was sufficient to prevent the acquisition of the right, however long such enjoyment might have continued.

Since the Prescription Act, where an easement is claimed under the Act, the effect of permission for the enjoyment having been given by the owner of the servient tenement has been considered in many cases.

A claim to an easement (other than light) under section 2 of the Act on the ground of an enjoyment for twenty years is defeated by an oral consent given at the beginning of and extending throughout the user.[35] If user has continued for forty years a claim will still be defeated by permission given during the period, but not by prior parol permission.[36] Once permission has been given, the user remains permissive and is not capable of ripening into a right (save where the permission is oral and the user has continued for forty years) unless and until, having been given for a limited period only, it expires or, being general, it is revoked, or there is a change of circumstances from which revocation may fairly be implied.[37] If the enjoyment was originally by permission, it is a question of fact, depending upon the evidence, and the inferences to be drawn therefrom, whether it has so continued.[38]

Where the easement of light is claimed under section 3 of the Act, it has been laid down in the House of Lords that enjoyment as of right need not be alleged or proved, and that the right is acquired by twenty years' enjoyment without interruption and without written consent.[39] A written consent would negative the effect of the enjoyment (see s. 3), but not a verbal consent.[40]

---

34 *Ward* v. *Kirkland* [1967] Ch. 194, 233–234.
35 *Healey* v. *Hawkins* [1968] 1 W.L.R. 1967 (considering and explaining dicta of Denman C.J. in *Tickle* v. *Brown* (1836) 4 Ad. & E. 369, 383, and Alderson B. in *Kinloch* v. *Nevile* (1840) 6 M. & W. 795, 806). See also *Reilly* v. *Orange* [1955] 2 Q.B. 112, 119.
36 *Gardner* v. *Hodgson's Kingston Brewery Co.* [1903] A.C. 229, affirming C.A. [1901] 2 Ch. 198; *Healey* v. *Hawkins* [1968] 1 W.L.R. 1967; and see *Tickle* v. *Brown* (1836) 4 A. & E. 369; *Beasley* v. *Clarke* (1836) 2 Bing.N.C. 705; *De La Warr (Earl)* v. *Miles* (1881) 17 Ch.D. 535, 596. Written permission, in order to defeat a claim based on an enjoyment for forty years, must be properly pleaded, a general traverse of enjoyment as of right being insufficient: *Tickle* v. *Brown, supra,* 383; see *Gardner* v. *Hodgson's Kingston Brewery Co.* [1900] 1 Ch. 594, *per* Cozens-Hardy J.; [1901] 2 Ch. 213, *per* Rigby L.J.; *Lowry* v. *Crothers* (1872) I.R. 5 C.L. 98.
37 *Healey* v. *Hawkins* [1968] 1 W.L.R. 1967, applying *Gaved* v. *Martyn* (1865) 19 C.B.(N.S.) 732.
38 *Gaved* v. *Martyn* (1865) 19 C.B.(N.S.) 732; *Healey* v. *Hawkins* [1968] 1 W.L.R. 1967. See " Prescription under the Statute " by P. St. J. Langan in 32 *Conveyancer* (N.S.) 40.
39 *Colls* v. *Home and Colonial Stores* [1904] A.C. 179, 205.
40 *London Corpn.* v. *Pewterers' Co.* (1842) 2 Moo. & R. 409; *Judge* v. *Lowe* (1873) I.R. 7 C.L. 291; see *Plasterers' Co.* v. *Parish Clerks' Co.* (1851) 6 Exch. 630; *Mallam* v. *Rose* [1915] 2 Ch. 222.

The rule that an enjoyment which is by permission is not an enjoyment as of right is illustrated by cases as to water rights. Thus, in the leading case of *Wood* v. *Waud* [41] it has been said that in that case the nature of an artificial watercourse showed that though the water in fact had flowed for sixty years, yet from the beginning it was only intended to flow so long as the coal-owners did not think fit otherwise to drain their mines, and so was precarious.[42] It was said also that the decision of the Court of Exchequer in the last-mentioned case was in fact a decision that an enjoyment for more than a statutable period is not an enjoyment as of right if during the period it is known that it is only permitted as long as some particular purpose is served.[43]

4. Enjoyment under a mistake

Where enjoyment takes place under a mistaken view of their rights entertained by both the dominant and servient owners, there is no enjoyment " as of right " upon which a prescriptive easement can be claimed. Thus, where Blackacre was demised to a tenant who during the lease made and enjoyed a watercourse on Blackacre for the benefit of an adjoining property of his own, the enjoyment being of a kind which the court assumed was not authorised by the lease, but both landlord and tenant being under the mistaken belief that it was so authorised, the Court of Appeal held that there was no enjoyment as of right.[44] Similarly it has been laid down that enjoyment must be attributed to the right claimed by the dominant owner and to no other. If the enjoyment originated in mistake and the dominant owner asserted his right to be grounded on some document which did not support it, then, however adversely the right may have been exercised, it cannot for the purposes of prescription be referred to any other ground than that which the dominant owner insisted on at the time.[45]

In *Thomas W. Ward Ltd.* v. *Alexander Bruce (Grays) Ltd.*[46] a grant for loading and unloading vessels was exceeded by breaking up vessels. There was no evidence that either party considered this to be within the grant and the dominant owner failed to discharge the onus of showing that the user was not *precario*.

---

[41] (1849) 3 Exch. 748.
[42] See *Mason* v. *Shrewsbury & Hereford Ry. Co.* (1871) L.R. 6 Q.B. 578, 584; *Schwann* v. *Cotton* [1916] 2 Ch. 459, 475, where Warrington L.J. explains the judgment (at 3 Exch. 779) in *Wood* v. *Waud, supra.*
[43] *Ibid.*, see *Staffordshire & Worcestershire Canal Co.* v. *Birmingham Canal Co.* (1866) L.R. 1 H.L. 254.
[44] *Chamber Colliery Co.* v. *Hopwood* (1886) 32 Ch.D. 559.
[45] *Att.-Gen.* v. *Horner* [1913] 2 Ch. 140, 169, 179, referring to *Campbell* v. *Wilson* (1803) 3 East 301; *Lord Rivers* v. *Adams* (1878) 3 Ex.D. 371.
[46] [1959] 2 Lloyd's Rep. 472. The Court of Appeal explained *De La Warr (Earl)* v. *Miles* (1881) 17 Ch.D. 535 (followed in the Irish case of *Dawson* v. *M'Groggan* [1903] 1 I.R. 92), which appears to be inconsistent with *Chamber Colliery Co.* v. *Hopwood* (1886) 32 Ch.D. 559, pointing out that in *De La Warr (Earl)* v. *Miles* there was no consensual element.

5. Knowledge of servient owner

The enjoyment must be one of which the servient owner has knowledge either actual or constructive.

This rule will be best illustrated in the first instance by the following statements of law made by judges in modern cases where easements were called in question.

In *Sturges* v. *Bridgman* [47] Thesiger L.J., in delivering the judgment of the Court of Appeal, used the following words:

" The law governing the acquisition of easements by user stands thus: Consent or acquiescence of the owner of the servient tenement lies at the root of prescription, and of the fiction of a lost grant, and hence the acts or user, which go to the proof of either the one or the other, must be, in the language of the civil law, *nec vi nec clam nec precario*; for a man cannot, as a general rule, be said to consent to or acquiesce in the acquisition by his neighbour of an easement through an enjoyment of which he has no knowledge, actual or constructive,[48] or which he contests and endeavours to interrupt, or which he temporarily licenses. It is a mere extension of the same notion, or rather it is a principle into which by strict analysis it may be resolved, to hold, that an enjoyment which a man cannot prevent raises no presumption of consent or acquiescence." [49]

Again, in delivering his opinion to the House of Lords in *Dalton* v. *Angus*,[50] Fry J. said:

" In my opinion, the whole law of prescription and the whole law which governs the presumption or inference of a grant or covenant rest upon acquiescence. The courts and the judges have had recourse to various expedients for quieting the possession of persons in the exercise of rights which have not been resisted by the persons against whom they are exercised, but in all cases it appears to me that acquiescence and nothing else is the principle upon which these expedients rest. It becomes then of the highest importance to consider of what ingredients acquiescence consists. In many cases, as, for instance, in the case of that acquiescence which creates a right of way, it will be found to involve, first, the doing of some act by one man upon the land of another; secondly, the absence of right to do that act in the person doing it; thirdly, the knowledge of the person affected by it that the act is done; fourthly, the power of the person affected by the act to prevent such act either by act on his part or by action in the

---

[47] (1879) 11 Ch.D. 852, 863. See also *per* Stirling L.J., *Roberts* v. *James* (1903) 89 L.T. 282, 287; and *per* Bray J., *Ambler* v. *Gordon* [1905] 1 K.B. 417, 424.

[48] See *Liverpool Corporation* v. *Coghill* [1918] 1 Ch. 307, 314.

[49] For a good example of a case where the owner of the servient tenement was held to have had either actual knowledge or constructive notice of the enjoyment of the easement claimed, see *Lloyds Bank* v. *Dalton* [1942] Ch. 466; see p. 180, *post.*

[50] (1881) 6 App.Cas. 740, 773.

courts; and lastly, the abstinence by him from any such interference for such a length of time as renders it reasonable for the courts to say that he shall not afterwards interfere to stop the act being done. In some other cases, as, for example, in the case of lights, some of these ingredients are wanting; but I cannot imagine any case of acquiescence in which there is not shown to be in the servient owner: 1, a knowledge of the acts done; 2, a power in him to stop the acts or to sue in respect of them; and 3, an abstinence on his part from the exercise of such power. That such is the nature of acquiescence and that such is the ground upon which presumptions or inferences of grant or covenant may be made appears to me to be plain, both from reason, from maxim, and from the cases."

Referring to the above opinions of Fry J., Lord Penzance, in his speech in the House of Lords in *Dalton* v. *Angus*, stated that he was in "entire accord" with that judge; the opinion being also described by Lord Blackburn as "a very able one."[1]   Lord Blackburn's own view seems to have been to base prescription not so much upon acquiescence as upon utility, *bono publico*.[2]   But later decisions appear to have followed rather the lines laid down by Fry J. than those laid down by Lord Blackburn. In *Union Lighterage Co.* v. *London Graving Dock Co.*[3] Vaughan Williams L.J. distinctly prefers the view of Fry J., stating, however, at the same time that actual knowledge is not essential to acquiescence, but that means of knowledge is sufficient.[4]   Romer L.J., in the Court of Appeal, also indicated that means of knowledge is sufficient.[5]

In *Lloyds Bank* v. *Dalton*,[6] Bennett J. found as a fact that the defendants, owners of dye-works which had in fact supported the plaintiff's yard and outbuilding, either must have known or must be taken to have had a reasonable opportunity of knowing that the said yard and outbuilding had been supported by the dye-works. The decision is clear authority for the view that constructive as opposed to actual knowledge is enough to prevent the owner of the servient tenement from setting up the defence that the enjoyment of the easement claimed was *clam*.

The cases in which the importance of knowledge on the part of the servient owner has been most frequently discussed are those where the servient tenement has during the enjoyment been in the possession

---

1   (1881) 6 App.Cas. 803, 823.
2   (1881) 6 App.Cas. 818, 826.
3   [1902] 2 Ch. 557.
4   *Ibid*. 568–569.   A servient owner who had been in possession of the servient tenement throughout was presumed to have notice, actual or constructive, of the use to which the servient land was being openly and continuously subjected: *Bower* v. *John Etherington Ltd.* (1965) 53 D.L.R. (2d) 338, Nova Scotia Supreme Court.
5   [1902] 2 Ch. 571.
6   [1942] Ch. 466.

of a tenant for life or years. And referring to these cases Mr. Gale wrote: The want of acquiescence of the owner of the inheritance of the neighbouring tenement may, it would seem, be inferred, either from the circumstance that he is not in possession, or from the nature of the enjoyment of the right, it being, in truth and in fact, out of the view and knowledge of such neighbouring owner, though he be in possession. With respect to the former question an important point arises, whether, if the knowledge in fact of the owner of the inheritance of the hostile enjoyment of an easement be shown, he is bound by it. Cases decided before the Prescription Act certainly lay down, that if knowledge in fact of the reversioner be shown, he would be bound; but in one of the cases a learned judge,[7] took a distinction between two divisions of easements, expressing an opinion to the effect that an enjoyment of a negative easement would not bind the reversioner, unless his knowledge were positively shown, though it would be otherwise of an affirmative easement. If it be taken as law, that a reversioner can be bound by his knowledge in fact of a user enjoyed during the time his land is in the possession of a tenant, as his acquiescence in such cases is inferred from his offering no opposition, it would seem that he must, by law, have some valid mode of preventing the right from vesting by the continuance of the user. With respect to a negative easement it is clear the user gives no right of action to any person; and even as to some positive easements, such as a right of way, it is doubtful whether the reversioner could maintain an action [8]; and during the continuance of the tenancy he may be unable either to interrupt the enjoyment or to compel his tenant to do so. Unless, therefore, some positive act, as a notice, intimating his dissent, be sufficient to obviate the effect of the user giving a right, he would not be brought into the condition of a *valens agere*, without which the prescription ought not to run against him.

Bracton, treating of the qualities of a possession necessary to confer a right, appears to consider that such notices, at all events if followed up by an action as soon as the party is in a condition to bring one, will amount to an interruption.

> " Continuam dico ita quod non sit interrupta; interrumpi enim poterit multis modis sine violentia adhibita, per denuntiationem et impetrationem diligentem, et diligentem prosecutionem, et per talem interruptionem, nunquam acquiret possidens ex tempore liberum tenementum." [9]

Moreover, in speaking of this precise case—of a particular estate existing in the servient tenement during the user of the easement—

---

[7] Le Blanc J. in *Daniel* v. *North* (1809) 11 East 372; and *semble* also Parke J. in *Gray* v. *Bond* (1821) 2 Brod. & Bing. 667.
[8] As to the power of the reversioner to sue, see *post*, p. 363.
[9] Lib. 2, f. 51b.

he seems to be clearly of opinion that such a prohibition will be sufficient to preserve his right.

" Si autem fuerit seisina clandestina, scilicet in absentia dominorum vel illis ignorantibus, et si scirent essent prohibituri, licet hoc fiat de consensu vel dissimulatione ballivorum, valere non debet." [10]

In *Daniel* v. *North*,[11] which was an action before the Prescription Act for obstructing ancient lights, the premises on which the obstruction was erected had been occupied during twenty years by a tenant at will, and there was no evidence that the owner of those premises was aware of such enjoyment. Lord Ellenborough observed, on the argument for a new trial:

" How can such a presumption be raised against the landlord, without showing that he knew of the fact when he was not in possession, and received no immediate injury from it at the time? "

In delivering his judgment his Lordship said:

" The foundation of presuming a grant against any party is, that the exercise of the adverse right on which such presumption is founded was against a party capable of making the grant; and that cannot be presumed against him unless there were some probable means of his knowing what was done against him. And it cannot be laid down as a rule of law, that the enjoyment of the plaintiff's windows during the occupation of the opposite premises by a tenant, though for twenty years, without the knowledge of the landlord, will bind the latter. And there is no evidence stated in the report from whence his knowledge should be presumed." [12]

As regards claims under the Prescription Act, Mr. Gale wrote that the Act had introduced two questions of difficulty upon the point how far the reversioner is bound by an enjoyment had during the continuance of a particular estate: First, supposing the reversioner, being aware of the fact, from time to time gives a parol or written notice of his dissent to the enjoyment of the easement, any active interference on his part being prevented by the existence of the particular estate; or secondly, supposing the reversioner be in total ignorance of any such enjoyment having been had during the continuance of the particular estate, and in consequence of such ignorance not to have availed himself of the exception in his favour contained in the statute—in either of these cases would a valid right to an easement be acquired?

---

10 Lib. 4, f. 221.
11 (1809) 11 East 372.
12 For the present rule where light is claimed under the statute, see *ante*, p. 149.

In the case of light the answer to this question is in the affirmative.[13]

In the case of other easements it would appear to depend upon whether the user is of twenty years or forty years, and, if of twenty years, whether the reversioner is entitled expectant on a term of years, or on a life tenancy. If the user is of twenty years the reversioner expectant on a life tenancy would not be bound, by reason of the exclusion of the period of disability under section 7. As, however, section 7 does not exclude the period during which the servient tenement shall have been in lease for a term of years, and section 8 applies only to the period of forty years, it would seem that, so far as the statute is concerned, he would be bound, if his reversion was expectant on a term of years. If the user is of forty years, he would be bound, unless he resisted within three years from the expiration of the term, under section 8; or unless the circumstances were such (as *e.g.* in *Kilgour* v. *Gaddes*[14]) as not to admit of the user having been " as of right " against him.

At all events, if the user of any easement had actually commenced before the property over which it was claimed passed into the possession of the lessee, the mere fact of such tenancy having continued during a period of twenty years will not, it seems, be sufficient to defeat the right acquired by the lapse of time, unless it be shown that the landlord, up to the time of granting the lease, was in ignorance that any such right was claimed.[15] Thus, in *Cross* v. *Lewis*,[16] where a house was proved to have been built thirty-eight years, during the whole of which time there had been windows towards the adjoining premises, and these premises had belonged for a number of years to a family residing at a distance, none of whom was proved to have ever seen them, and they had been occupied by the same tenant during the last twenty years—the court held that, after such a long enjoyment, the windows must be considered ancient windows, and that the plaintiff was consequently entitled to recover for their obstruction. Bayley J. in his judgment said[17]:

" The right is proved to have existed for thirty-eight years; the commencement of it is not shown. It is possible that the premises, both of the plaintiff and defendant, once belonged to the

---

13 See the cases cited *ante*, pp. 148–149. In particular, see *Morgan* v. *Fear* [1907] A.C. 425, where *Frewen* v. *Philipps* (1861) 11 C.B.(N.S.) 449 was approved. In his judgment in *Frewen* v. *Philipps* Pollock C.B. used the following words: " It may be that, if a man opens a light towards his neighbour's land, the reversioner may have no means of preventing a right thereto from being acquired by a twenty years' enjoyment, unless he can prevail upon his tenant to raise an obstruction, or is able to procure from the other party an acknowledgment that the light is enjoyed only by consent."
14 [1904] 1 K.B. 457 (*ante*, p. 167); and *Davies* v. *Du Paver* [1953] 1 Q.B. 184, *post*, p. 185.
15 But see *Davies* v. *Du Paver*, *supra*.
16 (1824) 2 B. & C. 686; and see now *Morgan* v. *Fear* [1907] A.C. 425.
17 (1824) 2 B. & C. 686, 689–690.

same person, and that he conferred on the plaintiff, or those under whom she claims, a right to have the windows free from obstruction. *Daniel* v. *North* [18] has been relied upon, to show that the tenancy rebutted the presumption of a grant; but this is a very different case; [the] tenancy was shown to have existed for twenty years, but the origin of the plaintiff's right was not traced."

Littledale J. added [19]:

" It was proved that the windows had existed for thirty-eight years, and [the] tenancy for twenty. How the land was occupied for eighteen years before that time did not appear. I think that quite sufficient to found the presumption of a grant." [20]

As the claim of an easement is in derogation of the ordinary rights of property, it lies upon the party asserting such claims, in opposition to common right, in all cases to support his case by evidence. In *Cross* v. *Lewis* [21] the absence of any evidence as to the earlier state of the windows was indeed held to operate in favour of the plaintiff— the party claiming the easement; but the substantial proof, *viz.*, of the user for a period of twenty years, had already been given by the claimant; and this, unrebutted by any evidence to take the case out of the ordinary rule, was of course sufficient to establish the easement. From the observations of the learned judge in the last-mentioned case, it would appear that, provided the existence of the easement prior to the commencement of the tenancy was shown, and a sufficient length of enjoyment had taken place to afford evidence of a grant, the burden of proof would be thrown upon the owner of the land sought to be made liable to the easement; and unless he could show such previous user to have taken place without his knowledge, the right to the easement would be established.[22] Indeed, it should seem from this case that proof of enjoyment for twenty years was in all cases prima facie evidence of a title which must be rebutted by the owner of the servient tenement; and where the servient tenement has been in the possession of a tenant for years, but an easement over it has been enjoyed for a long time, it has been laid down that the landlord may be presumed to have been aware of it.[23]

In *Pugh* v. *Savage* [24] the plaintiff was the owner in fee simple of a farm, which he had bought from R. in 1950. The farm included field A, which was approached from the highway along a lane, part of which bordered the plaintiff's land. A footpath ran from the highway along the lane into field A, across field A into field B, and across field B into field C. Until 1966 field B was owned by an estate

[18] (1809) 11 East 372.
[19] (1824) 2 B. & C. 686, 690.
[20] See *Palk* v. *Shinner* (1852) 18 Q.B. 568, *ante*, p. 157.
[21] (1824) 2 B. & C. 686.
[22] See *Gray* v. *Bond* (1821) 2 Brod. & B. 667.
[23] *Davies* v. *Stephens* (1836) 7 C. & P. 570.
[24] [1970] 2 Q.B. 373.

company, and field C formed an isolated part of another farm.   In
1966 the estate company bought field C and let it, together with field B
and a large field fronting onto the highway, to the defendant.   When
he took the tenancy the defendant was informed that he would be
entitled to a private right of way on foot and with vehicles over field
A and along the lane into the highway.   When, however, the defendant
purported to exercise that right, the plaintiff, while admitting that there
was a public footpath, denied the existence of any private way for
vehicles.   In 1968 the plaintiff ploughed up field A and partially
obstructed the lane with hedge-cuttings.   The defendant therefore took
his vehicles over other parts of the plaintiff's land to reach the highway.   The plaintiff claimed an injunction and damages for trespass,
and the defendant claimed a right of way across field A and along
the lane and counterclaimed for damages.   The defendant claimed that
such a right of way had been enjoyed without interruption by him and
his predecessors, the occupiers of field C, for over thirty years
immediately prior to the commencement of the proceedings.   At the
hearing of the action it was agreed that shortly after 1940 R. had
let the field to his son on an oral tenancy which was surrendered
when the plaintiff bought the farm in 1950.   The Court of Appeal,
applying *Cross* v. *Lewis* [25] and *Palk* v. *Shinner*,[26] held that where a
tenancy of a servient tenement came into existence during the course of
the period of user, the grant of the tenancy would not, in the absence
of evidence that the servient owner had no knowledge of the user
while the tenant was in possession, be a fatal objection to the presumption of a grant or to a claim made under the Prescription Act,
although it was a matter to be considered; and that where, as in the
case before the court, there had been long user of the way, the law
should support it and, in the absence of evidence to the contrary, it
should be presumed that the successive owners of field A between
1936 and 1950 knew of the user by the owner of field C, the dominant
tenement.   On the other hand, the court took the view that a distinction
was to be drawn between cases where the tenancy was in existence
at the beginning of the period of user and cases where the tenancy
came into existence in the course of the period of user.   In the former
case it might well be unreasonable to imply a lost grant by the owner
at the beginning of the user.   He might not have been able to stop
the user, even if he knew about it.

In *Davies* v. *Du Paver* [27] where a right of sheepwalk, based on user
for sixty years, was claimed by prescription at common law, alternatively under section 1 of the Act, over land which had been let during
all these years except a few towards the end, it was held that the onus
was on the plaintiff to show that the owner had some knowledge, or

[25] (1824) 2 B. & C. 686; see p. 183, *ante.*
[26] (1852) 18 Q.B. 568; 17 Jur. 372; see p. 157, *ante.*
[27] [1953] 1 Q.B. 184.

reasonable means of knowledge, of the user, and that in the absence of such evidence the claim failed, the plaintiff not showing user " as of right." Common local knowledge of the user was established, but, in the circumstances, this was considered not to extend to the owner.

6. Enjoyment must be capable of interruption

The enjoyment must be one which the servient owner could have prevented or interrupted.

This rule is well illustrated by the case of *Sturges* v. *Bridgman*.[28] There the question arose as regards two adjoining houses in London. One of these belonged to confectioners, who for more than sixty years before action had caused noise on their premises by the use of a pestle and mortar in their kitchen. The other house was purchased a few years before action by a doctor, who thereupon built a consulting room close to the kitchen. Shortly afterwards he brought an action against the confectioners to restrain them from causing the noise, which, on the evidence, the court held, amounted to a nuisance to the plaintiff's premises after the erection of his consulting room, but not before. The confectioners contended by way of defence that a right to cause the noise had been acquired by user, and that a grant should be presumed. The court, however, decided against the contention; holding that, before the erection of the consulting room, the noise could not have been legally prevented, either physically or by means of an action, and that accordingly there was no sufficient user from which a grant could be presumed. The same doctrine was applied where claims were made to the access of air to chimneys over an unlimited surface of the servient tenement[29] and to subterranean water percolating in unknown channels.[30] In neither of these cases could the servient owner have prevented the user.

In *Angus* v. *Dalton*[31] Cockburn C.J. and Mellor J. gave judgment against a claim of lateral support for buildings, partly upon the ground that the enjoyment of such support cannot be resisted or prevented by the adjoining owner by any means short of an excavation which may be destructive of his own tenement,[32] but the majority of the Court of Appeal, while conceding that an enjoyment physically incapable of interruption would confer no right,[33] held that the decided cases precluded them from applying the principle to the easement in question[34]; and their decision was upheld by the House of Lords.

---

[28] (1879) 11 Ch.D. 852.
[29] *Bryant* v. *Lefever* (1879) 4 C.P.D. 173.
[30] *Chasemore* v. *Richards* (1859) 7 H.L.C. 349.
[31] (1877) 3 Q.B.D. 85; (1878) 4 Q.B.D. 162; *sub nom. Dalton* v. *Angus* (1881) 6 App.Cas. 740.
[32] (1877) 3 Q.B.D. 117, 125 *et seq.*
[33] (1878) 4 Q.B.D. 175.
[34] (1878) 4 Q.B.D. 176–181.

" That power of resistance," said Lord Selborne,[35] " by interruption does and must in all such cases exist, otherwise no question like the present could arise. It is true that in some cases (of which the present is an example) a man acting with a reasonable regard to his own interest would never exercise it for the mere purpose of preventing his neighbour from enlarging or extending such a servitude. But, on the other hand, it would not be reasonably consistent with the policy of the law in favour of possessory titles, that they should depend, in each particular case, upon the greater or less facility or difficulty, convenience or inconvenience, of practically interrupting them. They can always be interrupted (and that without difficulty or inconvenience), when a man wishes, and finds it for his interest, to make such a use of his own land as will have that effect. So long as it does not suit his purpose and his interest to do this, the law which allows a servitude to be established or enlarged by long and open enjoyment, against one whose preponderating interest it has been to be passive during the whole time necessary for its acquisition, seems more reasonable, and more consistent with public convenience and natural equity, than one which would enable him, at any distance of time (whenever his views of his own interest may have undergone a change), to destroy the fruits of his neighbour's diligence, industry, and expenditure."

Lord Penzance concurred in the judgment, feeling himself bound by previous decisions; but his own opinion was that the enjoyment must, in order to confer a right, be capable of interruption " without extravagant and unreasonable loss or expense." [36]

With regard to a right to discharge a noxious effluent, time will not run against the servient owner during such time as the effluent remains harmless.[37]

The question what interruption will be sufficient to defeat a claim under the Act to an easement is considered in the cases quoted under section 4 of the Act, *ante*, p. 153.

7. Enjoyment as an easement

The enjoyment must have been an enjoyment of the easement in the character of an easement, distinct from the enjoyment of the land itself.

[35] (1881) 6 App.Cas. 796. Some of the judges even hinted that the enjoyment of lateral support was capable of being resisted by the simple method of bringing an action for trespass; and Lord Selborne appears to have concurred in this view, without making it the basis of his judgment. See *per* Lindley and Bowen JJ. at pp. 763, 784, and the contrary opinion of Fry J. at p. 775; Lord Selborne's opinion on this point is reported on p. 793, and Lord Watson's on p. 831.

[36] (1881) 6 App.Cas. 805. The opinions of the judges on this point will be found reported on pp. 749 (Pollock B.), 764 (Lindley J.), 774 (Fry J.), and 785 (Bowen J.).

[37] *Liverpool Corporation* v. *Coghill* [1918] 1 Ch. 307, *ante*, p. 176.

This rule has been so laid down as regards a right of way,[38] and also as regards the right of light [39]; and bears upon the case of unity of possession.[40] For where there is unity of possession of the dominant and servient tenements there is no enjoyment of an easement as an easement. The case of unity may also be referred to the preceding rule about prevention of enjoyment. Thus, where the same person has been in legal occupation as tenant of the servient and dominant tenements [41] it is obvious that the user of the servient tenement by the common occupier could not be prevented by the owner of that tenement.[42] The operation of the unity is to destroy the effect of the previous user by breaking the continuity of enjoyment.

8. Enjoyment must be definite and continuous

The enjoyment must be definite and sufficiently continuous in its character. Thus: " Non-user which would not be sufficient to establish an abandonment of a right acquired may be enough to prevent the acquisition of that right under the (Prescription) Act." [43]

Continuity may be interrupted by the act of the servient owner or by that of the person claiming the prescriptive right. In the first case the Prescription Act 1832, s. 4, will apply [44]; in the second case it is mainly a question of fact and degree whether the nature of a given enjoyment establishes an easement of an intermittent character or whether the enjoyment is so lacking in continuity as to be otiose. Thus it is not to be understood that the enjoyment of an easement must necessarily be incessant; although, in a great variety of cases, it would obviously be so—as in the case of windows, or rights to water. In those easements which require the repeated acts of man for their enjoyment, as rights of way, it would appear to be sufficient if the user is of such a nature, and takes place at such intervals, as to afford an indication to the owner of the servient tenement that a right is claimed against him—an indication that would not be afforded by a mere accidental or occasional exercise.[45]

The continuity of enjoyment may be broken either by the cessation to use, or by the enjoyment not being had in the proper manner.

" An enjoyment of an easement for one week," said Parke B. in

---

38 *Battishill* v. *Reed* (1856) 18 C.B. 702.
39 *Harbidge* v. *Warwick* (1849) 3 Exch. 552.
40 See *ante*, p. 160.
41 *Harbidge* v. *Warwick, supra.* See as to rights of way, *Damper* v. *Bassett* [1901] 2 Ch. 350; *Hulbert* v. *Dale* [1909] 2 Ch. 570.
42 See *Outram* v. *Maude* (1881) 17 Ch.D. 391, 405.
43 *Smith* v. *Baxter* [1900] 2 Ch. 138, *per* Stirling J. at p. 146; and see *Hulley* v. *Silversprings Bleaching and Dyeing Co.* [1922] 2 Ch. 268, 281; *Hollins* v. *Verney* (1884) 13 Q.B.D. 304, and other cases quoted under s. 4 of the Prescription Act, *ante*, p. 153.
44 See p. 152, *ante*.
45 *Per cur.* in *Bartlett* v. *Downes* (1825) 3 B. & C. 621; and in *Hollins* v. *Verney* (1884) 13 Q.B.D. 304, 315; as to light, see *Smith* v. *Baxter* [1900] 2 Ch. 138; *Andrews* v. *Waite* [1907] 2 Ch. 500; see also *Bower* v. *John Etherington Ltd.* (1965) 53 D.L.R. (2d) 338, Nova Scotia Supreme Court.

Monmouthshire Canal Co. v. *Harford*,[46] " and a cessation to enjoy it during the next week, and so on alternately, would confer no right." [47]

So, where the enjoyment has been had under permission asked from time to time, which, upon each occasion, amounts to an admission that the asker had then no right. Indeed, the very mode in which this enjoyment, under constantly renewed permission, operates in defeating the previous user is that it breaks the continuity of the enjoyment [48]; and it is expressly laid down by the Court of King's Bench, in their judgment in the case of *Tickle* v. *Brown*,[49] that the breaking of the continuity is inconsistent with the enjoyment during the periods of either twenty or forty years, and that for that reason evidence of the breaking of such continuity is admissible on a traverse of the enjoyment.

In a claim to sheep rights under section 1 of the Prescription Act, the claimant need not establish that the right has been exercised continuously, for the right, of its nature, would only be used intermittently. On the other hand the user must still be shown to have been of such a character, degree and frequency as to indicate an assertion by the claimant of a continuous right and of a right of the measure of the right claimed.[50]

Where a riparian owner claimed a prescriptive right to pollute the stream, it was held that a progressive increase, during the period relied on, in the plant of the polluting mill and in the volume of water polluted was " destructive of that certainty and uniformity essential for the measurement and determination of the user by which the extent of the prescriptive right is to be ascertained." [1]

9. Compliance with statute or custom

The enjoyment must not have been either contrary to the common law,[2] or to a statute of a public nature,[3] or inconsistent with a custom.[4]

---

46 (1834) 1 C.M. & R. 631.
47 This does not mean a cessation in the actual user, as, for instance, by reason of the claimant having no occasion to use the easement; otherwise a right to a way or other non-continuous easement could not be acquired. It means a cessation in the user as of right, as in the case cited in the text, where the asking of permission during the period, by admitting that the person asking had no right at that time, interrupted the continuity of the enjoyment as of right. See the question discussed in *Hollins* v. *Verney* (1884) 13 Q.B.D. 304, p. 153, *ante.*
48 *Monmouthshire Canal Co.* v. *Harford* (1834) 1 C.M. & R. 631, *per* Lord Lyndhurst.
49 (1836) 4 A. & E. 369, 383; *Beasley* v. *Clarke* (1836) 2 Bing.N.C. 705; *Gardner* v. *Hodgson's Kingston Brewery Co.* [1903] A.C. 229. See *ante*, pp. 176–178.
50 *White* v. *Taylor* (*No.* 2) [1969] 1 Ch. 160, 192–195.
1 *Hulley* v. *Silversprings Bleaching and Dyeing Co.* [1922] 2 Ch. 268, 281.
2 See p. 191, *post.*
3 " A lost grant cannot be presumed where such a grant would have been in contravention of a statute, and as title by prescription is founded on the presumption of a lost grant, if no grant could lawfully have been made no presumption of the kind can arise "; *per* Eve J., *Hulley* v. *Silversprings Bleaching and Dyeing Co.* [1922] 2 Ch. 268, 282, following *Neaverson* v. *Peterborough R.D.C.* [1902] 1 Ch. 557; *Green* v. *Matthews* (1930) 46 T.L.R. 206. As regards a statute of a private nature, a waiver may be presumed: *Goldsmid* v. *G.E. Railway* (1884) 25 Ch.D. 511; (1884)

---

4 For footnote see p. 190.

In deciding whether the enjoyment is contrary to statute the intention of the statute is relevant. Thus *Campbell* v. *Wilson*,[5] where it was held that the enjoyment of a way for twenty years was sufficient evidence from which to presume a grant or other lawful origin of a right of way (though an Act of Parliament had, prior to that enjoyment, extinguished a like right over the same land, so that the twenty years' enjoyment was in fact had by reason of the neglect of the owner of the servient tenement to avail himself of the provisions of the Act), is not at variance with the rule that a man cannot prescribe against a statute.[6] The object of the Inclosure Act in *Campbell* v. *Wilson*[5] was simply to benefit the owners of allotted lands, by exempting them from the burden of existing rights of way, but not to injure the allottees by restricting the power of each allottee to dispose of or burden his own land as he might think proper; and there was nothing in the statute prohibiting the creation of new rights. But where the acts of user relied upon are contrary to some statutory provision, so that an actual grant of the right which is sought to be established by user would be void, and it cannot possibly be referred to any legal origin, the common law rule prevails, and no right is acquired.[7]

4.—PRESCRIPTIVE RIGHT TO CAUSE NUISANCE

It is settled that many acts done upon a man's own property which are in their nature injurious to the adjoining land, and consequently actionable as private nuisances, are capable, at least in theory, of being legalised by prescription.[8] Thus, the right not to receive impure air is an incident of property, and for any interference with this right an action may be maintained; but by an easement acquired by his neighbour a man may, it appears, be compelled to receive the air from him in a corrupted state, as by the admixture of smoke or noisome smells. So, too, he may be compelled to submit to noises caused by the carrying on of certain trades. Again, with regard to flowing water, the right not to have impure water discharged on a man's land is one of the ordinary rights of property, the infringement of which can only be justified by an easement previously acquired by the party so discharging it.

---

9 App.Cas. 927. As to the statutory provisions for preventing the pollution of rivers, see p. 231, *post*.

4 *Wynstanley* v. *Lee* (1818) 2 Swans. 333; *Perry* v. *Eames* [1891] 1 Ch. 667.

5 (1803) 3 East 294.

6 Co.Litt. 115a.

7 *Rochdale* v. *Radcliffe* (1852) 18 Q.B. 287; *Race* v. *Ward* (1857) 7 E. & B. 384; *National Manure Co.* v. *Donald* (1859) 4 H. & N. 8; *Staffordshire & Worcestershire Canal Co.* v. *Birmingham Canal Co.* (1866) L.R. 1 H.L. 267, 278; *Neaverson* v. *Peterborough R.D.C.* [1902] 1 Ch. 557; *Hulley* v. *Silversprings Bleaching and Dyeing Co.* [1922] 2 Ch. 268; *Green* v. *Matthews* (1930) 46 T.L.R. 206.

8 A private nuisance may be legalised by implied grant: see *Lyttelton Times Co. Ltd.* v. *Warners Ltd.* [1907] A.C. 476, 481; *cf. Pwllbach Colliery Co.* v. *Woodman* [1915] A.C. 634; and see pp. 86–87, *ante*.

Thus, it is said in Viner's *Abridgment* [9] that an ancient brewhouse, though erected in Fleet Street or Cheapside, is not a nuisance. So, it seems that an ancient user may be a justification for the exercise of a noisy [10] or offensive trade, or for discharging water in an impure state upon the adjoining land, [11] or for discharging coal dust on a neighbour's wharf. [12]

From what period time runs

Until a nuisance arises, no one can complain, and no question of prescription can arise until a nuisance is first committed. [13] It follows that a right to carry on an offensive trade, or to pollute water with sewage, is not acquired merely by having carried on the trade or having polluted the water for twenty years; but it must be shown that the air over the plaintiff's land, or the water to which he is entitled, has been corrupted for that period, [14] and corrupted to the extent of the right claimed, [15] and so as to be actionable or preventable by the plaintiff or his predecessors. [16] The difficulties would usually be insuperable, and it does not seem that a contested claim to a prescriptive right to commit a nuisance by noise, smell or the like has ever, in fact, succeeded.

No prescription for a public nuisance

There can be no prescription to make a public nuisance, which is a prejudice to all people, because it cannot have a lawful beginning, by licence or otherwise, being against the common law. [17] Thus a prescription for the inhabitants of a town to lay logs in a highway was held void [18]; and so of a prescription to maintain in a navigable river a weir not erected before the time of Edward I [19]; similarly, a claim to a right to use a public footway for wheeled traffic after forty years' user for that purpose was held bad on the ground that the user was in its inception, and had been all along, a public nuisance. [20]

---

[9] Nusance, G.
[10] *Elliotson* v. *Feetham* (1835) 2 Bing.N.C. 134; *Crump* v. *Lambert* (1867) L.R. 3 Eq. 409, 413.
[11] *Wright* v. *Williams* (1836) 1 M. & W. 77; *Brown* v. *Dunstable Corpn.* [1899] 2 Ch. 378.
[12] *Royal Mail Steam Packet Co.* v. *George and Branday* [1900] A.C. 480.
[13] *Halsey* v. *Esso Petroleum Co. Ltd.* [1961] 1 W.L.R. 683, 702.
[14] *Flight* v. *Thomas* (1839) 10 A. & E. 590; *Murgatroyd* v. *Robinson* (1857) 7 E. & B. 391; *Goldsmid* v. *Tunbridge Wells Improvement Commissioners* (1866) 1 Ch.App. 349; see also *Liverpool Corporation* v. *Coghill* [1918] 1 Ch. 307.
[15] *Crossley & Sons Ltd.* v. *Lightowler* (1867) 2 Ch.App. 478; *Heather* v. *Pardon* (1878) 37 L.T. 393; *Hulley* v. *Silversprings Bleaching and Dyeing Co.* [1922] 2 Ch. 268. *Cf. Lemmon* v. *Webb* [1894] 3 Ch. 1; [1895] A.C. 1.
[16] *Sturges* v. *Bridgman* (1879) 11 Ch.D. 852.
[17] See *Butterworth* v. *West Riding Rivers Board* [1909] A.C. 57; *Mott* v. *Shoolbred* (1875) L.R. 20 Eq. 24. See also p. 189, *ante.*
[18] *Fowler* v. *Sanders* (1618) Cro.Jac. 446; *Dewell* v. *Sanders* (1618) Cro.Jac. 490; 2 Rolle Ab., 265; Vin.Ab., Prescription, F; Com.Dig. Praescription, F. 2.
[19] *Rolle* v. *Whyte* (1868) L.R. 3 Q.B. 286; *Leconfield* v. *Lonsdale* (1870) L.R. 5 C.P. 657.
[20] *Sheringham U.D.C.* v. *Holsey* (1904) 91 L.T. 225.

On the same ground a prescription to discharge sewage into a river was held bad.[21] As regards the right to discharge sewage into a tidal river or the sea, there is no such common law right,[22] but it seems that an easement in gross of this nature might be acquired by the corporation of a town (on behalf of the inhabitants), the right being based on a lost grant from the Crown,[23] or possibly on prescription at common law.[24]

---

[21] *Att.-Gen.* v. *Barnsley Corpn.* [1874] W.N. 37.
[22] *Foster* v. *Warblington Urban Council* [1906] 1 K.B. 665; *Hobart* v. *Southend-on-Sea Corpn.* (1906) 75 L.J.K.B. 305, compromised on appeal (1906) 22 T.L.R. 530.
[23] *Somersetshire Drainage Commissioners* v. *Bridgwater Corpn.* (1899) 81 L.T. 732.
[24] *Foster* v. *Warblington Urban Council* [1906] 1 K.B. 665.

CHAPTER 5

EASEMENTS AND REGISTERED LAND

Effect of registration of the dominant land

Upon the registration of any freehold or leasehold interest in land
with an absolute or good leasehold title, then subject to any entry to
the contrary on the register, any easement which is appurtenant to
that interest becomes appurtenant to the registered land in like manner
as if it had been granted to the proprietor who is so registered.[1] The
registration of a person as the proprietor of land, whether as first or
subsequent proprietor, passes the benefit of easements without mention
thereof on the register.[2]

Registration of an easement

The proprietor may, if he so wishes, apply (whether on first
registration or at any other time) to have a specific entry on the
register of any legal easement to which he may be entitled.[3] The
Registrar must thereupon give such notice (if any) to the person in
possession of the servient land as he may deem advisable.[4] If that land
is registered, he must give notice to the proprietor and to every person
appearing by the register to be interested, and he must, if he thinks fit,
enter notice of it against such land.[5] If the Registrar is satisfied that
there is a legal easement appurtenant to the land, he may enter it as
part of the description of the land in the Property Register, and the
effect of such entry is to confer an absolute, good leasehold, qualified
or possessory title to the easement, according to the nature of the title
to the land.[6] If the Registrar is not satisfied that the right is appurtenant he must enter it with such qualification as he deems advisable
or he may merely enter notice of the fact that the proprietor claims it.[7]

The benefit of an easement must not be entered on the register
except as appurtenant to a registered estate, and then only if it is a
legal easement.[8]

---

[1] Land Registration Act 1925, s. 72. See also *ibid.* ss. 5 and 9 which refer
specifically to registration as first proprietor; ss. 6 and 11 which refer to possessory
title; and ss. 7 and 12 which refer to qualified title.

[2] The Land Registration Rules 1925, S.R. & O. 1925 No. 1093, r. 251. The Land
Registration Act 1925, s. 3 (xxiv), defines "registered land" as including any
easement appurtenant thereto. See *Re Evans' Contract* [1970] 1 W.L.R. 583.

[3] Land Registration Rules 1925, r. 252.

[4] *Ibid.* r. 253 (1).   [5] *Ibid.* r. 253 (2).

[6] *Ibid.* r. 254 (1). This will be so even if there was, in fact, no title to the easement;
see *Peachey* v. *Lee* (1964) 192 E.G. 365.

[7] *Ibid.* r. 254 (2).

[8] *Ibid.* r. 257. See Land Registration Act 1925, s. 144 (1) (xx).

Registered disposition of land

On any registered disposition of the land or of a charge thereon, the benefit of the easement which has been entered on the register accrues, on registration, to the grantee as part of the registered estate, but without prejudice to any express exception or reservation.[9] Quite apart from easements entered on the register, a registered disposition will confer on the transferee or grantee all easements which are appurtenant to the registered land.[10] A person who has contracted to purchase registered land together with an easement appurtenant thereto cannot insist upon the vendor obtaining registration of the easement.[11]

Creation of easements by the proprietor

The proprietor of registered land may in the prescribed form expressly grant or reserve an easement thereover.[12] The easement must be entered on the register against the registered servient tenement.[13] If the easement is to be appurtenant to registered land it will not take effect as a legal interest until registered as such,[14] but where the dominant land is unregistered it is neither necessary nor possible to have the easement positively registered.[15]

General words

The general words implied in conveyances by virtue of section 62 of the Law of Property Act 1925 apply, so far as applicable thereto, to dispositions of a registered estate.[16] Therefore, in a transfer of registered land there are implied those rights and advantages which are enjoyed over the land retained by the registered proprietor. When the new proprietor is registered these rights will mature into legal easements, as on a conveyance of unregistered land.[17] Unlike the case where there is an express grant of an easement by a registered proprietor, there is here no requirement [18] for express registration of the easement or entry against the registered servient tenement. The creation of easements in this manner applies upon registration of the transfer irrespective of whether the land retained is registered or unregistered. If the vendor wishes to exclude the general words of section 62 of the Law of Property Act 1925, he should do so in the transfer, and an entry may be made on the register excluding them.[19]

---

[9] *Ibid.* r. 256.
[10] Land Registration Act 1925, ss. 20, 23, 72. Land Registration Rules 1925, r. 251.
[11] *Re Evans' Contract* [1970] 1 W.L.R. 583.
[12] Land Registration Act 1925, ss. 18 (1) (2), 21 (1).
[13] *Ibid.* ss. 19 (2), 22 (2).
[14] *Ibid.* ss. 19 (2), 22 (2). Until registration it will be an equitable easement.
[15] *Ibid.* ss. 19 (2), 22 (2), 141 (1) (xx). Land Registration Rules 1925, r. 257.
[16] Land Registration Act 1925, ss. 19 (3), 22 (3).
[17] *Ibid.* ss. 20 (1), 23 (1); Land Registration Rules 1925, r. 251.
[18] Registration of the easement may, if it is so desired, be obtained: Land Registration Rules 1925, rr. 252–254.
[19] Land Registration Act 1925, ss. 20 (1), 23 (1).

Implied grant

There is no clear provision which includes those rights which will pass by implication on a disposition of part of a tenement, in particular those quasi-easements which are discussed in *Wheeldon* v. *Burrows*.[20] In any event, such rights will normally be covered by the general words of section 62 of the Law of Property Act 1925. More important is the apparent lack of any provision for easements of necessity to be implied in a disposition of registered land.[21]

Implied reservation

There appears to be no provision by which a reservation of an easement will be implied in a disposition of registered land in those circumstances where a reservation would be implied in unregistered conveyancing, for example easements of necessity and those arising from the common intention of the parties.[22]

Of course, in the case of both implied grants and implied reservations the contract will contain the implication, and the purchaser or the vendor, as the case may be, can insist upon a transfer containing words sufficient to carry out the intention in the contract.

Prescription and registered land

Easements adversely affecting registered land may be acquired in equity by prescription in the same manner and to the same extent as if the land were not registered.[23] It is provided that if the easement so acquired is capable of taking effect at law it shall take effect at law also [24] and, being an overriding interest, the Registrar may, if he thinks fit, enter notice of it on the register.[25]

If a legal easement has been acquired by prescription for the benefit of registered land, it may, if the Registrar thinks fit, be registered as part of the description of the land.[26]

Overriding interests

Registered land is subject to " overriding interests," that is, those interests which are enforceable against a proprietor of registered land even though they do not appear on the register. Overriding interests include the following: " Right of common, drainage rights, customary

---

[20] (1879) 12 Ch.D. 31. In Curtis and Ruoff, *Registered Conveyancing*, 2nd ed., p. 115, it is stated that such quasi-easements are adequately covered by the wording in the Land Registration Act 1925, s. 20 (1), and the Land Registration Rules 1925, r. 251.
[21] Such easements would seem to be omitted from the Land Registration Act 1925, ss. 20 (1) and 23 (1), and from the Land Registration Rules 1925, r. 251, because they need not be appurtenant to the land nor would they necessarily pass under s. 62 of the Law of Property Act 1925, if the land were unregistered.
[22] There may be an express reservation: Land Registration Act 1925, ss. 18 (1) (*d*) (*e*), 18 (2), 20 (1) (*c*) (*d*).
[23] Land Registration Act 1925, s. 75 (5); Land Registration Rules 1925, r. 250 (1).
[24] Land Registration Rules 1925, r. 250 (2).
[25] *Ibid.* r. 250 (2) (*a*); Land Registration Act 1925, s. 70 (3).
[26] Land Registration Rules 1925, r. 250 (2) (*b*).

rights (until extinguished), public rights, *profits à prendre*, rights of sheepwalk, rights of way, watercourses, rights of water, and other easements not being equitable easements required to be protected by notice on the register." [27]   Legal easements [28] and *profits à prendre* will therefore bind registered land although not protected by entry on the register.[29]   An easement which was created before the land became registered will bind the first and subsequent registered proprietors of the land; and an easement properly created in registered land will bind the grantor and subsequent proprietors.[30]

A purchaser of registered land, therefore, may frequently be bound by easements and *profits à prendre* of which he had no knowledge and which were not discoverable by searching the register.   There are, however, certain provisions which envisage entry of these rights on the register.

Where at the time of first registration an easement or *profit à prendre* created by an instrument and appearing on the title adversely affects the land, the Registrar must enter a note thereof on the register.[31]   The status of such an easement or *profit à prendre* as an overriding interest is not affected if a note is not made.[32]

In any event, where the existence of an overriding interest is proved to the satisfaction of the Registrar or admitted, he may enter notice of the same or of a claim thereto on the register, but no claim to an easement or *profit à prendre* is to be noted against the title to the servient land if the proprietor of such land (after the prescribed notice is given to him) shows sufficient cause to the contrary.[33]

The grant by a registered proprietor of an easement or *profit à prendre* in his land, which is to be appurtenant to registered land, will not be effective to create a legal interest until the disposition has been completed by registration,[34] and in any event notice must be entered against the registered title of the servient land.[35]

---

[27] Land Registration Act 1925, s. 70 (1) (*a*).
[28] As to the question of whether equitable easements are overriding interests, see p. 72, *ante*. *Profits à prendre* seem to be overriding interests, whether legal or equitable.
[29] Land Registration Rules, r. 258.
[30] Where the dominant tenement is registered land the easement will not become a legal interest until registration; see p. 194, *ante*. A legal easement may be acquired by prescription in registered land without being registered; see p. 195, *ante*.
[31] Land Registration Act 1925, s. 70 (2).   There would appear to be a duty on the Registrar notwithstanding the Land Registration Rules 1925, rr. 41 and 199, which give him a discretion; see *Re Dances Way, West Town, Hayling Island* [1962] Ch. 490, 508, *per* Diplock L.J.
[32] *Re Dances Way, West Town, Hayling Island* [1962] Ch. 490, 507, *per* Upjohn L.J.
[33] Land Registration Act 1925, s. 70 (3); Land Registration Rules 1925, r. 41.
[34] See p. 194, *ante*.   Until registration the easement would seem to take effect in equity. As to whether this would be an overriding interest or requires to be protected by notice on the register, see p. 72, *ante*.
[35] Land Registration Act 1925, ss. 19 (2), 22 (2).   There would here seem to be no discretion in the Registrar to refuse to enter notice of the interest.

PART III

PARTICULAR EASEMENTS AND PARTICULAR NATURAL RIGHTS OF A SIMILAR CHARACTER

CHAPTER 6

RIGHTS IN RESPECT OF WATER

IN dealing with the rights of riparian owners in respect of the water
of a natural stream flowing through a defined channel, the first distinction
to be borne in mind is the distinction between natural rights and
acquired rights. The natural rights of a riparian owner, that is, the
owner of land intersected or bounded by a natural stream, may be
shortly defined as threefold: First, he has a right of user. He can use
the water for certain purposes connected with his riparian land.
Secondly, he has a right of flow. He is entitled to have the water come
to him and go from him without obstruction.[1] Thirdly, he has a right
of purity. He is entitled to have the water come to him unpolluted.
These common law principles relating to the abstraction of water must,
however, now be considered in the light of the Water Resources Act
1963.[2] In the present chapter a riparian owner's natural rights of user
and flow in a natural watercourse will be dealt with in section 1 and
the effect of the Act in section 2. Prescriptive rights of user and flow
will be considered in sections 3 and 4, artificial watercourses in section 5,
purity and pollution in section 6, the acquisition of water rights in section
7, and miscellaneous rights of riparian owners in section 8.

1.—NATURAL RIGHTS IN NATURAL WATERCOURSES

(1) *Surface Water : Defined Natural Channel*

Rules as to rights of riparian owners

In *Wood* v. *Waud*[3] the court held that a riparian owner has no
property in the water of a stream flowing through or past his land, but is
entitled only to the use of it as it passes along for the enjoyment of his
property, citing the law as laid down by the American Chancellor Kent,
thus[4]:

> " Every proprietor of lands on the banks of a river has naturally
> an equal right to the use of the water. . . . He has no property in
> the water itself, but a simple usufruct as it passes along."

[1] See *per* Lord Wensleydale in *Chasemore* v. *Richards* (1859) 7 H.L.C. 349, 382.
[2] The Act has been slightly amended by the Water Resources Act 1968.
[3] (1849) 3 Exch. 748, 775.
[4] Kent's *Commentaries on American Law*, 12th ed. (1896), Vol. III, p. 439.

Since then the rules as to the natural rights of riparian owners in water flowing through a natural watercourse having a defined and known channel have been successively stated by a series of great judges.

In 1851 Parke B. in *Embrey* v. *Owen*[5] laid down the law on this subject as follows:

" The right to have a stream to flow in its natural state without diminution or alteration is an incident to the property in the land through which it passes; but flowing water is *publici juris*, not in the sense that it is a *bonum vacans*, to which the first occupant may acquire an exclusive right, but that it is public and common in this sense only, that all may reasonably use it who have a right of access to it, that none can[6] have any property in the water itself, except in the particular portion which he may choose to abstract from the stream and take into his possession, and that during the time of his possession only. But each proprietor of the adjacent land has the right to the usufruct of the stream which flows through it.[7] This right to the benefit and advantage of the water flowing past his land, is not an absolute and exclusive right to the flow of all the water in its natural state . . ., but it is a right only to the flow of water, and the enjoyment of it, subject to the similar rights of all the proprietors of the banks on each side to the reasonable enjoyment of the same gift of Providence. It is only, therefore, for an unreasonable and unauthorised use of this common benefit that an action will lie. For such an use it will, even though there may be no actual damage to the plaintiff." [8]

In *Rawstron* v. *Taylor*[9] Parke B. said: " The right to have a stream running in its natural direction does not depend on a supposed grant, but is *jure naturae*."

In 1858 Lord Kingsdown said in *Miner* v. *Gilmour*[10]:

" By the general law applicable to running streams, every riparian proprietor has a right to what may be called the ordinary use of the water flowing past his land; for instance, to the reasonable use of the water for his domestic purposes and for his cattle, and this without regard to the effect which such use may have, in case of a deficiency, upon proprietors lower down the stream. But, further, he has a right to the use of it for any purpose, or what may be deemed the extraordinary use of it, provided that he does not thereby interfere with the rights of other proprietors either

[5] (1851) 6 Exch. 353, 369.
[6] Except by statute: *Medway Co.* v. *Romney (Earl)* (1861) 9 C.B.(N.S.) 575.
[7] *i.e.* to the reasonable use of the stream for ordinary purposes, *e.g.* for his domestic purposes and his cattle (*Miner* v. *Gilmour, infra*), but not for purposes foreign to or unconnected with his riparian tenement (*McCartney* v. *Londonderry and Lough Swilly Railway Co.* [1904] A.C. 301).
[8] See judgment in *Sampson* v. *Hoddinott* (1857) 1 C.B.(N.S.) 611, and 3 Kent's *Commentaries* 439–445, quoted in the judgment in *Embrey* v. *Owen*, 6 Exch. 353, 369–371.
[9] (1855) 11 Exch. 369, 382.   [10] (1858) 12 Moo.P.C. 131, 156.

above or below him. Subject to this condition, he may dam up the stream for the purpose of a mill, or divert the water for the purpose of irrigation. But he has no right to interrupt the regular flow of the stream, if he thereby interferes with the lawful use of the water by other proprietors, and inflicts upon them a sensible injury." [11]

In 1875 Lord Cairns again stated the law in *Swindon Waterworks Co.* v. *Wilts and Berks Canal Navigation Co.,*[12] where the appellants, being riparian owners on the bank of a stream, claimed the right to collect the water of the stream into a permanent reservoir for the supply of an adjacent town; and it was held that this was not a reasonable use of the water within the meaning of the above rules.

"Undoubtedly," said Lord Cairns L.C., "the lower riparian owner is entitled to the accustomed flow of the water for the ordinary purposes for which he can use the water, that is quite consistent with the right of the upper owner also to use the water for all ordinary purposes, namely, as has been said, *ad lavandum et ad potandum*, whatever portion of the water may be thereby exhausted and may cease to come down by reason of that use. But further, there are uses no doubt to which the water may be put by the upper owner, namely, uses connected with the tenement of that upper owner. Under certain circumstances, and provided no material injury is done, the water may be used and may be diverted for a time by the upper owner for the purpose of irrigation. That may well be done; the exhaustion of the water which may thereby take place may be so inconsiderable as not to form a subject of complaint by the lower owner, and the water may be restored after the object of irrigation is answered in a volume substantially equal to that in which it passed before. Again, it may well be that there may be a use of the water by the upper owner for, I will say, manufacturing purposes, so reasonable that no just complaint can be made upon the subject by the lower owner. Whether such a use in any particular case could be made for manufacturing purposes connected with the upper tenement would, I apprehend, depend upon whether the use was a reasonable one. Whether it was a reasonable use would depend, at all events in some degree, on the magnitude of the stream from which the deduction was made for this purpose over and above the ordinary use of the water."

[11] Buckley J. pointed out in *Rugby Joint Water Board* v. *Walters* [1967] Ch. 397, 419 that the final sentence of that passage is a wider statement of the law than that adopted in *Embrey* v. *Owen* (1851) 6 Exch. 353, and could be read as extending to permanent abstraction which caused no sensible injury; but the Privy Council was not concerned with permanent abstraction, and it is clear from the authorities reviewed by Buckley J. that permanent abstraction for extraordinary use is not permitted.

[12] (1875) L.R. 7 H.L. 697, 704. Lord Cairns' judgment has been said to have almost codified the law: *McCartney* v. *Londonderry and Lough Swilly Railway Co.* [1904] A.C. 301, 304.

In 1904, Lord Macnaghten dealt with the law in *McCartney* v. *Londonderry and Lough Swilly Railway Co.*,[13] where a railway line belonging to the respondents crossed a natural stream, and at the crossing abutted upon the stream for about eight feet on each side. The respondents inserted a pipe into the stream at the crossing, and by means of this pipe, which was laid along the strip of railway line, diverted water to other land belonging to them, about half a mile from the stream, and there consumed it in working their locomotive engines. The appellant, who was a lower riparian owner upon the stream, stopped the pipe, and thereupon the respondents brought their action for a declaration of their right to take the water through the pipe, and for an injunction. It was held, however, that the appellant was justified in the course taken by him and the action failed. Lord Macnaghten said [14]:

> " There are, as it seems to me, three ways in which a person whose lands are intersected or bounded by a running stream may use the water to which the situation of his property gives him access. He may use it for ordinary or primary purposes, for domestic purposes, and the wants of his cattle. He may use it also for some other purposes—sometimes called extraordinary or secondary purposes—provided those purposes are connected with or incident to his land, and provided that certain conditions are complied with. Then he may possibly take advantage of his position to use the water for purposes foreign to or unconnected with his riparian tenement. His rights in the first two cases are not quite the same. In the third case he has no right at all.
>
> " Now it seems to me that the first question your Lordships have to consider is, under what category does the proposed user of the railway company fall? Certainly it is not the ordinary or primary use of a flowing stream, nor is it, I think, one of those extraordinary uses connected with or incidental to a riparian tenement which are permissible under certain conditions. In the ordinary or primary use of flowing water a person dwelling on the banks of a stream is under no restriction. In the exercise of his ordinary rights he may exhaust the water altogether. No lower proprietor can complain of that. In the exercise of rights extraordinary but permissible, the limit of which has never been accurately defined and probably is incapable of accurate definition, a riparian owner is under considerable restrictions. The use must be reasonable. The purposes for which the water is taken must be connected with his tenement, and he is bound to restore the

---

13 [1904] A.C. 301, overruling *Sandwich* v. *G.N. Railway* (1878) 10 Ch.D. 707. *Cf. Orr-Ewing* v. *Colquhoun* (1877) 2 App.Cas. 839, 856; *Rameshur* v. *Koonj* (1878) 4 App.Cas. 121; *Roberts* v. *Richards* (1881) 50 L.J.Ch. 297; 51 L.J.Ch. 944; *Ormerod* v. *Todmorden Joint Stock Mill Co.* (1883) 11 Q.B.D. 155; *Kensit* v. *G.E. Railway* (1884) 27 Ch.D. 122; *Roberts* v. *Gwyrfai District Council* [1899] 2 Ch. 608; *Attwood* v. *Llay Main Collieries* [1926] Ch. 444.
14 [1904] A.C. 306, 307.

water which he takes and uses for those purposes substantially undiminished in volume and unaltered in character."

Mutual rights and liabilities

The rules set out in the above judgments relate to the user and flow of overground water in a defined natural stream, to which user and flow every riparian owner has a natural right. These rules were tersely expressed by Erle C.J. in *Gaved* v. *Martyn* [15] as follows: "The flow of a natural stream creates mutual rights and liabilities between all the riparian proprietors along the whole of its course. Subject to reasonable use by himself, each proprietor is bound to allow the water to flow on without altering the quantity or quality." To this may be added that as between himself and lower riparian owners the upper owner is not only bound to allow the water to flow on, but is entitled to insist that it shall flow on. "He has the right to have the natural stream come to him in its natural state, in flow, quantity and quality, and to go from him without obstruction." [16] Any obstruction by a lower riparian owner of such a character that it might reasonably be expected that injury would be caused to an upper riparian owner is actionable at the suit of the latter. [17]

User ordinary and extraordinary

The question what is a lawful user of the water by each riparian owner in the exercise of his natural rights depends on the circumstances of each case, and it is impossible to define precisely the limits which sever the permitted use of the water from its wrongful application. Thus, as regards the distinction drawn above by Lord Macnaghten between the ordinary or primary purposes and the extraordinary or secondary purposes to which the riparian owner may apply the water, this distinction may be different in different places and at different times. It has been said that the user which was at one time extraordinary might by changes in the condition of the property become ordinary; and also that a user which might be extraordinary in an agricultural district might not be extraordinary in a manufacturing district. [18]

Extraordinary user

Among purposes extraordinary but permissible Lord Cairns in *Swindon Waterworks Co.* v. *Wilts and Berks Canal Navigation Co.* [19]

---

[15] (1865) 19 C.B.(N.S.) 732, 759.

[16] *Per* Lord Wensleydale, *Chasemore* v. *Richards* (1859) 7 H.L.C. 349, 382.

[17] *Ambler (Jeremiah) & Son Ltd.* v. *Bradford (Mayor)* (1902) 87 L.T. 217; *M'Glone* v. *Smith* (1888) 22 L.R.Ir. 559; *Orr-Ewing* v. *Colquhoun* (1877) 2 App.Cas. 839, 856.

[18] *Per* Lord Esher in *Ormerod* v. *Todmorden Joint Stock Mill Co. Ltd.* (1883) 11 Q.B.D. 155, 168.

[19] (1875) L.R. 7 H.L. 697, 704; see p. 201, *ante*.

mentions manufacturing purposes, which were dealt with in *Dakin* v. *Cornish*,[20] where Alderson B. applied the test whether the same quantity of water continued to run in the river as if none of it had entered the manufacturing premises of the upper riparian owner. In dealing with the same user, Vaughan Williams L.J. in *Baily & Co.* v. *Clark, Son & Morland*[21] laid down that the riparian owner must not interfere with the lawful use of the water by owners above or below him or inflict on them a sensible injury. As has been seen, the right of a riparian owner to an extraordinary use does not enable a water company to divert water to supply a town,[22] nor does it enable a railway company which owns a tenement on a stream to divert water to a place outside that tenement and use it to supply locomotives along its line[23]; nor does it enable water to be diverted to supply a lunatic asylum and county jail.[24]

Swindon Waterworks Co. v. *Wilts and Berks Canal Navigation Co.*[25] and *McCartney* v. *Londonderry and Lough Swilly Railway Co.*[26] were applied by Lawrence J. in *Attwood* v. *Llay Main Collieries Ltd.*,[27] in which the defendant was held not to be entitled to draw water from a river in order to turn it into steam for working the defendant's colliery undertaking. Dealing with the right of a riparian owner to take water for extraordinary purposes, Lawrence J. said[28]:

> " . . . that he may also take and use the water for extraordinary purposes, if such user be reasonable and be connected with the riparian tenement, provided that he restores the water so taken and used substantially undiminished in volume and unaltered in character."

In *Rugby Joint Water Board* v. *Walters*[29] the plaintiff sought an injunction to restrain the defendant from abstracting water from the river Avon for the spray irrigation of his land. On occasion he took as much as 60,000 gallons a day. It was in evidence that, although the abstraction had no visible or measurable effect on the river, it amounted

---

20 Referred to by Alderson B. in *Embrey* v. *Owen* (1851) 6 Exch. 353, 360.
21 [1902] 1 Ch. 649, 665. See *Sharp* v. *Wilson* (1905) 93 L.T. 155, where the court held that for manufacturing purposes the defendants had dealt unreasonably with water.
22 *Swindon Waterworks Co.* v. *Wilts and Berks Canal Navigation Co.* (1875) L.R. 7 H.L. 697; see p. 201, *ante*; and see *Roberts* v. *Gwyrfai District Council* [1899] 2 Ch. 612; *Owen* v. *Davies* [1874] W.N. 175.
23 *McCartney* v. *Londonderry and Lough Swilly Railway Co.* [1904] A.C. 301; see p. 202, *ante*.
24 *Medway Co.* v. *Romney (Earl)* (1861) 9 C.B.(N.S.) 575.
25 (1875) L.R. 7 H.L. 697.
26 [1904] A.C. 301.
27 [1926] Ch. 444.
28 [1926] Ch. 458.
29 [1967] Ch. 397, disapproving *Lord Norbury* v. *Kitchin* (1863) 3 F. & F. 292 (as inconsistent with *McCartney* v. *Londonderry and Lough Swilly Railway Co.* [1904] A.C. 301) and *Earl of Sandwich* v. *Great Northern Railway Co.* (1878) 10 Ch.D. 707 (as not accurately reflecting the law as stated in *Embrey* v. *Owen* (1851) 6 Exch. 353). The plaintiff had statutory authority to take the whole flow of the river, but it sued as riparian owner.

to a considerable volume of water, only a very small part of which was returned to the river. Buckley J., holding that the defendant was not entitled to take water from the river for spray irrigation and granting an injunction, applied the dictum of Lord Macnaghten in *McCartney* v. *Londonderry & Lough Swilly Railway Co.*[30] and the decision of Lawrence J. in *Attwood* v. *Llay Main Collieries Ltd.*[31] that a riparian owner is not entitled to take water from a stream for extraordinary purposes without returning it to the stream in substantially unlimited quantity, a decision which Buckley J. found wholly consistent with the principles laid down in *Wood* v. *Waud*[32] and *Embrey* v. *Owen.*[33] If a riparian owner permanently abstracts water, he deprives other riparian owners of any use of the water so abstracted and thus infringes their rights. They are then entitled to complain, even without proof of damage.[34] The question whether the effect of the abstraction is such as to cause them sensible injury is consequently irrelevant.[35] Buckley J. observed[36] that no attempt had been made by judges in the past to define what uses can be regarded as "ordinary" uses, referred to by Lord Cairns in *Swindon Waterworks Co.* v. *Wilts and Berks Canal Navigation Co.*[37] as uses *ad lavandum et ad potandum.* That they extended to reasonable domestic uses and to watering cattle was clear. His Lordship said that, without attempting either to draw the line of demarcation between what are ordinary uses for this purpose and what extraordinary, or to suggest how it should be drawn, he felt no doubt that spray irrigation of the kind and upon the scale employed by the defendant could not be regarded as an ordinary use.

The decision in *Rugby Joint Water Board* v. *Walters*[38] does not, of course, mean that water can never be drawn from a river for irrigation. In *Swindon Waterworks Co.* v. *Wilts and Berks Canal Navigation Co.*[39] Lord Cairns mentions irrigation among extraordinary purposes. Parke B. in *Embrey* v. *Owen*[40] said that if the irrigation takes place, not continuously, but at intermittent periods when the river is full, and no damage is done thereby to the working of a mill on the stream, and the diminution of the water is not perceptible to the eye, it is not prohibited. In *Chasemore* v. *Richards*[41] Coleridge J. referred to irrigation as a perfectly legitimate mode of exercising the natural rights of

---

30 [1904] A.C. 301, 307; see p. 202, *ante.*
31 [1926] Ch. 444.
32 (1849) 3 Exch. 748; see p. 199, *ante.*
33 (1851) 6 Exch. 353; see p. 200, *ante.*
34 *Attwood* v. *Llay Main Collieries Ltd.* [1926] Ch. 444.
35 *Rugby Joint Water Board* v. *Walters* [1967] Ch. 397, 423.
36 [1967] Ch. 424.
37 (1875) L.R. 7 H.L. 697, 704; see p. 201, *ante.*
38 [1967] Ch. 397.
39 (1875) L.R. 7 H.L. 697, 704.
40 (1851) 6 Exch. 353, 372.
41 (1857) 2 H. & N. 150. See also *Sampson* v. *Hoddinott* (1857) 1 C.B.(N.S.) 603, *per* Cresswell J., in which case the question was as to the right to impede the flow by means of channels cut for irrigation.

an upper riparian owner if he thereby did not abridge the natural rights of a lower riparian owner—a result which would follow if the upper owner by irrigation exhausted the running stream.

Natural rights are part of fee simple

In dealing with riparian land it should not be forgotten that the natural rights above referred to are in law parts of the fee simple. Thus it was said by Parker J. in *Portsmouth Borough Waterworks Co.* v. *London Brighton and South Coast Railway* [42]:

> "When a riparian owner sells part of his estate, including land on the banks of a natural stream, it is not necessary to make any express provision as to the grant or reservation of the ordinary rights of a riparian proprietor. These rights are not easements to be granted or reserved as appurtenant to what is respectively sold or retained, but are parts of the fee simple and inheritance of the land sold or retained. If it be desired to alter or modify these rights, it can only be done by the grant or reservation of such rights in the nature of easements as the nature of the case may require. If no such rights are granted or reserved the vendor remains, and the purchaser becomes, a riparian owner, and retains or acquires all the ordinary rights of a riparian owner."

Where a riparian owner who had, or may have had, a prescriptive right to pollute the stream granted part of his land without any reservation, he could not as between himself and the grantee continue to pollute.[43]

Who are riparian owners

The question whether a particular piece of land sustains the character of a riparian tenement is a question of fact, and must be determined according to the special circumstances. In *Attwood* v. *Llay Main Collieries* Lawrence J. said [44]:

> "[The] expression ['riparian tenement'] in my opinion connotes, in addition to contact with the river, a reasonable proximity to the river bank. The proposition that every piece of land in the same occupation which includes a portion of the river bank and therefore affords access to the river is, in my opinion, far too wide. In order to test it, let me take an extreme case: nobody in their senses would seriously suggest that the site of Paddington Station and Hotel is a riparian tenement, though it may be connected with the river Thames by a strip of land many miles long; nor could it reasonably be suggested that the whole of a large estate of, say, 2,000 acres was a riparian tenement because a small portion of it was surrounded by a stream."

[42] (1909) 26 T.L.R. 175.
[43] *Crossley & Sons Ltd.* v. *Lightowler* (1866) 2 Ch.App. 478.
[44] [1926] Ch. 444.

It is settled that the rights of a riparian owner do not depend on his ownership of the soil of the stream.[45] To give rise to the existence of riparian rights it is necessary that the land in respect of which they are claimed should be in contact with the flow of the stream, but lateral contact is as good *jure naturae* as vertical,[46] that is to say, a man has as much right to water flowing past his land as he has to water flowing over his land. In the case of a tidal river the foreshore of which is left bare at low water, it was said that, although each bank is not always in contact with the flow of the stream, it is in such contact for a great part of every day in the regular course of nature; which fact is an amply sufficient foundation for a natural riparian right.[47] Where a riparian owner grants away a part of his land not abutting on the stream the grantee has no water rights in respect of such part.[48] Again, it has been held that a lessee of mines under land adjoining a stream, who also enjoys a grant from the surface owner of the use of the water for colliery purposes, is not as regards the user of the water a riparian owner.[49] The position of a person holding from a riparian owner a licence to use the water of the stream was dealt with in *Stockport Waterworks Co.* v. *Potter,*[50] *Ormerod* v. *Todmorden Joint Stock Mill Co.*[51] and *Kensit* v. *G.E. Railway,*[1] which are discussed, *post,* pp. 232 *et seq.*

First occupant acquires no right to divert

Reverting to the earlier cases in which the law as to water rights was stated, it seems that in discussing the question whether the right to receive the water is one of the ordinary incidents of the ownership of the soil, or an additional right claimed as an easement, a misconception formerly took place. The right to the corporeal thing, water itself, was confounded with the incorporeal right to have the stream flow in its accustomed manner.[2] Upon this a further error was founded—that the first occupant or appropriator of water had a right to continue to divert the stream to the extent of such appropriation, no matter how injurious such diversion might be to the rights of parties who should afterwards seek to use the stream. The question was debated—what nature of property existed by law, or could exist, in

---

45 *Lyon* v. *Fishmongers' Co.* (1876) 1 App.Cas. 673. In the case of land bounded by a non-navigable stream the ownership is presumed to extend *ad medium filum* of the soil of the stream (*City of London Commissioners* v. *Central London Railway* [1913] A.C. 379), even where the conveyance appears to exclude the soil (*Mellor* v. *Walmesley* [1905] 2 Ch. 179).
46 *North Shore Railway Co.* v. *Pion* (1889) 14 App.Cas. 621.
47 *Ibid.*
48 *Ormerod* v. *Todmorden Joint Stock Mill Co.* (1883) 11 Q.B.D. 155; *Stockport Waterworks Co.* v. *Potter* (1864) 3 H. & C. 326.
49 *Insole* v. *James* (1856) 1 H. & N. 243.
50 (1864) 3 H. & C. 300.
51 (1883) 11 Q.B.D. 155.
1 (1884) 27 Ch.D. 122.
2 *Mason* v. *Hill* (1833) 5 B. & Ad. 1.

air, light, and water. It was attempted to rest the right to the enjoyment of these elements upon the first occupancy of a common right.
Thus, Blackstone, in his chapter on " Title by Occupancy," after
remarking that a property in goods and chattels might be acquired
by occupancy—" the original and only primitive method of acquiring
any property at all " laid it down, that " the benefit of the elements—
light, air, and water—can only be appropriated by occupancy. If I
have an ancient window overlooking my neighbour's ground, he may
not erect any blind to obstruct the light; but if I build my house close
to his wall, which darkens it, I cannot compel him to demolish his wall,
for there the first occupancy is rather in him than in me. If my neighbour makes a tanyard, so as to annoy, and render less salubrious the
air of my house or gardens, the law will furnish me with a remedy; but
if he is first in possession of the air, and I fix my habitation near him,
the nuisance is of my own seeking, and may continue. If a stream be
unoccupied, I may erect a mill thereon, and detain the water, yet not
so as to injure my neighbour's prior mill or his meadow, for he hath
by the first occupancy, acquired a property in the current." [3] The last
two illustrations of Blackstone, however, are directly at variance with
the later decisions upon this subject.[4] And the question has since been
set at rest by the considered judgment of Lord Denman C.J. in *Mason* v.
Hill,[5] in which he laid it down that there is no authority in English law
for the proposition that the first occupant, though he may be proprietor
of the land above, has any right by diverting the stream to deprive the
owner of the land below of the natural flow of the water. " It has long
been established that the first occupant cannot acquire an exclusive right
to running water." [6]

No act of appropriation necessary

It was also at one time made a question whether the simple fact
of water running in a natural channel through land was sufficient to
confer upon the landowner the right to control his neighbour's interference, or whether there must be some tangible perception or active
appropriation by the landowner of the benefit of the water.[7] It is now
settled that no act of appropriation is necessary.[8] It has in effect been
decided that every proprietor of land along the stream has, without

---

3 2 Bl.Com. 402.
4 *Bliss* v. *Hall* (1838) 4 Bing.N.C. 183; *Mason* v. *Hill* (1833) 5 B. & Ad. 1; *Sturges*
   v. *Bridgman* (1879) 11 Ch.D. 852.
5 (1833) 5 B. & Ad. 1, where the earlier authorities are reviewed at length. See also
   Acton v. *Blundell* (1843) 12 M. & W. 324, p. 211, *post*, where Tindal C.J. compared
   the case of the stream running in its natural course over the surface with the case
   of an underground spring; *Wright* v. *Howard* (1823) 1 Sim. & St. 190.
6 *Per* Bowen L.J. in *Ormerod* v. *Todmorden Joint Stock Mill Co. Ltd.* (1883) 11
   Q.B.D. 155, 171.
7 See *Bealey* v. *Shaw* (1805) 6 East 208; *Saunders* v. *Newman* (1818) 1 B. & Ald.
   258; *Williams* v. *Morland* (1824) 2 B. & C. 910, and the considered judgment of
   Lord Denman in *Mason* v. *Hill* (1833) 5 B. & Ad. 1.
8 *Orr-Ewing* v. *Colquhoun* (1877) 2 App.Cas. 854.

ever having used the water, a right to maintain an action against any person who diverts it, unless the person so diverting it has acquired a legal title to do so, if the diversion diminishes the flow of water to an extent greater than that necessarily incident to the reasonable use of the water by the proprietor above in the exercise of his similar right. For instance, if a person erects a mill, and thereby interferes with the course of the stream to such an extent, he is liable to an action for such diversion at the suit of any proprietor of land lying lower down the stream, although the latter has never applied the water to a beneficial purpose, and brings an action only one day before the time requisite to give the owner of the mill a prescriptive right to a use of the water exceeding the natural right.[9]

(2) Surface Water: No Defined Channel

The natural right to the flow of water applies only to water flowing in some defined natural channel; and therefore the owner of land upon which there is surface water arising out of springy or boggy ground and flowing in no definite channel, or water arising occasionally at one spot but having no defined course, has a right to get rid of such water by draining the land or in any way he pleases, although, if not so disposed of, it might ultimately have reached the course of a natural stream.[10] The right of the riparian owner to the natural flow of water cannot extend further than the right to the flow of the stream itself and to the water flowing in some defined[11] natural channel, either subterranean or on the surface, communicating directly with the stream itself.[10] In Broadbent v. Ramsbotham[12] the owner of the soil was held not to be liable to an action for draining a pond the water of which occasionally, when it exceeded a certain depth, escaped and squandered itself over the surface, some of it augmenting a natural stream, but by no defined channel.

[9] See the judgments in Embrey v. Owen (1851) 6 Exch. 368, and Sampson v. Hoddinott (1857) 1 C.B.(N.S.) 611, where the action was by a reversioner; also Wood v. Waud (1849) 3 Exch. 772; Miner v. Gilmour (1858) 12 Moo.P.C. 156; and Crossley & Sons Ltd. v. Lightowler (1866) 2 Ch.App. 478; Roberts v. Gwyrfai District Council [1899] 2 Ch. 608; McCartney v. Londonderry and Lough Swilly Railway Co. [1904] A.C. 301; Sharp v. Wilson, Rotheray & Co. (1905) 93 L.T. 155; Attwood v. Llay Main Collieries Ltd. [1926] Ch. 444.

[10] Rawstron v. Taylor (1855) 11 Exch. 369.

[11] " A watercourse consists of bed, banks and water; yet the water need not flow continually, and there are many watercourses which are sometimes dry. There is, however, a distinction to be taken in law between a regular flowing stream of water, which at certain seasons is dried up, and those occasional bursts of water which, in times of freshet or melting of ice and snow, descend from the hills and inundate the country. To maintain the right to a watercourse or brook, it must be made to appear that the water usually flows in a certain direction and by a regular channel, with banks or sides. It need not be shown to flow continually, as stated above, and it may at times be dry; but it must have a well-defined and substantial existence ": Angell on Watercourses. Compare the explanation stated below of " defined channel." The elements of a watercourse are usefully considered in Lee v. Rural Municipality of Arthur (1964) 46 D.L.R. (2d) 448 (Manitoba Q.B.).

[12] (1856) 11 Exch. 602.

The defendant in *Rugby Joint Water Board* v. *Walters*,[13] in addition to drawing water for irrigation from the river Avon drew it from a reservoir which he constructed by enlarging a short length of a natural ditch which ran through his land into the river. The ditch, and hence the reservoir, was fed by piped overflows and drains, by surface water and by percolating water, but not by natural spring water. The water feeding the reservoir was not taken out of the old channel, but at the point at which it would have found its way into the channel. Buckley J. held that the defendant was entitled to impound the water at the point where it entered his reservoir, being the point at which if not intercepted the water would, before the construction of the reservoir, have passed from private ownership into a channel in which riparian rights would have attached to it, and to use it as he thought fit.

(3) *Underground Water : Channel Defined and Known*

If a natural stream flows through a defined underground channel, then, as soon as the channel is known, the owners of the land above it, and, if it continues on the surface, the riparian owners on each side of the continued channel, have the same rights, and the same rights of action for diversion or obstruction of water higher up in the channel, as they would have had if the stream were wholly above ground.[14]

" Defined " for this purpose means physically or actually defined; in other words a " defined channel " is a channel. A " known " channel is a channel whose course has become actually known, by excavation or otherwise, or can be gathered by reasonable inference from existing and observed facts in the natural or pre-existing condition of the surface of the ground; as, for instance, a stream, such as the river Mole, which disappears into the ground and reappears, presumably as the same stream, lower down.[15]

(4) *Underground Water : Channel Not Defined and Known*

Right to divert or appropriate

In the case of underground water flowing through undefined and unknown channels the above rules as to the natural rights of riparian owners do not apply. For it is settled by *Chasemore* v. *Richards* [16] that every man has the right to divert or appropriate all water of this

---

13 [1967] Ch. 397; see p. 204, *ante*, applying *Broadbent* v. *Ramsbotham* (1856) 11 Exch. 602 and *Chasemore* v. *Richards* (1859) 7 H.L.C. 349, *infra*.
14 *Dickinson* v. *Grand Junction Canal Co.* (1852) 7 Exch. 282, 301; *Chasemore* v. *Richards* (1859) 7 H.L.C. 374, 384; *Black* v. *Ballymena Township Commissioners* (1886) 17 L.R.Ir. 459; *Bradford Corporation* v. *Ferrand* [1902] 2 Ch. 655, 660; *Bleachers' Association Ltd.* v. *Chapel-en-le-Frith R.D.C.* [1933] Ch. 356.
15 *Black* v. *Ballymena Township Commissioners, supra*; *Bradford Corporation* v. *Ferrand, supra*; *Bleachers' Association Ltd.* v. *Chapel-en-le-Frith R.D.C., supra*.
16 (1859) 7 H.L.C. 376; applied in *Rugby Joint Water Board* v. *Walters* [1967] Ch. 397, 424, *supra*; see also p. 219, *post*.

nature which he can find on his own land.[17] "Percolating water below
the surface of the earth is a common reservoir in which nobody has
any property, but of which everybody has (as far as he can) the right
of appropriating the whole,"[18] and this right the landowner can exercise
notwithstanding that the stream which the neighbour owns may be
diminished in consequence of the diverted or appropriated water not
coming into it.[19] Again, it has been laid down that no action will lie
against a man who by digging in his own land drains his neighbour's
land, either by intercepting the flow of water percolating through the
soil, or by causing water already collected on his neighbour's soil to
percolate away.[20]

In *Acton* v. *Blundell*,[21] which decided that the owner of Blackacre
through which underground water percolates in an undefined channel
has no interest in such water which will enable him to maintain an action
against a neighbour, who, by mining in the usual manner in his own
land, lays dry a well on Blackacre, Tindal C.J. distinguished the case of
the stream running in its natural course and the case of an underground
spring as follows[22]:

> "The ground and origin of the law which governs streams run-
> ning in their natural course would seem to be this, that the right
> enjoyed by the several proprietors of the lands over which they
> flow is, and always has been, public and notorious: that the enjoy-
> ment has been long continued—in ordinary cases, indeed, time out
> of mind—and uninterrupted; each man knowing what he receives
> and what has always been received from the higher lands, and what
> he transmits and what has always been transmitted to the lower.
> The rule, therefore, either assumes for its foundation the implied
> assent and agreement of the proprietors of the different lands from
> all ages, or perhaps it may be considered as a rule of positive law
> (which would seem to be the opinion of Fleta and Blackstone), the
> origin of which is lost by the progress of time; or it may not be
> unfitly treated as laid down by Mr. Justice Story, in his judgment in
> the case of *Tyler* v. *Wilkinson*, in the courts of the United States,[23]
> as 'an incident to the land; and that whoever seeks to found an
> exclusive use must establish a rightful appropriation in some manner

---

[17] *Ballard* v. *Tomlinson* (1885) 29 Ch.D. 115, 123; *Salt Union* v. *Brunner* [1906] 2
K.B. 822; *English* v. *Metropolitan Water Board* [1907] 1 K.B. 588, 602. But an
express grant of all streams that might be found in certain closes prevented the
grantor from working mines under adjoining land so as to divert underground
water from wells in the closes: *Whitehead* v. *Parks* (1858) 2 H. & N. 870.

[18] *Ballard* v. *Tomlinson* (1885) 29 Ch.D. 115, 121, *per* Brett M.R.

[19] *Bradford Corporation* v. *Pickles* [1895] A.C. 587.

[20] *Ballacorkish Mining Co.* v. *Harrison* (1873) L.R. 5 P.C. 60, where this rule was
held to apply between a surface owner and the mine owner.

[21] (1843) 12 M. & W. 324. See *New River Co.* v. *Johnson* (1860) 2 E. & E. 435
(deciding that there is no distinction for this purpose between water already
collected in a well and water which would otherwise have flowed into it): *R.* v.
Metropolitan Board of Works (1863) 3 B. & S. 710.

[22] (1843) 12 M. & W. 324, 349–352.

[23] 4 Mason (U.S.) 401.

known and admitted by the law.' But in the case of a well sunk by
a proprietor in his own land, the water which feeds it from a neighbouring soil does not flow openly in the sight of the neighbouring
proprietor, but through the hidden veins of the earth beneath its
surface: no man can tell what changes these underground sources
have undergone in the progress of time: it may well be, that it is
only yesterday's date that they first took the course and direction
which enabled them to supply the well: again, no proprietor knows
what portion of water is taken from beneath his own soil: how
much he gives originally, or how much he transmits only, or how
much he receives: on the contrary, until the well is sunk, and the
water collected by draining into it, there cannot properly be said,
with reference to the well, to be any flow of water at all. In the
case, therefore, of the well, there can be no ground for implying
any mutual consent or agreement, for ages past, between the owners
of the several lands beneath which the underground springs may
exist, which is one of the foundations on which the law as to running streams is supposed to be built; nor, for the same reason, can
any trace of a positive law be inferred from long-continued
acquiescence and submission, whilst the very existence of the underground springs or of the well may be unknown to the proprietors
of the soil.

"But the difference between the two cases with respect to the
consequences, if the same law is to be applied to both, is still more
apparent. In the case of the running stream, the owner of the soil
merely transmits the water over its surface: he receives as much
from his higher neighbour as he sends down to his neighbour below:
he is neither better nor worse: the level of the water remains the
same. But if the man who sinks the well in his own land can
acquire by that act an absolute and indefeasible right to the water
that collects in it, he has the power of preventing his neighbour
from making any use of the spring in his own soil which shall interfere with the enjoyment of the well. He has the power, still further,
of debarring the owner of the land in which the spring is first found,
or through which it is transmitted, from draining his land for the
proper cultivation of the soil: and thus, by an act which is voluntary on his part, and which may be entirely unsuspected by his
neighbour, he may impose on such neighbour the necessity of bearing a heavy expense, if the latter has erected machinery for the
purposes of mining, and discovers when too late that the appropriation of the water has already been made. Further, the advantage
on one side, and the detriment to the other, may bear no proportion.
The well may be sunk to supply a cottage, or a drinking place for
cattle; whilst the owner of the adjoining land may be prevented from
winning metals and minerals of inestimable value. And lastly,

there is no limit of space within which the claim of right to an underground spring can be confined: in the present case the nearest coal-pit is at the distance of half a mile from the well: it is obvious the law must equally apply if there is an interval of many miles."

The principle of *Acton* v. *Blundell* [24] was applied in *Salt Union* v. *Brunner*,[25] although the underground liquid drawn off by the defendants in the course of pumping operations carried on by them on their own land was brine mainly formed by the dissolution of rock-salt in the plaintiffs' salt mines, and although it was found as a fact that the defendants had, by such operations, abstracted a large quantity of salt from the beds of rock-salt belonging to the plaintiffs, and that, if the defendants' brine-pumping were continued, more of the plaintiffs' rock would be dissolved, and the salt abstracted therefrom. Notwithstanding these facts it was held that the defendants were guilty of no actionable wrong. It is to be observed that, as pointed out by Pennycuick V.-C. in *Lotus Ltd.* v. *British Soda Co. Ltd.*,[26] the action was based upon the removal of salt by pumping and not upon any resulting subsidence.

The decision in *Grand Junction Co.* v. *Shugar*,[27] which seems inconsistent with the rule above stated as to percolating underground water, must be explained as relating to a direct tapping of an overground stream flowing in a defined channel, and not to a mere withdrawal of percolating underground water.[28]

The principles laid down in *Acton* v. *Blundell* [29] also apply where the surface and the mines beneath it belong to different owners, the surface having been granted and the mines retained. The owner of the mine is not responsible if, in working the mines, he drains the water from the surface. In *Ballacorkish Mining Co.* v. *Harrison* [30] Lord Penzance, delivering the advice of the Privy Council, said:

"The grant of the surface cannot carry with it more than the absolute ownership of the entire soil would include. The absolute ownership is held not to include a right to be protected from loss of water by percolation into openings made in the soil of the neighbouring owner. How then can the grant of the surface only be held to include such a protection? To hold otherwise might not

---

24 (1843) 12 M. & W. 324.
25 [1906] 2 K.B. 822. As to subsidence caused by the pumping of brine, see the Brine Pumping (Compensation for Subsidence) Act 1891. The functions under this Act of the Local Government Board were transferred to the Minister of Health by the Ministry of Health Act 1919, s. 3 (1) (*a*) (repealed) and are now vested in the Secretary of State discharging the functions of the Minister of Housing and Local Government (S.I. 1951, No. 753; S.I. 1970, No. 1681). As to the right of support which has been claimed from underground water, see *post*, p. 288.
26 [1971] 2 W.L.R. 7, 12; see p. 289, *post*.
27 (1871) 6 Ch.App. 483; see the report in 24 L.T. 402.
28 *Jordeson* v. *Sutton, Southcoates and Drypool Gas Co.* [1899] 2 Ch. 217, 251; *English* v. *Metropolitan Water Board* [1907] 1 K.B. 588, 601.
29 (1843) 12 M. & W. 324.
30 (1873) L.R. 5 P.C. 49, 63; see *Littledale* v. *Lonsdale* [1899] 2 Ch. 233n. As to a mine owner's rights in working his mines, see also the Scottish decision in *Scots Mines Co.* v. *Leadhills* (1859) 34 L.T. 34.

improbably result in rendering the reservation of mines and minerals wholly useless. Percolation of water into mines is an almost necessary incident of mining. And if the grant of the surface carries with it a right to be protected from any loss of surface water by percolation, the owner of the surface would hold the owner of the mines at his mercy; for he would be entitled by injunction to inhibit the working of mines at all. It is not at variance with this view that the case of *Whitehead* v. *Parks* [31] was decided, because in that case there was a lease and a distinct grant of the injured springs *eo nomine.*"

If, however, the grant of the surface were made for some express purpose necessarily and obviously requiring the continuance of a supply of surface water, the principle laid down in the above passage might come into conflict with the principle that a man may not derogate from his own grant. It is conceived, however, that even in such a case the surface owner could not claim a continuance of the surface water so as to prevent the working of the minerals. The reservation of the minerals would, it is thought, include all the natural and legal incidents consequent upon the working necessary to win them.

Surface springs

As will have been seen above, the rules regulating the right of flow laid down as to water flowing in an undefined channel differ from those which apply to defined channels. In the case of water flowing from surface springs there is often a difficulty in deciding whether they fall under the rules as to defined or undefined channels.[32] Where a natural defined stream issued from a springhead, it was held that the " stream " began at the springhead, and that the owner of the land could only take such water from either as was incident to his right as riparian owner.[33] The same principle applied even where at some remote period the springhead had been built round.[34]

2.—WATER RESOURCES ACT 1963

The Water Resources Act 1963 [35] provides for the establishment of " river authorities," each to administer an area of the country.[36] It is the general duty of each river authority to take action for the purpose of conserving, redistributing or otherwise augmenting water resources in

---

[31] (1858) 2 H. & N. 870.
[32] See *Ennor* v. *Barwell* (1860) 2 Giff. 423; *Briscoe* v. *Drought* (1860) 11 Ir.C.L.R. 250.
[33] *Dudden* v. *Clutton Union* (1857) 1 H. & N. 627; *Bunting* v. *Hicks* (1894) 70 L.T. 458; *Ewart* v. *Belfast Guardians* (1881) 9 L.R.Ir. 172; *Rugby Joint Water Board* v. *Walters* [1967] Ch. 397, 424.
[34] *Mostyn* v. *Atherton* [1899] 2 Ch. 360.
[35] The Act has been slightly amended by the Water Resources Act 1968.
[36] s. 3. An agreement entered into by a river authority for facilitating the performance of its functions may provide for registration of the agreement, in the case of unregistered land as a Class D (iii) land charge, and in the case of registered land under s. 59 (2) of the Land Registration Act 1925: Water Resources Act 1963, s. 81 (4) (5).

its area.[37] Part IV of the Act, which contains provisions for controlling the abstraction of water, affects rights and duties at common law.[38]

Basic rule

Section 23 (1) of the Act provides as follows:

". . . no person shall abstract water in a river authority area, or cause or permit any other person so to abstract any water, except in pursuance of a licence under this Act granted by the river authority and in accordance with the provisions of that licence."

Although there are exceptions, the general rule is that a licence is required to abstract [39] water from a source of supply. For the purposes of the Act, " source of supply " means any inland water or underground strata situated in a river authority area.[40]

In the case of an inland water the person entitled to apply for a licence must be either the occupier of land contiguous to that inland water at the proposed place of abstraction or a person having a right of access to such land.[41] In the case of underground strata the applicant must be the occupier of land consisting of or comprising those underground strata; and in a case where water contained in an excavation into underground strata is, by virtue of section 2 (2) (b) of the Act, to be treated as water contained in those underground strata, the applicant must have a right of access to land consisting of or comprising those underground strata.[42]

The river authority has a discretion as to whether to grant or refuse a licence, and may grant a licence containing such provisions as it considers appropriate.[43] There is a right of appeal to the Minister [44] and thence a limited right of appeal to the High Court.[45]

[37] s. 4.
[38] See " The Effect of the Water Resources Act 1963 on the Common Law Right to Abstract Water " by Mr. Michael Harwood (1969) 33 *Conveyancer* (N.S.) 14 for a full survey of the effect of the Act on the common law right to abstract water; also " Controls over the Use and Discharge of Water " by Mr. J. F. Garner (1963) 27 *Conveyancer* (N.S.) 489.
[39] " Abstract " in the Act means to remove water from a source of supply whereby it either ceases (either permanently or temporarily) to be comprised in the water resources of the area, or is transferred to another source of supply in the area: s. 135 (1).
[40] s. 2 (1). " Inland water " means *inter alia* any river, stream or other watercourse, whether natural or artificial and whether tidal or not, and any lake or pond, whether natural or artificial: s. 135 (1). " Source of supply," however, does not include a lake or pond which does not discharge to any other inland water, or one of a group of lakes or ponds where none of the groups discharges to any inland water outside the group: s. 2 (3). " Underground strata " means strata subjacent to the surface of any land: s. 135 (1). Water contained in any excavation into underground strata, where the level depends on water entering it from those strata, is to be treated as water contained in the underground strata: s. 2 (2) (b).
[41] s. 27 (2).
[42] s. 27 (3), as amended by the Water Resources Act 1968, s. 1 (1).
[43] s. 29 (8). For the factors which the river authority must take into account in dealing with an application, see s. 29 (3), (5), (6) and (7).
[44] s. 39. " The Minister " is now the Secretary of State for the Environment; see the Secretary of State for the Environment Order 1970 (S.I. No. 1681) made under the Ministers of the Crown (Transfer of Functions) Act 1946, s. 1, and the Ministers of the Crown Act 1964, s. 4.   [45] s. 117.

The licence must specify *inter alia* the period during which it is to remain in force and the quantity of water to be abstracted.[46]

Exceptional cases

There are several exceptional cases where a licence to abstract water is not necessary.[47] Three such cases are mentioned here.

A licence is not required for any abstraction of a quantity of water not exceeding 1,000 gallons, if it does not form part of a continuous operation, or a series of operations, whereby in the aggregate more than 1,000 gallons of water are abstracted.[48]

A licence is not required for any abstraction from an inland water for one or both of the following purposes, that is to say, the domestic purposes of the occupier's household and agricultural purposes other than spray irrigation. This exception is available only to an abstraction by or on behalf of the occupier of land contiguous to the inland water at the point of abstraction and only if the water abstracted is for use on a holding consisting of that land with or without other land held therewith.[49]

A licence is not required for the abstraction of water from underground strata, in so far as the water is abstracted by a person for the domestic purposes of his household.[50]

Effect on common law rights

Where a person abstracts water in pursuance of a licence he will not be liable in nuisance to another riparian owner even though he may have no defence at common law.[1]

Section 31 (1) of the Act provides as follows:

" . . . in any action brought against a person in respect of the abstraction of water from a source of supply, it shall be a defence for him to prove that the water was abstracted in pursuance of a licence under this Act, and that the provisions of the licence were complied with."

The grant of a licence, therefore, provides a statutory defence to the holder of the licence and, it seems, to any person whom he causes or

---

[46] s. 30. For succession to licences, see s. 32.

[47] The exceptions are contained in s. 24. In addition the river authority may apply to the Minister for an order exempting a source of supply from the licensing provisions of the Act: s. 25.

[48] s. 24 (1).

[49] s. 24 (2). The river authority has a power to determine what is the " holding " for the purposes of this subsection; see s. 55. " Spray irrigation " is defined in s. 135 (1).

[50] s. 24 (3).

[1] A licence does not provide a defence to an action for negligence or breach of contract: s. 31 (3). The statutory defence was not available to persons who abstracted water under a " licence of right " during a transitional period: ss. 31 (2), 56 (5). For " licences of right," see ss. 33–35. For " the relevant transitional period," see s. 56 (5). *Rugby Joint Water Board* v. *Walters* [1967] Ch. 397, see p. 204, *ante*, was a case arising during this period.

permits to abstract water in pursuance of the licence.[2] The terms of the licence must be complied with; the licence will not provide a partial defence where one of its terms is broken.

If this statutory defence is not available, that is, because there is no licence or one of its terms has been broken, there may nevertheless be a common law defence in respect of the abstraction, although there will be a statutory penalty.[3]

If a person abstracts water without a licence in one of the exceptional cases where no licence is required,[4] his defence to an action by a riparian owner depends entirely on the common law. The fact that he falls within one of the exceptions only exempts him from liability to a statutory penalty; it does not provide a defence to an action at common law. In such a case there seems to be nothing to prevent such a person from applying for a licence and thus obtaining a statutory defence under section 31 (1) of the Act.[5]

Liability of river authority

The river authority has a duty not to grant a licence authorising the abstraction of water so as to derogate from any rights which, at the time the application is determined, are " protected rights " under the Act.[6] If, however, the river authority, in breach of such duty, grants a licence, the grant is not invalid and cannot be restrained by prohibition or injunction, but the person having a " protected right " may sue the river authority in damages for breach of statutory duty.[7] A " protected right " is not necessarily the same as the common law right to restrain an abstraction of water, and is defined [8] as either (a) a right which the holder of a licence has to abstract water to the extent authorised by the licence and in accordance with its provisions or (b) a right which a person has by virtue of section 24 (2) or section 24 (3) of the Act to the extent specified in those subsections.[9]

The effect of this statutory duty is that the holder of a licence to abstract water has a right of action against the river authority if it grants another licence which prevents him from abstracting water to the extent authorised by his licence.[10] Similarly, a person who is in a position to abstract water without a licence by virtue either of subsection (2) of section 24 from an inland water (i.e. for domestic or agricultural purposes) or of subsection (3) of section 24 from underground strata (i.e. for domestic purposes) has a right of action against the river authority

---

[2] See s. 23 (1).
[3] s. 49.
[4] s. 24. See ante, p. 216.
[5] The statutory authority must not derogate from " protected rights " when granting a licence; but these rights do not necessarily correspond with common law rights. Infra.
[6] s. 29 (2).
[7] s. 50 (1). For defences available to the river authority, see s. 50 (3), (4).
[8] s. 26 (1).
[9] See ante, p. 216.
[10] s. 26 (1) (a), (2).

if he is prevented from exercising his right to the extent specified in those respective subsections by the granting of a licence to another person.[11]

3.—PRESCRIPTIVE RIGHTS IN NATURAL WATERCOURSES

Defined channel

In the case of water flowing through a natural watercourse with a defined channel, rights may be acquired by prescription which interfere with what would otherwise be the natural rights of other proprietors above and below.[12] A riparian owner may by user acquire a right to use the water in a manner not justified by his natural rights; but such acquired right has no operation against the natural rights of a landowner higher up or lower down, unless it affects the use such landowner has of the stream, or his power to use it, so as to raise the presumption of a grant, and so render the tenement above or below a servient tenement.[13] Before the Prescription Act 1832, twenty years' exclusive enjoyment of water in any particular manner afforded a strong presumption of right in the party so enjoying it derived from grant or Act of Parliament.[14] In *Prescott* v. *Phillips* [15] it was ruled " that nothing short of twenty years' undisturbed possession of water diverted from the natural channel, or raised by a weir, could give a party an adverse right against those whose lands lay lower down the stream and to whom it was injurious." The right of diverting water, which in its natural course would flow over or along the land of a riparian owner, can be created only by grant, or enjoyment from which a grant may be presumed, or by statute. Such an easement exists for the benefit of the dominant owner alone, and the servient owner acquires no right to insist on its continuance.[16]

A riparian owner may acquire a prescriptive right to pen back a stream,[17] or to divert part of a stream by means of a stone,[18] but he can acquire no such right in any navigable river.[19] So a lower riparian owner can acquire a right to place a hatch on the land of the upper owner to

---

[11] s. 26 (1) (*b*), (2). It is uncertain whether " extent " in relation to the purposes specified in section 24 (2) and (3) means the amount actually being used or capable of being used.

[12] *White (John) & Sons* v. *White* [1906] A.C. 72. What is said in this section of this chapter must be read in the light of the Water Resources Act 1963, as to which see section 2 of this chapter, *ante*.

[13] *Sampson* v. *Hoddinott* (1857) 1 C.B.(N.S.) 590.

[14] *Bealey* v. *Shaw* (1805) 6 East 208; *Cox* v. *Matthews* (1673) 1 Vent. 237; see *Dewhirst* v. *Wrigley* (1834) Coop.Pr.Cas. 329.

[15] (1798), cited in *Bealey* v. *Shaw*, 6 East 208, 213; *Mason* v. *Hill* (1833) 5 B. & Ad. 23.

[16] *Per* Cockburn C.J. in *Mason* v. *Shrewsbury and Hereford Railway* (1871) L.R. 6 Q.B. 578, 587. See, however, the opinion of Blackburn J. in the same case.

[17] *Cooper* v. *Barber* (1810) 3 Taunt. 110.

[18] *Holker* v. *Porritt* (1875) L.R. 10 Ex. 62.

[19] *Vooght* v. *Winch* (1819) 2 B. & Ald. 662.

regulate the flow of water [20] or for the latter purpose to go on the land of the upper owner and open lock gates.[21]   So the lower riparian owner can acquire a right to go on the land of an upper riparian owner and bank up the stream.[22]   Again, the right to a fishing weir may be acquired in non-navigable rivers by grant from other riparian owners, or by enjoyment, or by any means by which such rights may be constituted.[23] Even in a navigable river a riparian owner can acquire an interest in its water power as derived from a reservoir artificially formed by a dam across the channel.[24]   It should be noted here that the second section of the Prescription Act refers to a claim to a watercourse, words which have been held to include a claim to have water, which would otherwise flow down to the plaintiff's land, diverted over other land.[25]

No defined channel

In the case of water which percolates in an undefined course, no right to the uninterrupted flow can be acquired by prescription, for as regards this water no grant can be presumed.[26]   Similarly it has been held that a claim to have water percolate through the banks of a stream cannot be established by prescription.[27]

The principle governing these cases was settled by *Chasemore* v. *Richards*,[28] where the House of Lords approved and acted on the unanimous opinion of the judges, delivered by Wightman J.   The facts are set out in that opinion as follows [29]:

---

[20] *Wood* v. *Hewett* (1846) 8 Q.B. 913; *Moody* v. *Steggles* (1879) 12 Ch.D. 266; see *Greenslade* v. *Halliday* (1830) 6 Bing. 379.

[21] See *Simpson* v. *Godmanchester Corporation* [1897] A.C. 696.   Compare *Beeston* v. *Weate* (1856) 5 E. & B. 986, where A, a non-riparian owner, was held to have acquired an easement to go on the land of B, an adjoining riparian owner, to turn water from a natural stream into an artificial watercourse which passed from the stream across B's land to A's land, and to repair such watercourse.

[22] *Roberts* v. *Fellowes* (1906) 94 L.T. 279.

[23] *Rolle* v. *Whyte* (1868) L.R. 3 Q.B. 286; *Leconfield* v. *Lonsdale* (1870) L.R. 5 C.P. 657; *Barker* v. *Faulkner* [1898] W.N. 69.

[24] *Hamelin* v. *Bannerman* [1895] A.C. 237.

[25] *Mason* v. *Shrewsbury and Hereford Railway* (1871) L.R. 6 Q.B. 578.   See *Staffordshire and Worcestershire Canal Co.* v. *Birmingham Canal Co.* (1866) L.R. 1 H.L. 254.

[26] *Chasemore* v. *Richards* (1859) 7 H.L.C. 349, 370, 385.   There can be no express grant or reservation of water which percolates in an unidentified channel, because water is not the subject of property.   But although a grantor of land cannot reserve percolating water out of land conveyed by him, he can reserve the right to obtain water from such land: *Re Simeon* [1937] Ch. 525.   This case also decides that a covenant by the grantee, framed in such a way as to make the burden thereof run with the land conveyed, to the effect that the covenantor and his successors in title will not do anything on the land conveyed or any part or parts thereof whereby water now or hereafter obtained therefrom shall be diminished, is a covenant which will be enforced.   But in the absence of such special circumstances as existed in *Re Simeon* (*supra*), the owner of land containing underground water which percolates by undefined channels and flows to the land of a neighbour is entitled to divert or appropriate the percolating water within his own land so as to deprive his neighbour of it.   Whether or not by exercising such right he intends to injure his neighbour is immaterial: *Bradford Corpn.* v. *Pickles* [1895] A.C. 587.

[27] *Roberts* v. *Fellowes* (1906) 94 L.T. 281.

[28] (1859) 7 H.L.C. 349.

[29] (1859) 7 H.L.C. 349, 366.

"It appears by the facts that are found in this case, that the plaintiff is the occupier of an ancient mill on the River Wandle, and that for more than sixty years before the present action he and all the preceding occupiers of the mill used and enjoyed, as of right, the flow of the river for the purpose of working their mill. It also appears that the River Wandle is, and always has been, supplied, above the plaintiff's mill, in part by the water produced by the rainfall on a district of many thousand acres in extent, comprising the town of Croydon and its vicinity. The water of the rainfall sinks into the ground to various depths, and then flows and percolates through the strata to the River Wandle, part rising to the surface, and part finding its way underground in courses which continually vary. The defendant represents the members of the Local Board of Health of Croydon, who, for the purpose of supplying the town of Croydon with water, and for other sanitary purposes, sank a well in their own land in the town of Croydon, and about a quarter of a mile from the River Wandle, and pumped up large quantities of water from their well for the supply of the town of Croydon; and by means of the well and the pumping, the local board of health did divert, abstract, and intercept underground water, but underground water only, that otherwise would have flowed and found its way into the River Wandle, and so to the plaintiff's mill; and the quantity so diverted, abstracted, and intercepted was sufficient to be of sensible value towards the working of the plaintiff's mill. The question is, whether the plaintiff can maintain an action against the defendant for this diversion, abstraction, and interception of the underground water."

Having referred to *Embrey* v. *Owen*,[30] *Rawstron* v. *Taylor*,[31] *Broadbent* v. *Ramsbotham*[32] and *Acton* v. *Blundell*,[33] and having explained the apparently inconsistent cases of *Balston* v. *Bensted*[34] and *Dickinson* v. *The Grand Junction Canal Co.*,[35] Wightman J. said[36]:

"In such a case as the present, is any right derived from the use of the water of the River Wandle for upwards of twenty years for working the plaintiff's mill? Any such right against another, founded upon length of enjoyment, is supposed to have originated in some grant which is presumed from the owner of what is sometimes called the servient tenement. But what grant can be presumed in the case of percolating waters, depending upon the quantity of rain falling or the natural moisture of the soil, and in the

[30] (1851) 6 Exch. 353; see p. 200, *ante*.
[31] (1855) 11 Exch. 369; see p. 200, *ante*.
[32] (1856) 11 Exch. 602; see p. 209, *ante*.
[33] (1843) 12 M. & W. 324; see p. 211, *ante*.
[34] (1808) 1 Camp. 463.
[35] (1852) 7 Exch. 282.
[36] (1859) 7 H.L.C. 349, 370.

absence of any visible means of knowing to what extent, if at all, the enjoyment of the plaintiff's mill would be affected by any water percolating in and out of the defendant's or any other land? The presumption of a grant only arises where the person against whom it is to be raised might have prevented the exercise of the subject of the presumed grant; but how could he prevent or stop the percolation of water? "

Later he said [37]:

" The question then is, whether the plaintiff has such a right as he claims *jure naturae* to prevent the defendant sinking a well in his own ground at a distance from the mill, and so absorbing the water percolating in and into his own ground beneath the surface, if such absorption has the effect of diminishing the quantity of water which would otherwise find its way into the River Wandle, and by such diminution affects the working of the plaintiff's mill. It is impossible to reconcile such a right with the natural and ordinary rights of landowners, or to fix any reasonable limits to the exercise of such a right. Such a right as that contended for by the plaintiff would interfere with, if not prevent the drainage of land by the owner."

In the same case Lord Wensleydale said [38] with reference to the plaintiff's claim, as based on the possession of his mill for thirty or sixty years:

" I do not think that the principle on which prescription rests can be applied; it has not been with the permission of the proprietor of the land that the streams have flowed into the river for twenty years or upwards: ' *qui non prohibet quod prohibere potest, assentire videtur.*' But how here could he prevent it? He could not bring an action against the adjoining proprietor; he could not be bound to dig a deep trench in his own land to cut off the supplies of water, in order to indicate his dissent. It is going very far to say, that a man must be at the expense of putting up a screen to window lights, to prevent a title being gained by twenty years' enjoyment of light passing through a window. But this case would go very far beyond that. I think that the enjoyment of the right to these natural streams cannot be supported by any length of user if it does not belong of natural right to the plaintiff."

4.—MISCELLANEOUS PRESCRIPTIVE RIGHTS

To take water

Independently of the prescriptive rights of user and flow which are mainly called in question between riparian owners, other miscellaneous

[37] (1859) 7 H.L.C. 349, 370–371.
[38] (1859) 7 H.L.C. 349, 385–386.

rights may be mentioned. Thus a landowner can acquire by prescription the right to go on his neighbour's land and draw water there from a spring [39] or from a pump.[40] Similarly A, a non-riparian owner, was held to have acquired by prescription the right to go on the land of B, an adjoining riparian owner, to turn the water from a natural stream into an artificial channel which passed from the stream across B's land to A's land, and to repair such channel.[41]

To discharge water : eavesdrop

As regards discharging water upon adjoining land, it was said by Bowen L.J. in *Chamber Colliery Co.* v. *Hopwood* [42] that the mere discharge of water by A, an upper proprietor, on the land of B, a lower proprietor, may easily establish a right on the part of A to go on discharging, because so long as the discharge continues there is submission on the part of B to proceedings which indicate a claim of right on the part of A. But it is difficult for B " to establish a right to have the flow continued, just as it would be very difficult to make out that because for twenty years my pump has dripped on to a neighbour's ground, therefore he has the right at the end of twenty years to say that my pump must go on leaking."

In the case of eaves, it has been laid down that though everyone in building is bound so to construct his house as not to overhang his neighbour's property, and construct his roof in such a manner as not to throw the rain-water upon the neighbouring land,[43] yet according to our law a man may acquire a right, by user, to project his wall or eaves over the boundary line of his property, or discharge the rain running from the roof of his house upon the adjoining land. The case of projecting buildings over a boundary will be dealt with in a subsequent chapter.[44] The easement of eavesdrop is recognised by the Court of Exchequer in *Thomas* v. *Thomas.*[45] In *Pyer* v. *Carter* [46] there was an easement for the defendant to have the rain-water flow from his eaves on to the plaintiff's roof, and for the plaintiff to have such water, together with the water originally falling on his own roof, carried away by a drain on the defendant's land.

There are ancient decisions recognising similar easements in the case of a discharge of water onto the neighbouring land by means of a gutter or leaden pipe.[47] " If a man hath a sue, that is to say, a spout, above

---

[39] *Race* v. *Ward* (1855) 4 E. & B. 702.
[40] *Polden* v. *Bastard* (1865) L.R. 1 Q.B. 156.
[41] *Beeston* v. *Weate* (1856) 5 E. & B. 986.
[42] (1886) 32 Ch.D. 549, 558. See *ante*, pp. 53–55.
[43] Com.Dig. Action on the Case for a Nuisance, A.
[44] See *post*, Chap. 11.
[45] (1835) 2 C.M. & R. 34.
[46] (1857) 1 H. & N. 916.
[47] *Lady Browne's Case* (1572) 3 Dyer 319b, cited in *Sury* v. *Pigott* (1625) Palmer 446; Com.Dig. Action on the Case for a Nuisance, A; *Baten's Case* (1610) 9 Rep. 53b, recognised in *Fay* v. *Prentice* (1845) 1 C.B. 828.

his house, by which the water used to fall from his house, and another levies a house paramount the spout, so that the water cannot fall as it was wont but falls upon the walls of the house, by which the timber of the house perishes, this is a nuisance." [48] Where a man who had not acquired any easement of eavesdrop built his roof with eaves which discharged rain-water by a spout into adjoining premises, whereby the reversion in such premises was damaged, the reversioner could sue. [49] It was not necessary to prove that rain had actually fallen. [50]

The right of eavesdrop will not be lost by raising the house. [1] The occupier of a house who has a right to have the rain fall from the eaves of it upon another man's land cannot by spouts discharge it upon such land in a body. [2] For such an act trespass would not lie, but case. [3] The flow of water for twenty years from the eaves of a house will not give a right to the neighbour to insist that the house shall not be altered so as to diminish the quantity of water flowing from the roof. [4] It may be noted here that a legal origin was presumed for the right of discharging water from a highway through a pipe on to adjoining land. [5]

5.—ARTIFICIAL WATERCOURSES

Basis of rights

Artificial watercourses occur frequently, especially in parts of the country where mining is carried on. A common instance of an artificial watercourse is where a system of draining is created for a mine whereby the water is pumped up and flows away from the mining property through the lands of several neighbouring landowners to join some river or lake. [6] Another instance is where an artificial watercourse is constructed for diverting water from a natural stream for use at a mill not itself situate on the natural stream. [7] The rights in the water of artificial watercourses have been the subject of numerous judicial decisions.

Sir Montagu Smith, in delivering the advice of the Privy Council in *Rameshur* v. *Koonj*, [8] said:

"There is no doubt that the right to water flowing in a natural channel through a man's land and the right to water flowing to it through an artificial watercourse constructed on his neighbour's

---

48 Rolle, Abr. Nusans, G. 5, citing 18 Edw. 3, 22b; Vin.Abr. Nusance, G. 5.
49 *Tucker* v. *Newman* (1839) 11 A. & E. 40.
50 *Fay* v. *Prentice* (1845) 1 C.B. 828.
1 *Harvey* v. *Walters* (1872) L.R. 8 C.P. 162.
2 *Reynolds* v. *Clarke* (1725) 2 Ld.Raym. 1399.
3 *Reynolds* v. *Clarke, supra.*
4 *Wood* v. *Waud* (1849) 3 Exch. 748; *Greatrex* v. *Hayward* (1853) 8 Exch. 293, 294; *Arkwright* v. *Gell* (1839) 5 M. & W. 233.
5 *Att.-Gen.* v. *Copeland* [1902] 1 K.B. 690.
6 As in *Arkwright* v. *Gell* (1839) 5 M. & W. 233; *Wood* v. *Waud* (1849) 3 Exch. 748.
7 As in *Burrows* v. *Lang* [1901] 2 Ch. 502.
8 (1878) 4 App.Cas. 121, 126; a case in which disapproval was expressed of Lord Denman's ruling, in *Magor* v. *Chadwick* (1840) 11 A. & E. 586, that the law of natural and artificial watercourses was the same.

land, do not rest on the same principle. In the former case each successive riparian proprietor is prima facie entitled to the unimpeded flow of water in its natural course, and to its reasonable enjoyment as it passes through his land, as a natural incident to his ownership of it. In the latter, any right to the flow of the water must rest on some grant or arrangement, either proved or presumed, from or with the owners of the lands from which the water is artificially brought, or on some other legal origin."

Again, it was said by Vaughan Williams L.J. in *Baily & Co.* v. *Clark, Son & Morland* [9] that in the case of an artificial watercourse any right to the flow of the water must be based on some grant, whether in the nature of an easement or otherwise. The basis of every right to the flow of the water must be an agreement, expressed or presumed from the user, with the owners of the land through which the stream runs.

In ascertaining the rights in respect of an artificial watercourse, there must be taken into account, first, the character of the watercourse, whether it is temporary or permanent, secondly, the circumstances under which it was presumably created, and thirdly, the mode in which it has in fact been used and enjoyed. [10]

Permanent artificial watercourses

The court may conclude that the watercourse is a permanent one, [11] and in this case it is settled that prescriptive rights may be acquired. [12] The enjoyment on which the claim to such a prescriptive right is based must be " as of right," *i.e.* not by leave [13] or under a mistake. [14] There must also be a capable grantor of the easement. [15]

In the case of some artificial watercourses the origin of which is unknown the proper conclusion from the user of the water and other circumstances may be that the watercourse was originally constructed upon the condition that all the riparian owners should have the same rights as they would have had if the watercourse had been a natural one. [16] The result of such a conclusion would, it seems, be that not

---

[9] [1902] 1 Ch. 664.

[10] *Per* Stirling L.J., *Baily & Co.* v. *Clark, Son & Morland* [1902] 1 Ch. 668; applied in *Bartlett* v. *Tottenham* [1932] 1 Ch. 114.

[11] As in *Baily & Co.* v. *Clark, Son & Morland, supra*; *Lewis* v. *Meredith* [1913] 1 Ch. 571, 580. In *Gaved* v. *Martyn* (1865) 19 C.B.(N.S.) 732, the court held that the " lower launder " (one of the three streams in question in the action) was a good example of a stream artificially made but in its origin supplied by a natural spring, and subject to prescription, *i.e.* in effect, that this watercourse was a permanent one.

[12] *Ivimey* v. *Stocker* (1866) 1 Ch.App. 406, 409; *Rameshur* v. *Koonj* (1878) 4 App.Cas. 128; *Blackburne* v. *Somers* (1879) 5 L.R.Ir. 1; *Powell* v. *Butler* (1871) Ir.R. 5 C.L. 309.   [13] *Gaved* v. *Martyn* (1865) 19 C.B.(N.S.) 732.

[14] *Chamber Colliery Co.* v. *Hopwood* (1886) 32 Ch.D. 549.

[15] *McEvoy* v. *G.N. Railway* [1900] 2 I.R. 325.

[16] *Baily & Co.* v. *Clark, Son & Morland* [1902] 1 Ch. 665; *Whitmores (Edenbridge) Ltd.* v. *Stanford* [1909] 1 Ch. 427, 439; *Sutcliffe* v. *Booth* (1863) 32 L.J.Q.B. 136; *Roberts* v. *Richards* (1881) 50 L.J.Ch. 297. In *McCartney* v. *Londonderry & Lough Swilly Railway Co.*, the stream was in fact artificial, but the case was argued on the hypothesis that it was a natural one: see [1904] A.C. 303.

only could prescriptive rights be acquired, but also that the riparian owners would have in the water the ordinary rights known as natural rights.

Temporary artificial watercourses

On the other hand, the court may conclude that the watercourse is a temporary one, constructed for a temporary purpose,[17] as where a water-course was constructed and maintained for the purposes of a mill,[18] or for draining a mine.

The rules applicable to cases of this nature were discussed by Lord Abinger in delivering the judgment of the Court of Exchequer in *Arkwright* v. *Gell*.[19] That case turned upon the right of lower riparian owners, the occupiers of mills situate on a stream which drained a mine, to compel the mine-owners to continue such discharge. The court held that no such right existed. Lord Abinger, delivering the judgment of the court, said [20]:

> "The stream . . . was an artificial watercourse, and the sole object for which it was made was to get rid of a nuisance to the mines, and to enable their proprietors to get the ores which lay within the mineral field drained by it; and the flow of water through that channel was, from the very nature of the case, of a temporary character, having its continuance only whilst the convenience of the mine-owners required it, and, in the ordinary course it would most probably cease when the mineral ore above its level should have been exhausted. . . . What, then, is the species of right or interest which the proprietor of the surface, where the stream issued forth, or his grantees, would have in such a watercourse at common law, and independently of the effect of user under the recent statute 2 & 3 Will. 4, c. 71? He would only have a right to use it for any purpose to which it was applicable so long as it continued there. An user for twenty years, or a longer time, would afford no pre-sumption of a grant of the right to the water in perpetuity; for such a grant would, in truth, be neither more nor less than an obligation on the mine-owner not to work his mines by the ordinary mode of getting minerals, below the level drained by that sough, and to keep the mines flooded up to that level, in order to make the flow of water constant, for the benefit of those who had used it for some profitable purpose. How can it be supposed that the mine-owners could have meant to burthen themselves with such a servitude, so destruc-tive to their interests:—and what is there to raise an inference of such an intention? The mine-owner could not bring any action against the person using the stream of water, so that the omission to

17 As in *Hanna* v. *Pollock* [1900] 2 I.R. 664.
18 *Burrows* v. *Lang* [1901] 2 Ch. 502.
19 (1839) 5 M. & W. 203.
20 (1839) 5 M. & W. 203, 231–234. See also *ante*, p. 54.

bring an action could afford no argument in favour of the presumption of a grant; nor could he prevent the enjoyment of that stream of water by any act of his, except by at once making a sough at a lower level, and thus taking away the water entirely;—a course so expensive and inconvenient that it would be very unreasonable, and a very improper extension of the principle applied to the case of lights, to infer from the abstinence from such an act an intention to grant the use of the water in perpetuity as a matter of right. . . .

"It remains to be considered whether the statute 2 & 3 Will. 4, c. 71, gives to Mr. Arkwright and those who claim under him any such right, and we are clearly of opinion that it does not. The whole purview of the Act shews that it applies only to such rights as would before the Act have been acquired by the presumption of a grant from long user. The Act expressly requires enjoyment for different periods 'without interruption,' and therefore necessarily imports such a user as could be interrupted by someone 'capable of resisting the claim'; and it also requires it to be 'of right.' But the use of the water in this case could not be the subject of an action at the suit of the proprietors of the mineral field lying below the level of the Cromford Sough, and was incapable of interruption by them at any time during the whole period by any reasonable mode; and as against them it was not 'of right'; they had no interest to prevent it; and until it became necessary to drain the lower part of the field, indeed at all times, it was wholly immaterial to them what became of the water so long as their mines were freed from it."

After *Arkwright* v. *Gell*,[21] where the rights of lower riparian owners when asserted as against the creator of an artificial stream were discussed, there came before the same court *Wood* v. *Waud*,[22] where the question arose as to the same rights when asserted as against upper riparian owners. In the last-mentioned case water from the working of a colliery had for more than twenty years flowed through two artificial channels called the Bowling Sough and Low Moor Sough. The first passed directly through the plaintiffs' land. The second passed into a natural stream, which, so augmented, passed through the plaintiffs' land. The defendants, having works on each channel above the points where they respectively arrived at the plaintiffs' land and at the Bowling Sough, diverted the water of each. The channels were subterranean, but the court determined the question as it would have stood if they had been surface streams. Pollock C.B., delivering the judgment of the court, said[23]:

"The right to artificial watercourses, as against the party creating them, surely must depend upon the character of the water-

21 (1839) 5 M. & W. 203.
22 (1849) 3 Exch. 748.   23 (1849) 3 Exch. 748, 777–780.

course, whether it be of a permanent or temporary nature, and upon the circumstances under which it was created.[24] The enjoyment for twenty years of a stream diverted or penned up by permanent embankments clearly stands upon a different footing from the enjoyment of a flow of water originating in the mode of occupation or alteration of a person's property, and presumably of a temporary character and liable to variation.

" The flow of water for twenty years from the eaves of a house could not give a right to the neighbour to insist that the house should not be pulled down or altered, so as to diminish the quantity of water flowing from the roof. The flow of water from a drain for the purposes of agricultural improvements for twenty years could not give a right to the neighbour so as to preclude the proprietor from altering the level of his drains for the greater improvement of the land.[25] The state of circumstances in such cases show that one party never intended to give, nor the other to enjoy, the use of the stream as a matter of right. If, then, this had been a question between the plaintiffs and the colliery owners, it seems to us that the plaintiffs could not have maintained an action for omitting to pump water by machinery. . . . Nor, if the colliery proprietors had chosen to pump out the water from the pit, from whence the stream flowed continuously, and caused what is termed the natural flow to cease, could the plaintiffs, in our opinion, have sued them for so doing. But this case is different. The water has been permitted to flow in an artificial channel by the colliery owners, and for sixty years. And the question is one of more difficulty, whether the plaintiffs can sue another person, a proprietor and occupier of the land above and through which the sough passes not claiming under or authorised by them, for diverting the water.

" The case of the Bowling Sough differs from the Low Moor Sough in this, that the plaintiffs, in 1838 used the water of the Bowling Sough where it passes through their land, by making a communication to their reservoir, for working the mill. Have the plaintiffs a right to the water of this sough. . . . ? It appears to us to be clear that, as they have a right to the Bowling Beck [the natural stream] as incident to their property on the banks and bed of it, they would have the right to all the water which actually formed part of that stream, as soon as it had become part,[26] whether such water came by natural means, as from springs, or from the surface of the hills above, or from rains or melted snow, or was added by artificial means, as from the drainage of lands or

24 *Baily & Co.* v. *Clark, Son & Morland* [1902] 1 Ch. 649. See as to the case of a drowned mine, and the temporary support occasioned by the water, the observations of Wood V.-C. in *N.E. Railway* v. *Elliott* (1860) 1 J. & H. 145.
25 *Greatrex* v. *Hayward* (1853) 8 Exch. 291; *Hanna* v. *Pollock* [1900] 2 I.R. 664; *Bartlett* v. *Tottenham* [1932] 1 Ch. 114.
26 See *Dudden* v. *Clutton Union* (1857) 1 H. & N. 627.

of colliery works; and if the proprietors of the drained lands or of the colliery works augmented the stream by pouring water into it, and so gave it to the stream, it would become part of the current; no distinction could then be made between the original natural stream and such accessions to it.

" But the question arises with respect to an artificial stream not yet united to the natural one.

" The proprietor of the land through which the Bowling Sough flows has no right to insist on the colliery owners causing all the waters from their works to flow through their land. These owners merely get rid of a nuisance to their works by discharging the water into the sough, and cannot be considered as giving it to one more than another of the proprietors of the land through which that sough is constructed; each may take and use what passes through his land, and the proprietor of land below has no right to any part of that water until it has reached his own land—he has no right to compel the owners above to permit the water to flow through their lands for his benefit; and, consequently, he has no right of action if they refuse to do so.

" If they pollute the water, so as to be injurious to the tenant below, the case would be different.

" We think, therefore, that the plaintiffs have no right of action for the diversion of that water. The question as to the Low Moor Sough is less favourable to the plaintiffs, for this sough does not pass through their land at all.

" We are of opinion, that, if the plaintiffs would not be entitled to the water of the soughs if above ground, their being below ground in this case would probably make no difference. It does not certainly make a difference in favour of the plaintiffs." [27]

Of *Wood* v. *Waud* [28] it was said by Blackburn J. in *Mason* v. *Shrewsbury and Hereford Railway* [29] that this was in effect a decision that an active enjoyment in fact for more than the statutory period was not an enjoyment as of right, if during the period it was known that it was only permitted so long as some particular purpose was served. The nature of the sough showed that though the water had in fact flowed for sixty years, yet from the beginning it was only intended to flow so long as the coal owners did not think fit otherwise to drain their mine, and so was precarious.

In accordance with *Wood* v. *Waud*, [28] it was held in *Greatrex* v. *Hayward*, [30] that the flow of water for twenty years from a drain made for agricultural improvements did not give to the person through whose

[27] Cf. *Wardle* v. *Brocklehurst* (1859) 1 E. & E. 1058 at p. 1060; *Staffordshire and Worcestershire Canal Co.* v. *Birmingham Canal Co.* (1866) L.R. 1 H.L. 254; *Brymbo Water Co.* v. *Lester's Lime Co.* (1894) 8 R. 329.
[28] (1849) 3 Exch. 748.
[29] (1871) L.R. 6 Q.B. 578, 584.
[30] (1853) 8 Exch. 291.

land it flowed a right to the continuance of the flow, so as to preclude the proprietor of the land drained from altering his drains for improvement and so cutting off the supply.

Again, in *Bartlett* v. *Tottenham*,[31] it was held, in accordance with the two cases last cited, that no right could be acquired by prescription to receive water overflowing from a tank along an artificial watercourse constructed for a temporary purpose.

It follows from the above authorities that where the enjoyment of an artificial watercourse depends on temporary circumstances, no right to the uninterrupted flow of water can by prescription be acquired either against the creator of the stream [32] or against upper riparian owners through whose land the stream passes.[33]

Meaning of " temporary purpose "

As regards the question whether a watercourse should be held to have been constructed for a temporary purpose within the principle of the decision of *Arkwright* v. *Gell*,[34] it was said by Farwell J. in *Burrows* v. *Lang* [35] that the meaning of " temporary purpose " is not confined to a purpose that happens to last in fact for a few years only, but includes a purpose which is temporary in the sense that it may in the reasonable contemplation of the parties come to an end.

Watercourse not on neighbour's land

Again, it seems that it is more difficult to presume an agreement as to enjoyment when a watercourse is constructed entirely over the land of the creator than in the case of water pumped over the land of a neighbour.[36]

6.—PURITY AND POLLUTION

Purity

Every riparian owner on the banks of a natural stream is entitled as a natural right to have the stream flow past his land without sensible alteration in its character or quality.[37] He is accordingly entitled to insist that the water shall not be polluted by the refuse of a factory or the sewage of a town [38]; that very soft water shall not be made very hard water [39]; and that the water shall not be raised in temperature.[40] The right arises

---

31 [1932] 1 Ch. 114.
32 *Arkwright* v. *Gell* (1839) 5 M. & W. 203; *Burrows* v. *Lang* [1901] 2 Ch. 502.
33 *Wood* v. *Waud* (1849) 3 Exch. 748; *Mason* v. *Shrewsbury and Hereford Railway* (1871) L.R. 6 Q.B. 578.
34 (1839) 5 M. & W. 203.
35 [1901] 2 Ch. 508; see *Wright* v. *Macadam* [1949] 2 K.B. 744.
36 *Burrows* v. *Lang, supra*; see *McEvoy* v. *G.N. Railway* [1900] 2 I.R. 333.
37 *Young (John) & Co.* v. *Bankier Distillery Co.* [1893] A.C. 698.
38 *Crossley & Sons Ltd.* v. *Lightowler* (1867) 2 Ch.App. 478; *Jones* v. *Llanrwst U.D.C.* [1911] 1 Ch. 393; *Magor* v. *Chadwick* (1840) 11 A. & E. 571.
39 *Young (John) & Co.* v. *Bankier Distillery Co.* [1893] A.C. 698.
40 See *Tipping* v. *Eckersley* (1855) 2 K. & J. 264; *Pride of Derby and Derbyshire Angling Association* v. *British Celanese Ltd.* [1953] Ch. 149.

in respect of the ownership of the bank, independently of the ownership of the bed of the stream.[41]   Anyone who fouls the water infringes the riparian owner's right of property, and he can therefore maintain an action to restrain pollution without proving that there has been actual damage.[42]   The natural right to purity extends to underground water.[43] Again, it is settled that prima facie no man has a right to use his land in such a way as to be a nuisance to his neighbour.[44]   Accordingly, if a man puts poison or filth on his land, with the result that water percolating underground from his own to his neighbour's land is polluted, the neighbour has a right of action.[45]

The fact that the stream has already been polluted by A is not a defence to an action to restrain pollution by B.[46]   Again, if the acts of several persons which independently would not produce pollution result in producing pollution when combined, each of them may be restrained.[47]   The grantee of a right of fishing can obtain an injunction to restrain pollution without proving actual pecuniary loss, because the pollution is the disturbance of a legal right,[48] and the defendant in such an action is not in a position to set up *jus tertii* against a possessory title.[49]   On the other hand, an inhabitant of a town who, in common with other inhabitants, has been accustomed to take water from a river passing the town, cannot maintain an action for pollution; his only remedy is by indictment.[50]

Rights acquired by prescription

As in the case of the natural rights of user and flow, so in the case of the natural right of purity, rights may be acquired by prescription which interfere with the natural right.   The second section of the Prescription Act refers to claims which may be lawfully made by custom, prescription, or grant to any watercourse or the use of any water.   A claim to a watercourse within the section includes a claim to send through another's watercourse either polluted water [1] or sand and rubble,[2] and generally it is clear that a right may be acquired by

---

41 *Jones* v. *Llanrwst U.D.C.* [1911] 1 Ch. 393, 402.
42 *Ibid.*
43 *Hodgkinson* v. *Ennor* (1863) 4 B. & S. 229. As has been seen, p. 210, *ante*, every man has the right to appropriate all underground water percolating through an undefined channel on his land.
44 *Ballard* v. *Tomlinson* (1885) 29 Ch.D. 126.
45 *Ibid.* ; *Turner* v. *Mirfield* (1865) 34 Beav. 390.
46 *Crossley & Sons Ltd.* v. *Lightowler* (1867) 2 Ch.App. 478.
47 *Blair* v. *Deakin* (1887) 57 L.T. 522 ; *Pride of Derby and Derbyshire Angling Association Ltd.* v. *British Celanese Ltd.* [1952] 1 All E.R. 1326.
48 *Fitzgerald* v. *Firbank* [1897] 2 Ch. 96; *Nicholls* v. *Ely Beet Sugar Factory Ltd.* [1936] Ch. 343.
49 *Fitzgerald* v. *Firbank* [1897] 2 Ch. 96; *Nicholls* v. *Ely Beet Sugar Factory Ltd.* [1931] 2 Ch. 84.
50 *R.* v. *Bristol Dock Co.* (1810) 12 East 429.
 1 *Wright* v. *Williams* (1836) 1 M. & W. 77.
 2 *Carlyon* v. *Lovering* (1857) 1 H. & N. 784. Compare *Murgatroyd* v. *Robinson* (1857) 7 E. & B. 391.

prescription to pollute a stream,[3] but such a right can only be acquired by the continuance of perceptible injury for twenty years.[4] Householders may obtain a prescriptive right to discharge sewage into a local authority's sewers.[5]

There can, however, be no prescriptive right to justify a public nuisance [6]; and, as title by prescription is founded upon the presumption of a grant, if no grant could lawfully have been made, by reason of statutes passed to prevent pollution, no presumption can arise and a claim to a prescriptive right must fail.[7] The principal statutes now in force are the Rivers (Prevention of Pollution) Act 1951, the Clean Rivers (Estuaries and Tidal Waters) Act 1960 and the Rivers (Prevention of Pollution) Acts 1951 to 1961. Before the introduction by the Act of 1951 of the present system of control (now exercised by the river authorities established by the Water Resources Act 1963 [7a]) over the discharge of trade and sewage effluent, the Rivers Pollution Prevention Act 1876 [7b] prohibited the drainage of effluent into streams except where it was carried along a channel used, constructed or in the process of construction when that Act was passed on August 15, 1876. It follows that, so long as that Act was in force, a prescriptive right to pollute could seldom be established.[7c] By virtue of section 7 of the Act of 1951, however, a river authority can consent to the bringing into use of new or altered outlets for the discharge of trade or sewage effluent to streams and to the making of any new discharge of trade or sewage effluent to streams; and section 1 of the Act of 1961 extended the control to discharges not controlled as new discharges. In so far as effluent may now, by virtue of a consent having been given, be discharged into a stream without contravening any statute, a prescriptive right to discharge may be acquired to the detriment of lower riparian owners who fail to take the necessary steps to protect their interests.

Right acquired by agreement : Rights of licensees

As regards artificial watercourses, we have seen that in some cases the proper conclusion may be that the watercourse was originally constructed upon the condition that all the riparian owners should have the same rights as they would have had if the watercourse had been a

---

[3] *Baxendale* v. *McMurray* (1867) 2 Ch.App. 790; *McIntyre* v. *McGavin* [1893] A.C. 268, 274 (refuse from factory); *Att.-Gen.* v. *Dorking Guardians* (1882) 20 Ch.D. 595; *Brown* v. *Dunstable Corporation* [1899] 2 Ch. 378 (sewage).

[4] *Goldsmid* v. *Tunbridge Wells Improvement Commissioners* (1866) 1 Ch.App. 349; *Liverpool Corporation* v. *Coghill* [1918] 1 Ch. 307.

[5] *Harrington* v. *Derby Corporation* [1905] 1 Ch. 205, 219, *per* Buckley J.

[6] *Att.-Gen.* v. *Barnsley* [1874] W.N. 37; *Butterworth* v. *West Riding Rivers Board* [1909] A.C. 45, 57.

[7] *Hulley* v. *Silversprings Bleaching and Dyeing Co.* [1922] 2 Ch. 268, 282, *per* Eve J.

[7a] See p. 214, *ante.* Formerly the river boards exercised control.

[7b] ss. 3, 4 (repealed by the Rivers (Prevention of Pollution) Act 1951, s. 12 (2) and Sched. 3).

[7c] See *George Legge and Son Ltd.* v. *Wenlock Corporation* [1938] A.C. 204.

natural one.[8] In these cases it seems that the riparian owners would
have the natural right of purity. In other cases the proper conclusion
may be that the watercourse was a temporary one constructed for a
temporary purpose.[9] In these cases it seems that, apart from prescription, appropriation of the water by a person entitled to appropriate it
gives such a person the right to insist that the water shall not be polluted
to his injury.[10]

In *Whaley* v. *Laing* [10] the plaintiff, by permission of a canal company, made a communication from the canal to his own premises, by
which water was brought on to them, with which water he fed his
boilers. The defendant fouled the water in the canal, whereby the
water as it came into the plaintiff's premises was fouled, and by the use
of it his boilers were injured. The defendant had no permission from
the canal owners to do what he did. The Court of Exchequer gave
judgment for the plaintiff, on the ground that, as the defendant was
the cause of dirty water flowing on to the plaintiff's premises without
any right to do so, he was liable to an action. The court expressly
abstained from giving any opinion upon the question, whether an action
would have been maintainable against the defendant if the defendant
had diverted the water, or if the plaintiff had been obliged to go to the
canal and fetch the water instead of its flowing into his premises. In
the Exchequer Chamber the judgment was reversed, but for reasons
involving no dissent from the ground on which judgment in the court
below was based. The judgments in the Exchequer Chamber show,
however, that it was considered very doubtful whether a person, having
a mere permission from a riparian owner to take water out of a stream,
can maintain an action against a wrongdoer for diverting or fouling the
stream higher up.

The question as to the purity rights of a licensee from a riparian
owner was subsequently raised in the case of a natural stream.[11] In
Stockport Waterworks Co. v. *Potter* the plaintiff sued the defendant
for fouling the water of the Mersey, coming to its waterworks through
a tunnel which it had made under a grant from a riparian proprietor.
The Court of Exchequer held that it was not entitled to sue. The reason
of the decision is given in the judgment of Pollock C.B. and Channell B.
(in which Wilde B. concurred) as follows [12]:

"It is difficult to perceive any possible legal foundation for
a right to have the river kept pure in a person situate as this
company is.

"There seems to be no authority for contending that a riparian
proprietor can keep the land abutting on the river, the possession

---

8 *Ante*, p. 224.
9 *Ante*, p. 225.
10 *Whaley* v. *Laing* (1857) 2 H. & N. 476; (1858) 3 H. & N. 675.
11 (1864) 3 H. & C. 300.
12 (1864) 3 H. & C. 300, 326–327.

of which gives him his water rights, and at the same time transfer those rights or any of them, and thus create a right in gross by assigning a portion of his rights appurtenant.

" It seems to us clear that the rights which a riparian proprietor has with respect to the water are entirely derived from his possession of land abutting on the river. If he grants away any portion of his land so abutting, then the grantee becomes a riparian proprietor and has similar rights. But if he grants away a portion of his estate not abutting on the river, then clearly the grantee of the land would have no water rights by virtue merely of his occupation. Can he have them by express grant? It seems to us that the true answer to this is, that he can have them against the grantor,[13] but not so as to sue other persons in his own name for the infringement of them. The case of *Hill* v. *Tupper*,[14] recently decided in this Court, is an authority for the proposition that a person cannot create by grant new rights of property, so as to give the grantee a right of suing in his own name for an interruption of the right by a third party."

This case was approved in the Court of Appeal and treated as expressly deciding that a riparian owner cannot, except as against himself, confer on one who is not a riparian owner any right to use the water of the stream, and that any user of the stream by a non-riparian proprietor, even under a grant from a riparian proprietor, is wrongful if it sensibly affects the flow of the water by the lands of other riparian proprietors.[15]

In *McCartney* v. *Londonderry and Lough Swilly Railway Co.*[16] the House of Lords held that A, an upper riparian owner on a natural stream, had no right, as between himself and B, a lower riparian owner, to divert the water to a place outside A's tenement and there consume it for purposes unconnected with the tenement, although the damage suffered or likely to be suffered by B was small.

From *McCartney* v. *Londonderry and Lough Swilly Railway Co.*[17] it would appear that a lower riparian owner, even though his flow of water was not diminished or injured in quality (provided that the facts were not such as to bring the case within the maxim *de minimis non curat lex*), could prevent an upper riparian owner from permitting a third person to use the stream. Such user would be foreign to or unconnected with the tenement of the upper riparian owner, and the

[13] *Hamelin* v. *Bannerman* [1895] A.C. 237.
[14] (1863) 2 H. & C. 121; *ante*, p. 19.
[15] *Ormerod* v. *Todmorden Joint Stock Mill Co. Ltd.* (1883) 11 Q.B.D. 155.
[16] See [1904] A.C. 301, 310, 313, and p. 202, *ante*. See also the words of Bowen L.J.: " The only legitimate user by him [a riparian proprietor] of the water, other than such rights as he may have acquired by prescription, is for purposes connected with his ordinary occupation of the land upon the bank "; *Ormerod* v. *Todmorden Joint Stock Mill Co. Ltd.* (1883) 11 Q.B.D. 172.
[17] [1904] A.C. 301.

permission given would therefore be in excess of the rights of such owner.

In *Kensit* v. *G.E. Railway*[18] a person who held a licence from an upper riparian owner on a natural stream took water from the stream, and after using it for purposes unconnected with the riparian owner's tenement returned it to the stream unaltered in quality or quantity. A lower riparian owner having brought an action to restrain this user, the Court of Appeal refused an injunction. The grounds of their decision were thus stated by Cotton L.J.[19]:

> "The plaintiffs say, and they are right, that a riparian owner is in this position, that he can maintain an action for interference with his right, even although he does not show that at the time he has suffered any actual damage and loss. But then we must consider what the right of a riparian owner is as regards the lower riparian owners. It is this, that he has a right to take and use the water as it runs past him for all reasonable purposes. . . . Then, as against the upper proprietors, he has this right, he is entitled to have the flow of the water in the natural bed of the river coming down to him unaltered in quality and quantity, subject only to the right of the upper proprietors, such as he has against the proprietors below him, to take the water for reasonable purposes. Then he has this right, that where the stream comes opposite to or through his land it shall come in its ordinary and accustomed channel.
>
> "Now has that been interfered with? I am of opinion it has not. The quantity and quality of the stream when it comes into the plaintiff's land is the same as it always was."

And Lindley L.J. pointed out[20] that, so long as the defendant did only what he was then doing, there was no possibility of injury.

The theories applied by the House of Lords in *McCartney* v. *Londonderry and Lough Swilly Railway Co.*[21] and by the Court of Appeal in *Kensit* v. *G.E. Railway*[22] seem at first sight inconsistent. Lord Lindley was a party to both decisions, and they are to be reconciled (if at all) in the manner pointed out by him in his judgment in the House of Lords in *McCartney* v. *Londonderry and Lough Swilly Railway Co.*,[23] where he stated that the *ratio decidendi* in *Kensit* v. *G.E. Railway*[24] was that what was there complained of never could grow into a prescriptive title, inasmuch as all the water taken was returned unaltered in quantity or quality.

18 (1884) 27 Ch.D. 122.
19 (1884) 27 Ch.D. 122, 130.
20 *Ibid.* 135.
21 [1904] A.C. 301.
22 (1884) 27 Ch.D. 122.
23 [1904] A.C. 301, 313.
24 (1884) 27 Ch.D. 122.

7.—ACQUISITION OF WATER RIGHTS

Acquisition by express grant

Water rights may be acquired by express grant. As to the construction of an express grant, it has been laid down that the grant of a " watercourse " may mean (1) the right to the running water; or (2) the drain which contains the water; or (3) the land over which the water flows.[25] In the absence of words showing a contrary intention, a grant of a watercourse will be held to mean the grant of the right to the running water,[26] but the natural meaning of " watercourse " seems to be the channel, whether natural or artificial, through which a stream flows.[27] The reservation of a right to make a watercourse included the right to divert water and to use the water diverted.[28] A " spring of water " means a natural source of water of a definite and well-marked extent.[29] A " stream " is water which runs in a defined course, so as to be capable of diversion.[30] The same word was held not to include either the spring or water soaking through marshy ground.[31] In *Northam* v. *Hurley* [32] it was held, on the construction of the grant of a watercourse from the land of the grantor to the land of the grantee, that the grantor had acted wrongfully in altering the channel on his own land, although no damage had occurred to the grantee from such alteration. The effect of special words in an express grant or reservation of water was also considered in *Rawstron* v. *Taylor*,[33] *Lee* v. *Stevenson* [34] and *Finlinson* v. *Porter*.[35] A grant (in pursuance of a statute) of the exclusive right of drainage through a watercourse gave the grantee, not merely an easement, but (for the purpose of rating) possession of the watercourse.[36]

A grant of all streams of water that might be found in land, when at the time of the grant there were one stream and several wells, was held to include the underground water in the land; the grantor could not, nor could anyone claiming under him, do anything the effect of which could be to drain such underground water from the land.[37] On the other hand, a grant of an artificial watercourse as shown in a plan, with the stream and springs flowing into or feeding the same, was held to be a grant of the artificial channel and of the definite springs and streams feeding it, and of such other water as should run into and down

25 *Taylor* v. *St. Helens Corpn.* (1877) 6 Ch.D. 264, 271, where the effect of the grant of an artificial watercourse was considered.
26 *Taylor* v. *St. Helens Corpn.* (1877) 6 Ch.D. 264.
27 *Remfry* v. *Natal (Surveyor-General)* [1896] A.C. 558, 560; *Anderson* v. *Cleland* [1910] 2 I.R. 377; but see *Doe* d. *Egremont (Earl)* v. *Williams* (1848) 11 Q.B.D. 700.
28 *Remfry* v. *Natal (Surveyor-General)* [1896] A.C. 558.
29 *Taylor* v. *St. Helens Corpn.* (1877) 6 Ch.D. 264.
30 *Ibid.*
31 *McNab* v. *Robertson* [1897] A.C. 129.
32 (1853) 1 E. & B. 665.
33 (1855) 11 Exch. 369.
34 (1858) 27 L.J.Q.B. 263.   35 (1875) L.R. 10 Q.B. 188.
36 *Holywell Union* v. *Halkyn Drainage Co.* [1895] A.C. 117.
37 *Whitehead* v. *Parks* (1858) 2 H. & N. 870.

the channel as it stood, and not to justify the grantees in enlarging the channel so as to carry off more water.[38]

Acquisition by custom

Water rights may also be acquired by custom.[39]

8.—MISCELLANEOUS RIGHTS OF RIPARIAN OWNERS

To place erections on bed

It may be useful to add here some further decisions as to the rights of riparian owners. Thus it has been laid down that the owner of both banks of a non-tidal river may build on the bed, provided that he does not alter the natural flow of the water above or below his property.[40] Again, the owner of one bank only cannot as against the opposite owner build on his own moiety of the bed in such a manner as to interfere with the natural flow of the stream; and was restrained, although there was no proof that damage had been sustained or was likely to be sustained.[41] This principle has been extended to tidal navigable rivers.[42]

To divert flood water

As regards the rights of erection possessed by a riparian owner generally, it seems that he may erect a post for a ferry or for mooring a boat, or plant stakes to prevent poaching,[43] or place an erection on his own bank to protect it.[44] So it has been laid down that a riparian owner has a right to raise the banks upon his own land so as to prevent the water from overflowing his land, with this restriction, that he does not occasion injury to the property of others.[45] If an extraordinary flood is seen to be coming on land, the owner may, at least in the case of an artificial watercourse, protect his land from it without being responsible for the consequences, although his neighbour may be injured.[46] If, on the other hand, the flood has already come, the owner

---

[38] Taylor v. St. Helens Corpn. (1877) 6 Ch.D. 264; McNab v. Robertson [1897] A.C. 129.

[39] Bastard v. Smith (1837) 2 Mood. & R. 129; Gaved v. Martyn (1865) 19 C.B.(N.S.) 732 (customary right to divert); Carlyon v. Lovering (1857) 1 H. & N. 784 (customary right to pollute); Harrop v. Hirst (1868) L.R. 4 Exch. 43 (customary right to use of water).

[40] Orr-Ewing v. Colquhoun (1877) 2 App.Cas. 839; see Greyvensteyn v. Hattingh [1911] A.C. 359; Radstock Co-operative & Industrial Society Ltd. v. Norton-Radstock U.D.C. [1968] Ch. 605.

[41] Bickett v. Morris (1866) L.R. 1 H.L.Sc. & Div. 47.

[42] Att.-Gen. v. Lonsdale (Earl) (1868) L.R. 7 Eq. 377; Att.-Gen. v. Terry (1874) 9 Ch.App. 423; see Exeter Corpn. v. Devon (Earl) (1870) L.R. 10 Eq. 232.

[43] Withers v. Purchase (1889) 60 L.T. 821; compare Att.-Gen. v. Wright [1897] 2 Q.B. 318.

[44] Ridge v. Midland Railway (1888) 53 J.P. 55; see Bickett v. Morris, L.R. 1 H.L.Sc. & Div. 47.

[45] R. v. Trafford (1831) 1 B. & Ad. 874; Menzies v. Breadalbane (1828) 3 Bligh (N.S.) 414, 418; Att.-Gen. v. Lonsdale (Earl) (1868) L.R. 7 Eq. 377.

[46] Nield v. L. & N.W. Railway (1874) L.R. 10 Ex. 4; see Whalley v. Lancashire and Yorkshire Railway (1884) 13 Q.B.D. 131, 136, 140; Maxey v. G.N. Railway (1912) 106 L.T. 429. Compare the similar right on the seashore: R. v. Pagham (1828) 8 B. & C. 355.

must not, for the purpose of getting rid of the mischief, injure his neighbour.[47]

Navigable rivers

It may also be useful to notice some decisions as to navigable rivers. In the case of these rivers the public have a right to use the river for navigation similar to the right which they have to pass along a public highway through private land,[48] and an artificial navigable river may be dedicated as a public highway,[49] but the analogy between a navigable river and a public highway is not complete.[50] In the case of the soil of navigable rivers there may be also public rights incidental to the right of navigation, such as fixing moorings and anchoring.[51] As regards the right of access, it is settled that in general a riparian owner on a navigable river has, subject to the public right of navigation, the same right of access to the river as such an owner has on a non-navigable river.[52]

[47] *Whalley* v. *Lancashire and Yorkshire Railway* (1884) 13 Q.B.D. 131.
[48] *Orr-Ewing* v. *Colquhoun* (1877) 2 App.Cas. 839; see *Original Hartlepool Co.* v. *Gibb* (1877) 5 Ch.D. 713.
[49] *Att.-Gen.* v. *Simpson* [1901] 2 Ch. 673, 716; see *Simpson* v. *Att.-Gen.* [1904] A.C. 476, 494.
[50] *Att.-Gen.* v. *Simpson* [1901] 2 Ch. 673, 687; [1904] A.C. 476, 509.
[51] *Att.-Gen.* v. *Wright* [1897] 2 Q.B. 318; *Denaby* v. *Anson* [1911] 1 K.B. 171.
[52] *Lyon* v. *Fishmongers' Co.* (1876) 1 App.Cas. 662; *North Shore Railway Co.* v. *Pion* (1889) 14 App.Cas. 612; *Hindson* v. *Ashby* [1896] 2 Ch. 1, 30.

CHAPTER 7

RIGHT TO LIGHT

Acquisition of easement of light

The right to flowing water in a natural stream, it has already been shown, is an ordinary right of property requiring no length of time to fortify it. The right to light seems to depend, however, upon very different grounds. The passage of light over lands unincumbered by buildings must necessarily have existed from time immemorial: but the use of the light so passing, by means of windows in a house or otherwise, confers no right unless it has been continued during twenty years. The natural rights of the owner of property in this respect seem to be defined by the legal maxim, *cujus est solum ejus est usque ad coelum et ad inferos*, and the passage of light over adjoining lands affords *per se* no evidence of the enlargement of such right by an easement.

The right to the reception of light in a lateral direction without obstruction is an easement. The strict right of property entitles the owner to so much light only as falls perpendicularly on his land. He may build to the very extremity of his own land, and no action can be maintained against him for disturbing his neighbour's privacy by opening windows which overlook the adjoining property.[1] But it is competent to such neighbour to obstruct the windows so opened by building against them on his own land, at any time during twenty years after their construction, and thus prevent the acquisition of the easement of light[2]; if, however, that period is once suffered to elapse, his long acquiescence becomes evidence, as in the case of other easements, of a title, by the assent of the party whose land is subject to it.

In *Penwarden* v. *Ching*,[3] a case decided before the Prescription Act, a claim by the defendant to have light pass through a window which had been made twenty-one years before action was resisted by the plaintiff on the ground that the window was shown not to be an

---

[1] *Chandler* v. *Thompson* (1811) 3 Camp. 80; *Tapling* v. *Jones* (1865) 11 H.L.C. 290, 305; see *ante*, p. 26.
[2] See *per* Littledale J. in *Moore* v. *Rawson* (1824) 3 B. & C. 340; *Tapling* v. *Jones*, *ante*; and, as showing that a railway company has in this respect the same rights as an individual, see *Bonner* v. *G.W. Railway* (1883) 24 Ch.D. 1; *Foster* v. *London, Chatham & Dover Railway* [1895] 1 Q.B. 711.
[3] (1829) Moo. & Mal. 400.

ancient window. Tindal C.J. said: " The question is, not whether the window is what is strictly called ancient, but whether it is such as the law in indulgence to rights, has in modern times so called, and to which the defendant has a right."

Presumption of grant

The right to light can be claimed by prescription at common law or by lost grant (both of which methods existed before the Prescription Act 1832) as well as under the Act.[4] Where light is claimed in either of the two first-mentioned methods a grant must be presumed [5] and the enjoyment must be as of right [6]; but where light is claimed under section 3 of the Prescription Act 1832 it is not necessary to presume a grant,[7] or that the actual enjoyment should be as of right.[8]

The mode in which an easement may be acquired, namely, by grant, express or implied, or by prescription, has already been considered; but certain questions, peculiar to the easement of light, should be referred to in this place.

User in respect of vacant land

It is clear that the right to light cannot be acquired by user in respect of vacant land.

Where the right to light is claimed by prescription at common law or by lost grant, the last-mentioned rule is laid down in the reporter's marginal note to *Roberts* v. *Macord*,[9] which appears to be sound. The note runs as follows:

> " The use of an open space of ground in a particular way requiring light and air for twenty years does not give a right to preclude the adjoining owner from building on his land so as to obstruct the light and air." [10]

Where the right to light is claimed under the Prescription Act 1832, the enjoyment must have been had to and for a " building," in which there must be some aperture. This aperture may be a skylight,[11] or the glass roof and sides of a greenhouse,[12] but not an ordinary doorway.[13] The aperture defines the area which is to be kept free over the

---

4 *Aynsley* v. *Glover* (1874) 10 Ch.App. 283, *ante*, p. 133; *Tisdall* v. *McArthur & Co. (Steel and Metal) Ltd.* [1951] I.R. 228.
5 *Gardner* v. *Hodgson's Kingston Brewery Co.* [1903] A.C. 229, 239.
6 *Colls* v. *Home and Colonial Stores* [1904] A.C. 179, 206.
7 *Tapling* v. *Jones* (1865) 11 H.L.C. 290.
8 *Colls* v. *Home and Colonial Stores* [1904] A.C. 179, 205.
9 (1832) 1 Mood. & R. 230.
10 See *e.g. Potts* v. *Smith* (1868) L.R. 6 Eq. 311, 318; *Garritt* v. *Sharp* (1835) 3 A. & E. 325; *Scott* v. *Pape* (1886) 31 Ch.D. 554, 571; *Harris* v. *De Pinna* (1886) 33 Ch.D. 238.
11 *Harris* v. *Kinloch* [1895] W.N. 60; *Easton* v. *Isted* [1903] 1 Ch. 405; *Smith* v. *Evangelization Society (Incorporated) Trust* [1933] Ch. 515.
12 *Clifford* v. *Holt* [1899] 1 Ch. 698; *Born* v. *Turner* [1900] 2 Ch. 211.
13 *Levet* v. *Gas Light & Coke Co.* [1919] 1 Ch. 24.

servient tenement.[14]   But in the case of an alteration of the dominant tenement, the preservation of the right to light depends, not on identity of aperture, but upon identity of light.[15]

In assessing damages for obstruction of the light to a building, regard may be had to the potentialities of the dominant tenement as a building site.[16]

Actual user by building need not be shown

For the purpose of a claim under the Act no actual enjoyment (in the sense of user and occupation) of the light need be shown; it is sufficient that the aperture existed, and that the light might have been used at any time,[17] and the fact that a room has been used for a purpose requiring less than a normal quantity of light does not diminish the amount of light claimable therefor.[18]

Extent of right acquired by user

Considerable doubt formerly existed as to the extent of the right acquired by enjoyment—*viz.* whether the access of light through a window for the necessary period entitled the owner to object to *any* substantial diminution of the light which had been accustomed to pass through the window; or whether the adjoining owner might build so as substantially to diminish the light, provided that no actual nuisance is created.   After a long controversy the question was settled in the latter sense [19]; but some mention of the earlier authorities appears to be desirable.

In *Aldred's Case*,[20] an action on the case for building a pig-sty and obstructing lights, it was resolved that the action was well maintainable,

> " for in a house four things are desired, *habitatio hominis, delectatio inhabitantis, necessitas luminis et salubritas aeris*, and for nuisance done to three of them an action lies, *sc.* (1) to the habitation of a man, for that is the principal end of a house; (2) for hindrance of the light, for the ancient form of an action on the case was significant, *sc., quod messuagium horrida tenebritate obscuratum fuit*," etc.

[14] *Scott* v. *Pape* (1886) 31 Ch.D. 554, 575.
[15] *Andrews* v. *Waite* [1907] 2 Ch. 500.
[16] *Griffith* v. *Richard Clay & Sons Ltd.* [1912] 1 Ch. 291; *Wills* v. *May* [1923] 1 Ch. 317.
[17] *Courtauld* v. *Legh* (1869) L.R. 4 Exch. 126 (a case of an unfinished house); *Cooper* v. *Straker* (1888) 40 Ch.D. 21 (window with iron shutters only opened occasionally); *Collis* v. *Laugher* [1894] 3 Ch. 659 (window spaces opened, but no window sashes put in); *Smith* v. *Baxter* [1900] 2 Ch. 138 (windows obscured by shelves).
[18] *Price* v. *Hilditch* [1930] 1 Ch. 500.
[19] *Colls* v. *Home and Colonial Stores* [1904] A.C. 179; *Charles Semon & Co.* v. *Bradford Corpn.* [1922] 2 Ch. 737.
[20] (1611) 9 Co.Rep. 58b.

In *Fishmongers' Co.* v. *East India Co.*,[21] in refusing an application to restrain building so as to stop up lights, Lord Hardwicke said:

" As to the question of whether the plaintiffs' messuage is an ancient building so as to entitle them to the right of the lights, and whether the plaintiffs' lights will be darkened, I will not determine it here; for if it clearly appeared that what the defendants are doing is what the law considers as a nuisance, I would put it in a way to be tried. . . . But I am of opinion it is not a nuisance contrary to law; for it is not sufficient to say it will alter the plaintiffs' lights, for then no vacant piece of ground could be built on in the city; and here will be seventeen feet distance, and the law says it must be so near as to be a nuisance. It is true the value of the plaintiffs' house may be reduced by rendering the prospect less pleasant, but that is no reason to hinder a man from building on his own ground."

In *Back* v. *Stacey* [22] Best C.J. directed the jury that it was not sufficient to constitute an illegal obstruction that the plaintiff had in fact less light than before, nor that his warehouse, the part of his house principally affected, could not be used for all the purposes for which it might otherwise have been applied. In order to give a right of action and sustain the issue there must be a substantial deprivation of light, sufficient to render the occupation of the house uncomfortable and [23] to prevent the plaintiff from carrying on his accustomed business (that of a grocer) on the premises as beneficially as he had formerly done. His Lordship added that it might be difficult to draw the line, but the jury must distinguish between a partial inconvenience and a real injury to the plaintiff in the enjoyment of the premises.

In *Parker* v. *Smith* [24] Tindal C.J., in summing up, said:

" The question in this case is, whether the plaintiff has the same enjoyment now, which he used to have before, of light and air, in the occupation of his house; whether the alteration by carrying forward the wall to the height of ten feet has or has not occasioned the injury which he complains of. It is not every possible, every speculative exclusion of light which is the ground of an action; but that which the law recognises, is such a diminution of light as really makes the premises to a sensible degree less fit for the purposes of business. It appears that the defendants' premises had been injured by fire, and they re-erected them in a different manner. They have the right to re-erect in any way they please, with this single limitation, that the alteration which they make must not diminish the enjoyment by the plaintiff of light and air. It is

---

[21] (1752) 1 Dick. 163.
[22] (1826) 2 C. & P. 465.
[23] *Quaere* " or "; see *Dent* v. *Auction Mart Co.* (1866) L.R. 2 Eq. 238, 245.
[24] (1832) 5 C. & P. 438, 439–440; and see *Pringle* v. *Wernham* (1836) 7 C. & P. 377.

contended by the defendants that, on the whole, the light and air
are increased. If, as matters now stand, upon the evidence you have
heard, you think that this is a true proposition, then the plaintiff
will have no ground of action. But if, on the contrary, you think
that, in effect, these alterations (though they may certainly be
improvements), upon the whole diminish the quantity of light and
air, then you will find for the plaintiff with nominal damages; and
your verdict will have no other effect, than that of a notice to the
defendants, that they must pull down the building of which the
plaintiff complains."

In *Wells* v. *Ody* [25] Parke B. adopted the law as laid down by Tindal
C.J. in *Parker* v. *Smith*,[26] but left to the jury the question whether the
effect of the defendant's building was to diminish the light and air so as
sensibly to affect the occupation of the plaintiff's premises and make
them less fit for occupation.

Reviewing the authorities down to this point, it is noticeable that,
while in most of the earlier cases the question raised is whether the
effect of the building is to create a nuisance or not, in the cases from
Parker v. *Smith* [26] downwards more stress is laid on the diminution
of the light formerly enjoyed by the dominant owner.

In *Clarke* v. *Clark* [27] the defendant had erected a building which
undoubtedly diminished the amount of lateral light coming to the plaintiff's ancient window, and rendered the plaintiff's room less cheerful,
especially during the winter months. But Lord Cranworth refused an
injunction, saying that there was not such an obstruction of light as to
amount to a nuisance. He said [28]:

" The window in question still receives greatly more light than
falls to the lot of inhabitants of towns generally. . . . What the
plaintiff was bound to show was, that the buildings of the defendant
caused such an obstruction of light as to interfere with the ordinary
occupations of life. . . . The real question is not what is, scientifically estimated, the amount of light intercepted, but whether the
light is so obstructed as to cause material inconvenience to the
occupiers of the house in the ordinary occupations of life."

In *Yates* v. *Jack* [29] the same judge, holding that the defendant's
new buildings would materially interfere with the quantity of light
necessary or desirable for the plaintiffs in the conduct of their business,
restrained the defendant from building so as to darken, injure or
obstruct any of the ancient lights of the plaintiffs as the same were
enjoyed previously to the taking down by the defendant of his buildings

25 (1836) 7 C. & P. 410.
26 (1832) 5 C. & P. 438.
27 (1865) 1 Ch.App. 16. See also the discussion about this date of the alternative
   remedies of an injunction or damages in *Jackson* v. *Newcastle* (1864) 3 De G.J. &
   Sm. 275.
28 (1865) 1 Ch.App. 16, 20–21.
29 (1866) 1 Ch.App. 295.

on the opposite side of the street, and also from permitting to remain any buildings already erected which would cause any such obstruction. The judgment in this case indicates no intention on Lord Cranworth's part to depart from the rule laid down by him in *Clarke* v. *Clark*,[30] but the effect of the order (as set out above) was to preserve to the plaintiffs the whole of the light previously enjoyed by them, without any express reference to the question whether it could be diminished without causing a nuisance. The form of the order in *Yates* v. *Jack*,[31] which was in use for many years after that decision, and probably contributed to the uncertainty which existed as to the nature of the dominant owner's rights,[32] was in this respect modified in *Colls'* case.[33]

In *Durell* v. *Pritchard*,[34] *Curriers' Co.* v. *Corbett*[35] and *Robson* v. *Whittingham*,[36] Knight-Bruce and Turner L.JJ. followed *Clarke* v. *Clark*,[30] in each case refusing to grant an injunction on the ground that no material damage had been shown.

In *Kelk* v. *Pearson*[37] the principle was clearly stated by James L.J.

" On the part of the plaintiff," he says, " it was argued before us that this was an absolute right—that now, under the statute 2 & 3 Will. 4, c. 71, he had an absolute and indefeasible right by way of property to the whole amount of light and air which came through the windows into his house. . . . Now I am of opinion that the statute has in no degree whatever altered the pre-existing law as to the nature and extent of this right. The nature and extent of the right before the statute was to have that amount of light for a house which was sufficient, according to the ordinary notions of mankind, for the comfortable use and enjoyment of that house as a dwelling-house, if it was a dwelling-house, or for the beneficial use and occupation of the house if it was a warehouse, a shop, or other place of business. That was the extent of the easement—a right to prevent your neighbour from building upon his land so as to obstruct the access of sufficient light and air, to such an extent as to render the house substantially less comfortable and enjoyable ";

and he says that the absolute and indefeasible right given by the statute is not greater. Mellish L.J. laid down the rule in different terms; but it does not appear that he intended to differ from the above observations of James L.J.[38]

---

30 (1865) 1 Ch.App. 16.
31 (1866) 1 Ch.App. 295.
32 See *e.g.* the judgments in *Dent* v. *Auction Mart Co.* (1866) L.R. 2 Eq. 238; *Martin* v. *Headon* (1866) L.R. 2 Eq. 425; and *Calcraft* v. *Thompson* (1867) 15 W.R. 367, which cannot now be altogether relied upon as good law.
33 See *per* Lord Macnaghten [1904] A.C. 193.
34 (1865) 1 Ch.App. 244.
35 (1865) 4 De G.J. & Sm. 764.
36 (1866) 1 Ch.App. 442.
37 (1871) 6 Ch.App. 809, 811.
38 See *per* Lord Davey in *Colls'* case [1904] A.C. 200.

In *City of London Brewery Co.* v. *Tennant* [39] the same rule was repeated and applied, and an injunction was refused, Lord Selborne being a party to the decision. [40]

Summary of decisions as to right acquired by user

The judgments in *Clarke* v. *Clark*, [41] *Kelk* v. *Pearson*, [42] and *City of London Brewery Co.* v. *Tennant* [43] clearly laid down the rule that the court will not interfere to protect ancient lights unless there is such an obstruction of the light as to interfere with the comfortable use and enjoyment of the building according to the ordinary notions of mankind; in other words, unless a nuisance is caused. [44]

Some doubtful decisions

The impression derived from *Parker* v. *Smith* [45] and some of the succeeding cases, that the dominant owner was entitled to the whole of the light which had been accustomed to pass through his windows during the statutory period, was not finally removed even by the foregoing decisions. In *Scott* v. *Pape* [46] the repudiated doctrine reappeared in its most extreme form. In that case Cotton L.J. said [47]:

> " After twenty years the person who owns a dwelling-house, if he has used and enjoyed light, gets the absolute right to what he has used and enjoyed; and, in my opinion, the *quantum* of his enjoyment is defined by, and must depend on, the area of his windows, and also on the distance they are from other buildings. He acquires, in consequence of the position of other buildings and the size of the window, a right under this section [section 3 of the Prescription Act] to the enjoyment of that particular light which has come to his building. 'The access and use of light' depends upon the number of pencils of light which come directly or by refraction into that window."

Bowen L.J. was even more emphatic [48]:

> " Coming to the language of the section, what does it do? It seems to me that it creates an indefeasible right to the access of a specific quantity of light for the use of the house, workshop, or building."

In *Warren* v. *Brown* [49] the Court of Appeal, adopting a similar view, reversed a considered judgment of Wright J., [50] and granted an injunction,

---

39 (1873) 9 Ch.App. 212.
40 *Cf. Leech* v. *Schweder* (1874) 9 Ch.App. 463 (a case of grant).
41 (1865) 1 Ch.App. 16.
42 (1871) 6 Ch.App. 809.
43 (1873) 9 Ch.App. 212.
44 *Cf. Ecclesiastical Commissioners* v. *Kino* (1880) 14 Ch.D. 213.
45 (1832) 5 C. & P. 438.
46 (1886) 31 Ch.D. 554.
47 (1886) 31 Ch.D. 554, 568.
48 (1886) 31 Ch.D. 554, 571.
49 [1902] 1 K.B. 15.   50 [1900] 2 Q.B. 722.

notwithstanding that abundant light was left for purposes of ordinary habitation and business.

" If," said Romer L.J. in delivering the judgment of the court,[1] " ancient lights are interfered with substantially, and real damage thereby ensues to tenant or owner, then that tenant or owner is entitled to relief.

" With regard to the exact point arising in this case we think that, since the case of *Kelk* v. *Pearson*,[2] it is impossible to hold properly that the statutory right is not interfered with merely because after the interference the house may still come up to some supposed standard as to what a house ordinarily requires by way of light for the purposes of inhabitancy or business."

Colls v. Home and Colonial Stores

In *Colls* v. *Home and Colonial Stores*[3] the question was again raised, and carried to the House of Lords. Joyce J., before whom the action was tried, held that, if the plaintiffs were (as they contended) entitled to the full amount of light then enjoyed without appreciable diminution, they would have had a good cause of action upon the erection of the defendant's building. But he found as a fact that the plaintiffs' premises would, even after the erection of the defendant's building, be well and sufficiently lighted for all ordinary purposes of occupancy as a place of business; and, following the decision of Wright J. in *Warren* v. *Brown*[49] (which had not then been reversed), he dismissed the action. The Court of Appeal, following their own decision in *Warren* v. *Brown*,[49] reversed the decision of Joyce J. In the House of Lords, the decision of the Court of Appeal was reversed, and the judgment of Joyce J. restored, the decision of the Court of Appeal in *Warren* v. *Brown*[49] being at the same time overruled.

Lord Macnaghten considered that the principles governing the question were most clearly stated in *Back* v. *Stacey*[4] and *Parker* v. *Smith*.[5] The other learned Lords founded their judgments largely on the views expressed in *Clarke* v. *Clark*,[6] *Kelk* v. *Pearson*,[7] and *City of London Brewery Co.* v. *Tennant*,[8] of which they entirely approved. Lord Macnaghten said that the qualification of these views suggested by Bowen L.J. in *Scott* v. *Pape*[9] was not well founded. Lord Davey referred to the supposed inconsistency between Lord Cranworth's two judgments in *Clarke* v. *Clark*[6] and *Yates* v. *Jack*,[10] and said that the

1 [1902] 1 K.B. 15, 22.
2 (1871) 6 Ch.App. 809.
3 [1902] 1 Ch. 302; [1904] A.C. 179.
4 (1826) 2 C. & P. 465; see p. 241, *ante.*
5 (1832) 5 C. & P. 438; see p. 241, *ante.*
6 (1865) 1 Ch.App. 16; see p. 242, *ante.*
7 (1871) 6 Ch.App. 809; see p. 243, *ante.*
8 (1873) 9 Ch.App. 212; see p. 244, *ante.*
9 (1886) 31 Ch.D. 554; see p. 244, *ante.*
10 (1866) 1 Ch.App. 295.

language used by Lord Cranworth in the latter case was directed to the argument with which he was dealing. Lord Lindley pointed out that in *Yates* v. *Jack* [11] the plaintiff's right to light was clearly infringed, whether the measure of the light to which he was entitled was all that had come through his windows, or only so much as was reasonably necessary for business purposes.

In the speeches of the learned Lords in *Colls* v. *Home and Colonial Stores* [12] the whole question of the nature and extent of the prescriptive right to light was reviewed. It is proposed, therefore, to state shortly some of the conclusions which result from this decision, which is the leading case on the subject.

Measure of right to light

According to Lord Lindley, an owner of ancient lights is, generally speaking, entitled to sufficient light according to the ordinary notions of mankind for the comfortable use and enjoyment of his house as a dwelling-house if it is a dwelling-house, or for the beneficial use and occupation of the house if it is a warehouse, shop, or other place of business.[13] With this agrees Lord Davey, who describes the measure of the right to light through ancient windows as being that which is required for the ordinary purposes of inhabitancy or business of the tenement according to the ordinary notions of mankind.[14]

Nuisance must be proved

According to the House of Lords, the test of the right to bring an action to restrain an obstruction of light is whether the obstruction complained of is a nuisance.[15]

Unusually good light

From this it follows that no action on the footing of interference with an easement can be maintained to preserve the *quantum* of light passing to unusually well lighted premises if sufficient light remains for ordinary comfortable enjoyment,[16] but in a case of lease the right may be preserved on the ground that the lessor demised the premises with knowledge that they were to be used for a purpose requiring an

---

11 (1866) 1 Ch.App. 295.

12 [1904] A.C. 179.

13 [1904] A.C. 208.

14 [1904] A.C. 204.

15 *Per* Lord Halsbury [1904] A.C. 185; *per* Lord Davey, *ibid.* 204; *per* Lord Lindley, *ibid.* 210. See also *Paul* v. *Robson* (1914) 83 L.J.P.C. 304; *Ough* v. *King* [1967] 1 W.L.R. 1547.

16 See p. 253, *post*, and the opinions expressed by Farwell J. in *Higgins* v. *Betts* [1905] 2 Ch. 215; by Romer L.J. in *Kine* v. *Jolly* [1905] 1 Ch. 501; by Lord Robertson, *ibid.* [1907] A.C. 5; and by Lord Atkinson [1907] A.C. 7; and possibly by Lord Davey in *Colls* v. *Home and Colonial Stores* [1904] A.C. 196. But see the opinions expressed in *Kine* v. *Jolly* by Kekewich J. [1905] 1 Ch. 483; by Vaughan Williams L.J. [1905] 1 Ch. 494; by Cozens-Hardy L.J. [1905] 1 Ch. 503; by Lord James [1907] A.C. 4; and possibly by Lord Lindley in *Colls* v. *Home and Colonial Stores* [1904] A.C. 210.

unusually good light, and is in consequence bound by an obligation analogous to that imposed by a restrictive covenant.[17]

Nuisance

On the question of nuisance or no nuisance there are some further points which are clear. Thus the result of an inquiry whether there is a nuisance may differ according to the locality of the building affected. While in cases of nuisance by obstruction to ancient lights the question of locality is of very much less importance in determining whether such obstruction amounts to an actionable nuisance than in cases relating to other nuisances,[18] and it is probable that no variation in locality can justify the diminution of light below a minimum standard,[19] or afford grounds for reducing the light passing to a room in a manufacturing town to the standard of other inadequately lighted rooms in the neighbourhood, yet the court is entitled to have regard to the locality.[20]

Light from other sources

The court should have regard to light (including light from a skylight[21]), coming from sources other than that which has been obstructed, but only so far as this other light is light which the dominant owner is entitled by grant or prescription to enjoy; light of which such owner may be deprived at any time[22] ought not to be taken into account.[23] In this connection it should be pointed out that, as between the dominant and servient owners, the right to ancient light is a negative easement over the servient tenement considered as a whole; and where the

---

[17] See p. 43, ante.

[18] See Fishenden v. Higgs & Hill Ltd. (1935) 153 L.T. 128, 140 (per Romer L.J.) and 142, 143 (per Maugham L.J.). See also [1904] A.C. 183–185 (per Lord Halsbury), and 210 (per Lord Lindley); Kine v. Jolly [1905] 1 Ch. 480 (per Romer L.J.). In the case of nuisance other than obstructions to light, the question varies with locality: Rushmer v. Polsue & Alfieri Ltd. [1906] 1 Ch. 234, 250; [1907] A.C. 123.

[19] " The standard of lighting required to survive in order to eliminate the existence of a nuisance seems to be of necessity an absolute standard. The human eye requires as much light for comfortable reading or sewing in Darlington Street, Wolverhampton, as in Mayfair. True, no doubt it may be that as a rule buildings are more crowded together in manufacturing districts than in residential neighbourhoods. Lights have been obstructed, and no doubt where they have been ancient compensation has been accepted. True, no doubt it may be that an adequately lighted ground floor back room is a rare find in a manufacturing district. I can see, however, no reason in this for saying that a man whose room in such a locality has been turned into a room no longer adequately lighted for ordinary purposes has suffered no actionable wrong ": per Russell J., Hortons' Estate Ltd. v. James Beattie Ltd. [1927] 1 Ch. 75.

[20] Ough v. King [1967] 1 W.L.R. 1547.

[21] Smith v. Evangelization Society (Incorporated) Trust [1933] Ch. 515.

[22] Including, it seems, light reflected back into the plaintiff's window from a wall not belonging to him; see Price v. Hilditch [1930] 1 Ch. 500, 505, 506; Smith v. Evangelization Society (Incorporated) Trust [1933] Ch. 515, 523; and article in (1934) 20 Conveyancer 65.

[23] See the words of Lord Lindley [1904] A.C. 211; and the words in the judgments in Kine v. Jolly, used by Romer L.J. [1905] 1 Ch. 497; by Vaughan Williams L.J. [1905] 1 Ch. 493, and by Lord Atkinson [1907] A.C. 7. Since Colls v. Home and Colonial Stores it is doubtful whether the words of James V.-C. in Dyers' Co. v. King (1870) L.R. 9 Eq. 442, hold good to their full extent.

servient owner raised part of his tenement and lowered part, so that the net light was unaltered, it was held that the dominant owner could not complain.[24]

Glazed tiles

If an actionable nuisance is proved, it is not sufficient for the person who obstructs the light to offer to patch up the injury by putting glazed tiles in front of the windows in question. In *Dent* v. *Auction Mart. Co.*, Page Wood V.-C. said [25]:

> " A person who wishes to preserve his light has no power to compel his neighbour to preserve the tiles, or a mirror which might be better, or to keep them clean, nor has he covenants for these purposes that will run with the land, or affect persons who take without notice; and, therefore, it is quite preposterous to say, ' Let us damage you, provided we apply such and such a remedy.' "

Future use of dominant tenement

It was laid down by Cockburn C.J. in *Moore* v. *Hall* [26] that the court should consider not only the actual present use of the premises but also any purpose to which it may be reasonably expected that in the future they may be applicable. This rule was not altered by the decision in *Colls* v. *Home and Colonial Stores.*[27] Lord Davey said that regard might be had not only to the present use but also to any ordinary uses to which the dominant tenement is adapted, and that a man does not restrict his right by not using the full measure of light which the law permits [28]; and it was the opinion of Lord Lindley that if the dominant owner chooses to use a well-lighted room for a lumber-room for which little light is required, he does not lose his right to use at some future time the same room for some other purpose for which more light is required.[29]

In *Price* v. *Hilditch* [30] Maugham J. expressly adopted as the basis of his decision the observations of Lord Davey and Lord Lindley above referred to. The light received by a room in a residential house had by reason of the defendant's building operations been diminished to such an extent as no longer to be sufficient for the purposes of an ordinary room, although it was sufficient for the purposes of a scullery, for which the room had long been used. Maugham J. treated as irrelevant the

---

[24] *Davis* v. *Marrable* [1913] 2 Ch. 421.
[25] (1866) L.R. 2 Eq. 238, 251, 252. See *Black* v. *Scottish Temperance Assurance* [1908] I.R. 541.
[26] (1878) 3 Q.B.D. 181, 183; and see *Aynsley* v. *Glover* (1874) L.R. 18 Eq. 551, 554; *Dicker* v. *Popham, Radford & Co.* (1890) 63 L.T. 379.
[27] [1904] A.C. 179.
[28] [1904] A.C. 202, 203.
[29] [1904] A.C. 211. The decision in *Martin* v. *Goble* (1808) 1 Camp. 320, has been quoted in favour of the opposite view. The decision may be supported on a different ground : see [1904] A.C. 202.
[30] [1930] 1 Ch. 500.

use to which the room had been put, and, in regard to the observations of Lords Davey and Lindley, said [31]:

> " I respectfully adopt those views: and, for myself, I would add that the language of section 3 of the Prescription Act 1832 seems to support them, since the section begins with the words: ' When the access and use of light to and for any dwelling-house, workshop, or other building shall have been actually enjoyed therewith for the full period of twenty years, without interruption, the right thereto shall be deemed absolute and indefeasible.' Nothing is said to indicate that the right is to be measured by the internal arrangements of the building. . . . I think it is reasonably clear that the lost grant which juries were directed to presume before the Act must have been a grant of the access to and use of light over the servient tenement, knowingly permitted by the owners of it, to and for certain windows or lights in the dominant tenement, without any question at all as to the use for which the light had been used (as it is phrased, somewhat incorrectly) in the rooms which were lit from those windows. As was pointed out by Lord Lindley, the fact that a house has been unoccupied for twenty years, or that the shutters have been closed for a month at a time, does not prevent the easement being acquired; and this fact tends to support the view which I have adopted. The statute has created a fresh origin for the easement of light, and enjoyment as of right is not necessary under section 3; but the nature of the easement has not, in my opinion, been altered."

Cases subsequent to Colls v. Home and Colonial Stores

Shortly after the decision in *Colls* v. *Home and Colonial Stores* [32] the question was again considered in *Kine* v. *Jolly*,[33] which was argued successively in three courts. Kekewich J., in granting to the dominant owner an injunction against an obstruction, said [34]:

> " The great cause of complaint has been of the obstruction of light to what has been called the morning-room. . . . That there has been a large obstruction of light by the erection of the defendant's house is abundantly clear, and I think it is also clear that there has been a large interference with the cheerfulness of the room. . . . I am convinced that the character of the room is altered, and that though still a well-lighted room, it has lost in the obstruction of light one of its chief charms and advantages. . . . Having given all the circumstances full consideration, I have come to the conclusion that the obstruction of light to the morning-room is a nuisance within the meaning of the authorities on that subject."

[31] [1930] 1 Ch. 500, 508.
[32] [1904] A.C. 179.
[33] [1905] 1 Ch. 480; [1907] A.C. 1.
[34] [1905] 1 Ch. 480, 483.

This decision was affirmed by a majority of the Court of Appeal; and an appeal to the House of Lords also failed, the House being equally divided in opinion. Difficulty was caused by the learned judge's finding that the room was " still a well-lighted room "; but Lord Loreburn interpreted this as meaning that it was well lighted, not according to the standard to be expected in the actual locality and surroundings, but according to the standard of a crowded city.[35] It seems clear that the decision stood by reason of the express finding that there was a nuisance.

In *Sheffield Masonic Hall Co.* v. *Sheffield Corporation*,[36] Maugham J. held that, when a room in a building receives light through windows which have acquired a right to light under the Prescription Act, and are on different sides of the building, the owner of land on either side can as a general rule build only to such a height as, if a similar building were erected on the other side, would not deprive the room of so much light as to cause a nuisance.[37]

The effect of the authorities, down to and including *Colls* v. *Home and Colonial Stores*,[38] was stated by Farwell J. in *Higgins* v. *Betts* [39] as follows:

> " Apart from express contract or grant, the owner of a house has no right to any access of light to the windows thereof over his neighbour's land until he has acquired it by prescription or under the Act. When he has so acquired it, he has a house with an easement of light attached to it. Any substantial interference with his comfortable use and enjoyment of his house according to the usages of ordinary persons in that locality, is actionable as a nuisance at common law. His neighbour's brick burning or fried fish shop may be a nuisance in respect of smell, his pestle and mortar in respect of noise, and in like manner his neighbour's new building may be a nuisance in respect of interference with light. The difference between the right to light and the right to freedom from smell and noise is that the former has to be acquired as an easement in addition to the right of property before it can be

---

[35] [1907] A.C. 1, 3.
[36] [1932] 2 Ch. 17.
[37] The grounds were that the nature of the restrictive obligation imposed on the servient owners on each side is that they will not so build as by their joint action to cause a nuisance to the dominant owner. The proposition that the defendant, building on one side, was entitled to build to such an extent as, with the light coming from the other side, would leave sufficient light had to be qualified so as to preserve the right of the owner on the other side to a reasonable utilisation of his land (see pp. 22–23 of the report). The court cannot have been merely adjusting the rights of the servient owners *inter se*; for if the servient owner, building in excess of his quota, had derogated from the rights of the servient owner who was not, it would have been for the latter to complain; but damages were awarded to the plaintiff. It must follow that if the first servient owner exceeds his quota, the second remains entitled to build to the extent of his. A situation of some difficulty would arise if the first owner builds, without appreciable injury to or objection from the dominant owner, and the second owner builds, the combined result being to create a nuisance.
[38] [1904] A.C. 179.
[39] [1905] 2 Ch. 210, 214, 215.

enforced, the two latter are *ab initio* incident to the right of property. But the wrong done is in both cases the same, namely, the
disturbance of the owner in his enjoyment of his house. Inasmuch
as the acquisition of the easement was a necessary condition precedent to the right to sue, the courts appear in many cases to have
addressed themselves rather to the extent of the easement acquired
and the amount of such easement taken away by the defendant,
than to the sufficiency for ordinary purposes of the amount of light
left, so much so that many expressions can be found that lend
support to the argument that the right to light was a right of property for which trespass would lie. The dominant owner was never
entitled either by prescription or under the Act to all the light
that came through his windows. It was not enough to show that
some light had been taken, but the question always was whether so
much had been taken as to cause a nuisance. But for many years
the tendency of the courts had been to measure the nuisance by the
amount taken from the light acquired, and not to consider whether
the amount left was sufficient for the reasonable comfort of the
house according to ordinary requirement. If a man had a house
with unusually excellent lights, it was treated as a nuisance if he
was deprived of a substantial part of it, even although a fair amount
for ordinary purposes was left. It is in this respect that *Colls'* case [40]
has, to my mind readjusted the law. It is still, as it has always
been, a question of nuisance or no nuisance, but the test of nuisance
is not—How much light has been taken, and is that enough materially
to lessen the enjoyment and use of the house that its owner previously had? but—How much is left, and is that enough for the
comfortable use and enjoyment of the house according to the
ordinary requirements of mankind? "

Angle of forty-five degrees

Before *Colls* v. *Home and Colonial Stores* [40] some judges had been
inclined, in dealing with the easement of light, to establish a specific
test, and referred to the Metropolis Management Amendment Act
1862,[41] which contained the following clause:

" No building, except a church or chapel, shall be erected, on
the side of any new street of a less width than fifty feet, which shall
exceed in height the distance from the external wall or front of such
building to the opposite side of such street, without the consent in
writing of the Metropolitan Board of Works; nor shall the height of
any building so erected be at any time subsequently increased so as
to exceed such distance without such consent; and in determining

[40] [1904] A.C. 179.
[41] s. 85; repealed by the London Building Act 1894, and re-enacted (with modifications)
by s. 49 of that Act, now s. 53 of the London Building Act 1930. *Cf.* the by-law
of the Metropolitan Board given in *Theed* v. *Debenham* (1876) 2 Ch.D. 165, 168n.

the height of such building the measurement shall be taken from the level of the centre of the street immediately opposite the building up to the parapet or eaves of such building."

It would appear, both from the character of the statute and also from the direction to measure the distance in every case, not from the sill of any window, but from the level of the street, that the clause was primarily intended, not to protect the enjoyment of light in private houses, but to ensure the free passage of air and sunlight to the streets themselves. But in some cases it was suggested that a rule as to light was there laid down.[42] This question has now been set at rest by *Colls* v. *Home and Colonial Stores*,[43] where it was laid down that there is no hard-and-fast rule with regard to the angle of forty-five degrees.

"There is no rule of law," said Lord Lindley,[44] "that if a person has forty-five degrees of unobstructed light through a particular window left to him he cannot maintain an action for a nuisance caused by diminishing the light which formerly came through that window."

A person may be left with much less than forty-five degrees of light and yet have suffered no actionable diminution. Thus, where the defendants proposed to erect a building 73 feet high with a street 45 feet wide separating it from the plaintiffs' building, it was held that, as even the ground-floor windows of the plaintiffs' building would still be unusually well lighted, the plaintiffs could not sustain a *quia timet* action.[45]

"But experience shows," continues Lord Lindley,[46] "that it is, generally speaking, a fair working rule to consider that no substantial injury is done to him where an angle of forty-five degrees is left to him, especially if there is good light from other directions as well. Lord Justice Cotton pointed this out in *Ecclesiastical Commissioners* v. *Kino*." [47]

The question as to the angle of forty-five degrees had been previously dealt with by Lord Selborne in *City of London Brewery Co.* v. *Tennant*,[48] where he also discusses the evidence necessary to sustain an action to restrain lateral obstructions.

---

[42] *Hackett* v. *Baiss* (1875) L.R. 20 Eq. 494. See also *Beadel* v. *Perry* (1866) L.R. 3 Eq. 465; *City of London Brewery Co.* v. *Tennant* (1873) 9 Ch.App. 212; *Theed* v. *Debenham* (1876) 2 Ch.D. 165; *Ecclesiastical Commissioners* v. *Kino* (1880) 14 Ch.D. 213.

[43] [1904] A.C. 179.

[44] *Ibid.* 210.

[45] *Charles Semon & Co.* v. *Bradford Corpn.* [1922] 2 Ch. 737. The question as to what is sufficient light is exhaustively considered in this case.

[46] *Colls* v. *Home and Colonial Stores* [1904] A.C. 210.

[47] (1880) 14 Ch.D. 228. See also *Parker* v. *First Avenue Hotel Co.* (1883) 24 Ch.D. 282. The question of the angle of forty-five degrees was discussed very fully by Crossman J. in *Fishenden* v. *Higgs and Hill Ltd.* (1935) 153 L.T. 131–133, and his observations were approved by the Court of Appeal. As Maugham L.J. said (*ibid.* 143), "No hard-and-fast mathematical standards can be applied."

[48] (1873) 9 Ch.App. 220. See also, as to lateral obstructions, *Clarke* v. *Clark* (1865) 1 Ch.App. 16.

Evidence

A method employed by expert witnesses in some cases of measuring the obscuration of light caused by a new building is to estimate the amount of direct sky which will reach a hypothetical table two feet nine inches high in a particular room. In *Sheffield Masonic Hall Co.* v. *Sheffield Corporation* [49] Maugham J., while conceding the value of such expert evidence, said:

"I think it is safer to rely upon the view expressed in *Colls* v. *Home and Colonial Stores*,[50] and to consider whether, as a matter of common sense, there is such a deprivation of light as to render the occupation of the house uncomfortable in accordance with the ordinary ideas of mankind."

In *Ough* v. *King* [1] the so-called "Waldram" method was treated as not being decisive and the Court of Appeal held that it was admissible to have regard to the higher standards expected for comfort as the years go by. Lord Denning M.R. said [2] that he thought that it was very helpful for a judge in light cases to have a view of the premises.

Nature and extent of right

The language used by the judges in *Colls* v. *Home and Colonial Stores* [50] has further made it clear that the nature and extent of the prescriptive right to light acquired by user was not altered by the Prescription Act 1832, which was only concerned with the conditions or length of user.[3] The nature of the right is in fact the same whether it be claimed by prescription at common law, or under the statute,[4] or by lost grant, or by grant implied on a disposition by the owner of the two tenements,[5] or under a grant of "lights" among the general words of a deed.[6]

Extraordinary light

A question has from time to time arisen as to whether the owner of a tenement who for upwards of twenty years has carried on there a business requiring an extraordinary amount of light, and has in fact enjoyed such light, thereby acquires a prescriptive right to such extraordinary enjoyment. This question was discussed in *Lanfranchi* v. *Mackenzie*,[7] *Dickinson* v. *Harbottle*,[8] *Mackey* v. *Scottish Widows' Fund*

---

49 [1932] 2 Ch. 24.
50 [1904] A.C. 179.
1 [1967] 1 W.L.R. 1547. See also *McGrath* v. *The Munster and Leinster Bank Ltd.* (1959) 94 I.L.T.R. 110.
2 [1967] 1 W.L.R. 1547, 1552.
3 See the words of Lord Halsbury L.C. [1904] A.C. 179, 183, and of Lord Davey [1904] A.C. 179, 198, 199; and *Price* v. *Hilditch* [1930] 1 Ch. 500; *Sheffield Masonic Hall Co.* v. *Sheffield Corpn.* [1932] 2 Ch. 17.
4 [1904] A.C. 179; see *Kelk* v. *Pearson* (1871) 6 Ch.App. 809, 813.
5 *Leech* v. *Schweder* (1874) 9 Ch.App. 472, 474.
6 *Ibid.*
7 (1867) L.R. 4 Eq. 421.
8 (1873) 28 L.T. 186.

Assurance Society,[9] *Cartwright* v. *Last,*[10] *Theed* v. *Debenham,*[11] *Lazarus* v. *Artistic Photographic Co.,*[12] and *Parker* v. *Stanley* [13]; and was finally decided in the negative in *Ambler* v. *Gordon.*[14] Bray J., in giving judgment in the last-mentioned case, referred [15] to words of Lord Davey in *Colls* v. *Home Colonial Stores,* where he says [16]:

> " It is agreed on all hands that a man does not lose or restrict his right to light by non-user of his ancient lights, or by not using the full measure of light which the law permits.[17] . . . If the actual user is not the test where the use falls below the standard of what may reasonably be required for the ordinary uses of inhabitancy and business, why (it may be asked) should it be made a test where the use has been of a special or extraordinary character in excess of that standard? "

In the case of leases, however, the court has protected special light required for the business for which the premises were let.[18]

Bad light

In the course of the argument in *Colls'* case [19] Lord Robertson said:

> " Can a man by making one window where there should be five to give proper light, and living twenty years in this cave, prevent his neighbour from building a house which would have done no harm to the light if there had been five windows? "

A question of this nature may hereafter arise; but there is no doubt that in many cases a window having what is called " a bad light " has received even greater protection from the courts than the window of a well-lighted room.[20]

Custom of London

By the custom of London, a man might rebuild his house, or other edifice, upon the ancient foundation to what height he pleased, though

---

9 (1877) Ir.R. 11 Eq. 541.
10 [1876] W.N. 60.
11 (1876) 2 Ch.D. 165.
12 [1897] 2 Ch. 214.
13 (1902) 50 W.R. 282.
14 [1905] 1 K.B. 417. See also *Browne* v. *Flower* [1911] 1 Ch. 219, 226. In *Newham* v. *Lawson* (1971) 115 S.J. 446 Plowman J. doubted whether church authorities who had a prescriptive right of light through church windows were entitled to claim any greater degree of protection if the windows were of stained glass than if they were of clear glass; the evidence failed to show that the erection of the defendants' building would prevent the comfortable use of the church according to the ordinary requirements of people attending church and the plaintiffs accordingly were not entitled to relief.
15 [1905] 1 K.B. 417, 424.
16 [1904] A.C. 179, 203.
17 See *Price* v. *Hilditch* [1930] 1 Ch. 500.
18 See *Herz* v. *Union Bank of London* (1854) 2 Giff. 686, *ante,* p. 89.
19 [1904] A.C. 179, 181.   20 See *O'Connor* v. *Walsh* (1908) 42 I.L.T.R. 20.

thereby the ancient windows or lights of the adjoining house were stopped, if there were no agreement in writing to the contrary.[21]

This custom remains binding where the light is claimed by prescription at common law. But where the right is claimed under the Prescription Act 1832, a justification of a disturbance by force of this custom is taken away by the express enactment,[22] " any local custom or usage notwithstanding." [23]

---

[21] Com.Dig.London, N. (5); *Wynstanley* v. *Lee* (1818) 2 Swan. 333, 339.
[22] s. 3.
[23] *Perry* v. *Eames* [1891] 1 Ch. 667. See *Salters' Co.* v. *Jay* (1842) 3 Q.B. 109; *Truscott* v. *Merchant Tailors' Co.* (1856) 11 Exch. 855; *Cooper* v. *Hubbuck* (1862) 12 C.B.(N.S.) 456.

CHAPTER 8

AIR

Right to light and to air

At one time it had become usual in referring to decisions upon the access to light to describe them as cases of light and air, and a formula of this description had crept into both pleadings and evidence.[1] This, however, is inaccurate. For the grounds upon which the court will restrain the obstruction of light may differ widely from the grounds upon which it will restrain the obstruction of air.[2] Generally speaking, however, the modes in which a right to the access of light and a right to the access of defined air can be acquired are similar.[3]

No right to the passage of air over an unlimited surface

The old authorities mention a singular case of a claim to the access of air which might have the effect of imposing very extensive restrictions upon the owners of the neighbouring land. Winch J. said that " where one erected a house so high that the wind was stopped from the wind-mills in Finsbury Fields, it was adjudged that it should be broken down." [4] And again, " in an assize of nuisance, brought because *levavit domum ad nocumentum* of his mill, by which the wind is stopped to come at his mill, so that he cannot grind, etc., and the jury find that the defendant has erected a house *de novo*, and that only two yards of the top of the house is to the nuisance: this is found for the plaintiff; for here the declaration is not falsified (*falsifié*)[5] but only abridged; and the judgment shall be that the two yards be dejected " (M. 11 James I, inter

---

[1] *Bryant* v. *Lefever* (1879) 4 C.P.D. 172; *City of London Brewery Co.* v. *Tennant* (1873) 9 Ch.App. 221; see *Dent* v. *Auction Mart Co.* (1866) L.R. 2 Eq. 252.

[2] *City of London Brewery Co.* v. *Tennant, supra*; *Baxter* v. *Bower* (1875) 44 L.J.Ch. 625.

[3] *Cable* v. *Bryant* [1908] 1 Ch. 263.

[4] Viner's Abridg. Nusance, G. pl. 19, taken from Winch's Reports, 3, where, in what professes to be a report of the proceedings of the Court of Common Pleas in E. 19 James I, it is said: " Winch said it was adjudged in this court that where one erected a house so high in Finsbury Fields by the windmills that the wind was stopped from them, it was adjudged in this case that the house shall be broken down." These reports professing to be a translation of the judge's own notes, it seems strange that, instead of reporting a case, he should record an anecdote told by himself in court, and speak of himself in the third person. This is explained by the fact, mentioned in the preface to Benloe and Dalison, that Winch's Reports are improperly ascribed to that learned judge.

[5] This is erroneously printed " satisfied " in Viner, Nusance, N. 2, pl. 6.

256

Goodman and Gore and others, adjudged).[6] In view of the later decisions, these authorities can no longer be considered good law. The more recent cases establish that a general right to the access of air passing over the unlimited surface of neighbouring land cannot be acquired by prescription. The ground of the rule is that a right cannot be acquired against others by a user which they cannot interrupt.[7]

In *Webb* v. *Bird*,[8] the plaintiff's windmill was built in 1829. The defendant, in 1860, built a schoolhouse within twenty-five yards from the mill, which obstructed the currents of air that would otherwise have

[6] 2 Rolle's Abr. 704, Triall, C. pl. 23. The case referred to by Rolle is reported in Godb. 221 as *Trahern's Case* (C.P. 11 James), where, in an assize of nuisance, the plaintiff showed that he had a windmill, and that the defendant built a house so as it hindered his mill. The jury found that the defendant built the house, but that only two feet of it did hinder the plaintiff's mill, and was a nuisance. The court (Hobart C.J.) was of opinion that but part of the house should be abated, *viz.* that which was found to be a nuisance.

In *Goodman and Gore's Case* (C.P. 10 James, Godb. 189), Goodman brought an assize against Gore and others for erecting two houses to the west end of his windmill, *per quod ventus impeditur, etc.* It was given in evidence that the houses were about eighty feet from the mill, in height did extend above the top of the mill, and in length were twelve yards from the mill; and, notwithstanding, the court (Coke C.J.) directed the jury to find for the defendant (see 10 C.B.(N.S.) 273n.).

On the cases in Rolle and Winch, Willes J. observes that there was a distinction between ordinary mills and the prescriptive right which the lord of a manor had to compel all residents within the manor to grind their corn at his mill. Privileged mills of that description had peculiar rights: 10 C.B.(N.S.) 285.

These three windmill cases may perhaps be reduced to one, and that a case considered by the lawyers of the time as of no authority on the subject of easements. The first was tried before Coke C.J. in 10 James I, reported by Godb. 189 as *Goodman* v. *Gore and others*. It will be seen by the report that Lord Coke displayed a disposition to trip the plaintiff up on a point of form, a circumstance consistent with the fact of the house being built contrary to a royal proclamation which he would not directly oppose, as he was then on his preferment, being then Chief Justice of the Common Pleas, and soon after appointed Chief Justice of the King's Bench. His opinion of these proclamations may be seen in 3 Inst. 201, "Of Buildings," where he says: "We have not read of any *Act of Parliament* now in force made against the excess of building, or touching the order or manner of building; but it is a wasting evil whereunto some wise men are subject." Also in 12 Rep. 74. The second case was tried the following year before Hobart C.J. and brought to a more successful issue. It is cited by Rolle as *Goodman* v. *Gore*; the same as that given to the first by Godbolt. Rolle does not refer to Godbolt, and probably took the case from his own notes before Godbolt was published. Godbolt was published in 1652, when Rolle was Chief Justice of the Upper Bench. Winch, eight years afterwards, says that such a case had been adjudged in the Common Pleas, and his description of the case fits the cases in Godbolt. As to the authority of the windmill case, it is mentioned neither by Coke nor Hobart. Coke, in his chapter on buildings (3 Inst. 201), says: "Also the common law prohibits the building of any edifice to the common nuisance or to the nuisance of any man in his house, as the stopping up of *his light*, or to any other prejudice or annoyance of him." Rolle does not abridge it under the head of "*Nusans*," where he abridges the judgment of Wray C.J. in *Aldred's Case*, as to the stoppage of air to windows, but under the head of "*Trial*," as an authority for the position that where a plaintiff declares that a whole building is a nuisance, and the jury find part only to be so, the action shall not entirely fail.

In old maps of London a row of windmills appears on the heights to the north of London. Probably in the time of King James it was thought an alarming circumstance, as affecting the supply of food to the city, that anyone should build so near them as to take the wind from their sails.

[7] *Harris* v. *Da Pinna* (1886) 33 Ch.D. 238, 262 (a claim to the uninterrupted access of air to a structure for storing timber).

[8] (1861) 10 C.B.(N.S.) 268; (1862) 13 C.B.(N.S.) 841; referred to as stating the law by Lord Denning M.R. in *Phipps* v. *Pears* [1965] 1 Q.B. 76, 83.

passed to the mill; and for the obstruction an action was brought which failed. The Court of Exchequer Chamber held that the plaintiff's claim could not be supported upon the presumption of a grant, which only arose where the person against whom the right was claimed might have prevented the exercise of the subject of the supposed grant; and in the case of the windmill such prevention would be, if not absolutely impossible, yet so difficult that no presumption of a grant could be founded upon non-prevention. Blackburn J. said that he wished to guard against its being supposed that anything in the judgment affected the common law right that might be acquired to the access of air through a window.

In *Bryant* v. *Lefever*[9] the plaintiff and the defendants were occupiers of adjoining houses, which had remained in the same condition for thirty years. The defendants, in rebuilding, raised their house, thereby causing the plaintiff's chimney to smoke. The plaintiff having brought an action claiming a right to have the free access of air to his chimneys, the Lords Justices held that the action failed. There was no natural right to such access; for the establishment of such a right would prevent every adjoining owner from making a reasonable use of his land. Neither could the right be acquired by prescription, for the claim was vague and uncertain, and the enjoyment incapable of being interrupted by any reasonable means. Cotton L.J. added that it was unnecessary to say whether, if the uninterrupted flow of air through a definite aperture or channel over a neighbour's property had been enjoyed as of right for a sufficient period, a right by way of easement could be acquired.

Air through a defined aperture or channel

While, as appears from the authorities above referred to, a general right to the access of air passing over the unlimited surface of neighbouring land cannot be acquired by prescription, on the other hand a right to the access of air can be acquired where such access is enjoyed either through a definite aperture in the dominant tenement or through a definite channel over adjoining property.[10]

In *Gale* v. *Abbott*[11] and *Dent* v. *Auction Mart Co.*[12] injunctions were granted to remove and prevent impediments to ventilation. In the first case the defendant was ordered to remove a skylight which he had placed over his yard, and which materially impeded the passage of air to the window of the plaintiff's kitchen. In the second case Page Wood V.-C. said[13]:

---

9 (1879) 4 C.P.D. 172.

10 *Bass* v. *Gregory* (1890) 25 Q.B.D. 481, where the plaintiff succeeded in establishing a prescriptive right to ventilate a cellar by a shaft communicating with a disused well. See also *Moseley* v. *Bland*, 2 Roll.Abr. 141, Nusans, G. pl. 16 (cited in *Aldred's Case* (1611) 9 Rep. 58); *Aldin* v. *Latimer Clark, Muirhead & Co.* [1894] 2 Ch. 437, 446; *Chastey* v. *Ackland* [1895] 2 Ch. 402; *Cable* v. *Bryant* [1908] 1 Ch. 264. It is not sufficient for the plaintiff to prove only a casual and temporary obstruction depending on the direction of the wind: *Johnson* v. *Wyatt* (1863) 2 De G.J. & S. 17, 26.   11 (1862) 8 Jur.(N.S.) 987.

12 (1866) L.R. 2 Eq. 238.   13 (1866) L.R. 2 Eq. 252.

" There is a staircase lighted in a certain manner by windows which, when opened, admit air. The Defendants are about to shut up these windows, as in a box with the lid off, by a wall about eight or nine feet distant, and some forty-five feet high; and in that circumscribed space they purpose to put three water-closets. There are difficulties about the case of air as distinguished from that of light; but the Court has interfered to prevent the total obstruction of all circulation of air; and the introduction of three water-closets into a confined space of this description is, I think, an interference with air which this Court will recognise on the ground of nuisance."

In *Hall* v. *Lichfield Brewery Co.*[14] the plaintiff, who had for thirty years enjoyed a free access of air to his slaughter-house through two apertures, brought an action for the obstruction of this air. Fry J. said that the right to have an access of air to an aperture in the building could undoubtedly be acquired at law, and that for this purpose the court would imply a covenant. In the case of a dwelling-house the covenant to be implied would be not to interrupt the free use of salubrious air. In the case of a slaughter-house the covenant to be implied would be not to interrupt the free access of air suitable for a slaughter-house. Fry J. said that the right to defined air could not be claimed by grant, and therefore not by prescription; and he referred to the words of Littledale J. in *Moore* v. *Rawson*[15] to the effect that such a right more properly arises by covenant. It would seem, however, that a right to the passage of defined air is a negative easement, or a right *ne facias*; and as such may be the subject of a grant, and therefore claimable by prescription.[16]

It was at one time suggested that a right to the access of air was not an easement within section 2 of the Prescription Act.[17] Where, however, the right is claimed through a definite aperture or through a definite channel, it seems that it may be an easement within section 2.[18]

Derogation from grant

On the principle that a grantor may not derogate from his grant, it has been held that where land is expressly granted for carrying on a particular business the grantor cannot interrupt air so as to interfere with that business.[19] Similarly, where there was an express grant of land with a stable on it (which stable was ventilated by defined apertures) the grantor could not subsequently erect anything

14 (1880) 49 L.J.Ch. 655.
15 (1824) 3 B. & C. 332.
16 See *Dalton* v. *Angus* (1881) 6 App.Cas. 740, 794, 823; *ante*, pp. 23–25.
17 *Chastey* v. *Ackland* [1895] 2 Ch. 389, 402.
18 *Simpson* v. *Godmanchester Corpn.* [1897] A.C. 696, 709; *Dalton* v. *Angus* (1881) 6 App.Cas. 740, 798; *Bass* v. *Gregory* (1890) 25 Q.B.D. 483; *Harris* v. *De Pinna* (1886) 33 Ch.D. 251; *Cable* v. *Bryant* [1908] 1 Ch. 259, 263.
19 *Aldin* v. *Latimer Clark, Muirhead & Co.* [1894] 2 Ch. 437, *ante*, p. 89.

on his adjoining property which by interfering with the air prevented
the use of the stable as a stable.[20] A grantee may have an implied
easement of necessity to go onto the grantor's land to erect an air-duct
without which the grantee's business cannot be carried on legally.[21]

Right to prevent access of impure air not an easement

It may be observed here that the right to a lateral passage of
air, as to a flow of water, superadds a privilege to the ordinary
rights of property, and is quite distinct from that right which every
owner of a tenement, whether ancient or modern, possesses to prevent
his neighbour transmitting to him air or water in impure condition;
this latter right is one of the ordinary incidents of property, requiring
no easement to support it, and can be countervailed only by the
acquisition of an easement for that purpose by the party causing the
nuisance.

In *Curriers' Co.* v. *Corbett* [22] it was argued, from air not being
mentioned in section 3 of the Prescription Act, that the custom of
London, as to building on an ancient foundation, was not affected
by it so far as it related to the obstruction of air, and on this ground
a formal objection was made to a decree of the Vice-Chancellor for an
injunction. Turner L.J. said that he should not be disposed to
come to any decision in the absence of evidence that the custom
applied to air, as well as to light.

20 *Cable* v. *Bryant* [1908] 1 Ch. 259, *ante*, p. 90.
21 *Wong* v. *Beaumont Property Trust Ltd.* [1965] 1 Q.B. 173; see p. 121, *ante*.
22 (1865) 4 De G.J. & Sm. 764.

CHAPTER 9

RIGHTS OF WAY

1.—NATURE OF RIGHTS OF WAY

Different kinds of ways

Rights of way are at once the most familiar and important of the class of affirmative easements, which impose upon the owner of the servient tenement the obligation to submit to something being done within the limits of his own property.

Rights of this nature are susceptible of almost infinite variety: they may be limited as to the intervals at which they may be used— as a right to be exercised during daylight,[1] or (formerly) as a way for a parson to carry away his tithe.[2] Again, they may be limited as to the actual extent of user authorised—as a foot-way, horse-way, carriage-way, or drift-way. Or they may be limited as to the purposes for which they may be exercised; thus there may be a way for agricultural purposes only,[3] or for the carriage of coals only,[4] or for the carriage of all articles except coals.[5]

There may be both a private right of way and a public highway over the same road.[6] A private right of way is not necessarily destroyed either by the public acquiring a right of way over the same road[7] or by a public highway over the same road being extinguished by an order of quarter sessions under section 91 of the Highway Act 1835 (now repealed)[8] or by a private Act.[9]

2.—EXTENT OF RIGHTS OF WAY ACQUIRED BY USER

Mode of user

Rights of way are usually acquired by user or by grant, express or implied. In the former case, as the user is not continuous and may vary

---

[1] *Collins* v. *Slade* (1874) 23 W.R. 199.
[2] *James* v. *Dods* (1834) 2 Cr. & M. 266.
[3] *Reignolds* v. *Edwards* (1741) Willes 282.
[4] *Iveson* v. *Moore* (1700) 1 Ld.Raym. 486.
[5] *Stafford* v. *Coyney* (1827) 7 B. & C. 257. See also *Jackson* v. *Stacey* (1816) Holt N.P.C. 455; *Tomlin* v. *Fuller* (1681) 1 Mod. 27; *Bidder* v. *North Staffordshire Ry.* (1878) 4 Q.B.D. 412.
[6] *Brownlow* v. *Tomlinson* (1840) 1 Man. & G. 484; *Att.-Gen.* v. *Esher Linoleum Co. Ltd.* [1901] 2 Ch. 647; *Pullin* v. *Deffel* (1891) 64 L.T. 134.
[7] *Duncan* v. *Louch* (1845) 6 Q.B. 904; *R.* v. *Chorley* (1848) 12 Q.B. 515.
[8] *Walsh* v. *Oates* [1953] 1 Q.B. 578. See now Highways Act 1959, s. 108.
[9] *Wells* v. *London, Tilbury and Southend Rail Co.* (1877) 5 Ch.D. 126.

at different times, great difficulties are presented both in law and in fact in determining the amount of right conferred by it; though the maxim, " *Omne majus continet in se minus,*" seems equally applicable here as in other cases. The real difficulty is to ascertain what constitutes the relative *majus* and *minus* in rights of this nature. A man may allow the passage of foot passengers and carriages near his house, and yet refuse permission to drive cattle along the same road.

Coke, citing the authority of Fleta and Bracton,[10] says: " There are three kinds of ways: first, a foot-way, which is called *iter, quod est jus eundi vel ambulandi homini*; and this was the first way. The second is a foot-way and a horse-way, which is called *actus, ab agendo*; and this vulgarly is called pack and prime way, because it is both a foot-way, which was the first or prime way, and a pack or drift-way also. The third is *via,* or *aditus,* which contains the other two, and also a cart-way, etc.; for this is *jus eundi, vehendi, et vehiculum et jumentum ducendi.*" [11]

The distinctions here taken by Coke, which, in the terms used at all events, correspond with the definitions of the civil law, appear to be of no practical utility. If this division into three classes were rigorously observed, the second comprehending the rights peculiar to the first class, and the third those both of the second and first, it is obvious that the establishment of a right to do any one of the things comprised in a superior class would at the same time establish a right to do, not only all the acts comprised in the inferior classes, but also all the other acts comprehended in that class of which it forms but a single instance. Such is clearly not the case by the law of England. In *Ballard* v. *Dyson* [12] it was expressly decided that a right which, adopting Coke's definition, is of the highest class, as, for instance, a right to drive carts, does not of necessity include the right to drive cattle, ranged by him in the subordinate class. The general rule is that where a right of way is acquired by user, the extent of the right must be measured by the extent of the user.[13] Where a prescriptive right is founded upon evidence of user in some particular manner, the question which arises is whether there was a right of user in some other manner which would have equally served the purposes of the dominant tenement during the period of user.

In *Ballard* v. *Dyson,*[14] which was an action of replevin, the defendant avowed taking a heifer damage feasant, and issue was

10 Co.Litt. 56a.
11 The text of the civil law is as follows: *Iter* est jus eundi ambulandi homini, non etiam jumentum agendi (vel vehiculum). *Actus* est jus agendi vel jumentum vel vehiculum. Ita qui habet iter, actum non habet; qui actum habet, et iter habet (eoque uti potest), etiam sine jumento. *Via* est jus eundi et agendi et ambulandi; nam et iter et actum via in se continet.—Inst. 2, 3, praef.
12 (1808) 1 Taunt. 279; and see *Cowling* v. *Higginson* (1838) 4 M. & W. 250; *Higham* v. *Rabett* (1839) 5 Bing.N.C. 622; *British Railways Board* v. *Glass* [1965] Ch. 538.
13 *Finch* v. *Great Western Railway* (1879) 5 Ex.D. 254, 258.
14 (1808) 1 Taunt. 279.

joined upon a plea in bar of " a right of way to pass and repass with cattle from a public street through and along a certain yard and way adjoining to the said place in which, etc., towards and unto certain premises in the plaintiff's occupation as appurtenant thereto." On the trial it appeared that the plaintiff's building had anciently been a barn, but had not been used as such for a great many years; that the folding-doors of it opened, not to the plaintiff's yard, but to a highway; for many years it had been converted to the purposes of a stable; the last preceding occupier, who was a pork butcher, had used it as a slaughter-house for slaughtering his hogs; and the present occupier, who was a butcher, used it as a slaughter-house for slaughtering oxen. The yard in question, along which the right of way to these premises was claimed, was a narrow passage bounded by a row of houses on each side, the doors of which opened into it: when a cart and horse was driven through it, the foot passengers could not pass the carriage, but were compelled, on account of the narrowness, to retreat into the houses; and they would be exposed to considerable danger if they were to meet horned cattle driven through it. It was in evidence that the preceding occupier had been accustomed to drive fat hogs that way to his slaughter-house: and that the plaintiff had been accustomed to drive a cart, the only carriage which he possessed, usually drawn by a horse, but in one or two instances by an ox, along this passage to this barn, where he kept his cart; there was then no other way to it. He had lately begun to drive fat oxen that way to the premises for the purpose of killing them there; but there was no evidence of any other user than this of the way for cattle. No deed of grant was produced. The defendant produced no evidence that he had ever interrupted the occupiers of the plaintiff's premises in driving cattle there, or that they had been usually possessed of horned cattle which had not been driven that way; he admitted that there was sufficient evidence of a right of way for *all manner of carriages*. It did not appear at what period the houses adjoining the way had been built. For the plaintiff it was contended that a right of way for all manner of carriages necessarily included a right of way for all manner of cattle, and therefore proved the prescription.

Mansfield C.J. told the jury that, inasmuch as this was a private and not a public way, they were not to conclude that a man might not grant a right of way to pass with horses and carts, and yet preclude the grantee from passing with all manner of cattle; and the degree of inconvenience which would attend the larger grant in this case furnished an argument against the probability of it. He directed them, therefore, to say whether there was sufficient evidence of a right of way to drive cattle loose, or whether they would consider the grant or prescription as only co-extensive with the use that had been made of it. The jury found a verdict for the defendant, that is, against the right to use the way for cattle.

The court, after taking time to consider, discharged a rule for a new trial. Mansfield C.J. said [15]:

> "I have always considered it as a matter of evidence, and a proper question for a jury, to find whether a right of way for cattle is to be presumed from the usage proved of a cart-way. Consequently, although in certain cases a general way for carriages may be good evidence from which a jury may infer a right of this kind, yet it is only evidence; and they are to compare the reasons which they have for forming an opinion on either side."

His Lordship went on to instance cases when it would be highly inconvenient to the grantor of a right of carriage-way if the grant also comprehended a way for cattle, and said that he could find no case in which it had been decided that a carriage-way necessarily implied a drift-way, though it appeared sometimes to have been taken for granted. Heath J. said [16] that "a carriage-way includes a horse-way, but not a drift-way." Lawrence J. seems to have proceeded on the general ground that a grant not being shown, the extent of the right could only be shown from the use, from which he inferred that proof of a use of a carriage-way and of a way for pigs afforded no evidence of a way for horned cattle.[17] Chambre J. in a dissenting judgment said [18]:

> "I never thought that a carriage-way necessarily included a drift-way; but I think it is prima facie evidence, and strong presumptive evidence, of the grant of a drift-way. Undoubtedly a person may restrict his grant as he pleases, and when he has so limited it, the pleadings must be adapted to the particular grant; which accounts for the variety in the entries. But it rests with the grantor to prove the restriction of the grant; otherwise it must be intended to be of the usual extent."

Ballard v. *Dyson* [19] was applied by the Court of Appeal in *British Railways Board* v. *Glass*,[20] a case where there was an express grant, the court taking the view that the words "with all manner of cattle" enlarged rather than limited the nature of the right granted, a drift-way for cattle being a more onerous right than a mere right of way with horses and carts. This decision runs directly contrary to Coke's definition [21] into *iter*, *actus* and *via*, in ascending order of importance.

It appears, then, that there is not in English law any positive division of rights of way into distinct classes. Applying the general principle that every easement is a restriction of the rights of property of the

15 (1808) 1 Taunt. 279, 284.
16 *Ibid.* 285.
17 *Ibid.* 286.
18 *Ibid.* 287.
19 (1808) 1 Taunt. 279.
20 [1965] Ch. 538.
21 See p. 262, *ante*.

party over whose lands it is exercised, the real question appears to be, on the peculiar facts of each case, whether proof has been given of a right co-extensive with that amount of inconvenience sought to be imposed by the right claimed. It is obvious that, in some cases, a right to drive cattle might be productive of greater inconvenience than a right to drive carts, and vice versa. It will, therefore, be for the jury, or the court acting as a jury, to infer the extent of the supposed grant from the actual amount of injury proved under all circumstances attending it. If it appeared that the way had been used for all the purposes required by the claimant, there would be strong evidence of a general right, while, on the other hand, proof that the party, having occasion for a particular use, had not made that use of the way in question, would be almost conclusive evidence that he had not a right of way for that particular purpose.

This doctrine is supported by *Cowling* v. *Higginson* [22] where it was held that proof of user for farming purposes did not necessarily prove a right of way for the purpose of conveying coal, the produce of a mine lying under the defendant's land. In the course of the argument Lord Abinger C.B. observed [23]:

"The extent of the right must depend upon the circumstances. If a road led through a park, the jury might naturally infer the right to be limited; but if it went over a common, they might infer that it was a way for all purposes. Using a road as a foot-path would not prove a general right; nor proof that a party had used a road to go to church only. Some analogy should be shewn between farming and mining purposes."

Parke B. said [24]:

"If it had been shewn, that from time immemorial it had been used as a way for all purposes that were required, would not that be evidence of a general right of way? . . . If they shew that they have used it time out of mind, for all the purposes that they wanted, it would seem to me to give them a general right. . . . You must generalise to some extent. If your argument is to be taken strictly, it must be confined to the identical carriages that have previously been used upon the road, and would not warrant even the slightest alteration in the carriage or the loading, or the purpose for which it was used."

Lord Abinger C.B., in his judgment, said [25]:

"I do not give any opinion upon the effect of the evidence; but I should certainly say that it is not a necessary inference of law, that a way for agricultural purposes is a way for all purposes,

22 (1838) 4 M. & W. 245.
23 (1838) 4 M. & W. 252.
24 (1838) 4 M. & W. 251–254.
25 *Ibid*. 256.

but that is a question for the jury in each particular case. . . .
If a way has been used for several purposes, there may be a
ground for inferring that there is a right of way for all purposes;
but if the evidence shews a user for one purpose, or for particular
purposes only, an inference of a general right would hardly be
presumed."

Parke B. said [26] :

" To make out this plea, it is necessary to shew an enjoyment
of the way generally as of right, for the period during which the
plea states it to have been used; he must have used it for all
purposes as of right; and such user, for all purposes for which
it was wanted, would be evidence to go to the jury of a general
right. Under a plea of prescription of a way, it was necessary to
shew a user of it for all purposes time out of mind, according to
the usual terms in which such a plea is pleaded. If it is shewn that
the defendant, and those under whom he claimed, had used the way
whenever they had required it, it is strong evidence to shew that
they had a general right to use it for all purposes, and from which
a jury might infer a general right. In this particular case, I think
the user is evidence to go to the jury that the defendant had a
right to a way for all purposes for twenty years. As to the effect
of such evidence, it is unnecessary to offer any opinion. If the
way is confined to a particular purpose, the jury ought not to
extend it, but if it is proved to have been used for a variety of
purposes, then they might be warranted in finding a way for all.
You must generalise to some extent, and whether in the present
case to the extent of establishing a right for agricultural purposes
only, is a question for the jury." [27]

It is settled that proof of user with horses and carts will establish
a right of user with mechanically propelled vehicles.[28]

Purposes of user : Alteration of dominant tenement

Questions have also arisen whether proof of user, over a long period,
for the purposes of the dominant tenement as it was during that period
establishes a right of user for additional or new purposes required, for
instance, by some alteration in the dominant tenement. Speaking
generally, and subject to considerations of degree, the answer appears
to be in the negative. In *Williams* v. *James*,[29] which was a case of

26 *Ibid.* 257.
27 *Cf. Dare* v. *Heathcote* (1856) 25 L.J.Ex. 245.
28 *Lock* v. *Abercester Ltd.* [1939] Ch. 861. The grounds of this decision, though not
the decision itself, may be respectfully questioned; for it appears to have been
decided or assumed that a right to use with horses and carts was sufficiently established, for the purposes of s. 2 of the Prescription Act, by proof of user for a period
ending, not at the commencement of the action, but about eight years before.
Contrast *R. C. P. Holdings Ltd.* v. *Rogers* [1953] 1 All E.R. 1029, 1031; and
see *ante*, pp. 134, 152; *post*, p. 346.
29 (1867) L.R. 2 C.P. 577. *Cf. Bradburn* v. *Morris* (1876) 3 Ch.D. 812.

alleged excessive user of a prescriptive way, the decision being that user for the purpose of carting hay grown on land adjoining the dominant tenement was not, in the circumstances, colourable or excessive, Bovill C.J. said [30]:

> " In all cases of this kind which depend on user the right acquired must be measured by the extent of the enjoyment which is proved. When a right of way to a piece of land is proved, then that is, unless something appears to the contrary, a right of way for all purposes according to the ordinary and reasonable user to which that land might be applied at the time of the supposed grant. Such a right cannot be increased so as to affect the servient tenement by imposing upon it any additional burthen."

Willes J. said [31]:

> " I agree . . . that where a way has to be proved by user, you cannot extend the purposes for which the way may be used, or for which it might reasonably be inferred that parties would have intended it to be used. To be a legitimate enjoyment of the right of way, it must be used for the enjoyment of the nine acre field, and not colourably for other closes. I quite agree also with the argument that the right of way can only be used for the field in its ordinary use as a field. The right could not be used for a manufactory built upon the field. The use must be the reasonable use for the purposes of the land in the condition in which it was while the user took place."

In *Wimbledon and Putney Commons Conservators* v. *Dixon*,[32] where the user proved was a user for farming purposes only—except for two or three slight circumstances, the enlargement of a farmhouse, the replacing of a mud cottage by a brick cottage, and apparently the taking away of gravel—the court declined to presume a grant of a way for all purposes, and restrained the defendant from carting building materials for a new house. The Lords Justices, affirming Jessel M.R., held that the property could not be so changed as substantially to increase or alter the burden upon the servient tenement. James L.J. said [33]:

> " I am satisfied that the true principle is, . . . that you cannot, from evidence of user of a privilege connected with the enjoyment of property in its original state, infer a right to use it, into whatsoever form or for whatever purpose that property may be changed, that is to say, if a right of way to a field be proved by evidence of user, however general, for whatever purpose, *qua* field,

30 (1867) L.R. 2 C.P. 580.
31 *Ibid.* 582.
32 (1875) 1 Ch.D. 362. *Cf.* the dicta of North J. in *New Windsor (Mayor)* v. *Stovell* (1884) 27 Ch.D. 665, 672.
33 (1875) 1 Ch.D. 368.

the person who is the owner of that field cannot from that say, I have a right to turn that field into a manufactory, or a town, and then use the way for the purposes of the manufactory or town so built."

Mellish L.J.[34] expressed an opinion that Parke B., in giving judgment in *Cowling* v. *Higginson*,[35] had not present to his mind the question of a change in the dominant tenement. He preferred the language of Lord Abinger,[36] and added that user of a way for purposes connected with the occupation of the land in its existing state might be considered to be a user for Lord Abinger's "particular purposes."

Where, however, a right of way to a dwelling-house had been acquired by user, there was no excess of user by opening a small shop.[37]

The question came again before the court in *R. C. P. Holdings Ltd.* v. *Rogers*.[38] There the plaintiff sought to restrain the defendant from trespassing on a track passing over the plaintiff's golf course to the defendant's field. The defendant had recently established on this field, and was about to enlarge, a camping site for caravans. The defendant proved that from about 1880 down to a few years before the commencement of the action the track had been used for the ordinary agricultural purposes of the field, and on this ground [39] he established a right of way by prescription at common law. The question then arose whether this right was a right to use the track for agricultural purposes only, or a right to use it for all purposes, including the purposes of the camping site. Harman J., after considering *Cowling* v. *Higginson*,[40] *Williams* v. *James* [41] and *Wimbledon and Putney Commons Conservators* v. *Dixon*,[42] decided against the plaintiff. He said [43]:

"It seems to me as a result of these three authorities that the question of the extent of the right is one which I as a juryman have got to determine, but that I am not to conclude from the mere fact that while the property was in one state the way was for all purposes for which it was wanted, therefore, that is a general right exercisable for totally different purposes which only came into existence at a later date. Sitting as a juryman I can feel no doubt that the way here was a way limited to agricultural purposes, and that to extend it to the use proposed would be an unjustifiable increase of the burden of the easement."

[34] *Ibid.* 371.
[35] (1838) 4 M. & W. 245; see p. 265, *ante.*
[36] (1838) 4 M. & W. 256; see p. 265, *ante.*
[37] *Sloan* v. *Holliday* (1874) 30 L.T. 757.
[38] [1953] 1 All E.R. 1029.
[39] *Ante,* p. 133.
[40] (1838) 4 M. & W. 245.
[41] (1867) L.R. 2 C.P. 577.
[42] (1875) 1 Ch.D. 362.
[43] [1953] 1 All E.R. 1035.

In *British Railways Board* v. *Glass* [44] the Court of Appeal by a majority (Harman and Davies L.JJ., Lord Denning M.R. dissenting) held that the defendant had acquired a prescriptive right to use a level-crossing over the plaintiff's railway for the purposes of a caravan site which was situate in a field on the north side of the railway line. The plaintiff on the pleadings admitted that the whole of the field constituted the site. Over the years there had been a substantial increase in the number of caravans using the site, but Harman and Davies L.JJ. held, applying *Williams* v. *James*,[45] that, no radical change having occurred in the character of the dominant tenement, the mere increase in the number of caravans using the site and the consequent increase in the user of the crossing did not amount to an excessive user of the prescriptive right, and there had been no such increase in the burden of the easement as would justify the plaintiff in seeking an injunction. Saying that if there were a radical change in the character of the dominant tenement, then the prescriptive right would not extend to it in that condition, Harman L.J.[46] instanced a change of a small dwelling-house to a large hotel.

In *Woodhouse & Co. Ltd.* v. *Kirkland (Derby) Ltd.*[47] Plowman J. found that the plaintiff had established a prescriptive right of way over a passageway owned by the defendant for the plaintiff's reasonable business purposes and that this extended to, *inter alia*, use by its customers, the identity of the persons using the passage for such business purposes being immaterial. The user by the plaintiff's customers had greatly increased, but Plowman J. held, applying *British Railways Board* v. *Glass*,[48] that there had been no excessive user, since the user had not been of a different kind or for a different purpose. His Lordship found it unnecessary on the facts to consider whether an increase in user, if very great, could ever of itself amount to excessive user.

3.—EXTENT OF RIGHTS OF WAY ACQUIRED BY GRANT

In the case of an express grant the language of the instrument can be referred to. It is for the court to construe that language in the light of the circumstances,[49] and, in the absence of any clear indication of the intention of the parties, the maxim that a grant must be construed most strongly against a grantor must be applied.[50] In particular, in construing a grant the court will consider (1) the *locus in quo* over which the way is granted; (2) the nature of the *terminus ad quem*; and (3) the purpose for which the way is to be used.[1]

[44] [1965] Ch. 538.
[46] [1965] Ch. 562.
[48] [1965] Ch. 538.
[49] *Callard* v. *Beeney* [1930] 1 K.B. 353.
[50] *Williams* v. *James* (1867) L.R. 2 C.P. 577, 581; *Wood* v. *Saunders* (1875) 10 Ch.App. 584n.
[1] See *Cannon* v. *Villars* (1878) 8 Ch.D. 415; *Bulstrode* v. *Lambert* [1953] 1 W.L.R. 1064, and *Sketchley* v. *Berger* (1893) 69 L.T. 754.

[45] (1867) L.R. 2 C.P. 577.
[47] [1970] 1 W.L.R. 1185.

Quality of user

It seems that, subject to any qualifying words in the grant, the authorised mode or quality of user (with or without vehicles, etc.) is as general as the physical capacity of the *locus in quo* at the time of the grant will admit, unless in any particular case (which must be rare) some limitation on mode of user can be gathered from the surrounding circumstances. The following passage from the judgment of Jessel M.R. in *Cannon* v. *Villars*,[2] where the court was considering the extent of an implied right of way arising under an agreement to grant a lease of premises for the purpose of a business, is often quoted:

"As I understand, the grant of a right of way *per se* and nothing else may be a right of footway, or it may be a general right of way, that is a right of way not only for people on foot but for people on horseback, for carts, carriages, and other vehicles. Which it is, is a question of construction of the grant, and that construction will of course depend on the circumstances surrounding, so to speak, the execution of the instrument. Now one of those circumstances, and a very material circumstance, is the nature of the *locus in quo* over which the right of way is granted. If we find a right of way granted over a metalled road with pavement on both sides existing at the time of the grant, the presumption would be that it was intended to be used for the purpose for which it was constructed, which is obviously the passage not only of foot-passengers, but of horsemen and carts. Again, if we find the right of way granted along a piece of land capable of being used for the passage of carriages, and the grant is of a right of way to a place which is stated on the face of the grant to be intended to be used or to be actually used for a purpose which would necessarily or reasonably require the passing of carriages, there again it must be assumed that the grant of the right of way was intended to be effectual for the purpose for which the place was designed to be used, or was actually used.

"Where you find a road constructed so as to be fit for carriages and of the requisite width, leading up to a dwelling-house, and there is a grant of a right of way to that dwelling-house, it would be a grant of a right of way for all reasonable purposes required for the dwelling-house, and would include, therefore, the right to the user of carriages by the occupant of the dwelling-house if he wanted to take the air, or the right to have a waggon drawn up to the door when the waggon was to bring coals for the use of the dwelling-house. Again, if the road is not to a dwelling-house but to a factory, or a place used for business purposes which would require heavy weights to be brought to it, or to a wool warehouse which would require bags or packages of wool to be brought

2 (1878) 8 Ch.D. 415, 420, 421.

to it, then a grant of a right of way would include a right to use it for reasonable purposes, sufficient for the purposes of the business, which would include the right of bringing up carts and waggons at reasonable times for the purpose of the business.[3] That again would afford an indication in favour of the extent of the grant. If, on the other hand, you find that the road in question over which the grant was made was paved only with flagstones, and that it was only four or five feet wide, over which a waggon or cart or carriage ordinarily constructed could not get, and that it was only a way used to a field or close, or something on which no erection was, there, I take it, you would say that the physical circumstances showed that the right of way was a right for foot-passengers only. It might include a horse under some circumstances, but could not be intended for carts or carriages. Of course where you find restrictive words in the grant, that is to say, where it is only for the use of foot-passengers, stated in express terms, or for foot-passengers and horsemen, and so forth, there is nothing to argue. I take it that is the law. Prima facie the grant of a right of way is the grant of a right of way having regard to the nature of the road over which it is granted and the purpose for which it is intended to be used; and both those circumstances may be legitimately called in aid in determining whether it is a general right of way, or a right of way restricted to foot-passengers, or restricted to foot-passengers and horsemen or cattle, which is generally called a drift-way, or a general right of way for carts, horses, carriages, and everything else."

In *Todrick* v. *Western National Omnibus Co.*[4] it was held that the grant of a right of way, with or without vehicles, over a road supported by a retaining wall, seven feet nine inches wide at its entrance, and clearly not intended for heavy vehicles, did not authorise user by motor buses.

In *Cousens* v. *Rose*[5] a grant in a lease of " free liberty and right of way and passage, and of ingress, egress and regress for [the lessees], their workmen and servants, and all persons by their authority or permission," over a strip of land described as a roadway or passage was held, on the facts, to be a foot-way only.

In *Watts* v. *Kelson*[6] and *Robinson* v. *Bailey*[7] it was admitted that a grant in general terms of " a right of way " authorised user with vehicles; and it is submitted that the true principle appears in the passage in the judgment of Jenkins J. in *Kain* v. *Norfolk*,[8] where he says:

3 See *Bulstrode* v. *Lambert* [1953] 1 W.L.R. 1064.
4 [1934] Ch. 190; reversed on other grounds [1934] Ch. 561; explained on this point in *Robinson* v. *Bailey* [1948] 2 All E.R. 791. See further p. 280, *post.*
5 (1871) L.R. 12 Eq. 366.   6 (1870) 6 Ch.App. 166, 170n.
7 [1948] 2 All E.R. 791, 793.
8 [1949] Ch. 163, 168. The decision in the case, which raised the question whether the grantee in 1919 of a right of way " with or without horses carts and agricultural machines and implements " was entitled to convey sand in lorries from a gravel pit subsequently opened on the dominant tenement, was not founded on the passage quoted, but on the fact that the grant, properly construed, included the right of carting loads, with any kind of " cart," including a motor lorry. See p. 281, *post.*

" [Counsel] says, and I think he is supported by authority, that a right given to the grantee of property at all times hereafter to go, pass and repass over and along a certain way without any reference to horses, carriages, carts or anything else, will, *per se*, unelaborated as it is, give a right of way for all purposes, that is to say, a right to pass with vehicles as well as on foot, provided that the way to which the grant refers is a way suitable at the date of the grant for use by vehicles. I think that accords with the statement of the law contained in the judgment of Jessel M.R. in *Cannon* v. *Villars*." [9]

In *Bulstrode* v. *Lambert*,[10] a conveyance of a house and a passage or yard running alongside it and leading to a building retained by the vendor and used as an auction mart reserved a right, for the vendor, his tenants and workmen and others authorised by him, to pass and repass with or without vehicles over and along the passage or yard for the purpose of obtaining access to the auction mart. Upjohn J. held that the vendor's successor in title had the right to bring vans and pantechnicons over the yard for the purpose of transporting furniture and other chattels to and from the auction mart; also the right (without causing undue inconvenience to the servient owner) to bring these vehicles to a point in the yard beyond which it was physically impossible for them to pass, and to carry the goods thence into the mart by hand; and also the right (as to which there was no previous authority) to halt the vehicles in the yard (which was a cul-de-sac) as often and for so long as might be necessary for the purpose of loading and unloading. This last-mentioned right was necessary for the enjoyment of the right reserved.[11]

In *Keefe* v. *Amor* [12] Russell L.J., delivering the leading judgment of the Court of Appeal, observed [13] that the terms of the grant in *Bulstrode* v. *Lambert* [14] were " very particular." In *Keefe* v. *Amor* [15] the particular considerations present in the language in *Bulstrode* v. *Lambert* [14] were absent, but the Court of Appeal nevertheless held that on the construction of the transfer of a dwelling-house " together also with a right of way over " a strip of land some twenty feet wide and coloured brown on the plan annexed to the transfer, the right extended to vehicular traffic of any sort and was not limited by the physical characteristics of the site at the time of the grant. At that time (1930) there was at the frontage to the highway a continuous wall, except for a gap four feet six inches wide between two brick pillars. Inside a gravelled strip eight feet wide, in appearance like a footpath rather than a roadway, led to a doorway

---

9 (1878) 8 Ch.D. 415; see p. 270, *ante*.
10 [1953] 1 W.L.R. 1064. See also *V.T. Engineering Co. Ltd.* v. *Richard Barland and Co. Ltd.* (1968) 19 P. & C.R. 890.
11 See *ante*, p. 44.
12 [1965] 1 Q.B. 334. The Court of Appeal considered its decision in *Dyer* v. *Mousley* (1962) unreported, Bar Library transcript No. 315.
13 [1965] 1 Q.B. 346.
14 [1953] 1 W.L.R. 1064.
15 [1965] 1 Q.B. 334.

three feet wide to the plaintiff's property and to a gap some seven feet wide leading to the remainder of the defendant's property. In 1962 the defendant had widened the entrance from the highway to about seven feet six inches wide by rehanging the original gate and hanging another, three feet wide, alongside, which she kept locked, claiming to be entitled to do so.

In *McIlraith* v. *Grady* [16] there had been a grant in 1901 " with or without horses carts and carriages to pass and repass through over and along " a yard leading from a main road to the back of shop premises. In 1953 the shopkeeper built a small wall at the back of his premises so that thereafter vehicles stopped in the yard to load and unload. The Court of Appeal held that, just as in *Bulstrode* v. *Lambert*,[17] there was by implication a right to halt and unload, so in the present case there was necessarily imported, in addition to an actual right to pass and repass, a right to stop for a reasonable time for the purpose of loading and unloading.

It has been held in Ireland that the grant of a right of way on foot over a passage does not authorise the grantee to have carried through the passage burdens not ordinarily carried by foot passengers in the use of a footway.[18]

Under a grant of a free and convenient horse and foot-way, and for carts, etc., " to carry stones, timber, coals and other things whatsoever," it was held that the grantee could lay a framed way along the land for carrying coals, but not a transverse way.[19] Where in 1630 land was granted, excepting and reserving out of the grant all mines of coal with sufficient wayleave to the said mines, and with liberty of sinking pits, it was held that the right was not confined to such ways as were in use at the time of the grant, and that it included the right to instal steam engines and other machinery necessary for draining the pits off.[20] Where, however, A granted land, reserving a wagon or cart road of the width of eighteen feet, to be at all times thereafter kept in repair at his own cost, it was held that this reservation did not enable A to lay down a railroad for carrying coals from his neighbouring colliery.[21]

Where a right of way was granted " as at present enjoyed," the words quoted were held to refer to the quality, and not to the purpose or extent, of the user.[22]

Quantity and purpose of user

It appears now to be settled that, subject to any restriction to be gathered from the words of the grant or the surrounding circumstances,

[16] [1968] 1 Q.B. 468.   [17] [1953] 1 W.L.R. 1064.
[18] *Austin* v. *Scottish Widows' Fund Assurance Society* (1881) 8 L.R.Ir. 385.
[19] *Senhouse* v. *Christian* (1787) 1 T.R. 560.
[20] *Dand* v. *Kingscote* (1840) 6 M. & W. 174; see *Newcomen* v. *Coulson* (1877) 5 Ch.D. 133, 139.   [21] *Bidder* v. *North Staffordshire Railway* (1878) 4 Q.B.D. 412.
[22] *Hurt* v. *Bowmer* [1937] 1 All E.R. 797. In *Collins* v. *Slade* (1874) 23 W.R. 199, the same words were held to refer to the time of user, *i.e.* during specified daylight hours only, the servient owner being entitled to block the way at night.

a right of way may be used, in the manner authorised by the grant,[23] for any purpose and to any extent for the time being required for the enjoyment of the dominant tenement or any part of it, irrespective of the purpose for which the dominant tenement was used at the date of the grant.[24] It would seem, also, that user of an authorised kind, *e.g.* with vehicles, may be had, at least if that particular kind of user is expressly authorised, to any increased extent which the physical state of the *locus in quo* will for the time being allow.[25] It is still a question, however, whether a description, in the grant, of the *terminus ad quem* limits the dominant owner to user for the purposes of that terminus as it was at the time.

In *Allan* v. *Gomme*,[26] which was an action of trespass, it appeared that the defendant, having by express reservation a right of way over the plaintiff's premises to a stable and loft on his own land, and to a " space or opening under the said loft and then used as a wood-house," converted the loft and the space thereunder into a cottage, and claimed to use the way as appurtenant to the cottage. A verdict having been found for the plaintiff, the defendant obtained a rule *nisi* for a nonsuit, which was discharged by the Exchequer Chamber. The judgment of the court was delivered by Lord Denman C.J., who, while conceding that the words " now used as a wood-house " were to be taken merely as ascertaining the place where the open space of ground was, was of opinion that the defendant was confined to the use of the way

" to a place which should be *in the same predicament* as it was at the time of the making the deed. We do not mean to say that he could only use it to make a deposit of wood there, for we consider the words ' now used as a wood-house ' merely used for the ascertaining the locality and identity of the place called a space or opening under the loft; and we think he might have the benefit of the way to make a deposit of any articles, or use it in any way he pleased, provided it continued in the state of open ground. But we think he could only use it for purposes which were compatible with the ground being open, and that, if any buildings were erected upon it, it was no longer to be considered as open for the purpose of this deed. Suppose that this piece of ground, instead of being a small quantity, had been a field of many acres, and that Browne had sold off the part above mentioned to the plaintiff, reserving to himself this right of way to the land, calling it a field then in pasture, or in corn, and had subsequently filled the land with small cottages or

23 See p. 269, *ante.*
24 *White* v. *Grand Hotel, Eastbourne Ltd.* (1912) 106 L.T. 785; [1913] 1 Ch. 113; *Robinson* v. *Bailey* [1948] 2 All E.R. 791.
25 *Bulstrode* v. *Lambert, ante,* p. 272, where the vehicles the use by which of the yard was expressly authorised were not confined to such as could originally have passed through a gate, with a bar over it, which was inside the entrance to the yard at the date of the reservation and had been removed before the dispute in the action arose.
26 (1840) 11 A. & E. 759.

had built a factory, or established gas works, it surely never could be contended that it was the meaning of either of the parties to the deed that there should be a right of way over the yard to those buildings."

His Lordship referred to *Luttrel's* case,[27] and concluded:

" The court [in *Luttrel's* case] appears to have put the case on whether the alteration of the thing, in respect of which the right was claimed, was of the substance and not merely of the quality of the thing.[28] Now the alteration of a piece of vacant ground into a cottage is certainly an alteration of the substance, and not merely of the quality."

Allan v. *Gomme*[29] was admittedly a case of first impression; in the course of the argument in *Henning* v. *Burnet*[30] Parke B. said that the law appeared to him to have been laid down too strictly.

" No doubt," he added, " if a right of way be granted for the purpose of being used as a way to a cottage, and the cottage is changed into a tanyard, the right of way ceases; but if there is a general grant of all ways to a cottage, the right is not lost by reason of the cottage being altered."

In *South Metropolitan Cemetery Co.* v. *Eden*,[31] Jervis C.J. remarked:

" If I grant a man a way to a cottage which consists of one room, I know the extent of the liberty I grant; and my grant would not justify the grantee in claiming to use the way to gain access to a town he might build at the extremity of it. Here the grant is general,—to use the road for the purpose of going to or returning from the land conveyed, or any part thereof; it is not defined, as in the case referred to."

The decision in *Allan* v. *Gomme*[29] has often been quoted to support the view that the right to use a way is confined to the use of it for the purposes of the dominant tenement in the condition in which such tenement was at the time of the grant. It is clear, however, that there is no such general rule, and that *Allan* v. *Gomme*[29] can be applied, if at all, only where the grant appears to be of a way to some particular building or thing.

Finch v. *Great Western Railway Co.*[32] was a case of an award under an Inclosure Act; here the way in question (twenty feet wide) was to " remain a private carriage-road and drift-way for the use of the respec-

27 (1601) 4 Rep. 86a; where it was held that a prescriptive right to the flow of water to a mill was not affected by a change in the character of the mill. See *post*, p. 320.
28 *i.e.* the substance and not merely the quality of the mill. In *White* v. *Grand Hotel, Eastbourne Ltd.* [1913] 1 Ch. 113, 117, Hamilton L.J., commenting on this case, translated " thing " into " right," or " enjoyment." He is variously reported.
29 (1840) 11 A. & E. 759.
30 (1852) 8 Ex. 187, 192.
31 (1855) 16 C.B. 42, 57.
32 (1879) 5 Ex.D. 254.

tive owners and occupiers for the time being of the allotment over which the same passes, and of several old inclosed meadows and woodlands belonging to [A], a meadow called Broadmead, belonging to [B], and the said inclosed meadow, belonging to [C], to which the same passes." A part of the " allotment over which the " road passed, which had been pasture land, was converted by the defendant company into a cattle-pen for storing cattle in transit, the user of the road being much increased; and, an action having been brought, the court held that the new user could be justified. The court thought that *Allan* v. *Gomme* [29] established no general rule, but turned on the construction of the particular deed referred to; and that the principle was established " that, where there is an express grant of a private right of way to a particular place,[33] to the unrestricted use of which the grantee of the right of way is entitled, the grant is not to be restricted to access to the land for the purposes for which access would be required at the time of the grant."

Newcomen v. *Coulson* [34] was also the case of an award under an Inclosure Act. The award directed that each of the allottees, " and the owner or owners for the time being of the lands hereby to them respectively allotted, shall for ever hereafter have and enjoy a way-right and liberty of passage for themselves and their respective tenants and farmers of the said lands and grounds, as well on foot as on horseback, and with their carts and carriages, and to lead and drive their horses, oxen and other cattle, as often as occasion shall require," over a certain property therein specified; and that, if the allottees or any of them, or any of the owners for the time being of their respective allotments, should " street out " the way, it should be made eleven yards broad at the least between the quick-sets. The allotments were merely agricultural land. The owners of one of the allotments having commenced to build upon their land a number of villa residences, and to metal the road for the purpose of being used with the residences, the owner of the soil of the road and of the adjoining property interfered, and insisted that the way could not be used except for access to agricultural property. His action, and the appeal, were dismissed. Malins V.-C. distinguished *Allan* v. *Gomme*,[35] being of opinion that this was not the case of an easement, but of an arrangement between the owners of the land enclosed for the formation and enjoyment of a way, which meant a way for all purposes. The Court of Appeal held that it was a case of easement, and relied on the fact that the way was granted as appurtenant to " land," which meant the land and all buildings from time to time to be erected upon it or any part of it.

In *United Land Co.* v. *Great Eastern Railway Co.*[36] a railway company had been empowered to make a railway through Crown lands by

---

33 The words " to a particular place," if emphatic, tend to negative *Allan* v. *Gomme*
    (1840) 11 A. & E. 759.   34 (1877) 5 Ch.D. 133.
35 (1840) 11 A. & E. 759.
36 (1873) L.R. 17 Eq. 158.

an Act which required the company to make such convenient crossings where the railway traversed the Crown lands as should in the judgment of certain Commissioners, be " necessary for the convenient enjoyment and occupation of the lands." In accordance with this provision, the company agreed with the Commissioners to make " four level crossings " at certain specific points, " with proper approaches thereto from the lands on the other side," three of the crossings to be thirty feet wide each, and the remaining one twenty feet wide. The crossings were made substantially in accordance with this agreement. The land in question was, at the date of the Act, marsh or pasture land, and was subject to a statute which prevented building. The land was subsequently sold free from this restriction and advertised for resale in building lots, and the defendants, successors in title of the original railway company, objected to the crossings being used for access to the houses. The objection was overruled by Malins V.-C., who distinguished the case before him from a grant of a private right of way on the ground that it was a case of compulsory sale, and that a railway company dividing land into lots was bound to render it as useful for all purposes as if no severance had been made. He thought that the width of the crossings showed that they had not been intended to be used merely for agricultural purposes. The nature of the communications agreed upon had no doubt reduced the amount of compensation paid.

On appeal,[37] the Court of Appeal in Chancery affirmed this decision, chiefly for the special reasons given by the Vice-Chancellor, but Mellish L.J. added some words on the general principle.

> " No doubt," he said,[38] " there are authorities that, from the description of the lands to which the right of way is annexed, and of the purposes for which it is granted, the Court may infer that the way was intended to be limited to those purposes. But if there is no limit in the grant, the way may be used for all purposes."

James L.J. said [39] that there was nothing in the circumstances of the case, or in the situation of the parties, or in the situation of the land, to prevent the words in the Act from having their full operation. Farwell J. evidently had this passage in the judgment of James L.J. in mind when he said in *Todrick* v. *Western National Omnibus Co. Ltd.*[40]:

> " In considering whether a particular use of a right of this kind is a proper use or not, I am entitled to take into consideration the circumstances of the case, the situation of the parties and the situation of the land at the time when the grant was made: see *United Land Company* v. *Great Eastern Railway Company*, *per* James L.J.[39]; and in my judgment a grant for all purposes means for all

---

[37] (1875) 10 Ch.App. 586.
[38] (1875) 10 Ch.App. 586, 590–591.
[39] (1875) 10 Ch.App. 590.
[40] [1934] Ch. 190, 206; this part of Farwell J.'s judgment was approved by the Court of Appeal [1934] Ch. 561.

purposes having regard to the consideration which I have already mentioned. It would be ridiculous to suppose that merely because the grant was expressed to be for all purposes it entitled the owner of the dominant tenement to attempt to use it for something for which obviously it could not be used."

Farwell J. held that the grant of a right of way, with or without vehicles, over a road supported by a retaining wall, seven feet nine inches high at its entrance, and clearly not intended for heavy vehicles, did not authorise use by motor buses.

In *Jelbert* v. *Davis* [41] agricultural land had been conveyed " together with the right of way at all times and for all purposes over the drive-way . . . leading to the main road in common with all other persons having the like right." The Court of Appeal held that although the wide terms of the grant permitted use of the driveway for vehicular traffic of a kind different from that contemplated at the time of the grant, and therefore for caravans, excessive user of the way such as would interfere with the rights of " other persons having the like right " or cause a legal nuisance would be outside the terms of the grant, looked at in the cir-cumstances at the date it was made. On the evidence, the proposed user of the driveway for 200 camping units (consisting of caravans and/or tents) on the dominant land would be excessive. Lord Denning M.R. referred [42] to the passage in the judgment of Farwell J. in *Todrick* v. *Western National Omnibus Co. Ltd.*[43] referred to above as having stated the law on this subject.

In *Watts* v. *Kelson* [44] the plaintiff was, by express words contained in the conveyance of his premises, entitled to " a right of way " through the defendant's gateway and close " to a wicket-gate to be erected by the plaintiff leading into the hereinbefore described piece or part of garden ground." The plaintiff's premises contained, beside the garden, a cot-tage, a number of stalls for feeding cattle, a yard and outbuildings, and a few acres of land. The defendant's gate would admit carriages. The plaintiff did not erect a wicket-gate, but erected a cart-shed on the same spot, and brought carts to it. The defendant having obstructed the way, Lord Romilly M.R. granted an injunction. The defendant contended that the way was granted for so long only as the part of the plaintiff's premises nearest to the proposed wicket-gate should continue to be used as a garden, quoting *Allan* v. *Gomme* [45]; but Lord Romilly, without giving reasons, rejected this contention.

In *White* v. *Grand Hotel, Eastbourne,*[46] where the dominant tenement had been converted (in effect) from a private dwelling-house into an hotel,

41 [1968] 1 W.L.R. 589.
42 [1968] 1 W.L.R. 595.
43 [1934] Ch. 190, 206.
44 (1870) 6 Ch.App. 166.
45 (1840) 11 A. & E. 759.
46 (1912) 106 L.T. 785; [1913] 1 Ch. 113 (C.A.); varied in H.L. on another point
    sub nom. *Grand Hotel, Eastbourne Ltd.* v. *White* (1913) 110 L.T. 209.

and the court had to consider an oral, and apparently general, grant of a
right of way, it was decided that user for the purposes of the hotel was
justified. Joyce J.[47] accepted the proposition laid down in *Finch* v.
Great Western Railway [48] that "where there is an express grant of a
right of way to a particular place, to the unrestricted use of which the
grantee of the right of way is entitled, the grant is not to be restricted to
access to the land for the purposes for which access would be required
at the time of the grant." His decision was affirmed by the Court of
Appeal, who considered the law to be settled by *United Land Co.* v.
Great Eastern Railway [49] with which Farwell L.J.[50] thought *Allan* v.
Gomme [1] to be inconsistent. Cozens-Hardy M.R. said [2]:

> " The plaintiff's main point was . . . that it was only a right of
> way for what I may call domestic purposes as distinct from trade
> purposes; and that it was only for such use as could reasonably be
> expected to be in the contemplation of the parties at the time when
> the defendants' house, St. Vincent Lodge, was a private residence,
> and ought not to be altered now that St. Vincent Lodge is turned
> into a [hotel-] garage. We heard that point fully argued by counsel
> for the appellants and we have come to the conclusion that there
> is no ground for limiting the right of way in the manner suggested.
> It is not a right of way claimed by prescription. It is a right of way
> claimed under a grant, and, that being so, the only thing the Court
> has to do is to construe the grant; and unless there is some limita-
> tion to be found in the grant, in the nature of the width of the road
> or something of that kind, full effect must be given to the grant,
> and we cannot consider the subsequent user as in any way sufficient
> to cut down the generality of the grant."

In *South Eastern Railway* v. *Cooper* [3] the predecessors in title of the
defendant had owned land through part of which the plaintiff company
constructed its railway under statutory powers in 1844, so that
the remainder of the defendant's land was completely cut off from the
highway which had adjoined the land before the construction of the
railway. In order to restore access to the highway, the company made
a level-crossing from the defendant's land to the highway, and granted
a right of way in general terms. For many years after 1844 the owners
of the land had used the crossing for agricultural purposes only; but in
1920 the defendant opened a sandpit upon the land and sold out of it
large quantities of sand for commercial purposes, so that the burden of
the easement was much increased. The plaintiff company having
brought an action to restrain the defendant from using the crossing in

47 (1912) 106 L.T. 788.
48 (1879) 5 Ex.D. 254; see p. 275, *ante*.
49 (1873) L.R. 17 Eq. 158; see p. 276, *ante*.
50 [1913] 1 Ch. 115.
 1 (1840) 11 A. & E. 759.
 2 [1913] 1 Ch. 116.
 3 [1924] 1 Ch. 211.

excess of the extent to which it was used when the easement was granted, the Court of Appeal held that, the grant being a grant of a general right of way for all purposes and not merely a grant of an "accommodation way" under section 68 of the Railway Clauses Act 1845,[4] the user was not restricted to that contemplated when the grant was made.

South Eastern Railway v. *Cooper*[5] was applied by the Court of Appeal (Harman and Davies L.JJ., Lord Denning M.R. dissenting) in *British Railways Board* v. *Glass*.[6] In that case a conveyance of land to a railway company was expressed to except a right of crossing the railway and the majority of the Court of Appeal construed the conveyance as operating as a grant of a right of way for all purposes, not limited to the user contemplated when the grant was made. Hence the way was not limited to the agricultural purposes in the contemplation of the parties and could be used for access to a caravan site in the defendant's field.

In *Robinson* v. *Bailey*[7] a limitation on the permitted quantity and purpose of user was sought to be established by inference from the surrounding circumstances. The Court of Appeal, affirming Harman J. whose judgment is not reported, recognised that surrounding circumstances can affect the construction of a grant, but considered that they had no limiting effect in that case. The defendant, who was a builder, had bought from the plaintiff a plot on a new building estate, together with "a right of way" over an adjacent roadway, about twenty-five feet wide, leading to the public highway. At the date of the conveyance this roadway was laid out in a rudimentary fashion, and in the conveyance the plaintiff covenanted to make up and maintain it until it should be taken over as a public road by the local authority. The whole estate in the hands of the plaintiff was subject to a restrictive covenant, which was assumed to be enforceable against the defendant, prohibiting the erection of buildings other than private dwelling-houses and the carrying on of any trade or business on any part. Under a local town planning scheme, building was restricted to residential houses. The defendant covenanted with the plaintiff that only one house should be erected on his plot. The plaintiff sought to establish that the defendant was not entitled, under the grant to him of "a right of way," to use the roadway for the passage of heavy lorries engaged in carrying to and from the plot builders' materials for which the defendant, who was prevented by current conditions from building a house, was using the plot as a store in connection with his business. The plaintiff admitted that user by lorries was in itself an authorised mode of user, but contended that, in

---

[4] As to the limited permissible use of such ways, see *Great Western Railway* v. *Talbot* [1902] 2 Ch. 759; *Taff Vale Railway* v. *Gordon Canning* [1909] 2 Ch. 48; *British Railways Board* v. *Glass* [1965] Ch. 538, 553–554, *per* Lord Denning M.R., 558, 559, *per* Harman L.J.
[5] [1924] 1 Ch. 211.
[6] [1965] Ch. 538; see p. 269, *ante*.
[7] [1948] 2 All E.R. 791.

the circumstances, the right granted must be confined inferentially to user for the purposes of a house, and that the persistent use of the road by lorries carrying builders' materials was excessive. It was said that, having regard to the restrictions existing at the time of the grant, the parties must have contemplated that the plot, and consequently the roadway, would be used only for the purposes of a residential house; but the court pointed out that, as between the parties, the authorised use of the plot was not confined to residential use; that the restrictions imposed on the plaintiff, and by the town planning scheme, were not necessarily permanent or immutable; and that the effect of the plaintiff's covenant to maintain the road until it should be taken over as a public road was, if anything, to confirm the view that the road was intended to be used as fully as a public road might be; and they concluded that there was nothing in the surrounding circumstances that limited the unqualified terms of the grant.

In *Kain* v. *Norfolk* [8] where the defendant, grantee of a right of way " with or without horses carts agricultural machines and implements " was held entitled to use the way for lorries carrying sand from a sand-pit recently opened on the dominant land, which at the date of the grant was agricultural, it was conceded that the right was not confined to user for agricultural purposes. The contention was that the words quoted were restrictive, and that " carts " did not include motor-lorries.

In *Selby* v. *Crystal Palace Gas Co.* [9] it was held that a covenant that the occupiers of lands conveyed should have the full use and enjoyment of all roads " in as full, free, complete, and absolute a manner to all intents and purposes whatsoever as if the same were public roads " entitled them not only to the use of the roads for the purpose of transit or for the purposes for which public roads could be used at the date of the deed, but also to authorise a gas company to open one of the roads for the purpose of laying a gas main to serve the houses of the occupiers.

Implied grants

In *Milner's Safe Co. Ltd.* v. *Great Northern and City Railway*, [10] the question arose as to the extent of a way to be implied over a common passage which ran along the back of certain houses into a side street. The plaintiff was the owner of two of these houses, deriving title under one limitation in the will, made in 1828, of a testator who died in 1832, and the defendant was the owner of the site of two others of the houses, deriving title under another limitation. The will contained no express provision as to any right of way over the passage. The defendant pulled down the houses on its land and constructed a railway station having one of its entrances opening into the passage which it claimed to use as a thoroughfare for its passengers. Kekewich J. held that, as in the case

8 [1949] Ch. 163.
9 (1862) 4 De G.F. & J. 246.
10 [1907] 1 Ch. 208.

of a way acquired by prescription, the extent of the right ought to be measured by the user at the time of the grant.[11] He inferred, from evidence of subsequent user, that the passage was at the relevant time used for ordinary business purposes only, and concluded that its user by railway passengers was excessive.[12]

4.—MISCELLANEOUS INCIDENTS

User confined to purposes of the dominant tenement

In *Harris* v. *Flower & Sons* Romer L.J. said [13]: " If a right of way be granted for the enjoyment of close A, the grantee, because he owns or acquires close B, cannot use the way in substance for passing over close A to close B." It need hardly be said that the mere fact that the grantee uses the way to enter close A does not make close B incapable of access from A; the question must always be whether the ostensible use of the way for the purposes of the dominant tenement is genuine or colourable.[14] If land is granted with a right of way, the fact that the way is expressed to be to a particular point or place in the land does not necessarily or usually prevent the right from being annexed to all the land.[15] The question of the identification of the dominant tenement has already been considered.[16]

Who may use the way

It is submitted that a way may be used, with the authority of the person entitled to possession of the dominant tenement, by anyone whose user is not inconsistent with the quantity and purpose [17] of user envisaged by the grant. In *Hammond* v. *Prentice Brothers Ltd.* Eve J. said [18]: " After all, the grant is appurtenant to the dominant tenement, and in my opinion in the absence of special circumstances ought to be so construed as to secure to the grantee all that is necessary for the reasonable enjoyment of the dominant tenement." Words in a grant mentioning certain persons as entitled to use, *e.g.* tenants, visitors, and the like, are generally regarded as illustrative, and not as restrictive.[19]

In *Baxendale* v. *North Lambeth Liberal and Radical Club Ltd.*[20] it was held that a grant, contained in a lease, of full right " for the

---

11 Whether the relevant date for this purpose was the date of the will or the date of the death was not decided; see [1907] 1 Ch. 222.

12 An appeal against this decision was compromised: [1907] 1 Ch. 229.

13 (1905) 74 L.J.Ch. 127, 132; see also Rolle's Abr., Chemin private, A pl. 1; *Gamble* v. *Birch Island Estates Ltd.* (1971) 13 D.L.R. (3d) 657.

14 *Harris* v. *Flower & Sons, supra*; *Skull* v. *Glenister* (1864) 16 C.B.(N.S.) 81; and note (a) to *Lawton* v. *Ward* (1697) 1 Ld.Raym. 75.

15 *Callard* v. *Beeney* [1930] 1 K.B. 353; see *ante*, p. 9.

16 See pp. 8 *et seq., ante.*

17 See *ante*, p. 273.   18 [1920] 1 Ch. 201, 216.

19 *Cf.* the argument on an analogous point, which the court was inclined to accept, in *Kain* v. *Norfolk* [1949] Ch. 163, 168.

20 [1902] 2 Ch. 427. See also *Mitcalfe* v. *Westaway* (1864) 34 L.J.C.P. 113 (" assigns, officers, servants and workmen " held not restrictive). As to somewhat similar words in a grant of a *profit à prendre*, see *Reynolds* v. *Moore* [1908] 2 I.R. 641, and *cf. Re Vickers' Lease* [1947] Ch. 420

lessee, his executors, administrators and assigns, undertenants and servants, at all times for all purposes connected with the use and enjoyment of the premises," to use a way, extended to members and honorary members of, and all other persons going lawfully to and from, a workmen's club afterwards established on the premises. Swinfen Eady J. said that it could not be doubted that, in the ordinary case of a right of way to a house and premises which could only be used as a private dwelling-house, the right would extend not only to the grantee, but to members of his family, servants, visitors, guests and tradespeople, even though none of those persons was expressly mentioned in the grant; and that the necessary or reasonable user of the club premises as a club required that there should be liberty of passing over the way in question for the persons and vehicles shown to have used it.

Similarly, in *Hammond* v. *Prentice Brothers Ltd.*[21] a grant of a right of way for " the grantees, their heirs and assigns, and their servants, customers and workmen, and the tenants and occupiers " of the dominant tenement was held to extend to licensees of the dominant owners, and not to be limited to the persons mentioned. Eve J. said [22]:

> " Parties may, of course, so frame the grant as to demonstrate their intention that it is to be limited in its application to particular objects; but when the grant is in general terms, and there are no circumstances subsisting at the date of the grant and nothing in the grant itself sufficient to point in an opposite direction, I think the proper inference is that the added words are not intended to be read as exhaustive, but rather as illustrative of the individuals or classes of individuals entitled to use the way. In this case, unless I adopt this view, no visitor, no doctor, no tradesman, no traveller, and no apprentice can approach the defendant company's premises under this grant."

In *Thornton* v. *Little* [23] where a right of way was granted, so as to be annexed to premises then used as a school, to the grantee, her administrators and assigns, and her and their tenants, visitors and servants, to the intent that the right should be appurtenant to the premises for all purposes connected with the use, occupation and enjoyment of the same, Kekewich J. seemed inclined to regard the enumeration of permitted persons as exhaustive, but he held that, construing the grant in the light of the circumstances, " visitors " included pupils.

In *Keith* v. *Twentieth Century Club Ltd.*[24] the sites of certain houses then being built round a London " square " garden had been conveyed to A, with a grant to A, his heirs, executors, administrators and assigns, and his and their lessees and sub-lessees or tenants, being occupiers for the time being of the houses then in course of erection or thereafter to be

21 [1920] 1 Ch. 201.
22 [1920] 1 Ch. 216.
23 (1907) 97 L.T. 24.
24 (1904) 73 L.J.Ch. 545.

erected immediately adjoining the garden, and for his and their families and friends, in his and their company or without, of free use and right of ingress, egress and regress at all times into, out of and upon the garden, he and they conforming to such rules as should be ordered by the vendor, his heirs or assigns, or the committee (if any) of residents to whom the management of the garden should be committed, and also paying an annual subscription for the maintenance of the garden. Some of the houses having been acquired by the defendant and converted into a residential club, certain adjoining residents, who were entitled to the same right, sought to restrain the defendant from allowing its members to use the garden. The owner of the garden was not a party. Two preliminary points of law, namely, whether resident members of the club were entitled as of right to use the garden, and whether the defendant was entitled to authorise its members, resident or non-resident, to use it, were answered by Buckley J. in the negative, on the ground that members of the defendant's club were not tenants or friends of the defendant. The learned judge evidently felt that the user of the garden was intended to be confined to owners and occupiers of residential houses adjoining it, and their families and friends, and that, as there was nothing to prevent the houses round the square from being used otherwise than as private dwelling-houses, the words of enumeration in the grant ought to be considered as exhaustive.

Physical extent of the way

A right of way should, generally speaking, have a *terminus a quo* and a *terminus ad quem*, so as to be bounded and circumscribed to a place certain,[25] but in *Wimbledon and Putney Commons Conservators* v. *Dixon*,[26] the Court of Appeal was of the opinion that the fact that the occupiers of a tenement to which a way by user was claimed had used, not a definite road marked out between the termini, but a number of tracks indifferently, did not prevent the right from being acquired. Again, on the taking of a lease of land in Ireland the court implied a grant by the lessor to the lessee of a right of way across the lessor's other land by such route as the lessor should from time to time point out.[27]

Questions have arisen, on the construction of particular grants, as to whether a right of way over a road mentioned is a right over its whole length, or over a part only.[28]

If the site of a way over which a right is granted is not physically

25 *Albon* v. *Dremsall* (1610) 1 Brownl. 216; Yelv. 163; Com.Dig.Chemin, D.2.
26 (1875) 1 Ch.D. 362.
27 *Donnelly* v. *Adams* [1905] 1 I.R. 154.
28 *Wood* v. *Stourbridge Railway* (1864) 16 C.B.(N.S.) 222; *Knox* v. *Sansom* (1877) 25 W.R. 864; *Randall* v. *Hall* (1851) 4 De G. & Sm. 343. For a case of mutual mistake in describing a staircase, see *Cowen* v. *Truefitt Ltd.* [1898] 2 Ch. 551; [1899] 2 Ch. 309.

apparent, it is for the servient owner to indicate where it is to be.[29] Once he has done so, or the way has been defined by usage, it cannot (except by agreement) be altered.[30]

Amount of way to which grantee entitled

There is this distinction between a private and a public right of way, that the former is not necessarily, as the latter is, over every part of the land along which the right exists.[31] The grant of a private right of way along " the passage coloured blue " on a plan confers, it has been said,[32] a prima facie right to the reasonable use of every part of the passage, but an action for disturbance will not lie unless there is a real substantial interference with the enjoyment.[33] Accordingly, where there was granted to the plaintiff a right to use a forty-foot road, it was held that he could not maintain an action in respect of a portico which projected two feet into the carriage-way but left ample space for the convenient enjoyment by the plaintiff of the way.[34] The question is whether practically and substantially the right of way can be exercised as conveniently as before.[35] In *Pettey* v. *Parsons*,[36] the dominant owner was held entitled to place a gate, to be kept open during business hours and never to be locked, at one end of the way, and to fence in a small portion of it at its wider end.

In *Strick (F. C.) & Co. Ltd.* v. *City Offices Ltd.*[37] the defendants granted to the plaintiffs a lease of offices in a block of buildings. No mention was made in the lease of any right of access from the entrance hall, but it was admitted that the plaintiffs had such right. At the date of the lease the hall was of large dimensions, and the defendants subsequently proposed to diminish the size. The plaintiffs claiming a right of way over every part of the hall, it was held that no such right existed, the plaintiffs being entitled only to a reasonable user.

---

[29] *Deacon* v. *South Eastern Railway* (1889) 61 L.T. 377; *Bolton* v. *Bolton* (1879) 11 Ch.D. 968.

[30] *Deacon* v. *South Eastern Railway, supra.* See, however, as to the alteration of an easement of necessity, *Wynne* v. *Pope* (1960) 3 S.A. 37, and p. 117, *ante.*

[31] *Hutton* v. *Hamboro* (1860) 2 F. & F. 218, 219; *Pettey* v. *Parsons* [1914] 2 Ch. 653. A grant of a right to pass over certain roads " in the same manner and as fully as if the same were public roads " was held to entitle the grantee to the use of the whole of the roads; *Nicol* v. *Beaumont* (1883) 53 L.J.Ch. 853; *cf. Selby* v. *Crystal Palace Gas Co.* (1862) 4 De G.F. & J. 246. A grantee is entitled to have vertical " swing-space," that is, to have the way free from obstruction to such a height as is reasonable, but there is no implied right of lateral " swing-space " which would prevent the servient owner from building on either side of the way; *V.T. Engineering Ltd.* v. *Richard Barland & Co. Ltd.* (1968) 19 P. & C.R. 890.

[32] *Sketchley* v. *Berger* (1893) 69 L.T. 754.

[33] *Pettey* v. *Parsons, supra.*

[34] *Clifford* v. *Hoare* (1874) L.R. 9 C.P. 362.

[35] *Hutton* v. *Hamboro, supra*; *Robertson* v. *Abrahams* [1930] W.N. 79.

[36] [1914] 2 Ch. 653. A question as to the right of the servient owner to make a gate into the way arose, on peculiar facts, in *Guilford (Earl)* v. *St. George's Golf Club Trust* (1916) 85 L.J.Ch. 669.

[37] (1906) 22 T.L.R. 667.

Access from dominant tenement

Pickford L.J. in *Pettey* v. *Parsons* [38] said that " It is a question of construction, in a deed granting a right of way, whether the way that is granted is a way so that the grantee may open gates, or means of access to the way, at any point of his frontage, or whether it is merely a way between two points, a right to pass over the road, and is limited to the modes of access to the road existing at the date of the grant," and that, assuming the right of access from every part of the land from which access is required to every part of the way, such access should be given as will give reasonable opportunity for the exercise of the right.

Right to deviate

If an obstruction, not easy of removal, is placed across a way by the servient owner or occupier (or *semble*, by any other person) [39] who is entitled to adjoining land, the person entitled to use the way may, so long as the obstruction continues, deviate into the adjoining land in order to connect the two parts of the way on each side of the obstacle. [40] If the obstructing party holds the adjoining land for a particular estate, the right of deviation is limited to the duration of that estate. [40] There is, it seems, no other right to deviate. [41]

Remedy for excessive user

Where user of a right of way is excessive the dominant owner will be liable in trespass and may be restrained by injunction. [42] Where it is impossible to sever proper user of an easement from excessive user, the servient owner may stop the whole user. [43] It has been held, [44] in the case of a right of way, that if the excessive user cannot be abated without obstructing the whole user, the servient owner may obstruct the whole of that user.

---

[38] [1914] 2 Ch. 653, 667, 669; and see *Cooke* v. *Ingram* (1893) 68 L.T. 671; *Sketchley* v. *Berger* (1893) 69 L.T. 754; *South Metropolitan Cemetery Co.* v. *Eden* (1855) 16 C.B. 42.

[39] *Stacey* v. *Sherrin* (1913) 29 T.L.R. 555.

[40] *Selby* v. *Nettleford* (1873) 9 Ch.App. 111.

[41] *Bullard* v. *Harrison* (1815) 4 M. & S. 387; *Taylor* v. *Whitehead* (1781) 2 Doug.K.B. 745; and see 1 Wms.Saund. (1871 ed.) 565, note (3), where it is pointed out that the proposition in Com.Dig.Chemin, D.6, that a right to deviate arises if the way becomes impassable through lack of repair, is applicable only to highways. As to the repair of ways, see *ante*, pp. 44 *et seq.*

[42] *Milner's Safe Co. Ltd.* v. *Great Northern and City Railway Co.* [1907] 1 Ch. 208, 229.

[43] See *post*, pp. 346, 347.

[44] *Bernard and Bernard* v. *Jennings and Hillaire* (1968) 13 W.I.R. 501, Trinidad and Tobago C.A.

CHAPTER 10

SUPPORT

Right to support

The right to support from the adjacent or subjacent soil may be claimed in respect of land in its natural state, or in respect of land subjected to an artificial pressure by means of buildings or otherwise. A further right to support may be claimed for one building from adjacent or subjacent buildings.

1.—Natural Support to Land

If every proprietor of land were at liberty to dig and mine at pleasure on his own soil, without considering what effect such excavations must produce upon the land of his neighbours, it is obvious that the withdrawal of the lateral support would, in many cases, cause the falling in of the land adjoining. As far as the mere support to the soil is concerned, such support must have been afforded as long as the land itself has been in existence; and in all those cases, at least, in which the owner of land has not, by buildings or otherwise, increased the lateral pressure upon the adjoining soil, he has a right to the support of it, not as an easement but as an ordinary right of property, necessarily and naturally attached to the soil. The leaning of the courts appears to have been in favour of this doctrine from a very early period: thus, in 2 Rolle's Abridgment,[1] it is laid down: " It seems that a man who has land closely adjoining my land cannot dig his land so near mine that mine would fall into his pit; and an action brought for such an act would lie."

Prima facie rule as to support

Questions as to support have arisen where the title to land A has been severed from the title to land B which is subjacent to land A vertically; or from the title to land C which is adjacent to land A laterally. The prima facie rule in these cases is that (independently of the result of any facts or instruments connected with the severance) the owner of land A is of common right entitled to have it supported vertically by land B [2] and laterally by land C.[3] But the obligation to support land A

---

[1] Trespass, Justification, I, pl. 1.

[2] *Humphries* v. *Brogden* (1850) 12 Q.B. 739; *Caledonian Railway* v. *Sprot* (1856) 2 Macq. 449; *Backhouse* v. *Bonomi* (1861) 9 H.L.C. 503; *N.E. Railway* v. *Elliott* (1860) 1 J. & H. 145.

[3] *Hunt* v. *Peake* (1860) John. 705; *Davis* v. *Treharne* (1881) 6 App.Cas. 460, 466, *per* Lord Blackburn; *Dalton* v. *Angus* (1881) 6 App.Cas. 808, 809, *per* Lord Blackburn.

laterally only binds that portion of the adjacent land C, the existence of
which in its natural state is necessary for the support of land A.[4]

Support from water, silt and liquid pitch

The natural right does not extend to the enjoyment of the support of
any underground water which may be in the soil, so as to prevent the
adjoining owner from draining his soil; the presence of the water in
the soil being an accidental circumstance, the continuance of which the
landowner has no right to count upon.

In *Popplewell* v. *Hodkinson*,[5] land was granted for building subject
to a chief rent, and cottages were built upon it, and the owner afterwards granted the adjacent land to the builders of a church, whose
excavations so far drained the land on which the cottages stood that the
soil subsided and they became cracked and damaged. The church
builders, however, were held not responsible. Delivering the judgment
of the Court of Exchequer Chamber, Cockburn C.J. said [6]:

> " Although there is no doubt that a man has no right to with-
> draw from his neighbour the support of adjacent soil, there is nothing
> at common law to prevent his draining that soil, if, for any reason
> it becomes necessary or convenient for him to do so. It may be,
> indeed, that when one grants land to another for some special pur-
> poses, for building purposes, for example, then, since according to
> the old maxim a man cannot derogate from his own grant, the
> grantor could not do anything whatever with his own land which
> might have the effect of rendering the land granted less fit for the
> special purpose in question than it otherwise might have been."

The Court held that there was nothing in the grant to the plaintiff to
warrant the inference of an implied condition to prevent the defendant
from doing with the adjacent land what was incidental to its ordinary
use, *viz.* draining it in order to render it more capable of being adapted
to building purposes.

Popplewell v. *Hodkinson* [5] was applied by Plowman J. in *Langbrook
Properties Ltd.* v. *Surrey County Council.*[7] The plaintiff company
claimed damages for nuisance and negligence against the defendants,
alleging that, by pumping out excavations on land in the vicinity of the
plaintiff's land, the defendants had abstracted water percolating beneath
the plaintiff's land, causing settlement of the buildings on that land. A
preliminary issue was ordered to be tried whether, on the facts pleaded
in the statement of claim, the plaintiff had any cause of action against
the defendants by reason of any withdrawal of water by the pumping of
it from beneath the surface of the land in the vicinity of the plaintiff's
land, and Plowman J., after an extensive review of the cases on the

---

4 *Birmingham Corporation* v. *Allen* (1877) 6 Ch.D. 284.
5 (1869) L.R. 4 Ex. 248.
6 (1869) L.R. 4 Ex. 251, 252.
7 [1970] 1 W.L.R. 161.

withdrawal of percolating water, held that they established that a man may abstract the water under his land which percolates in undefined channels to whatever extent he pleases, notwithstanding that this may result in the abstraction of water percolating under the land of his neighbour and, thereby, cause him injury. In such circumstances the principle of *sic utere tuo ut alienum non laedas* did not operate and the damage was *damnum sine injuria*. There was no room for the law of nuisance or the law of negligence to operate.

There may, however, be a right of support from silt or liquid pitch or brine. Thus, in *Jordeson* v. *Sutton, Southcoates and Drypool Gas Co.*[8] the defendants carried out excavation works upon their property, which adjoined the plaintiff's property, and in the course of such excavation cut through a stratum of running silt, with the result that the plaintiff's houses erected upon his adjoining property subsided. The evidence was conflicting as to whether the stratum of silt could truly be considered to be muddy water or wet sand, and in effect the decision turned upon the view taken by a majority of the Court of Appeal as to the conclusion to be drawn from this evidence; Sir Nathaniel Lindley M.R. and Rigby L.J. holding that the plaintiff's land was supported, not by a stratum of water, but by a bed of wet sand, whilst Vaughan Williams L.J. came to the conclusion that the withdrawal of subterranean water support had caused the subsidence. The decision of a majority of the court was therefore based upon the ordinary law with regard to the right to support. In *Trinidad Asphalt Co.* v. *Ambard*[9] the subsidence of the plaintiff's land was caused by the oozing and escape of pitch, which formed the main ingredient of the plaintiff's land, consequent upon excavations on the defendant's adjacent lands. The judgment of the Privy Council was in favour of the plaintiff, but the grounds of the decision were based upon the conclusion that the pitch or asphalt which escaped from beneath the plaintiff's land was not water, but a mineral.

Jordeson v. *Sutton, Southcoates and Drypool Gas Co.*[10] was applied by Pennycuick V.-C. in *Lotus Ltd.* v. *British Soda Co. Ltd.*[11] The defendants engaged in wild brine pumping, that is to say, the extraction from beneath their land of saturated brine resulting from the dissolution of rock salt by water. As the defendants extracted the brine, more water flowed under the plaintiff's land and dissolved further salt and the resulting brine was pumped away to be replaced by yet more water. In consequence the plaintiff's land subsided and serious damage was caused to buildings on the land. Pennycuick V.-C. said that there was no difference in principle between the removal *in specie* of a support such as wet sand and an operation which consisted, first, in causing a solid support to liquefy and then removing the resultant liquid. As the threat

8 [1899] 2 Ch. 217. See the Brine Pumping (Compensation for Subsidence) Act 1891, and *cf. Salt Union* v. *Brunner* [1906] 2 K.B. 822, which is ·onsidered at p. 213, *ante*.
9 [1899] A.C. 594.
10 [1899] 2 Ch. 217.
11 [1971] 2 W.L.R. 7.

of subsidence was a continuing one, the plaintiff was entitled to an injunction which it claimed restraining further pumping.

Nature of the right

A right of support, whether natural or acquired, possessed by the owner of land A is not a right to have the whole or any part of the adjacent or subjacent soil left in its natural state, but simply a right not to have land A appreciably affected by anything done, however carefully,[12] in the adjoining soil subjacent or adjacent.[13] Hence, if on the working of the adjacent or subjacent soil a subsidence is prevented by the use of artificial means of support, no cause of action arises.[14] And as no cause of action arises until actual injury is caused to land A, time does not begin to run under the Limitation Act until then.[15] Where there are successive subsidences, each creates a separate cause of action.[16] A person in possession of the dominant land at the time of subsidence is not liable if this is the result of some act of his predecessor.[17]

The obligation of the servient owner is negative, namely, to refrain from any act which will diminish support; he is not obliged to take active steps to maintain the thing that gives support.[18]

No action lies for subsidence caused by the operation of nature on adjoining land after this has been used in a normal manner not itself diminishing support.[19]

2.—SUPPORT OF BUILDINGS BY LAND

No natural right

There is no natural right to the support of a building *per se*; thus it was said by Lord Selborne in *Dalton* v. *Angus*[20]: "Support to that which is artificially imposed upon land cannot exist *ex jure naturae* because the thing supported does not itself so exist."

If, however, land has been affected by the withdrawal of support, and a building on it has also been affected, and it is shown that the withdrawal of support would have affected the land in its natural state,

---

12 *Hunt* v. *Peake* (1860) John. 705, 710; *Humphries* v. *Brogden* (1850) 12 Q.B. 739, 757.
13 *Dalton* v. *Angus* (1881) 6 App.Cas. 740, 808; *Bonomi* v. *Backhouse* (1858) E.B. & E. 622, 657; *Att.-Gen.* v. *Conduit Colliery Co.* [1895] 1 Q.B. 301, 313.
14 *Bower* v. *Peate* (1876) 1 Q.B.D. 321, 327; *Rowbotham* v. *Wilson* (1857) 8 E. & B. 123, 157.
15 *Backhouse* v. *Bonomi* (1861) 9 H.L.C. 503; *West Leigh Colliery Co.* v. *Tunnicliffe & Hampson Ltd.* [1908] A.C. 27.
16 *Darley Main Colliery Co.* v. *Mitchell* (1886) 11 App.Cas. 127; *Crumbie* v. *Wallsend Local Board* [1891] 1 Q.B. 503; *Hall* v. *Norfolk (Duke)* [1900] 2 Ch. 493, 503; *Redland Bricks Ltd.* v. *Morris* [1970] A.C. 652, 664.
17 *Greenwell* v. *Low Beechburn Coal Co.* [1897] 2 Q.B. 165; *Hall* v. *Norfolk (Duke)* [1900] 2 Ch. 493; distinguished on the facts in *Manley* v. *Burn* [1916] 2 K.B. 121.
18 *Sack* v. *Jones* [1925] Ch. 235; *Bond* v. *Nottingham Corporation* [1940] Ch. 429, 438; *Macpherson* v. *London Passenger Transport Board* (1946) 175 L.T. 279.
19 *Rouse* v. *Gravelworks Ltd.* [1940] 1 K.B. 489 (erosion caused by rain-water in a gravel-pit on adjoining land being blown on to the plaintiff's land).
20 (1881) 6 App.Cas. 740, 792; see *Ray* v. *Fairway Motors (Barnstaple) Ltd.* (1968) 20 P. & C.R. 261 (C.A.).

in other words, that the land has been deprived of its natural right of support, damages may be recovered for the consequent injury to the building.[21]

The rule negativing any natural right of support as regards buildings appears to have been acted upon in early cases. Thus it was laid down in *Wilde* v. *Minsterley* [22]:

> " If A is seised in fee of copyhold land closely adjoining the land of B, and A erect a new house upon his copyhold land, and any part of his house is erected on the confines of his land adjoining the land of B, if B afterwards dig his land so near to the foundation of the house of A, but not in the land of A, that by it the foundation of the messuage, and the messuage itself, fall into the pit, still no action lies by A against B, inasmuch as it was the fault of A himself that he built his house so near the land of B, for he cannot by his (own) act prevent B from making the best use of his land that he can."

In *Wyatt* v. *Harrison* [23] the declaration stated that the plaintiff was possessed of a certain dwelling-house; that the defendant in rebuilding his dwelling-house adjoining, dug so negligently, carelessly, and improperly into the soil and foundation of his own dwelling-house, and so near the soil and foundation of the said dwelling-house of the plaintiff, that by reason thereof the plaintiff's wall gave way and was damaged. To so much of this declaration as " related to the defendant's digging into the soil and foundation of the said dwelling-house of him the defendant, so near to the soil and foundation of the said dwelling-house of the plaintiff, that by reason thereof," etc., the defendant demurred. Lord Tenterden said [24]:

> " The question reduces itself to this, whether, if a person builds to the utmost extremity of his own land, and the owner of the adjoining land digs the ground there, so as to remove some part of the soil which formed the support of the building so erected, an action lies for the injury thereby occasioned? Whatever the law might be if the damage complained of were in respect of an ancient messuage possessed by the plaintiff at the extremity of his own land, which circumstance of antiquity might imply the consent of the

---

21 *Brown* v. *Robins* (1859) 4 H. & N. 186; *Hunt* v. *Peake* (1860) John. 705; *Hamer* v. *Knowles* (1861) 6 H. & N. 454; *Richards* v. *Jenkins* (1868) 18 L.T. 437; *Att.-Gen.* v. *Conduit Colliery Co.* [1895] 1 Q.B. 301, 312. *Smith* v. *Thackerah* (1866) L.R. 1 C.P. 564, which appears to throw some doubt on the principle, is commented on in *Att.-Gen.* v. *Conduit Colliery Co.*, *supra*, 313, and it is noticeable that in that case *Hamer* v. *Knowles* does not appear to have been cited. Damages may also be recovered for letting down a modern house where the person excavating in the adjoining land is not the owner, but a trespasser; *Jeffries* v. *Williams* (1850) 5 Exch. 792; *Bibby* v. *Carter* (1859) 4 H. & N. 153; or a contractor having no proprietary interest therein; *Keegan* v. *Young* [1963] N.Z.L.R. 720.
22 (1640) 2 Rolle's Abr. 564, Trespass, Justification (I) pl. 1.
23 (1832) 3 B. & Ad. 871.
24 *Ibid.* 875, 876.

adjoining proprietor, at a former time, to the erection of the building in that situation, it is enough to say in this case that the building is not alleged to be ancient, but may, as far as appears from the declaration, have been recently erected; and if so, then, according to the authorities, the plaintiff is not entitled to recover. It may be true that if my land adjoins that of another, and I have not by building increased the weight upon my soil, and my neighbour digs in his land so as to occasion mine to fall in, he may be liable to an action; but if I have laid an additional weight upon my land, it does not follow that he is to be deprived of the right of digging his own ground because mine will then become incapable of supporting the artificial weight which I have laid upon it. And this is consistent with 2 Rolle's Abridgment Trespass (I.) pl. 1. The judgment will therefore be for the defendant."

In *Ray* v. *Fairway Motors (Barnstaple) Ltd.*[25] the defendant company's land was excavated in such a way that a wall on the plaintiff's land collapsed but without there being any interference with the natural right of support. The Court of Appeal held that, in the absence of an easement of support (which in this case there was), an owner of land could do what he liked, even if the result was the collapse of his neighbour's building; and there was no room, at least so far as the Court of Appeal was concerned, for a duty to exercise reasonable care: *Donoghue* v. *Stevenson*[26] has not affected this rule of law. Fenton Atkinson L.J. suggested, however,[27] that the position might have been different if the plaintiff could have shown something beyond the mere removal of soil, or omission to take active steps to prevent its effect; *e.g.* the adoption of an unnecessarily dangerous method of removal.

Acquisition of right to support

Although the surface owner where he has incumbered the surface by building has no natural right to the additional support which has become necessary, it is settled by the decision of the House of Lords in the leading case of *Dalton* v. *Angus*[28] that an enjoyment of such additional support for not less than twenty years will be sufficient to confer a right, subject only to the conditions which limit all acquisitions of rights by length of enjoyment only. The action was brought by the owners in fee of a coach factory at Newcastle upon Tyne, to recover damages for injuries to their factory caused by the defendant Commissioners, and by their contractor, the defendant Dalton, in excavating the soil of the adjoining property, on which the Probate Office was to be built. It appeared that the plaintiffs' building and the adjoining building on the

25 (1968) 20 P. & C.R. 261.
26 [1932] A.C. 562.
27 (1969) 20 P. & C.R. 275.
28 *Angus & Co.* v. *Dalton and the Commissioners of Her Majesty's Works and Public Buildings* (1877) 3 Q.B.D. 85; (1878) 4 Q.B.D. 162; *sub nom. Dalton* v. *Angus* (1881) 6 App.Cas. 740.

defendants' land were estimated to be upwards of a hundred years old; that up to the year 1849, being about twenty-seven years before the accident, both houses had been occupied as dwelling-houses; that in that year the plaintiffs' predecessor in title had converted his house into a coach factory, in such a manner as to increase the pressure on the borders of his own soil and consequently on the adjoining property; that this had been done without the express assent of the defendants' predecessor, but openly and without any attempt at concealment; that the defendants had pulled down their house and the wall dividing the two properties without injury to the factory; but that, in excavating in their land for the purpose of providing cellarage (which had not previously existed) for the offices to be built, they had dug below the foundations of the plaintiffs' building without leaving sufficient support, and had thus brought the whole building to the ground.

At the trial Lush J. directed a verdict for the plaintiffs for the damages claimed, but left them to move for judgment in order to have the questions of law determined.

On motion for judgment it was argued for the defendants, first, that the plaintiffs' factory was not entitled to the support claimed; and, secondly, that the Commissioners were not responsible for the negligence of their contractor.

Upon the second point the court considered itself bound by the decision in *Bower* v. *Peate* [29] to find against the defendants; and this ruling was ultimately affirmed by the Court of Appeal and the House of Lords.

On the first point, which raised the whole question of the law of support, the judges differed. Lush J., adhering in substance to the view which he had taken at the trial, thought that the plaintiffs ought to succeed; and rested his opinion partly on the doctrine of the presumption of a grant after twenty years' uninterrupted enjoyment and partly on an analogy to the Statutes of Limitation. He thought that the decision in *Bonomi* v. *Backhouse* [30] involved the very point in question. But Cockburn C.J. held that, if any presumption of a grant were derived from twenty years' user, it was open to be rebutted, and that, when it was proved or admitted that no grant or assent was in fact made or given, the presumption was at an end; and further that, the enjoyment not being capable of being interrupted by any reasonable means, no presumption in fact arose. Mellor J. agreed with the Lord Chief Justice, and accordingly judgment was given for the defendants. All the judges agreed that the right to support was not an easement within the Prescription Act. On appeal [31] Brett L.J. agreed with the majority of the court below; but Cotton and Thesiger L.JJ., being of the contrary opinion, the decision was reversed.

[29] (1876) 1 Q.B.D. 321.
[30] (1859) E.B. & E. 655; (1861) 9 H.L.C. 503.
[31] (1878) 4 Q.B.D. 162.

Thesiger L.J., while admitting that the presumption of a lost grant was a presumption, not " juris et de jure," but liable to be rebutted, held that it could not be rebutted by mere proof by the owner of the servient tenement that no grant was in fact made either at the commencement or during the continuance of the enjoyment; in fact, it " is in the nature of an estoppel by conduct, which, while it is not conclusive so far as to prevent denial or explanation of the conduct, presents a bar to any simple denial of the fact, which is merely the legal inference drawn from the conduct." [32]   The cases of *Barker* v. *Richardson*,[33] *Webb* v. *Bird* [34] and *Chasemore* v. *Richards*,[35] in which a presumption of this nature had been held to be rebutted,

> " as direct authorities go no further than to shew that a legal
> incompetence as regards the owner of the servient tenement to
> grant an easement, or a physical incapacity of being obstructed as
> regards the easement itself, or an uncertainty and secrecy of enjoy-
> ment putting it out of the category of all ordinary known easements,
> will prevent the presumption of an easement by lost grant; and
> on the other hand indirectly, they tend to support the view, that
> as a general rule, where no such legal incompetence, physical
> incapacity, or peculiarity of enjoyment, as was shewn in those
> cases, exists, uninterrupted and unexplained user will raise the
> presumption of a grant, upon the principle expressed by the maxim,
> ' Qui non prohibet quod prohibere potest assentire videtur.' " [36]

As to the alleged impossibility or extreme difficulty of obstructing the enjoyment of the right of support, he pointed out that this only exists where the servient tenement, being itself covered with buildings, enjoys a reciprocal benefit from the dominant tenement; and in any case he held himself bound by the authorities not to admit the argument as sufficient.

The judgment of Cotton L.J. was to the same effect. None of the Lords Justices adopted the view expressed by Lush J., that the period of twenty years might be limited for the acquisition of a right to support by analogy to the Limitation Acts [37]; and none of them seems to have considered that the right might be an easement within the Prescription Act.[38]

But although, upon the main question, the majority of the Court of Appeal decided in favour of the plaintiffs' contention, the Court was unanimously of opinion that, the construction of the plaintiffs' factory being somewhat unusual, the jury should have been asked to determine whether the weight which had been put upon the adjoining soil was such as the owner of the soil could be reasonably expected to be aware

32 (1878) 4 Q.B.D. 173.
33 (1821) 4 B. & Ald. 579.
34 (1863) 13 C.B.(N.S.) 841.
35 (1859) 7 H.L.C. 349.
36 (1878) 4 Q.B.D. 162, 175.
37 See *per* Thesiger L.J. (1878) 4 Q.B.D. 170, and *per* Brett L.J., *ibid*. 199.
38 *Ibid*. 170, 196.

of, and, on this ground, directed the defendants to elect within fourteen days whether they would take a new trial.[39] The option was not exercised; and, judgment having been entered for the plaintiffs for damages assessed by a special referee, the defendants appealed to the House of Lords.

The appeal [40] was, in the House of Lords, twice argued, the second time before seven judges of the High Court who had not yet been parties to any decision in the case.[41] The judges, in answering the questions put to them by the House, were unanimous in advising that the judgment of the Court of Appeal was justified by the authorities; and two only of them [42] disapproved of the principle underlying the authorities, but the reasons on which their opinions were based were very diverse. Pollock B. and Field and Manisty JJ. did not refer the right to support to any presumption of grant or acquiescence, but treated it as a proprietary right, to be acquired by a *de facto* enjoyment for twenty years; and the first-named expressly approved of the conclusion arrived at by Lush J. at the trial, that the rule might be derived by analogy from the Statutes of Limitation. On the other hand, Lindley J. (with whom Lopes J. agreed) was of opinion that support was an easement which, after twenty years' open and uninterrupted enjoyment, the court would presume to have been granted, even though it should be proved or admitted that no sealed or written grant had in fact been executed; and that the law which required the servient owner to remove his soil in order to preserve his unrestricted right to let down his neighbour's house, though it did not " commend itself to common sense," was completely established by authority. Fry J. felt the same difficulty in approving of the principles of the decisions, holding that " an excavation for the sole purpose of letting down a neighbour's house is of so expensive, so difficult, so churlish a character, that it is not reasonably to be required in order to prevent the acquisition of a right " [43]; and adding that, as the servient owner cannot, " except by a trespass or an impertinence," ascertain the nature of his neighbour's structure, the incidence of its burden on the soil, or the depth and character of its foundations, the enjoyment is so secret that no right ought to be founded upon it; but he also thought the authorities conclusive against this view being adopted in practice. Lastly, Bowen J., reverting to some extent to the opinions of the Lord Chief Justice and Brett L.J., treated the twenty years' rule as a " canon of evidence," and held that twenty years' user, peaceful, open, and as of right, was sufficient ground for inferring a lawful origin of the user, and that the inference could only be met by showing that there was no such lawful origin, either at law (as by grant or covenant), or in equity (as by agreement or acquiescence); he thought the decisions showed that

[39] (1878) 4 Q.B.D. 162, 187, 204.
[40] (1881) 6 App.Cas. 740.
[41] Pollock B. and Field, Lindley, Manisty, Lopes, Fry and Bowen JJ.
[42] Lindley and Fry JJ.
[43] (1881) 6 App.Cas. 775.

the enjoyment was capable of interruption. As to the question of notice, upon which the plaintiffs had obtained from the Court of Appeal the option to have the case retried, Lindley, Lopes and Bowen JJ. thought that this should have gone to the jury, while the remaining judges considered the question immaterial.

It should be added that Lindley J., in the course of his opinion,[44] discussed the important question whether the enjoyment of support is not after all rather affirmative than negative, and so capable of interruption by the short method of an action of trespass, and, in the absence of interruption, ripening into an easement under section 2 of the Prescription Act. He said[45]:

> " Support, even when lateral, involves pressure on and an actual use of the laterally supporting soil. . . . No trace is to be found in our law books of any action at law or suit in equity based upon any wrong done to the owner of the servient tenement; and the general opinion certainly is that in the absence of actual damage to the soil, no such action or suit could be maintained. Upon principle, I confess I do not see why this should be so. If a person builds so near the edge of his own land as to use his neighbour's land to support his house without his neighbour's consent, I do not see why such neighbour should have no cause of action. The enjoyment of light coming across adjoining land and the enjoyment of the use of such land for support, are in some respects entirely different; for no use is made of a man's property by opening a window on other property near it; and a right not to be overlooked is not recognised by our law. At the same time in every case in which the right to lateral support is alluded to, it is treated as analogous to the right to light, and the difference to which I have drawn attention has not been dwelt upon or treated as material. Nevertheless, whatever my own opinion would be, looking at the matter theoretically, I am not prepared to say that an action for damages, or an injunction, could be maintained in such a case as I have supposed. The authority against it, although purely negative, would, in my judgment, be considered as too strong to be got over. If, however, your Lordships should be of a different opinion, I apprehend that it would follow that the Prescription Act[46] would apply to and include an easement of lateral support; and the law upon this important subject would then be contained in the provisions of that statute. But all the Judges before whom this case has come concur in holding the Prescription Act not to apply; and, in the absence of authority to the contrary, I am not prepared to differ from them."

[44] (1881) 6 App.Cas. 740, 764.
[45] (1881) 6 App.Cas. 740, 763, 764.
[46] 2 & 3 Will. 4, c. 71, s. 2.

On the same subject Fry J. made the following observations in a contrary sense [47]:

"It has been argued at your Lordships' Bar that the doctrine [48] applies in its simplest form to the right in question; for it has been contended that the act of building a house on one piece of land which derives lateral support from the adjoining soil of a different owner is both actionable and preventible, and that, therefore, time constitutes a valid bar. Is such a building actionable? I think not. The lateral pressure of a heavy building on soft ground which causes an ascertainable physical disturbance in a neighbour's soil would no doubt be trespass; but no one ever heard of an action for the mere increment caused by reason of a new building to the pre-existing lateral pressure of soil on soil, producing no ascertainable physical disturbance. If that were the law no one could rightly build on the edge of his land, unless he built upon a rock; and yet the building of walls and other structures on the borders of land is universally recognised as lawful. Nay more, any erection of a house would give a right of action not only to the adjoining neighbours, but to every owner of land within the unascertainable area over which the increase of pressure must, according to the laws of physics, extend. Such an increase of pressure when unattended with unascertainable physical consequences, is, in my opinion, one of those minima of which the law takes no heed. The distinction between the principles applicable to water collected into visible streams and that running in invisible ones through the ground, affords a very good analogy to the distinction which I draw between the pressure of an adjoining house which produces a visible displacement of the soil, and that which produces no visible or ascertainable result, but is only a matter of inference from physical science or subsequent experiment."

Bowen J.'s observations on the same point [49] appear to indicate that he agreed in principle with Lindley J.

The House of Lords [50] unanimously dismissed the appeal; and it is of importance to notice the grounds upon which their Lordships' opinions in favour of this course proceeded.

Lord Selborne L.C., after showing that the right to support to buildings was not a natural but a conventional or acquired easement, expressed his agreement with the views of Lindley J. and Bowen J.,

"that it is both scientifically and practically inaccurate to describe it as one of a merely negative kind. What is support? The force of gravity causes the superincumbent land, or building, to press

---

[47] (1881) 6 App.Cas. 775.
[48] *Sc.* qui non prohibet quod prohibere potest assentire videtur.
[49] (1881) 6 App.Cas. 784.
[50] The Lords present were Lord Selborne L.C. and Lords Coleridge, Penzance, Blackburn and Watson.

downward upon what is below it, whether artificial or natural; and it has also a tendency to thrust outwards, laterally, any loose or yielding substance, such as earth or clay, until it meets with adequate resistance. Using the language of the law of easements, I say that, in the case alike of vertical and of lateral support, both to land and to buildings, the dominant tenement imposes upon the servient a positive and a constant burden, the sustenance of which, by the servient tenement, is necessary for the safety and stability of the dominant. It is true that the benefit to the dominant tenement arises, not from its own pressure upon the servient tenement, but from the power of the servient tenement to resist that pressure, and from its actual sustenance of the burden so imposed. But the burden and its sustenance are reciprocal, and inseparable from each other, and it can make no difference whether the dominant tenement is said to impose, or the servient to sustain, the weight." [1]

From these considerations it followed that the right to support was to some extent affirmative, and so properly the subject, not of covenant only,[2] but of grant. It was also capable of interruption, if not by action, at least by the removal of the supporting soil; and if in some cases it did not suit the purpose of the supporting owner to exercise this right of removal, it was the policy of the law that his inaction (whether due to negligence or to his own preponderating interest) should in time confer a possessory title upon his neighbour. The right of support then, being an easement, not purely negative, capable of being granted and also capable of being interrupted, was within section 2 of the Prescription Act; and the question of grant or no grant was excluded. And, even though the Prescription Act should not apply, the presumption of a lost grant could not be rebutted by showing that no grant had in fact been made. As to the question of notice, a landowner who sees building operations, or alterations of an existing building, in progress upon the borders of his property, must have imputed to him the knowledge that the building will require fresh support from the adjoining land; and, if everything is done honestly and (as far as possible) openly, he must be fixed with knowledge of the amount of support enjoyed. No question need therefore have been submitted to the jury.

Lord Penzance expressed the opinion that, if the matter were *res integra*, it might properly be held that a building owner acquired, immediately upon erecting a house, the right to have it supported by the adjacent soil; but he agreed with Fry J. in thinking that length of enjoyment could only confer a title through the acquiescence of another, and that an enjoyment which was both secret and incapable of being interrupted without an unreasonable waste of labour and expense was no evidence of acquiescence, and should not on principle be made the basis

---

1 (1881) 6 App.Cas. 793.
2 See *per* Littledale J. in *Moore* v. *Rawson* (1824) 3 B. & C. 332, 340; *ante*, p. 23.

of any right. However, he considered that the ruling of Lush J. was entirely supported by the authorities, and that the appeal on this ground should be dismissed.

Lord Blackburn thought that the fiction of a lost grant, however introduced, was not a rule of evidence which a jury might or might not conform to, but an established doctrine of the court; and that to refuse to administer such a rule, when established, was at least as much a usurpation of legislative authority as it was at first to introduce it. He did not consider that acquiescence or laches was the sole, or indeed the chief, principle on which prescriptive rights were founded. Prescription, or *usucapio*, was a matter, not of natural justice, but of positive law, differing in different countries; and the authorities showed that the English law conferred a right after twenty years' enjoyment. The servient owner had notice that some support was required; and this was enough to put him on inquiry.

Lord Blackburn thought it unnecessary to decide the question whether support was within the Prescription Act. But, incidentally, he supplied an answer to the argument drawn by Fry J.[3] from the impossibility of pushing the doctrine of Lindley J. to its extreme limits. Lord Blackburn said[4]:

" The distinction between a right to light and a right of prospect, on the ground that one is a matter of necessity and the other of delight, is to my mind more quaint than satisfactory. A much better reason is given by Lord Hardwicke in *Att.-Gen.* v. *Doughty*,[5] where he observes that if that was the case there could be no great towns. I think this decision, that a right of prospect is not acquired by prescription, shews that, whilst on the balance of convenience and inconvenience, it was held expedient that the right to light, which could only impose a burthen upon land very near the house, should be protected when it had been long enjoyed, on the same ground it was held expedient that the right of prospect, which would impose a burthen on a very large and indefinite area, should not be allowed to be created, except by actual agreement. And this seems to me the real ground on which *Webb* v. *Bird*[6] and *Chasemore* v. *Richards*[7] are to be supported. The rights there claimed were analogous to prospect in this, that they were vague and undefined, and very extensive. Whether that is or is not the reason for the distinction the law has always, since *Bland* v. *Moseley*,[8] been that there is a distinction; that the right of a window to have light and air is acquired by prescription, and that a right to have a prospect can only be acquired by actual agreement."

3 (1881) 6 App.Cas. 775; see p. 297, *ante*.
4 (1881) 6 App.Cas. 824.
5 (1788) 2 Ves.Sen. 453.
6 (1861) 10 C.B.(N.S.) 268; (1862) 13 C.B.(N.S.) 841.
7 (1859) 7 H.L.C. 349.
8 (1587), cited in 9 Co.Rep. 58a.

Lord Watson agreed with Lord Selborne in holding that the right
of support to a building, whether lateral or vertical, was a positive
easement; being, as he said, probably influenced by the consideration
that a decision that the easement was negative would form an unsatis-
factory precedent in Scotland, where positive servitudes alone are
capable of being acquired by prescription. He thought that no question
of fact need have been submitted to the jury. Lord Coleridge did not
deliver a detailed opinion, but expressed his concurrence in the judgments of Lords Selborne and Blackburn. He did not say whether he
agreed with the former in holding the easement to be a positive one.

The decision of the House of Lords in *Dalton* v. *Angus* [9] may be
taken as establishing the rule that twenty years' enjoyment of support
to a building, whether from the adjacent or from the subjacent land,
being peaceable, open and as of right, will (either by a right springing
out of the enjoyment at the common law, or under the Prescription Act,
or under the doctrine of lost grant) confer the right to have the support
continued; that, if the right is based on the presumption of a grant
founded on the enjoyment, the presumption is absolute and cannot be
rebutted by showing that no grant has in fact been made; and that, in
the absence of any wilful fraud or concealment, the outward appearance
of the building is sufficient notice to all persons concerned of the amount
of support which it requires.[10]

Acquisition of right of support for buildings by grant

Apart from a title resulting from enjoyment, a title to the easement
of support for buildings may be made in other ways. Thus, it follows
from the judgments in *Dalton* v. *Angus* [11] that where the title to land
A, on which a building has been or is about to be erected, is severed
from the title to the subjacent or adjacent land, the right to have such
building supported by the subjacent or adjacent land may be acquired by
grant whether express or implied. When acquired the right is precisely
the same as that of support for land.[12]

Under the Coal-Mining (Subsidence) Act 1957, the National Coal
Board is obliged, subject to certain conditions, to make good or pay
compensation for damage occurring to land or buildings as the result
of the withdrawal of support in working coal.[13]

3.—SUPPORT OF BUILDINGS BY BUILDINGS

A question of equal practical importance arises where the owner of one
house claims a right to have it supported by the adjoining house belong-

---

9 (1881) 6 App.Cas. 740.
10 See *Union Lighterage Co.* v. *London Graving Dock Co.* [1902] 2 Ch. 557; *Lloyds
   Bank Ltd.* v. *Dalton* [1942] Ch. 466.
11 (1881) 6 App.Cas. 792, 809. As to implied grants and reservations of the right to
   support, see also p. 100, *ante*.
12 *Ibid*.
13 For the creation of easements by statute, see p. 75, *ante*.

ing to his neighbour.[14] There is no natural right to such support [15]; but it may in the case of buildings belonging to different owners be claimed by prescription,[16] in which case the enjoyment must have been as of right,[17] and therefore open [18]; or by implied grant or reservation.[19] The nature of the right has been summarised as follows by Sir Wilfrid Greene M.R. in *Bond* v. *Nottingham Corporation* [20] :

" The owner of the servient tenement is under no obligation to repair that part of his building which provides support for his neighbour. He can let it fall into decay. If it does so, and support is removed, the owner of the dominant tenement has no cause for complaint. On the other hand, the owner of the dominant tenement is not bound to sit by and watch the gradual deterioration of the support constituted by his neighbour's building. He is entitled to enter and take the necessary steps to ensure that the support continues by effecting repairs, and so forth, to the part of the building which gives the support. But what the owner of the servient tenement is not entitled to do is, by an act of his own, to remove the support without providing an equivalent. There is the qualification upon his ownership of his own building that he is bound to deal with it, and can only deal with it, subject to the rights in it which are vested in his neighbour."

If a servient building becomes subject to a clearance order made under section 44 of the Housing Act 1957 [21] and so is required to be demolished, but the order does not extend to the dominant building, the demolishing servient owner or local authority is bound to provide equivalent support for the dominant building.[22]

14 The subject is discussed in " Rights of Support for Buildings and Flats " by Mr. E. H. Bodkin in (1962) 26 *Conveyancer* (N.S.) 210 *et seq.*
15 See *Southwark and Vauxhall Water Co.* v. *Wandsworth Board of Works* [1898] 2 Ch. 603, 612. In the absence of an easement, the pulling-down owner must be careful to interfere as little as possible with the adjoining house, but he is not bound to take active steps for its protection, or to mitigate a mischief which follows inevitably on the reasonable exercise of his own rights (*per* Collins L.J. 612, 613).
16 *Lemaitre* v. *Davis* (1881) 19 Ch.D. 281; *Waddington* v. *Naylor* (1889) 60 L.T. 480; *Selby* v. *Whitbread & Co.* [1917] 1 K.B. 736, 751.
17 *Tone* v. *Preston* (1883) 24 Ch.D. 739.
18 *Lemaitre* v. *Davis, supra*; *Solomon* v. *Vintners' Co.* (1859) 4 H. & N. 601; *Gately* v. *Martin* [1900] 2 I.R. 269; *Union Lighterage Co.* v. *London Graving Dock Co.* [1902] 2 Ch. 557; *Lloyds Bank Ltd.* v. *Dalton* [1942] Ch. 466.
19 See *ante*, p. 100. Where the owner of building A and building B, which is subjacent to A and supports it, demises A, he cannot withdraw the support, but no covenant is implied by him to repair B; *Colebeck* v. *Girdlers' Co.* (1876) 1 Q.B.D. 234, 243.
20 [1940] Ch. 429, 438.
21 Re-enacting s. 26 of the Housing Act 1936.
22 *Bond* v. *Nottingham Corporation* [1940] Ch. 429. In *Grimley* v. *Minister of Housing and Local Government* [1971] 2 Q.B. 96 John Stephenson J. held that on the compulsory purchase of the servient tenement the owner of the dominant tenement, which enjoyed an easement of support, was not entitled to notice under para. 3 (1) (*b*) of Schedule 1 to the Acquisition of Land (Authorisation Procedure) Act 1946, as the dominant owner was not the owner of land comprised in the order within the meaning of s. 8 (1) of that Act and s. 3 (2) of the Liverpool Corporation (General Powers) Act 1966.

CHAPTER 11

PARTY-WALLS, BANKS, AND BOUNDARY TREES AND BUILDINGS

1.—PARTY-WALLS

Meaning of party-wall

Before 1926 the term " party-wall " (in relation to a wall separating two properties) might mean—(1) a wall of which the two adjoining owners were tenants in common; or (2) a wall divided longitudinally into two portions, one belonging to each adjoining owner; or (3) a wall belonging entirely to one adjoining owner, but subject to an easement in the other to have it maintained as a dividing wall; or (4) a wall divided longitudinally into two portions, each portion being subject to a cross-easement in favour of the owner of the other.[1]

A wall could (and still can) be a party-wall up to a certain point, namely, so far as it divides two buildings of unequal height, and an external wall above that point[2]; and a pilaster or portico, or a fascia, which appears to form an integral portion of one house, may be parcel of and pass on a conveyance of another house.[3]

Before 1926 the primary meaning of " party-wall " was a wall of which the two adjoining owners were tenants in common.[1] Such owners were prima facie tenants in common where there had been common user of the wall.[4] And the same conclusion might result where it was not known under what circumstances the wall was built.[5] But where the quantity of land which each adjoining owner contributed to the site of the wall is known, the property in the wall follows the property in the land, and each party is the owner of so much of the wall as stands upon his own land.[6]

Walls held in common before 1926, or declared after 1925 to be party-walls

As a result of the Law of Property Act 1925 a legal estate in an undivided share in land or buildings cannot exist,[7] and it is by that Act provided that where, immediately before 1926, a party-wall or other

---

[1] *Watson* v. *Gray* (1880) 14 Ch.D. 192, 194.
[2] *Weston* v. *Arnold* (1873) 8 Ch.App. 1084; *Drury* v. *Army & Navy Auxiliary Co-operative Society* [1896] 2 Q.B. 271.
[3] *Thrupp* v. *Scruton* [1872] W.N. 60; *Fox* v. *Clarke* (1874) L.R. 9 Q.B. 565; *Francis* v. *Hayward* (1882) 22 Ch.D. 177. Cf. *Laybourn* v. *Gridley* [1892] 2 Ch. 53.
[4] *Cubitt* v. *Porter* (1828) 8 B. & C. 257; *Standard Bank of British S. America (Africa)* v. *Stokes* (1878) 9 Ch.D. 71.
[5] *Wiltshire* v. *Sidford* (1827) 1 Man. & Ry.K.B. 404.
[6] *Matts* v. *Hawkins* (1813) 5 Taunt. 20. See *Murly* v. *M'Dermott* (1838) 8 A. & E. 138; *Irving* v. *Turnbull* [1900] 2 Q.B. 129.　　　　　　[7] s. 1 (6).

party structure was held in undivided shares,[8] or where, under a disposition or other arrangement which, if a holding in undivided shares had been permissible, would have created a tenancy in common, a wall or other structure is or is expressed to be made a party-wall or structure,[9] that structure is to be severed vertically as between the respective owners, and the owner of each part has rights of support and user over the rest of the structure corresponding to those which could have subsisted if a valid tenancy in common had been created, or, if it existed at the commencement of the Act, had continued. Walls which, apart from the Act, would have been in the first class, above-mentioned, are thus transferred to the fourth. Rights of support have already been considered.[10]

Other party-walls

Where a wall was held in severalty before 1926, or its ownership becomes divided after 1925 and it is not declared to be a party-wall (in which case the statutory provisions last mentioned will not apply), there seems no authority for saying that the rights of the respective owners of the portions of the wall differ from those of the proprietors of any other two walls which abut on each other. Unless prevented by some easement having been acquired, either party would be at liberty to pare away or even entirely to remove his portion, notwithstanding the other half might be unable to stand without the support of it.[11] In *Cubitt* v. *Porter* Bayley J. said [12]:

> " If the wall stood partly on one man's land and partly on another's, either party would have a right to pare away the wall on his side, so as to weaken the wall on the other, and to produce a destruction of that which ought to be the common property of the two."

At the utmost, the fact of the close union of the walls could only impose a duty of greater caution than might otherwise be required in removing the materials. Reasonable care should be used in removing any portion of the wall.[13] And trespass will lie if one adjoining owner in rebuilding goes beyond his own boundary.[14]

---

8 First Sched., Pt. V, para. 1.   9 s. 38.
10 *Ante*, p. 300. S. 38 (1) of the Law of Property Act 1925 refers to " rights to support and user." The significance of the words " and user " is not clear. *Upjohn* v. *Seymour Estates Ltd.* [1938] 1 All E.R. 614, which suggests that there is a right to protection from the elements, cannot, it seems, be considered as being any longer good law, in view of the decision of the Court of Appeal in *Phipps* v. *Pears* [1965] 1 Q.B. 76; see p. 24, *ante*.
11 *Wigford* v. *Gill* (1592) Cro.Eliz. 269; *Peyton* v. *London Corpn.* (1829) 9 B. & C. 725.
12 (1828) 8 B. & C. 257, 264. See, on this point, *Bradbee* v. *Christ's Hospital* (1842) 4 Man. & G. 714, 761.
13 *Kempston* v. *Butler* (1861) 12 Ir.C.L.R. 516; *Southwark and Vauxhall Water Co.* v. *Wandsworth Board of Works* [1898] 2 Ch. 612. See *Hughes* v. *Percival* (1883) 8 App.Cas. 443.   14 *Mayfair Property Co.* v. *Johnston* [1894] 1 Ch. 508.

London

In the Administrative County of London party-walls are regulated by the London Building Acts (Amendment) Act 1939.[15] Rights acquired under this Act supersede all rights acquired under the general law.[16]

2.—BANKS, HEDGES AND DITCHES

In the case of banks or hedges separating fields, the ownership is thus determined: If two fields are separated by an artificial ditch and a bank or hedge, the bank or hedge and the ditch, prima facie and in the absence of proof to the contrary,[17] are presumed to belong to the owner of the field immediately adjoining the bank or hedge [18]; but if there be a bank with ditches at each side of it, then there is no presumption as to the ownership of the bank, and the question must be determined by acts of ownership.[19]

Where parcels on the Ordnance Survey map are bounded by a hedge, it is the invariable practice of the Ordnance Survey Office, of which the court will take judicial notice,[20] to run the boundary through the centre of the hedge. Consequently, if parcels so bounded are conveyed by reference to the Ordnance Survey map, their boundary will be in the centre of the hedge, and any presumption to the contrary will be rebutted.[21]

3.—BOUNDARY TREES AND BUILDINGS

Boundary trees

As regards boundary trees, there is no authority in the English law that an easement can be acquired to compel a man to submit to the invasion of his land by the roots or branches of a tree planted on his neighbour's soil. The principal objections to the acquisition of such an easement by user consist in the perpetual change in the

---

[15] 2 & 3 Geo. 6, c. xcvii, replacing earlier Acts; and see London Government Act 1963, s. 43.

[16] *Selby* v. *Whitbread & Co.* [1917] 1 K.B. 736. See " Party Walls in London " by Mr. Desmond Wright in (1954) 18 *Conveyancer* (N.S.) 347 *et seq.*

[17] *Marshall* v. *Taylor* [1895] 1 Ch. 641; *Craven* v. *Pridmore* (1902) 18 T.L.R. 282; *Henniker* v. *Howard* (1904) 90 L.T. 157; *Simcox* v. *Yardley* (1905) 69 J.P. 66.

[18] *Noye* v. *Reed* (1827) 1 Man. & Ry.K.B. 63, 65; *Guy* v. *West* (1808) cited in 2 Selwyn N.P., 13th ed., 1244. See the explanation given by Lawrence J. in *Vowles* v. *Miller* (1810) 3 Taunt. 137, 138; and, for a review of the cases, see *per* Scrutton L.J. in *Collis* v. *Amphlett* [1918] 1 Ch. 232, 259–260. The rule seems to have been applied in *Weston* v. *Lawrence Weaver Ltd.* [1961] 1 Q.B. 402, in which the defendant's property was separated from a private road by a ditch, bank and hedge.

[19] *Guy* v. *West, supra.* So-called " fencing easements " are referred to at pp. 37 *et seq., ante,* where rights analogous to easements are considered.

[20] *Davey* v. *Harrow Corporation* [1958] 1 Q.B. 60.

[21] *Fisher* v. *Winch* [1939] 1 K.B. 666; *Rouse* v. *Gravelworks Ltd.* [1940] 1 K.B. 489; *Davey* v. *Harrow Corporation, supra.* Where a ditch does not pass by conveyance, because the plan refers to the boundaries as on the Ordnance Survey map, it cannot pass under s. 62 (1) of the Law of Property Act 1925; *Jarvis* v. *Aris* (July 14, 1961, unreported: see 232 L.T.Jour. 229).

quantity of inconvenience imposed by it, and, in the case of penetrating roots, the secrecy in the mode of enjoyment. It is now settled that the encroachment of boughs or roots of trees (whether planted or self-growing) over and within the land of the adjoining owner is not a trespass or occupation which by lapse of time can become a right, but is (or may be) a nuisance.[22]

Overhanging branches

The owner or occupier of land which is overhung by the branches of a tree growing on adjoining land is entitled, without notice, if he does not trespass on the adjoining land, to cut the branches, however old they may be, so far as they overhang[23]; but this right does not carry with it a right to appropriate the severed branches or the fruit growing thereon.[24] If the overhanging branches are not in fact doing damage it may be that the only right is to cut back the overhanging portions.[25] But an action lies where the overhanging branches are actually doing damage, *e.g.* through interfering with the growth of fruit trees,[25] or poisoning cattle.[26] On the other hand, the owner or occupier has no right of action if his cattle eat poisonous leaves on the branches on the adjoining land, not overhanging his own land,[27] nor possibly if poisonous leaves from branches which do not overhang fall on to his own land.[28]

In *Cheater* v. *Cater*[29] where A had let a farm which was overhung by yew trees standing on A's adjoining land, and the tenant's mare died as a result of eating the yew branches, it was held by the Court of Appeal (following the judgment of Mellish L.J. in *Erskine* v. *Adeane*[30]) that, as the tenant had taken the farm with the yew trees overhanging, he must abide the consequences, and had no cause of action. What the position of the tenant would have been if the danger had first arisen after the date of the lease was not decided.

Encroaching roots

The rights of the owner or occupier of land which is invaded by the roots of a tree growing on adjoining land appear to be exactly

22 *Lemmon* v. *Webb* [1894] 3 Ch. 1, 24; [1895] A.C. 1; *Davey* v. *Harrow Corporation* [1958] 1 Q.B. 60; *Morgan* v. *Khyatt* [1964] 1 W.L.R. 475. It seems that the ownership of a tree goes with the land in which the tree was first planted, and that the place where it was planted may be a matter of inference. On this obscure subject, see *Holder* v. *Coates* (1827) 1 Moo. & M. 112; *Masters* v. *Pollie* (1620) 2 Roll.Rep. 141; *Anon,* 2 Roll.Rep. 255; *Waterman* v. *Soper* (1697) 1 Ld.Raym. 737; *Lemmon* v. *Webb* [1894] 3 Ch. 1, 20; *Hetherington* v. *Galt* (1905) 7 F. (Ct. of Sess.) 706. 23 *Lemmon* v. *Webb, supra.*
24 *Mills* v. *Brooker* [1919] 1 K.B. 555.
25 *Smith* v. *Giddy* [1904] 2 K.B. 451; 73 L.J.K.B. 894.
26 *Crowhurst* v. *Amersham Burial Board* (1878) 4 Ex.D. 5.
27 *Ponting* v. *Noakes* [1894] 2 Q.B. 281.
28 *Smith* v. *Giddy* (1904) as reported in 73 L.J.K.B. 894, 896; *cf. Wilson* v. *Newberry* (1871) L.R. 7 Q.B. 31; *Giles* v. *Walker* (1890) 24 Q.B.D. 656; but see *Davey* v. *Harrow Corporation* [1958] 1 Q.B. 60.
29 [1918] 1 K.B. 247. The principle was recognised in *Shirvell* v. *Hackwood Estates Co.* [1938] 2 K.B. 577. 30 (1873) 8 Ch.App. 756, 761.

the same as his right in respect of overhanging branches [31] (see above). Where damage has occurred, damages have been awarded,[32] and an injunction has been granted restraining the defendant from causing or permitting the roots to encroach so as to cause a nuisance.[33]

Building projecting over boundary

Speaking generally, the ownership of a building includes the airspace above it.[34] While, however, the grant of a building may well include parts of it which project beyond its apparent boundary,[35] such a grant will not normally include anything above or below the projecting part.[36]

After some conflict of authority, it appears to be settled that the invasion of air-space by projecting buildings, advertising signs or the like constitutes a trespass, actionable whether actual damage is caused or not.[37] The right to maintain such a projection may, it seems, be acquired as an easement.[38]

---

[31] Butler v. Standard Telephones and Cables Ltd. [1940] 1 K.B. 399; Lemmon v. Webb [1894] 3 Ch. 1; [1895] A.C. 1; McCombe v. Read [1955] 2 Q.B. 429. See "Liability for Damage Caused by Tree Roots" by Mr. Edward F. George in (1963) 27 Conveyancer (N.S.) 179 et seq.

[32] Butler v. Standard Telephones and Cables Ltd., supra; McCombe v. Read, supra.

[33] McCombe v. Read, supra. In this case it was stated in evidence that the roots of a poplar normally extend to one and a half times the height of the tree.

[34] According to the maxim cujus est solum ejus est usque ad coelum. Kelsen v. Imperial Tobacco Co. (of Great Britain and Ireland) Ltd. [1957] 2 Q.B. 334.

[35] Francis v. Hayward (1882) 22 Ch.D. 177; Truckell v. Stock [1957] 1 W.L.R. 161 (projecting footings and eaves); cf. Laybourn v. Gridley [1892] 2 Ch. 53 (overhanging part of building included in a lease of the building, but also in subsequent conveyance of the property overhung).

[36] Corbett v. Hill (1870) L.R. 9 Eq. 671 (first floor room projecting over ground floor of adjoining house); Truckell v. Stock, supra. Contrast Gifford v. Dent [1926] W.N. 336.

[37] Kelsen v. Imperial Tobacco Co. (of Great Britain and Ireland) Ltd., supra; Lemmon v. Webb [1894] 3 Ch. 1, 18.

[38] Harris v. De Pinna (1885) 33 Ch.D. 238, 260; Lemmon v. Webb, supra.

PART IV

EXTINGUISHMENT OF EASEMENTS

As regards the extinguishment of easements Mr. Gale wrote as follows:

"The modes by which easements may be lost correspond with those already laid down for their acquisition: 1. Corresponding to the express grant is the express renunciation; 2. To the disposition by the owner of two tenements, the merger by the union of them; 3. To the easement of necessity, the permission to do some act which of necessity destroys it; 4. And to the acquisition by prescription, abandonment by non-user."

Mr. Gale proceeded to discuss the extinguishment of easements under the heads of "express release" and "implied release."

In the ninth edition Mr. Carson adopted a somewhat different arrangement, which was as follows: Easements may be extinguished —(1) by operation of law, under which head may be conveniently placed the effect upon an easement of the union of ownership (whether for absolute or partial interest) of the dominant and servient tenements; (2) by statute; (3) by express release; (4) by implied release. This arrangement is adhered to in the present edition.

CHAPTER 12

EXTINGUISHMENT OF EASEMENTS BY OPERATION
OF LAW

How an easement may be extinguished by operation of law

An easement may be extinguished by operation of law. Thus, it
has been said that a way of necessity is limited by the necessity which
created it, and when such necessity ceases the right of way is extinguished.[1] Again, where an easement is created by grant for a certain
period, when that period has elapsed the easement comes to an end.[2]

So, again, an easement will be extinguished where the purpose for
which it was created has come to an end. Thus, where a statute
conferred upon a company the right to take water to supply a canal,
the right ceased when the canal was abandoned.[3]

Extinguishment by unity of ownership

As an easement is a charge imposed upon the servient for the
advantage of the dominant tenement, when these are united in the
same owner, the easement is extinguished; the special kind of property
which the right to the easement conferred, so long as the tenements
belonged to different owners, is now merged in the general rights of
property.[4]

In order, however, that the easement should be entirely extinguished,
it is essential that the owner of the two tenements should have an
estate in fee simple in both of them of an equally perdurable nature.

"Where the tenant," says Littleton, " hath as great and as
high an estate in the tenements as the lord hath in the seigniory,
in such case, if the lord grant such services to the tenant in fee,
this shall enure by way of extinguishment. *Causa patet*." [5]

Upon which Coke observes [6]:

"Here Littleton intendeth not only as great and high an estate,
but as perdurable also, as hath been said, for a disseisor or tenant

---

[1] *Holmes* v. *Goring* (1824) 2 Bing. 76. See *ante*, p. 120.
[2] *Beddington* v. *Atlee* (1887) 35 Ch.D. 323. See *ante*, pp. 77, 111.
[3] *National Guaranteed Manure Co.* v. *Donald* (1859) 4 H. & N. 8.
[4] The following cases decide that a man cannot have an easement over his own land:
Metropolitan Ry. v. *Fowler* [1892] 1 Q.B. 165; *Kilgour* v. *Gaddes* [1904] 1 K.B.
461; *Roe* v. *Siddons* (1888) 22 Q.B.D. 236. See *ante*, p. 20.
[5] s. 561.
[6] Co.Litt. 313b.

in fee upon condition hath as high and great an estate, but not so perdurable an estate as shall make an extinguishment."

In a previous section, speaking of seigniories, rents, *profits à prendre*, etc., he says:

"They are said to be extinguished when they are gone for ever, *et tunc moriuntur,* and can never be revived, that is, when one man hath as high and as perdurable an estate in the one as in the other." [7]

Unless this be the case, the easement, of whatever species it be, is suspended only so long as the unity of ownership continues, and revives again upon the separation of the tenements.

"Suspense cometh of *suspendeo,* and, in legal understanding, is taken when a seigniory, rent, *profit à prendre,* etc., by reason of unity of possession of the seigniory, rent, etc., and of the land out of which they issue, are not in esse for a time, *et tunc dormiunt,* but may be revived or awaked." [8]

So strictly has this doctrine been construed that no extinguishment was held to have taken place where the king was seised of one tenement "of a pure fee simple indeterminable," *jure coronae,* and of the other of an estate in fee simple, determinable on the birth of a Duke of Cornwall.[9]

Extent of application of doctrine

As regards the extent of application of the doctrine that extinguishment results from the union in the same owner of absolute interests in the dominant and servient tenements, it was said by Alderson B. in *Pheysey* v. *Vicary* [10] that no easement of absolute necessity to the dominant tenement is extinguished by unity of ownership. The doctrine, however, appears to be applicable to rights in the nature of easements, *e.g.* the right to have a fence repaired.[11] It is also applicable to various sorts of easements. Thus, where the absolute owner of Blackacre, who has a right of way over Whiteacre, purchases an absolute interest in Whiteacre, the right of way is extinguished by the unity of ownership.[12] So as regards prescriptive rights in water, if the same person becomes absolute owner of the land from which a stream of water flows and also of the land into which it flows, the easement which the latter might have claimed is extinguished.[13]

---

[7] Co.Litt. 313a.   [8] *Ibid.*

[9] *R.* v. *Hermitage* (1692) Carth. 239. See also *James* v. *Plant* (1836) 4 A. & E. 749, 766, where it was held that the momentary seisin of a release to uses was insufficient to work a merger by unity of seisin.

[10] (1847) 16 M. & W. 484, 490.

[11] See Dyer 295b, pl. 19; *Sury* v. *Pigot* (1625) Palm. 444; *Boyle* v. *Tamlyn* (1827) 6 B. & C. 329.

[12] *Heigate* v. *Williams* (1607) Noy 119; *James* v. *Plant* (1836) 4 A. & E. 749.

[13] *Ivimey* v. *Stocker* (1866) 1 Ch.App. 396, 407. Consider *Holland* v. *Deakin* (1828) 7 L.J.(o.s.)K.B. 145; and see *Pheysey* v. *Vicary* (1847) 16 M. & W. 484, 489.

With respect of natural rights in water, the question of the effect of unity of ownership was raised and discussed in the early case of *Sury* v. *Pigot*,[14] which was an action for stopping a natural water-course. According to the report in Popham, the judgment of Whitlock C.J. contained the following: " Where the thing hath its being by prescription, unity will extinguish it; but where the thing hath its being *ex jure naturae* it shall not be extinguished." [15]   In the report of this case in Latch it is said: " Rent shall be extinguished by unity, and also a way, because it does not exist durant the unity; but it is otherwise of a thing which exists, notwithstanding the unity." A case of warren is cited from 35 Hen. 6, ff. 55, 56.

The above decisions as to the effect of unity in extinguishing an existing easement should be compared with the decisions referred to above [16] as to the effect of unity during the prescriptive period upon the acquisition of an easement.

Effect of severance

When two tenements become completely united, and, as it were, fused into one, the owner may modify the previous relative position of the different parts at his pleasure. If he exercise this right so that the part which previously served the other no longer does so—as, for instance, by changing the direction of a spout which emptied the rain-water of one house on the adjoining one—it has never been doubted that on subsequent severance no easement will revive.[17]

It has been contended that if he neglect to do so, and again sever the tenements, all easements having the qualities of being both continuing and apparent, as well as those which existed by necessity, will be revived upon the severance. In the 11th Hen. 7 [18] it was decided, " that a customary right in the city of London to have a gutter running in another man's land was not extinguished by unity of possession." It was argued that if the purchaser of both tenements had destroyed the gutter, the right would not have revived; to which Danvers J. replied: " If the matter were so, it might have been pleaded specially: it would be a good issue."

It will be found that the classes of easements with respect to which revivor is supposed to take place correspond with those already considered, as being acquired by the implied grant resulting either from the disposition of the owner of the two tenements, or from the easement being of necessity. It is practically immaterial whether the foundation of the right be a new grant or a revival of the old right; but the former

---

[14] (1625) Pop. 166; Lat. 153; 3 Bulst. 339; Palm. 444.
[15] See *Wood* v. *Waud* (1849) 3 Ex. 748, 775, where the above was approved by the Court of Exchequer.
[16] p. 160.
[17] 11 Hen. 7, f. 25; *Lady Browne's Case*, cited in *Sury* v. *Pigot* (1625) Palm. 446.
[18] Fol. 25.

is the more correct view of the title to them, and it is certainly more in harmony with the general principles of the law of easements.[19]

Vesting in one owner having different estates

The particular case where the dominant and servient tenements become vested in the same owner for different estates or interests has been dealt with by many judges. Thus, Page Wood V.-C. in *Simper* v. *Foley*[20] expressed the opinion that the effect of such a union of ownership was not to extinguish an easement, but merely to suspend it so long as the union of ownership continued; and that upon the severance of the ownership the easement revived. Again, it was said by Bayley B. in *Canham* v. *Fisk*[21] that a unity of possession merely suspends; there must be a unity of ownership to destroy the prescriptive right. Again, it was said by Alderson B. in *Thomas* v. *Thomas*[22]:

> "If I am seised of freehold premises, and possessed of lease-hold premises adjoining, and there has formerly been an easement enjoyed by the occupiers of the one as against the occupiers of the other, while the premises are in my hands, the easement is necessarily suspended, but it is not extinguished, because there is no unity of seisin; and if I part with the premises, the right, not being extinguished, will revive."

The application of the above rules to individual cases is not always easy. Three principles should be borne in mind, *viz.*: (1) No one can derogate from his own grant[23]; (2) The law does not allow the co-existence in the same ownership of (a) a right to an easement (*e.g.* a right of way) over Whiteacre, and (b) an interest in possession in Whiteacre[24]; (3) If two such rights or interests become vested in the same owner, and he continues to exercise his right of way, the law will attribute this exercise to his interest in possession in Whiteacre, and not to his easement.[25]

Upon this subject there have been the following decisions. Where the owner in fee of the dominant tenement acquired an outstanding lease in the servient tenement but subsequently parted with the lease, it was held in effect that during the union of ownership the easement of light was not extinguished, and that upon a severance of the ownership the easement revived.[26] Again, where A, the owner in

---

19 *Holmes* v. *Goring* (1824) 2 Bing. 76.
20 (1862) 2 J. & H. 555, 563–564.
21 (1831) 2 Cr. & J. 126.
22 (1835) 2 C.M. & R. 41. See also the judgment of Eyre C.J. in *Whalley* v. *Tompson* (1799) 1 Bos. & P. 375, and the opinion of the Court of Common Pleas in *Buckby* v. *Coles* (1814) 5 Taunt. 314.
23 *Browne* v. *Flower* [1911] 1 Ch. 224.
24 *Ladyman* v. *Grave* (1871) 6 Ch.App. 763, 768.
25 *Bolton* v. *Bolton* (1879) 11 Ch.D. 971. See *Bright* v. *Walker* (1834) 1 C.M. & R. 219.
26 *Simper* v. *Foley* (1862) 2 J. & H. 555.

fee of the dominant tenement, granted a lease thereof to X and subsequently sold his reversion in fee to B, who was the owner in fee in possession of the servient tenement, it was held in effect that during X's term the easement of light continued, there being no extinguishment. A could not derogate from his grant so as to interfere with X's right to the easement, nor could B standing in the place of A.[27]   In such a case on the falling in of X's lease extinguishment would of course follow.

---

[27] *Richardson* v. *Graham* [1908] 1 K.B. 39 (see the judgment of Kennedy L.J., 46).

CHAPTER 13

EXTINGUISHMENT OF EASEMENTS BY STATUTE

Expressly or by implication

An easement may be extinguished by statute. The extinguishment may have resulted from express words, *e.g.* from the words of section 8 of the Inclosure (Consolidation) Act 1801 [1] or section 68 of the Inclosure Act 1845, providing that "ways shall be for ever stopped up and extinguished " [2]; or from the words of the special Act of a railway company.[3] The extinguishment may also result by necessary implication from a statute. Thus, where the Legislature distinctly authorises the doing of a thing which is physically inconsistent with the continuance of an existing right, the right is gone.[4] Generally speaking, where a statute which extinguishes a right is repealed, the repeal will not revive the right.[5]

As regards the extinguishment of private rights of way under the Inclosure Acts, it should be mentioned that a proviso in section 8 of the Inclosure Act 1801 required an order of two justices for stopping up an "old or accustomed road." It seems that this proviso only applied to public roads, and not to private ones.[6] Where the road is stopped up under the Inclosure Act 1845 no order of the justices is required.[7] As to the effect of an order under the Highways Act 1959, see *ante*, p. 261.

Lands compulsorily taken

Where lands compulsorily taken under one of the numerous statutes giving compulsory powers are subject to an easement which is disturbed in exercise of statutory powers, the person entitled to the easement cannot in general bring an action for disturbance; nor is he

[1] s. 8; repealed by the Commons Act 1899, s. 23, Sched. 2.
[2] s. 68; *Turner* v. *Crush* (1879) 4 App.Cas. 221.
[3] See *Att.-Gen.* v. *Great Central Railway* [1912] 2 Ch. 124.
[4] *Yarmouth Corpn.* v. *Simmons* (1878) 10 Ch.D. 518, where it was shown that the construction of a pier authorised by statute would be physically inconsistent with the existence of a public right of way.
[5] Interpretation Act 1889, s. 38 (2) (*a*); *Gwynne* v. *Drewitt* [1894] 2 Ch. 616 (the case of a public right of way).
[6] *White* v. *Reeves* (1818) 2 Moore 23.
[7] See ss. 62–68. The "old inclosures " referred to in these sections are discussed and explained in *Hornby* v. *Silvester* (1888) 20 Q.B.D. 797. As to the construction of local Inclosure Acts giving powers to stop up roads, see, further, *Logan* v. *Burton* (1826) 5 B. & C. 513; *R.* v. *Hatfield* (1835) 4 A. & E. 156.

entitled to notice to treat. His remedy is by claiming compensation as for lands injuriously affected.[8]

Where a railway company's private Act extinguished, without compensation, " all rights of way in, over, and affecting " certain " footways," the clause affected only public rights, and did not extinguish a private right of way.[9]

The London Building Acts do not affect easements. The provisions which authorise the raising of party-walls confer no authority to raise them to the prejudice of a neighbour's right to light.[10]

The Housing Act 1957 [11] enacts that upon the purchase of land by a local authority pursuant to Part III of the Act dealing with clearance and re-development, all private rights of way and all rights of laying down, erecting, continuing, or maintaining any pipes, sewers, drains, wires or cables on, under or over that land, and all other rights or easements in or relating to that land shall be extinguished, subject to the payment of compensation. Comparable provisions are contained in the Town and Country Planning Act 1971,[12] the Requisitioned Land and War Works Act 1948,[13] the Civil Aviation Act 1949 [14] and the New Towns Act 1965.[15]

Statutory title

In the event of an easement already acquired by prescription vesting in the owner of the dominant tenement by statutory authority, the prescriptive title will merge in the statutory title, and if the operation of the statute be limited to a period the easement will be lost on the expiration of the period.[16] In *New Windsor Corporation* v. *Taylor* Lord Davey said [17]:

> " I hold it to be an indisputable proposition of law that where an Act of Parliament has according to its true construction, to use the language of Littledale J., ' embraced and confirmed ' a right which had previously existed by custom or prescription, that right becomes henceforward a statutory right, and that the lower title by custom or prescription is merged in and extinguished by the higher title derived from the Act of Parliament."

8 See, under the Lands Clauses Act 1845, *Eagle* v. *Charing Cross Railway* (1867) L.R. 2 C.P. 638; *Bedford* v. *Dawson* (1875) L.R. 20 Eq. 353; *Wigram* v. *Fryer* (1887) 36 Ch.D. 87; *Kirby* v. *Harrogate School Board* [1896] 1 Ch. 437; *M.S. & L. Railway* v. *Anderson* [1898] 2 Ch. 394; *Long Eaton* v. *Midland Railway* [1902] 2 K.B. 574.
9 *Wells* v. *London, Tilbury and Southend Railway* (1877) 5 Ch.D. 126.
10 See, *e.g.* on 14 Geo. 3, c. 78, *Titterton* v. *Conyers* (1813) 5 Taunt. 465, and *Wells* v. *Ody* (1836) 1 M. & W. 452; on 18 & 19 Vict. c. 122, ss. 83, 85, *Crofts* v. *Haldane* (1867) L.R. 2 Q.B. 194; and, on a Bristol Improvement Act, *Weston* v. *Arnold* (1873) 8 Ch.App. 1084. The London Building Acts (Amendment) Act 1939, s. 54, contains an express provision to the like effect.
11 s. 64 (3), replacing s. 46 (3) of the Housing Act 1936.
12 ss. 117–127. 13 s. 7.
14 s. 26. 15 s. 19.
16 *New Windsor Corpn.* v. *Taylor* [1899] A.C. 41; *Manchester Corpn.* v. *Lyons* (1882) 22 Ch.D. 287.
17 [1899] A.C. 41, 49.

CHAPTER 14

EXTINGUISHMENT OF EASEMENTS BY RELEASE

1.—EXPRESS RELEASE

Form of release

An easement may be extinguished by express release. It would appear that, in the case of easements, as of other incorporeal rights, an express release, to be effectual at law, must be under seal.[1] This rule, however, must not be taken to exclude a written instrument not under seal, or even a parol declaration, as evidence to show the character of any act done, or any cessation of enjoyment. And in equity an easement may be lost or modified by agreement.[2]

It seems that a release by deed " which is the act of the party shall be taken most strongly against himself." [3]

2.—IMPLIED RELEASE

(1) *Licence given by the Owner of the Dominant Tenement to the Owner of the Servient Tenement*

Licence to obstruct

If the owner of the dominant tenement authorises an act of a permanent nature to be done on the servient tenement, the necessary consequence of which is to prevent his future enjoyment of the easement, it is thereby extinguished.[4] Provided that the authority is exercised, it is immaterial whether it was given by writing or by parol.[5]

(2) *Extinguishment by Cessation or Alteration of User*

Generally

As the acquisition of an easement is an addition to the ordinary rights of property of the dominant and a corresponding diminution

---

[1] Co.Litt. 264b; Com.Dig. Release (A. 1), (B. 1). See judgment of Willes J. in *Lovell* v. *Smith* (1857) 3 C.B.(N.S.) 127; but see *Norbury* v. *Meade* (1821) 3 Bli. 241. In *Poulton* v. *Moore* [1915] 1 K.B. 400, a release of a right of way resulted from a deed operating by estoppel.

[2] *Davies* v. *Marshall* (1861) 10 C.B.(N.S.) 710; *Fisher* v. *Moon* (1865) 11 L.T. 623; *Waterlow* v. *Bacon* (1866) L.R. 2 Eq. 514. *Cf. Salaman* v. *Glover* (1875) L.R. 20 Eq. 444, where a lease was held to be controlled by the terms of a prior agreement.

[3] Co.Litt. 265a.

[4] *Davies* v. *Marshall* (1861) 10 C.B.(N.S.) 697; *Winter* v. *Brockwell* (1807) 8 East 308; *Liggins* v. *Inge* (1831) 7 Bing. 682; *Johnson* v. *Wyatt* (1863) 9 Jur.(N.S.) 1333; *Armstrong* v. *Sheppard & Short Ltd.* [1959] 2 Q.B. 384, 399–401, *per* Lord Evershed M.R.; see also " The Executed Licence " by Mr. Maurice C. Cullity in (1965) 29 *Conveyancer* (N.S.) 19 *et seq.*

[5] *Liggins* v. *Inge* (1831) 7 Bing. 682.

of those rights of the servient tenement, so the loss of the easement, when once acquired, by restoring both tenements to their natural state, is an addition to the rights of the servient and a corresponding diminution of those of the dominant. Hence, though the law regards with less favour the acquisition and preservation of these accessorial rights than of those which are naturally incident to property, and, therefore, does not require the same amount of proof of the extinction as of the original establishment of the right,[6] yet as an easement, when once created, is perpetual in its nature, being attached to the inheritance and passing with it, some acquiescence on the part of the absolute owner of the dominant tenement is necessary to give effect to any act of abandonment. In *Tehidy Minerals Ltd.* v. *Norman*[7] the Court of Appeal held that abandonment of an easement or a *profit à prendre* can only be treated as having taken place where a person entitled to it has demonstrated a fixed intention never at any time thereafter to assert the right himself or to attempt to transmit it to anyone else. In that case the subjection by commoners of their rights of grazing to the control of an association was, as the Court of Appeal found, only a temporary and terminable arrangement, not sufficient to infer abandonment.

It is the policy of the law, favouring the freedom of property, that no restriction should be imposed upon one tenement without a corresponding benefit arising from it to another, and hence it is that it is essential to the validity of an easement that it should conduce to the more beneficial enjoyment of the dominant tenement. If, therefore, any alteration be made in the disposition of the dominant tenement, of such a nature as to make it incapable any longer of the perception of the particular easement, the status of the dominant tenement, to which the easement was attached, and which is an inherent condition of its existence, is determined. Such alteration must, of course, be of a permanent character, evincing an intention of ceasing to take the particular benefit, or otherwise an easement might be lost by the mere pulling down of the tenement for the purposes of necessary repair.[8]

The question of the extinguishment of easements by the dominant owner ceasing or altering the user may be conveniently further considered by distinguishing between two classes of easements. First, continuous easements, *viz.* those of which the enjoyment is or may

---

6 The Prescription Act 1832 is silent as to the mode by which easements may be lost. Its enactments as to interruption and disabilities apply in terms only to their acquisition.

7 [1971] 2 Q.B. 528, 553. The doctrine of the extinction of easements by unity of ownership (see p. 137, *ante*) proceeds on the ground that the loss of an easement is a permanent injury to the inheritance, and can therefore only result from unity when the person in whom the union occurs is the owner of the fee simple of both servient and dominant tenements.

8 *Luttrel's Case* (1601) 4 Rep. 86; *Staight* v. *Burn* (1869) 5 Ch.App. 163; *Ecclesiastical Commissioners* v. *Kino* (1880) 14 Ch.D. 213. *Cf. per* Fry J. in *National Provincial Co.* v. *Prudential Co.* (1877) 6 Ch.D. 757, 764.

be continuous without the necessity of interference by man; such as a right to light. These easements require for their enjoyment a permanent adaptation of the dominant tenement. Secondly, discontinuous easements, *viz.* those of which the enjoyment can only be had by the interference of man; such as a right of way. These easements require no permanent adaptation of the dominant tenement. In the case of both these classes of easements questions arise as to the effect in law of (1) the actual cessation of enjoyment, and (2) an alteration in the mode of user, whether accompanied or not by an alteration of the dominant tenement. Under the last head must be considered those difficult cases where, instead of there being an intention to relinquish the right, an attempt has been made to usurp a greater right than the dominant owner was entitled to, or to enjoy it in a different manner; and here it may be pointed out that in the case of continuous easements it may often be a matter of great difficulty to ascertain the extent of the usurpation or excess, in other words, to sever the increased burden attempted to be imposed on the servient tenement. In the case of discontinuous easements the extent of the acts of usurpation or excess can usually be easily ascertained; in other words, the increased burden can be severed.

(a) *Continuous Easements*

Intention to abandon right

The cases in which this question has most frequently been raised have been cases relating to the easement of light, where there has been an actual cessation for a longer or shorter period of the old enjoyment. It appears from these cases that the law has fixed no precise time during which this cessation must continue. The material inquiry must always be whether there was an intention to abandon the right.

Certain acts will clearly show the intention to abandon; *e.g.* the shutting up of windows with bricks and mortar for twenty years.[9] Again, in the leading case of *Moore* v. *Rawson*,[10] the plaintiff pulled down his wall, in which there were some ancient windows, and rebuilt it as a blank wall. Fourteen years later the defendant erected a building in front of this blank wall. Three years afterwards the plaintiff opened in the blank wall a window in the place of one of the ancient windows, and sued the defendant for obstruction. The action failed, the court holding that the plaintiff had abandoned his right. In his judgment in that case it was said by Littledale J. that if a man pulls down a house and does not make any use of the land for two or three years, or converts it into tillage, he may be taken

---

[9] *Lawrence* v. *Obee* (1814) 3 Camp. 514.
[10] (1824) 3 B. & C. 332.

to have abandoned all intention of rebuilding the house, and consequently the right to the light has ceased.[11]

On the other hand, the mere alteration of a building containing ancient lights does not imply abandonment.[12] Nor, again, does the mere pulling down of a building destroy the right. Thus, in *Ecclesiastical Commissioners* v. *Kino*,[13] a church became vested in the Commissioners upon trust to pull it down and sell the site. The church having been pulled down, but not yet sold, the defendant commenced to build upon the adjoining land in a way which would have obstructed the light to the ancient church windows had they still been subsisting. In an action brought by the Commissioners, the defendant was restrained from obstructing the lights of any building to be erected on the site of the church, so far as such lights occupied the same position as the lights of the church. The Court of Appeal thought that the Commissioners were entitled to sell the land with the right to rebuild. James L.J. said [14]:

> "It appears to me that when a building, in which there are ancient lights, has been taken down, though the actual enjoyment of the light has been suspended, there is nothing to prevent the owner from applying to the Court for an injunction to restrain an erection which would interfere with the easement of the ancient lights, where the Court is satisfied that he is about to restore the building with its ancient lights. That was so decided by Lord Justice Giffard in *Staight* v. *Burn*." [15]

Onus of proving intention

The question turning upon intention, there has been discussion as regards the onus of proving this intention. It seems that where a house is rebuilt shortly after it has been pulled down, and rebuilt in such a way that the new windows will receive a considerable portion of the light which went into the old windows, it is unnecessary to give further evidence of intention to preserve the right.[16]

On the other hand, in *Moore* v. *Rawson* [17] Abbott C.J. said:

> "It seems to me that, if a person entitled to ancient lights pulls down his house and erects a blank wall in the place of a wall in which there had been windows, and suffers that blank wall to remain for a considerable period of time, it lies upon him at least to show, that, at the time when he so erected the blank

[11] *Ibid.* 341. See also the judgment of Tindal C.J. in *Liggins* v. *Inge* (1831) 7 Bing. 682, 693.
[12] *Greenwood* v. *Hornsey* (1886) 33 Ch.D. 471. See *Stokoe* v. *Singers* (1857) 8 E. & B. 31.
[13] (1880) 14 Ch.D. 213.
[14] (1880) 14 Ch.D. 219.
[15] (1869) 5 Ch.App. 163.
[16] *Smith* v. *Baxter* [1900] 2 Ch. 138, 142; *Scott* v. *Pape* (1886) 31 Ch.D. 554, 567.
[17] (1824) 3 B. & C. 332, 336.

wall, and thus apparently abandoned the windows which gave light and air to the house, that was not a perpetual, but a temporary abandonment of the enjoyment; and that he intended to resume the enjoyment of those advantages within a reasonable period of time. I think that the burden of showing that lies on the party who has discontinued the use of the light. By building the blank wall, he may have induced another person to become the purchaser of the adjoining ground for building purposes, and it would be most unjust that he should afterwards prevent such a person from carrying those purposes into effect."

Necessity for act by owner of servient tenement

From the language of the judges in cases before *Stokoe* v. *Singers*,[18] it does not appear to be necessary, where a building containing ancient lights has been altered, that after the alteration the servient owner should have done any act on the faith that the easement had been extinguished. In *Stokoe* v. *Singers*,[18] on the other hand, there are dicta to the effect that in order to make out an extinguishment of the easement such an act is essential; but these dicta have never been followed. While there appears to be no sufficient authority in our law for requiring any such act as the condition of the extinguishment of an easement, yet such an act, unopposed by the owner of the dominant tenement, as in the case of *Moore* v. *Rawson*,[19] would be almost conclusive evidence that there was no intention to preserve the easement.

Alteration in mode of user : general rule

In cases where there has been no actual cessation of user of the continuous easement, but there is an alteration in the mode of user, whether accompanied or not by an alteration of the dominant tenement, the rule seems to be that where the alteration does not impose any additional burden on the servient tenement, there is no extinguishment of the easement. On the other hand, an alteration which imposes an additional burden may destroy the easement altogether.[20]

In 1601 this question came before the court in *Luttrel's Case*,[21] which has ever since been treated as a leading authority. There an action was brought for the diversion of water. The declaration stated that the plaintiff, on the 4th of March in the 40th year of Elizabeth, was seised in fee of two old and ruinous fulling-mills, and that from time whereof, etc., *magna pars aquae cujusdam rivuli* ran

---

18 (1857) 8 E. & B. 31.
19 (1824) 3 B. & C. 332.
20 For the first branch of the rule, see the cases quoted, *post*, pp. 322, 323; for the second branch, see *post*, pp. 323, 324 *et seq.*; and compare the cases as to discontinuance easements *post*, pp. 337 *et seq.*
21 (1601) 4 Rep. 86a, recognised and applied in modern cases—*e.g. Colls* v. *Home and Colonial Stores* [1904] A.C. 179, 202; *Att.-Gen.* v. *Reynolds* [1911] 2 K.B. 888, 896.

from a place called Hod Weir to the said mills; and that for all the said time there had been a bank to keep the water within the current; and that afterwards the plaintiff, on the 8th October, 41 Eliz., pulled down the said fulling-mills, and in June, 42 Eliz., in place of the said fulling-mills erected two mills to grind corn, and the said water ran to the said mills until the 10th September next following; and the same day the defendants *foderunt et fregerunt* the bank, and diverted the water from his mills, etc.

The defendants pleaded not guilty, and it was found against them, on which the plaintiff had judgment; upon which the defendant brought a writ of error in the Exchequer Chamber, on which two errors were assigned. The principal of these was, that, by the breaking and abating of the old fulling-mills, and by the building of new mills of another nature, the plaintiff had destroyed the prescription and could not prescribe to have any watercourse to grist-mills: " As if a man grants me a watercourse to my fulling-mills, I cannot, as it was said, convert them to corn-mills, *nec e contra*." One of the cases cited in argument was from 10 Hen. 7, 13 a, b, and 16 Hen. 7, 9 a, b, " where the abbot of Newark granted by fine to find three chaplains in such a chapel of the conusee; afterwards the said chapel fell, and there *tenetur*, during the time there is no chapel, the divine service shall cease, for it ought to be done in a decent and reverend manner, and not at large, *sub dio*; but *tenetur*, if the chapel is rebuilt in the same place where the old stood, then he ought to do the divine service again "; but (it was collected) if it is built in another place, then the grantee is not bound to do divine service there.

It was contended in argument, that the alteration from fulling-mills to corn-mills might be injurious to the grantor, because he might have corn-mills himself, the proximity of others to which might injure him; and it was further contended that a man may not preserve an easement by rebuilding on the same spot, and in the same manner, unless the previous destruction has been caused by some act of God, as by tempest or lightning.

> " But it was resolved that the prescription did extend to these new grist mills; for it appears by the register, and also by Fitz.Nat. Brev. that if a man is to demand a grist mill, fulling mill, or any other mill, the writ shall be general, *de uno molendino*, without any addition of grist or fulling. . . . So that the mill is the substance, and thing to be demanded, and the addition of grist, or fulling, are but to shew the quality or nature of the mill, and therefore if the plaintiff had prescribed to have the said watercourse to his mill generally (as he well might) then the case would be without question, that he might alter the mill into what nature of a mill he pleased, provided always that no prejudice should thereby arise, either by diverting or stopping

G.E.—11

of the water, as it was before, and it should be intended that the grant to have the watercourse was before the building of the mills, for nobody will build a mill before he is sure to have water, and then the grant of a watercourse being generally to his mill, he may alter the quality of the mill at his pleasure, as is aforesaid: so if a man has estovers either by grant or prescription to his house, although he alter the rooms and chambers of this house, as to make a parlour where it was the hall, or the hall where the parlour was, and the like alteration of the qualities, and not of the house itself, and without making new chimnies, by which no prejudice accrues to the owner of the wood, it is not any destruction of the prescription, for then many prescriptions will be destroyed, and although he builds new chimney, or makes a new addition to his old house, by that he shall not lose his prescription, but he cannot employ or spend any of his estovers . . . in the part newly added; the same law of conduits and water-pipes, and the like: so if a man has an old window to his hall and afterwards he converts the hall into a parlour or any other use, yet it is not lawful for his neighbour to stop it, for he shall prescribe to have the light in such part of his house: and although in this case the plaintiff has made a question, forasmuch as he has not prescribed generally to have the said water-course to his mills generally, but particularly to his fulling mill, yet forasmuch as in general the mill was the substance, and the addition demonstrates only the quality, and the alteration was not of the substance, but only of the quality or the name of the mill, and that without any prejudice in the watercourse to the owner thereof; for these reasons it was resolved, that the prescription remained."

A further case [22] is mentioned of a grant to a corporation, who were afterwards incorporated by another name; it was held, that they retained all their franchises and privileges, because no person would be prejudiced thereby.

In *Saunders* v. *Newman*,[23] where the claim in the declaration was for a mill generally, the right to the discharge of water was held not to be lost by an alteration in the dimensions of the mill-wheel. Abbott J. said [24]:

"The owner [of a mill] is not bound to use the water in the same precise manner or to apply it to the same mill; if he were, that would stop all improvements in machinery. If, indeed, the alterations made from time to time prejudice the right of the lower mill, the case would be different."

In *Hall* v. *Swift* [25] the plaintiff had a right to water flowing from

---

[22] 14 Hen. 6, 12.   [23] (1818) 1 Barn. & Ald. 258.
[24] (1818) 1 Barn. & Ald. 258, 261.
[25] (1838) 4 Bing.N.C. 381 (a case of an alteration in the enjoyment of a natural right).

the defendant's land across a lane to his own land. Previously the stream had meandered down the lane before it flowed into the plaintiff's land. But the plaintiff varied the course by making a straight cut to his own premises. This, it was contended, negatived the right. Tindal C.J. said [26]:

"I think that these objections to the verdict ought not to prevail . . . If so, any alteration, however slight, would destroy the right, however long established. No authority has been cited in support of such a proposition and I think it cannot be maintained."

In *Hale* v. *Oldroyd* [27] the plaintiff had a right to a flow of surplus water to an ancient pond. Instead of using the water to supply that pond, he had during thirty years past used it to supply three more recent ponds. It was held he had not abandoned or lost his right to the flow of water by such user. Rolfe B. said [28]:

"If the plaintiff had even filled up the [old] pond, that would not in itself amount to an abandonment, although, no doubt, it would be evidence of it."

Parke B. said [29]:

"The use of the old pond was discontinued only because the plaintiff obtained the same or a greater advantage from the use of the three new ones. He did not thereby abandon his right, he only exercised it in a different spot; and a substitution of this nature is not an abandonment."

In *Watts* v. *Kelson* [30] the right to a watercourse which had been used to supply cattle-sheds was held not to be lost by the erection of cottages in their place.

Eavesdropping

The easement of eavesdropping might be extinguished by an alteration of the projection of the roof from which it could be inferred that the dominant owner meant to direct the rain-water into a different channel. Where, however, a greater burden is not thrown on the servient tenement, such an easement will not be lost either by increasing the projection [31] or by raising the house.[32]

Additional burden imposed on servient tenement

Of the rule set out previously at page 320, the second branch (which states that an alteration of the dominant tenement which imposes an additional burden on the servient tenement may destroy the continuous

---

[26] (1838) 4 Bing.N.C. 383.
[27] (1845) 14 M. & W. 789. *Cf. Davis* v. *Morgan* (1825) 4 B. & C. 8.
[28] (1845) 14 M. & W. 789, 793.
[29] (1845) 14 M. & W. 789, 793.
[30] (1870) 6 Ch.App. 166.
[31] *Thomas* v. *Thomas* (1835) 2 C.M. & R. 34.
[32] *Harvey* v. *Walters* (1872) L.R. 8 C.P. 162.

easement altogether) is illustrated by *Angus* v. *Dalton*,[33] where it was pointed out that any easement of lateral support which might have attached to the plaintiffs' premises as they originally were had been lost by the taking down of the old house and substituting a building of an entirely different construction,[34] but the cases in which the suggestion has been most frequently made that the continuous easement has been destroyed are cases relating to the easement of light.[35] These decisions are numerous, and for a long time there was much doubt about the doctrine. In view of the importance of the questions raised, some of the decisions must now be referred to.

One of the most important of the early decisions was *Martin* v. *Goble*,[36] where a building having been used for upwards of twenty years as a malt-house was converted into a dwelling-house. In an action for obstruction of light, the question for the jury was held to be whether, if the building had remained in the condition of a malt-house, a proper degree of light for making malt was prevented entering the windows by the obstruction. Macdonald C.B. said that the converting of the building from a malt-house to a dwelling-house could not affect the rights of the owner of the adjoining ground, for " no man could by any act of his, suddenly impose a new restriction upon his neighbour." [37] This decision has been much criticised,[38] but may be supported on the ground that (to use the language of *Luttrel's Case*) " the alteration affected the substance and not only the quality of the tenement." [39]

Extinguishment of easements by encroachment

Commenting upon the above decisions, Mr. Gale observed that it was directly admitted in many of the cases, and in none was it denied, that the right of the owner of the dominant tenement to make alterations in the mode of his enjoyment was, in all cases,

---

[33] (1877) 3 Q.B.D. 85, 102 (see *ante*, p. 292); *cf. Ray* v. *Fairway Motors (Barnstaple) Ltd.* (1968) 20 P. & C.R. 261.

[34] Contrast *Lloyds Bank Ltd.* v. *Dalton* [1942] Ch. 466, 471 *et seq.*

[35] See Lord Davey's words in *Colls* v. *Home and Colonial Stores* [1904] A.C. 202: " It would be contrary to the principles of the law relating to easements that the burden on the servient tenement should be increased or varied from time to time at the will of the owner of the dominant tenement. . . . I do not propose to discuss at length the question how far a variation in a tenement will destroy an easement appurtenant to it. The law on that subject is as old as *Luttrel's Case.*"

[36] (1808) 1 Camp. 320. See also *Cherrington* v. *Abney* (1709) 2 Vern. 646; *East India Co.* v. *Vincent* (1740) 2 Atk. 83.

[37] (1808) 1 Camp. 320, 323.

[38] See *Moore* v. *Hall* (1878) 3 Q.B.D. 178; *Dent* v. *Auction Mart Co.* (1866) L.R. 2 Eq. 238, 250.

[39] (1601) 4 Rep. 86a. See *Colls* v. *Home and Colonial Stores* [1904] A.C. 202; see also *Cotterell* v. *Griffiths* (1801) 4 Esp. 69, *per* Lord Kenyon; *Chandler* v. *Thompson* (1811) 3 Camp. 80, in which the judgment of Le Blanc J. appears to be in accordance with the view afterwards adopted in the House of Lords; *Garritt* v. *Sharp* (1835) 3 A. & E. 325, *per* Lord Denman. It is doubtful how far *Blanchard* v. *Bridges* (1835) 4 A. & E. 176 can now be relied on: see *Scott* v. *Pape* (1886) 31 Ch.D. 554, *per* North J. 561, and *per* Bowen L.J. 573.

subject to the condition that no additional restriction or burden be thereby imposed on the servient tenement; and that although, where the amount of excess could be ascertained and separated, as in the case of estovers,[40] such excess alone was bad, and the original right would nevertheless remain, yet, in those cases where the original and excessive uses were so blended together that it would be impossible, or even difficult, to separate them, and to impede the one without at the same time affecting the enjoyment of the other, the right to enjoy the easement at all appeared to be lost, so long as the dominant tenement remained in its altered form. It was admitted by the Court of King's Bench in *Garritt* v. *Sharp* [41] that " a party may so alter the mode in which he has been permitted to enjoy [an easement] . . . as to lose the right altogether "; and it would seem, on principle, that this consequence should ensue, at all events to the above extent, wherever a material injury is caused to the owner of the servient tenement by the alteration, and the original and usurped enjoyments are so mixed together as to be incapable of being separately opposed.[42]

Alterations in windows

In several subsequent decisions including *Renshaw* v. *Bean* [43] and *Hutchinson* v. *Copestake* [44] it was laid down that where an owner of the dominant tenement altered his ancient lights, or opened additional lights, he had not necessarily lost or suspended his admitted right; but that the alterations or the opening of the additional lights justified the owner of the servient tenement in obstructing the ancient lights, if in fact the doing so was unavoidable in the exercise of his right to obstruct the new lights. Accordingly it was held in equity that in such a case an injunction would not be granted to restrain the obstruction, except upon the terms of the plaintiff blocking up the new lights and restoring the ancient lights to their previous position.[45]

The whole subject was reviewed in *Tapling* v. *Jones*,[46] a case which was carried to the House of Lords. This was an action for obstructing the lights of the house of the plaintiff, who had altered the size and position of his lower windows, which were ancient, so that the new windows occupied parts only of the old apertures. He had also added upper windows in such a position that it was impossible for the adjoining owner to obstruct them without also obstructing the

---

40 See *Luttrel's Case* (1601) 4 Rep. 86a; *ante,* p. 320.
41 (1835) 3 A. & E. 325, 330.
42 These comments of Mr. Gale occur in the second edition of the present treatise (published in 1848) at p. 373.
43 (1852) 18 Q.B. 112.
44 (1861) 9 C.B.(N.S.) 863. See also *Binckes* v. *Pash* (1861) 11 C.B.(N.S.) 324; *Davies* v. *Marshall* (1861) 1 Dr. & Sm. 557; *Wilson* v. *Townend* (1860) 1 Dr. & Sm. 324; *Turner* v. *Spooner* (1861) 1 Dr. & Sm. 467; *Curriers' Co.* v. *Corbett* (1865) 2 Dr. & Sm. 355.
45 *Cooper* v. *Hubbuck* (1860) 30 Beav. 160; *Weatherley* v. *Ross* (1862) 1 H. & M. 349.
46 (1861) 11 C.B.(N.S.) 283; affirmed (1862) 12 C.B.(N.S.) 826; affirmed (1865) 20 C.B.(N.S.) 166; 11 H.L.C. 290.

ancient portion of the new lower windows. The defendant, who was tenant of the adjoining property, built thereon a wall which obstructed the whole of the plaintiff's windows. Subsequently the plaintiff restored his lower windows to their original size and position, blocked up his new upper windows, and called on the defendant to pull down his wall, but the defendant refused. At the trial a verdict was found for the plaintiff subject to a special case which was argued before the Court of Common Pleas. There was much difference of opinion, but in the result judgment was entered for the plaintiff.[47] This was affirmed in the Exchequer Chamber, where there was also much difference of opinion.[48] The House of Lords affirmed the Exchequer Chamber. The question in dispute turned on the nature of the right to light acquired under the Prescription Act; and the theory of this right was discussed by the judges in the House of Lords.[49]

Lord Westbury, after citing section 3 of the Act,[50] observed that the right to light now depended upon positive enactment, and did not require, and therefore ought not to be rested on, any presumption of grant, or fiction of a licence having been obtained from the adjoining proprietor. He said [1]:

"The right is declared by the statute to be absolute and indefeasible, and it would seem therefore that it cannot be lost or defeated by a subsequent temporary intermission of enjoyment, not amounting to abandonment. Moreover this absolute and indefeasible right which is the creation of the statute is not subject to any condition or qualification; nor is it made liable to be affected or prejudiced by any attempt to extend the access or use of light beyond that which, having been enjoyed uninterruptedly during the required period, is declared to be not liable to be defeated."

He could not accept the reasoning on which the decisions in *Renshaw* v. *Bean* [2] and *Hutchinson* v. *Copestake* [3] were founded. He said [4]:

"Upon examining the judgments [in those cases] it will be seen that the opening of the new windows is treated as a wrongful act done by the owner of the ancient lights, which occasions the loss of the old right he possessed; and the Court asks whether he can complain of the natural consequence of his own act. I think two erroneous assumptions are involved in or underlie this reasoning; first, that the act of opening the new windows was a wrongful one; and secondly, that such wrongful act is sufficient in law to deprive the party of his right under the statute."

---

47 (1861) 11 C.B.(N.S.) 283.
48 (1862) 12 C.B.(N.S.) 826.
49 *Tapling* v. *Jones* (1865) 11 H.L.C. 290.
50 See p. 147, *ante*.
1 (1865) 11 H.L.C. 290, 304–305.
2 (1852) 18 Q.B. 112.
3 (1861) 9 C.B.(N.S.) 863.   4 (1865) 11 H.L.C. 290, 307.

His Lordship's opinion was that the defendant's wall, so far as it obstructed the access of light to the plaintiff's ancient unaltered window, was an illegal act from the beginning.

Lord Cranworth gave similar reasons for his judgment, and expressed his dissent from the reasoning in *Renshaw* v. *Bean*.[2] Lord Chelmsford said that he did not see that the defendant's case would be benefited if it were established, contrary to the express words of the statute, that the right to the enjoyment of light rested on the footing of a grant. He stated the law to be that the right acquired by user must necessarily be confined to the exact dimensions of the opening through which the access of light and air had been permitted. As to anything beyond, the parties possessed exactly the same relative rights which they had before. The owner of the privileged window did nothing unlawful if he enlarged it, or made a new window in a different situation. The adjoining owner was at liberty to build upon his own ground so as to obstruct the addition to the old window, or shut out the new one; but he did not acquire his former right of obstructing the old window, which he had lost by acquiescence; nor did the owner of the old window lose his absolute and indefeasible right to it, which he had gained by length of user. The right continued uninterruptedly until some unequivocal act of intentional abandonment was done by the person who had acquired it, which would remit the adjoining owner to the unrestricted use of his own premises. Lord Chelmsford said[5]:

"It will, of course, be a question in each case, whether the circumstances satisfactorily establish an intention to abandon altogether the future enjoyment and exercise of the right. If such an intention is clearly manifested, the adjoining owner may build as he pleases upon his own land; and should the owner of the previously existing window restore the former state of things, he could not compel the removal of any building which had been placed upon the ground during the interval; for a right once abandoned is abandoned for ever."

On the other hand a person, by endeavouring to extend a right, could not manifest an intention to abandon it; he evinced his determination to retain it, and acquire something more; and the enlarging an ancient window would be no cause of forfeiture, because the act was not unlawful. Lord Chelmsford also thought that *Renshaw* v. *Bean*[6] could not be supported.

The decision of the House of Lords in *Tapling* v. *Jones*[7] has been uniformly followed since it was given.[8] With respect, however, to

---

[5] (1865) 11 H.L.C. 290, 319.   [6] (1852) 18 Q.B. 112.
[7] (1865) 11 H.L.C. 290.
[8] See *Martin* v. *Headon* (1866) L.R. 2 Eq. 425, 433; *Staight* v. *Burn* (1869) 5 Ch.App. 163; *Newson* v. *Pender* (1884) 27 Ch.D. 43; *Scott* v. *Pape* (1886) 31 Ch.D. 554; *Smith* v. *Baxter* [1900] 2 Ch. 138. It may be observed, however, that the question of nuisance or no nuisance was not considered in *Tapling* v. *Jones*

its bearing on earlier decisions, it has been pointed out by Sir A. Hobhouse, when delivering the judgment of the Privy Council in *Frechette* v. *La Compagnie Manufacturière de St. Hyacinthe*,[9] that the plaintiff in *Tapling* v. *Jones*[7] succeeded in getting protection for nothing but his old lights; and that it may be inferred from the judgments that, if the plaintiff had so mixed up his old lights with his new ones that they could not be distinguished, he would have failed. He said [10] :

> " It is true that in that case the protection given to the ancient light carried with it incidentally protection to the new lights. But the only reason why it did so was that the new lights could not be obstructed without obstruction to the ancient light. New lights are no encroachment, nor did the plaintiff's decree aggravate the defendant's servitude, for he was only prevented from building so as to obstruct the ancient lights."

Increase in size of window

It has been seen that in *Colls* v. *Home and Colonial Stores* [11] it was laid down that an obstruction to be actionable must amount to a nuisance. Since that decision it seems that an increase in the size of an ancient window will not increase the burden of the servient tenement, seeing that any obstruction which would be a nuisance to the enlarged window would *a fortiori* have been a nuisance to the original window.

Decrease in size of window

It would seem clear that, after an alteration in an ancient window whereby its size was decreased, the dominant proprietor would not be entitled to prevent the erection of buildings which, though obstructing the altered window, would not, before the alteration, have caused an illegal obstruction within the rule laid down in *Colls'* case.[11] This principle was applied in *Ankerson* v. *Connelly*.[12] There an easement of light had been acquired in respect of ancient windows, but the dominant tenement was amply lighted by means of light other than that which came through the ancient windows. The defendant, who was the dominant owner, rebuilt his tenement so as practically to

---

(1865) 11 H.L.C. 290, and that the tacit assumption that when the building was altered a right to light had been actually acquired under s. 3 of the Prescription Act appears (having regard to s. 4) to have been incorrect. See *Colls* v. *Home and Colonial Stores* [1904] A.C. 179, 189.

[9] (1883) 9 App.Cas. 170. The judgment of Farwell J. in *News of the World* v. *Allen Fairhead & Sons* [1931] 2 Ch. 402, 405, 406, is to the same effect; see p. 330, *post.*

[10] (1883) 9 App.Cas. 185, 186.

[11] [1904] A.C. 179; see p. 245, *ante.*

[12] [1906] 2 Ch. 554; [1907] 1 Ch. 678. The foregoing part of the paragraph was inserted in the eighth edition of this work by Mr. (afterwards Judge) Roope Reeve; and his words were cited with approval by Sargant J. in *Bailey* (*W. H.*) & *Son Ltd.* v. *Holborn and Frascati Ltd.* [1914] 1 Ch. 598, 602–603.

exclude all light other than that coming through the ancient windows. The plaintiff, who was the servient owner, erected an obstruction which prevented any access of light to the ancient windows, which obstruction the defendant pulled down. The plaintiff thereupon applied for a declaration that the defendant was not entitled to any easement of light over the plaintiff's land. The evidence showed that, after the rebuilding, the plaintiff's obstruction would materially interfere with the access of light to the defendant's ancient windows, whereas before the rebuilding it would not have caused such an interference as, since *Colls'* case,[11] would have justified an injunction. In the result the plaintiff succeeded. The Court of Appeal laid down that in the case of alteration there must be substantial identity between the altered premises and the old ones before the protection of ancient lights can be obtained, and held that as a matter of fact the reconstruction had destroyed this identity. They also held that what the servient owner had done would not have been the subject of an injunction prior to the alterations made by the dominant owner.

After *Ankerson* v. *Connelly*[13] the question was further considered in *Bailey (W. H.) & Son Ltd.* v. *Holborn and Frascati Ltd.*[14] That was a case, not of the dominant owner decreasing the size of his window, but of his consenting to an obstruction of light coming over one of several servient tenements, by which obstruction his light had been diminished. From the judgment of Sargant J.[15] it seems that in his opinion a decrease by the dominant owner in the size of his window would not entirely negative his right to an easement of light, though it would not give him any further right so as to prevent the erection of a building which he could not have prevented had the size of the window not been decreased.

The difficulty in these cases arises in defining and applying under the altered circumstances the rights of the owner of the old easement. It has been pointed out that in many cases where lights have been altered it may, since *Colls* v. *Home and Colonial Stores*,[16] be a matter of extreme difficulty to show that an interference with light is capable of legal remedy, having regard to the great difficulty of showing whether what is existing under the present conditions would have been a nuisance under the conditions formerly existing.[17]

The dominant owner is strictly speaking entitled to his old easement, but to nothing more; and if in any particular case the evidence enables the court to distinguish between the interference which, having regard to his old easement, the dominant owner can prevent, and that which he cannot prevent, the old easement can be protected accordingly.

---

13 [1906] 2 Ch. 554; [1907] 1 Ch. 678.
14 [1914] 1 Ch. 598.
15 [1914] 1 Ch. 602, 603.
16 [1904] A.C. 179.
17 *Andrews* v. *Waite* [1907] 2 Ch. 510, where the evidence enabled the court to surmount this difficulty.

If, however, the evidence does not enable the court to make this distinction—in other words, if it be impossible to sever any increased burden—then the question will arise whether the old easement has or has not been lost. In *Ankerson* v. *Connelly*,[18] Warrington J. decided that in such a case the old easement had been lost; but the Court of Appeal refused to deal with the question.

News of the World Ltd. v. *Allen Fairhead & Sons Ltd.*[19] was a case where the evidence did not enable the court to make this distinction. The plaintiff company was the lessee of certain buildings in the City of London which were entitled to receive light over the defendant's property. In 1925 the plaintiff's buildings were pulled down, and a new building was erected with numerous windows fronting the defendant's buildings (the servient tenement). At the trial no proper survey plan was produced showing the partial coincidence between the old and the new windows, and it was clear that the plaintiff's architect had never considered the question of preserving ancient lights. Such partial coincidences as did exist were not the result of any intention on the part of the plaintiff or its architect to preserve ancient lights, but were purely fortuitous. After the plaintiff's new buildings had been completed, the defendant pulled down its existing buildings and began to erect in their place new buildings of much greater height. In 1931 the plaintiff, fearing that its light would be obstructed, sued for an injunction and damages.

Farwell J. dismissed the action. He held that the mere lack of evidence of any intention to preserve the ancient lights was not by itself sufficient to prove an intention to abandon them, even though the amount of coincidence between the old and new windows was comparatively very small. On the ground floor, moreover, there were undoubtedly substantial coincidences between new apertures and the old windows, and the plaintiff still had a right to ancient lights in regard to these particular apertures. In these circumstances Farwell J. had to consider whether the defendant's new building would obstruct the plaintiff's ancient lights to a sufficient extent to cause a nuisance.

The learned judge began his judgment by referring to the well-known observations of Farwell J. in *Higgins* v. *Betts*,[20] pointing out that the test of nuisance is: How much light is left, and is that enough for the comfortable use and enjoyment according to the ordinary requirements of mankind? The learned judge then dealt with the question how, in applying that test, he was to ascertain whether there was a nuisance or not. The plaintiff had contended that the right way to apply this test was to treat the windows as only consisting of the portion through which the ancient light passed, and to treat the

---

18 [1906] 2 Ch. 549; [1907] 1 Ch. 682.
19 [1931] 2 Ch. 402.
20 [1905] 2 Ch. 210, 215. The judge in *Higgins* v. *Betts* was Sir George Farwell; the judge in *News of the World Ltd.* v. *Allen Fairhead & Sons* (*supra*) was Sir Christopher Farwell.

remaining portion as blocked up. The court should then, according to the plaintiff's argument, have ascertained whether the obstruction to the window so treated was such as to cause a nuisance. Dealing with this argument of the plaintiff, Farwell J. said [21]:

"They rely on *Colls* v. *Home and Colonial Stores* [22] where Lord Lindley said: 'As regards light from other quarters, such light cannot be disregarded; for, as pointed out by James V.-C. in the *Dyers' Co.* v. *King*,[23] the light from other quarters, and the light the obstruction of which is complained of, may be so much in excess of what is protected by law as to render the interference complained of non-actionable. I apprehend, however, that light to which a right has not been acquired by grant or prescription, and of which the plaintiff may be deprived at any time, ought not to be taken into account.'

"The plaintiffs say that in applying that principle, in order to see whether there is a nuisance, I must exclude all light except that passing through those portions of the new apertures which correspond with the old. They say that *Tapling* v. *Jones* [24] is to the same effect.

"If that is so, I am bound to give effect to those decisions, but I cannot accept the view either that *Tapling* v. *Jones* [24] decided anything of the kind, or that Lord Lindley ever intended to suggest that it did."

The learned judge, after pointing out that the question in *Tapling* v. *Jones* [24] was whether the alteration and reinstatement of the plaintiff's building had amounted to abandonment, and explaining that Lord Lindley was clearly speaking of light to which a right had not been acquired and of which the plaintiff could be deprived at any time, said [25]:

"I can well understand that if a man has a room lighted, both by ancient lights and by non-ancient lights, obstructible by outsiders, then, if an obstruction is threatened to the ancient lights, the Court cannot say to the plaintiff, 'you are at present getting enough light from the other windows to prevent this obstruction being a nuisance, and therefore you cannot complain' since the result might be that if the obstructible windows were subsequently blocked the plaintiff might be left with a room wholly unsuitable for ordinary occupation.

"But on the other hand it cannot be right that anything the plaintiff himself does should increase the burden on the servient tenement, and I cannot believe that the learned Lords in *Tapling* v. *Jones*,[24] or

---

[21] [1931] 2 Ch. 402, 405, 406.
[22] [1904] A.C. 179, 210.
[23] (1870) L.R. 9 Eq. 438.
[24] (1865) 11 H.L.C. 290, *ante*, p. 325.
[25] [1931] 2 Ch. 402, 406, 407.

Lord Lindley in the *Colls* case,[26] ever contemplated that a plaintiff could pull down his old building and put up a new building totally different in every respect, except for some slight coincidences in the old and new window spaces, and then say to the Court, ' Treat all my present light facilities as blocked out, leaving me nothing but a comparatively small peephole of ancient light, and then give me relief because that very inadequate amount of ancient light space will be made more inadequate by the defendants' proposed acts.' If that were the law, the plaintiff by his own acts would have greatly increased the burden on the servient tenement.

" The true view is this. If the plaintiff pulls down the building with ancient light windows and erects a new building totally different in every respect, but having windows to some extent in the same position as the old windows, he cannot require the servient owners to do more than see that the ancient lights, if any, to which he is still entitled are not obstructed to the point of nuisance. He cannot require them not to obstruct non-ancient light merely because a portion of the window through which that non-ancient light enters his premises also admits a pencil of ancient light. If the obstruction of the pencil itself causes a nuisance the plaintiff is entitled to relief, but if taking the building as it stands, the pencil obstruction causes no nuisance at all, the plaintiff will not be entitled to relief."

After referring to observations of Warrington J. in *Ankerson* v. *Connelly*,[27] Farwell J. said that in the case before him it was also impossible to determine the exact result of the threatened obstruction.

Farwell J.'s decision appears to establish clearly that the principle that a dominant owner is not entitled to increase the burden on the servient tenement by altering the size and position of ancient buildings is paramount to the consideration that obstructible light is not to be taken into account in estimating whether the servient owner's obstruction amounts to an actionable nuisance.

Alteration of plane of window

Alterations may be made, not only in the size or area of a window, but in its plane and inclination; and the question whether an alteration of this latter kind would suffice to extinguish an easement of light has been much discussed. It is now settled that alterations of this kind stand on the same footing as alterations of size, and do not, unless they are of such a character as substantially to change the nature of the easement [28] amount to abandonment.

Thus, in *National Provincial Plate Glass Insurance Co.* v. *Prudential Assurance Co.*,[29] a building containing ancient lights had been pulled

---

26 [1904] A.C. 179.
27 [1906] 2 Ch. 544, 548, 549.
28 See p. 336, *post*.
29 (1877) 6 Ch.D. 757.

down and rebuilt; and the old dormer window of three faces, which lighted the ground floor, had been converted into a skylight partially co-extensive with the old window, but of a different shape. The defendants having obstructed the light to this skylight, the plaintiffs brought their action. On the motion for an injunction Jessel M.R., while refusing the interlocutory injunction on the ground that the obstruction was complete before action brought, expressed his opinion that the easement formerly belonging to the ground floor window had not been lost; for, although the plane or direction of the glass had been altered, the aperture remained substantially the same.[30] At the trial, Fry J. awarded damages for the obstruction of the ground floor window. He said[31]:

" It is said that the access of light to the dwelling-house must be identical, and that the right claimed and the enjoyment which has existed must be of access of light through identical apertures. Now in its breadth that proposition is not true, because the case of *Tapling* v. *Jones*[32] has shewn that you may destroy the identical aperture by taking away the surrounding lines of that aperture and yet leave your right to light intact. Furthermore, I find nothing whatever in the statute which refers expressly to a window or aperture. I find in the statute a reference to the access of light, and in my view the access of light might be described as being the freedom with which light may pass through a certain space over the servient tenement; and it appears to me that, wherever for the statutory period a given space over the servient tenement has been used by the dominant tenement for the purpose of light passing through that space, a right arises to have that space left free so long as the light passing through it is used for or by the dominant tenement.[33] I come to that conclusion for this reason—that you do not want a statute to give you a right of access in your own premises to light through your own aperture. The statute is wanted to assure your right in the space over the servient tenement.

" But then it is said that the cases have to a large extent proceeded upon the form and size of the aperture or window; and that is perfectly true, because, of course, the opening in the dominant tenement is the limit which defines the boundaries of the space over the servient tenement. It is for that reason that in all the cases the Court has had regard to the aperture in the dominant tenement by means of which the space over the servient tenement has been useful to the dominant tenement."

---

[30] His Lordship also thought that the windows in the upper floors, which had been set back about five feet eight inches, were no longer the same windows so as to retain their right to light; but it appeared on the hearing that these windows were not affected by the defendant's building, and the case cannot therefore be regarded as a decision on this point. See and consider the cases next quoted.

[31] (1877) 6 Ch.D. 757, 764.   [32] (1865) 11 H.L.C. 290.

[33] Since *Colls* v. *Home and Colonial Stores* [1904] A.C. 179, expressions to this effect must not be taken literally, but must be taken to refer to the right as defined by that decision; and see *Ambler* v. *Gordon* [1905] 1 K.B. 417.

To the same effect is *Barnes* v. *Loach*,[34] where a wall containing ancient windows had been set back, and windows had been made in the new wall of the same size and in the same relative positions as those in the old wall, but in a different plane; and it was held that the right to light remained. It was also held in the same case that the dominant owner had not, by erecting a wall and a window in it, outside and at an angle with an ancient window, lost the easement of light attached to the ancient window.

Again, in *Bullers* v. *Dickinson*,[35] the plaintiff's premises stood on the site of an old toll-house which had projected obliquely into the street, and had enjoyed an easement of light for the windows on the ground floor; the toll-house had recently been pulled down, the site of the projecting part being sold for widening the street, and the plaintiff's premises being forthwith erected on the remainder. The plaintiff's ground floor window, for which he claimed protection, was substantially on the same level as the old window; but it stood further back, and, of course, at a different angle to the street. On an action being brought to restrain an interference with the new window, the defendant objected that the plaintiff had lost or abandoned his right; but Kay J. overruled the objection.

In *Scott* v. *Pape* [36] the whole question as to the effect of an alteration in a building was fully considered. The plaintiff, who was the owner of buildings having ancient lights looking into a lane, had pulled down his buildings within twenty years before action brought, and erected larger buildings on the site. The new buildings contained windows on all the floors. Parts of six windows on the first floor of the new building occupied a large portion of the area formerly covered by three ancient lights; and for this portion of such area the plaintiff claimed protection. It was a material element in the case that the plaintiff, in rebuilding, had slightly advanced his wall into the lane, the gain varying from a foot to three feet five inches. Upon these facts North J., who heard the action, declined to infer abandonment, and granted an injunction

> "restraining the defendant from permitting to remain erected any wall, etc., so as to darken, injure, or obstruct any of the ancient lights of the plaintiff's premises, as the same were enjoyed by means of those portions of the windows on the first floor of the plaintiff's old buildings which had not been blocked up in the rebuilding of the plaintiff's premises."

This was affirmed by the Court of Appeal. Cotton L.J., after referring to section 3 of the Prescription Act, continued [37]:

> "What alteration, then, will deprive the Plaintiff of his right, this right which can be claimed only in respect of a dwelling-house,

34 (1879) 4 Q.B.D. 494.   35 (1885) 29 Ch.D. 155.
36 (1886) 31 Ch.D. 554.   37 (1886) 31 Ch.D. 554, 569, 570.

workshop, or other building? Will the alteration of the purpose or object for which the building is to be used, as the conversion of a workshop into a house, or of a house into a workshop, have this effect? It will not: that is definitely settled by the case of *Ecclesiastical Commissioners* v. *Kino*.[38] The old building there was a church, and that which was to be built on the site of the church was a warehouse, an entire alteration of the purposes and of the character of the building. Then will moving back the plane of the wall deprive the Plaintiff of his right? In my opinion, no. It is difficult to see how the mere fact of moving back can do so, and in fact there is authority against such a proposition. Then if moving it back will not, will simply moving it forward have this effect? In my opinion, both the moving back and the moving forward may destroy the right, because the new building when constructed may, either by being substantially advanced or substantially set back, be so placed that the light which formerly went into the old windows will not go into the new. If a building is set back, say 100 feet, it will not enjoy the same cone of light that was enjoyed before, but will have an entirely different cone, and it may be moved so far forward that it will not enjoy the same light as that enjoyed by the old building. In my opinion the question to be considered is this, whether the alteration is of such a nature as to preclude the Plaintiff from alleging that he is using through the new aperture in the new wall the same cone of light, or a substantial part of that cone of light, which went to the old building. If that is established, although the light must be claimed in respect of a building, it may be claimed in respect of any building which is substantially enjoying a part, or the whole, of the light which went through the old aperture."

Bowen L.J., developing the same principle, said [39]:

"The measure of the enjoyment and the measure of the right acquired are not the windows and apertures themselves, which would involve a continuing structural identity of the windows, but the size and position of the windows, which necessarily limit and define the amount of light which arrives ultimately for the house's use."

Fry L.J. added his opinion that the "access of light" referred to in the Prescription Act was not access through the aperture or window, but access or freedom of passage over the servient tenement; and that the "right thereto," which is by the statute rendered "absolute and indefeasible," is a right to the same access and use of light to and for *any* dwelling-house, workshop, or other building. The Act, he said, was silent as to identity of aperture, as it was silent as to identity of building.

The above judgments are misleading in so far as they suggest that

[38] (1880) 14 Ch.D. 213; see p. 319, *ante*.
[39] (1886) 31 Ch.D. 572.

the right acquired under the Prescription Act is a right to the whole of
"that particular light which has come to" a building.[40]   As has been
already seen, since the decision in *Colls* v. *Home and Colonial Stores* [41]
it is established that the right acquired is a right only to freedom from
nuisance by obstruction. With this qualification the decision in *Scott* v.
Pape [42] has put the law as to the effect upon an easement of light of an
alteration in the dominant tenement on a clear and definite footing; and
it must now be taken that, if and so long as the dominant tenement
continues to enjoy the same or some part of the same light formerly
enjoyed, no abandonment will be inferred.[43]   In *Andrews* v. *Waite*
Neville J. said [44]:

> "It seems to me that the question which has to be determined
> is, whether proof is necessary of identity of the window or aperture
> through which the light claimed has been admitted to the dominant
> building, or whether the true matter for investigation is the identity
> of the light which has been so admitted. . . .   I think the real test
> is, as I said before, identity of light and not identity of aperture, or
> entrance for the light."

Present rule as to inferring abandonment

Where the alteration is such that none of the existing windows
can be said substantially to correspond with an ancient window, even
though part of the space occupied by each may be identical, no difficulty
arises; and, as it cannot be proved that any window in respect of which
a right had been acquired has been in fact obstructed, abandonment may
be inferred.[45]   The case of *Hutchinson* v. *Copestake*,[46] above quoted,
may be referred to this principle, and, so interpreted, may stand even
without *Renshaw* v. *Bean*.[47]   To the same effect are *Heath* v. *Bucknall*,[48]
where the new windows did not cover more than one-fourth of the
former area, and the opinions of the judges in *Newson* v. *Pender*,[49] where
the whole question was discussed.

In any case, it is essential to the preservation of the right that the
dominant owner, when affecting the alteration, should preserve clear
and definite evidence of the size and position of the former windows.[50]

40 See *Colls* v. *Home and Colonial Stores* [1904] A.C. 179, 189, *per* Lord Macnaghten.
41 [1904] A.C. 179; *ante*, p. 245.
42 (1886) 31 Ch.D. 554.
43 *Greenwood* v. *Hornsey* (1886) 33 Ch.D. 471; *Smith* v. *Baxter* [1900] 2 Ch. 138;
    Andrews v. *Waite* [1907] 2 Ch. 500; *cf. Raper* v. *Fortescue* [1886] W.N. 78;
    Re London and Tilbury Railway (1889) 24 Q.B.D. 326
44 [1907] 2 Ch. 500, 509.
45 *Pendarves* v. *Monro* [1892] 2 Ch. 611; *cf. Ankerson* v. *Connelly* [1906] 2 Ch. 544;
    [1907] 1 Ch. 678; *News of the World* v. *Allen Fairhead & Sons* [1931] 2 Ch. 402.
46 (1861) 9 C.B.(N.S.) 863; *ante*, pp. 325, 326.   47 (1852) 18 Q.B. 112.
48 (1869) L.R. 8 Eq. 1.   49 (1884) 27 Ch.D. 43.
50 *Fowlers* v. *Walker* (1881) 51 L.J.Ch. 443; *Scott* v. *Pape* (1886) 31 Ch.D. 554;
    Pendarves v. *Monro* [1892] 2 Ch. 611. In *Arcedeckne* v. *Kelk* (1858) 2 Giff. 683;
    Staight v. *Burn* (1869) 5 Ch.App. 163; *Bourke* v. *Alexandra Hotel Co.* [1877] W.N.
    30; and *Dyer's Co.* v. *King* (1870) L.R. 9 Eq. 438, it was held that a plaintiff
    who obscured the light of his house, but left a substantial part unaffected, was not
    thereby disentitled to an injunction.

Restoration after alteration

Upon the question whether a party who has lost his rights by altering his tenement is still at liberty to restore his tenement to its former condition and recur to his former enjoyment, it would seem on principle that the party so altering his tenement would have no such right, as he would have clearly evinced an intention to relinquish his former mode of enjoyment.[1] In addition to the actual encroachment, the uncertainty caused by the attempted extension of the right would of itself impose a heavier burden upon the owner of the servient tenement, if such return to the original right were permitted.

(b) *Discontinuous Easements*

Cessation of user

There seems to be no doubt that discontinuous easements may be lost by mere non-user, provided such cessation to enjoy be accompanied by the intention to relinquish the right. From the very nature, however, of the enjoyment, and from the circumstance that the cessation of enjoyment may take place without any alteration in the dominant tenement, it must always be difficult to lay down any precise rule to determine when a cessation of user shall be taken to have the characteristics requisite to make it amount to an abandonment of the right.[2]

In considering this part of the subject two questions appear to arise:

First, supposing there to have been simply a cessation of user, has the law presented any fixed period to raise the presumption of a release or abandonment of the easement?

Secondly, if any such period be fixed, can a shorter period suffice, if there be clear evidence of intention to relinquish the right?

Coke appears to have been of opinion that, when a title by prescription was once acquired, it could only be lost by non-user during a period equal to that required for its acquisition. " It is to be known that the title being once gained by prescription or custom cannot be lost by interruption of the possession for ten or twenty years." [3] At this time the analogy to the statute of James I had not been introduced into the law.

In *Doe* d. *Putland* v. *Hilder*,[4] Abbott C.J., in delivering the judgment of the court, said:

" One of the general grounds of a presumption is, the existence of a state of things, which may most reasonably be accounted for, by supposing the matter presumed. Thus the long enjoyment of a

---

[1] See the judgment of Lord Chelmsford in *Tapling* v. *Jones* (1865) 11 H.L.C. 319; the judgment of Pollock C.B. in *Jones* v. *Tapling* (1862) 12 C.B.(N.S.) 864. See also *Moore* v. *Rawson* (1824) 3 B. & C. 332; *Garritt* v. *Sharp* (1835) 3 A. & E. 325; *South Metropolitan Cemetery Co.* v. *Eden* (1855) 16 C.B. 42.
[2] As to the effect of the alteration of a building to which a right of way has been granted, see pp. 273 *et seq.*, *ante*.
[3] Co.Litt. 114b.
[4] (1819) 2 B. & Ald. 782, 791.

right of way by A. to his house or close, over the land of B., which
is a prejudice to the land, may most reasonably be accounted for,
by supposing a grant of such right by the owner of such land : and
if such right appears to have existed in ancient times, a long for-
bearance to exercise it, which must be inconvenient and prejudicial
to the owner of the house or close, may most reasonably be
accounted for, by supposing a release of the right. In the first
class of cases, therefore, a grant of the right, and in the latter, a
release of it, is presumed."

Littledale J., in the case of *Moore* v. *Rawson*,[5] though he did not
cite the above authority, expressed an opinion in accordance with it,
that easements of this character could only be lost by cessation of
enjoyment during twenty years; the learned judge distinguished between
these easements and a right to light and air, principally on the ground
that the former, as far as their acquisition by prescription was concerned,
could only be acquired by enjoyment accompanied with the consent of
the owner of the land, while the enjoyment of the latter required no such
consent, and could only be interfered with by some obstruction. He
said [6] :

   " According to the present rule of law a man may acquire a
   right of way, or a right of common, (except, indeed, common
   appendant) upon the land of another, by enjoyment. After twenty
   years' adverse enjoyment, the law presumes a grant made before
   the user commenced, by some person who had power to grant.
   But if the party who has acquired the right by grant ceases for a
   long period of time to make use of the privilege so granted to him,
   it may then be presumed he has released the right. It is said,
   however, that as he can only acquire the right by twenty years'
   enjoyment, it ought not to be lost without disuse for the same
   period; and that as enjoyment for such a length of time is necessary to found a presumption of a grant, there must be a similar
   non-user, to raise a presumption of a release. And this reasoning,
   perhaps, may apply to a right of common or of way."

In *Holmes* v. *Buckley*,[7] where there had been a grant of a watercourse through two pieces of land, with a covenant by the grantor to
cleanse the same, the court decreed the party claiming the land under
the grantor to cleanse the stream, although the grantee had cleansed it
at his own expense during forty years.

The precise period requisite to extinguish a right of way, by mere
non-user, does not appear to have been determined by any express
decision of the English courts. In *Bower* v. *Hill*,[8] Tindal C.J. indeed

---

5 (1824) 3 B. & C. 332, 339 *et seq.*   6 (1824) 3 B. & C. 332, 339.
7 (1691) 1 Eq.Cas.Abr. 27; there are some observations on this case, as bearing on
  the law of covenants running with the land, in *Austerberry* v. *Corporation of
  Oldham* (1885) 29 Ch.D. 750, 777, 782; see *ante*, p. 48.
8 (1835) 1 Bing.N.C. 555. *Cf. Drewett* v. *Sheard* (1836) 7 C. & P. 465.

said that an obstruction to a way of a permanent character, if acquiesced in for twenty years, would be evidence of a renunciation and abandonment of the right, but the weight of authority is against this dictum. In the earlier case of *Seaman* v. *Vawdrey*,[9] where a right of access to mines had been reserved by a conveyance of 1704, but had never been exercised, it had been held that the right had not been released by this non-user. " The non-user of this right proves nothing," said Grant M.R. In *Dogherty* v. *Beasley*,[10] where the plaintiff brought an action against the defendant for obstructing the plaintiff's right of way over the defendant's close, and the defendant pleaded in effect that the plaintiff had not used the way for twenty years, Joy C.B. said that the question really came to this: Was the plaintiff obliged to use the way, and if he did not make use of it for twenty years, was he to be excluded by a plea such as the defendant's? He said [11]: " We think not. The question is not whether the non-user may not be evidence . . . but whether it is *per se* an absolute bar. We think that we must allow the demurrer."

In *Cook* v. *Bath*,[12] Malins V.-C. held that thirty years' non-user without more was insufficient to extinguish a right of way.

Cessation of user : no indication of intention to abandon

The following cases elucidate the doctrine that a mere intermittence of the user, or a slight alteration in the mode of enjoyment, when unaccompanied by any intention to renounce the right, does not amount to an abandonment.

In *Payne* v. *Shedden* [13] issue was taken upon a plea of right of way; and it appeared that, by agreement of the parties, the line and direction of the way used had been varied, and at certain periods wholly suspended. Patteson J. was of opinion [14] that the occasional substitution of another track might be considered as substantially the exercise of the old right and " evidence of the continued enjoyment of it," and that the suspension by agreement was not inconsistent with the right.

In *R.* v. *Chorley* [15] the defendants were indicted for obstructing a public footway by driving carts in a lane through which there was a public footway. The lane was so narrow that carts could not pass without damage to persons on foot. The defence was that the defendants had a private right of way with carts, etc., to a malthouse, etc., situated in the lane, and that the public right of footway had been acquired subsequently to the private right, and was qualified by or subject to it [16]:

---

[9] (1810) 16 Ves. 390.
[10] (1835) 1 Jones Exch.Rep.(Ir.) 123.
[11] (1835) 1 Jones Exch.Rep.(Ir.) 123, 129.
[12] (1868) L.R. 6 Eq. 177.
[13] (1834) 1 Mood. & R. 382. The defendant failed to establish any right of way. See also *Hale* v. *Oldroyd* (1845) 14 M. & W. 789; and *Carr* v. *Foster* (1842) 3 Q.B. 581.
[14] (1834) 1 Mood. & R. 382, 383.
[15] (1848) 12 Q.B. 515.
[16] See *Brownlow* v. *Tomlinson* (1840) 1 Man. & G. 484; *Elwood* v. *Bullock* (1844) 6 Q.B. 383; *Morant* v. *Chamberlin* (1861) 6 H. & N. 541.

and the question was, whether the privilege was extinguished by the acquiescence of the dominant owners in the user of the way by the public—a user which was inconsistent with its use as a cartway by the defendants. The learned judge at the trial told the jury that nothing short of twenty years' user by the public, in a way inconsistent with the private user, would destroy the right. Lord Denman C.J., on making a rule absolute for a new trial for misdirection, after saying [17] that if

> "the learned judge had done no more than remark that, if a *mere* ceasing to use the private way, or a *mere* acquiescence in the interruption by the public were relied on, it would be prudent in them not to rely on such mere cesser or acquiescence unless shewn for twenty years, we think such a remark . . . would have been no misdirection,"

proceeded as follows [18]:

> "As an express release of the easement would destroy it at any moment, so the cesser of use coupled with any act clearly indicative of an intention to abandon the right would have the same effect without reference to time. For example, this being a right of way to the defendant's malthouse, and the mode of user by driving carts and waggons to an entrance from the lane into the malthouse yard, if the defendant had removed his malthouse, turned the premises to some other use, and walled up the entrance, and then for any considerable period of time acquiesced in the unrestrained use by the public, we conceive the easement would have been clearly gone. It is not so much the duration of the cesser as the nature of the act done by the grantee of the easement, or of the adverse act acquiesced in by him, and the intention in him which either the one or the other indicates, which are material for the consideration of the jury." [19]

In *Ward* v. *Ward* [20] a right of way was held not to have been lost by mere non-user for a period much longer than twenty years, it being shown that the way was not used, because the owner had a more convenient mode of access through his own land. Alderson B. said [21]:

> "The presumption of abandonment cannot be made from the mere fact of non-user. There must be other circumstances in the case to raise that presumption. The right is acquired by adverse enjoyment. The non-user, therefore, must be the consequence of something which is adverse to the user."

[17] (1848) 12 Q.B. 518.
[18] (1848) 12 Q.B. 519.
[19] The court, it will be seen, expressed no distinct opinion on the point left open in *Stokoe* v. *Singers* (1857) 8 E. & B. 31, *ante*, p. 320, whether or not, to make out an abandonment, the servient owner should have done some act on the faith that the easement had been abandoned, but in the latter case Lord Campbell said of *R.* v. *Chorley* (1848) 12 Q.B. 515: "It is an authority that an abandonment is effectual if communicated and acted upon. It goes no further."
[20] (1852) 7 Exch. 838.
[21] (1852) 7 Exch. 839.

In *Lovell* v. *Smith* [22] the owner of a right of way had, about thirty years before the action, agreed with the servient owner to use, in lieu of part of the old way, a new way over the servient owner's land, and therefore he discontinued to use the old way, and used the new. The court held that the mere non-user of the old way and the user of the new one for more than twenty years, under such circumstances, furnished no evidence of an intention to abandon the old right.

In *Cook* v. *Mayor and Corporation of Bath* [23] there had formerly been a right of way through a back door, which had been closed for thirty years, and then opened and used for four years before the obstruction. Malins V.-C. held that there had been no abandonment. He said [24]:

> "It is always a question of fact, to be ascertained by a jury, or by the Court, from the surrounding circumstances, whether the act amounts to an abandonment, or was intended as such. If in this case the defendants had commenced building before this back-door had been re-opened, I should have been of opinion that the Plaintiff had, by allowing it to so remain closed, led them into incurring expense, and therefore could not prevent them acting on the impression that he intended to abandon his right."

In *James* v. *Stevenson* [25] it was held that mere non-user of some of the roads over which a right of way existed, where no occasion for user had arisen, coupled with the use by the servient owner of those parts of the roads for farm purposes, did not constitute abandonment; and to the same effect is *Cooke* v. *Ingram*.[26]

In *Midland Railway* v. *Gribble*,[27] on the other hand, where, on the intersection of land by a railway, a crossing had been provided for the purpose of communication between the severed parts, it was held that, on the alienation by the owner of the part on one side of the railway without reserving any right of way over it, the right to use the crossing was finally abandoned.

In *Young* v. *Star Omnibus Co.*,[28] the plaintiffs claimed, and were held entitled to, a right of way over a strip of land ten feet wide in the occupation of the defendants. Some years prior to the commencement of the action the plaintiffs erected on their land a summer-house which projected over the strip of land to the extent of two feet four inches. The defendants having obstructed the way, this action was brought, and the defendants pleaded extinguishment or abandonment on the part of the plaintiffs. It was held that the erection of the

---

22 (1857) 3 C.B.(N.S.) 120. See *Hulbert* v. *Dale* [1909] 2 Ch. 570.
23 (1868) L.R. 6 Eq. 177.
24 (1868) L.R. 6 Eq. 179.
25 [1893] A.C. 162.
26 (1893) 68 L.T. 671.
27 [1895] 2 Ch. 827.
28 (1902) 86 L.T. 41.

summer-house was at best only a partial abandonment, and constituted no defence to the action.

In *Hall* v. *Swift*,[29] where it appeared that about forty years since a stream of water from natural causes ceased to flow in its accustomed course, and did not return to it until nineteen years before the action was brought, the court held that the right to the flow of water was not lost. Tindal C.J. said [30]:

> " It is further objected that the right claimed has been lost by desuetude, the water having many years since discontinued to flow in its accustomed channel, and having only recommenced flowing nineteen years ago. That interruption, however, may have been occasioned by the excessive dryness of seasons or from some other cause over which the plaintiff had no control. But it would be too much to hold that the right is therefore gone; otherwise, I am at a loss to see why the intervention of a single dry season might not deprive a party of a right of this description, however long the course of enjoyment might be." [31]

In *Gotobed* v. *Pridmore* [32] the Court of Appeal held that abandonment of an easement is not lightly to be inferred. Mere abstinence from the use of a right of way was not enough to establish an intention to abandon. What was required was conduct by the owner of the dominant tenement which made it clear that neither he nor any successor in title of his would afterwards make use of the way.

Indication of intention to abandon

In *Crossley & Sons Ltd.* v. *Lightowler* [33] the plaintiffs were carpet manufacturers, and had carried on business on the banks of the River Hebble from 1840 to 1864. A supply of pure water was necessary for their business. The defendants claimed a right to foul the stream with the refuse of dye-works, which had been carried on before 1839, but had then been shut up and abandoned, and re-opened by the defendants in 1864. Page Wood V.-C. said [34]:

> " The question of abandonment, I quite concede to the counsel for the Defendants, is a very nice one. On that a great number of authorities have been cited, which appear to me to come to this, that the mere non-user of a privilege or easement of this description, is not, in itself, an abandonment that in any way concludes the claimant; but the non-user is evidence with reference to abandonment. The question of abandonment is a question of fact that

29 (1838) 6 Scott 167; 4 Bing.N.C. 381. See observations on this case by Patteson J. in *Carr* v. *Foster* (1842) 3 Q.B. 586. *Hall* v. *Swift* is a case of a natural right, not an easement, but the same principle applies in both types of case.
30 (1838) 6 Scott 167, 170.
31 *Cf. Hale* v. *Oldroyd* (1845) 14 M. & W. 789.
32 (1970) 115 S.J. 78; see also *Costagliola* v. *English* (1969) 210 E.G. 1425.
33 (1866) L.R. 3 Eq. 279; (1867) 2 Ch.App. 478.
34 (1866) L.R. 3 Eq. 279, 292.

must be determined upon the whole of the circumstances of the case. . . . It has always been held to be of considerable importance, that a person in possession of a certain right, and leaving the right wholly unused for a long period of time, and having given so far an encouragement to others to lay out their money, on the assumption of that right not being used, should not be allowed at any period of time to resume his former right, to the damage and injury of those who themselves have acquired a right of user, which the recurrence to this long disused easement will interfere with."

On appeal Lord Chelmsford L.C. said [35]:

"The authorities upon the subject of abandonment have decided that a mere suspension of the exercise of a right is not sufficient to prove an intention to abandon it. But a long continued suspension may render it necessary for the person claiming the right to shew that some indication was given during the period that he ceased to use the right of his intention to preserve it. The question of abandonment of a right is one of intention, to be decided on the facts of each particular case. Previous decisions are only so far useful as they furnish principles applicable to all cases of the kind. The case of R. v. Chorley,[36] shews that time is not a necessary element in a question of abandonment as it is in the case of the acquisition of a right."

His Lordship, on the facts, held that, the ancient dye-works having been dismantled without any intention of erecting others, the right had been abandoned.

In Swan v. Sinclair [37] the Court of Appeal (Warrington and Sargant L.JJ., Pollock M.R. diss.) held that abandonment might be inferred where there was non-formation or non-user of the way and continuous obstruction of the way for more than fifty years. All the judges accepted the dictum of Alderson B. in Ward v. Ward,[38] but the two Lords Justices held, while the Master of the Rolls was unable to hold, that in the present case, as distinguished from Ward v. Ward,[38] there were facts, other than the mere non-user, which raised the presumption of abandonment. This decision was affirmed on other grounds by the House of Lords,[39] Viscount Cave L.C. remarking,[40] however, that even if the right of way had been effectively granted, the non-user of the way, coupled with acquiescence in the continuance of walls running across it, and (since 1883) in the additional obstruction caused by the filling up of the strip of land comprising one of the lots, would, according to the decisions of Moore v. Rawson,[41] Bower v. Hill [42] and R. v. Chorley,[43]

35 (1867) 2 Ch.App. 478, 482.
36 (1848) 12 Q.B. 515; ante, p. 339.
37 [1924] 1 Ch. 254.
38 (1852) 7 Exch. 838; see p. 340, ante.
39 [1925] A.C. 227.
40 [1925] A.C. 237.
41 (1824) 3 B. & C. 339; p. 338, ante.
42 (1835) 1 Bing.N.C. 555; p. 338, ante.
43 (1848) 12 Q.B. 515, p. 339, ante.

have afforded good ground for inferring a release or abandonment of the easement. The effect of the transactions was, however, at most to create a contractual relationship under which the several purchasers might have been called upon to clear the land and form the road; until that had been done there would be no effectual creation of the easement of passage. In fact no right of way ever came into existence. Viscount Finlay said [44]:

> " The scheme contemplated that it should come into existence when the road at the back of the premises had been made and the other provisions of the conditions had been complied with. As this never took place, the right of way remained a mere possibility of the future."

Lord Shaw of Dunfermline said [45]:

> " All the arguments as to non-use of a subject which is *res mere facultatis* can find no place in the present case. For there was no *res*, no right, and the physical basis of the right, including the very construction of the road over which the right of way was to run, has never yet been in existence."

Where a cessation to enjoy has been accompanied by indications of an intention to abandon the right, as by a disclaimer, there is authority for saying that a shorter period than that of the non-user in *Swan* v. *Sinclair* [46] will be sufficient to extinguish the right. Such direct evidence of intention appears to have been treated in the same manner as the similar indications afforded by a change in the status of the dominant tenement. Such non-user, accompanied by confessions that the party had no right, would at all events be strong evidence, and in effect almost conclusive evidence, that he never had any such right.

In *Norbury* v. *Meade* [47] Lord Eldon L.C. said:

> " In the case of a right of way over the lands of other persons, being an easement belonging to lands, if the owner chooses to say ' I have no right of way over those lands,' that is disclaiming that right of way; and though the previous title might be shown, a subsequent release of the right might be presumed."

In *Howton* v. *Hawkins* [48] lessees, to whom had been granted rights of way over land retained by the lessor by mutual agreement, enclosed within the gardens of their respective properties parts of the retained land so that the whole was enclosed. The lessor, who had not objected to the enclosure for forty years, was held to have no right to do so, even if he did not know of it. Therefore when the reversion was sold the lessor was obliged to accept that the retained land had been added to the gardens of the properties concerned.

[44] [1925] A.C. 240.
[46] [1924] 1 Ch. 254; [1925] A.C. 227.
[47] (1821) 3 Bligh 211, 241–242.
[48] (1966) 110 S.J. 547.

[45] [1925] A.C. 243.

Partial user

Where the extent of the right is known, and does not (as in the case of a right claimed by prescription) have to be gathered from user, user to something less than the full extent does not prejudice the full right.[49]

Effect of Prescription Act 1832

A question upon this point under the Prescription Act 1832 was suggested in the first edition of this work,

> "Whether, in all cases where an easement is claimed by prescription, the user must possess all the qualities requisite to confer a title down to the very commencement of the suit; and therefore, although the right may have clearly existed at an earlier period, it is destroyed by a subsequent user not possessing those essential qualities."[50]

It has been already seen that, by the statute, the period of user to acquire an easement must be that immediately preceding the commencement of an action,[1] and, if the statute had been held to be obligatory in all cases upon parties to proceed under it, many ancient rights would have been lost on grounds which at the common law would have been insufficient to produce that result, and which the legislature, in framing the statute, did not appear to contemplate. For example, where, within the period requisite to confer an easement, there has been a unity of possession of the dominant and servient tenements, no right under the statute can be acquired, according to the cases cited *ante*, pages 147, 160; and supposing the right to be ancient, the incidental operation of the statute would have been, in such a case, to destroy it. So of any other failure of the requisite qualities of the user.

Another anomaly would also have arisen as to the mode of losing an easement, which would be different in the case of an easement claimed by express grant and by prescription. Thus, a right of way by express grant would not be determined by unity of possession, as it would have been if claimed by prescription.

This inconvenience has been obviated by considering this as an affirmation statute, which does not take away the common law.[2] In *Onley* v. *Gardiner*[3] where the defendant failed in proving a sufficient title under the statute in consequence of a unity of possession, the court allowed the defendants to amend by pleading a right by prescription generally. In *Richards* v. *Fry*,[4] where it was suggested in argument that if "a party had a right three years ago, which he released, and

---

[49] *Keewatin Power Co. Ltd.* v. *Lake of the Woods Milling Co. Ltd.* [1930] A.C. 640, 657; *Bulstrode* v. *Lambert* [1953] 1 W.L.R. 1064, 1068.

[50] See *e.g. Hyman* v. *Van den Bergh* [1907] 2 Ch. 516; affd. [1908] 1 Ch. 167 (a case of light).

[1] See p. 152, *ante*.

[2] Bacon Ab., Stat.G.

[3] (1838) 4 M. & W. 496.

[4] (1838) 3 Nev. & P.K.B. 67.

then that an action was brought against him for a trespass committed before the release, if he pleads according to the letter of the statute, *i.e.* a user for thirty years before the commencement of the suit, he would be defeated, although the act in question was perfectly justifiable at the time," Patteson J. observed [5]: " He might not be able to avail himself of the statute, but he would have a defence at common law."

In accordance with this view, statements occur in several later cases to the effect that the Prescription Act has not taken away any of the methods of claiming easements which existed before that Act was passed. The rule has been so laid down by Mellish L.J. in *Aynsley* v. *Glover*,[6] by Lord Blackburn in *Dalton* v. *Angus*,[7] by Stirling J. in *Smith* v. *Baxter*,[8] and by Lord Lindley in *Gardner* v. *Hodgson's Kingston Brewery Co.*[9] Again, as regards *profits à prendre*, Lord Hatherley in 1871 [10] held that rights of common could be established by prescription at common law independently of the statute.

It should be remembered, however, that by the combined effect of section 1, section 2 or section 3 and section 4 of the Prescription Act, a right under the Act is not established by user for the prescribed period in gross, but remains inchoate until it is brought into question by action [11]; and consequently, in many of the cases referred to in this chapter, where a tenement had been altered after enjoying a right for the prescribed period, the question would seem to have been, not whether the right, supposed to have been acquired under the Act, had been abandoned, but whether, having regard to the alteration, a right had been acquired at all. In *Andrews* v. *Waite*,[12] a light case where a building had enjoyed light since 1879 but had been altered in 1888 and 1895, Neville J. expressed the opinion that no distinction can be drawn between what, in the way of alteration, involves the loss of the right to light when once indefeasibly acquired, and what is sufficient to prevent the acquisition of the right during the twenty years.

Effect of excessive user

In the case of discontinuous easements the previously existing right will not be affected by acts of excessive user or usurpation, if (as is usually the case) the extent of the excess can be ascertained. Thus, if a party having a right of footway were to use it as a carriageway, though he might thereby become liable to an action for such trespass, he might nevertheless sustain an action for any disturbance of his footway. The right thus sought to be usurped would, in the mode of its enjoyment, be altogether distinct from the previous easement. It has been held,[12a]

[5] *Ibid.* 72.   [6] (1875) 10 Ch.App. 283, 285.
[7] (1881) 6 App.Cas. 740, 814.   [8] [1900] 2 Ch. 138.
[9] [1903] A.C. 229, 238. [10] *Warrick* v. *Queen's College, Oxford* (1871) 6 Ch.App. 716.
[11] See *ante*, p. 152.
[12] [1907] 2 Ch. 500, 509.
[12a] *Bernard and Bernard* v. *Jennings and Hillaire* (1968) 13 W.I.R. 501, Trinidad and Tobago C.A.

in a case where a dominant owner having a right of footway claimed an unlimited right of way, that if the excessive user of an easement cannot be abated without obstructing the whole user, the owner of the servient tenement may obstruct the whole of that user, and the servient owner was therefore entitled to block the way and erect a fence in order to prevent the dominant owner from exercising an unlimited right of way.

In *Harris* v. *Flower & Sons* [13] the excessive user by which it was attempted to impose an additional burden on the servient tenement consisted in the use of a right of way for obtaining access to buildings erected partly on the land to which the right of way was appurtenant and partly on other land. A claim was put forward on behalf of the plaintiffs that the right of way had been abandoned, on the ground that, as it was practically impossible to separate the lawful from the excessive user, the right of way could not be used at all. This contention failed, however, the court holding that there had been no abandonment, but that the user of the way for access to the buildings so far as they were situate upon land to which the right of way was not appurtenant was in excess of the rights of the defendants, and a declaration was made accordingly, with liberty to apply.

It may, however, happen that an alteration of the dominant tenement, accompanied by a claim to use an easement in excess of the old right, will result in its suspension or extinguishment. In *Milner's Safe Co. Ltd.* v. *G. N. & City Railway* [14] the case of a right of way, a house which was the dominant tenement had been pulled down and a railway station erected on the site, and a claim by the dominant owner to use the way for access to the station failed. It was further argued for the servient owner that the dominant tenement had been so altered that the dominant owner could not help exceeding the right if it used it at all, and, the good user not being severable from excess of user, the right was suspended. Kekewich J. gave effect to the argument, saying [15]: "It may be correct to say that the right is suspended, for I suppose it is presumably capable of being revived, but what I hold is that it is not under present circumstances exercisable at all." So, again, where a person who has a right to send down clean water through a drain sends down foul water, so that it is impossible to sever the good user from the excessive user, the servient owner may stop the whole discharge. [16] Where, however, a right had been acquired to pollute water by a certain manufacture, it was said that the right would not be destroyed by altering the materials used. [17]

[13] (1905) 74 L.J.Ch. 127.
[14] [1907] 1 Ch. 215, *ante*, p. 281. See also, as to the extinguishment of a right of way by alteration of the dominant tenement, *Allan* v. *Gomme* (1840) 11 A. & E. 772; *Henning* v. *Burnet* (1852) 8 Ex. 191; *ante*, pp. 274, 275.
[15] [1907] 1 Ch. 215, 227–228.
[16] *Cawkwell* v. *Russell* (1856) 26 L.J.Ex. 34; *Charles* v. *Finchley Local Board* (1883) 23 Ch.D. 775; *Hill* v. *Cock* (1872) 26 L.T. 185.
[17] *Baxendale* v. *MacMurray* (1867) 2 Ch.App. 790, 794.

PART V

DISTURBANCE OF EASEMENTS

CHAPTER 15

WHAT AMOUNTS TO A DISTURBANCE

Nuisance and disturbance compared

There is a distinction as to the foundation of the right of action for a private nuisance, properly so called, and an action for the disturbance of an easement. No proof of any right in addition to the ordinary right of property is required in the case of the former; for example, where an action is brought for corrupting the air, or establishing an offensive trade. On the other hand, to maintain an action for a disturbance of an easement to receive air by a window, proof of the accessorial right must be given.[1] Yet the incidents of the two classes of rights, as far as concerns the remedies for any infringement of them, are similar.

> " A man has no need to prescribe to do a thing which he may do of common right, as to distrain for rent, rent service, etc.; or if I would prescribe that, when a man builds a house so that from his house the water runs upon my land, I have been used to abate that which causes the water to run upon my land, this prescription is void, for by the common law I can do that as well." [2]

In many cases an action may be founded on both these rights; thus, in *Aldred's Case* [3] the plaintiff complained of the stoppage of his windows, and that the defendant had erected a wooden building and kept hogs therein, by means of which his easement of light was obstructed, and his enjoyment of his messuage diminished by the smell of the hogs. Both injuries are called nuisances, and the same principles as to the nature of the remedies for them apply indiscriminately to both.

Sensible diminution of enjoyment

It is not every interference with the full enjoyment of an easement that amounts in law to a disturbance; there must be some sensible abridgment of the enjoyment of the tenement to which it is attached, although it is not necessary that there should be a total destruction of the easement. The injury complained of must be of a substantial nature, in the ordinary apprehension of mankind, and not

---

[1] *Paine & Co. Ltd.* v. *St. Neots Gas and Coke Co. Ltd.* [1938] 4 All E.R. 492; [1939] 3 All E.R. 812.

[2] *Per* Choke J., 8 Edw. 4, 5, pl. 14; *Tenant* v. *Goldwin* (1705) 1 Salk. 360.

[3] (1611) 9 Co.Rep. 57b.

arising from the caprice or peculiar physical constitution of the party aggrieved.

Watercourses

It is said in *Aldred's Case*[4]:

> " So if a man had a watercourse running in a ditch from the river to his house, for his necessary use; if a glover sets up a lime-pit for calf-skins and sheep-skins so near the said watercourse that the corruption of the lime-pit has corrupted it, for which cause his tenants leave the said house, an action on the case lies for it, as it is adjudged, 13 Hen. 7, 26b."

So, also, the driving of stakes into a watercourse, or otherwise diverting it, whereby there is no longer sufficient water for a mill[5] is actionable; even if the stream be choked up for want of cleansing,[6] or by the roots of trees growing into it.[7] An action will also lie for affixing a small pipe and thereby taking water from a larger one,[8] or for diverting part of the water only,[9] or for opening a drain into a sewer made by another on my land under a reservation of right to make it for the purpose of carrying off his drainage.[10]

> " Item," says Bracton, " si quis aliquid fecerit quominus ad fontem, etc., ire possit, vel haurire, vel de fonte aquae non tantum aquam ducere vel haurire, tales cadere possunt in assisam." [11]

Private rights of way

As regards the disturbance of private rights of way, it has been laid down that in a public highway any obstruction is a wrong if appreciable, but in the case of a private right of way the obstruction is not actionable unless it is substantial.[12] Again, it has been said that for the obstruction of a private way the dominant owner cannot complain unless he can prove injury; unlike the case of trespass, which gives a right of action though no damage be proved.[13] In *Hutton* v. *Hamboro*,[14] where the obstruction of a private way was alleged, Cockburn C.J. laid down that the question was whether practically and substantially the right of way could be exercised as conveniently as before. In *Keefe* v. *Amor*[15] Russell L.J. said that the grantee of a right of way could only object to such activities of the owner of the land, including retention of obstructions, as substantially

4 (1611) 9 Co.Rep. 57b.   5 2 Rolle, pl. 8, 9.
6 *Bower* v. *Hill* (1835) 1 Bing.N.C. 549.
7 *Hall* v. *Swift* (1838) 4 Bing.N.C. 381.
8 *Moore* v. *Browne* (1572) Dyer 319b, pl. 17.
9 *Anon.* (1566) Dyer 248b, pl. 80; see also *R.* v. *Tindall* (1837) 6 A. & E. 143.
10 *Lee* v. *Stevenson* (1858) E.B. & E. 512.
11 Bracton, Lib. 4, f. 233.
12 *Pettey* v. *Parsons* [1914] 2 Ch. 662. See *Pullin* v. *Deffel* (1891) 64 L.T. 134.
13 *Thorpe* v. *Brumfitt* (1873) 8 Ch.App. 650, 656.
14 (1860) 2 F. & F. 218.
15 [1965] 1 Q.B. 334, 347.

interfered with the use of the land in such exercise of the defined right as for the time being was reasonably required. It must not be forgotten that the grant of a private way ordinarily speaking confers only a right to a reasonable use of the way by the grantee in common with others [16]; and the question what is a reasonable use has been said to be a question for the jury.[17] In deciding what is a substantial interference with the dominant owner's reasonable user of the way, all the circumstances must be considered; for example, the reciprocal rights of the persons entitled to use the way [18]; also the case of persons carrying burdens along the way.[19] Certain acts by the servient owner have been held to be obstruction, e.g. building on the way [20]; or ploughing up the way, which makes it not so easy as it was before [21]; or erecting a building so as to leave a tunnel only ten feet high.[22]

The owner of a right of way cannot recover damages for physical damage to the servient tenement. The right to damages lies in the unlawful interference with the right to use the way, and if there is no substantial interference there is no cause of action.[22a]

Gates

With respect to the particular disturbance of a private right of way caused by the servient owner erecting a gate across the way, the following dictum by Jones J. occurs in his report of *James* v. *Hayward* [23]:

"If a private man has a way across the land of J.S. by prescription or grant, J.S. cannot make a gate across the way; and if on a private way a gate cannot be made, *a multo fortiori* it cannot be made on a highway which would be prejudicial to many."

In *Andrews* v. *Paradise* [24] the plaintiff recovered judgment against the defendant for breach of covenant for quiet enjoyment, the breach consisting of the erection of a gate across a way. The case was argued on demurrer, which admitted the plaintiff's allegation that the defendant had erected a gate across the way, *per quod* the plaintiff's tenant was obstructed. In *Kidgill* v. *Moor* [25] a declaration by the plaintiff (owner

[16] *Clifford* v. *Hoare* (1874) L.R. 9 C.P. 362, 371. See *Harding* v. *Wilson* (1823) 2 B. & C. 96; *Strick* v. *City Offices* (1906) 22 T.L.R. 667; *Robertson* v. *Abrahams* [1930] W.N. 79.
[17] *Hawkins* v. *Carbines* (1857) 27 L.J.Ex. 46.
[18] *Shoesmith* v. *Byerley* (1873) 28 L.T. 553. And see especially the remarks of Jessel M.R. as to reasonable user, in *Original Hartlepool Co.* v. *Gibb* (1877) 5 Ch.D. 713 (access to a wharf on a navigable river, which is a public highway).
[19] *Austin* v. *Scottish Widows Fund Assurance Society* (1881) 8 L.R.Ir. 385.
[20] *Lane* v. *Capsey* [1891] 3 Ch. 411. See *Phillips* v. *Treeby* (1862) 3 Giff. 632.
[21] 2 Rolle, Ab., Nusans, G. 1. See *Nicol* v. *Beaumont* (1883) 50 L.T. 112.
[22] *V.T. Engineering Ltd.* v. *Richard Barland & Co. Ltd.* (1968) 19 P. & C.R. 890.
[22a] *Weston* v. *Lawrence Weaver* [1961] 1 Q.B. 402.
[23] (1631) Sir W. Jones 222; Cro.Car. 184. The words of Jones J. do not occur in Croke's report.
[24] (1724) 8 Mod. 318.
[25] (1850) 9 C.B. 364.

in reversion of the dominant tenement) against the defendant for fastening a gate made across a private way was held good after verdict.

Modern cases have placed the law on a clearer footing. It has been held in the Court of Appeal in England that a gate is not necessarily an interference with a private right of way. To be actionable the interference must be substantial.[26] And it has been held in Ireland that whether a gate is or is not an interference with the right is a matter of fact.[27] In both the last-mentioned cases the erection of a gate across a private way was held to be no interference with the right, proper facilities being given to the dominant owner,[28] who, on his part, is under an obligation to shut after him a gate which has been left unlocked for his convenience.[29] If a gate across a private way is locked, it is not necessarily an answer to a complaint of the obstruction to say that keys will be supplied.[30]

Light

To maintain an action for obstructing light it is not sufficient to show that the light is less than before. The plaintiff must show that the obstruction complained of is a nuisance.[31] The measure of the right to light laid down by the House of Lords and the matters to which the court should have regard in deciding the question of nuisance or no nuisance have already been stated and discussed.[32] In particular, it has been pointed out that the court should have regard to light coming from sources other than that which has been obstructed, but only so far as this other light is light which the dominant owner is entitled by grant of prescription to enjoy.[33]

Assuming, for example, a room having windows in walls facing both east and west, the windows in either wall being amply sufficient to light the room without the assistance of the light coming through the windows in the other wall; assuming, also, the windows in the eastern wall to have enjoyed the access of light for more than twenty years, and those in the western wall to have been open for less than the statutory period. In such a case, in an action for obstruction to the ancient windows in the eastern wall, could regard be had to

---

[26] *Pettey* v. *Parsons* [1914] 2 Ch. 662, 666; see also *Lister* v. *Rickard* (1969) 113 S.J. 981.

[27] *Flynn* v. *Harte* [1913] 2 I.R. 327.

[28] See also *Deacon* v. *S.E. Ry.* (1889) 61 L.T. 377, where the erection of gates across a private right of way was held justifiable. And gates may even be placed across public highways. "You may, as a matter of law, have a gate upon a public highway," said Scrutton J. in *Att.-Gen.* v. *Meyrick & Jones* (1915) 79 J.P. 515; but it must not be locked: *Guest* v. *Milner, infra.*

[29] *Geoghegan* v. *Henry* [1922] 2 I.R. 1. In *Lister* v. *Rickard* (1969) 113 S.J. 981 it was held that the servient owner was not bound to close the gates, for it was not reasonably necessary for the enjoyment of the dominant owner's land that the gates should be kept closed.

[30] *Guest Estates Ltd.* v. *Milner's Safes Ltd.* (1911) 28 T.L.R. 59; *cf. Johnstone* v. *Holdway* [1963] 1 Q.B. 601.

[31] *Colls* v. *Home and Colonial Stores* [1904] A.C. 179.

[32] See *ante*, p. 247 *et seq.*

[33] See *ante*, p. 247.

the light enjoyed through the windows in the western wall, of which the owner of the building would be liable to be deprived at any moment? The answer to this question should, in accordance with the words of the judges referred to above,[34] be in the negative. It should be pointed out, however, that in practice it may be difficult to limit the light coming from other sources to light to which the dominant owner has acquired a right. For such a qualification might and probably would involve questions of the rights of third persons. Moreover, as regards a claim to light under the Prescription Act, it is now settled that even after twenty years' enjoyment the right remains inchoate until some action is commenced in which the right is called in question.[35]

It is no answer to an action for disturbance of light that the plaintiff has himself slightly diminished the light.[36] It is otherwise if the result of the plaintiff's act is to render the burden on the servient tenement more onerous; as, for example, if the plaintiff, by altering his premises, so diminishes the light coming to them by means other than through the ancient windows as to cause an obstruction, which before the alteration would have been immaterial, to effect a substantial diminution in his light.[37]

Disturbance of secondary easements

An action lies as well for a disturbance of the secondary easements, without which the primary one cannot be enjoyed, as for a disturbance of the primary easement itself.

> "Item," says Bracton, "si quis ire ad fontem prohibetur, habet actionem, 'Quare quis obstruxit'; quia cui conceditur haustus, ei conceditur iter ad fontem et accessus." [38]

[34] *Ante,* p. 247.
[35] *Hyman* v. *Van den Bergh* [1908] 1 Ch. 167; *ante,* p. 152.
[36] See *Arcedeckne* v. *Kelk* (1858) 2 Giff. 683; *Staight* v. *Burn* (1869) 5 Ch.App. 163; *Barnes* v. *Loach* (1879) 4 Q.B.D. 494.
[37] *Ankerson* v. *Connelly* [1906] 2 Ch. 554; [1907] 1 Ch. 678; *News of the World* v. *Allen, Fairhead & Sons* [1931] 2 Ch. 402. See *Bailey (W. H.) & Son Ltd.* v. *Holborn and Frascati Ltd.* [1914] 1 Ch. 602.
[38] Lib. 4, f. 233; *Race* v. *Ward* (1857) 7 E. & B. 384. And see *Peter* v. *Daniel* (1848) 5 C.B. 568.

CHAPTER 16

REMEDIES FOR DISTURBANCE

Kinds of remedy

The remedies for any disturbance of an easement are of two kinds:
(1) By act of the party aggrieved; and (2) By act of law.

1.—REMEDIES BY ACT OF THE PARTY

Abatement

It is a general rule of law that a person who suffers a nuisance is
entitled to abate it. He may enter on to his neighbour's land in order
to put an end to the nuisance.[1] Thus, if there is a disturbance of an
easement the owner of the dominant tenement may exercise this right
of abatement.

So, in *R. v. Rosewell*,[2] it is laid down: "If H. builds a house so near
mine that it stops my lights, or shoots the water upon my house, or is
in any other way a nuisance to me, I may enter upon the owner's soil
and pull it down. . . ."

In *Raikes v. Townsend*[3] where the disturbance complained of was
the obstruction of a rivulet, by means whereof the defendant's cattle
could not obtain water so plentifully as before, and the defendant
entered upon the soil of the plaintiff and abated the mill-dam, after
judgment for the defendant an unsuccessful motion was made to enter
judgment for the plaintiff *non obstante veredicto*. It was held that the
defendant's trespass was justified. Previous cases where trespass had
been justified to end a nuisance to a mill, a house or land were only
instances of a general rule.

Abatement in the case of ways

In the case of private ways the courts have recognised the common
law right of the dominant owner to apply the remedy of abatement, and
himself to remove an obstruction, even though it be a house which is
inhabited.[4] Where the obstructing house is in the possession of the
court's receiver leave to abate may still be given.[5] Leave will be granted

---

[1] *Baten's Case* (1610) 9 Rep. 54b; *Perry v. Fitzhowe* (1845) 8 Q.B. 757, 775; and
  see examples in 2 Rolle, Ab., Nusans S.W.
[2] *R. v. Rosewell* (1699) 2 Salk. 459.
[3] (1804) 2 Smith 9.
[4] *Davies v. Williams* (1851) 16 Q.B. 546; *Lane v. Capsey* [1891] 3 Ch. 411.
[5] *Lane v. Capsey, supra.*

unless it is clear that there is no foundation for the claim.[6] The owner in fee of a dominant tenement can abate even if the tenement be in the occupation of a tenant.[7] The party in possession may abate although the nuisance existed before his entry.[8]

Water

A party entitled to a watercourse may enter the land of a person who has occasioned a nuisance to a watercourse to abate it; but he can only interfere so far as his interference is positively necessary[9]; and if there are two methods of abating he must choose the least mischievous,[10] for he is bound to abate the nuisance in the most reasonable manner.[11] In several cases abatements have been held reasonable.[12]

Light

In the case of rights of light, if the servient owner erects a building so near the house of the dominant owner that it stops his lights, the dominant owner may enter upon the servient tenement and pull the building down.[13]

Previous request to abate

It is not entirely settled when the dominant owner must give notice of his intention to abate before actually entering on to the servient land. It is clear that notice is necessary where abatement involves pulling down an inhabited house.[14] Again, notice is necessary where the land on which the nuisance arose has since passed into the possession of a person not responsible for the nuisance,[15] except in a case of emergency, when notice is not necessary before entry is made.[16]

There are dicta to the effect that except in the case of emergency, notice is always necessary before entering on to the servient tenement,[17] at least if it involves a trespass thereon; but these have probably not affected earlier authorities where it has been said that notice is not necessary if the person in occupation created the nuisance.[18]

It is certainly the law that (except in the case of emergency) notice is

---

6 *Randfield* v. *Randfield* (1861) 3 De G.F. & J. 771.
7 *Proud* v. *Hollis* (1822) 1 B. & C. 8.
8 *Brent* v. *Haddon* (1620) Cro.Jac. 555.
9 *Roberts* v. *Rose* (1865) L.R. 1 Exch. 82; *Greenslade* v. *Halliday* (1830) 6 Bing. 379.
10 *Roberts* v. *Rose* (1865) L.R. 1 Exch. 82.
11 *Hill* v. *Cock* (1872) 26 L.T. 186.
12 *e.g. Roberts* v. *Rose, supra*; *McCartney* v. *Londonderry and Lough Swilly Railway Co.* [1904] A.C. 301.
13 *R.* v. *Rosewell* (1699) 2 Salk. 459; *Thompson* v. *Eastwood* (1852) 8 Ex. 69.
14 *Perry* v. *Fitzhowe* (1846) 8 Q.B. 757; *Davies* v. *Williams* (1851) 16 Q.B. 546; *Jones* v. *Jones* (1862) 1 H. & C. 1; *Lane* v. *Capsey* [1891] 3 Ch. 411.
15 *Penruddock's Case* (1598) 5 Rep. 100b; *Jones* v. *Williams* (1843) 11 M. & W. 176.
16 In both *Penruddock's Case, supra*, and *Jones* v. *Williams, supra*, an exception is made in cases of immediate danger; and see *Lemmon* v. *Webb* [1894] 3 Ch. 1, 13.
17 *Lemmon* v. *Webb* [1895] A.C. 1, per Lord Herschell 5, per Lord Davey 8. In the case of a right of way entry on to the servient tenement would not be a trespass.
18 *Jones* v. *Williams* (1843) 11 M. & W. 176, per Parke B. 181, cited by the Court of Appeal with apparent approval in *Lemmon* v. *Webb* [1894] 3 Ch. 1; see also *Earl of Lonsdale* v. *Nelson* (1823) 2 B. & C. 302, per Best J. 312; and *Job Edwards* v. *Birmingham Navigations* [1924] 1 K.B. 341, per Scrutton L.J. 355.

necessary when the occupier of the servient tenement is not responsible for the creation or continuance of the nuisance,[19] and possibly in all cases where he has not created it.[20]

When a request is necessary it may be made to the lessor who created the nuisance or to the lessee, for the continuance is a nuisance by the lessee, against whom an action well lies.[21]

In the case of nuisance caused by overhanging branches no entry on to another's land is necessary in order to abate and therefore notice is not required.[22]

Care in abating

In abating a private nuisance a party is bound to use reasonable care that no more damage be done than is necessary for effecting his purpose [23] without injury to third parties.[24] On the other hand, in abating a public nuisance, it seems doubtful whether the same degree of caution is required.[25] Thus, in *Lodie* v. *Arnold* [26] it is said that "The Court seemed to agree . . . That when H. has a right to abate a public nuisance, he is not bound to do it orderly, and with as little hurt, in abating it, as can be."

In the case of *James* v. *Hayward* [27] the defendant might have opened the gate without cutting it down, yet the cutting was lawful; and the court denied *Hill* v. *Prideaux*,[28] that matter of aggravation needed to be answered. It does not appear that the gate was fastened, but rather the contrary.[29]

---

[19] *Jones* v. *Williams* (1843) 11 M. & W. 176.
[20] *Earl of Lonsdale* v. *Nelson* (1823) 2 B. & C. 302, *per* Best J. 311.
[21] *Brent* v. *Haddon* (1620) Cro.Jac. 555.
[22] *Lemmon* v. *Webb* [1895] A.C. 1.
[23] Com.Dig. Action on the Case for a Nuisance, D. 4; *Perry* v. *Fitzhowe* (1846) 8 Q.B. 757; *Greenslade* v. *Halliday* (1830) 6 Bing. 379; *Davies* v. *Williams* (1851) 16 Q.B. 546.
[24] *Roberts* v. *Rose* (1865) L.R. 1 Exch. 82.
[25] In Comyns' *Digest* it is stated "That a man may justify pulling down a house with violence, whereby the materials are lost." The only authority cited for this proposition, if it means that such damage may be caused by unnecessary violence, is the case of *Lodie* v. *Arnold, infra*, which is an authority for it at all events only in the case of an abatement of a public nuisance.
[26] (1698) Salk. 458.
[27] (1631) Cro.Car. 184; Rolle, Ab., Nusans, T.; Jones, W., 221, S.C.
[28] (1595) Cro.Eliz. 384.
[29] The origin of the doubt above expressed, whether the same care is required in abating a public and a private nuisance, appears to be the extra-judicial opinion which, in the passage above cited, is attributed to the court in *Lodie* v. *Arnold, supra*. That opinion appears from the context to have been founded on *James* v. *Hayward, supra*. In *James* v. *Hayward*, however, the question was not as to the manner of abating the nuisance, but whether the gate was a nuisance, and, if so, could be abated. The opening of the gate would not have abated the nuisance. The old precedents of justification on the ground of the removal of a public nuisance allege that no unnecessary damage was done by the defendant in the removal (see 3 Chit. on Pl. (7th ed.) 353); and in *Colchester Corpn.* v. *Brooke* (1845) 7 Q.B. 339, the court put the cases of private and public nuisances on the same footing with regard to the care to be used in removing them. According to the latter case, and *Dimes* v. *Petley* (1850) 15 Q.B. 283, an individual is not justified in abating a public nuisance, unless it does him a special injury; and, in the case of a nuisance in a public highway " he can only interfere with it as far as is

Disposal of materials

In the case of *Lodie* v. *Arnold* [26] it appears from the report that the materials of the house pulled down rolled into the sea, but not that the defendant threw them there. In *James* v. *Hayward* [27] it is laid down, that

> " a (public) nuisance must be abated, in such a convenient manner as it can be; if a house be levied to the nuisance (of another), the whole house shall be abated; if a part, that part only shall be abated; but, as to the house, when the nuisance is abated, it is not lawful to destroy the materials, but they shall, after the abatement, remain to the owners of them, and to him who did the nuisance."

According to *Rea* v. *Sheward*,[30] goods wrongfully placed by the plaintiff on the defendant's land might lawfully be removed to and deposited on the plaintiff's own land; and an action of trespass was dismissed.

Law does not favour abatement

The law does not favour abatement by a private individual. The burden is therefore on him to prove that he has not exceeded his right to abate. In *Lagan Navigation Co.* v. *Lambeg Bleaching, Dyeing and Finishing Co.*[31] cutting away banks to allow flood water to escape was held to be unjustifiable even upon the supposition that the works which had caused the floods constituted a nuisance, for the abator had failed to prove that he had not done any unnecessary damage and that there was no alternative method.

Abatement after court proceedings

When the dominant owner brings an action and a mandatory injunction is refused, it is uncertain whether he still has a right to abate the nuisance. In *Lane* v. *Capsey* [32] where a house, which was obstructing rights of way, was in the possession of the court's receiver, Chitty J., after refusing a mandatory injunction, gave leave to the dominant owner to pursue such lawful remedies as there might be notwithstanding that the house was in the receiver's possession, but he expressly left open the question whether the right to abate still existed. The decision, therefore, is not strictly authority in favour of the right of abatement continuing. If the dominant owner has been awarded damages in lieu of an injunction, under Lord Cairns' Act, he must lose his right of abatement for he has in effect received compensation for a permanent

necessary to exercise his right of passing along the highway . . . and cannot justify doing any damage to the property of the person who has improperly placed the nuisance in the highway, if, avoiding it, he might have passed on with reasonable convenience." In *Bateman* v. *Bluck* (1852) 18 Q.B. 876, Lord Campbell C.J. goes so far as to say that he cannot justify unless " there was no way in which he could exercise his right without the removal."

30 (1837) 2 M. & W. 424.
31 [1927] A.C. 226.
32 [1891] 3 Ch. 411.

infringement of his rights.[33]　As it was said in one case,[34] "To refuse to aid the legal right by injunction and to give damages instead is in fact to compel the plaintiff to part with his easement for money."

Effect of abatement

It has been said [35] that the effect of exercising the right to abate is to destroy the right to bring an action for damages in respect of the nuisance. This, however, is probably not so, the dominant owner still having the right to sue for any damage he has suffered before the abatement.[36] The old action *quod permittat posternere*, which claimed abatement by order of the court, would not lie after abatement,[37] and an action will not now lie for the purpose of abating a nuisance through the medium of the court.[38]

Apprehended injury

The occupier of land cannot abate an apprehended nuisance. In 1617 it was said by Croke J.:

> "If the boughs of your tree grow over my land, I may cut them off; but I cannot justify cutting them before they grow over my land, for fear they should grow over." [39]

Again it was said by Coke C.J.:

> "Whether the defendant may pull down the nuisance before the house is made, and so come to be a nuisance; I do much doubt of this; here it is only said *conatus fuit* to edifice this house, and rear up the timber, the defendant hath no hurt by this, for he may afterwards leave off again; the defendant is not to pull this down . . . for his intent only." [40]

Generally, some injury must have been sustained before redress can be had. Thus, if a party intending to build a house, which will obstruct ancient lights, erects fences of timber for the purpose of building, there is no right to pull them down. However, a nuisance may exist although no actual damage has accrued: "if a house be built the eaves of which project over my land, I need not wait till any water actually falls from them, but may pull them down at once." [41]

---

33 See *e.g. Shelfer* v. *City of London Electric Lighting Co.* [1895] 1 Ch. 287, 315–316, 322; *Cowper* v. *Laidler* [1903] 2 Ch. 337, 341; *Woollerton and Wilson Ltd.* v. *Richard Costain Ltd.* [1970] 1 W.L.R. 411, 414; *Morris* v. *Redland Bricks Ltd.* [1967] 1 W.L.R. 967, 980.

34 *Cowper* v. *Laidler* [1903] 2 Ch. 337, *per* Buckley J. 341.

35 Blackstone, 21st ed., Vol. 3, pp. 219–220; *Lagan Navigation Co.* v. *Lambeg Bleaching, Dyeing and Finishing Co.* [1927] A.C. 226, *per* Lord Atkinson 244.

36 *Kendrick* v. *Bartland* (1679) 2 Mod.Rep. 253; and see *Job Edwards* v. *Birmingham Navigations* [1924] 1 K.B. 341, *per* Scrutton L.J. 356; *Lemmon* v. *Webb* [1894] 3 Ch. 1, 24; *Smith* v. *Giddy* [1904] 2 K.B. 448.

37 *Baten's Case* (1610) 9 Co.Rep. 54b, 55a.

38 *Lane* v. *Capsey* [1891] 3 Ch. 411, 416.

39 *Norris* v. *Baker* (1617) 1 Rolle 393, 394.

40 *Per* Coke C.J. in S.C., 3 Bulst. 197, *sub nom. Morrice* v. *Baker*. See *Penruddock's Case* (1598) 5 Co.Rep. 101.

41 2 Rolle, Ab., 145, Nusans U.; *Fay* v. *Prentice* (1845) 1 C.B. 828.

Mere threats unaccompanied by any act do not amount to a disturbance.[42]

2.—REMEDIES BY ACT OF LAW

Action in High Court

The remedy by act of law for the disturbance of an easement is by an action for nuisance.[43] Damages may be recovered, and the court may grant a mandamus or an injunction " in all cases in which it appears to the court to be just or convenient so to do." [44]

Action in county court

By the County Courts Act 1959,[45] the county courts have jurisdiction to try any action in which the title to an easement or licence comes in question, if the net annual value for rating of the hereditament in respect of which the easement or licence is claimed, or on, through, over or under which the easement or licence is claimed, does not exceed four hundred pounds.

(1) *Parties to Actions*

Who may sue

As an easement is a benefit attached to the dominant tenement, the party in possession of that tenement may sue for any interference with its enjoyment; and if such interference be of a permanent nature, and injurious to the inheritance, the reversioner may also sue. It is conceived that any person who would be entitled to sue for a nuisance affecting a particular piece of land is entitled to sue for a nuisance constituted by the disturbance of an easement annexed to that land, at least if the defendant is not the lawful owner or occupier of the servient tenement; such a defendant could not impugn the plaintiff's title to the dominant tenement.[46] On the other hand, if the lawful owner or occupier of the servient tenement is being sued for his disturbance of an easement he can probably raise the defence of *jus tertii*, putting the plaintiff to proof of his title.[46] It is probably otherwise in the case of a natural

---

[42] *Earl of Shrewsbury's Case* (1610) 9 Co.Rep. 46b.

[43] *Paine & Co.* v. *St. Neots Gas & Coke Co.* [1939] 3 All E.R. 812, 823.

[44] Judicature Act 1925, s. 45.

[45] s. 51, as amended by the County Courts (Jurisdiction) Act 1963. *Quaere* whether the decision in *R.* v. *Judge Drucquer* [1939] 2 K.B. 588, that the jurisdiction is ousted if the annual value of either the dominant or the servient tenement exceeds the financial limit, applies to s. 51 of the 1959 Act. The decision dealt with the slightly different wording of s. 51 (*a*) of the County Courts Act 1934. The plain meaning of s. 51 would appear to give the court jurisdiction if either the dominant or the servient tenement does not exceed the £400 limit. But in *Wong* v. *Beaumont Property Trust Ltd.* [1965] 1 Q.B. 173, Lord Denning M.R. 181–182 appears to assume that neither the dominant nor the servient tenement must have a rateable value exceeding £400.

[46] See *Salmond on Torts*, 15th ed., p. 94.

right, *e.g.* of support for land, where even a possessory title will carry a right to enjoyment against the lawful servient owner.[47]

Licensees without possession cannot sue in nuisance,[48] and therefore cannot sue for the disturbance of rights appurtenant to the land. Where, however, a licence carries with it possession of land [49] the licensee may have a right to sue for the disturbance of easements annexed to that land.

Occupiers. An injunction to restrain an obstruction to light has been granted at the suit of a yearly tenant [50] and of a tenant whose lease had expired after the obstruction, but who had agreed to renew [1]; and in *Jones* v. *Chappell* [2] Jessel M.R. said that so far as he was aware, it had never been decided that a weekly tenant could not have an injunction, and if a weekly tenant and his landlord were to join in a suit to restrain a nuisance he would not find the slightest difficulty in granting an injunction. In *Jacomb* v. *Knight*,[3] where a yearly tenant filed a bill against adjoining tenants holding under the same landlord to restrain a slight obstruction to light, and the landlord after the filing of the bill gave the plaintiff notice to quit, so that at the time of the hearing less than eight months of the tenancy remained unexpired, Romilly M.R. granted a mandatory injunction; but the Court of Appeal, taking into consideration the extent of the plaintiff's interest, and the balance of convenience and inconvenience, dismissed the bill without costs, and without prejudice to an action for damages. The owner of a house, who has no intention of residing there, may have an injunction against an obstruction to the windows simply on the ground of the effect of such an obstruction on the value of the property.[4] The court may grant damages in lieu of an injunction under Lord Cairns' Act on the ground that the plaintiff has only a limited interest.[5]

It seems, accordingly, that an injunction to restrain a nuisance may be obtained by a tenant who holds by the year [50] or by the week.[6] But in such a case the injunction may be limited to the duration of the plaintiff's tenancy,[7] or may be refused without prejudice to a claim for damages.[8] Tenants have been added as co-plaintiffs by amendment at the trial.[9] The respective owners or occupiers of adjoining buildings

---

[47] See *Newcastle-under-Lyme Corpn.* [1947] Ch. 93, where Evershed J. held that a person with possession could sue the servient owner for disturbance of the natural right of support. This proposition was not affected on appeal, [1947] Ch. 472.
[48] *Malone* v. *Laskey* [1907] 2 K.B. 141.
[49] *e.g.* as in *Inwards* v. *Baker* [1965] 2 Q.B. 79.
[50] *Inchbald* v. *Robinson* (1869) 4 Ch.App. 388.
[1] *Gale* v. *Abbott* (1862) 8 Jur.(N.S.) 987.
[2] (1875) L.R. 20 Eq. 539.
[3] (1863) 32 L.J.Ch. 601.
[4] *Wilson* v. *Townend* (1860) 1 Dr. & Sm. 324.
[5] *McGrath* v. *The Munster and Leinster Bank Ltd.* (1959) 94 I.L.T.R. 110. See p. 388, *post.*
[6] *Jones* v. *Chappell* (1875) L.R. 20 Eq. 539.
[7] *Simper* v. *Foley* (1862) 2 J. & H. 555.
[8] *Jacomb* v. *Knight* (1863) 32 L.J.Ch. 601.
[9] *House Property and Investment Co.* v. *H. P. Horse Nail Co.* (1885) 29 Ch.D. 190.

will not, as a general rule, be allowed to join in one action for relief in respect of the obstruction of light.[10]

Reversioners. As already mentioned, if the interference be injurious to the reversion, the reversioner may also have an action for the same disturbance.[11]

The action by a landlord for an injury to land in the possession of his tenant may be traced to very early times. There are several cases in the Year Books where such actions have been maintained, not only for a permanent damage or destruction of the land,[12] but also for transient acts commencing and ending during the tenancy, but which occasioned loss to the landlord. Such acts are: ousting a tenant [13]; menacing tenants at will, whereby they determined their tenancies [14]; improperly setting up a court, and, by frequent distresses on the tenants for not attending the court, impoverishing them so that they were unable to pay their rent [15]; fouling water with the refuse of a lime-pit, in which the defendant steeped calves' skins and sheep-skins, which caused the plaintiff's tenants to leave his houses [16]: or, taking toll of a tenant who was exempt from toll.[17]

The rule laid down in Com.Dig., Action on the Case for a Nusance, B., on the authority of *Bedingfield* v. *Onslow* [18] and *Jesser* v. *Gifford*,[19] is,

" If the nuisance is to the damage of the inheritance, he in the reversion shall have an action for it."

The authorities relied on by the court in *Bedingfield* v. *Onslow* [18] were 19 Hen. 6, 45; 12 Hen. 6, 4; 2 Rolle, Ab. 551; and the following note of *Love* v. *Pigott* [20]:

" It was said there are divers precedents, that if a lessee for years be sued in Court-Christian for tythes, he in the reversion may have a prohibition."

---

10 *Bendir* v. *Anson* [1936] 3 All E.R. 326.
11 Com.Dig. Action on the Case for a Nusance, B.; *Jackson* v. *Pesked* (1813) 1 M. & S. 234; 14 R.R. 417; *Alston* v. *Scales* (1832) 9 Bing. 3. See also *Hopwood* v. *Schofield* (1837) 2 Mood. & R. 34; *Tucker* v. *Newman* (1839) 11 A. & E. 40; *Fay* v. *Prentice* (1845) 1 C.B. 828; *Kidgill* v. *Moor* (1850) 9 C.B. 364; *Metropolitan Association* v. *Petch* (1858) 5 C.B.(N.S.) 504.
12 As in 19 Hen. 6, 45, where land in the possession of a tenant at will was subverted by a stranger, and it was held that the tenant at will should have an action of trespass, because he could not have the profit of the land, and the landlord another action of trespass for the destruction of the land: Bro.Ab. Trespas. pl. 131; 2 Rolle, Ab., 551, Trespas. N. pl. 3.
13 12 Hen. 6, 4.
14 9 Hen. 7, 7; 1 Rolle, Ab., 108, pl. 21; Com.Dig. Action on the Case for Misfeasance, A. 6; cited by Holt C.J., *Keeble* v. *Hickeringill* (1809) 11 East 576; *Bell* v. *Midland Railway* (1861) 10 C.B.(N.S.) 307.
15 *Earl of Suffolk's Case*, 13 Hen. 4, 11; 1 Rolle, Ab., 107, pl. 7; Com.Dig. Action on the Case for a Disturbance, A. 6; cited by Willes J. in *Bell* v. *Midland Railway, supra*.
16 *Prior of Southwark's Case*, 13 Hen. 7, 26; cited by Wray C.J. in *Aldred's Case* (1611) 9 Rep. 59a.
17 43 Edw. 3, 29; 2 Rolle, Ab. 107, pl. 8.
18 (1685) 3 Lev. 209.
19 (1767) 4 Burr. 2141.
20 Cro.Eliz. 56.

According to the modern authorities, an interference will be injurious to the reversion if (1) it be something which will in the future continue to the time when the reversion falls into possession, or if (2) it be something which in the present operates as a denial of the right of the reversioner.

As regards the first head of injury, it was laid down by Cotton L.J. in *Rust* v. *Victoria Graving Dock Co.*[21] that as a general rule a reversioner cannot get any damages for a wrongful act unless the damage is one which will endure and be continuing when the reversion becomes an estate in possession. And the rule has been more recently stated by Parker J. in *Jones* v. *Llanrwst U.D.C.*[22] as follows:

> "It is reasonably certain that a reversioner cannot maintain actions in the nature of trespass, including, I think, actions for infringement of natural rights arising out of his ownership of land, without alleging and proving injury to the reversion. If the thing complained of is of such a permanent nature that the reversion may be injured, the question of whether the reversion is or is not injured is a question for the jury: *Simpson* v. *Savage.*[23] I take ' permanent,' in this connection, to mean such as will continue indefinitely unless something is done to remove it. Thus, a building which infringes ancient lights is permanent within the rule, for, though it can be removed before the reversion falls into possession, still it will continue until it be removed. On the other hand, a noisy trade, and the exercise of an alleged right of way, are not in their nature permanent within the rule, for they cease of themselves, unless there be someone to continue them. . . . It is not a case only of the present intention of the defendants, but of the necessary consequences of the physical conditions, if nothing is done to alter them."

Under the second of the above heads of injury to the reversion there fall the following decisions. Where a reversioner sued on the ground that the defendant had erected a roof to the obstruction of an ancient light, Lord Tenterden held that the reversioner had a good cause of action, because it was an injury to the right; and the effect of letting the obstruction stand might be that from the death of witnesses the evidence of its erection might be lost, and so the injury become permanent.[24] In the case of the same obstruction a second action was brought for its continuance, and the court held that if the erection were in the first instance an injury to the reversion, the continuance must be so likewise. Such continuance would render the proof of the title more difficult at a future time. Lord Tenterden said in the first action that

---

21 *Rust* v. *Victoria Graving Dock Co.* (1887) 36 Ch.D. 132.
22 [1911] 1 Ch. 393, 404, followed by Sargant J. in *White* v. *London General Omnibus Co.* [1914] W.N. 78. As to the meaning of " permanent," see *Shelfer* v. *City of London Electric Lighting Co.* [1895] 1 Ch. 287, 299–317.
23 (1856) 1 C.B.(N.S.) 347.   24 *Shadwell* v. *Hutchinson* (1829) 3 C. & P. 615.

the injury might "become permanent," not that it was so; and the recovery of damages in the second action shows that judgment in the first was given for the past obstruction, not for its permanence.[25] So, again, a reversioner could sue for obstruction to an ancient light caused by a hoarding which might have been put up " in denial of the plaintiff's right." [26] In such cases, said Jessel M.R., there was an injury to the right which might be lost if the reversioner were not able to institute proceedings.[27]

Again, it was said that such an obstruction, if acquiesced in for a sufficient time, would be evidence of the abandonment of the right.[28] With this should be compared the case where a stranger entered on demised land in exercise of an alleged right of way, and it was said that such acts would be no evidence of right against the reversioner, who accordingly could not sue.[29]

It seems doubtful whether a reversioner can sue for a wrongful act on the sole ground that such act lessens the selling value of the reversion.[30]

Having regard to the above rules, the right of a reversioner to sue is considered in the case of actions for the disturbance of easements; in the case of actions for the disturbance of natural rights; and in the case of actions for trespass.

Reversioner's action for disturbance of easements

Of a reversioner's action for the disturbance of easements the books contain the following instances. Where ancient lights had been obstructed by the erection of a permanent structure, a reversioner had a good right of action.[31] Again, where rights in respect of a watercourse had been disturbed, a reversioner sued.[32] Again, where a private way had been permanently obstructed, a reversioner was held to have a good right of action.[33]

---

25 *Shadwell* v. *Hutchinson* (1831) 4 C. & P. 334.
26 *Metropolitan Association* v. *Petch* (1858) 5 C.B.(N.S.) 504.
27 *Mott* v. *Shoolbred* (1875) L.R. 20 Eq. 22, 24.
28 *Bower* v. *Hill* (1835) 1 Bing.N.C. 549, 555.
29 *Baxter* v. *Taylor* (1832) 4 B. & Ad. 72.
30 See, on the one hand, the opinion of Cotton L.J. in *Rust* v. *Victoria Graving Dock Co.* (1887) 36 Ch.D. 113, 132; and, on the other hand, *Jesser* v. *Gifford* (1767) 4 Burr. 2141; *Dobson* v. *Blackmore* (1847) 9 Q.B. 1004, and *Simpson* v. *Savage* (1856) 1 C.B.(N.S.) 347.
31 *Jesser* v. *Gifford* (1767) 4 Burr. 2141; *Shadwell* v. *Hutchinson* (1829) 3 C. & P. 615; S.C. (1831) 4 C. & P. 334; *Metropolitan Association* v. *Petch* (1858) 5 C.B. (N.S.) 504; *Wilson* v. *Townend* (1860) 1 Dr. & Sm. 324. See also the words of Jessel M.R. in *Mott* v. *Shoolbred, supra,* and of Parker J. in *Jones* v. *Llanrwst U.D.C.* [1911] 1 Ch. 404, quoted *supra.*
32 *Peter* v. *Daniel* (1848) 5 C.B. 568; *Bedingfield* v. *Onslow* (1685) 3 Lev. 209. See *Egremont* v. *Pulman* (1829) Mood. & M. 404; *Bell* v. *Twentyman* (1841) 1 Q.B. 766.
33 *Bower* v. *Hill* (1835) 1 Bing.N.C. 549; *Bell* v. *Midland Railway* (1861) 10 C.B.(N.S.) 287. See *Hopwood* v. *Schofield* (1837) 2 Mood. & R. 34; *Kidgill* v. *Moor* (1850) 9 C.B. 364. As to a reversioner suing in respect of rights connected with a public highway, see *Dobson* v. *Blackmore* (1847) 9 Q.B. 1004; *Mott* v. *Shoolbred* (1875) L.R. 20 Eq. 22.

Reversioner's action for disturbance of natural rights

Of a reversioner's action for the disturbance of natural rights there are also some examples. Where the water of a natural stream had been polluted (the right of purity being infringed), and the pollution would not cease unless and until something was done to divert it, a reversioner had a good cause of action.[34] In the case of nuisances arising from noise and smoke, a reversioner was held to have no right of action, on the ground that the nuisances might cease at any moment[35]; but where a house was structurally injured by vibration caused by the adjoining owner, the reversioner could sue.[36]

It is to be observed that in *Baxter* v. *Taylor*[37] Taunton and Parke JJ. held that the act complained of would not be evidence of right against the reversioner; and that in *Mumford* v. *Oxford, etc., Railway*,[38] and in *Simpson* v. *Savage*,[39] the act was not a disturbance of an easement (the onus of establishing which, if disputed, would be on the plaintiff), but an injury, not of a permanent kind, to a natural right. A natural right would prima facie subsist after the determination of the term; and, unless the reversioner suffered the injurious acts to continue after the end of the term,[40] they would not be likely to afford an obstacle, by way of evidence, to the maintenance of the right. For the evidence afforded by them might be rebutted by proof of the subsistence of the tenancy during the continuance of them; whereas in the case of the disturbance of an easement the proof of its existence is equally affected by acts of interference with the enjoyment of it, whether the dominant tenement has been under lease or not.[41]

Reversioner's action for trespass

Where an adjoining owner had committed a trespass of a permanent nature by building a wall on the demised land the reversioner could sue.[42] So where the defendant had built a wall on the demised land and placed timber thereon overhanging a yard.[43] Again, where the adjoin-

---

[34] *Jones* v. *Llanrwst U.D.C.* [1911] 1 Ch. 393.

[35] *Mumford* v. *Oxford Railway* (1856) 1 H. & N. 34; *Simpson* v. *Savage* (1856) 1 C.B.(N.S.) 347; *Jones* v. *Chappell* (1875) L.R. 20 Eq. 539; *Cooper* v. *Crabtree* (1882) 20 Ch.D. 589; *House Property and Investment Co.* v. *H. P. Horse Nail Co.* (1885) 29 Ch.D. 190; *White* v. *London General Omnibus Co.* [1914] W.N. 78.

[36] *Shelfer* v. *City of London Electric Lighting Co.* [1895] 1 Ch. 287; *Colwell* v. *St. Pancras Borough Council* [1904] 1 Ch. 707. See *Kirby* v. *Chessum* (1914) 30 T.L.R. 660, where the reversioner's wall was in danger from adjoining excavation.

[37] (1832) 4 B. & Ad. 72.

[38] (1856) 1 H. & N. 34; see p. 367, *post.*

[39] (1856) 1 C.B.(N.S.) 347; see p. 367, *post.*

[40] As to the effect of which, see *Palk* v. *Shinner* (1852) 18 Q.B. 575.

[41] See *Crump* v. *Lambert* (1867) L.R. 3 Eq. 409; *Johnstone* v. *Hall* (1856) 2 K. & J. 414; *Mott* v. *Shoolbred* (1875) L.R. 20 Eq. 22; *Jones* v. *Chappell* (1875) L.R. 20 Eq. 539. *Cooper* v. *Crabtree* (1881) 19 Ch.D. 193, where the reversioner failed, was a simple case of trespass.

[42] *Mayfair Property Co.* v. *Johnston* [1894] 1 Ch. 508.

[43] *Jackson* v. *Pesked* (1813) 1 M. & S. 234. See *Alston* v. *Scales* (1832) 9 Bing. 3; *Raine* v. *Alderson* (1838) 4 Bing.N.C. 702.

ing owner had erected a roof with eaves projecting over the demised land and discharging rain-water on to it.[44] In the case, however, of a simple trespass (as where a stranger entered in exercise of an alleged right of way) the reversioner had no right of action.[45]

Earlier decisions on reversioner's right to sue

The following discussion of earlier decisions on the right of a reversioner to sue was contained in some of the former editions of this treatise, and is retained here.

To enable a reversioner to maintain the action, said Parke J. in *Baxter* v. *Taylor*,[46]

" it was necessary for him to allege and prove that the act complained of was injurious to his reversionary interest, or that it should appear to be of such a permanent nature as to be necessarily injurious. A simple trespass, even accompanied with a claim of right, is not necessarily injurious to the reversionary estate."

Baxter v. *Taylor* [47] was acted upon in *Simpson* v. *Savage*,[48] in which the court held that no action lies by a reversioner for a smoke nuisance caused by lighting fires in a factory and causing smoke to issue so as to be a nuisance to the reversioner's tenants and make them give notice to quit; and a very similar point was decided in *Mumford* v. *Oxford Railway*,[49] where the complaint was for causing loud noises, and the court held that the action would not lie. It would be foreign to the subject of this book to discuss the question how far these cases can be reconciled with the old authorities referred to by the court in *Bell* v. *Midland Railway* [50] as to the right of action for causing tenants to leave their tenements. In both cases the court relied upon the fact that the injury complained of was not of a permanent character, although unquestionably the repetition of such acts would furnish evidence against the reversioner, whether he might be able to rebut it or not. In *Kidgill* v. *Moor*,[1] Maule J., referring to the dictum of Parke J. in *Baxter* v. *Taylor*,[47] said: " My brother Parke does not say that it would not be evidence, if the party claimed a right of way, and meant to assert it "; and in *Tickle* v. *Brown* [2] Patteson J. said: " Before the statute, the acts of tenants might be evidence against the reversioners, yet their naked declarations were not so."

In *Palk* v. *Shinner*,[3] there being a user of twenty years, during the first fifteen years of which the premises were under lease, Erle J. said:

[44] *Tucker* v. *Newman* (1839) 11 A. & E. 40.
[45] *Baxter* v. *Taylor* (1832) 4 B. & Ad. 72.
[46] (1832) 4 B. & Ad. 76. See *Damper* v. *Bassett* [1901] 2 Ch. 350.
[47] (1832) 4 B. & Ad. 76.
[48] (1856) 1 C.B.(N.S.) 352.
[49] (1856) 1 H. & N. 34.
[50] (1861) 10 C.B.(N.S.) 287.
[1] (1850) 9 C.B. 364, 372.
[2] (1836) 4 A. & E. 378.
[3] (1852) 18 Q.B. 575.

" If this case had arisen before the statute, there would have been good evidence to go to the jury, notwithstanding the existence of the tenancy, and the question is still to be left to the jury in the same way." [4]

It seems unjust to deprive the reversioner of an immediate remedy in respect of acts which may at a future time furnish evidence against him, and which, though he may possibly in many cases be able then to rebut, must in all cases involve him in trouble and expense, by affecting the evidence of his right. The point is akin to that which is raised in an action by a reversioner for obstructions by others to the enjoyment of easements by his tenants, the ground of which action is that the evidence of the right of the reversioner to the easement is affected, as his acquiescence in the obstruction would furnish evidence against him of a renunciation and abandonment of it.[5]

In *Kidgill* v. *Moor* [6] the plaintiff sued for the locking of a gate across a way to which the tenants of the plaintiff were entitled in respect of the tenement of which he was the reversioner, and it was objected, on motion in arrest of judgment, that the act complained of was not of a permanent character; but the court held that the declaration was good, as such an act *might* operate as an injury to the reversionary interest, and that the question whether the plaintiff is injured in his reversionary estate is one of fact for the jury. Maule J. said:

" I cannot doubt that there might be such a locking and chaining of a gate as would amount to as permanent an injury to the plaintiff's reversionary interest as the building of a wall. The meaning of the allegation, that . . . the plaintiff was greatly injured in his reversionary estate and interest, is . . . an allegation of a matter of fact, . . . which is for the jury to find, or not, according to the evidence."

In *Metropolitan Association* v. *Petch* [7] a declaration in an action by a reversioner for obstructing ancient lights by the erection of a hoarding was sustained, the court holding that such an erection might be an injury to the reversion, and that it was for the jury to determine. In that case also the judges laid down that the way in which the act might injure the reversioner would be by *affording evidence in denial of the right.* According to the last class of cases, the jury might find for the plaintiff if the act complained of would furnish any evidence in denial of the right. It is difficult to discover any principle upon which the reversioner should be without remedy by action in respect of a series of separate acts of obstruction furnishing evidence in denial of the right, while he has such action in the case of the wooden hoarding intervening,

---

[4] And see the judgments in *Daniel* v. *North* (1809) 11 East 372; *Lineham* v. *Deeble* (1859) 9 Ir.C.L.R. 309; *Cooper* v. *Crabtree* (1882) 20 Ch.D. 589; *Hanna* v. *Pollock* [1900] 2 Ir.R. 664.
[5] See *per* Tindal C.J. in *Bower* v. *Hill* (1835) 1 Bing.N.C. 549.
[6] (1850) 9 C.B. 364.
[7] (1858) 5 C.B.(N.S.) 504.

or why a series of trespasses in the assertion of a right of way should not give a right of action to a reversioner.

Continuing disturbance

If the disturbance be continued, a fresh action may be maintained from time to time by the persons filling the situation of tenant in possession or reversioner.[8]

Parties liable to be sued

The party creating the disturbance is liable to an action, whether he be the owner of the servient tenement or not.[9] He remains liable for all consequential damage even though he is no longer in possession and is unable to prevent the damage continuing.[10] Thus, if the person in possession has leased the premises he remains liable,[11] and if a contractor erects a building on another's land he remains liable if it is a nuisance.[12]

For the continuance of a disturbance each successive owner in occupation of the servient tenement is liable, though it may have been begun before his estate commenced.[13]

Where, however, the party was not the original creator of the disturbance, a request must be made to remove it before any action is brought; but it is sufficient if such request is made to the party in possession, though he be only lessee.[14]

The acts of two or more persons may, taken together, constitute such a nuisance that the court in separate actions will restrain each of them from doing the acts constituting the nuisance, although the act of one taken alone would not amount to a nuisance.[15]

Landlord and tenant

If the owner of land on which a nuisance exists lets the land, an action for the continuance will lie, at the option of the party injured,[16]

---

8 *Penruddock's Case* (1598) 5 Rep. 101; *Shadwell* v. *Hutchinson* (1831) 2 B. & Ad. 97; *Battishill* v. *Reed* (1856) 18 C.B. 696; *Wilson* v. *Peto* (1821) 6 Moore 47; *Darley Co.* v. *Mitchell* (1886) 11 App.Cas. 127; *Crumbie* v. *Wallsend Local Board* [1891] 1 Q.B. 503.

9 Com.Dig. Action on the Case for a Nuisance, B.; *Wettor* v. *Dunk* (1864) 4 F. & F. 298; *Thompson* v. *Gibson* (1841) 7 M. & W. 456. See *Corby* v. *Hill* (1858) 4 C.B.(N.S.) 556; *Wilson* v. *Peto* (1821) 6 Moore (C.P.) 47.

10 *Rosewell* v. *Prior* (1701) 12 Mod. 635, 639.

11 *Ibid.*

12 *Thompson* v. *Gibson* (1841) 7 M. & W. 456.

13 *Broder* v. *Saillard* (1876) 2 Ch.D. 692; *White* v. *Jameson* (1874) L.R. 18 Eq. 303; see also *Manley* v. *Burn* [1916] 2 K.B. 121.

14 *Penruddock's Case* (1598) 5 Rep. 101; *Brent* v. *Haddon* (1620) Cro.Jac. 555. A request to a former occupier while in possession will suffice: *Salmon* v. *Bensley* (1825) Ry. & M. 189. There appears to be no recent authority in favour of the proposition in the text.

15 *Lambton* v. *Mellish* [1894] 3 Ch. 163, where there were several actions; *Blair* v. *Deakin* (1887) 57 L.T. 522, where there was one action against one such person. And see *Nixon* v. *Tynemouth* (1888) 52 J.P. 504.

16 *i.e.* if he be a stranger, and not the tenant or his licensee: *Robbins* v. *Jones* (1863) 15 C.B.(N.S.) 240.

either against the tenant [17] or (subject to the following remarks) against the landlord.[18]

No action for the continuance of a nuisance lies against the landlord for an act of his tenant done during the tenancy [19] unless it be done by the landlord's authority.[20] And no such action lies against the landlord for an injury due to the dangerous condition of the premises if he has taken from the tenant a covenant to repair; for in such a case he does not authorise the continuance of the nuisance.[21]

Generally speaking, a landlord is liable for a nuisance on premises occupied by his tenant—(1) where he takes from the tenant a covenant to do things which result in the nuisance [22]; (2) where he lets the premises for a purpose likely to result and resulting in the nuisance [23]; (3) where he relets the premises after a nuisance upon them has been created [24]; (4) if he lets the premises and has either undertaken the duty to repair or reserved the right to enter and do repairs. It would seem that the defendant's knowledge or means of knowledge have no relevance to the question of his liability in this last type of case.[25]

It seems to have been held that a tenant for years, occupying a house which was an obstruction to light, erected before his tenancy, was not liable to be sued for damages for its continuance; for he had no authority to abate it.[26]

Where the landlord was not made a party the court has refused to grant against a lessee a mandatory injunction to pull down buildings which infringed a right of light.[27]

Liability for act of stranger

In all cases the defendant must be shown to be in some sense responsible for the continuance of the act complained of. The occupier

---

[17] *Broder* v. *Saillard* (1876) 2 Ch.D. 692. Unless, *semble,* the tenant neither knew nor ought to have known of the nuisance; *Sedleigh-Denfield* v. *O'Callaghan* [1940] A.C. 880; *Wilkins* v. *Leighton* [1932] 2 Ch. 106.

[18] *Christian Smith's Case* (1633) Sir W. Jones 272; *Rosewell* v. *Prior* (1701) 12 Mod.Rep. 635; *R.* v. *Pedly* (1834) 1 A. & E. 822; *Todd* v. *Flight* (1860) 9 C.B.(N.S.) 377, in which the previous authorities are reviewed; *Att.-Gen.* v. *Bradford Canal Proprietors* (1866) L.R. 2 Eq. 71; and *Mason* v. *Shrewsbury Railway* (1871) L.R. 6 Q.B. 585.

[19] *Cheetham* v. *Hampson* (1791) 4 T.R. 318; *Rich* v. *Basterfield* (1847) 4 C.B. 783; *Bishop* v. *Bedford Charity* (1859) 1 E. & E. 697; *R.* v. *Pedly* (1834) 1 A. & E. 827, *per* Littledale J.; *Preston* v. *Norfolk Railway* (1858) 2 H. & N. 735; *Bartlett* v. *Baker* (1864) 3 H. & C. 153. As to a tenancy from year to year, see *Gandy* v. *Jubber* (1864) 5 B. & S. 485; 9 B. & S. 15; *Bowen* v. *Anderson* [1894] 1 Q.B. 164; *cf. Kieffer* v. *Le Seminaire de Quebec* [1903] A.C. 85, where it was held that under Canadian Law the landlord was not liable.

[20] *Harris* v. *James* (1876) 45 L.J.Q.B. 545; *Phillips* v. *Thomas* (1890) 62 L.T. 793.

[21] *Pretty* v. *Bickmore* (1873) L.R. 8 C.P. 401; *Gwinnell* v. *Eamer* (1875) L.R. 10 C.P. 658. But see *Mint* v. *Good* [1951] 1 K.B. 517, 528.

[22] *Burt* v. *Victoria Graving Dock Co.* (1882) 47 L.T. 378.

[23] *Winter* v. *Baker* (1887) 3 T.L.R. 569; *Jenkins* v. *Jackson* (1888) 40 Ch.D. 77.

[24] *Sandford* v. *Clarke* (1888) 21 Q.B.D. 398; *Bowen* v. *Anderson* [1894] 1 Q.B. 164.

[25] See *Nelson* v. *Liverpool Co.* (1877) 2 C.P.D. 311; *Gwinnell* v. *Eamer, supra*; *Wilchick* v. *Marks and Silverstone* [1934] 2 K.B. 56, 66; *Heap* v. *Ind Coope and Allsopp Ltd.* [1940] 2 K.B. 476; *Wringe* v. *Cohen* [1940] 1 K.B. 229; *Mint* v. *Good* [1951] 1 K.B. 517.

[26] *Ryppon* v. *Bowles* (1615) Cro.Jac. 373.   [27] *Barnes* v. *Allen* [1927] W.N. 217.

of land on which is something, not done or placed there by himself, which causes a nuisance to other land is liable if he continues the nuisance, that is, if with knowledge or presumed knowledge of its existence he fails to take reasonable means to bring it to an end when he has ample time to do so; or if he adopts the nuisance by making any use of the erection or artificial structure which constitutes it.[28]

Liability for acts of contractor

The further question, how far an owner who employs a contractor to perform work for him is liable for the consequences of the contractor's negligent or wrongful acts, has been much discussed.

Where the work contracted to be done is itself unlawful, or necessarily involves the doing of some unlawful act, the employer is clearly liable.[29]

Where the act contracted to be done is in itself lawful, and involves no special risk or duty which the employer has neglected, it is equally clear that the employer is not liable.[30]

But where the work contracted to be done is hazardous to third persons, or is otherwise of such a nature as to cast a duty upon the person undertaking it, the employer is bound to see that proper and reasonable precautions are taken, and is liable for any omission in this respect. Nor is it sufficient that, by the contract between employer and contractor, it is stipulated that the precautions shall be taken by the contractor; the employer must also take care that the stipulation is carried out.[31] Delivering the judgment of the court in *Pickard* v. *Smith*,[32] Williams J. said:

"Unquestionably, no one can be made liable for an act or breach of duty, unless it be traceable to himself or his servant or servants in the course of his or their employment. Consequently, if an independent contractor is employed to do a lawful act, and in the course of the work he or his servants commit some casual act of wrong or negligence, the employer is not answerable. To this effect are many authorities which were referred to in the argument. That rule is, however, inapplicable to cases in which the act which occasions the injury is one which the contractor was employed to do; nor, by a parity of reasoning, to cases in which the contractor is intrusted with the performance of a duty incumbent upon his employer, and neglects its fulfilment, whereby an injury is occasioned. Now, in the present case, the defendant

28 *Sedleigh-Denfield* v. *O'Callaghan* [1940] A.C. 880.
29 *Ellis* v. *Sheffield Co.* (1853) 2 E. & B. 767.
30 *Quarman* v. *Burnett* (1840) 6 M. & W. 499; *Reedie* v. *L. & N.W. Railway* (1849) 4 Ex. 244; *Knight* v. *Fox* (1850) 5 Ex. 721; *Gayford* v. *Nicholls* (1854) 9 Ex. 702; *Kiddle* v. *Lovett* (1885) 16 Q.B.D. 605.
31 *Hole* v. *Sittingbourne Railway* (1861) 6 H. & N. 488; *Gray* v. *Pullen* (1864) 5 B. & S. 970; *Pickard* v. *Smith* (1861) 10 C.B.(N.S.) 470; *Holliday* v. *National Telephone Co.* [1899] 2 Q.B. 392; *The Snark* [1900] P. 105.
32 (1861) 10 C.B.(N.S.) 470, 480.

employed the coal merchant to open the trap in order to put in the coals; and he trusted him to guard it whilst open, and to close it when the coals were all put in. The act of opening it was the act of the employer, though done through the agency of the coal merchant; and the defendant, having thereby caused danger, was bound to take reasonable means to prevent mischief. The performance of this duty he omitted; and the fact of his having intrusted it to a person who also neglected it, furnishes no excuse, either in good sense or law."

In *Bower* v. *Peate*,[33] where the defendant was held liable for the act of his contractor in letting down a house entitled to support, the rule was put even more strongly by Cockburn C.J., thus:

"A man who orders a work to be executed, from which, in the natural course of things, injurious consequences to his neighbours must be expected to arise, unless means are adopted by which such consequences may be prevented, is bound to see to the doing of that which is necessary to prevent the mischief, and cannot relieve himself of his responsibility by employing someone else—whether it be the contractor employed to do the work from which the danger arises or some independent person— to do what is necessary to prevent the act he has ordered to be done from becoming wrongful. There is an obvious difference between committing work to a contractor to be executed from which, if properly done, no injurious consequences can arise, and handing over to him work to be done from which mischievous consequences will arise unless preventive measures are adopted. While it may be just to hold the party authorizing the work in the former case exempt from liability for injury, resulting from negligence which he had no reason to anticipate, there is, on the other hand, good ground for holding him liable for injury caused by an act certain to be attended with injurious consequences if such consequences are not in fact prevented, no matter through whose default the omission to take the necessary measures for such prevention may arise."

The first part of the passage above quoted was, in *Hughes* v. *Percival*,[34] objected to by Lord Blackburn as being so broadly stated as to appear to conflict with *Quarman* v. *Burnett*,[35] but the substance of the law is quite clear, and was in fact applied in *Hughes* v. *Percival* [36] itself. There the defendant, having authorised a contractor to perform some building operations which involved a use of the party-wall between his premises and the plaintiff's, and a risk to the plaintiff's

[33] (1876) 1 Q.B.D. 321, 326. The decision was approved by the House of Lords in *Dalton* v. *Angus* (1881) 6 App.Cas. 740, 791, 829.
[34] (1883) 8 App.Cas. 443, 447.
[35] (1840) 6 M. & W. 499 (a case concerned with vicarious liability: see p. 371, *ante*).
[36] (1883) 8 App.Cas. 443.

premises themselves, was held liable for damage caused to the plaintiff's premises in the course of the operations by workmen employed by the contractor. Lord Fitzgerald said [37]:

> " The law has been verging somewhat in the direction of treating parties engaged in such an operation as the defendant's as insurers of their neighbours, or warranting them against injury. It has not, however, reached quite to that point. It does declare that under such a state of circumstances it was the duty of the defendant to have used every reasonable precaution that care and skill might suggest in the execution of his works, so as to protect his neighbours from injury, and that he cannot get rid of the responsibility thus cast on him by transferring that duty to another. He is not in the actual position of being responsible for injury, no matter how occasioned, but he must be vigilant and careful, for he is liable for injuries to his neighbour caused by any want of prudence or precaution, even though it may be *culpa levissima.*" [38]

(2) *Title to the Easement*

Where a landowner is enjoying the *de facto* benefit of an easement, for instance, of support for his buildings, but has no title to an easement, he cannot of course sue the lawful owner of the land providing the *de facto* benefit for its disturbance. Where, however, something is done on property A, to the detriment of property B, by X, a stranger to A, the owner or occupier of B can sue X without alleging or proving any easement, even though, *vis-à-vis* the owners and occupiers of A, B has no natural right of immunity against the consequences of the thing done by X.[39] This proposition, however, cannot be regarded with certainty as a general statement of the law. Each of the authorities which supports it [39] concerns action against a stranger (*i.e.* not the owner or occupier of the quasi-servient tenement) for the disturbance of *de facto* support enjoyed by buildings on the quasi-dominant tenement. There is one authority which suggests that even against a stranger title to the easement must be shown.[40]

---

[37] (1883) 8 App.Cas. 443, 455.
[38] *Cf.* as to the liabilities of local authorities for the default of their contractors, *Smith* v. *West Derby Board* (1878) 3 C.P.D. 423; *Hardaker* v. *Idle Council* [1896] 1 Q.B. 335; *Penny* v. *Wimbledon Council* [1898] 2 Q.B. 212; [1899] 2 Q.B. 72; *Hill* v. *Tottenham Council* (1899) 79 L.T. 495.
[39] *Jeffries* v. *Williams* (1850) 5 Exch. 792; *Bibby* v. *Carter* (1859) 4 H. & N. 153; *Richards* v. *Jenkins* (1868) 18 L.T. 437, 443–444; *Keegan* v. *Young* [1963] N.Z.L.R. 720.
[40] *Paine & Co.* v. *St. Neots Gas & Coke Co.* [1938] 4 All E.R. 592; [1939] 3 All E.R. 812, *per* Goddard L.J. at first instance, and, on appeal, *per* Luxmoore L.J.; Scott and Finlay L.JJ. expressing no opinion. In *Keegan* v. *Young* [1963] N.Z.L.R. 720, however, the decision was distinguished. In *Salmond on Torts*, 6th ed., p. 312, Sir John Salmond suggested that as against a stranger *de facto* possession of an easement was sufficient if the disturbance produced harmful effects to the dominant tenement, but where the act complained of produced no such harmful effects a legal right had to be proved even against a stranger. Thus, a landowner could sue

On the other hand, it is quite clear that the person in actual enjoyment of a *profit à prendre* can maintain an action of trespass against any person who disturbs his enjoyment,[41] save the owner of the servient tenement and persons holding under him; as against the latter a good title to the *profit à prendre* must be shown. The reason given for the distinction from easements in this respect is that a *profit à prendre* is an interest capable of existing in gross and is protected by an action in trespass; possession, therefore, is all that need be proved.[42] On the other hand, an easement is protected by an action in nuisance and it depends for its existence upon being attached to a dominant tenement; its mode of origin must therefore be proved.[43]

Where a landowner has a right in the nature of an easement arising from an application of equitable principles,[44] he may sue the owner of the servient tenement for a disturbance of this right and obtain an injunction.[45] The right will bind a successor in title to the servient tenement[46]; and a stranger to the servient tenement may be sued for a disturbance of the right.

(3) *Pleadings*

Allegation of title

Whenever a party claims more than he is entitled to of common right, he must allege in his pleading that he ought to have that which he demands.[47]

In early authorities a distinction is taken as to the mode of alleging title in actions against strangers and in actions against the terre-tenant of the servient tenement: in the former case it was admitted that a general allegation, " that he had and ought to have the right claimed," was sufficient; whilst in the latter case it was said that a title by grant or prescription must be shown, it being an attempt to " put a charge upon " the defendant.[48] By subsequent decisions it appears to have been held that in all actions for disturbance of an easement, whether the action be brought against the servient owner or a stranger,

a stranger for interfering with *de facto* support to buildings, for blocking up his windows, or for interfering with his water supply, but not for interfering with his use of a right of way across another's land. This distinction, however, may not be valid since *Paine & Co.* v. *St. Neots Gas & Coke Co., supra*, where an interference with a *de facto* water supply was held not actionable.

41 *Fitzgerald* v. *Firbank* [1897] 2 Ch. 96.
42 *Paine & Co.* v. *St. Neots Gas & Coke Co.* [1938] 4 All E.R. 592, 597; [1939] 3 All E.R. 812, 823.
43 *Ibid.* [1938] 4 All E.R. 592, 598; [1939] 3 All E.R. 812, 823–824.
44 See *e.g. Ward* v. *Kirkland* [1967] Ch. 194; *E. R. Ives Investments Ltd.* v. *High* [1967] 2 Q.B. 379.
45 *Ward* v. *Kirkland* [1967] Ch. 194.
46 *E. R. Ives Investments Ltd.* v. *High* [1967] 2 Q.B. 379.
47 *Wyatt* v. *Harrison* (1832) 3 B. & Ad. 871; *Tebbutt* v. *Selby* (1837) 6 A. & E. 786; *Laing* v. *Whaley* (1858) 3 H. & N. 675, 901.
48 *St. John* v. *Moody* (1687) 3 Keb. 528; S.C. 531; *Blockley* v. *Slater* (1693) 1 Lut. fol. 119; *Winford* v. *Wollaston* (1689) 3 Lev. 266. *Cf. Bullard* v. *Harrison* (1815) 4 M. & S. 387.

a general allegation of right was sufficient.[49] Where, however, the defendant justified his act by virtue of an easement he was obliged to set out the particular title upon which he relied, whether by grant or prescription.[50]

Pleadings after the Prescription Act 1832

In the case of actions brought after the Prescription Act 1832 modifications in pleading were introduced by section 5 of the Act.[1] Under this section it is necessary to allege enjoyment " as of right " in claiming a prescriptive right of way,[2] but not in claiming a prescriptive right to light [3]; enjoyment as of right meaning an enjoyment *nec vi, nec clam, nec precario*.[4]

The concluding words of the fifth section provide that " any cause or matter of fact or of law not inconsistent with the simple fact of enjoyment shall be specially alleged and set forth."

" The simple fact of enjoyment " was explained in the judgments quoted below to mean a continuous enjoyment as of right, and as an easement. Having regard to these words, the courts held that it was necessary to allege specially things consistent with such enjoyment, *e.g.* a tenancy for life,[5] or a licence extending over the whole period,[6] or such facts as that during the first part of the period of enjoyment the user was in exercise of a statutory right; and the statutory right having ceased, the enjoyment was continued for the rest of the period [7]; but that it was not necessary to allege specially things inconsistent with such enjoyment—*e.g.* unity of ownership, or stealth, or leave given during the period [8]; all of which could be given in evidence under a general traverse.

In *Tickle* v. *Brown* [9] it was held that where a defendant justifies under an enjoyment of twenty or forty years, if the plaintiff relies upon a licence covering the whole of that period he must plead such licence specially, but a licence granted and acted upon during the period may

---

49 *Sands* v. *Trefuses* (1640) Cro.Car. 575; *Villers* v. *Ball* (1689) 1 Show. 7; *Tenant* v. *Goldwin* (1705) 1 Salk. 360; S.C. 2 Ld.Raym. 1089; *Rider* v. *Smith* (1790) 3 T.R. 766; 2 Wms.Saund. 113a, note; 2 Notes to Saund. 361; Com.Dig. Pleader (C. 39); see also *Trower* v. *Chadwick* (1836) 3 Scott 699; 3 Bing.N.C. 334; *Paine & Co.* v. *St. Neots Gas & Coke Co.* [1939] 3 All E.R. 812, 823; [1938] 4 All E.R. 592, 598.
50 See Com.Dig. Chimin, D. 2; 1 Wms.Saund. 624; *Bird* v. *Dickinson* (1701) 2 Lut. 1526; *Grimstead* v. *Marlowe* (1792) 4 T.R. 717; *Bailey* v. *Appleyard* (1838) 8 A. & E. 167.
1 See p. 154, *ante*.
2 *Holford* v. *Hankinson* (1844) 5 Q.B. 584. For a modern example, see *Copeland* v. *Greenhalf* [1952] Ch. 488, 490.
3 See *Colls* v. *Home and Colonial Stores* [1904] A.C. 179, 205.
4 See *Gardner* v. *Hodgson's Kingston Brewery* [1903] A.C. 229, 238.
5 *Pye* v. *Mumford* (1848) 11 Q.B. 666; *Warburton* v. *Parke* (1857) 2 H. & N. 64. See s. 7 of the Act, *ante*, p. 155.
6 *Tickle* v. *Brown* (1836) 4 A. & E. 369, 382.
7 *Kinloch* v. *Nevile* (1840) 6 M. & W. 795.
8 *Onley* v. *Gardiner* (1838) 4 M. & W. 496; *Beasley* v. *Clarke* (1836) 2 Bing.N.C. 705; *Monmouth Canal Co.* v. *Harford* (1834) 1 C.M. & R. 614.
9 (1836) 4 A. & E. 369.

be given in evidence under the general traverse of the enjoyment "during the period alleged, showing that there was not, at the time when the agreement was made, an enjoyment as of right; and so the continuity is broken, which is inconsistent with the simple fact of enjoyment during the forty or twenty years."

In *Beasley* v. *Clarke* [10] Tindal C.J. said:

> "Under a plea denying that the Defendant had used the way for forty years, as of right and without interruption, the Plaintiff is at liberty to shew the character and description of the user and enjoyment of the way during any part of the time; as that it was used by stealth, or in the absence of the occupier of the close and without his knowledge, or that it was merely a precarious enjoyment by leave or licence, or any other circumstances which negative that it is an user or enjoyment under a claim of right; the words of the fifth section, 'not inconsistent with the simple fact of enjoyment,' being referable, as we understand the statute, to the fact of enjoyment as before stated in the Act, *viz.* an enjoyment claimed and exercised 'as of right.'"

In *Onley* v. *Gardiner* [11] the Court of Exchequer decided that unity of actual possession was inconsistent with the simple fact of enjoyment as of right, and, therefore, need not be specially pleaded. The simple fact of enjoyment, referred to in section 5, is an enjoyment as of right; and proof that there was an occasional unity of actual possession is as much in denial of that allegation as the occasionally asking permission would be; because the enjoyment during the unity of possession could not be an enjoyment as of an easement.

The disabilities and exceptions mentioned in sections 7 and 8 must be alleged in answer to a pleading claiming an easement under the Act [12]; so must the fact that the enjoyment was under a statutory right which ceased before the expiration of the required period of enjoyment [13]; or that the servient owner and his agents were absent from the neighbourhood and ignorant of the enjoyment during the whole period; or, in short, any other facts which would rebut the inference of a right by prescription or grant. Sections 7 and 8 only apply to the easements included in section 2, so that those sections cannot be set up in answer to a claim to an easement of light by virtue of twenty years' enjoyment.

Pleading prescriptive rights under the Judicature Acts

Section 5 of the Prescription Act and the decisions under it must now be read in connection with the rules of pleading established

[10] (1836) 2 Bing.N.C. 705.
[11] (1838) 4 M. & W. 498.
[12] *Pye* v. *Mumford* (1848) 11 Q.B. 666. As to pleading where a tenancy for life is alleged, see *ibid.*; also *Clayton* v. *Corby* (1842) 2 Q.B. 813.
[13] *Kinloch* v. *Nevile* (1840) 6 M. & W. 795.

under the Judicature Acts. R.S.C., Order 18 provides[14] that every pleading shall contain, and contain only, a statement in a summary form of the material facts on which the party pleading relies; and, further,[15] that a party must raise by his pleading all matters which show the action or counterclaim not to be maintainable, and all such grounds of defence or reply as, if not raised, would be likely to take the opposite party by surprise: and, further,[16] that in a defence or reply a general denial shall not be sufficient, but the party must deal specifically with each allegation of fact of which he does not admit the truth. Pleadings need not state inferences of law.[17]

It would seem from Order 18 that the general allegations and denials which were sufficient within section 5 of the Prescription Act 1832 are now insufficient.

Accordingly in an action to restrain the obstruction of an alleged private right of way, the plaintiff was held bound in pleading to state the title by which he claimed, and whether by grant or by prescriptive user.[18] Where in trespass the defendants pleaded that the *locus in quo* was a highway, they were ordered to show the mode in which they claimed that it had become a highway, and to give particulars of dedication.[19]

Under the present system of pleading, it is conceived that, whether the action be brought against the servient owner or a stranger, a party cannot safely allege his right to an easement generally, but should state specifically the manner in which he claims title to the easement, whether by grant (actual or lost), prescription at common law, or under the Prescription Act[20]; and in many cases it is advisable to plead, alternatively, a title by all three methods.[21]

As the right to an easement exists in respect of the dominant tenement, the pleading usually states the possession of the tenement by the party, and that by reason thereof he was entitled to the right in question.

A pleading under the Prescription Act was required to state the enjoyment to have been without interruption.[22] Under a plea of

---

[14] r. 7.
[15] r. 8.
[16] r. 13.
[17] *Hanmer* v. *Flight* (1876) 24 W.R. 347.
[18] *Harris* v. *Jenkins* (1882) 22 Ch.D. 481; *Farrell* v. *Coogan* (1890) 12 L.R.Ir. 14. See *Pledge* v. *Pomfret* [1905] W.N. 56.
[19] *Spedding* v. *Fitzpatrick* (1888) 38 Ch.D. 410.
[20] *Harris* v. *Jenkins* (1882) 22 Ch.D. 481; and see *Smith* v. *Baxter* [1900] 2 Ch. 138, 146; *Hyman* v. *Van den Bergh* [1907] 2 Ch. 516, 524; [1908] 1 Ch. 167, 169, 176; *cf. Spedding* v. *Fitzpatrick* (1888) 38 Ch.D. 410; *Pledge* v. *Pomfret* [1905] W.N. 56.
[21] In *Tehidy Minerals* v. *Norman* [1971] 2 Q.B. 528, 543, the Court of Appeal expressed the view that the co-existence of three separate methods of prescribing was anomalous and undesirable, for it resulted in much unnecessary complication and confusion. The court expressed the hope that it might " be possible for the Legislature to effect a long-overdue simplification in this branch of the law."
[22] *Per* Patteson J. in *Richards* v. *Fry* (1838) 7 A. & E. 698, 701.

forty years' user, according to the statute, evidence of what took place before that period was admissible as showing the state of things at the commencement of the forty years' enjoyment.[23] The necessity of giving particulars of a claim to an easement by prescription is less strict in the county court.[24]

Pleading grant

According to modern practice, a lost grant, if relied upon, should be pleaded[25]; but claims based on lost grant have been added by amendment at the trial.[26] Formerly, the names of the parties to, and the date of, the supposed grant had to be stated[27]; but on averment that the deed had been lost profert was excused.[28] The statement of date and parties is no longer necessary,[29] but a statement whether the supposed grant was before or after a private Act was required.[30]

There appears to be no precedent of a pleading of an easement arising from the disposition of the owner of two tenements; but it seems that, as in the case of easements of necessity, the right must be pleaded as arising by implied grant from the joint owner at the time of severance. The pleading might allege the joint ownership and subsequent conveyance, and aver the apparent and continuous nature of the easement, and its existence at the period of severance.

A pleading of an easement of necessity must, in like manner, allege the joint ownership at the time of the conveyance, and that the easement is essential to the full enjoyment of the principal thing conveyed or reserved.[31]

The party should describe in his pleading the nature of the right in question. Thus, in an action for the disturbance of a way, he should state the *terminus a quo* and *ad quem*, and the kind of way he claims, as a footway, etc.[32] A precise local description, as by alleging the land to be in any particular place, is not, however, requisite; and it is not necessary, although it is convenient, to give the intervening closes.[33]

---

[23] *Lawson* v. *Langley* (1836) 4 A. & E. 890.
[24] See *Pugh* v. *Savage* [1970] 2 Q.B. 373.
[25] *Smith* v. *Baxter* [1900] 2 Ch. 147.
[26] *Brown* v. *Dunstable Corpn.* [1899] 2 Ch. 380, 387; *Gardner* v. *Hodgson's Kingston Brewery Co.* [1900] 1 Ch. 601.
[27] *Hendy* v. *Stephenson* (1808) 10 East 55. See *Livett* v. *Wilson* (1825) 3 Bing. 115; *Doe* d. *Fenwick* v. *Reed* (1821) 5 B. & Ald. 232.
[28] *Read* v. *Brookman* (1789) 3 T.R. 151.
[29] See the pleadings in *Norfolk* (*Duke*) v. *Arbuthnot* (1879) 4 C.P.D. 293; *Brown* v. *Dunstable Corpn.* [1899] 2 Ch. 380. Particulars of a lost grant will not be ordered: *Wade & English Ltd.* v. *Dixon & Cardus Ltd.* [1937] 3 All E.R. 900.
[30] *Palmer* v. *Guadagni* [1906] 2 Ch. 494.
[31] *Proctor* v. *Hodgson* (1855) 10 Ex. 824; *Bullard* v. *Harrison* (1815) 4 M. & S. 387.
[32] *Vide* Com.Dig. Action on the Case for a Disturbance, B. (1); Chimin, D. (2); *Harris* v. *Jenkins* (1882) 22 Ch.D. 481.
[33] *Simpson* v. *Lewthwaite* (1832) 3 B. & Ad. 226; *Harris* v. *Jenkins* (1882) 22 Ch.D. 481.

Pleading damage

As regards the allegation and proof of damage, the rule should be borne in mind that actual perceptible damage is not indispensable as the foundation of an action. It is sufficient to show the violation of " a right," in which case the law will presume damage.[34] Again, wherever any act injures another's rights and would be evidence in future in favour of the wrongdoer, an action may be maintained for the invasion of the right without proof of specific injury.[35] These rules have been applied in the case of actions of trespass to land [36]; in the case of actions for diversion of water (where it has been pointed out that the defendant might by the diversion acquire a right injurious to the plaintiff [37]); in the case of actions for pollution of water [38]; and in the case of actions for the disturbance of rights of way.[39]

In applying these rules, however, it is necessary to bear in mind the distinction between various " rights." Thus, where water was taken from a river by the licensee of an upper riparian owner, a lower riparian owner was refused an injunction on the ground that the water taken was returned undiminished in quantity and undeteriorated in quality, so that the acts of the licensee could never grow into a prescriptive title, and the right of the lower riparian proprietor was not in fact interfered with.[40] Again, as regards support, a landowner has the right to insist that his land shall not be let down by his neighbour's excavation. But supposing the neighbour to excavate, the landowner has no right of action at law unless and until subsidence follows.[41]

In the case of an action for diversion of water, the principle that to sustain the action actual damage need not be alleged or proved applies not only in the case of natural rights, but also where rights in respect of water have been acquired by grant or user,[42] or arise under a statute.[43]

---

34 *Per* Parke B. in *Embrey* v. *Owen* (1851) 6 Ex. 353, 368; *per* Littledale J. in *Williams* v. *Morland* (1824) 2 B. & C. 910, 916.
35 1 Wms.Saund. 626.
36 See the judgment of Lord Holt C.J. in *Ashby* v. *White*, 1 Sm.L.C. (13th ed.), p. 253; (1703) 2 Ld.Raym. 938.
37 *Wilts & Berks Canal Navigation Co.* v. *Swindon Waterworks Co.* (1874) 9 Ch.App. 457, 458; *Roberts* v. *Gwyrfai D.C.* [1899] 2 Ch. 610. See *Embrey* v. *Owen, supra*; *Harrop* v. *Hirst* (1868) L.R. 4 Ex. 47; *McCartney* v. *Londonderry Co.* [1904] A.C. 313; *Bickett* v. *Morris* (1866) L.R. 1 H.L.Sc. 60.
38 *Jones* v. *Llanrwst U.D.C.* [1911] 1 Ch. 402.
39 *Bower* v. *Hill* (1835) 1 Bing.N.C. 555; *Clifford* v. *Hoare* (1874) L.R. 9 C.P. 372.
40 *Kensit* v. *G.E. Railway* (1884) 27 Ch.D. 130. See *McCartney* v *Londonderry Co., supra.* Compare *Ormerod* v. *Todmorden Joint Stock Mill Co.* (1883) 11 Q.B.D. 155; and see *ante,* pp. 232–234.
41 *Backhouse* v. *Bonomi* (1861) 9 H.L.C. 503.
42 *Northam* v. *Hurley* (1853) 1 E. & B. 665; *Rawstron* v. *Taylor* (1855) 11 Ex. 369; *Harrop* v. *Hirst* (1868) L.R. 4 Ex. 47.
43 *Rochdale Co.* v. *King* (1849) 14 Q.B. 122.

Allegation of breach of duty

In *Mersey & Irwell* v. *Douglas*,[44] an action on the case for a disturbance, it was held sufficient to allege a disturbance generally, without showing the particular manner of the disturbance.[45]

In *Tebbutt* v. *Selby*,[46] however, Patteson J. appears to have doubted whether such a general allegation of obstruction would be sufficient, and nowadays particulars would undoubtedly be ordered.

In a pleading by the reversioner he must show that he sues in that capacity, and allege that the disturbance is to the injury of his reversionary estate.[47]

(4) *Remedy by Injunction*

Powers of court

The remedy which was afforded at common law for the continuous disturbance of easements or other nuisances, by an indefinite series of actions for damage, was obviously, in many cases, quite inadequate; and the Court of Chancery always exercised, and the High Court still exercises, the power of interfering, by injunction, to stop the whole mischief complained of.[48]

The foundation of the plaintiff's right in such cases being a right at common law, the Court of Chancery, before finally granting equitable relief, at one time required that the legal right of the person seeking relief should be established in a proceeding at law.[49] Now, by the Judicature Act 1925, replacing the Judicature Act 1873, the jurisdiction both of the Court of Chancery and of the common law courts is vested in the High Court of Justice, which has power to entertain legal and equitable claims and defences alike.

Perpetual injunctions

Before a perpetual injunction can be granted to restrain a private nuisance or the disturbance of an easement, the court as a general rule requires the party to establish his legal right and the fact of its violation. But when these things have been established, then, unless there be something special in the case, the party is entitled as of

---

44 (1802) 2 East 497.
45 Com.Dig. Action on the Case for a Disturbance, B. (1); *Anon.* (1566) 3 Leon. 13; *Dawney* v. *Dee* (1620) Cro.Jac. 605.
46 (1837) 6 A. & E. 793.
47 *Jackson* v. *Pesked* (1813) 1 M. & S. 234.
48 *Robinson* v. *Byron* (1785) 1 Bro.C.C. 588 (watercourse); *Thorpe* v. *Brumfitt* (1873) 8 Ch.App. 650 (way); *Arcedeckne* v. *Kelk* (1858) 2 Giff. 683; *Herz* v. *Union Bank of London* (1854) 2 Giff. 686, and *Wilson* v. *Townend* (1860) 1 Dr. & Sm. 324 (light); *Hunt* v. *Peake* (1860) John. 705 (natural right of support); *N.E. Railway* v. *Elliott* (1863) 10 H.L.C. 333 (easement of support).
49 See judgments in *Imperial Gas Light & Coke Co.* v. *Broadbent* (1859) 7 H.L.C. 600; *Cardiff Corpn.* v. *Cardiff Waterworks Co.* (1859) 4 De G. & J. 596; *Eaden* v. *Firth* (1863) 1 H. & M. 573; *Roskell* v. *Whitworth* (1870) 5 Ch.App. 459. It never was a ground of demurrer that the legal right had not yet been tried, though it was a ground for not granting interlocutory injunctions.

course to an injunction to prevent the recurrence of that violation.[50] An easement is a legal right. The remedy by injunction is in aid of that legal right. The owner of the right is entitled to an injunction, not in the discretion of the court, but of course; unless there is something special in the case, *e.g.* laches, or the fact that the disturbance is only trivial or occasional.[1] The cost to the defendant of complying with a negative injunction is not a factor to be taken into account.[2] The grounds on which the court acts in granting an injunction were thus stated by Page Wood L.J. in *Attorney-General* v. *Cambridge Consumers' Gas Co.*[3]:

> " Where the Court interferes by way of injunction to prevent an injury in respect of which there is a legal remedy, it does so upon two grounds, which are of totally distinct character; one is that the injury is irreparable, as in the case of cutting down trees; the other, that the injury is continuous, and so continuous that the Court acts upon the same principle as it used in older times with reference to bills of peace, and restrains the repeated acts which could only result in incessant actions, the continuous character of the wrong making it grievous and intolerable. As an illustration of this class of case, I may refer to *Soltau* v. *De Held*,[4] where the annoyance from the ringing of the bell was in itself slight, but it was so continuous that the Court thought fit to arrest the nuisance *brevi manu* and save the complainant all further annoyance."

" Irreparable injury " has been referred to as meaning injury which cannot be compensated in damages.[5]

To obtain an injunction, proof of actual damage is not necessary where a right of property has been infringed[6]; or where the parties to a contract for valuable consideration with their eyes open have contracted that a particular thing shall not be done.[7] Again, where the wrong is of a recurring nature an injunction may be obtained even though the actual damage is slight.[8] The court, however, will not interfere by injunction where the violation of a legal right is

---

50 *Imperial Gas Co.* v. *Broadbent* (1859) 7 H.L.C. 612; *Fullwood* v. *Fullwood* (1878) 9 Ch.D. 176; *Martin* v. *Price* [1894] 1 Ch. 285.

1 *Cowper* v. *Laidler* [1903] 2 Ch. 339, 341.

2 *Redland Bricks Ltd.* v. *Morris* [1970] A.C. 652, 664.

3 (1868) 4 Ch.App. 71, 80.

4 2 Sim.(N.S.) 133.

5 *Mogul Steamship Co.* v. *M'Gregor* (1885) 15 Q.B.D. 486; *Att.-Gen.* v. *Hallett* (1847) 16 M. & W. 581.

6 *Jones* v. *Llanrwst U.D.C.* [1911] 1 Ch. 393, 402 (where Parker J. refers to other authorities); *Thorpe* v. *Brumfitt* (1873) 8 Ch.App. 656; *Pennington* v. *Brinsop Hall Coal Co.* (1877) 5 Ch.D. 772.

7 *Doherty* v. *Allman* (1873) 3 A.C. 709, 719.

8 *Clowes* v. *Staffordshire Potteries Waterworks Co.* (1872) 8 Ch.App. 142.

trivial,[9] nor will it interfere by injunction to restrain actionable wrongs for which damages are the proper remedy.[10]

Mandatory injunction

The jurisdiction to grant a mandatory injunction, even on interlocutory motion, has often been asserted.[11] A distinction was taken in some early cases between those injunctions which merely prevent the doing of an act and those the consequence of which, either directly or indirectly, will be to compel a party to do some act, as to fill up a ditch,[12] or pull down a wall [13]; the former being granted on motion, the latter only at the trial. This distinction, however, though recognised, does not appear to have been strictly adhered to; indeed, in one case,[14] Lord Eldon, though he refused the order, as prayed, " to restrain the defendant from continuing to keep certain roads out of repair," purposely made an order in such a form as to have the same effect, by making it difficult for the defendant to avoid completely repairing his works. And in commenting on this case, in *Blakemore* v. *Glamorganshire Canal Navigation*,[15] Lord Brougham said [16]:

> " . . . if this court has this jurisdiction, it would be better to exercise it directly and at once; and I will further take leave to add, that the having recourse to a roundabout mode of obtaining the object seems to cast doubt upon the jurisdiction."

The court has now departed from the " roundabout mode," and where an injunction is granted, the effect of which is to require the performance of a certain act, such as the pulling down and removal of buildings, the order is made in a direct mandatory form, and not in the indirect form formerly in use.[17]

Such an injunction may order the pulling down of work done or erected after the commencement of an action, or after notice given

---

[9] *Coulson* v. *White* (1743) 3 Atk. 21; *Att.-Gen.* v. *Sheffield Gas Consumers' Co.* (1853) 3 De G.M. & G. 304; *Swaine* v. *G.N. Railway* (1864) 10 Jur.(N.S.) 191; *Durell* v. *Pritchard* (1865) 1 Ch.App. 244; *Cooke* v. *Forbes* (1867) L.R. 5 Eq. 166; *Att.-Gen.* v. *Cambridge Consumers' Gas Co.* (1868) 4 Ch.App. 71; *Llandudno Urban Council* v. *Woods* [1899] 2 Ch. 705; *Behrens* v. *Richards* [1905] 2 Ch. 614; *Armstrong* v. *Sheppard & Short Ltd.* [1959] 2 Q.B. 384.

[10] *London and Blackwall Railway* v. *Cross* (1886) 31 Ch.D. 369; *Wood* v. *Sutcliffe* (1851) 2 Sim.(N.S.) 165.

[11] *Mexborough* v. *Bower* (1843) 7 Beav. 127; *Hervey* v. *Smith* (1855) 1 K. & J. 389; *Westminster Brymbo, etc. Co.* v. *Clayton* (1867) 36 L.J.Ch. 476; *Beadel* v. *Perry* (1866) L.R. 3 Eq. 465; *Shepherd Homes* v. *Sandham* [1971] Ch. 340; and see *post*, p. 387.

[12] *Robinson* v. *Byron* (1785) 1 Bro.C.C. 588.

[13] *Ryder* v. *Bentham* (1750) 1 Ves.Sen. 543.

[14] *Lane* v. *Newdigate* (1804) 10 Ves. 192.

[15] (1832) 1 My. & K. 154.

[16] *Ibid.* 184; *cf.* the observations of Jessel M.R. in *Smith* v. *Smith* (1875) L.R. 20 Eq. 500, 504; and *Bidwell* v. *Holden* (1890) 63 L.T. 104.

[17] *Jackson* v. *Normanby Brick Co.* [1899] 1 Ch. 438; Seton's *Judgments and Orders* (7th ed.), pp. 369, 539.

to the defendant that his erecting it will be objected to,[18] even where
the work or erection was completed before the writ was issued.[19]
On the question of granting such an injunction it is important to
see if the defendant knew he was doing wrong.[20] Further, it may not
be granted if the injury to the plaintiff can be estimated and sufficiently
compensated by an award of damages,[21] and is restricted to cases
where extreme or very serious damage would ensue from not granting
it [22]; although these are now factors which may justify an award of
damages in lieu of an injunction under Lord Cairns' Act rather than
a refusal of an injunction *ab initio*.[23]

Unlike a prohibitory injunction, a mandatory injunction is entirely
discretionary and can never be granted " as of course," every case
depending upon its own particular circumstances.[24]

There must be no delay or acquiescence on the part of the plaintiff
if he is to be granted a mandatory injunction,[25] unless this can be
adequately explained.[26]

For the principles upon which mandatory injunctions are granted
quia timet, see *infra*.

Quia timet injunction

There may arise a situation where it is apprehended that there
may be injury to an easement or natural right, although the injury
has not so far occurred. In such a case an injunction may be obtained
in a *quia timet* action. Such an action is broadly applicable in two
types of cases [27] : first, where the defendant has as yet done no
hurt to the plaintiff but is threatening to do works which will render
irreparable harm to him or his property if carried to completion.
These cases are normally, though not always, concerned with negative
injunctions. The second type of case arises where the plaintiff has
been fully recompensed in law and in equity for the damage he
has suffered (*e.g.* by an award of damages and an injunction restraining the defendant from further activity) but where he alleges that
the earlier actions of the defendant may lead to future causes of
action, for example, where the defendant has withdrawn support from
his neighbour's land or where he has so acted in depositing his soil
from his mining operations, as to constitute a menace to the plaintiff's

---

18 *Smith* v. *Day* (1880) 13 Ch.D. 651; *Kelk* v. *Pearson* (1871) 6 Ch.App. 809;
   Clifford v. *Holt* [1899] 1 Ch. 698.
19 *Lawrence* v. *Horton* (1890) 62 L.T. 749.
20 *Smith* v. *Smith* (1875) L.R. 20 Eq. 500, 503; *Lawrence* v. *Horton* (1890) 62 L.T. 749.
21 *Isenberg* v. *East India House Estate Co. Ltd.* (1863) 3 De G.J. & S. 263.
22 *Durell* v. *Pritchard* (1865) 1 Ch.App. 244.
23 See p. 388, *post*.
24 *Smith* v. *Smith* (1875) L.R. 20 Eq. 500, 503; *Gaskin* v. *Balls* (1879) 13 Ch.D. 324;
   Shiel v. *Godfrey* [1893] W.N. 115.
25 See *e.g. Baxter* v. *Bower* (1875) 23 W.R. 805.
26 *Redland Bricks Ltd.* v. *Morris* [1970] A.C. 652, 665.
27 *Redland Bricks Ltd.* v. *Morris* [1970] A.C. 652, 665.

land.[28] Here the court has jurisdiction to grant a mandatory injunction ordering the defendant to carry out positive works. These two types of case will now be considered in turn:

(1) The defendant may be carrying on an activity which, when completed, may infringe the rights of the plaintiff, for example, by erecting a building which threatens to obstruct a right of light[29] or way, or by so mining his land as to threaten to interfere with the support of the land of the plaintiff.[30] If an injunction to restrain the activity is to be granted there must be a strong probability that the activity will cause injury to the plaintiff.[31] Although it has sometimes been said that the apprehended injury must be irreparable,[32] this is probably not so, it being necessary to show only that an actionable injury be apprehended.[33]

The alleged intention of the defendant to interfere with the rights of the plaintiff must normally be accompanied and evidenced by some activity,[34] for example laying the foundations of a house which when built would interfere with a right to light. But this is unnecessary if the avowed intentions of the defendant are to commence the activity, provided that there is a real probability that he will carry out such intentions.[35]

Instead of granting an injunction the court may make a declaration that the defendant cannot carry on his activity to its fulfilment and may give liberty to apply for an injunction.[36]

(2) In the second type of case the conditions for the grant of a *quia timet* injunction, that is, when mandatory, are far more stringent. In *Redland Bricks Ltd.* v. *Morris*[37] the principles upon which the court's discretion should be exercised were considered. The respondents owned and farmed some eight acres of land which was valued at £12,000 or thereabouts. The appellants used adjoining land to excavate clay for their brick-making business. Due to this activity support to the respondents' land was withdrawn and it started to slip into the appellants' land. Despite remedial works carried out by the appellants the slipping continued. The respondents began proceedings in the county court and the judge found that there was a strong possibility

---

[28] *Kennard* v. *Cory Bros. & Co. Ltd.* [1922] 1 Ch. 265; *Redland Bricks Ltd.* v. *Morris* [1970] A.C. 652.
[29] *Litchfield-Speer* v. *Queen Anne's Gate Syndicate* [1919] 1 Ch. 407, where it was said that the decision in *Colls* v. *Home and Colonial Stores* [1904] A.C. 179 had not abrogated the right to relief in a *quia timet* action.
[30] *Siddons* v. *Short and Harley & Co.* (1877) 2 C.P.D. 572.
[31] *Pattisson* v. *Gilford* (1874) L.R. 18 Eq. 259; *Fletcher* v. *Bealey* (1884) 28 Ch.D. 688, 698; *Att.-Gen.* v. *Manchester Corporation* [1893] 2 Ch. 87, 92; *Litchfield-Speer* v. *Queen Anne's Gate Syndicate* [1919] 1 Ch. 407, 411.
[32] See *e.g. Fletcher* v. *Bealey* (1884) 28 Ch.D. 688, *per* Pearson J. 698; *Litchfield-Speer* v. *Queen Anne's Gate Syndicate* [1919] 1 Ch. 407, *per* P. O. Lawrence J. 411.
[33] *Siddons* v. *Short and Harley & Co.* (1877) 2 C.P.D. 572.
[34] See *e.g. Phillips* v. *Thomas* (1890) 62 L.T. 793.
[35] *Cf. Lord Cowley* v. *Byas* (1877) 5 Ch.D. 944.
[36] *Litchfield-Speer* v. *Queen Anne's Gate Syndicate* [1919] 1 Ch. 407.
[37] [1970] A.C. 652.

of further slips with serious loss to the respondents. It was agreed that to prevent further slipping would cost the appellants up to £35,000. The judge, in addition to awarding damages to the respondents for damage already suffered and granting an injunction restraining further excavations, ordered the appellants to "take all necessary steps to restore the support" to the respondents' land. The appellants appealed to the Court of Appeal who upheld the decision of the county court judge, but a further appeal to the House of Lords was allowed. Lord Upjohn, delivering a judgment with which the remainder of the House agreed, set out [38] the principles applicable to the grant of mandatory injunctions *quia timet* which may be summarised as follows:

(1) The plaintiff must show a very strong probability that grave damage will accrue to him in the future.

(2) Damages will not be a sufficient or adequate remedy if such damage does happen.[39]

(3) The cost to the defendant to do works to prevent or lessen the likelihood of a future apprehended wrong is an element to be taken into account. Where the defendant has acted without regard to his neighbour's rights, or has tried to steal a march on him or has tried to evade the jurisdiction of the court or, to sum it up, has acted wantonly and quite unreasonably in relation to his neighbour he may be ordered to repair his acts by doing positive work to restore the *status quo* even if the expense to him is out of all proportion to the advantage thereby accruing to the plaintiff.[40] Where, however, the defendant has acted reasonably, the cost of remedying by positive action his earlier activities is important for two reasons: first, because no legal wrong has yet occurred (for which the plaintiff has not been recompensed in law and in equity) and may never occur again, or at least only on a smaller scale than anticipated; secondly, because if damage does occur he has his action in law and remedies in equity. Considering these factors, the court must balance the amount to be expended under a mandatory order by the defendant against the anticipated possible damage to the plaintiff in deciding whether it is unreasonable to inflict such expenditure on a potential wrongdoer. The court can order works to be done which will merely lessen the likelihood of further injury.[41]

(4) If a mandatory injunction is granted, the defendant must know exactly what he has to do as a matter of fact.[42]

On the facts of the case the House of Lords held that the decision

---

[38] [1970] A.C. 665–667.
[39] This is a general principle of equity. It has nothing to do with Lord Cairns' Act; see *post*, p. 388 *et seq.*
[40] *Woodhouse* v. *Newry Navigation Co.* [1898] 1 I.R. 161.
[41] *Kennard* v. *Cory Bros. & Co. Ltd.* [1922] 1 Ch. 265, 274; affd. [1922] 2 Ch. 1.
[42] *Att.-Gen.* v. *Staffordshire County Council* [1905] 1 Ch. 336, 342; *Fishenden* v. *Higgs & Hill Ltd.* (1935) 153 L.T. 128, 142.

of the county court judge could not stand. Although the respondents had satisfied conditions (1) and (2) above, they had failed under (3) and (4). The appellants had not behaved unreasonably but only wrongly. Moreover, the terms of the order imposed upon the appellants an unqualified obligation to restore support without giving them any indication of what was to be done. It would have cost at least £30,000 to prevent further damage and this offended condition (3).

Interlocutory injunction

The question whether the court will grant an interlocutory injunction before the plaintiff's right is decided one way or the other by a trial is one depending upon the discretion of the court, having regard to all the circumstances, including the clearness, extent and amount of the plaintiff's right, the injury which he is likely to sustain, his promptness in complaining, and a comparison of the injury likely to result to the plaintiff or defendant respectively, in case the ultimate issue should be in his favour, by reason of the refusal or the granting of the injunction, as the case may be.[43]

The provision in section 25 (8) of the Judicature Act 1873, which empowered the court to grant an interlocutory injunction "in all cases in which it shall appear to the court to be just or convenient that such an order should be made," was not intended to disturb the settled principles on which injunctions had been formerly granted or refused.[44] The provision, which is, in substance, repeated in section 45 of the Judicature Act 1925, enabled the court to grant injunctions, for example, in trespass, where in practice it previously did not do so,[45] but not where there was previously no jurisdiction.[46] Lord Brougham in *Blakemore* v. *Glamorganshire Canal Navigation*,[47] said:

> "The leading principle then on which I proceed in dealing with this application, the principle which, as I humbly conceive, ought, generally speaking, to be the guide of the Court, and to limit its discretion in granting injunctions, at least where no very special circumstances occur, is, that only such a restraint shall be imposed as may suffice to stop the mischief complained of, and where it is to stay further injury, to keep things as they are for the present."

It is not necessary, in order that an interlocutory injunction may be

---

[43] See Daniell's *Chancery Practice* (8th ed.), p. 1405; and *Wynstanley* v. *Lee* (1818) 2 Swan. 336; *Hilton* v. *Granville* (1841) Cr. & Ph. 297; *Newson* v. *Pender* (1884) 27 Ch.D. 43.
[44] See *Beddow* v. *Beddow* (1878) 9 Ch.D. 89; *Day* v. *Brownrigg* (1878) 10 Ch.D. 307, *per* James L.J.; *Gaskin* v. *Balls* (1879) 13 Ch.D. 324; *Fletcher* v. *Rodgers* (1878) 27 W.R. 97.
[45] *Cummins* v. *Perkins* [1899] 1 Ch. 20.
[46] *Smith* v. *Day* (1880) 13 Ch.D. 651. *Cf. Aynsley* v. *Glover* (1874) L.R. 18 Eq. 544, 553, *per* Jessel M.R.; *Mackey* v. *Scottish Widows' Fund Assurance Society* (1876) Ir.R. 10 Eq. 113; *Greenwood* v. *Hornsey* (1886) 33 Ch.D. 471.
[47] (1832) 1 My. & K. 154, 185.

obtained, that the evidence of right shall be conclusive. The party applying must, however, make a prima facie case, and satisfy the court that there is a question to be tried at the hearing.[48] He must also show that, unless an interlocutory injunction be granted, he will sustain irreparable injury, *i.e.* such an injury as cannot be compensated in damages.[49]

A mandatory injunction may be granted on interlocutory motion. Thus, where a defendant hurries up a building after receiving a writ[50] or a letter of complaint,[1] a mandatory injunction may be granted to pull down the building.[2] As a general rule, however, a stronger case must be made out for a mandatory than for a prohibitory injunction on motion.[3]

Undertaking as to damages

Where the plaintiff obtains an interlocutory injunction, an undertaking by him to abide by an order which the court may make as to damages, in case the court should afterwards be of opinion that the defendants have sustained any, by reason of the order, which the plaintiff ought to pay, is inserted in the order as a matter of course[4]; and where an interlocutory injunction has been granted on such an undertaking, and afterwards at the trial the plaintiff does not obtain an injunction, an inquiry as to damages may be directed, even though the plaintiff obtained the order without misrepresentation, concealment, or default.[5]

Undertaking to pull down

In some cases the court has ordered a motion for an interim injunction to stand over until the trial, on the defendant undertaking to abide by any order which may be made at the trial as to pulling down the additional buildings to be erected[6]; but no such undertaking is required in order to found the jurisdiction of the court over buildings erected after the commencement of the action.[7]

---

[48] *Preston* v. *Luck* (1844) 27 Ch.D. 497, 506, *per* Cotton L.J.; *Challender* v. *Royle* (1887) 36 Ch.D. 425; *Peru Republic* v. *Dreyfus Bros. & Co.* (1888) 38 Ch.D. 362.

[49] *Att.-Gen.* v. *Hallett* (1847) 16 M. & W. 581; *Mogul Steamship Co.* v. *M'Gregor* (1885) 15 Q.B.D. 486; *J. T. Stratford & Son Ltd.* v. *Lindley* [1965] A.C. 269, 338; and see *Cordell* v. *Second Clanfield Properties Ltd.* [1969] 1 Ch. 9, where an injunction was refused because completion of the buildings would not interfere any further with the plaintiff's right of way.

[50] *Daniel* v. *Ferguson* [1891] 2 Ch. 27.

[1] *Von Joel* v. *Hornsey* [1895] 2 Ch. 774.

[2] *Von Joel* v. *Hornsey* [1895] 2 Ch. 774; *Keeble* v. *Poole* (1898) 42 S.J. 791.

[3] *Shepherd Homes* v. *Sandham* [1971] Ch. 340; *Hounslow London Borough Council* v. *Twickenham Garden Developments Ltd.* [1971] Ch. 233.

[4] *Chappell* v. *Davidson* (1856) 8 De G.M. & G. 1; *Graham* v. *Campbell* (1878) 7 Ch.D. 490.

[5] *Griffith* v. *Blake* (1884) 27 Ch.D. 474, where the Lords Justices dissented from an opinion to the contrary expressed by Jessel M.R. in *Smith* v. *Day* (1882) 21 Ch.D. 421.

[6] *Wilson* v. *Townend* (1860) 1 Dr. & Sm. 324.

[7] *Smith* v. *Day* (1880) 13 Ch.D. 651. *Cf. Aynsley* v. *Glover* (1874) L.R. 18 Eq. 544, 553, *per* Jessel M.R.; *Mackey* v. *Scottish Widows' Fund Assurance Society* (1876) Ir.R. 10 Eq. 113; *Greenwood* v. *Hornsey* (1886) 33 Ch.D. 471.

Delay

As regards delay, it has been held that, even though there has
been no such acquiescence as to amount to the constructive grant of
a right, a party may be barred by delay from obtaining an injunction.[8]
There may be a difference between the acquiescence which will justify
the refusal of an interlocutory and of a perpetual injunction.[9]

Lord Cairns' Act

The question whether for any particular disturbance of an easement a party could obtain damages, or an injunction, or both,
depended for a long time on the different jurisdictions of the courts
of common law and equity. In some cases a party came into a
court of equity for an injunction and was sent to a court of law to
recover damages, being thus bandied about from one court to another.[10]
Section 2 of the Chancery Amendment Act 1858,[11] commonly known
as Lord Cairns' Act, provided as follows:

"In all cases in which the Court of Chancery has jurisdiction
to entertain an application for an injunction against a breach of
any covenant, contract, or agreement, or against the commission
or continuance of any wrongful act, or for the specific performance of any covenant, contract, or agreement, it shall be lawful for
the same Court, if it shall think fit, to award damages to the party
injured, either in addition to or in substitution for such injunction
or specific performance; and such damages may be assessed in such
manner as the Court shall direct." [12]

This Act was discussed in many cases, the effect of which was
stated in *Cowper* v. *Laidler* [13] as follows: The Act gives jurisdiction
to substitute damages for an injunction where the plaintiff asks
for a mandatory injunction, or for an injunction to restrain a continuing nuisance, but where an injunction is asked to restrain a
threatened injury the jurisdiction is doubtful. The last point had
been doubtful for many years, and it was not finally decided until
1924. In one case decided under Lord Cairns' Act, *Krehl* v. *Burrell*,[14]
the plaintiff claimed a mandatory injunction to restrain building on

8 *Wicks* v. *Hunt* (1859) John. 372; *Cooper* v. *Hubbuck* (1860) 30 Beav. 160; *Gaskin*
   v. *Balls* (1879) 13 Ch.D. 324; *Young* v. *Star Omnibus Co.* (1902) 86 L.T. 41.
   See *Hogg* v. *Scott* (1874) L.R. 18 Eq. 444; *Smith* v. *Smith* (1875) L.R. 20 Eq. 503.
9 *Johnson* v. *Wyatt* (1863) 2 De G.J. & S. 18; *Turner* v. *Mirfield* (1865) 34 Beav. 390.
10 See *Ferguson* v. *Wilson* (1866) 2 Ch.App. 77.
11 21 & 22 Vict. c. 27.
12 This enactment was repealed by the Statute Law Revision and Civil Procedure Act
   1883, s. 3, but the jurisdiction conferred by it was preserved by the proviso contained in s. 5. S. 5 of the Act of 1883 was itself repealed by the Statute Law
   Reform Act 1898, but the proviso in s. 1 of the Act of 1898, coupled with s. 16
   of the Judicature Act 1873 (now s. 18 of the Supreme Court of Judicature (Consolidation) Act 1925), kept alive the jurisdiction under s. 2 of the Act of 1858.
   (See *Leeds Industrial Co-operative Society* v. *Slack* [1924] A.C. 861–862, *per* Lord
   Finlay.)
13 [1903] 2 Ch. 337, 339, *per* Buckley J.
14 (1878) 7 Ch.D. 551, 555; affd. 11 Ch.D. 146.

a passage over which he had a right of way, and the defendant contended that only damages should be given. Sir George Jessel M.R. granted a mandatory injunction, saying:

> "If I acceded to this view, . . . I should add one more to the number of instances which we have from the days in which the Bible was written until the present moment, in which the man of large possessions has endeavoured to deprive his neighbour, the man with small possessions, of his property, with or without adequate compensation."

In *Dreyfus* v. *Peruvian Guano Co.* [15] Bowen, Cotton and Fry L.JJ., although differing on other points, all agreed that the court had no power to award damages for an injury only threatened and not yet committed. In *Martin* v. *Price*, [16] however, Lindley L.J., in delivering the judgment of himself and of the other two members of the court (A. L. Smith and Davey L.JJ.), described the point as being by no means free from difficulty, but did not feel called upon to decide it. In *Litchfield-Speer* v. *Queen Anne's Syndicate* [17] P. O. Lawrence J. expressed the opinion that it was extremely doubtful whether the court had power in a *quia timet* action to give damages in lieu of an injunction. With the law in this unsettled state, the case of *Slack* v. *Leeds Industrial Co-operative Society* [18] came before Romer J. on an application by the plaintiff for an injunction restraining the defendants from carrying out their admitted intention of erecting a building which would be an infringement of the plaintiff's ancient lights. Romer J. held that the infringement of the plaintiff's rights would be small, and could be adequately compensated by damages; but conceiving himself to be bound by *Dreyfus* v. *Peruvian Guano Co.*, [19] he decided that he had no jurisdiction to grant damages in lieu of an injunction; and the Court of Appeal (Lord Sterndale M.R. and Warrington L.J.; Younger L.J. dissenting) held that his decision was right. The House of Lords [20] (Lord Birkenhead, Lord Finlay, and Lord Dunedin; Lord Sumner and Lord Carson dissenting) disapproved of *Dreyfus* v. *Peruvian Guano Co.*, [21] reversed the decisions of Romer J. and of the Court of Appeal, and decided that the court has jurisdiction to award damages in lieu of an injunction in the case of an injury which is merely threatened. On the case being remitted to the Court of Appeal it was held that, as there was evidence to support the findings of Romer J., the injunction granted by him (contrary to his own inclination) should be discharged and an inquiry ordered as to damages. [22]

---

[15] (1889) 43 Ch.D. 316.
[16] [1894] 1 Ch. 276.
[17] [1919] 1 Ch. 407.
[18] [1923] 1 Ch. 431.
[19] (1889) 43 Ch.D. 316.
[20] *Sub nom. Leeds Industrial Co-operative Society* v. *Slack* [1924] A.C. 851.
[21] *Supra.*
[22] [1924] 2 Ch. 475.

The decision of the House of Lords has, of course, determined once and for all the question that the jurisdiction exists, but the question as to the circumstances in which the jurisdiction should be exercised is quite another matter. On that point the words of Sir George Jessel in *Krehl* v. *Burrell*,[23] quoted above, should be borne in mind: so also should the words of Lindley L.J. in *Shelfer* v. *City of London Electric Lighting Co.*,[24] where he said:

> "Ever since Lord Cairns' Act was passed the Court of Chancery has repudiated the notion that the Legislature intended to turn that Court into a tribunal for legalizing wrongful acts; or in other words, the Court has always protested against the notion that it ought to allow a wrong to continue simply because the wrong-doer is able and willing to pay for the injury which he may inflict ";

and so again should the words of Buckley J. in *Cowper* v. *Laidler*[25]:

> "The Court has affirmed over and over again that the jurisdiction to give damages where it exists is not so to be used as in fact to enable the defendant [in an action for disturbance of an easement] to purchase from the plaintiff against his will his legal right to the easement."

As Lord Finlay said in *Leeds Industrial Co-operative Society* v. *Slack*[26]:

> "these passages bring out very clearly the scope of the Act and the care taken to prevent abuse of its powers."

Disregard of them and of other such dicta would lead up to a practice under which the court would, as Lord Sumner said in the same case,[27]

> "fix the price at which an intending tortfeasor should be judicially licensed to violate the rights of another," and would "allow the big man . . . to have his way, and to solace the little man for his darkened and stuffy little house by giving him a cheque that he does not ask for."

Since the Judicature Act 1873 each Division of the High Court has had full power, apart from Lord Cairns' Act, to do complete justice by granting either an injunction or damages. It is not now necessary to have recourse to Lord Cairns' Act,[28] for the High Court has a much larger power than it had under Lord Cairns' Act.[29]

Should the remedy be injunction or damages?

The appropriateness of the comparative remedies of an injunction or damages was discussed in a long line of cases (chiefly relating to the

---

23 (1878) 7 Ch.D. 551, 555; see p. 389, *ante*.
24 [1895] 1 Ch. 287, 315.
25 [1903] 2 Ch. 337, 341.
26 [1924] A.C. 851, 861.
27 [1924] A.C. 851, 871–872.
28 *Sayers* v. *Collyer* (1884) 28 Ch.D. 108; *Serrao* v. *Noel* (1885) 15 Q.B.D. 559.
29 *Elmore* v. *Pirrie* (1887) 57 L.T. 335.

easement of light), and the effect of many of these cases was thus stated in the eighth edition of this treatise:

Where the defendant has erected or substantially erected his building, either after action brought, or otherwise with notice of the plaintiff's right and in defiance of his protests, the judges have absolutely refused to allow him to compensate the plaintiff with damages, but have forced him to pull down his buildings.[30] But, except for such cases of wilful breach of duty, the courts have declined to fetter their discretion by laying down any absolute rule, and have considered each case upon its own circumstances. The tendency of the earlier decisions[31] was to award damages in preference to a mandatory injunction whenever the injury to the plaintiff could be reasonably estimated in money—whenever, in fact, the injury was not " irreparable " except by the restoration of the status quo ante. But, at a later period, the inclination of the judges was to exercise the discretion only in cases where the damage to the plaintiff, although not so trifling as to exclude the jurisdiction altogether, was yet small in amount and capable of being amply compensated by a money payment, or when there were special circumstances which would make it oppressive to grant an injunction.[32] It seems also that damages might be awarded even for injury done after the issue of the writ,[33] and possibly for injury which may be expected to accrue after judgment.[34]

The cases before Colls v. Home and Colonial Stores[35] had laid down the following principles to guide the court in the exercise of its discretion whether to grant an injunction or to award damages:

Where a legal right has been established, the plaintiff is prima facie entitled to an injunction[36]; and in cases of continuing actionable nuisance the jurisdiction to award damages ought only to be exercised in very exceptional circumstances.

In Shelfer v. City of London Electric Lighting Co.[37] an injunction was granted to restrain a continuing nuisance by noise and vibration.

---

[30] Smith v. Smith (1875) L.R. 20 Eq. 500; Gaskin v. Balls (1879) 13 Ch.D. 324; Greenwood v. Hornsey (1886) 33 Ch.D. 471; Lawrence v. Horton (1890) 59 L.J.Ch. 440; 38 W.R. 555; Parker v. Stanley (1902) 50 W.R. 282.

[31] Johnson v. Wyatt (1863) 2 De G.J. & S. 18; Isenberg v. East India House Estate Co. (1863) 3 De G.J. & S. 263; Bowes v. Law (1870) L.R. 9 Eq. 636; Ball v. Derby (1874) referred to by Jessel M.R. in Aynsley v. Glover, L.R. 18 Eq. 544, 555, and by Kekewich J. in Dicker v. Popham, Radford & Co., 63 L.T. 379, 381; Stanley of Alderley (Lady) v. Shrewsbury (Earl) (1875) L.R. 19 Eq. 616; National Co. v. Prudential Co. (1877) 6 Ch.D. 757; Holland v. Worley (1884) 26 Ch.D. 578.

[32] Senior v. Pawson (1866) L.R. 3 Eq. 330; Aynsley v. Glover (1874) L.R. 18 Eq. 544; Smith v. Smith (1875) L.R. 20 Eq. 500; Allen v. Ayres [1884] W.N. 242; Dicker v. Popham (1890) 63 L.T. 379; Young v. Star Omnibus Co. (1902) 86 L.T. 41.

[33] Davenport v. Rylands (1865) L.R. 1 Eq. 302; Fritz v. Hobson (1880) 14 Ch.D. 542; Chapman v. Auckland Union Guardians (1889) 23 Q.B.D. 298.

[34] See Dicker v. Popham (1890) 63 L.T. 379.

[35] [1904] A.C. 179.

[36] Martin v. Price [1894] 1 Ch. 285; Shelfer v. City of London Electric Lighting Co. [1895] 1 Ch. 287; Jordeson v. Sutton, Southcoates and Drypool Gas Co. [1899] 2 Ch. 217. See Cowper v. Laidler [1903] 2 Ch. 337, 341.

[37] [1895] 1 Ch. 287.

It was a case where damages would have been an entirely inadequate remedy.[38]   In the course of his judgment, Lindley L.J. said [39]:

" Without denying the jurisdiction to award damages instead of an injunction, even in cases of continuing actionable nuisances, such jurisdiction ought not to be exercised in such cases except under very exceptional circumstances. I will not attempt to specify them, or to lay down rules for the exercise of judicial discretion. It is sufficient to refer, by way of example, to trivial and occasional nuisances: cases in which a plaintiff has shewn that he only wants money; vexatious and oppressive cases; and cases where the plaintiff has so conducted himself as to render it unjust to grant him more than pecuniary relief. In all such cases as these, and in all others where an action for damages is really an adequate remedy—as where the acts complained of are already finished—an injunction can be properly refused."

In the same case, however, A. L. Smith L.J., in the course of his judgment, indicated the principles which, in his opinion, should guide the court in the exercise of its discretion. His observations, which were *obiter dicta*,[40] were as follows [41]:

" Many judges have stated, and I emphatically agree with them, that a person by committing a wrongful act . . . is not thereby entitled to ask the Court to sanction his doing so by purchasing his neighbour's rights, by assessing damages in that behalf, leaving his neighbour with the nuisance, or his lights dimmed, as the case may be.

" In such cases the well-known rule is not to accede to the application, but to grant the injunction sought, for the plaintiff's legal right has been invaded, and he is prima facie entitled to an injunction."

The Lord Justice, after pointing out that there were cases in which this rule might be relaxed, and in which damages might be awarded in substitution for an injunction, and mentioning that a plaintiff might by his acts or laches disentitle himself, continued as follows:

" In my opinion it may be stated as a good working rule that—
(1) If the injury to the plaintiff's legal rights is small,
(2) And is one which is capable of being estimated in money,
(3) And is one which can be adequately compensated by a small money payment,
(4) And the case is one in which it would be oppressive to the defendant to grant an injunction;

then damages in substitution for an injunction may be given.

---

38 See *Fishenden* v. *Higgs and Hill Ltd.* (1935) 153 L.T. 128, 144, *per* Maugham L.J.
39 [1895] 1 Ch. 316, 317. *Cf. Colls* v. *Home and Colonial Stores* [1904] A.C. 179, 212.
40 See *Fishenden* v. *Higgs and Hill Ltd.* (1935) 153 L.T. 128, 144.
41 [1895] 1 Ch. 322–323.

" There may also be cases in which, though the four above-mentioned requirements exist, the defendant by his conduct, as, for instance, hurrying up his buildings so as if possible to avoid an injunction, or otherwise acting with a reckless disregard to the plaintiff's rights, has disentitled himself from asking that damages may be assessed in substitution for an injunction.

" It is impossible to lay down any rule as to what, under the differing circumstances of each case, constitutes either a small injury, or one that can be estimated in money, or what is a small money payment, or an adequate compensation, or what would be oppressive to the defendant."

It would seem that, when this frequently quoted " working rule " is read in its proper context, A. L. Smith L.J. did not really differ from Lindley L.J. and that, although he went further than Lindley L.J. in formulating principles to guide the court in subsequent cases, he was anxious so to express himself as not to fetter the court in the exercise of its discretion.

In *Colls* v. *Home and Colonial Stores* [42] the rule to be followed by the court in granting damages or an injunction where the easement of light is in question was laid down by Lord Macnaghten as follows:

" In some cases, of course, an injunction is necessary—if, for instance, the injury cannot fairly be compensated by money—if the defendant has acted in a high-handed manner—if he has endeavoured to steal a march upon the plaintiff or to evade the jurisdiction of the Court. . . . But if there is really a question as to whether the obstruction is legal or not, and if the defendant has acted fairly and not in an unneighbourly spirit, I am disposed to think that the Court ought to incline to damages rather than an injunction. It is quite true that a man ought not to be compelled to part with his property against his will, or to have the value of his property diminished, without an Act of Parliament. On the other hand, the Court ought to be very careful not to allow an action for the protection of ancient lights to be used as a means of extorting money."

In *Kine* v. *Jolly* [43] Cozens-Hardy L.J. said that the tendency of the speeches in *Colls* v. *Home and Colonial Stores* [44] was to go a little further than was done in *Shelfer* v. *City of London Electric Lighting Co.* [45] and to indicate that, as a general rule, the court ought to be " less free in granting mandatory injunctions than it was in years gone by." Nevertheless in *Slack* v. *Leeds Industrial Co-operative Society* [46] the " good working rule " was applied by the Court of Appeal, and again,

[42] [1904] A.C. 179, 193.   [43] [1905] 1 Ch. 496, 504.
[44] [1904] A.C. 179.
[45] [1895] 1 Ch. 287.
[46] [1924] 2 Ch. 475.   The case had been remitted to the Court of Appeal by the House of Lords, who had decided by a majority that the court had jurisdiction to award damages in lieu of an injunction in a *quia timet* action. See p. 389, *ante*.

in *Price* v. *Hilditch*,[47] Maugham J. declined to grant a mandatory injunction and ordered an inquiry as to damages.

In *Fishenden* v. *Higgs and Hill Ltd*.[48] the scope of the " good working rule " was fully considered by Crossman J. and the Court of Appeal (Lord Hanworth M.R., Romer and Maugham L.JJ.). Crossman J. found as a fact, and the Court of Appeal agreed with him, that a building which was being erected by the defendants would, when completed, cause a nuisance by interference with the plaintiffs' ancient lights. Crossman J., after reviewing the authorities, came to the conclusion that the " good working rule " obliged him to grant an injunction unless all the conditions mentioned by A. L. Smith L.J. existed. He treated the " good working rule " as a rule which had to be applied in its entirety in every case and decided that in the case before him, the " good working rule " had not been complied with because (a) he was not satisfied that the injury to the plaintiffs' rights was small within the meaning of the rule; (b) he could not say that it was capable of being estimated in money; (c) he did not think it was capable of being compensated by a small money payment; and (d) he did not think the case was one where it would be oppressive to the defendants to grant an injunction.

The Court of Appeal refused to treat the *Shelfer* case[49] as laying down any inflexible rule which might hamper the court in the exercise of its discretion. Lord Hanworth M.R.,[50] after referring to a number of authorities, including the speeches of Lords Macnaghten and Lindley in *Colls* v. *Home and Colonial Stores*[1] and the judgments of Vaughan Williams and Cozens-Hardy L.JJ., in *Kine* v. *Jolly*,[2] said:

> " It seems to me, therefore, that those rules in the *Shelfer* case[49] must now be taken with the concomitant passages to which I have referred in later cases, in *Colls*[1] and in *Kine* v. *Jolly*,[2] and that we ought to incline against an injunction if possible."

Romer L.J. said[3]:

> " Where the four conditions enunciated by A. L. Smith L.J. are fulfilled, I do not doubt that a court will grant damages in lieu of an injunction. But it by no means follows that A. L. Smith L.J. intended to say or did say or in fact could say that in all cases in which these four conditions do not prevail, the injunction must be granted; he could not have intended to have fettered the discretion imposed upon the court by Lord Cairns' Act. The fact that he did not do that is apparent, I think, from the judgment of Lindley L.J. in the same case."

47 [1930] 1 Ch. 500.
48 (1935) 153 L.T. 128.
49 [1895] 1 Ch. 287.
50 (1935) 153 L.T. 139.
1 [1904] A.C. 179.
2 [1905] 1 Ch. 480.   3 (1935) 153 L.T. 141.

The Lord Justice then read the passage from the judgment of
Lindley L.J. already quoted and part of the above-quoted observations
of Lord Macnaghten in *Colls* v. *Home and Colonial Stores.*[4]

Maugham L.J.[5] expressed the opinion that the " working rule " was
not a universal or even a sound rule in all cases of injury to light and
said that he agreed with the rule as propounded by Lindley L.J.[6]

Romer L.J. said[7] that in his opinion the case was one where the
interference was small and could be compensated in damages and that
it would be oppressive to grant an injunction. In other words, even if
the " good working rule " was applicable, the plaintiff ought not to
obtain an injunction.

The Court of Appeal refused an injunction and the case was sent
back to the trial judge for damages to be assessed by him. But, in
view of the observations of the Court of Appeal, it seems at best doubtful whether the " good working rule " can be applied to any case where
an alleged injury to lights is in question and that the court has a discretion which should be exercised in the broad principles laid down by
Lindley L.J. in the *Shelfer* case[8] and by Lords Macnaghten and
Lindley in *Colls* v. *Home and Colonial Stores.*[9] Possibly the nearest
approach to a working rule is the explanation of the observations of
A. L. Smith L.J., given by Romer L.J. in *Fishenden* v. *Higgs and Hill
Ltd.*[10]

The non-joinder of a necessary party may make damages the only
remedy which can be given.[11]

(5) *Injunctions in Particular Cases*

The cases in which the remedy by way of injunction has been applied
by the court include cases of (1) interference with rights of light; (2)
interference with rights in respect of air; (3) interference with rights of
way, or with rights of water, or with rights of support.

1. Interference with rights of light

In *Dent* v. *Auction Mart Co.*[12] Page Wood V.-C. referred to earlier
authorities and adopted the form of injunction settled by Lord Cran-

---

4 [1904] A.C. 179, 193.   5 (1935) 153 L.T. 144.
6 [1895] 1 Ch. 316, 317, quoted p. 392, *ante.*   7 (1935) 153 L.T. 142.
8 [1895] 1 Ch. 287, 316–317, *ante*, p. 392.   9 [1904] A.C. 179.
10 (1935) 153 L.T. 141, *ante*, p. 394. In *McGrath* v. *The Munster and Leinster Bank
Ltd.* (1959) 94 I.L.T.R. 110 the dictum of Lord Macnaghten was applied in granting
damages in lieu of an injunction to the plaintiff, a lessee, who sued for an interference with light. In *Mathias* v. *Davies* (1970) 114 S.J. 268 the same dictum was
applied by the Court of Appeal when granting an injunction to restrain an interference with light where the defendant had built in the face of protests from the
plaintiff; Russell L.J. said that there was no arguable case to oppose the injunction
because of the " high-handed manner of the defendant." In *Prow* v. *Chaplin*
(1964) 108 S.J. 463 the interference with the plaintiffs' light would have been
estimable in money, but Widgery J. granted an injunction because the plaintiffs had
protested and it would be unfair to force them to move from their house.
11 *Barnes* v. *Allen* [1927] W.N. 217.
12 (1866) L.R. 2 Eq. 238.

worth in 1866 in *Yates* v. *Jack*.[13] This order (the form of which was followed until 1904) restrained the defendant

> " from erecting any building so as to darken, injure, or obstruct any of the ancient lights of the Plaintiffs as the same were enjoyed previously to the taking down by the Defendant of his buildings on the opposite side of the street, and also from permitting to remain any buildings already erected which will cause any such obstruction."

Lord Cranworth, in the same case, following *Stokes* v. *City Offices Co.*,[14] added a proviso enabling the parties to come before the chief clerk in order to have it ascertained whether any proposed addition to the building would or would not be a violation of the injunction; but this proviso was not inserted as a matter of course in subsequent orders.

Since it was definitely laid down in *Colls* v. *Home and Colonial Stores* [15] that the easement of light confers only the " right to be protected against a particular form of nuisance," and not the right to the whole of the light as it was previously enjoyed, the form of the order in *Yates* v. *Jack* [16] is not appropriate as it stood. It was disapproved as a common form order in *Colls'* case,[17] and suggestions for an alteration in the form of order were made by Lord Macnaghten [18]:

> " The common form of injunction which has been in use since the case of *Yates* v. *Jack* [16] is not, I think, altogether free from objection. I think it would be better that the order, when expressed in general terms, should restrain the defendant from erecting any building so as to cause a nuisance or illegal obstruction to the plaintiff's ancient windows, as the same existed previously to the taking down of the house which formerly stood on the site of the defendant's new buildings. If the action is brought to a hearing before the defendant's new buildings are completed, and there seems to be good ground for the plaintiff's apprehensions, an order, I think, might be conveniently made in that form with costs up to the hearing, and liberty to the plaintiff within a fixed time after completion to apply for further relief by way of mandatory injunction or damages, as he may be advised."

In *Anderson* v. *Francis*,[19] Swinfen Eady J. followed the above suggestions of Lord Macnaghten, and the form so suggested has now been adopted as the common form order.[20]

---

13 (1866) 1 Ch.App. 295; *ante*, p. 242.
14 (1865) 2 H. & M. 650.
15 [1904] A.C. 179.
16 (1866) 1 Ch.App. 295.
17 [1904] A.C. 193, *per* Lord Macnaghten; *per* Lord Davey 201; *per* Lord Lindley 207.
18 [1904] A.C. 193–194.
19 [1906] W.N. 160.
20 See the orders made in *Higgins* v. *Betts* [1905] 2 Ch. 217; *Andrews* v. *Waite* [1907] 2 Ch. 500, 510; and *Vere* v. *Minter* [1914] W.N. 89. Other forms of injunctions dealing with the obstruction of ancient lights are given in Seton (7th ed.), pp. 553 *et seq.*

Reference to experts

There are cases [21] where the court, after deciding that there is an obstruction to be restrained, has, by consent of the parties, referred it to a surveyor to say what alteration will be sufficient to remedy the obstruction. Thus, in *Abbott* v. *Holloway*,[22] an order was by consent made to refer it to an independent surveyor to determine whether the erection of the defendants' buildings, having regard to the increased height thereof, would depreciate to any and what extent the value of the plaintiffs' premises; the defendants to pay to the plaintiffs the sum (if any) so determined; the surveyor to be agreed upon by the parties, or in default to be appointed by the judge and his fees to be borne by the parties equally; the defendants to pay the plaintiffs' taxed costs of the action; the surveyor not to be attended by anyone on behalf of the parties, or to take evidence.

It was said not to be the practice of the court on interlocutory motion to appoint an expert to report to the court at the trial of the action.[23]

In *Colls* v. *Home and Colonial Stores*,[24] Lord Macnaghten made the following observations [25]:

" It will be observed that in *Back* v. *Stacey* [26] the learned judge told the jury who had viewed the premises that they were to judge rather from their own ocular observation than from the testimony of any witnesses, however respectable, of the degree of diminution which the plaintiffs' ancient light had undergone. Now a judge who exercises the functions of both judge and jury cannot be expected to view the premises himself, even if he considers himself an expert in such matters. But I have often wondered why the Court does not more frequently avail itself of the power of calling in a competent adviser to report to the Court upon the question. There are plenty of experienced surveyors accustomed to deal with large properties in London who might be trusted to make a perfectly fair and impartial report, subject,

---

[21] *Jessel* v. *Chaplin* (1856) 2 Jur.(N.S.) 931; *Att.-Gen.* v. *Merthyr Tydfil Local Board of Health* [1870] W.N. 148; but see *Att.-Gen.* v. *Colney Hatch Lunatic Asylum* (1868) 4 Ch.App. 146.

[22] [1904] W.N. 124.

[23] *Stokes* v. *City Offices Co.* (1865) 13 W.R. 537; *Baltic Co.* v. *Simpson* (1876) 24 W.R. 390, where Jessel M.R. pointed out that in *Kelk* v. *Pearson* (1871) 6 Ch.App. 809, the motion was treated as the hearing, and said that this was probably so in *Cartwright* v. *Last* [1876] W.N. 60. The order in the last-mentioned case was made upon motion, but concluded: " and it is ordered that the further hearing of the said motion do stand over until after such report as aforesaid shall have been made, when any of the parties are to be at liberty to apply to have this action disposed of, and at such further hearing of the said motion, or hearing of the said action, both parties are to be at liberty to examine the said referee viva voce." See *Leech* v. *Schweder* (1874) 9 Ch.App. 463, where at the trial a surveyor was appointed to report; and see R.S.C., Ord. 29, rr. 2, 3; Ord. 33, r. 16.

[24] [1904] A.C. 179.

[25] [1904] A.C. 192. See also *Fishenden* v. *Higgs & Hill* (1935) 153 L.T. 128, 144, *per* Maugham L.J.

[26] (1826) 2 C. & P. 465.

of course, to examination in Court if required. I am not in the least surprised that the plaintiffs in the present case objected to a report from a disinterested surveyor, but in my opinion the Court ought to have obtained such a report for its own guidance."

It has been doubted whether a judge should himself visit the premises in question and use his own senses to ascertain whether an injury has been committed; for he may be mistaken, and it is his duty to decide on sworn evidence.[27] He is, however, expressly authorised by R.S.C., Ord. 35, r. 8, to inspect the premises.[28]

2. Interference with rights in respect of air

It is improper in injunctions to restrain interference with rights of light to couple as a general rule injunctions to restrain interference with rights of air. For an injunction to protect air is not granted unless a separate case be made for it.[29] Where, however, a separate case is made in respect of air, injunctions have been granted by the courts.[30]

3. Interference with rights of way, water or support

Forms of injunctions against interference with rights of way will be found in Seton (7th ed.), p. 574; against interference with a party's rights in respect of the flow or user of water, Seton, p. 582; and in respect of his right to purity of water, Seton, p. 605. Forms of injunctions against interference with the right of support are given in Seton, 7th ed., p. 565.

---

[27] *Jackson* v. *Newcastle (Duke)* (1864) 3 De G.J. & S. 275; *Leech* v. *Schweder* (1874) 22 W.R. 292. In *Ough* v. *King* [1967] 1 W.L.R. 1547, 1552, Lord Denning M.R. said it was helpful for the judge to have a view in light cases.

[28] See *Buckingham* v. *Daily News Ltd.* [1956] 2 Q.B. 534; *Kine* v. *Jolly* [1905] 1 Ch. 480, 499.

[29] See *ante*, p. 256.

[30] *Chastey* v. *Ackland* [1895] 2 Ch. 391, 392; *Cable* v. *Bryant* [1908] 1 Ch. 260; *Dent* v. *Auction Mart Co.* (1866) L.R. 2 Eq. 238, 255.

INDEX

ABANDONMENT. *See* EXTINGUISHMENT OF EASEMENTS.

ABATEMENT, 356–361.
apprehended injury, whether justifies, 360–361
care required in, 358.
court proceedings, after, 359–360.
damages, does not destroy right to, 360.
disposal of material after, 359.
effect of, 360.
law does not favour, 359.
light, in the case of, 357.
notice, whether necessary to give, 357–358.
watercourses, in the case of, 357.
ways, in the case of, 356–357.

ACQUIESCENCE,
equitable easements arising from, 61–67. *See also* EQUITABLE EASEMENTS.
in interruption, under Prescription Act, 153–154, 173–174

ACQUISITION OF EASEMENTS.
See also GENERAL WORDS; GRANT; GRANTEE; GRANTOR; PRESCRIPTION; RESERVATION.
agreement, in equity. *See also* EQUITABLE EASEMENTS.
actual, 61, 67–69
imputed, 61–67
enfranchisement, by, 76
implication, by, 82–122
common intention, from, 86–88, 108–110
continuous and apparent. *See* Wheeldon v. Burrows, RULE IN.
description in parcels, from, 84–86
estoppel, arising by, 85
lease, on grant of, 112–117
necessity. *See* NECESSITY, EASEMENTS OF.
reciprocal right, 106–107
reservation, 106–110. *See* RESERVATION.
simultaneous dispositions, on, 110–112
special circumstances, from, 86–88
special immunities. *See* DEROGATION FROM GRANT.
summary of, 82–83
inter partes, 76–82
prescription, by. *See* PRESCRIPTION.
public bodies, by, 76
registration, by, 76
statute, by, 75–76
will, by, 61, 82, 111

ACTIONS. *See also* INJUNCTION; PARTIES TO ACTION FOR DISTURBANCE.
county court, in, 361
damages,
in lieu of injunction, 388–395
undertaking as to, 387
dominant tenement, whether title must be proved, 361–362
easement, whether title must be proved to, 373–374
High Court, in, 361
parties to, 361–373. *See also* PARTIES TO ACTION FOR DISTURBANCE.
pleadings, 374–380. *See also* PLEADINGS.
who may be sued, 369–373.
creator of disturbance, 369
landlord and tenant, 369–370
liability for contractor, 371–373
occupiers, 369
who may sue, 361–369
occupiers, 362–363, 370–371
reversioners, 363–369

ADVERTISEMENTS,
right to post, 19 n., 20, 34, 108–110
implication, whether arising by, 108–110

AGREEMENT,
construed as grant, 23
equitable easements arising from. *See also* EQUITABLE EASEMENTS.
actual, 61, 67–69, 83, 112
imputed, 61–67

AIR, 256–260
chimney, passage of, to, 258
custom of London may not apply to, 260
defined aperture or channel, through, 258–259
general flow of, no right to, 25–26, 256–258
light, distinguished from, 256
necessity, arising by, 121–122
non-derogation from grant, doctrine of, arising by, 259–260
pollution of, natural right to prevent, 260
right to, possibly rests on implied covenant, 23–24
windmill, passage of, to, 256–258

ALTERATION OF DOMINANT TENEMENT,
effect of, 57, 58, 266–269, 274–282, 320–337, 347

ANCILLARY EASEMENTS, 44–45
disturbance of, 355
electric lines, support for, 44
enter and repair, right to, 44–45
interference with, 45
included where necessary, 44

399

ANCILLARY EASEMENTS—*cont.*
sheep, water troughs for, 44
vehicles, right to halt, 44 n.

ARTIFICIAL WATERCOURSE, 223–229
permanent, 224–225
prescriptive rights may be acquired in, 224
rights in may be equivalent to natural rights, 224–225
right to receive, whether, 53–55, 222, 224–229
rights in, basis of, 223–224
temporary, 225–229
no prescriptive right to receive, 225–229
" temporary purpose," meaning of, 229

ASSENT,
easement, of, giving effect to devise, 61, 82, 112

BANKS,
separating fields, ownership of, 304

BOUNDARY,
branches overhanging, 305
building projecting over, 306
fields separated by ditch, 304
Ordinance Survey Map, presumption as to, 304
roots encroaching beyond, 305–306
trees encroaching beyond, 304–305

BRINE PUMPING,
whether actionable, 213, 288–289

BUILDING. *See also* SUPPORT, RIGHT OF.
projecting over boundary, 306
pulling down, effect on easement, 58
support for,
adjoining land, by, 290–300
another building, by, 300–301

BURIAL,
right of, 14–15

BUSINESS PURPOSES. *See also* ADVERTISEMENTS.
whether easement may be acquired for, 19, 20

CANAL,
right to use, whether easement, 19

CHANNEL FOR WATERCOURSE,
defined and known in order to give right, must be, 209–214

CHICKEN COOPS,
right to keep, 32

CHURCH LAND,
easements, granted over, 77
prescription against, 167

COALSHED,
right to use, as easement, 33, 126–127

COMMON LAW,
prescription at, 133–137, 162–163
absolute owner, enjoyment must be against, 162–163
length of time for, 133–136
presumption from long enjoyment, 133–134
statutes of limitation, effect of, 134–136
time of legal memory, 133
unity of possession, effect of, 136–137

CONTRACT,
easements implied in, 83, 95–96, 98–99, 111–112
equitable easements arising from, 61, 67–69, 83, 112. *See also* EQUITABLE EASEMENTS.

CONVEYANCE,
dominant tenement, of, easements pass on, 4, 8
general words in. *See* GENERAL WORDS.
servient tenement, of, subject to easements, 4

COPYHOLDER,
grazing by, not reputed rights, 129
prescription by, 21

CORPORATION,
power of, to grant easements, 76
prescription against, 167–169
[prescription] by, 169

COST,
repair and maintenance, of. *See* REPAIR.

COVENANT. *See also* RESTRICTIVE COVENANT.
grant, operating as, 23
rent for easement, to pay, 49
repair of servient tenement, for,
dominant owner, by, 46–47
servient owner, by, 48–49

CREATION OF EASEMENTS. *See* ACQUISITION OF EASEMENTS.

CUSTOM,
prescription must not be contrary to, 189–190

DAMAGES. *See* ACTIONS; INJUNCTION.

DEED,
easement, creation of, by, 61, 79
profit à prendre, creation of, by, 69

DEROGATION FROM GRANT,
rule against, 43, 88–92, 259–260
air, in case of, 259–260
physical interference, not confined to, 90
restrictive covenants, compared with, 89, 90–91
rights may be wider than easements, 89

DEVISE,
   easement, creation of, by, 61, 82,
   111

DISTURBANCE OF EASEMENTS, 351–355.
   See also PARTIES TO ACTION FOR
   DISTURBANCE.
   action for, and for nuisance, distinguished, 351
   light, right to, 354–355. *See also*
   LIGHT, RIGHT TO.
   remedies for. *See* ABATEMENT;
   ACTIONS; INJUNCTION.
   right of repair, 45
   secondary easements, 355
   sensible diminution of enjoyment,
   must be, 351–352
   threats of injury are not, 360–361
   watercourses, 352
   way, rights of, 352–354
      gates across, 353–354

DITCHES,
   separating fields, ownership of, 304

DIVERSION OF STREAM. *See also*
   ARTIFICIAL WATERCOURSE; WATER
   RESOURCES ACT 1963.
   acquisition of right to, 218–219
   first occupant acquires no right to,
   207–208
   increase in, 57
   qualified, may be, 37
   servient owner cannot insist on, 55,
   218
   undefined underground channel, not
   actionable in case of, 210–214
   unreasonable user, may be, 201–203,
   204

DOMINANT OWNER,
   entitled to repair, 44–45
   need not use easement, 53–55
   not bound to repair, 45
      except to prevent nuisance, 45–46
   stipulation for repair by, effect of,
   46–47

DOMINANT TENEMENT. *See also* ALTER-
   ATION OF DOMINANT TENEMENT.
   accommodated, must be, 16–20
   alteration of, 57, 58
   contiguous with servient tenement,
   need not be, 20
   conveyance of, easements pass on,
   4, 8
   corporeal and incorporeal hereditaments, may consist of, 14
   easement cannot be separated from,
   8
   enjoyment of, alteration in, 57, 58,
   266–269
   extrinsic evidence of, 8–12
   identification of, 8–13
   incorporeal hereditament, whether
   capable of being, 13–14
   minerals as, 13–14
   necessity of, 7–8
   pipes as, 14
   registration of, includes easements,
   193

DRAIN. *See also* PIPE.
   dominant owner, not obliged to use,
   53–55

EASEMENTS,
   acquisition of. *See also* ACQUISITION
   OF EASEMENTS; DEROGATION
   FROM GRANT; PRESCRIPTION.
   agreement, in equity, 61–69. *See
   also* EQUITABLE EASEMENTS.
   general words, by. *See* GENERAL
   WORDS.
   implied grant, by. *See* WHEELDON
   v. BURROWS, RULE IN.
   statute, by, 75–76
   will, by, 61
   ancillary, 44–45. *See also* ANCIL-
   LARY EASEMENTS.
   appurtenant to land, must be, 7, 8,
   61
   characteristics, essential, of, 6–34
      1. Must be a dominant and a
      servient tenement, 7–16
      2. Easement must accommodate
      the dominant tentment, 16–20
      3. Dominant and servient owners
      must be different, 20–22
      4. Easement must be a right cap-
      able of being granted, 22–34,
      127, 128
      general flow of air, 25–26
      jus spatiandi, 27–29
      negative rights, 23–25
      positive rights, 22–23
      prospect and privacy, 26
      protection from weather, 25, 26–
      27
      recreation and amusement, 29–
      30
      usurpation or sharing of posses-
      sion, 30–34
   class of, not closed, 34
   creation of. *See* ACQUISITION OF
   EASEMENTS.
   deed necessary for grant of, 61, 79
   definition of, 3, 4, 5
   disturbance of. *See also* DISTUR-
   BANCE OF EASEMENTS.
   remedies for, 356–398. *See also*
   REMEDIES.
   what amounts to, 351–355
   dominant tenement. *See also*
   DOMINANT TENEMENT.
   cannot be separated from, 8
   must accomodate, 16–20
   equitable. *See* EQUITABLE EASE-
   MENTS.
   examples of, 35–37. *See also* AIR;
   LIGHT, RIGHT TO; SUPPORT, RIGHT
   OF; WATER; WATERCOURSE; WAY,
   RIGHTS OF.
   exclusive use of land, contrasted
   with, 5
   extent of, 57–59. *See also* WAY,
   RIGHTS OF.

EASEMENTS—*cont.*
　extinguishment of. *See* EXTINGUISH-
　　MENT OF EASEMENTS.
　fencing, 37–42. *See also* FENCES.
　grant of, 79–81
　incidents of, 43–55. *See also* INCI-
　　DENTS OF EASEMENTS.
　in common, 37
　in gross, cannot exist, 7, 8
　　ways, possible exception, 42–43
　mode of enjoyment of, 57–59. *See
　　also* WAY, RIGHTS OF.
　natural rights, distinguished from,
　　3–4
　negative. *See* NEGATIVE EASEMENTS.
　persons entitled to use, 8, 282–284
　positive. *See* POSITIVE EASEMENTS.
　possessory rights, contrasted with, 5
　profits à prendre, contrasted with, 4
　purchasers without notice, enforce-
　　able against, 4, 25, 113
　qualified, 37
　registered land. *See* LAND REGISTRA-
　　TION ACT 1925.
　rent for, 49
　reservation of, 80–81
　restrictive covenants, distinguished
　　from, 25
　rights analogous to, 37–43
　　duty to repair fences, 37–42
　　non-derogation from grant, 43
　　ways in gross, 42–43
　rule against perpetuities and, 49–53
　user of, purpose of, 8. *See also* WAY,
　　RIGHTS OF.
　vague grant of, 25–27
　who may use, 8, 282–284
　will, creation by, 61, 82, 111

EAVESDROP,
　extinguishment of, 323
　prescriptive right of, 222–223

EQUITABLE EASEMENTS, 61–72
　acquiescence, arising from, 61–67
　actual agreement, arising from, 61,
　　67–69, 83, 112
　devolution of, 69–72
　　registered land, in, 71–72
　dominant tenement, run with, 69
　estoppel, arising by, 65
　mutual benefit and burden, arising
　　by, 65
　purchaser for value without notice,
　　not binding on, 69–70, 79
　registrable, whether, 70–72

ESTOPPEL. *See also* EQUITABLE EASE-
　MENTS; GRANTOR.
　description in parcels, arising from,
　85

EXCESSIVE USER, 57–58, 286, 346–347

EXTENT OF EASEMENTS, 57–59. *See also*
　WAY, RIGHTS OF.

EXTINGUISHMENT OF EASEMENTS, 309–
　347
　1. By operation of law, 309–313
　　unity of ownership of absolute
　　　interests, 309–311
　　　severance, effect of, 311–312
　2. By statute, 314–315
　3. By express release, 316
　4. By implied release, 316–347
　　cessation or alteration of user,
　　　from, 316–347
　　　continuous easements, 318–337
　　　discontinuous easements, 337–
　　　　347
　　licence to obstruct, from, 316
　alteration of dominant tenement, by,
　　320–337, 347
　continuous easements, 318–337
　　alteration of user, 320–325
　　cessation of user, 318–320
　discontinuous easements, 337–347
　　cessation of user, 337–344
　　excessive user, effect of, 346–347
　intention to abandon, 318–319, 342–
　　344
　　onus of proving, 319–320
　light, right to, 318–320, 324, 325–
　　336
　pollute, right to, 342–343, 347
　Prescription Act, effect of, 345–346
　support, right of, 324
　way, rights of, 338–342, 343–344,
　　346–347

FASCIA,
　adjoining building, may be a part of,
　34

FENCES,
　obligation to repair, 37–42
　　Law of Property Act, s. 62, may
　　　arise under, 40–42
　　prescription, arises by, 38, 39, 40
　　whether capable of being granted,
　　　40–42

FLUE,
　right to use, 69–70, 108

FORESHORE,
　easement over, 32

FRAUDS, STATUTE OF,
　agreement for easement, applies to, 68

GARDEN,
　right to use, whether easement, 6–7,
　　16–19, 27, 28

GATE,
　easement to open, 19
　obligation to close, whether, 354
　right of way, whether disturbance
　　of, 353–354

GENERAL WORDS,
　disposition of registered land, apply
　　on, 194

GENERAL WORDS—*cont.*
grant of easement by, 40–42, 122–132
Law of Property Act 1925, s. 62 . . ., 122–132
continuous and apparent quasi-easements, whether limited to, 125–126
contrary intention, 130–131
" conveyance," meaning of, 95, 123, 126
definitions of terms in, 123–124
diversity of occupation, whether necessary, 125–126
" enjoyed with," meaning of, 125, 128
" land," meaning of, 123
legal grant, must be capable of, 128
permissive user, includes, 126–128
rectification, 131–132
reputed rights, 129
tenant, conveyance to, 126
reservation, by, 80–81

GRANT. *See also* DEROGATION FROM GRANT; EASEMENTS; GRANTEE; GRANTOR; RESERVATION.
construction of, 58. *See also* WAY, RIGHTS OF.
doctrine of lost. *See* LOST GRANT, DOCTRINE OF.
easement must be susceptible of, 22–34, 127, 128
inter vivos, 79–81
easement, of,
covenant or agreement may operate as, 23
deed necessary, 61, 79
implied. *See* ACQUISITION OF EASEMENTS.
light and air, of, possibly rests on implied covenant, 23–24
rights of way, of. *See* WAY, RIGHTS OF.
water, rights in, of, 235–236
wide and vague rights, of, 25–27
will, by, 82
words of limitation not necessary for, 80

GRANTEE,
competent, who is, 79
for prescription purposes, 169–170
equitable owner, 79
lessee, 79
Settled Land Act 1925, under, 79

GRANTOR,
church land, over, 77
commoners, 77
competent, who is, 76–79
contract to sell servient land, whether bound by, 78–79, 111–112
corporation, 76
estoppel, bound by, 78
incompetent, for prescription purposes, 167–169
lessee, 78
mortgagee, 76
personal representatives, 77

GRANTOR—*cont.*
Settled Land Act 1925, under, 77
trustees for sale, 77
vendor of servient land, 78–79

HEDGES,
separating fields, ownership of, 304

HOUSE. *See* BUILDING.

IMPLICATION, CREATION OF EASEMENTS BY. *See* ACQUISITION OF EASEMENTS; DEROGATION FROM GRANT; *Wheeldon* v. *Burrows*, RULE IN.

INCIDENTS OF EASEMENTS, 43–55. *See also* ANCILLARY EASEMENTS; REPAIR.
ancillary rights, 44–45
repair, right of dominant owner to, 44–45
dominant owner not bound to use easement, 53–55
Limitation Act, 43
perpetuities, rule against, 49–53
rent, payment of, 49
repair, obligation to,
dominant owner, 45–47
servient owner, 47–49
way, rights of. *See* WAY, RIGHTS OF.

INCORPOREAL HEREDITAMENT,
dominant tenement, as, 13–14

INFANT,
disability of, under Prescription Act, 156

INJUNCTION, 380–398
damages in lieu of, 388–395
delay, effect of, 388
forms of, 395–398
interlocutory, 386–387
buildings, undertaking to pull down, 387
undertaking as to damages, 387
mandatory, 382–383
delay or acquiescence, may be barred by, 383
discretionary, 383
interlocutory motion, may be granted on, 382, 387
quia, timet, 383–386
perpetual, 380–382
cost to defendant, not a consideration, 381
damage, proof of, unnecessary, 381
dominant owner entitled to, as of course, 381
powers of Court, 380
quia, timet, 383–386
apprehended injury, in case of, 384
further injury, to prevent, 384–386
tenant for years may obtain, 362

INTERFERENCE WITH EASEMENTS. *See* DISTURBANCE OF EASEMENTS.

IRRIGATION,
whether lawful user of water, 204–206

Jus Spatiandi, 27–29

Kitchen,
    right to use, as easement, 31

Land Charges Act 1925,
    contract to sell servient land, regis-
        tration under, 78–79
    registration of equitable rights
        under, 70–72

Land Registration Act 1925. See
    also Equitable Easements.
    creation of easements by registered
        proprietor, 194
    easement, registration of, under, 193
    appurtenant to registered estate,
        must be, 193, 194
    effect of conferring title, 76, 193
    first registration, on, adverse ease-
        ments and profits should be noted,
        196
    general words apply on disposition,
        194
    implied grant or reservation, no clear
        provision for, 195
    overriding interests, 195–196
        equitable easements, whether, 71–
            72
        legal easements and profits are, 196
        may be noted, 196
    prescription in registered land, 195
    purchaser cannot insist upon registra-
        tion of easement, 194
    registered disposition, easements pass
        on, 194
    registration of equitable rights under,
        71–72
    registration of land under,
        easements acquired by, 76, 193

Lavatory,
    right to use, as easement, 31

Law of Property Act 1925, s. 62. See
    General Words.

Lease,
    easements implied on grant of, 112–
        117
    easements pass with, 8
    effect of, on forty-year period under
        Prescription Act, 157–159, 160–161
    prescription during currency of, 149,
        157–159, 160–161, 164–165, 166–
        167, 181–186

Lessee. See Tenant for Years.

Lessor. See Reversioner.

Licence, 55–57
    disturbance of, liability for, 19, 56
    executed, 56
    personal, not assignable, 56
    revocable, whether, 56
    river authorities, by, to abstract
        water. See Water Resources
        Act 1963.

Licence—cont.
    stranger, whether liable to grantee
        of, 19, 56
    successor in title, whether binding
        on, 56–57

Light, Right to, 238–255. See also
    Wheeldon v. Burrows; Rights
    of Light Act 1959.
    abatement of obstruction to, 357
    acquisition of. See also Acquisition
        of Easements.
    doctrine of non-derogation, under,
        89, 90–91, 246–247.
    equitable, by agreement, 63, 67
    implication, by, 101–105
    prescription, by, 238–244, 246,
        249–250
    angle of forty-five degrees, rule as to,
        251–252
    not a rule of law, 252
    custom of London, 254–255
    damages in lieu of injunction, 393–
        395
    disturbance of, 354–355
    dominant tenement, future use of,
        taken into account, 248–249
    evidence of diminution in, 253
    experts, reference to, 253, 397–398
    extent of, 240–244, 246, 250–251, 253
    extinguishment of, 318–320, 324, 325–
        336
    extraordinary amount of, no claim
        to, 253–254
    except under doctrine of non-
        derogation, 246–247
    glazed tiles, offer to put in, no de-
        fence, 248
    implied covenant, probably rests on,
        23–24
    increase in, 57
    injunction in case of, 395–398
    locality, court may have regard to,
        247
    measure of, 246, 250–251, 253
    nature and extent of, 253
    nuisance, obstruction to be action-
        able must amount to, 242, 243,
        244, 246, 247, 249–251, 354
    obstruction of, 240–244, 354–355
        light from other sources, effect of,
            247–248, 354–355
        locality, effect of, 247
        nuisance, must amount to, 242,
            243, 244, 246, 247, 249–251, 354
    other sources, court may have re-
        gard to, 247–248, 354–355
    poor, how far protected, 254
    prescriptive, 238–244, 246, 249–250.
        See also Prescription.
        actual user need not be shown,
            240, 248–249
        extent of, 240–244, 246, 249, 250–
            251, 253
        vacant land, cannot be over, 239–
            240
    view of premises, useful for judge
        to have, 253

LIGHT, RIGHT TO—*cont.*
"Waldram" method of measuring diminution, 253
windows,
alterations in, 325–328, 336
decrease in size of, 328–332
increase in size of, 328
plane of, alteration of, 332–336

LIMITATION ACT,
support, withdrawal of, time runs from injury, 290
title acquired under,
does not include implied rights, 43
subject to easements, 43

LORD CAIRNS' ACT, 388–395

LOST GRANT, DOCTRINE OF, 137–143, 163–165
absolute owner, whether enjoyment must be had against, 163–165
application of, 142–143
evidence required to rebut, 138–142
examples of, 142–143
length of time for, 137–143
lessee, enjoyment may be had against, 164–165
objections to, 138
purpose of, 137
support, in the case of, 292–300

LUNATIC,
disability of, under Prescription Act, 156

MAINTENANCE. *See* REPAIR.

MEMORANDUM,
indorsement of, on document of title, 82

MILL,
alteration of, 57, 58
whether watercourse extinguished by, 320–322

MORTGAGEE,
easements, power to grant, 76

NECESSITY, EASEMENTS OF, 117–122
legally necessary, may be, 121–122
reservation, in, 107–108, 117–120
ventilation duct, in case of, 121–122
ways, in case of, 117–121
extent of, decided at time of grant, 119–120
line chosen by grantor, 117
may not survive the necessity, 120–121
meaning of necessity, 118–119
what may be, 107–108, 121–122

NEGATIVE EASEMENTS, 3, 23–25, 34, 35–36
class of, probably now closed, 24–25, 34
examples of, 36–37
implication, arising by, 99–106
support, whether included, 24

NOISE, 186, 191

NUISANCE. *See also* POLLUTION OF WATER.
easement to create, 3, 22, 23, 190–191
arising in equity, 63
legalisation of, by grant, 86–87
prescriptive right to commit, 190–192
examples, 190–191
extent of, must be proved, 191
period of time for, 191
public nuisance, not included in, 191–192

OCCUPIER,
dominant tenement, title to, may not be put to proof of, 361–362
easement, whether title need be proved to, 373–374
liable for continuance of disturbance of easement, 369, 370–371
may sue for disturbance of easement, 362

OVERRIDING INTERESTS. *See* LAND REGISTRATION ACT 1925.

OWNERSHIP,
unity of, 20–22
effect on prescription, 136–137, 147, 148, 188
extinguishment of easements by, 309–313

PARK,
right to use, whether easement, 6–7, 16–19, 27–30

PARKING,
cars, of, whether within statutory general words, 128–129

PARTIES TO ACTION FOR DISTURBANCE, 361–373. *See also* REVERSIONER.
defendant,
contractor, liability for, 371–373
creator of disturbance, 369
landlord and tenant, 369–370
occupier, 369, 370–371
stranger, liability for, 370–371
plaintiff,
dominant tenement, may need to prove title to, 361–362
easement, may not need to prove title to, 373–374
interest of, what is sufficient to sustain action, 361–362
licensee with possession, 362
occupier, 362–363
reversioner, 363–369
successive occupiers or reversioners may sue for continuing disturbance, 369

PARTY-WALLS, 302–304

PERCOLATING WATER, 210–214
no property in, 210–214
rights cannot be acquired in, 219–221
support from, no right of, 288–289

406

PERPETUITIES, RULE AGAINST, 49–53
ancillary rights, may not apply to, 52
Law of Property Act 1925, s. 162...52
Perpetuities and Accumulations Act
1964 applies, 50
PIPE,
diversion of stream by, 202
dominant owner,
repair, may be practically obliged
to, 45–46
repair, no duty to, 45
dominant tenement, as, 14
escape of water from, liability for,
45–46
ownership of, 15–16, 30, 100
prescriptive right to discharge water
from, 222–223
repair, right to, 44–45, 46
interference with, 45
right to use, 15, 16, 30
arising by implication, 99–100, 107,
108
arising in equity, 64, 66
servient tenement, as, 15, 16
soil surrounding, ownership of, 30
support for, 16
PLEADINGS, 374–380
breach of duty, 380
damage, 379
grant, 378
Judicature Acts, under, 376–378
prescription, 154–155, 169, 375–378
Prescription Act, under, 154–155,
375–376, 377, 378
title, allegation of, 374–375
POLLUTION OF WATER, 229–235
alteration in mode of, 58–59
extinguishment of right to, 342–343,
347
increase in, 57
natural rights in respect of, 229–230
prescriptive rights as to, 230–231
public nuisance, cannot justify, 231
trade and sewage effluent, 231
rights as to,
licensees, of, 231–234
prescription, acquired by, 230–231
POSITIVE EASEMENTS, 3, 22–23, 35–36
examples of, 35–36
implication, arising by, 95–99
POSSESSION,
right of exclusive or joint, whether
easement, 30–34
unity of, 22
effect on prescription, 136–137,
147, 148, 188
POSSESSORY RIGHT,
easement is not, 5
PRESCRIPTION. See also COMMON LAW;
LOST GRANT, DOCTRINE OF; PRE-
SCRIPTION ACT.
against whom enjoyment must be
had, 161–169
common law, at, 162–163
incompetent grantors, whether,
167–169

PRESCRIPTION—cont.
against whom enjoyment must be
had—cont.
lost grant, under doctrine of, 163–
165
Prescription Act, under, 149, 165–
167
by whom enjoyment must be had,
169–170
church land, against, 167
copyhold tenant, by, against another
tenant or lord, 21
corporation, against, 167–169
definition of, 133
fence, duty to repair, arising by, 38,
39, 40
grantee, competence of, 169–170
incompetent grantors, against, 167–
169
landlord or tenant of landlord,
against, 21, 149, 162–163, 165, 166,
167
length of time for,
common law, at, 133–137
lost grant, under doctrine of, 137–
143
under Prescription Act, 144–161
modes of, 133
nuisance, legislation of, by. See
NUISANCE.
qualities and character of enjoyment,
170–190
as of right, must be, 170–171, 172–
173
capable of interruption, 186–187
compliance with statute or custom, 189–190
definite and continuous, 188–189
knowledge, actual or constructive,
of servient owner, 171, 175–176,
179–186
nec clam, 171–172, 174–176
nec precario, 171–172, 176–178
nec vi, 171–172, 173–174
under a mistake, 178
registered land, in, 195
unity of possession or ownership,
effect of, 136–137, 147, 148, 188
PRESCRIPTION ACT, 144–161, 165–167
against whom enjoyment must be
had,
forty years' enjoyment, 166–167
light, in the case of, 149
twenty years' enjoyment, 165–166
extinguishment, effect of, 345–346
interruption and acquiescence, 153–
154, 173–174
length of time for prescription under,
144–161
long title and preamble of, 145
purpose and effect of, 144–145, 160–
161
s. 1, profits à prendre, 145, 160
profits in gross, does not apply to,
145n., 155
s. 2, ways and other easements, 146–
147, 160
claim under, how defeated, 147

PRESCRIPTION ACT—*cont.*
s. 2, ways and other easements—*cont.*
length and mode of user, 146–147
light, does not apply to, 146
negative easements, whether applicable to, 146
rights of way and water, not confined to, 146
support, whether applicable to, 296, 297, 298
s. 3, light, 144, 147–152, 161. *See also* RIGHTS OF LIGHT ACT 1959.
" building," meaning of, 147–148, 239
consent or agreement excluding, 149–150, 177
Crown not bound by, 147
enjoyment may be against lessee or limited owner, 149
interruption, 148–149
mode of user, 148
quantum, 148
Rights of Light Act 1959, purpose and effect of, 150–152
user need not be of right, 148
s. 4, computation of time, 144–145, 152–154, 173–174
acquiescence, 154
interruption, 153–154
period immediately preceding the action, 152–153
user throughout period, 153, 173–174
s. 5, pleadings, 154–155, 375–376, 377–378
s. 6, no presumption from less than statutory period, 155
s. 7, disabilities, 155–156, 160
prolongs specified period, 156, 160–161, 183
s. 8, extension of longer period by lease or life tenancy, 157–159, 160–161, 166–167, 183
support, whether applicable to, 296, 297, 298
unity of possession defeats claim under, 147, 148
water and watercourses. *See* ARTIFICIAL WATERCOURSE; POLLUTION OF WATER; WATER; WATERCOURSE.
way, rights of. *See* WAY, RIGHTS OF.

PRIVACY,
no easement of, 26

PROCEEDINGS. *See* ACTIONS.

PROFITS À PRENDRE, 4–5, 59–60, 145, 155
claims to, under Prescription Act, 145, 155
not applicable to profits in gross, 155
classification of, 59–60
deed, creation by, 69
definition of, 4
easements, contrasted with, 4, 59
equitable, 69
devolution of, 69–72
examples of, 4

PROFITS À PRENDRE—*cont.*
registered land. *See* LAND REGISTRATION ACT 1925.
title to, whether proof necessary of, 374

PROSPECT,
no easement of, 26, 299

PURCHASER FOR VALUE WITHOUT NOTICE,
easement, of, not bound by prior contract, 78–79
easements, enforceable against, 4, 25, 113
equitable easement, does not bind, 69–70, 79
rectification, not bound by right of, 132

PURITY OF WATER. *See* POLLUTION OF WATER.

QUASI-EASEMENTS, 21, 81, 92–106

QUI SENTIT COMMODUM SENTIRE DEBET ET ONUS, 46

RAILWAY,
embankment, status of, 30–31
right to pass over, 75–76

RECREATION AND AMUSEMENT, 29–30

RECTIFICATION,
right to, not binding on purchaser for value without notice, 132
where general words too wide, 131–132

REGISTERED LAND. *See* LAND REGISTRATION ACT 1925.

REGISTRATION. *See* LAND CHARGES ACT 1925; LAND REGISTRATION ACT 1925.

RELEASE. *See* EXTINGUISHMENT OF EASEMENTS.

REMEDIES. *See also* ABATEMENT; ACTIONS; INJUNCTION.
act of party, 356–361
injunction, 380–398
legal proceedings, 361–398

RENT,
easements, for, 49

REPAIR. *See also* COVENANT.
common parts, duty of lessor to, 47
dominant owner, 44–47
express duty to, 46–47
may be practically obliged to, 45–46
no general duty to, 45
right of, 44–45, 301
fences, of, 37–42
interference with right to, 45
servient owner,
express duty to, 47–49
no general duty to, 47, 301

REPAIR—*cont.*
servient tenement, of, covenant for,
dominant owner, by, 46–47
servient owner, by, 48–49
RESERVATION,
easements, of, 80–81, 106–110
grantor, construed against, 80
implication, by, 106–110
operates at law, 80
general words, from, 80–81
implication, by, 106–110
common intention, 108–110
lease, on grant of, 112–117
necessity. *See* NECESSITY, EASE-
MENTS OF.
reciprocity, 106–107
simultaneous dispositions, on, 110–
112
RESTRICTIVE COVENANTS,
easements distinguished from, 25
REVERSIONER,
action by, 363–369
easements, for disturbance of, 365
natural rights, for disturbance of,
366
trespass, for, 366–367
what must be proved, 363–365,
367–369
disturbance of easement, may be
liable for, 369–370
user during limited interest, when
bound by, 157–159, 160–161, 164–
165, 166–167, 181–186
RIGHTS OF LIGHT ACT 1959...150–152
certificate of Lands Tribunal, 151
effect of notice, 151
notional obstruction, 151–152
purpose of, 150
registration of notice, 151
statutory period for prescription, extension of, 150–151
RIPARIAN OWNERS,
first occupant acquires no right to
divert stream, 207–208
licensee of, whether natural rights
may be transferred to, 231–234
miscellaneous rights of, 236–237
divert flood water, to, 236–237
navigable rivers, access to, 237
place erections on river bed, to, 236
natural overground stream,
mutual rights and liabilities, 203
natural rights of user and flow
in, 199–203
purity, natural rights as to, 229–230
who are, 206–207
RIVER AUTHORITIES. *See* WATER RE-
SOURCES ACT 1963.
ROOTS OF TREES,
encroachment by, 305–306

SERVIENT OWNER,
knowledge, actual or constructive, of
prescriptive enjoyment, must have,
171, 175–176, 179–186

SERVIENT OWNER—*cont.*
no right to have easement continued,
53–55
not bound to repair, 47
permission of, generally defeats prescription, 176–178
stipulation for repair by, effect of,
47–49
SERVIENT TENEMENT,
conveyance of, subject to easements,
4
identification of, 15–16
increase of burden on, 57
necessity of, 7–8, 15
registration of, subject to easements,
196
SETTLED LAND ACT 1925,
easements,
power to acquire under, 79
powers to grant, under, 77
prescription by tenant for life, 169–
170
user under Prescription Act against
tenant for life, 156
SEWER. *See* PIPE.
SHEEP,
water troughs for, right to place on
servient land, 44, 88
SILT,
right to maintain, in a dock, not
an easement, 32
withdrawal of support from, 289
SIMULTANEOUS DISPOSITIONS,
implied grant or reservation of easements, on, 110–112
STATUTE,
creation of easements by, 75–76. *See
also* LAND REGISTRATION ACT 1925.
extinguishment of easements by,
314–315
general words in. *See* GENERAL
WORDS.
prescription must not be contrary to,
189–190
STORAGE,
right of, as easement, 31
unlimited right of, not an easement,
32–33
STREAM. *See* DIVERSION OF STREAM.
SUBTERRANEAN WATER,
in defined and known channel only,
right to, 210–214
no right of support from, 288–289
SUPPORT, RIGHT OF, 287–301
ancillary, 44, 76
extinguishment of, 324
for buildings by adjoining land, 290–
300
acquisition of, 292–300
grant, express or implied, by, 300
Prescription Act, 296, 297, 298
twenty years' user, by, 292–300
National Coal Board, obligations
of, 300

SUPPORT, RIGHT OF—*cont.*
for buildings by adjoining land—*cont.*
not a natural right, 290–292
exception for trespasser or contractor, 291n.
whether negative easement, 24, 296, 297, 298
for buildings by buildings, 300–301
clearance order, 301
dominant owner may enter to repair, 301
not a natural right, 301
servient owner need not repair, 301
for land by adjoining or subjacent land, 287–290
consequential damage to buildings, 290–291
nature of the right explained, 290
right of property not an easement, 287
servient owner, negative obligation of, 290
silt or brine, from, 289–290
underground water, does not extend to, 288–289
implication, arising by, 100–101, 106, 300, 301
mandatory injunction to prevent further damage, 384–386
prescriptive enjoyment, capable of interruption, 187
secrecy of prescriptive enjoyment, 174–176
statute of limitation, when time begins to run under, 290

SURFACE,
right to let down, 23, 37
not necessarily an easement, 37

TENANT FOR LIFE. *See* SETTLED LAND ACT 1925.

TENANT FOR YEARS,
continuing disturbance of easement, may be liable for, 369–370
grantee of easement, 79
grantor of easement, 78
may sue for disturbance of easement, 362
permission of, defeats prescription under s. 2 of Prescription Act, 176–177
prescribing against landlord or tenant of same landlord, 21, 165, 166, 167
prescription by, 170
prescriptive enjoyment against, 149, 157–159, 160–161, 164–165, 166–167, 181–186
lost grant, under doctrine of, 164–165
Prescription Act, under, 157–159, 160–161, 166–167
under s. 3 of Prescription Act, 149

TREES,
encroaching roots of, 305–306

TREES—*cont.*
overhanging branches of, 305
notice to abate unnecessary, 358
roots and branches of, whether easement to encroach, 304–305

TRUSTEE,
whether can have easement for or over land held beneficially, 22

TUNNEL,
right to use, whether easement or corporeal right, 5

UNITY,
of ownership and possession, 20–22
effect on prescription, 136–137, 147, 148, 188
extinguishment of easements by, 309–313

USE OF WATER,
in defined overground channel, what is lawful, 203–206

VEHICLES,
park, right to, 128–129
right to halt on way, 44n., 272, 273
unlimited storage of, not an easement, 32–33

VESSELS,
easement to break up, in a dock, 32

VIEW,
unobstructed, no easement of, 26
useful for judge in light cases to have, 253

WALL. *See also* PARTY-WALLS.
right to maintain, as easement, 33–34

WATER, 199–237. *See also* ARTIFICIAL WATERCOURSE; POLLUTION OF WATER; RIPARIAN OWNERS; WATERCOURSE; WATER RESOURCES ACT 1963.
acquisition of rights in,
custom, by, 236
express grant, by, 235–236
channel,
" defined," 210
" known," 210
diversion of. *See* DIVERSION OF STREAM.
equitable right to, 62–63
escape of, from pipe, 45–46
extraordinary user of, 203–206
fee simple, natural rights are part of, 206
irrigation, whether lawful user of, 204–206
natural rights in natural stream,
defined channel, in,
overground, 199–209
underground, 210

WATER—*cont.*
  natural rights in natural stream—*cont.*
    undefined channel, in,
      overground, 209–210
      underground, 210–214
  percolating, 210–214. *See also* PER-
    COLATING WATER.
  prescriptive right. *See also* ARTI-
    FICIAL WATERCOURSE.
    discharge, to, 222–223
    divert, to, 218–219
    take, to, 221–222
  right to compel continuance of dis-
    charge, whether, 53–55, 222
  riparian owners, who are, 206–207
  subterranean. *See* SUBTERRANEAN
    WATER.
  surface springs, 214

WATERCOURSE. *See also* ARTIFICIAL
  WATERCOURSE; POLLUTION OF
  WATER; RIPARIAN OWNERS; WATER;
  WATER RESOURCES ACT 1963.
  abatement of nuisance to, 357
  appropriation not necessary to
    acquire natural rights in, 208–209
  channel, enlargement of 58
  discharge on servient tenement, right
    of,
    increase in, 58
    sewage, may not include, 58
    whether bound to continue, 53–55,
    222
  disturbance of right to, what is, 352
  diversion of. *See* DIVERSION OF
    STREAM.
  express grant of, construction of,
    235–236
  extinguishment of right to, 320–323
  flow of, increase in, 57
  lawful use of, what is, 203–206
  natural rights in, part of fee simple,
    206
  prescriptive rights in,
    defined channel, 218–219
    undefined channel, 219–221
  user of, increase in, 57

WATER RESOURCES ACT 1963 . . ., 214–
  218
  abstraction of water, licence gener-
    ally required for, 215
  licence,
    abstraction of water, generally
      required for, 215
    common law rights, effect on, 216
    conditions, may be subject to, 215
    discretionary, grant of, 215
    nuisance, defence to, 216
    penalty for abstraction without,
      217
    where not required, 216
    who may apply for, 215
  river authorities,
    agreements by, registrable, 214n.
    discretion of, 215
    duties of, 214–215
    liability of, 217–218
    protected rights, must not derogate
      from, 217

WAY, RIGHTS OF, 261–286
  abatement of obstruction to, 356–
    357
  access from dominant tenement, 286
  acquisition of. *See also* ACQUISITION
    OF EASEMENTS.
    continuous and apparent, as, 95–
      99
    description in parcels, from, 84–86
    doctrine of non-derogation, under,
      91–92
    grant of lease, on, 113–114, 116–
      117
    in equity, 64–65, 68–69
    necessity, arising by, 117–121
    statutory general words, under,
      125–128, 129, 130
  amount of way to which dominant
    owner is entitled, 285
  construction of particular grants of,
    269–286
  deviate, right to, 286
  disturbance of, 352–354
  dominant tenement, alteration of,
    266–269, 274–282
  excessive user of, effect of, 286, 346–
    347
  extent of,
    grant, arising by, 269–282
      dominant tenement, alteration
        of, 274–282
      quality of user, 270–273
      quantity and purpose of user,
        273–281
    implied grant, arising by, 281
    prescription, arising by, 261–269
      dominant tenement, alteration
        of, 266–269
      mode of user, 261–266
      purpose of user, 265–269
  extinguishment of, 338–342, 343–344,
    346–347
  incidents of, 282–286
  in gross, 42–43
  kinds of, 261
  physical extent of, 284–285
  remedy for excessive user of, 286,
    346–347
  user of, confined to dominant tene-
    ment, 282
  who may use, 282–284

WEATHER, PROTECTION FROM,
  no such easement, 25, 26–27

WHEELDON *v.* BURROWS, RULE IN, 92–
  106
  negative easements,
    light, 101–105
    support, 100–101
    water supply, 99–100
  positive easements, 95–99
    drainage, 99
    rights of way, 95–99
    support, right to withdraw, 99

WILL,
  easement, creation of, by, 61, 82, 111

WINDMILL,
  passage of air to, 256–258